ideal marriage p143.

hope p132

children - faith
p116

church hospitality
p110

renewing our vows
p118

marriage & family p125-26

safe place p63
(turned out as a battle place

communion set p231

Two coins p201
one for god

Mother-In-law p91

with a little help p313

How you are remade
p89

patience p303

helping each other p317
cooperation

pray for education
p164

an old tale about
a wild goose
p193

ordinary person
→ extraordinary
living

chinese Xians
before & after class p99

commitment
card charge course
lighthouse p122

strong family p125

funeral service p145

The Ministers Manual for 1994

SIXTY-NINTH ANNUAL ISSUE

THE MINISTERS MANUAL

1994 EDITION

Edited by

JAMES W. COX

HarperSanFrancisco
A Division of HarperCollins*Publishers*

Editors of THE MINISTERS MANUAL

G. B. F. Hallock, D.D., 1926–1958
M. K. W. Heicher, Ph.D., 1943–1968
Charles L. Wallis, M.A., M.Div., 1969–1983
James W. Cox, M.Div., Ph.D.

Translations of the Bible referred to and quoted from in this book may be indicated by their standard abbreviations, such as NRSV (New Revised Standard Version) and NIV (New International Version). In addition, some contributors have made their own translations and others have used a mixed text.

Other acknowledgments are on page 324.

FIRST EDITION

Library of Congress Catalog Card Number
25–21658
ISSN 0–06–061619–9

93 94 95 96 97 HAD 10 9   8 7 6 5 4 3 2 1

This edition is printed on acid-free paper that meets the American National Standards Institute Z39.48 Standard.

CONTENTS

PREFACE

What are sermons made of? Surely a sermon has to do with the Bible, one would believe! But such is not always the case. And when it is not the case, the sermon suffers and the congregation is deprived. This does not mean that the sermon has to have a specific biblical text to be authentic preaching. In fact, a sermon without a text may be biblical, while a sermon with a text may be unbiblical. Biblical preaching, as defined by Professor John Knox, is preaching that stays close to the great themes of the Bible, "the characteristic and essential biblical ideas."

Within the parameters of those great themes are vital concerns of biblical import. The ancient text must come alive in the context of contemporary life and need. The sermons in *The Ministers Manual* are presented with that intention. Some of the sermons are expository and some topical—all of them, it is hoped, *biblical*. In any case, the preacher will find material to edify, confirm, challenge, and perhaps provoke disagreement. But what is new and strange about that?

I have found that six categories serve to identify the types of sermons that form and build up the people of God. *Evangelistic* sermons put individuals in touch with the redeeming grace of God. *Expository* sermons ground these believers in a knowledge and understanding of salvation history as contained in the Bible. *Doctrinal/theological* sermons help those who are thus participants in salvation history to get a systematic perspective on the often-confusing mass of biblical material. *Ethical* sermons present the practical implications of the great truths of Scripture. *Pastoral* sermons endeavor to give sympa-

thetic encouragement and direction in living out the demands of a vital faith. *Devotional* sermons promote private and public worship of God, primarily to give God his due, but also to point to spiritual resources needed to live victoriously. Of course, expository sermons themselves can—depending on the particular text and the special purpose of the preacher—fulfill any of the several other objectives of the sermon. Pastoral preaching, likewise, can make use of four of these objectives. Therefore, the reader can find a wide variety of sermon types and aims in *The Ministers Manual.*

I continue to be grateful for the contributions of many individuals who provide me with materials from their own reading and ministry that go into *The Ministers Manual.* I wish to express gratitude also for the practical encouragement given by the Southern Baptist Theological Seminary and to thank publishers for permission to quote from their material. Clara McCartt, C. Neil Strait, and Lee R. McGlone over many years have made special contributions for which I am grateful. Alicia Gardner, office service supervisor, and Keitha Brasler, who typed the manuscript, also have my profound gratitude for their care in producing this volume. I am most appreciative of the faithful attention and work of the editorial staff at Harper San Francisco.

James W. Cox
The Southern Baptist Theological Seminary
2825 Lexington Road
Louisville, Kentucky 40280

SECTION I.
General Aids and Resources
Civil Year Calendars

1994

JANUARY	FEBRUARY	MARCH	APRIL

JANUARY

S	M	T	W	T	F	S
						1
2	3	4	5	6	7	8
9	10	11	12	13	14	15
16	17	18	19	20	21	22
23	24	25	26	27	28	29
30	31					

FEBRUARY

S	M	T	W	T	F	S
		1	2	3	4	5
6	7	8	9	10	11	12
13	14	15	16	17	18	19
20	21	22	23	24	25	26
27	28					

MARCH

S	M	T	W	T	F	S
		1	2	3	4	5
6	7	8	9	10	11	12
13	14	15	16	17	18	19
20	21	22	23	24	25	26
27	28	29	30	31		

APRIL

S	M	T	W	T	F	S
					1	2
3	4	5	6	7	8	9
10	11	12	13	14	15	16
17	18	19	20	21	22	23
24	25	26	27	28	29	30

MAY

S	M	T	W	T	F	S
1	2	3	4	5	6	7
8	9	10	11	12	13	14
15	16	17	18	19	20	21
22	23	24	25	26	27	28
29	30	31				

JUNE

S	M	T	W	T	F	S
			1	2	3	4
5	6	7	8	9	10	11
12	13	14	15	16	17	18
19	20	21	22	23	24	25
26	27	28	29	30		

JULY

S	M	T	W	T	F	S
					1	2
3	4	5	6	7	8	9
10	11	12	13	14	15	16
17	18	19	20	21	22	23
24	25	26	27	28	29	30
31						

AUGUST

S	M	T	W	T	F	S
	1	2	3	4	5	6
7	8	9	10	11	12	13
14	15	16	17	18	19	20
21	22	23	24	25	26	27
28	29	30	31			

SEPTEMBER

S	M	T	W	T	F	S
				1	2	3
4	5	6	7	8	9	10
11	12	13	14	15	16	17
18	19	20	21	22	23	24
25	26	27	28	29	30	

OCTOBER

S	M	T	W	T	F	S
						1
2	3	4	5	6	7	8
9	10	11	12	13	14	15
16	17	18	19	20	21	22
23	24	25	26	27	28	29
30	31					

NOVEMBER

S	M	T	W	T	F	S
		1	2	3	4	5
6	7	8	9	10	11	12
13	14	15	16	17	18	19
20	21	22	23	24	25	26
27	28	29	30			

DECEMBER

S	M	T	W	T	F	S
				1	2	3
4	5	6	7	8	9	10
11	12	13	14	15	16	17
18	19	20	21	22	23	24
25	26	27	28	29	30	31

1995

JANUARY

S	M	T	W	T	F	S
1	2	3	4	5	6	7
8	9	10	11	12	13	14
15	16	17	18	19	20	21
22	23	24	25	26	27	28
29	30	31				

FEBRUARY

S	M	T	W	T	F	S
			1	2	3	4
5	6	7	8	9	10	11
12	13	14	15	16	17	18
19	20	21	22	23	24	25
26	27	28				

MARCH

S	M	T	W	T	F	S
			1	2	3	4
5	6	7	8	9	10	11
12	13	14	15	16	17	18
19	20	21	22	23	24	25
26	27	28	29	30	31	

APRIL

S	M	T	W	T	F	S
						1
2	3	4	5	6	7	8
9	10	11	12	13	14	15
16	17	18	19	20	21	22
23	24	25	26	27	28	29
30						

MAY

S	M	T	W	T	F	S
	1	2	3	4	5	6
7	8	9	10	11	12	13
14	15	16	17	18	19	20
21	22	23	24	25	26	27
28	29	30	31			

JUNE

S	M	T	W	T	F	S
				1	2	3
4	5	6	7	8	9	10
11	12	13	14	15	16	17
18	19	20	21	22	23	24
25	26	27	28	29	30	

JULY

S	M	T	W	T	F	S
						1
2	3	4	5	6	7	8
9	10	11	12	13	14	15
16	17	18	19	20	21	22
23	24	25	26	27	28	29
30	31					

AUGUST

S	M	T	W	T	F	S
		1	2	3	4	5
6	7	8	9	10	11	12
13	14	15	16	17	18	19
20	21	22	23	24	25	26
27	28	29	30	31		

SEPTEMBER

S	M	T	W	T	F	S
					1	2
3	4	5	6	7	8	9
10	11	12	13	14	15	16
17	18	19	20	21	22	23
24	25	26	27	28	29	30

OCTOBER

S	M	T	W	T	F	S
1	2	3	4	5	6	7
8	9	10	11	12	13	14
15	16	17	18	19	20	21
22	23	24	25	26	27	28
29	30	31				

NOVEMBER

S	M	T	W	T	F	S
			1	2	3	4
5	6	7	8	9	10	11
12	13	14	15	16	17	18
19	20	21	22	23	24	25
26	27	28	29	30		

DECEMBER

S	M	T	W	T	F	S
					1	2
3	4	5	6	7	8	9
10	11	12	13	14	15	16
17	18	19	20	21	22	23
24	25	26	27	28	29	30
31						

Church and Civic Calendar for 1994

JANUARY

 1 New Year's Day
   The Name of Jesus
 5 Twelfth Night
 6 Epiphany
 9 The Baptism of Jesus
17 Martin Luther King, Jr.,
   Day
19 Robert E. Lee's Birthday
25 Conversion of St. Paul

FEBRUARY

 1 National Freedom Day
 2 Groundhog Day
   Presentation of Jesus in
   the Temple
 3 Four Chaplains Memorial
   Day
12 Lincoln's Birthday
13–20 Brotherhood/Sisterhood
   Week
14 St. Valentine's Day
15 Shrove Tuesday
   Susan B. Anthony Day
16 Ash Wednesday
20 First Sunday in Lent
21 Presidents' Day
22 Washington's Birthday
25 Purim
27 Second Sunday in Lent

MARCH

 4 World Day of Prayer
 6 Third Sunday in Lent
13 Fourth Sunday in Lent
17 St. Patrick's Day
19 Joseph, Husband of Mary
20 Fifth Sunday in Lent
   Passion Sunday
25 The Annunciation
27–4/2 Holy Week
27 Palm Sunday
   Passion Sunday (alternate)
   Pesach (First day of
   Passover)
31 Maundy Thursday

APRIL

 1 Good Friday
 3 Easter
   Daylight Saving Time
   begins
14 Pan American Day
25 St. Mark, Evangelist
29 Arbor Day

MAY

 1 Law Day
   Loyalty Day
   May Day
   St. Philip and St. James,
   Apostles
   Easter (Orthodox)
1–8 National Family Week
 3 National Teacher Day
 5 National Day of Prayer
 8 Mother's Day
   Festival of the Christian
   Home
12 Ascension Day
15 Rural Life Sunday
16 First day of Shavuot
22 Pentecost (Whitsunday)
   National Maritime Day
23 Victoria Day (Canada)
29 Trinity Sunday
30 Memorial Day
31 Visitation of the Virgin
   Mary

JUNE

12 Children's Day
14 Flag Day
19 Father's Day
24 Nativity of St. John the
   Baptist
29 St. Peter and St. Paul,
   Apostles

JULY

 1 Canada Day
 4 Independence Day
22 St. Mary Magdalene
25 St. James the Elder

AUGUST

1 Civic Holiday (August)
6 The Transfiguration
15 Mary, the Mother of Jesus
19 National Aviation Day
24 St. Bartholomew, Apostle

SEPTEMBER

4 Labor Sunday
5 Labor Day
6 Rosh Hashanah
8 Birth of the Virgin Mary
11 Grandparents' Day
   Rally Day
15 Yom Kippur
17 Citizenship Day
20 First day of Sukkot
21 St. Matthew, Apostle and
   Evangelist
23 Native American Day
25 Christian Education
   Sunday
27 First day of Shemini
   Atzerer
29 St. Michael and All Angels

OCTOBER

2 World Communion
  Sunday
3 Child Health Day
9 Laity Sunday
10 Columbus Day
   Thanksgiving Day
   (Canada)
15 World Poetry Day
18 St. Luke, Evangelist
24 United Nations Day
28 St. Simon and St. Jude,
   Apostles
30 Reformation Sunday
   Daylight Saving Time ends
31 Halloween

National UNICEF Day
Reformation Day

NOVEMBER

1 All Saints' Day
4 World Community Day
5 Sadie Hawkins Day
8 Election Day
11 Armistice Day
   Remembrance Day
   (Canada)
   Veterans Day
12 Elizabeth Cady Stanton
   Day
13 Stewardship Sunday
20 Bible Sunday
   Christ the King
   Thanksgiving Sunday
21 Presentation of the Virgin
   Mary in the Temple
24 Thanksgiving Day
27 First Sunday of Advent
28–12/5 Hanukkah
30 St. Andrew, Apostle

DECEMBER

4 Second Sunday of Advent
11 Third Sunday of Advent
15 Bill of Rights Day
17 Wright Brothers Day
18 Fourth Sunday of Advent
21 Forefathers' Day
   St. Thomas, Apostle
24 Christmas Eve
25 Christmas
27 Boxing Day (Canada)
   St. Stephen, Deacon and
   Martyr
27 St. John, Apostle and
   Evangelist
28 The Holy Innocents,
   Martyrs
31 New Year's Eve
   Watch Night

The Common Lectionary for 1994

The following Scripture lessons are commended for use in public worship by various Protestant churches and the Roman Catholic church and include first, second, Gospel readings, and Psalms, according to Cycle B from January 2 to November

24 and according to Cycle C from November 27 to December 25. (Copyright 1992 Consultation on Common Texts.)

January 2: Jer. 31:7–14 (alt.); Sir. 24:1–12 (alt.); Ps. 147:12–20 (alt.); Wis. 10:15–21 (alt. resp.); Eph. 1:3–14; John 1:(1–9) 10–18

EPIPHANY SEASON

January 9: Is. 60:1–6; Ps. 72:1–7, 10–14; Eph. 3:1–12; Matt. 2:1–12 and Baptism of the Lord: Gen. 1:1–5; Ps. 29; Acts 19:1–7; Mark 1:4–11
January 16: 1 Sam. 3:1–10 (11–20); Ps. 139:1–6, 13–18; 1 Cor. 6:12–20; John 1:43–51
January 23: John 3:1–5, 10; Ps. 62:5–12; 1 Cor. 7:29–31; Mark 1:14–20
January 30: Deut. 18:15–20; Ps. 111; 1 Cor. 8:1–13; Mark 1:21–28
February 6: Is. 40:21–31; Ps. 147:1–11, 20c; 1 Cor. 9:16–23; Mark 1:29–39
February 13: 2 Kings 5:1–14; Ps. 30; 1 Cor. 9:24–27; Mark 1:40–45

LENT

February 16 (Ash Wednesday): Jl. 2:1–2, 12–17 (alt.); Is. 58:1–12 (alt.); Ps. 51:1–17; 2 Cor. 5:20b–6:10; Matt. 6:1–6, 16–21
February 20: Gen. 9:8–17; Ps. 25:1–10; 1 Pet. 3:18–22; Mark 1:9–15
February 27: Gen. 17:1–7, 15–16; Ps. 22:23–31; Rom. 4:13–25; Mark 8:31–38 (alt.); Mark 9:2–9 (alt.)
March 6: Ex. 20:1–17; Ps. 19; 1 Cor. 1:18–25; John 2:13–22
March 13: Num. 21:4–9; Ps. 107:1–3, 17–22; Eph. 2:1–10; John 3:14–21
March 20: Jer. 31:31–34; Ps. 51:1–12 (alt.); Ps. 119:9–16 (alt.); Heb. 5:5–10; John 12:20–33
March 27 (Palm/Passion Sunday): Mark 11:1–11 (alt.) (palms); John 12:12–16 (alt.) (palms); Ps. 118:1–2, 19–29 (palms); Is. 50:4–9a; Ps. 31:9–16; Phil. 2:5–11; Mark 14:1–15:47 (alt.); Mark 15:1–39 (40–47) (alt.)
March 28 (Monday): Is. 42:1–9; Ps. 36:5–11; Heb. 9:11–15; John 12:1–11

March 29 (Tuesday): Is. 49:1–7; Ps. 71:1–14; 1 Cor. 1:18–31; John 12:20–36
March 30 (Wednesday): Is. 50:4–9a; Ps. 70; Heb. 12:1–3; John 13:21–32
March 31 (Maundy Thursday): Ex. 12:1–4 (5–10) 11–14; Ps. 116:1–10, 12–19; 1 Cor. 11:23–26; John 13:1–17, 31b–35
April 1 (Good Friday): Is. 51:13–53:12; Ps. 22; Heb. 10:16–25 (alt.); Heb. 4:14–16; 5:7–9 (alt.); John 18:1–19:42
April 2 (Holy Saturday): Job 14:1–14 (alt.); Lam. 3:1–9, 19–24 (alt.); Ps. 31:1–4, 15–16; 1 Peter 4:1–8; Matt. 27:57–66 (alt.); John 19:38–42 (alt.)

SEASON OF EASTER

April 1–3 (Easter Vigil): Gen. 1:1–2:4a; Ps. 136:1–9, 23–26; Gen. 7:1–5, 11–18; 8:6–18; 9:8–13; Ps. 46; Gen. 22:1–18; Ps. 16; Ex. 14:10–31; 15:20–21; Ex. 15:1b–13, 17–18 (resp.); Is. 55:1–11; Is. 12:2–6 (resp.); Bar. 3:9–15, 32–4:4 (alt.); Prov. 8:1–8, 19–21; 9:4–6 (alt.); Ps. 19; Ezek. 36:24–28, Pss. 42 & 43; Ezek. 37:1–14; Ps. 143; Zeph. 3:14–20; Ps. 98; Rom. 6:3–11; Ps. 114; Mark 16:1–8
April 3 (Easter Sunday): Acts 10:34–43 (alt.); Is. 25:6–9 (alt.); Ps. 118:1–2, 14–24; 1 Cor. 15:1–11 (alt.); Acts 10:34–43 (alt.); John 20:1–18 (alt.); Mark 16:1–8 (alt.) and Easter evening: Is. 25:6–9; Ps. 114; 1 Cor. 5:6b–8; Luke 24:13–49
April 10: Acts 4:32–35; Ps. 133; 1 John 1:1–2:2; John 20:19–31
April 17: Acts 3:12–19; Ps. 4; 1 John 3:1–7; Luke 24:36b–48
April 24: Acts 4:5–12; Ps. 23; 1 John 3:16–24; John 10:11–18
May 1: Acts 8:26–40; Ps. 22:25–31; 1 John 4:7–21; John 15:1–8
May 8: Acts 10:44–48; Ps. 98; 1 John 5:1–6; John 15:9–17
May 12 (Ascension): Acts 1:1–11; Ps. 47 (alt.); Ps. 93 (alt.); Eph. 1:15–23; Luke 24:44–53
May 15: Acts 1:15–17; 21–26; Ps. 1; 1 John 5:9–13; John 17:6–19

SEASON OF PENTECOST

May 22: Acts 2:1–21 (alt.); Ezek. 37:1–14 (alt.); Ps. 104:1a, 24–34, 35b; Rom. 8:22–27 (alt.); Acts 2:1–21 (alt.); John 15:26–27; 16:4b–15

May 29 (Trinity Sunday): Is. 6:1–8; Ps. 29; Rom. 8:12–17; John 3:1–17

June 5: 1 Sam. 8:4–11 (12–15) 16–20 (11:14–15); Ps. 138; 2 Cor. 4:13–5:1; Mark 3:20–35

June 12: 1 Sam. 15:34–16:13; Ps. 20; 2 Cor. 5:6–10 (11–13) 14–17; Mark 4:26–34

June 19: 1 Sam. 17:(1a, 4–11, 19–23) 32–49 (alt.); 1 Sam. 17:57–18:5 (10–16) (alt.); Ps. 9:9–20 (alt.); Ps. 133 (alt.); 2 Cor. 6:1–13; Mark 4:35–41

June 26: 2 Sam. 1:1, 17, 23–27; Ps. 130; 2 Cor. 8:7–15; Mark 5:21–43

July 3: 2 Sam. 5:1–5, 9–10; Ps. 48; 2 Cor. 12:2–10; Mark 6:1–13

July 10: 2 Sam. 6:1–5, 12b–19; Ps. 24; Eph. 1:13–14; Mark 6:14–29

July 17: 2 Sam. 7:1–14a; Ps. 89:20–37; Eph. 2:11–22; Mark 6:30–44, 53–56

July 24: 2 Sam. 11:1–15; Ps. 14; Eph. 3:14–21; John 6:1–21

July 31: 2 Sam. 11:26–12:13a; Ps. 51:1–12; Eph. 4:1–16; John 6:24–35

August 7: 2 Sam. 18:5–9, 15, 31–33; Ps. 130; Eph. 4:25–5:2; John 6:35, 41–51

August 14: 1 Kings 2:10–12; 3:3–14; Ps. 111; Eph. 5:15–20; John 6:51–58

August 21: 1 Kings 8:1, 6, 10–11, 22–30, 41–43; Ps. 84; Eph. 6:10–20; John 6:56–69

August 28: Song 2:8–13; Ps. 45:1–2, 6–9; Jas. 1:17–27; Mark 7:1–8, 14–15, 21–23

September 4: Prov. 22:1–2, 8–9, 22–23; Ps. 125; Jas. 2:1–10 (11–13) 14–17; Mark 7:24–37

September 11: Prov. 1:20–33; Ps. 19 (alt.); Wis. 7:26–8:1; Jas. 3:1–12; Mark 8:27–38

September 18: Prov. 31:10–31; Ps. 1; Jas. 3:13–4:3, 7–8a; Mark 9:30–37

September 25: Est. 7:1–6, 9–10; 9:20–22; Ps. 124; Jas. 5:13–20; Mark 9:38–50

October 2: Job 1:1; 2:1–10; Ps. 26; Heb. 1:1–4; 2:5–12; Mark 10:2–16

October 9: Job. 23:1–9, 16–17; Ps. 22:1–15; Heb. 4:12–16; Mark 10:17–31

October 16: Job 38:1–7 (34–41); Ps. 104:1–9, 24, 35c; Heb. 5:1–10; Mark 10:35–45

October 23: Job. 42:1–6, 10–17; Ps. 34:1–8 (19–22); Heb. 7:23–28; Mark 10:46–52

October 30: Ru. 1:1–18; Ps. 146; Heb. 9:11–14; Mark 12:28–34

November 1 (All Saints): Wis. 3:1–9 (alt.); Is. 25:6–9 (alt.); Ps. 24; Rev. 21:1–6a; John 11:32–44

November 6: Ru. 3:1–5; 4:13–17; Ps. 127; Heb. 9:24–28; Mark 12:38–44

November 13: 1 Sam. 1:4–20; 1 Sam. 2:1–10 (resp.); Heb. 10:11–14 (15–18) 19–25; Mark 13:1–8

November 20 (Reign of Christ): 2 Sam. 23:1–7; Ps. 132:1–12 (13–18); Rev. 1:4b–8; John 18:33–37

November 24: Jl. 2:21–27; Ps. 126; 1 Tim. 2:1–7; Matt. 6:25–33

ADVENT

November 27: Jer. 33:14–16; Ps. 25:1–10; 1 Thess. 3:9–13; Luke 21:25–36

December 4: Bar. 5:1–9 (alt.); Mal. 3:1–4 (alt.); Luke 1:68–79 (resp.); Phil. 1:3–11; Luke 3:1–6

December 11: Zeph. 3:14–20; Is. 12:2–6 (resp.); Phil. 4:4–7; Luke 3:7–18

December 18: Mic. 5:2–5a; Luke 1:47–55 (alt. resp.); Ps. 80:1–7 (alt.); Heb. 10:5–10; Luke 1:39–45 (46–55)

CHRISTMAS SEASON

December 25 (Christmas Day): Is. 9:2–7; Ps. 96; Tit. 2:11–14; Luke 2:1–14 (15–20); Is. 62:6–12; Ps. 97; Tit. 3:4–7; Luke 2:(1–7) 8–20; Is. 52:7–10; Ps. 98; Heb. 1:1–4 (5–12); John 1:1–14; 1 Sam. 2:18–20, 26; Ps. 148; Col. 3:12–17; Luke 2:41–52

Four-Year Church Calendar

	1994	1995	1996	1997
Ash Wednesday	February 16	March 1	February 21	February 12
Palm Sunday	March 27	April 9	March 31	March 23
Good Friday	April 1	April 14	April 5	March 28
Easter	April 3	April 16	April 7	March 30
Ascension Day	May 12	May 25	May 16	May 8
Pentecost	May 22	June 4	May 26	May 18
Trinity Sunday	May 29	June 11	June 2	May 25
Thanksgiving	November 24	November 23	November 28	November 27
Advent Sunday	November 27	December 3	December 1	November 30

Forty-Year Easter Calendar

1994 April 3	2004 April 11	2014 April 20	2024 March 31
1995 April 16	2005 March 27	2015 April 5	2025 April 20
1996 April 7	2006 April 16	2016 March 27	2026 April 5
1997 March 30	2007 April 8	2017 April 16	2027 March 28
1998 April 12	2008 March 23	2018 April 1	2028 April 16
1999 April 4	2009 April 12	2019 April 21	2029 April 1
2000 April 23	2010 April 4	2020 April 12	2030 April 21
2001 April 15	2011 April 24	2021 April 4	2031 April 13
2002 March 31	2012 April 8	2022 April 17	2032 March 28
2003 April 20	2013 March 31	2023 April 9	2033 April 17

Traditional Wedding Anniversary Identifications

1 Paper	7 Wool	13 Lace	35 Coral
2 Cotton	8 Bronze	14 Ivory	40 Ruby
3 Leather	9 Pottery	15 Crystal	45 Sapphire
4 Linen	10 Tin	20 China	50 Gold
5 Wood	11 Steel	25 Silver	55 Emerald
6 Iron	12 Silk	30 Pearl	60 Diamond

Colors Appropriate for Days and Seasons

White. Symbolizes purity, perfection, and joy and identifies festivals marking events, except Good Friday, in the life of Jesus: Christmas, Epiphany, Easter, Eastertide, Ascension Day; also Trinity Sunday, All Saints' Day, weddings, funerals. Gold may also be used.

Red. Symbolizes the Holy Spirit, martyrdom, and the love of God: Good Friday, Pentecost, and Sundays following.

Violet. Symbolizes penitence: Advent, Lent.

Green. Symbolizes mission to the world, hope, regeneration, nurture, and growth: Epiphany season, Kingdomtide, Rural Life Sunday, Labor Sunday, Thanksgiving Sunday.

Blue. Advent, in some churches.

Flowers in Season Appropriate for Church Use

January. Carnation or snowdrop.
February. Violet or primrose.
March. Jonquil or daffodil.
April. Lily, sweet pea, or daisy.
May. Lily of the valley or hawthorn.
June. Rose or honeysuckle.

July. Larkspur or water lily.
August. Gladiolus or poppy.
September. Aster or morning glory.
October. Calendula or cosmos.
November. Chrysanthemum.
December. Narcissus, holly, or poinsettia.

Historical, Cultural, and Religious Anniversaries in 1994

Compiled by Kenneth M. Cox

1984 (10 years). *January 1*: Breakup of giant American Telephone and Telegraph Company takes effect. *January 10*: United States and the Vatican restore full diplomatic relations, after a century interruption. *March 5*: U.S. Supreme Court rules in *Lynch v. Donnelly* that public financing of a nativity scene does not necessarily violate the First Amendment's Establishment Clause. *October 19*: Polish priest Rev. Jerzy Popieluszko is kidnapped and later found slain. *October 31*: India's Prime Minister Indira Gandhi is assassinated.

1969 (25 years). *July 19*: Body of Mary Jo Kopechne is retrieved from water off Chappaquiddick Island bridge in car driven by Sen. Edward Kennedy, who comes forward the next day. *July 20*: Neil Armstrong steps down from Apollo 11's lunar module "Eagle" to become first man to walk on the moon. *August 10*: Seven persons die in L.A.'s Tate-LaBianca murders, for which Charles Manson and cult members are later found guilty. *September 3*: North Vietnamese leader Ho Chi Minh dies. *October 16*: Baseball's "Miracle" Mets of New York win their first World Series title. *Debuts*: Concorde supersonic jet; Frosted Mini Wheats; "Sesame Street"; *Penthouse* magazine.

1954 (40 years). Korean evangelist Sun Myung Moon founds the Unification Church. *May 6*: Englishman Roger Bannister runs world's first sub-four-minute mile. *May 17*: U.S. Supreme Court hands down 9-0 decision in *Brown v. Board of Education*, declaring racial segregation in public schools unconstitutional, overturning "separate but equal" doctrine set forth in *Plessy v. Ferguson* in 1897. *June 14*: President Eisenhower orders modification of U.S. pledge of allegiance from "one nation indivisible" to "one nation under God, indivisible." *December 2*: U.S. Senate votes to condemn Senator Joseph McCarthy for misconduct in Communist spy hearings. *December 31*: Dow Jones Industrial Average finally passes the 381.17

high of 1929. *Debuts*: Open-heart surgery; *Sports Illustrated*.

1944 (50 years). *April 3*: U.S. Supreme Court in *Smith v. Allwright* declares that Americans cannot be denied the right to vote because of race. *June 6*: D-Day: 176,000 Allied troops land on Normandy beaches in France, under command of General Dwight Eisenhower. *June 22*: Congress passes G.I. Bill of Rights to finance educations for millions of U.S. war veterans. *August 25*: Paris liberated from Germans. *Debuts*: French newspaper *Le Monde*; *Seventeen* magazine.

1919 (75 years). *January 25*: Versailles Peace Conference delegates create League of Nations, as 27 post-war victors unite to protect each other from aggression. *March 3*: U.S. Supreme Court Justice Oliver Wendell Holmes in *Schenck v. U.S.* articulates "clear and present danger" test to define conditions under which freedom of speech may be abridged. *June 20*: Congress approves Nineteenth Amendment, to grant women suffrage, and sends it to states for ratification. *June 28*: Treaty of Versailles is signed, as Germany accepts responsibility for the Great War and agrees to pay reparations and give land back to France. *July 4*: Jack Dempsey, the "Manassa Mauler," knocks out Jess Willard to win the heavyweight boxing crown. *September 24*: First meeting of Roman Catholic hierarchy of U.S. begins in Washington. *September 25*: President Wilson is paralyzed by a stroke. *Debut*: Dial telephones.

1894 (100 years). Economic depression and strikes, including the Pullman railroad strike, cripple the U.S. *May 26*: Henry Preserved Smith of Lane Theological Seminary in Cincinnati, Ohio, is convicted in heresy trial by the General Assembly of the Presbyterian Church. *July 4*: Republic of Hawaii is proclaimed. *December 22*: French army captain Alfred Dreyfus is court-martialed for providing military secrets to Germany, causing a wave of anti-Semitism in France, though he later is absolved. *Debuts*: Hershey chocolate bar; Labor Day; Radcliffe College for Women.

1869 (125 years). Pope Pius IX declares abortion of any kind an excommunicatory sin. *February 26*: Congress approves Fifteenth Amendment, to guarantee that the right to vote shall not be denied because of race, color or previous condition of servitude, and sends it to states for ratification. *May 10*: First transcontinental rail link is completed at Promonotory Point near Ogden in Utah Territory, as the Union Pacific and Central Pacific railroads meet. *September 24*: Financiers Gould and Fisk unsuccessfully attempt to corner the gold market on Wall Street's first "Black Friday." *November 17*: Suez Canal opens to traffic, linking the Mediterranean Sea with the Gulf of Suez at the head of the Red Sea. *December 8*: First Vatican Council, the first general council of the Roman Catholic Church since Trent three centuries earlier, begins and doctrine of papal infallibility is proclaimed. *Debuts*: Term "ecology"; margarine; rickshaw; washing machine.

1844 (150 years). Karl Marx writes in *Introduction to a Critique of the Hegelian Philosophy of the Right*: "Religion is the sigh of the oppressed creature, the feelings of a heartless world, just as it is the spirit of unspiritual conditions. It is the opium of the people." *May 24*: Samuel Morse transmits first telegraph message, from U.S. Capitol in Washington to Baltimore: "What God hath wrought." *Debut*: Young Men's Christian Association.

1819 (175 years). Boston Congregationalist pastor William Ellery Channing founds Unitarianism, which denies the holiness of the Trinity, believing in only one divine being. *March 6*: U.S. Court rules in *McCulloch v. Maryland* that no state may tax any instrumentality of the federal government. *June 30*: U.S. ship *Savannah*, in the first transatlantic crossing assisted by steam propulsion, arrives in Liverpool. *Debut*: Stethoscope.

1794 (200 years). Whiskey Rebellion takes place in western Pennsylvania. First of three parts of Thomas Paine's *The Age of Reason, Being an Investigation of True and Fabulous Theology* is published. *March 14*: Eli Whitney receives a patent for his cotton gin. *March 22*: Congress passes law forbidding U.S. citizens from engaging in foreign slave trade. *June 8*: Ending the cult of reason in France, Robespierre establishes himself as high priest of a new Festival of the Supreme Being, ushering in the height of the Reign of Terror, which ends in July with his execution by guillotine.

Anniversaries of Hymn Writers and Hymn-Tune Composers in 1994

Compiled by Hugh T. McElrath

25 *years* (1969). *Death* Walter Russell Bowie (b. 1882), author "O holy city, seen of John"; Clarence Dickinson (b. 1873), har. HERR, NUN HEB ("Lord, we cry to thee for help"); Grace Noll Crowell (b. 1877), author "Because I have been given much"; Harry Emerson Fosdick (b. 1878), author "God of grace and God of glory."

50 *years* (1944). *Birth* Carl Daw, Jr., author "God, our author and creator," "How lovely is Thy dwelling place" and others; Les Garrett, author/composer "This is the day," THIS IS THE DAY; Nobuaki Hanaoka, tr. "Jesus, my friend, is great"; Norm Jockman, composer HO-SEA ("O my people, turn to me"), TRANSFIGURATION ("Christ upon the mountain peak"); Stephen Leddy, author/composer, "Worthy is the Lamb," WORTHY LAMB; Russell Schulz-Widmar, author "Your love, O God, has called us here."

Death Henry Coward (b. 1849), composer NORFOLK PARK ("Saviour, blessed Saviour"); Cleland B. McAfee (b. 1866), author/composer "Near to the heart of God," MCAFEE; Thomas John Williams (b. 1869), composer EBENEZER ("Once to every man and nation," "O the deep, deep love of Jesus" and others); Maurice Frank Campbell Willson (b. 1884), author "Upon Thy table, Lord, we place"; Frederick Luke Wiseman (b. 1858), composer ALL HALLOWS ("None other Lamb") and others.

75 years (1919). *Birth* Brian Foley, author "Holy Spirit, come, confirm us," "With wonder, Lord, we see your works," and others; John W. Grant. tr. "O Holy Ghost, by whose breath"; Austin Lovelace, composer THREEFOLD GIFTS ("Of all the Spirit's gifts to me") and others; Marie J. Post, author "Praise and thanksgiving"; James Quinn, author "Blessed by the God of Israel," "Give thanks to God the Father," "here in Christ we gather" and others; Jaroslav John Vajda, author "Up through endless ranks of angels," "Now the silence" and others; David H. Williams, composer VERMONT ("My singing is a prayer") and others; Gordon Young, author/ composer, "Praise ye the name of the Lord," PRAISE YE.

Death Arthur Campbell Ainger (b. 1841), "God is working his purpose out" and others; Henry Collins (b. 1827), author, "Jesus, my Lord, my God, my all"; Louis Hartsough (b. 1828), author/ composer "I hear thy welcome voice," WELCOME VOICE; Elijah E. Hoss (b. 1849), author "O God, great Father, Lord and King"; Julia H. Johnston (b. 1849), author "Grace greater than our sin"; Henry Williams Mozley (b. 1842), author "Lord, who fulfillest thus anew" and others; John H. Sammis (b. 1846), author "Trust and obey"; Narayan Vaman Tilak (b. 1862), author orig. of "One who is all unfit to count"; Daniel B. Towner (b. 1850), composer CALVARY ("Years I spent in vanity and pride"), MOODY ("Marvellous grace of our loving Lord"), TRUST AND OBEY ("When we walk with the Lord"); W. G. Whinfield (b. 1865), composer WYCHBOLD ("Christ above all glory seated," "Praise to God, almighty maker").

100 years (1894). *Birth* Albert A. Ketchum, author/composer "Why do I sing about Jesus," KETCHUM; Rhea F. Miller (d. 1966), author "I'd rather have Jesus."

Death William John Blew (b. 1808), tr. "Let sighing cease and woe"; Matthew Bridges (b. 1800), author "Crown Him with many crowns"; Oliver Wendell Holmes (b. 1809), author "Lord of all being, throned afar"; William D. Longstaff (b. 1822), author "Take time to be holy"; Christina G. Rossetti (b. 1830), author "In the bleak mid-winter," "Love came down at Christmas," "What can I give Him" and others.

125 years (1869). *Birth* Hugh P. Allen (d. 1946), composer KINGLEY VALE ("Thanks to God whose word was spoken"); Henry Walford Davies (d. 1941), composer TEMPLE ("O King enthroned on high"), FIRMAMENT ("The spacious firmament on high"), GOD BE IN MY HEAD ("God be in my head and in my understanding"); Henry Ernest Hardy (d. 1946), author "O dearest Lord, Thy sacred head"; Civilla D. Martin (d. 1948), author "God will take care of you"; Ernest O. Sellers (d. 1952), author "There is never a day so dreary" and others; Grant Colfax Tullar (d. 1950), composer FACE TO FACE ("Face to face with Christ, my Saviour"); Thomas John Williams (d. 1944), composer EBENEZER ("Jesus, lover of my soul," "O the deep, deep love of Jesus").

Death Charlotte A. Barnard (b. 1830), composer BARNARD ("Jesus was a loving teacher"); Elizabeth C. Clephane (b. 1830), author "Beneath the cross of Jesus," "The ninety and nine" and others; Louis Moreau Gottschalf (b. 1829), composer MERCY ("Holy Spirit, with light divine"); Gilbert Rorison (b. 1821), author "Three in one and one in three"; John B. Wilkes (b. 1785), arr. MONKLAND ("let us with a gladsome mind").

150 years (1844). *Birth* John Frederick Bridge (d. 1924), composer SPEAN ("Brightest and best of the sons of the morning"); Robert Seymour Bridges (d. 1930), tr. "Ah, holy Jesus, how hast Thou offended?", "The duteous day now closeth," "All my hope on God is founded," "O gladsome light" and others; Joseph E. Carpenter (d. 1927), author "Eternal God, whose changeless will"; Constance Coote (d. 1926), author "In the quiet consecration"; Palmer Hartsough (d. 1932), author "I am resolved no longer to linger"; Gerard Manley Hopkins (d. 1889), author orig. of "The word of God proceeding forth"; James Ashcraft Noble (d. 1896), author "Lord Jesus in the days of old"; J. S. Norris (d. 1907), composer NORRIS ("Where He leads me I will follow"); Frederick C. Maker (d. 1927), composer REST or ELTON ("Dear Lord and Father of mankind"), ST. CHRISTOPHER ("Beneath the cross of Jesus"), WENTWORTH ("My God, I thank Thee"); George C. Martin (d. 1916), composer HOLY FAITH ("Jesus, my Lord, my God, my all"), CHILTON FOLIAT ("Almighty Father of all things that be"); James Mountain (d. 1933), composer WYE VALLEY ("Like a river glorious"), EVERLASTING LOVE ("I am His, and he is mine"); Albert Lister Peace (d. 1912), composer ST. MARGARET ("O love that wilt not let me go").

Death Thomas Campbell (b. 1777), composer SAGINA ("And can it be that I should gain"); Oliver Holden (b. 1765), composer CORONATION ("All hail the power of Jesus' name") and others.

175 years (1819). *Birth* Thomas H. Gill (d. 1906), author "Lord, Thou hast been our dwelling place," "Lord, in the fulness of Thy might," "We come unto our fathers' God" and others; James Hamilton (d. 1890), author "Praise, O praise the Lord of harvest"; James Russell Lowell (d. 1891), author "Once to every man and nation"; Mary Fawler Maude (d. 1913), author "Thine forever God of love"; Joseph Scriven (d. 1866), author "What a friend we have in Jesus"; William T. Sleeper (d. 1904), author "Out of my bondage, sorrow and night," "Ye must be born again"; Benjamin Webb (d. 1885), tr. "O Love, how deep, how broad"; Joseph P. Webster (d. 1875), composer SWEET BY AND BY ("There's a land that is fairer than day"); Richard Storrs Willis (d. 1900), composer CAROL ("It came upon the midnight clear"), arr. CRUSADER'S HYMN or ST. ELIZABETH ("Fairest Lord Jesus"); James Ellor (d. 1899), composer DIADEM ("All hail the power of Jesus' name").

Death John Bakewell (b. 1721), author "Hail, Thou once despised Jesus."

200 years (1794). *Birth* Julia Ward Howe (d. 1910), author "Mine eyes have seen the glory"; Charles Kinsley (d.

1875), author "From Thee all skill and science flow"; Samuel Longfellow (d. 1892), author "Holy Spirit, truth divine," "Again as evening's shadows fall" and others; Edwin George Monk (d. 1900), composer ANGEL VOICES ("Angel voices, ever singing"); William B. Tappan (d. 1849), author "'Tis midnight, and on Olive's brow"; Henry Ware, Jr. (d. 1843), author "Happy the home when God is there."

225 years (1769). *Birth* Benjamin Carr (d. 1831), arr. MADRID ("Come, Christians, join to sing"); Thomas Kelly (d. 1855), author "Look, ye saints! the sight is glorious," "The head that once was crowned with thorns" and others.

Death Christian F. Gellert (b. 1715), author orig. of "Jesus lives!"; James Merrick (b. 1720), author "Eternal God, we look to Thee," "The festal morn, O God, we come"; Gerhardt Tersteegen (b. 1697), author orig. of "God Himself is with us," "Lo, God is here, let us adore!" and others.

275 years (1719). *Birth* Thomas Cotterill (d. 1823), author "Hail the day that sees Him rise"; Ignaz Franz (d. 1790), author orig. "Holy God, we praise your name."

Death Joseph Addison (b. 1672), author "The spacious firmament on high," "When all Thy mercies, O my God."

300 years (1694). *Death* John Mason (b. 1645), author "How shall I sing that majesty" and others.

325 years (1669). *Birth* Jeremiah Clarke (d. 1707), composer ST. MAGNUS ("The head that once was crowned with thorns," "The Lord will come and not be slow" and others).

Death John Austin (b. 1613), author "Lord, now the time returns," "Hark my soul, how everything."

375 years (1619). *Birth* Tobias Clausnitzer (d. 1684), author orig. of "We all believe in one true God"; Johann Rosenmuller (d. 1684), composer WURTEMBERG ("Christ the Lord is risen again").

400 years (1594). *Birth* John Cosin (d. 1672), tr. "Come, Holy Ghost, our souls inspire"; Matthaus Apelles von Lowenstern (d. 1648), author orig. of "Lord of our life, and God of our salvation." *Death*

William Kethe (b. c. 1530), author "All people that on earth do dwell"; Giovanni P. da Palestrina (b. 1525), composer VICTORY ("The strife is o'er").

500 years (1494). *Death* Jean Tisserand (b. c. 1440), author orig. of "O sons and daughters, let us sing!"

Quotable Quotations

1. The mill cannot grind with water that's past.—George Herbert

2. God pursues us like a persistent mother searching for a lost child, like a compassionate baker seeking out the starving in order to give them bread, like a thoughtful clown looking for a hospital ward in which to make sad people laugh. We cannot get away from God.—Welton Gaddy

3. Your neighbor is the man who needs you.—Elbert Hubbard

4. He that demands mercy, and shows none, ruins the bridge over which he himself is to pass.—Thomas Adams

5. Life is the art of drawing sufficient conclusions from insufficient premises.—Samuel Butler

6. Wisdom entereth not into a malicious mind.—Rabelais

7. When sex and spirit are separated, sex either becomes superficial, casual, recreational, or a means of domination, intimidation, threat.—Richard Groves

8. This is the punishment of a liar: He is not believed, even when he speaks the truth.—Babylonian Talmud: Sanhedrin

9. Those who hate you don't win unless you hate them—and then you destroy yourself.—Richard Nixon

10. Evil is life turned backwards.—Peter Kreeft

11. Obedience means marching right on whether we feel like it or not. Many times we go against our feelings. Faith is one thing; feeling is another.—D. L. Moody

12. Man is a god in ruins.—Ralph Waldo Emerson

13. Experience is the comb that Nature gives us when we are bald.—Belgian proverb

14. Some people think that doctors and nurses can put scrambled eggs back into the shell.—Dorothy Canfield Fisher

15. There is nothing so bad but it can masquerade as moral.—Walter Lippmann

16. The earth will never know quiet and security and goodness except it stands right with its Maker, for he will upset every accursed happiness that is not based on his will.—Elizabeth Achtemeier

17. Destiny, n.: a tyrant's authority for crime and a fool's excuse for failure.—Ambrose Bierce

18. If we are not our brother's keep, let us at least not be his executioner.—Marlon Brando

19. Those who bring sunshine to the lives of others cannot keep it from themselves.—James M. Barrie

20. Habit is overcome by habit.—Thomas à Kempis

21. Abstinence is as easy to me as temperance would be difficult.—Samuel Johnson

22. Of all days, the day on which one has not laughed is surely the most wasted.—Sebastien Chamfort

23. We can stand affliction better than we can prosperity, for in prosperity we forget God.—D. L. Moody

24. Few people can be happy unless they hate some other person, nation, or creed.—Bertrand Russell

25. Character is always known. Thefts never enrich; alms never impoverish; murder will speak out of stone walls.—Ralph Waldo Emerson

26. Advice is a drug in the market; the supply always exceeds the demand.—Josh Billings

27. Death is not the greatest loss in life. The greatest loss is what dies inside us while we live.—Norman Cousins

28. Faith justifies the person, and works justify his faith.—Elisha Coles

29. Of all the countless people who have lived before our time on this planet,

not one is known in history or legend as having died of laughter.—Max Beerbolm

30. There is no such thing as a great talent without great will power.—Honoré de Balzac

31. Hating people is like burning your own house down to get rid of a rat.—Harry Emerson Fosdick

32. Marriage is an edifice that must be rebuilt every day.—André Maurois

33. I like the dreams of the future better than the history of the past.—Thomas Jefferson

34. In Hollywood all marriages are happy. It's trying to live together afterwards that causes problems.—Shelly Winters

35. Soldiers win battles but generals get the credit.—Napoleon

36. I thought when I became a Christian I had nothing to do but just to lay my oars in the bottom of the boat and float along. But I soon found that I would have to go against the current.—D. L. Moody

37. I don't know the key to success, but the key to failure is trying to please everybody.—Bill Cosby

38. I have never found anyone, however religious and devout, who did not sometimes experience withdrawal of grace, or feel a lessening of devotion.—Thomas à Kempis

39. Growth is the only evidence of life.—Cardinal Newman

40. Life is to be fortified by many friendships. To love, and to be loved, is the greatest happiness of existence.—Sydney Smith

41. Can there be a love which does not make demands on its object?—Confucius

42. Most men's anger against religion is as if two men should quarrel for a lady they neither of them care for.—Lord Halifax

43. God is an infinite circle whose center is everywhere and whose circumference is nowhere.—Augustine of Hippo

44. Love is what you've been through with somebody.—James Thurber

45. Rumor is a loud liar, like a snowball that gathereth as it goeth.—John Trapp

46. The religion of the atheist has a God-shaped blank at its heart.—H. G. Wells

47. If we ever stopped to look at it, we could see that we often use noble causes and even religious activities to shield us from the harder and more demanding task of helping those who are closest to us.—Mark Trotter

48. One of the signs of passing youth is the birth of a sense of fellowship with other human beings as we take our place among them.—Virginia Woolf

49. A man may be so much of everything that he is nothing of anything.—Samuel Johnson

50. We never know what ripples of healing we set in motion by simply smiling on one another.—Henry Drummond

51. A teacher affects eternity; he can never tell where his influence stops.—Henry Adams

52. There is little hope of children who are educated wickedly. If the dye have been in the wool, it is hard to get it out of the cloth.—Jeremiah Burroughs

53. The goal in marriage is not to think alike, but to think together.—Robert C. Dodds

54. The church must be reminded that it is not the master or the servant of the state, but rather the conscience of the state.—Martin Luther King, Jr.

55. The three great apostles of practical atheism that make converts without persecuting, and retain them without preaching, are health, wealth, and power.—Charles Caleb Colton

56. If you shut your door to all errors truth will be shut out.—Rabindranath Tagore

57. He who passively accepts evil is as much involved in it as he who helps to perpetrate it. He who accepts evil without protesting against it is really co-operating with it.—Martin Luther King, Jr.

58. Believe me, every man has his secret sorrows, which the world knows not; and oftentimes we call a man cold when he is only sad.—Longfellow

59. Injustice anywhere is a threat to justice everywhere.—Martin Luther King, Jr.

60. The most important thing a father can do for his children is to love their mother.—Theodore Hesburgh

61. I shall tell you a great secret, my friend. Do not wait for the last judgment, it takes place every day.—Albert Camus

62. The only people who seem to have nothing to do with the education of the children are the parents.—G. K. Chesterton

63. What mean and cruel things men do for the love of God.—W. Somerset Maugham

64. Humanitarianism consists in never sacrificing a human being for a purpose.—Albert Schweitzer

65. Human beings are perhaps never more frightening than when they are convinced beyond doubt that they are right.—Laurens Van Der Post

66. A comprehended God is no God at all.—Gerhard Tersteegen

67. God's story is probably better documented than that of all the history books, all the philosophy books, all the books of religious experience ever written.—John Killinger

68. There is no security on this earth; there is only opportunity.—General Douglas MacArthur

69. Success is that old A B C—ability, breaks and courage.—Charles Luckman

70. It is much easier to be critical than to be correct.—Benjamin Disraeli

71. Down in their hearts, wise men know this truth: the only way to help yourself is to help others.—Elbert Hubbard

72. Many people are working and working, like children on a rocking horse—it is a beautiful motion, but there is no progress.—D. L. Moody

73. A decent provision for the poor is the true test of civilization.—Samuel Johnson

74. Heaven goes by favor. If it went by merit, you would stay out and your dog would go in.—Mark Twain

75. The throne of glory never lacks for saints. It's this poor world that needs them! The cry goes out today, we need worldly saints! We need good and holy saints who believe in the world and who will move around in it with boldness and love.—W. Sibley Towner

76. Let me tell you the secret that has led me to my goal. My strength lies solely in my tenacity.—Louis Pasteur

77. They lose nothing who gain Christ.—Samuel Rutherford

78. Valour can do little without discretion.—John Ray

79. Life consists not simply in what heredity and environment do to us but in what we make out of what they do to us.—Harry Emerson Fosdick

80. Happiness in this world, when it comes, comes incidentally. Make it the object of pursuit, and it leads us a wild-goose chase, and is never attained.—Hawthorne

81. The Resurrection means that God is always a factor in our human situation, a God who intervenes and who will have the last word in life and the world.—A. Leonard Griffith

82. I thank God for my handicaps, for, through them, I have found myself, my work, and my God.—Helen Keller

83. Laws are not made for the good.—Socrates

84. A good deed never goes unpunished.—Gore Vidal

85. Money is a terrible master but an excellent servant.—P. T. Barnum

86. Fear God, and where you go men will think they walk in hallowed cathedrals.—Ralph Waldo Emerson

87. I have three chairs in my house: one for solitude, two for friendship, three for company.—Henry David Thoreau

88. Come hurricane, come earthquake, come freeway pileup, come old age, come death, come disease, the promise of God in Jesus Christ is the promise of God in the psalmist's song. God will preserve us from all evil. We shall live forever.—Ronald D. Sisk

89. Good theology is "poetry plus," rather than "science minus."—Krister Stendahl

90. Time makes more converts than reason.—Tom Paine

91. Many blush to confess their faults, who never blush to commit them.—William Secker

92. Grace is not a commodity to be hoarded or rationed. It is to be lavished upon any willing to receive it. We ought to celebrate wherever, whenever, and upon whomever it may be poured.—David R. Wilkinson

93. The world is equally shocked at hearing Christianity criticized and seeing it practiced.—D. Elton Trueblood

94. If a man cannot be a Christian where he is, he cannot be a Christian anywhere.—Henry Ward Beecher

95. You can make more friends in two months by becoming interested in other people than you can in two years by trying to get other people interested in you.—Dale Carnegie

96. No morality can be founded on authority, even if the authority were divine.—A. J. Ayer

97. Every war is a national calamity whether victorious or not.—General Von. Moltke

98. All truths are half-truths.—Alfred North Whitehead

99. God has two dwellings—one in heaven and the other in a thankful heart.—Izaak Walton

100. There is just one way to bring up a child in the way he should go, and that is to travel that way yourself.—Abraham Lincoln

Questions of Life and Religion

These questions may be useful to prime homiletic pumps, as discussion starters, or for study and youth groups.

1. Is the sense of "the absence of God" sometimes a part of the life of faith?

2. In what various ways does the Bible speak of "the Word of God"?

3. Is work a moral issue?

4. What are the necessary ingredients in sound decision-making?

5. How does faith mature?

6. Can we separate the physical and the spiritual, the secular and the sacred?

7. When are we assured of God's forgiveness?

8. How is our forgiveness of others related to God's forgiveness of us?

9. In what ways are church and state related, and in what respects should they be separate?

10. Is every Christian a minister?

11. Why do crucifixion and resurrection belong together?

12. When is it right to be angry?

13. How should we relate the Ten Commandments to the teaching "justification by faith alone"?

14. What does the Bible teach about suicide?

15. Can we reconcile human tragedy and God's providence?

16. Does doubt play a role in spiritual growth?

17. What can we cite as examples of modern idolatry?

18. How does God guide us?

19. What does Christian love (agape) say to envy and jealousy?

20. Why should Christians try to convert people from other faiths?

21. Is wealth opposed to God?

22. What is the kingdom of God?

23. Does the sacrifice of Jesus Christ free us from the obligation of sacrifice?

24. What are the guidelines for our financial stewardship?

25. Is the church an extension of the incarnation?

26. How is Christ's Second Coming related to his First Coming?

27. In what ways are the scriptures authoritative?

28. What will help us understand the Bible?

29. Under what circumstances, if any, should abortion be allowable?

30. What purposes were served by the miracles of the Bible?

31. How are we created in the image of God?

32. Is God in control of everything?

33. How can we explain the apparent injustice of God's ways?

34. When do children know God?

35. How can we fulfill our stewardship of the environment?

36. Does patience have its limits?

37. How much of our faith must we leave to the realm of mystery?

38. Do monastic disciplines suggest helpful models for our devotional life?

39. Is Christian hope more than wishful thinking?

40. What is special about *agape* love?

41. What support do the scriptures give to the equality of women?

42. Does prayer change things?

43. Is it always helpful to be honest?

44. What is eternal life?

45. What does it mean to be "in Christ"?

46. Is there salvation outside the church?

47. How can we know God?

48. What can we do to build community?

49. In what ways is Mary the mother of Jesus important in the church?

50. How does the Bible define sin?

51. Does the Trinity contradict the unity of God?

52. How does conversion happen?

53. When is divorce permissible?

54. How does the Bible describe heaven?

55. When is conscience a fallible guide?

56. When is a feeling of guilt appropriate?

57. Where can we place the blame for human suffering?

58. How should self-control rate as a Christian virtue?

59. Can temptation be avoided?

60. To what extent should the situation or context modify ethical behavior?

61. Is there justification for war?

62. Why is humility rated high as a Christian virtue and pride as the first of the Seven Deadly Sins?

63. What should be the attitude of Christians toward their Jewish neighbors?

64. What are the forms of addiction that harm individuals and society?

65. How is God revealed to us?

66. In what ways is the family a paradigm of the people of God?

67. How can the different words used by Christians for the Lord's Supper enrich our understanding of it?

68. In what sense is the Bible inspired?

69. Why does sex get so much attention?

70. How can we as believers unleash the power of blessing upon others?

71. Does God give to all and each a special vocation?

72. How important is tradition for our understanding of the "faith once delivered to the saints"?

73. Is capital punishment a deterrent to crime?

74. What is the biblical understanding of "peace"?

75. If obedience is a virtue whom or what should we obey?

76. Are creation and evolution compatible?

77. How is grace given and received?

78. What are the functions of the Holy Spirit?

79. How do we know truth?

80. How are knowledge and wisdom related in the Bible?

81. Could Jesus be both divine and human?

82. Can we explain evil?

83. In what ways does God enter the human grief process?

84. What contributions do the aged and the process of aging make to the Christian community?

85. How does a sinful human being become justified in the eyes of God?

86. What stages does a person go through when death is imminent?

87. How is repentance related to faith?

88. What is salvation in its several dimensions?

89. How can we "justify the ways of God to man"?

90. Can the "precious promises" in the Bible play a significant role in courageous living?

91. Can a career in politics fulfill a genuine Christian vocation?

92. What is the cure for worry?

93. Why is racism a sin?

94. Is baptism necessary?

95. What can be done to halt increasing contempt for marriage?

96. Is worship an indispensable factor in genuine religious experience?

97. How does the word *equal* apply to all human beings?
98. What is the basis of justice and liberation?

99. Is poverty a virtue?
100. Is confession essential to spiritual progress?

Biblical Benedictions and Blessings

The Lord watch between me and thee, when we are absent from one another.—Gen. 31:49.

The Lord bless thee, and keep thee; the Lord make his face to shine upon thee, and be gracious unto thee; the Lord lift up his countenance upon thee, and give thee peace.—Num. 6:24–26.

The Lord our God be with us, as he was with our fathers; let him not leave us, nor forsake us; that he may incline our hearts unto him, to walk in all his ways, and to keep his commandments, and his statutes, and his judgments, which he commanded our fathers.—1 Kings 8:57–58.

Let the words of my mouth, and the meditation of my heart, be acceptable in thy sight, O Lord, my strength, and my redeemer.—Ps. 19:14.

Now the God of patience and consolation grant you to be likeminded one toward another according to Christ Jesus; that ye may with one mind and one mouth glorify God, even the Father of our Lord Jesus Christ. Now the God of hope fill you with all joy and peace in believing, that ye may abound in hope, through the power of the Holy Ghost. Now the God of peace be with you.—Rom. 15:5–6, 13, 33.

Now to him that is of power to establish you according to my gospel and the preaching of Jesus Christ, according to the revelation of the mystery, which was kept secret since the world began, but now is manifest, and by the scriptures of the prophets, according to the commandment of the everlasting God, made known to all nations for the obedience of faith: to God only wise, be glory through Jesus Christ for ever.—Rom. 16:25–27.

Grace be unto you, and peace, from God our Father, and from the Lord Jesus Christ.—1 Cor. 1:3.

The grace of the Lord Jesus Christ and the love of God, and the communion of the Holy Ghost, be with you all.—2 Cor. 13:14.

Peace be to the brethren, and love with faith, from God the Father and the Lord Jesus Christ. Grace be with all them that love our Lord Jesus Christ in sincerity.—Eph. 6:23–24.

And the peace of God, which passeth all understanding, shall keep your hearts and minds through Christ Jesus. Finally, brethren, whatsoever things are true, whatsoever things are honest, whatsoever things are just; whatsoever things are pure, whatsoever things are lovely, whatsoever things are of good report; if there be any virtue, and if there be any praise, think on these things. Those things, which ye have both learned and received, and heard, and seen in me, do; and the God of peace shall be with you.—Phil. 4:7–9.

Wherefore also we pray always for you, that our God would count you worthy of this calling, and fulfill all the good pleasure of his goodness, and the work of faith with power; that the name of our Lord Jesus Christ may be glorified in you, and ye in him, according to the grace of our God and the Lord Jesus Christ.—2 Thess. 1:11–12.

Now the Lord of peace himself give you peace always by all means. The Lord be with you all. The grace of our Lord Jesus Christ be with you all.—2 Thess. 3:16–18.

Grace, mercy, and peace, from God our Father and Jesus Christ our Lord.—1 Tim. 1:2.

Now the God of peace, that brought again from the dead our Lord Jesus, that great shepherd of the sheep, through the blood of the everlasting covenant, make you perfect in every good work to do his will, working in you that which is well-pleasing in his sight, through Jesus Christ, to whom be glory for ever and ever.—Heb. 13:20–21.

The God of all grace, who hath called us unto his eternal glory by Christ Jesus, after that ye have suffered a while, make you perfect, establish, strengthen, settle you. To him be glory and dominion for ever and ever. Greet ye one another with a kiss of charity. Peace be with you all that are in Christ Jesus.—1 Pet. 5:10–11, 14.

Grace be with you, mercy, and peace, from God the Father, and from the Lord Jesus Christ, the Son of the Father, in truth and love.—2 John 3.

Now unto him that is able to keep you from falling, and to present you faultless before the presence of his glory with exceeding joy, to the only wise God our Savior, be glory and majesty, dominion and power, both now and ever.—Jude 24–25.

Grace be unto you, and peace, from him which was, and which is to come; and from the seven Spirits which are before his throne; and from Jesus Christ, who is the faithful witness, and the first begotten of the dead, and the prince of the kings of the earth. Unto him that loved us, and washed us from our sins in his own blood, and hath made us kings and priests unto God and his Father; to him be glory and dominion for ever and ever.—Rev. 1:4–6.

SECTION II.
Sermons and Homiletic and Worship Aids for Fifty-two Sundays

SUNDAY: JANUARY SECOND

SERVICE OF WORSHIP

Sermon: When God Moves In

TEXT: John 9:25; 21:24

Every religious conception was a throbbing experience long before it crystallized into a creed or a doctrine. So the Apostle John concludes his gospel by saying, "We speak whereof we know." The young man to whom Jesus restored his sight stood against his tormentors, stubbornly insisting: "Whether he be a sinner, I know not; one thing I know, that, whereas I was blind, now I see."

The entire New Testament revolves around this conviction, that when God comes in to our live something happens. This conviction moves with terrific acceleration: Men and women experience a new birth; they find a new and living way. God will make all things new. He who surrenders himself to God and his Christ will be a new creature. This is the mystery and the glory of the New Testament. Something happens in the lives of men when God takes hold upon them. He takes a Peter and leads him from indecision and half-heartedness to resolute living. He takes a Paul and changes his cold, defiant nature into something gentle and redeeming. He drives the conscience of a Zaccheus to the sticking point. He leads a Mary Magdalene from a life of sin and makes her a redeeming power in her community.

And perchance, some of us, remembering how God came into our lives, touched something within us, can say

humbly and sincerely: "One thing I know, that, whereas I was blind, now I see."

Well, what precisely does happen when God moves into our lives? Three things.

I. To begin with, we have reconciled to the contradictions in the person of God. These contradictions disturb us. At one time or another, we have found them stumbling blocks to a firmer faith. Thinking that we must come to his defense, we have at times endeavored to reconcile these contradictions, or said that they are only apparent and not real. But they are real!

(a) Have you ever looked deeply into the life of Jesus? What did you see there? No contradictions? Did he not say, "Suffer the little children to come unto me, for of such is the kingdom of heaven"? Did he not also say, "Who so shall offend one of these little ones which believe in me, it were better for him that a millstone were hanged about his neck, and he were drowned in the depth of the sea"? Is that no contradiction? Is there not love here, and hatred?

(b) We are troubled because we read that God is a God of comfort but also a God of anger. How can he be both? Of course, he is the God of comfort. But must we not also say that God is a God of anger? If he is not that, how can we believe in him? Shall we say there is no anger in the divine soul, and shall we say that this anger must not be reflected within our own souls? We look at those who degrade life, cheapen the sanctity of

18

marriage, lower our moral standards, and by their excesses, indecencies, and filth find their way onto the front pages of our newspapers, and we say, "When will somebody do something about that?" I must confess that I am not greatly concerned about when somebody will do this or that. What concerns me is when we will do something about it. When will we be done with our apathy? How can we say—how dare we say—we love our children and not let our wrath fall upon those who mock every decency? When God moves into our lives, we become reconciled to the great contradictions in him, for they are the mark of his divinity. He loves—truly he loves—but he hates that which destroys love.

II. In the second place, when God comes into our hearts, we come to a growing awareness that life must be a matter of sharp antagonisms.

(a) Of course, we do not want to hear this sort of thing. It is like a hair shirt on our conscience. We want our tempers soothed; we want our emotions quieted; we want to be told that our faith in God smooths out the ripples of life.

(b) The cheapest way to escape into moral indifference is to rationalize all life into tolerance, but there is no room for moral lameness in the Christian religion. There are no pastel shades in the Christian ethic. Here the distinctions are clear, acute, and cutting. It is this or that; it is one thing or the other. The difference is as sharp as black and white, as midnight and high noon. In matters of morals, the Christian cannot say, "It makes little difference"; nor can he say, "It depends upon circumstances."

(c) When God moves into our lives we become aware of moral absolutes: absolute right and absolute wrong, absolute decency and absolute indecency, absolute virtue and absolute sin. The great achievement in Christian faith is not to arrive at a place where there is no longer any moral conflict, but where we know where we will stand in the conflict.

III. The last thing we must say comes as an inevitable consequence. We ought to know that when God moves into our lives we will want to find his will for us.

(a) Surely, this is the will of God: in all things to live in the spirit of Christ. Any man and any woman may find that. More often than not, it is that we do not wish to know his will. We do not want to tear ourselves loose from our own desires. We have marked a road for ourselves, and that is the road we will want to take.

(b) But we must also know that this stubborn insistence leads nowhere except into the misery of a far country, and there is no loneliness or remorse greater than that which we experience when at long last we come to that. It is not enough to say, "I will live life as best I can." It is not enough to insist, "This is the decent thing to do." It is not enough to say, "This is what everyone else does." The question—at times the terrible question, always the searching question—is, "What is God's will for me in this instance?"

(c) Once you find the answer to your question and know what God's will is for you, it will have far-reaching implications. It will go beyond you to others, until you are persuaded that all of life must ultimately come under the judgment and the will of God. Isn't that the question we need to ask ourselves today? In the face of our world situation, we can no longer be complacent and say superficially that the problems which beset us are only political or economic. Once we know the will of God, we also know that these problems are deeper than that.

(d) The final question belongs in another category altogether. When God moves into our lives and something is to happen, will we let it happen? Will we yield ourselves? Will we submit ourselves? Will we be guided by his hand and led by his will? Or, as we have done before, will we shut the door?—Arnold H. Lowe

Illustrations

LIFE-UNIQUENESS.   In our efforts to listen to God's words to us, we often neglect what might be called his "first word" to us. This is the gift of ourselves to ourselves: our existence, our nature, our personal history, our uniqueness, our identity. All that we have, and indeed our very existence, is one of the unique and never-to-be-repeated ways God has chosen to express himself in space and time.—Mother Teresa, in *Leadership*

GREATNESS.   Perhaps some lives are marked by sharp contradictions because they are great. In fact, the greater a man the more obvious are the contradictions. The little man can be pigeonholed; the great man is not easily classified. It is the great man who has conflicting moods. It is the great man who is patient today and impatient tomorrow. It is the great man who works feverishly at one time and lazily at another time. It is the great man who makes enemies as readily as he makes friends. It is the great man who stirs some people to relentless opposition and others to sacrificial loyalty. It is the great man who has warm affections and at other times fatal antipathies. This probably is the reason why some say that it is so difficult to live with a great man and equally difficult to live without him.—Arnold H. Lowe

Sermon Suggestions

BECAUSE OF GOD'S CONSTANT LOVE. TEXT: Jer. 31:7–14. (1) God will reverse the ill fortunes of his people, verses 7–11. (2) His people will rejoice in his goodness, verses 11–14.

WHAT WE HAVE IN CHRIST.   TEXT: Eph. 1:3–14, especially verse 10. (1) Election. (2) Redemption. (3) Forgiveness. (4) An inheritance.

Worship Aids

CALL TO WORSHIP.   "The Lord is in his Holy Temple: let all the earth keep silence before Him" (Hab. 2:20).

INVOCATION.   We praise you, O God, for your mighty deeds for our salvation. Your mighty grace delivered the children of Israel from their bondage in Egypt and now in these last days you come in the person of your only Son, Jesus of Nazareth, declaring a grace in him suffi-

cient, yea, more than sufficient, to deliver us from the bondage of all our sin.

For Christ's gift of the Church to keep alive the story and to mediate the grace of your mighty deeds, we are indeed grateful. We praise you for the blessed fellowship of your Church in this time and place and the opportunities for worship, learning and ministry that it offers. Praise be to you—Father, Son and Holy Spirit.—John Thompson

OFFERTORY SENTENCE.   "This is the thing which the Lord commanded, saying, 'Take ye from among you an offering unto the Lord: whosoever is of a willing heart, let him bring it, an offering of the Lord'" (Exod. 35:4–5).

OFFERTORY PRAYER.   We know, Lord God, that your perception exceeds our keenest vision; that telescopes and microscopes, though they be the products of our finest achievement and technology, seem unimportant and insignificant when we pause to consider the ways in which you can look into the human heart—or behold the vastness of your creation. Look, we pray, into our own hearts—those places and recesses of our being where we form our values and set our priorities. Prevent us from measuring the quality of life by the quantity of our possessions, and help us to keep our perspective, lest in gaining this whole world, we lose your love.—Robert F. Langwig

PRAYER.   Our eyes have seen the glory of your coming!

That you are the God who comes with light and life—that you are turned toward us in the eternity of your love—that you have identified with us in the flesh and blood of our common humanity—that you are here in the light of your presence in these moments and in every moment in the greatest way you can be—that your Spirit which is holy—whole, complete, lacking nothing—is present in our minds and hearts and persons quickening and renewing life. We praise you: Father, Son, and Holy Spirit.

We praise you for the new birth of freedom that has touched the lives of so many in this great season and pray for direction that their longings and yearnings and aspirations for a new life may be fulfilled.

That our coming and our going—our birthing and our dying; that our successes and our failures—our joys and our sorrows are embraced in the loving intimacy of this community of faith, we are grateful. To include in the embrace of your love we reach out to those who, in the weakness of mind, of body, or of spirit need the ministry of your grace to make whole. In all the relationships of each day grant to us the faith, the courage, the love to follow him who was the man for others, and so teaches us to pray:

O you who sent your only son among us that the Word become flesh, bless with your favor and encouragement us in our high calling to "flesh out" your love in our time and our place.

When the song of the angels is still,
When the star in the sky is gone,
When the kings and princes are home,
When the shepherds are back with
   their sheep,
The work of Christmas begins:
To find the lost,
To heal the broken,
To feed the hungry,
To release the prisoner,
To rebuild the nations,
To bring peace among all peoples
To make music in the heart.

We pray through him who is our faith, our hope, our joy, our peace and teaches us to pray together: "Our Father . . . ."—John Thompson

LECTIONARY MESSAGE

Topic: The Word, Eternal Among Us

TEXT: John 1:1–9, 10–18

Poetry is beautiful indeed. And when the poet can also offer a commentary on his poetry and thus bring more meaning to the verse, its beauty is only enhanced. That is exactly what John, the poet and author of the Fourth Gospel, does for us. He weaves in a powerful commentary between lines of verse that illuminates our thinking.

These verses attempt to define the essential character of the Divine Word whom we know as Jesus. John shows us that he is eternal, personal, and divine. But John also comments on the role of the witness who points others to the Word.

I. The Word is eternal (verse 2). The Rock of Gibraltar, long a symbol of permanence, endurance, and an anchor against life's shifting sands, had a beginning, at creation. And it will have an end one day when time is no more. Not so, says John, of the eternal Word. None other was with God in the beginning, except the Word, Jesus.

The Word did not come into beginning but has always been in fellowship with the Father. Thus the emphasis in verse one on was rather than became. For people who need something to hold on to, to anchor them in this life, John gives the answer. The divine Word has always been and will always be. This Word is eternal light and life that has always shone and will continue to shine long after the mountains fall into the sea.

II. The Word requires a witness (verse 6). One of the greatest privileges a person has is to show another the way back when he is turned around, confused, and lost. God's gifts to his children include the opportunity to show others the way.

Christian witnessing takes on a simpler definition as one points others to Jesus, the divine Word. In our zeal we often make witnessing complicated. Some reluctantly witness because they see it as only a duty; something they are commanded to do; as a difficult task. But for John it was opportunity, opportunity to point others in the right direction who would open their hearts and willingly receive him. Witnessing becomes the telling of a story of who he is and what he has done in our lives.

III. The Word dwells with us (verse 14). An old saying admonishes us to never criticize a person until we have walked a mile in his shoes. It is difficult to know people from afar. We have to get close to them to know really who they are. We learn even more about someone when we live with them. The sound of their voice, the look in their eyes, and their manner of life, tells us much about them.

The eternal Word has chosen to pitch his tent with us, to walk before us, to demonstrate the Father's love to us, and to help us know the grace of God in our lives. John juxtaposes the law of Moses and grace in Jesus. This grace in Jesus compounds itself in love. The law reminds us of cold legalism, of separateness, of distance. But grace points us to warmth, acceptance, and nearness. And the grace of God that dwells among his people is not temporary. His dwelling does not end but continues through the Spirit who walks daily with those who have been redeemed. These three characteristics make it clear to those who see Jesus that they have also seen God.—Ronald W. Johnson

SUNDAY: JANUARY NINTH

SERVICE OF WORSHIP

Sermon: Star Over Bedlam

Texts: Isa. 60:1, 3; 49:1, 12–13; Zech. 2:10–11

I. I have come to this particular study from my twenty-first overseas preaching mission and the vision of the coastlands and far places looking to God as their hope is especially vivid to me just now. The dimensions of Epiphany are the dimensions of the Christian faith, revealing the world-wide love of the God whose coming in Christ is the foundation of hope for every people. Epiphany charges us with letting all men know they are included in the love of God—"to make all men see what is the plan of the mystery hidden for ages in God" (Eph. 3:9). "All men," whether near or far, whether affluent or indigent, of whatever race or color, have the right to know that God so loved the world that he gave his only Son. Here is the dynamic for evangelistic witness, social compassion, missionary outreach, and the happy worship of praise.

Matthew 2:1–12 is the basic Epiphany story that is the keynote of the Sundays in January and February. January 6 is the traditional day of the Epiphany, the showing forth of the infant Jesus to the Wise Men, who represent the Gentile world. We thrill to the story of that star of hope, bringing the Wise Men from afar. It is the logical outcome of Christmas that, since God has given good tidings of great joy for all people, then all people should know the good news of the birth of a Saviour.

II. The star of hope could well be described as "Star Over Bedlam," for our needy world is such a scene of mad confusion. "Bedlam" is the name of a hospital in England for the mentally deranged, but it is also a variation of "Bethlehem." The star shone over Bedlam to reveal how God's love meets man's need.

The story of the Wise Men begins in the middle and we find them, after an arduous journey, at Jerusalem. What could be worse? For Jerusalem was the city of Herod the Great, as villainous a king as ever ruled. This infamous man was both clever and cruel. He was known as a great builder, and indeed he built a temple in Jerusalem far greater than Solomon's Temple. Yet he trusted no one, murdered his own family, betrayed his friends, and ordered the Massacre of the Innocents. This was the man into whose presence the foreigners came, innocently inquiring, "Where is he who has been born king of the Jews?" To Herod this meant a threat to his rule and immediately his crafty mind went to work, to be confounded at last only by the grace of God.

III. For God put the star in the sky, and God is able to take care of his own, who like the Wise Men, venture forward in faith. So the star over Bedlam became the Star over Bethlehem. The story of faith being rewarded and evil being caught in its own cleverness is not only stranger than fiction, but also truer to life than we sometimes think. For the Wise Men did get the needed information that guided them to Jesus, and faith had its reward.

For these were men of faith. They did not ask *if* a king had been born, but "*where* is he?" In such simple faith, they had followed the star of hope, not knowing where they were going. We, too, may not know *what* life's meaning is, but we can have faith *that* it is, and when God puts a star in our sky, we dare to venture forward.

It isn't far to Bethlehem, from Jerusalem about six miles. But could this be journey's end—a hillside cave and a newborn babe? As I stood in front of a cave in Bethlehem and meditated on the Epiphany story, I marvelled at the faith that could see God's eternal purpose for all the world in so humble a scene. If the Wise Men were disappointed, there is no hint of it in the Bible story. To paraphrase Julius Caesar, "They came, they saw, they were conquered." They worshipped the Babe of Bethlehem. They placed before him gifts of love. They were able to recognize in small things the mighty workings of God.

IV. But the danger was not yet past, for they had been ordered to return to report to Herod. But God spoke to them in a dream, warning them to return home another way. What courage! For they risked their lives by defying Herod the king. They took that chance without hesitation, men of faith, insight and courage, guided of God.

Yet these were but heathen, not God's chosen people, but outsiders and Gentiles. They had not had the benefit of the great religious heritage of God's people. But how beautifully their lives, their spirit, their faith, their courage shine in this wonderful story. They followed the star in the sky, because there was a star in their hearts. There is hope in every Bedlam because God has given a light to every man who comes into this world. There is no place from which wise men cannot make their way to Jesus Christ!

This is the good news Epiphany proclaims to all, that every man can follow the star to Christ and at journey's end, find a glory in the light of which he can live joyously forever after.

The star still shines. If we follow its light, it will lead us to the Saviour. So God will give us our own Epiphany, and we shall want to make known God's saving love to all men everywhere.—Lowell M. Atkinson

Illustrations

NEW LIFE. It is said that when Starr Daily was 16, his ambition was to establish a reputation as a dangerous criminal. After his first arrest, he spent 14 years in penal farms, chain gangs, and penitentiaries. In his last imprisonment he was condemned to solitary confinement in "the hole" for plotting an escape using a warden as a hostage.

For 14 days he survived the agony of "the hole," filled with hate toward those who put him there. Finally he lapsed into a state of delirium and disconnected dreams. Then the dreams began to take on shape. He was in a garden and Jesus Christ was coming toward him. With piercing eyes the Lord stood face to face with Daily. This resulted in the conversion of Daily and the beginning of a new life of service to many.—John C. Howell

WITH YOU IN TROUBLE. C. Roy Angell, one of Southern Baptists' greatest storytellers, described an experience of Richard H. Hutton while Hutton and a companion were traveling through Scotland on foot and bicycle. An innkeeper told them that Lake Lochy, the most beautiful lake in Scotland, was only four miles away on a circular pathway. When asked if there was a shorter way, he said there was, but it was called "The Dark Mile" and nobody ever traveled it by choice.

The two decided to do so and found it to be a treacherous and difficult trail. But suddenly at the very bottom, they saw the stars above them in the broad daylight. They remembered the old adage, "when it is dark enough, you can see the stars."

When the beauty of Lake Lochy finally burst upon their sight, they agreed that they would never have appreciated the beauty of the lake if they had not traveled the Dark Mile. So the promise of God's presence encourages us as we travel our dark miles.—John C. Howell

Sermon Suggestions

"ARISE, SHINE!"   TEXT: Isa. 60:1–6, especially verse 1. (1) It is God's will that his people collectively and individually reflect his glory. Cf. Matt. 5:16. (2) Many things make this difficult: a. sin; b. injustice; c. possible discouragement in waiting. See chapter 59. (3) When God's time for action arrives, the "impossible" can become reality.

THE BOUNDLESS RICHES OF CHRIST. TEXT: Eph. 3:1–12. (1) The news came by revelation. (2) The news came to the Gentiles. (3) The news brought and brings to all access to God "in boldness and confidence" through faith in Christ.

Worship Aids

CALL TO WORSHIP.   "From the rising of the sun to its setting my name is great among the nations" (Mal. 1:11 RSV).

INVOCATION.   Lord, may what we do here affect all else we do, so that the world becomes a better place because of our worship. In Christ's name, we pray.—E. Lee Phillips

OFFERTORY SENTENCE.   "Give unto the Lord the glory due unto his name: bring an offering, and come before him: worship the Lord in the beauty of holiness" (1 Chron. 16:29).

OFFERTORY PRAYER.   Lord, we might have kept some of this offering, but we know of no better use for it. Reach with its light where we had not thought to reach that the light of Christ may shine all the more brightly.

PRAYER.   That you are the God who calls men and women, youth, boys and girls to serve through your church in every generation, we praise you. May we hear your call in this time and place and respond according to our opportunity.

We are grateful for the sense of mission that pervades our life as a congregation: challenges to be not only disciples, those who come to learn, but to be apostles, those sent into all the world and all the world of people—for that great army of missionaries who in this day and in previous generations have lovingly and faithfully obeyed your marching orders.

For every intimation that the Church exists by mission as fire exists by burning, may we be grateful. Without that sense of mission to which you are calling us in Christ, we may be a cozy enclave of like-minded people but not your church—you who so love the world that you give your only Son.

Deliver us, O God, from any parochialism, denominationalism, nationalism, racism, party spirit that denies you as Father of us all and betrays our calling to be brothers and sisters to one another. For those who lead us, and those who aspire to lead us, we pray for the vision of your Kingdom that embraces all people as your children. Save us from the subterfuge, intrigue, deceit that can destroy us, for "except the Lord build the house they labor in vain who build it, except the Lord keep the city, or the nation, the watchman wakes but in vain."

We pray, O Father, not only for this household of faith and all members of its family, broken and whole, weak and strong, young and old—but for the Church universal, the Body of Christ to be given for the life of the world as Christ gave and is giving himself.

Make us loving, make us strong, make us faithful for this high calling through him who as your eternal Word is among us.—John Thompson

LECTIONARY MESSAGE

Topic: The Purpose and Power of Prophecy

TEXT: Matthew 2:1–12

The events described in our text are a remarkable demonstration of the fulfillment of all of God's prophecies concerning his relation to his people, and of all his prophetic presence in the world.

The purpose of prophecy is the guidance and protection of God's people, in order to bring to pass the eventual blessing of all the world through God's son. In this passage we see the realization of several lines of Old Testament prophecies, which may be fulfilled in our lives today as well.

I. The coming of the Messiah was foretold in many forms from the very beginning of God's revelation, as in Genesis 3:15, to which Paul refers in Romans 16:20. Many Messianic prophecies are well known, and all come together here: Genesis 49:10, pertaining to the time of fulfillment for the tribe of Judah, whose purpose was to maintain a special witness until the tribe could transfer its leadership into the hands of the ideal ruler; although Judah kept its own government, as witnessed by the calling to Bethlehem for taxation/enrollment of the holy family, it did not survive as an entity after the resurrection of Jesus.

The prophecy of Numbers 24:17, ". . . There shall come a star out of Jacob, and a scepter shall rise out of Israel," refers not to a sidereal event but to the birth of the true "star" of God, Jesus Christ. The expectation that a great ruler would appear in Israel was well known worldwide, and his coming was marked by a sidereal star.

Psalm 72:10 and 2 Chronicles 9:23, 24 speak of a tribute even larger than that brought to King Solomon, so that we may take the coming of the Magi as its true fulfillment. Isaiah 40 in its entirety describes the coming, the work, and the blessings of Christ as the Holy One of Israel.

II. One aspect of the guiding purpose of prophecy is seen in the direction of the Magi as they sought to find the One who had come. They had a purpose of heart whose origin no one can certainly ascertain, and they were given their direction by a distinct physical manifestation, a sidereal event which occurred once in all time. They reported seeing it at its rising in the east, and following it to the city where other definite guidance could be given them. God's prophecy was their evidence that God was leading them.

Even a secular (not to say profane) ruler such as Herod the King knew that there was a storehouse of prophecy preserved by the peculiar people of God. When Herod summoned the chief priests and scribes, they cited a small prophetic book, not very important except that it had God's truth for his people at the right time. They found in Micah 5:2 the prophecy of a place, the name of a small, obscure town, Bethlehem of Judea, which was to be raised into eternal prominence as the birthplace of the King of all the ages, "whose goings forth have been from of old, from eternity."

III. The protection of God has always been afforded to his people in his word. He protected the royal worshipers by warning them in a dream that Herod had evil plans, and they went by a different route to their own country. God's power extended through this form of guidance also, to thwart the evil designs of those who would usurp his place in the world.

We cannot see each particular occurrence or event of history as an isolated instance. This passage, this account of the tribute brought to Jesus by non-Israelite wise men, or kings as tradition has it, is a particular link forged into a chain binding all humanity to the purposes of God. It is another evidence that the truth of God is not hidden, but that seekers in any part of the world could learn God's truths, whether from people of Israel living there, or by other acquaintance with his manifold revelation. We cannot doubt that if we seek Jesus still, God will reveal our most blessed direction to us, and give us the protection we need. —John R. Rodman

SUNDAY: JANUARY SIXTEENTH

SERVICE OF WORSHIP

Sermon: The Depth That Is in Christ

TEXT: John 1:1–18

One of the most interesting things about our use of words is the way we often use the same word to mean quite different things.

If you speak about the depth of the sea, you are talking about a distance in space that can be measured. But if you say of a portrait, "That portrait has depth," you are not talking about space or distance; you are saying that the artist has caught the quality of that particular person's inner life and revealed it in a way no candid camera ever could. The portrait, in other words, has depth.

Speaking of portraits brings us a little closer to the subject of this chapter. The artists, if we may refer to them as such, were Matthew, Mark, Luke, and John. Each artist painted the same figure, and the figure is always unmistakably the same in each of the four portraits, but each one approached that figure from a peculiar, personal angle of vision.

John caught something that the others appreciated but not with the same intensity. He caught the more elusive quality that we have called depth. His is a portrait of the same figure, with all the power, authority, and compassion of the others, but his portrait has a depth that the others do not have.

That is what I should like you to look at now, and with these two things especially in mind. As you look at this portrait, you may appreciate more than you have before the unique contribution of St. John to our knowledge of Christ, and also, as you look at it, you yourself may perceive more clearly and enter more fully than you have before into the depth that is in Christ Jesus.

I. You do not appreciate the depth of anything the first time you see it. You have to live with it. This is true of a place. A tourist in Boston sees the city and gets a rough impression of what it is like. But he does not grasp the depth of Boston, he does not know what Boston is really like, not in one visit. You have to live in it for that.

(a) If that is true of a place, it is certainly far more true of a person. The first time you meet a person you see a great deal. You see what he looks like; you get a general impression of the kind of person he is. But you do not get the depth of a person simply by seeing him once. You have to live with him, be near him, over a long period of time, before you appreciate his real quality.

(b) St. John the Evangelist caught the depth of Christ because he had lived with him so long. The picture that John gives us of Christ could only be drawn by someone who not only lived with him as a companion, walking with him over the dusty roads of Judaea, but who in some way lived in him the way a man's body lives in the air. So John lived in Christ decade after decade. He walked in his light through all the dark ways of his own personal existence. What he wrote, therefore, was the fruit of this lifelong association.

(c) You will never appreciate the depth of Christ on any casual acquaintance. To do that you must live with him, think about him, do your work—whatever it is—for his sake; try to be more and more like him even though you realize that you can never come anywhere near him, but try, nevertheless, to be more and more like him in your character and in your nature, in your sensitiveness to the needs of men and your willingness to try to meet them.

II. When you once see the depth of anything, you are almost bound to describe it in symbolic language, simply because there is no other language available.

This is essentially what John did in his portrait of Christ. The others told the facts, and perhaps told them more accurately and in more perfect chronological order than he did. The others called Jesus the Messiah, which was a good, familiar Hebrew title, coming right up out of the land and soil. It was the name of the person who would deliver the nation from the enemy. John kept it, but he went further than that.

(a) He said that Jesus is the Bread of Life. His life is to a man's soul what bread is to a man's body. He is not one of the luxuries of life; he is one of the necessities. Without him, without his life and love, your life will wither away. Jesus is the Light of the World, not like the light of the sun which as it rises puts to flight the darkness; he is more like a searchlight that sends a shaft of light through the darkness, driving it back farther and farther on either side so you can find your way through the night. John knew that because he had walked in that light.

(b) Jesus, John said, is the Fountain of living water. He is not one of the wells that run dry. There is in him inexhaustible energy and sustenance for the people who come to him to drink of the living water of life. He is the Resurrection and the Life. He can raise people from the dead. He can take a life that is withering away and bring it back so that it flowers again. He is the Way, the Truth, and the Life.

(c) John did not stop there. He went on to say that Jesus is the Good Shepherd. He is the Love of God looking for you, searching for you because he cares for you, wanting to draw you back into his flock, not against your will but because you wish to come home. He is the Vine; we are the branches. He is the life and if we are cut off from him, we are lifeless. He is in the Father and the Father is in him; he and the Father are one.

III. Do you see how the depth is growing? You may be beyond your depth at this point, but follow me. The climax he reached in the beginning, in the very first chapter of his Gospel, when he said, Jesus, the local carpenter of Nazareth who died on Calvary, is the Word of God—the express purpose, intention, and will of God—made flesh. You cannot go much deeper than that.

(a) John then took the facts about Jesus and used them to fill out and give flesh to these great themes; he rearranged them to suit his purpose, included what would amplify it and left out what would not. As you read his Gospel, you begin to get a glimpse of the depth that one man found in Christ.

(b) Then with this portrait in your hands, you can go your way, trying to live with Jesus so that more and more, every day of your life, you will be able to say, "He and the Father are one, and through him and in him I see God; he is God; apart from him I can do nothing."—Theodore Parker Ferris

Illustrations

GOD—THE "THOU." In so far as I understand my faith not only as assent, or as subjective emotion, but as life in decision and responsibility (which means life in personal terms) I must always reckon with God as personal: in this situation God has always become for me the "thou" by whom I stand confronted. And it must be understood that this is not primarily a theological notion, it is the wholly original, existential self-understanding of the life of faith. Faith, seen as existence in decision and responsibility, contains implicitly the "thou" of the Other who stands over against it.—Heinrich Ott

GOING FAR ENOUGH. People, both young and old, constantly say to me, I can't understand the divinity of Christ, and I don't really believe it. My suggestion to them is that they change their approach. Instead of beginning with a proposition about the nature of Christ, begin with John's Gospel and try to see the depth that is in Christ. If they go far enough, they will come to the depth which is the ground of all being, namely, God.—Theodore Parker Ferris

Sermon Suggestions

HOW TO HEAR GOD SPEAK. TEXT: 1 Sam. 3:1–10 (11–20). (1) Samuel was in God's house. (2) Samuel heeded (finally) the counsel of a servant of God. (3) Samuel went directly to God in submission.

FREE—FOR WHAT? TEXT: 1 Cor. 6:12–20. (1) Not to become a slave to anything. (2) Not to bring the name of Christ into disrepute. (3) But to glorify God in your body.

Worship Aids

CALL TO WORSHIP.   "I was glad when they said unto me, Let us go into the house of the Lord" (Ps. 122:1).

INVOCATION.   Thank you, God, for the church, and for the genuine needs that come to it, most of them unspoken, some of the deepest from people we never see. Deliver us from busyness and vanity, and from fear of censure and of change. Center us down in the very few things that matter, and teach us to live for others, that our life together may be purposeful, simple, and may be acceptable in your sight.—Peter Fribley

OFFERTORY SENTENCE.   "And he said to them all, If any man will come after me, let him deny himself, and take up his cross daily, and follow me" (Luke 9:23).

OFFERTORY PRAYER.   Lord, give us joy in our giving that we may be cheered by the spread of the gospel and the possible nurture of many in the faith that abides forever.—E. Lee Phillips

PRAYER.   O God, we beseech thee to save us this day from the distractions of vanity and the false lure of inordinate desires. Grant us the grace of a quiet and humble mind, and may we learn of Jesus to be meek and lowly of heart. May we not join the throng of those who seek after things that never satisfy and who draw others after them in the fever of covetousness. Save us from adding our influence to the drag of temptation. If the fierce tide of greed beats against the breakwaters of our soul, may we rest at peace in thy higher contentment. In the press of life may we pass from duty to duty in tranquillity of heart and spread thy quietness to all who come near.—Walter Rauschenbusch

LECTIONARY MESSAGE

Topic: God's Final Revelation
TEXT: John 1:43–51
God is one who reveals himself. His person and his purpose are beyond the ken of human beings. From the beginning of his conversation with Adam and Eve in the garden, the Bible tells the story of God's revelation. Jesus, like his Father, was intent on revealing himself. At the beginning of his ministry he called for helpers who would share that revelation with him and with others. Already, before our scripture reading begins, he had called Andrew and another disciple and Simon Peter. They were to grow in their perception of God's revelation.

I. Son of Joseph. He called Philip and, as is his intention, saw Philip call another to follow. Philip's witness to Jesus was simple: we have found him of whom Moses and the prophets wrote, Jesus of Nazareth, son of Joseph. Andrew had found Simon, his brother. Philip found Nathaniel, his friend. Perhaps all claimed Capernaum as their home.

Here is Philip's conception of God's final revelation. He was foretold by Moses: God will raise up a prophet like myself. He was promised by the prophets: Isaiah and Micah. What could Philip say about Jesus? He was from Nazareth. The place of one's home helps to identify him. But not for Philip! He, along with many Galileans, despised Nazareth: "Can anything good come out of Nazareth?" It still isn't very much, but it has outlived Capernaum!

Perhaps Philip realized that the Nazareth origin did not impress Nathaniel. He added another descriptive phrase: He's the son of Joseph. Perhaps Nathaniel knew Joseph of Nazareth. He made no disparaging remark. But for us—who is Joseph? There must have been many bearing that name.

II. Son of God. Philip persisted, much as Jesus himself had spoken in John 1:39. You must taste the revelation, you must will to see it, before its fullness comes. Now, from doubtful cynicism concerning the place of origin, Nathaniel moves toward curiosity. Jesus began to reveal himself in his declaration describing Nathaniel as "an Israelite in whom is no guile." Nathaniel betrayed something of his ego in his response, How did you know me? Jesus played along, I saw you before Philip called you. It was enough for

Nathaniel—you are the Son of God. How much he perceived at that time we do not know, but it was quite a confession. Perhaps even more striking was his statement, you are King of Israel. This identified him with the nation in all its weakness and perils. It was all that Philip could manage.

III. Son of Man. "So Jesus answered . . ." He continued the progressive revelation as Nathaniel was able to understand it, and more. Beyond human testimony offered by Philip and the extent of Nathaniel's confession, Jesus spoke. Beyond mystifying experience suggested by Jesus' recognition of Nathaniel, Jesus spoke. "You will see greater things than these." This vision will become a part of yourself.

You will share in a vision like that of Jacob at Bethel. God will continually reveal himself to you in your relationship to me. The angels of God will ascend and descend upon the Son of Man—down where Nathaniel lived—and Philip . . . "Son of Man."

In him is the Amen to all the promises of God (2 Cor. 1:20). At the end of a long series of revelations, God at the end of these days spoke in his Son. Here is God's truth incarnate. Here is God's grace incarnate. Here is God's power incarnate. Son of Joseph . . . Son of God . . . Son of man.—J. Estill Jones

SUNDAY: JANUARY TWENTY-THIRD

SERVICE OF WORSHIP

Sermon: The Healing of Old Wounds

TEXT: John 5:1–9

"Time heals all wounds," they say. "Time heals all wounds." I've heard it all my life as you have, but it isn't so. Time does *not* heal all wounds. More than time is needed to heal many of our wounds.

I suspect that there are those of us here today who need to have old wounds healed; we need to have old wounds of the spirit healed. Those old wounds down deep inside still hurt when they are touched, still cause us pain, continually remind us that we are not whole.

How do we cope when our spirits are sore? How *can* we cope when that dimension of who we are—which is not only our essence, but also our source of energy and strength—is long-wounded and will not heal? Well, Jesus heals those kinds of wounds if we want to be well. Isn't that the point of the healing miracle which Jesus performed at the pool of Bethzatha?

I. Of course, that poor old guy at the pool had been sick for thirty-eight years, and his illness was of the physical variety—not a wounded spirit, we think as we read quickly through the story. So, those of us with old emotional wounds don't have much to learn from this story—right? Not so fast!

(a) The man had been ill for thirty-eight years. For many of those years, he had been brought to his pool beside the Sheep Gate—on the northern side of the Jerusalem Temple—where he, with so many others, waited to be healed. Though he had those who helped transport him put him close to the edge of the pool, he had never been the first one in after the angelic stirring of the waters. But he still came there with regularity hoping to be healed, hoping that someone would help him in or even push him in if need be—first thing.

(b) He was known as an invalid—and an astoundingly unlucky one at that. Can you detect any emotional wounds by looking at his face? Look more closely. The evidence is there. The truth is that the physical impairment wasn't nearly so crippling after all these years as his emotional wounds—his sense of helplessness; his feelings of abandonment, worthlessness, shame. Remember also that he had been taught to believe that all infirmity was God's doing; just think how well you would be able to regard yourself if you were inclined to believe that Almighty God had it in for you.

II. This man whose name we never know has all kinds of wounds—all kinds of wounds, thirty-eight-year-old wounds, inside and out; and Jesus walks up to him and asks, "Do you want to be made well?"

(a) "Do you want to be made well?" Jesus asks again, which—at first—seems about as useless a question as when somebody asks the proprietor of a clock shop if she knows the time. But the question was not for Jesus' information; it was for the sick man. Jesus could not be certain that the man had considered it, but he had to consider this question if he seriously wanted to be well. Jesus knew, you see, that old wounds are tender to touch, and sometimes we'd rather pretend to be all well, denying our infirmities, than to have them handled—even by a healer.

(b) The invalid answered, but not the question Jesus asked. He responded by explaining his plight which, as with many of us, is a rationalization for why we have not sought healing for ourselves, and that often means finding someone else to blame. "Mister," the man said to Jesus, "I don't have anybody to get me into the pool after the angel stirs up the water. Somebody else always beats me there. Only the first one in is healed, you know."

(c) Jesus asks us if we want to be made well, and we may miss the chance for wholeness by trying to shield ourselves from his concern, from his loving acceptance of us that feels almost unbearable to souls not warmed by love, not even a memory of love.

III. Coming to church for worship may be like a Bethzatha for some of us. We come here just as we are, and for many of us, that means with our wounds. Sometimes, these wounds are in the forefront; they are the basis on which we relate to others. We are more comfortable with than we are without our old wounds so we come here, sometimes halfheartedly hoping for a kind of healing.

(a) Some of us have found the healing we seek; others of us have not. We've never been healed. Never! We've been coming here for years—faithfully, too.

And there are still those old wounds deep down inside us which have not been healed. We haven't given up all hope—no, not all hope; but we've become at least a little skeptical about the honest prospects for healing.

(b) We watch as others seem to benefit from angelic stirrings in worship on the other side of the sanctuary or down front where Baptists fear to tread or sit; there are those who seem actually to move toward wholeness, and we are envious of them. We wonder when and if we will ever be able to connect somehow with the invisible presence of the Divine.

IV. To the invalid at Bethzatha, Jesus said: "'Stand up, take your mat and walk.' And at once the man was made well, and he took his mat and began to walk." This is powerful stuff!

(a) Jesus doesn't ignore our pain though he may have little patience with our excuses—especially when we become more preoccupied with our limitations than we are with him. After thirty-eight years of feeling helpless and dependent, embarrassed and abused, worthless and frustrated, the man—in a moment's time—stood up and walked away from Bethzatha. His physical malady was cured, and—no doubt—the wounds of his soul even began to heal that day.

(b) This incidence of healing was not simply a matter of making the man believe that he could be better—though that was a part of the dynamic of his healing in this situation. His healing came about because, at some level, he obviously wanted to be well and because of the power of Jesus' words spoken forth forcefully and yet in love.

(c) We can know wholeness we had thought almost inconceivable for us. The key is this: begin by believing that the healing of your old wounds is possible—even the touchy, painful ones you can't ever remember not having with you. You have to believe that healing for yourself is possible. Beyond that, listen for the voice of Jesus speaking to you. In the love of Jesus Christ, our Lord, and the power of his word, even old wounds can be healed. In fact, they are being healed right now.—David Albert Farmer

Illustrations

FRESH WOUNDS. Fresh wounds—treated with some sense of immediacy—have a much better chance of healing properly than do wounds that go unattended. That's why my great-grandmother used to rush for the Clorox™ and the baking soda when my sister or I stepped on a bumblebee hidden in thick clumps of clover. That's why emergency room nurses and doctors and physicians' assistants get, as soon as possible, to the business of irrigating a wound. Wounds that aren't cleaned and dressed suitably tend to fester and become infected. And haven't you heard of orthopedic physicians re-breaking bones once broken in order to reset them properly? Old wounds are harder to heal than new ones.—David Albert Farmer

COUNTERPRODUCTIVE ANGER. I somewhat identify with an experience related by my friend Barry Bailey. A man driving home late one night took a shortcut and had a flat tire. At 1:00 in the morning, he discovered that his jack did not work. Looking down the strange road, he saw a dark farmhouse. He hated to awaken the people who lived there, but maybe they owned a jack. The man started walking toward the house. As he stepped along through the night, his mind took over. These were his thoughts: "I'm probably going to make that man mad by knocking on his door at this late hour. Likely, I will awaken him from his sleep. Even if he does own a jack, probably he will be so furious with me that he will not let me use it." He reached the farmhouse and knocked on the door. When the farmer opened the door to meet him, the motorist shouted in his face: "Keep your old jack!"—Welton Gaddy

Sermon Suggestions

THE SECOND CHANCE. TEXT: Jonah 3:1–5, 10. (1) Jonah's second chance. (2) Nineveh's second chance.

DRASTIC DECISIONS. TEXT: 1 Cor. 7:29–31, especially verse 31b. Because the present world is not our permanent home: (1) In ordinary times, our daily attitude and conduct will be different. (2) In extraordinary times our response will reflect a radical faith and commitment.

Worship Aids

CALL TO WORSHIP. "Let the words of my mouth, and the meditation of my heart, be acceptable in thy sight, O Lord, my strength and my redeemer" (Ps. 19:14).

INVOCATION. O Lord, help us to make the prayer of the Psalmist our very own, to the end that we may offer acceptable worship this day and acceptable service in the days ahead.

OFFERTORY SENTENCE. "And he said unto them, Take heed what ye hear: with what measure ye mete, it shall be measured to you; and unto you that hear shall more be given" (Mark 4:24).

OFFERTORY PRAYER. Allow, O Lord, that we may be faithful givers in season and out, for when we have much we should share and when we have little we would share, for sharing in Jesus' name is part and parcel of what we believe life is all about.—E. Lee Phillips

PRAYER. We come to you, dear God, as though we were peering through a veil of tears, saddened by a world in which we cannot seem to get our priorities aligned with your creative intentions.

You created us to be in harmony with you and thus at peace with each other. But we have sought our own slice of the pie and eaten selfishly not only from our own plates, but from those of others as well. We have fattened our self-indulgences and sacrificed families and friendships, communities and covenants.

Help us, O Lord, with our problems of vision. Let us perceive that when we see double for ourselves, we are not truly focused on our return to new creation in Jesus Christ. We have died in Adam and

Eve and not been made alive in Jesus the Christ.

Renew a right heart within each of us, O Lord, so that the continual flow of your saving love may bring us to a new resurrection experience. Bring us to that moment when we may proclaim, "Not our wills, O Lord, but yours be done, on earth as it is in heaven."

Then let us walk in such heavenly light that our pathways will never be dark and we will see in all creation the reflection of your great and good presence through Jesus Christ our Lord. Let the fresh winds of your Holy Spirit part the veil of sorrow and open us to the light of your Son, in whose name we pray.—John M. Thompson

LECTIONARY MESSAGE

Topic: God's Victory

Text: Mark 1:14–20

Many will be able to identify with the frustration and confusion that must have been felt by the followers of John the Baptist at the time of his arrest. The general acceptance of his ministry, the public approval of his preaching and the numbers who followed him seemed to indicate what would generally be called success. Yet, all this was ended with his arrest. Secular power, once again, seemed to have been all powerful.

One commentator has suggested that Mark intended to imply that there was a parallel between the experience of John the Baptist and that of Jesus. It certainly is possible. The crowds from all Judea and Jerusalem seemed to rush out to hear John and then the crushing news, "John was arrested." Close to that experience would be the acclaim of Jesus, particularly on Palm Sunday, and then so soon, he too was arrested.

I. The time is fulfilled. The real lesson, however, is that the success of evil is only illusory and for the present. Even in the time of the seeming defeat of the prophet, Jesus comes with the announcement, "The time is fulfilled, the kingdom of God is at hand."

The message of Jesus reminds us that God's time is different from human appearances and expectations. Even when events give evidence of defeat, God still works. In fact, he would seem to say, God's work begins when the work of others for him must be abandoned.

II. The kingdom appears. Even the end of the ministry of John the Baptist must be interpreted in the light of the events in Jesus' life and death. God's kingdom appears when one in faith turns from dependence on everything else and learns that utter dependence on God and his purpose is the only source of victory in one's life. The followers of Jesus learned in the dark days following the Crucifixion that God's victory comes when God is trusted completely.

C. H. Dodd was correct when he insisted the kingdom had come "already but not yet." Those who trust in the power of God already have the basis for overcoming evil. The final victory may yet see struggles with the powers of darkness, but the victory of the kingdom of God is assured.

III. The kingdom requires participation. Those who would experience the victory must "Repent, and believe in the Gospel." The call of Jesus to Simon, Andrew and the sons of Zebedee (1:17, 20) also further illustrates that those who are to be a part of God's reign must actively participate in the declaration of that kingdom.

The call of the fishermen and their response clearly shows that God's reign requires a change in values and new allegiances.

The immediate response of the two pairs of brothers established the pattern of discipleship. The response must be decisive and the commitment radical. The illustration in the life of the early close followers set the pattern and described the requirements expected of those who would follow Jesus, both during his earthly ministry and in the centuries to follow.—Arthur L. Walker

SUNDAY: JANUARY THIRTIETH

SERVICE OF WORSHIP

Sermon: It's About Time

TEXT: Nehemiah 8:1–4a, 5–6, 8–10; Luke 4:14–30

I am interested in those polls that show that something like 95 percent of Americans believe the Bible is the Word of God, but only about 25 percent can name the first book of the Bible. It seems to indicate that though we believe it is important, we don't read the Bible. That's the case, I suspect, not because we're lazy, but because it is such difficult reading. Even though we read it in a modern translation in our own language, its meaning for our personal life, its relevance for the world in which we live today, does not immediately seem to be apparent.

We believe scripture is the Word of God, and the lesson that you heard read from the Book of Nehemiah this morning illustrates when scripture became that.

I. The story begins with the Jews returning from one hundred years of exile in Babylon about four hundred years before Christ. They are not like they were when they left. The Exile has changed them forever, and changed the way they will look upon their religion.

(a) When they were in Babylon, they were away from all these familiar places, especially from Jerusalem, and the most holy of places, the Temple. They didn't have holy places in which to worship God in Babylon, but they had something else. They took with them their scripture, the Torah, what we know as the first five books of our Bible. They met together to read the Bible, and discovered that God spoke to them through the scripture. That's when scripture came to be known as the Word of God.

(b) That's why Jewish religion was never the same after the Babylonian exile. Oh, they returned to Jerusalem, they rebuilt the Temple, but now scripture is central, the Torah is central, not sacrifice. And what's more, the Temple is not the only place Jews could worship. Now

synagogues, which are meeting halls in which scripture is read and interpreted, appear in the country towns. The central part of the worship in the synagogue is the reading of the text.

II. It began in this scene described in Nehemiah. He describes a ceremony, probably a dedication ceremony for the rebuilding of the Temple. Ezra, the priest, comes out carrying the scrolls in his arms. The people stand out of respect for the Word of God.

(a) Ezra begins reading, starting with Genesis. His voice gives out and he turns it over to somebody else. This is the first recorded Bible reading marathon. They read the whole thing, all the way through, until noon time.

(b) The most important part of that passage is, ". . . they read from the book . . . with interpretation; and they gave the sense, so that the people understood the reading." Scripture is to be interpreted. There is a sense to a text. There is a point, there is some meaning in the text that cannot be grasped simply by a cursory reading. It has to be studied. It has to be interpreted.

III. Now go to the New Testament lesson. It's a synagogue at Nazareth, in Jesus' hometown, the place where people gathered to hear the Word read and interpreted.

(a) According to Luke, right after the baptism there were forty days in the desert, and then Jesus headed for Galilee, for Nazareth, for his hometown. It was a homecoming, that's what it was. He was coming home after a long absence. The Sabbath came, he went to the synagogue. They noticed him there. They asked, "Will you read the scripture?" They poke each other as he goes up to the desk to read. "Remember when he was this high? Remember when he used to walk his younger brothers and sisters home from Hebrew school? Remember him?"

(b) The text for that morning was from Isaiah, a prophesy of the coming of the Messiah, the time when God is going to bring relief to the poor, free the captives, heal the sick. They had heard this many, many times. They could probably recite it as the rabbi read it. They knew it by heart. It's a wonderful prophesy. "The spirit of the Lord is upon me, for he has anointed me to preach good news to the poor, to proclaim release to the captives, recovering of sight to the blind, to set at liberty those who are oppressed, to proclaim the acceptable year of the Lord."

(c) Jesus read well. They were real proud of him. "Wasn't that good?" Then he paused. There should always be a pause between reading the scripture and the interpretation. They expected to hear what others had said about this text, that it's a prophecy about what is going to happen one of these days. They thought it was a "one of these days" prophecies. Jesus said it is a "today" prophecy. "Today this scripture has been fulfilled in your presence."

They were shocked. "Is this not Joseph's son? What is he talking like that for? Maybe it's just youthful enthusiasm. Wait til he gets his first church. That'll humble him. He won't be so optimistic after that."

(d) He ruined their homecoming. They wanted it to be nostalgic. They wanted to reminisce. They wanted a nice occasion, nothing provocative, something inspirational laced with a little humor. Certainly nothing that was going to challenge the way they thought, the way they saw things in this world, which was the way their parents had seen things before them, and their grandparents.

IV. This text is about time. What time is it? When does God act? "Today this scripture is fulfilled." And if that is true, if God is acting today, then scripture is God's itinerary. Scripture is where you can find where God is today. Just follow Jesus through the scripture, that's the best method. It's right there.

(a) God is at work today wherever there is great need, where people are suffering and oppressed, where you find the wretched poor of the world. The problem with the folk at Nazareth was that that was at Capernaum, someplace else, another country. According to this rab-

bi's interpretation, if you are looking for God, you will find him at Capernaum.

(b) If we believe the Bible is the Word of God, if we believe that God speaks to us through the Bible, then it's about time. When does God speak? "Today this scripture is fulfilled in your presence." Today this scripture is about me. So I have to decide, where am I in this story? Am I among those in Capernaum, or am I among those in the synagogue at Nazareth? It makes a difference, you know, in how you hear the word of God.—Mark Trotter

Illustrations

VISION FOR COMBAT. It was David Thoreau who said that it takes about three years before a man's pants start fitting him, and something of this holds of this, the armor of God. It grows on us; it fits itself to us; it accommodates itself to us by daily use. Let us wear that armor of God. Let us not turn to self-analysis. Let us write the words that Luther wrote on the table before him in those dreadful moments of solitary despair: *Baptizatus sum!* "I have been baptized!" That is a present perfect. When God took hold of my life and made me his own, he did it for keeps. He clothed me in that armor. "This is my body, this is my blood," our Lord has said, for keeps. These are weapons.—Martin H. Franzmann

HOMETOWN BOY. I think I know what it was like on that Sabbath day in Nazareth, because I grew up in one church, left there when I was sixteen, and after fifteen years I came back. I was ordained now, and they asked me to preach. It was the first time I had been back in fifteen years to that old church. And oh my, they were impressed. They sat there transfixed throughout the whole service, rapt attention, watching everything I did.

They didn't hear a word I said. I could have said anything to them. They were just dumbfounded that I was up there doing it, this overgrown kid, the one they were sure wouldn't amount to anything, the youngest one, you know, what's his name? They were just amazed. That's what happens when you go back to the home church. They don't come to hear a sermon, they come to celebrate a homecoming. They come to remember old times. They feel proud. It's one of our kids. Look at him up there.—Mark Trotter

Sermon Suggestions

THE TRUE PROPHET. TEXT: Deut. 18:15–20. (1) *Situation*: We all need divine guidance. (2) *Complication*: We are tempted to go to the wrong sources for the help we need. (3) *Resolution*: a. Clarifying our motives. b. Testing the authenticity of the one who presumes to speak for God.

BEYOND ARROGANCE. TEXT: 1 Cor. 8:1–13. (1) The arrogance of biblical and theological knowledge. (2) The arrogance of ethical freedom. (3) The graciousness of concern for the spiritual well-being of the last and least soul for whom Christ died.

Worship Aids

CALL TO WORSHIP. "For thus saith the high and lofty One that inhabiteth eternity, whose name is Holy; I dwell in the high and holy place, with him also that is of a contrite and humble spirit, to revive the spirit of the humble, and to revive the heart of the contrite ones" (Isa. 57:15).

INVOCATION. "O God of peace, who hast taught us that in returning and rest we shall be saved, in quietness and in confidence shall be our strength; by the might of thy Spirit lift us, we pray thee, to thy presence, where we may be still and know that thou art God.—*Book of Common Prayer*

OFFERTORY SENTENCE. "Therefore, my beloved brethren, be ye steadfast, unmovable, always abounding in the work of the Lord, forasmuch as ye know that your labor is not in vain in the Lord" (1 Cor. 15:58).

OFFERTORY PRAYER. Holy God, as we give this portion, we wish it were more, for in giving to the church we know we place our money where it will do the most good, and for that good and your glory we humbly pray.—E. Lee Phillips

PRAYER. Almighty Father of us all, we thank thee for these associations and rejoicings and psalms of praise, and for this place of prayer. We rejoice that we are all understood here by One whose eye never faileth, whose pity is everlasting, and whose sympathy is as large as all the universe dominated by the throne of our great Father, our God.

We are here this morning with so many needs, such intricate ways, such complex and serious problems that only the divine hand may touch our wound in safety; only the divine kindness that moves amidst many sicknesses with stillness; only a love that remembers our griefs and would not make them more agonizing; only the power to redeem that may save the lowliest—only this we ask for, the presence of thyself, O God, in Christ Jesus, our Lord.—Frank W. Gunsaulus

LECTIONARY MESSAGE

Topic: New Authority; New Commitment

TEXT: Mark 1:21–28

One of the most difficult parts of maturing is the realization that one cannot erase previous experience and its consequences. Both of these continue to have a nagging presence in our life even when we wish to change them.

The contrast between previous experience and the consequence of a new religious commitment can be both a lesson and a reinforcement of the value of the new experience.

I. New commitments must be based on previous experience. Those who heard Jesus teach could never escape their earlier religious experience. They constantly compared Jesus with other religious teachers they had known. The authority of the earlier teachers always came from those from whom they, in turn, had learned. It was impossible both for the earlier teachers, and those who heard them, to understand that as Jesus spoke his very identity gave new authority to his words.

Even a new commitment must be based on previous experience. It is not surprising, therefore, that the people constantly contrasted Jesus' teaching with that of the teachers they had previously known. Their earlier experience only made more difficult the acceptance of one with such a new message.

II. New commitments require a new authority. The man possessed of an evil spirit recognized the source of the difference in the teaching he heard from Jesus. He was able to recognize the new authority reflected. This authority also identified the messenger as one coming from God.

The recognition of the new authority required a new commitment. A new authority and a new commitment inevitably raise questions. These questions are always the same: What will it require of me? What will be the result?

The new requirements always result in a greater commitment and new expectations. The resulting change also requires, at least, that some of the existing conditions must be changed and perhaps destroyed. The cry of the changed man, "Are you here to destroy us?" (RSV), is a universal one for those cleansed by the Christ.

III. New commitments require cleansing. The experience teaches that a new commitment always requires a cleansing, the changing of experiences. The truth is that one cannot continue to be what he or she previously was if there is a new loyalty. The cleansing of the man was an illustration of both the requirement of a new authority and of a new approach to life. In fact, if one does acknowledge his identity and authority, contact with Jesus does destroy both what the person has been previously and the previous basis for authority in that person's life.

This acknowledgement may well be the most difficult decision in today's society. Few wish to change life as radically as is required by a new religious authority and a new commitment for living. Most wish to hold on both to some of the earlier experiences and the consequence of these. This is the impediment to "the new teaching" in religious life.—Arthur L. Walker

SUNDAY: FEBRUARY SIXTH

SERVICE OF WORSHIP

Sermon: Who Gets the Glory?

TEXT: Exodus 40:34–38

For Israel, Mount Sinai was definitely God's address. The cloud which had symbolized God's presence and protection of his people during their exodus hovered perpetually over the mountain top. And occasionally, they even heard God's voice behind the cloud. But the mountain was not God's permanent address.

During their final months at Sinai, the Israelites built the first church—the tabernacle. It was God's house, a majestic reproduction of an ordinary dwelling. It was a place of personal encounter where worshipers could meet with God.

The text represents the climax of the construction project. The cloud covered the Tent as it had covered Mount Sinai, and the glory of God, symbolizing his presence, immediately occupied and filled the tabernacle. From now on, God would live with his people—wherever they could be found.

All of us have a deep yearning to know where God lives. In these troubled and threatening times, our restless hearts keep looking for some evidence that he really is still in control of the world. We look for the cloud over our heads—or out there in front of us—as evidence of his presence. We listen for his voice for some reassurance that we are not alone. We desperately want his glory to fill the places where we live and worship.

I. None of us ever likes to admit there are times when we are afraid that God is absent. But the truth is, even in the most saintly life, there are always spaces—vacant places of the heart when God seems far away and remote.

(a) A part of the reason that God sometimes seems absent—or at least, far removed from our hurts and circumstances—is because of who he is. "My thoughts are not your thoughts," he said, "neither are your ways my ways" (Isa. 55:8). God is bigger than our concepts, our ideals, and our understanding of doctrine and righteousness. He is bigger than our church or denomination. We can't tame, control, or domesticate God.

(b) At other times, God seems absent from our life because of who we are—rebellious, hard headed, and selfish. Admit it, there are periods when our prayers, even our churches, our worship, our programs are so full of ourselves—our wants, our plans, our feelings—that there is simply no room left for God.

(c) Another reason God sometimes seems absent to us is because of our affluence, apathy, and comfort. We simply don't need God as much as those who are suffering, the hungry and homeless, or those enduring persecution or oppression.

(d) A final reason God seems absent to us is because there are frankly some places God will not go. Let me illustrate from the Bible. The tabernacle was always placed in the center of the camp. But inside the tabernacle—in the Holy of Holies, the inner sanctum—was kept the Ark of the Covenant.

The Ark had an incredible power connected with it. In fact, it was generally assumed that Israel was invulnerable in military campaigns because of the presence of the Ark. Once, however, something really bad happened (see 1 Sam. 2:12–36; 4:1–22). Eli was the high priest at the time. His two sons were to assume his priestly vocation when he became unable to function in that role. However, they had lost personal touch with God and completely ignored the standards of holiness imposed upon priests.

Israel was at war with the Philistines. Eli's sons carried the Ark onto the battle field itself. But they were killed, Israel was defeated, the Ark was impounded by the enemy, and Eli dropped dead from the shock of the news. The whole, tragic thing occasioned the naming of a baby with one of the most horrible names ever given to a child: Ichabod.

For Israel, the glory of the Lord was his presence—symbolized by the Ark of the Covenant. And the truth is that God's glory had temporarily departed—but not because the Ark had been taken. God's glory was gone because of the sin of his people. But it's important for us to know that the absent glory did not reveal an absent God. Even when the sin of his people rendered them impotent and spiritually empty, God was never absent. He never abandoned his people!

II. God was and is still alive and ready to display his power! He's simply searching for those who will meet his conditions: that worship must be placed at the center of all that we do!

(a) Our worship ought to be an enjoyable experience. Do you remember that one of the primary charges against Jesus was that he was "a glutton and a drunkard" (Matt. 11:19)? His critics were shocked by how much he enjoyed God and people. But do you also remember Jesus' explanation? "When the bridegroom arrives for the wedding party, do the guests look sad? No! The bridegroom is here. Let the party begin!" (Luke 5:34–35, AP)

(b) Our worship, our praise, our joy is because the glory of the Lord is here among us! Let me tell you something about joy. You don't just decide to be joyful. Rather, it is the fitting response to the actions of someone else.

It's as spontaneous as the "Ah!" that rises from our lips when we see a rocket explode during a Fourth of July fireworks display. It's as sudden as the stillness that comes over us when we stand on the mountain summit and look across a Smoky Mountain valley. It's as unexpected as the tears that come to our eyes when we hold our child for the very first time. To be here in God's presence is to put ourselves where joy, real spontaneous joy, is possible!

(c) It's amazing to me how many people feel guilty about their worship. "I can't keep my mind on what's going on," some say. "My mind wanders to what I am supposed to do—or where I'm supposed to go—after the service, or to what we are having for lunch." "I can't concentrate on the prayers or the sermon. I find myself just going through the motions, not really thinking about what I am doing."

Let me help you! Relax! Enjoy it! You are here simply to glorify God and to enjoy him forever. There's something about worship that is ruined if you have to work at it too hard.—Gary C. Redding

Illustrations

CONFESSING AND AFFIRMING.   I cannot demonstrate the existence of the Christian God. I can only confess my own faith in the God and Father of our Lord Jesus Christ. I can only affirm that in place of the restless quest which drives us from one tentative faith to another, in Jesus Christ I have met the God who has himself taken the initiative, who does not wait to be found but comes out in search of us. I can only affirm that in place of the compulsive search for a meaningful intimacy with life I have met, in Jesus Christ, the God who—incredibly—cared enough about human life to share it, and thus overcome the cosmic loneliness which often threatens to undo us. I can only affirm that in place of the disappointment which comes in the repeated discovery that we have put our trust in weak and empty things I have met, in Jesus Christ, the God whose defeat of death discloses his mastery over life.—Lloyd J. Averill

POWER IN SUFFERING.   Several years ago, the Methodist Bishop of Angola visited several seminaries and divinity schools in America. At every stop he was asked how the Christian church was surviving under a communist government. He reported that most Christian churches were actually thriving—growing by 10 percent or more each year.

Someone asked what would happen if the government became strong enough to shut down the churches. "We will keep meeting," he said. "It is their job to be the government, our job to be the church. Our church had its most rapid growth during the revolution when so many of our members were in jail. Jail is a wonderful opportunity for evangelism."

Then, he said something quite remarkable. "Don't worry about us, brothers and sisters. We are doing fine in Angola. Frankly, I would find it much more difficult to be a pastor in the United States." Maybe it is too easy for us!—Gary C. Redding

Sermon Suggestions

THE LONG WAIT.   TEXT: Isa. 40:21–31. (1) God is incomparably great and all-knowing. (2) However, our circumstances sometimes seem to deny that truth. (3) Nevertheless, if we wait for the Lord, a. the impossible becomes possible, b. the difficult becomes easy, c. the ordinary is no burden.

"FOR THE SAKE OF THE GOSPEL."   TEXT: 1 Cor. 9:16–23. (1) Paul's obligation—to share the gospel. (2) Paul's pride—preaching without compensation. (3) Paul's strategy—resourceful service. (4) Paul's reward—sharing in the blessings of the gospel.

Worship Aids

CALL TO WORSHIP.   "O send out thy light and thy truth: let them lead me; let them bring me unto thy holy hill, and to thy tabernacles" (Ps. 43:3).

INVOCATION.   Father of the human family, giver of life to each one of us, we gather here this morning in the quiet of this sacred place to worship you in Spirit and in truth. We know that you are never far from us, but there are too many times in our life journey when we find ourselves far from you. Call us again into your nearer presence. Make us keenly aware of the higher values that make life great. Restrict for a moment the tumult, the task, the strife of the world about us and give us peace. Indeed, make our hearts to shine with your glory. Build your altar in our lives and on that altar kindle a fire that will at least light the way for us in the darkness that surrounds, as well as the darkness that invades the lives of others who occupy the segment of the world that we call ours. Fill us now, even as you did those whom Jesus taught to pray: (Lord's Prayer)—Henry Fields

OFFERTORY SENTENCE. "So then every one of us shall give account of himself to God" (Rom. 14:12).

OFFERTORY PRAYER. Lord of life, we saturate this offering in prayer and believe it can be multiplied to bless many lives through the miraculous love and power of God. Thanks be to God!

PRAYER. Almighty and everloving God, thou who hast given thine all for us, wilt thou teach us to give our all for thee. Thou who hast come personally into our world that we might be fitted for citizenship in thine eternal world, may thy blessing be upon our lives. Thou who has given us the gospel through Jesus Christ that we might in our own day be a means of blessing to the world in thy name, wilt thou make us instruments of thy will and of thy peace. We thank thee for the glad good news with which we are entrusted. May we learn to know it, may we learn to share it and give it to others.

We ask that thou wilt bless our worship through the strengthening of our souls and spirits to the invigoration of our total life. We ask that thou wilt widen our horizons with such understanding of the world's possibilities and the world's needs as can be seen only in the light of thy truth. We pray that thou wilt deepen our convictions that they may rest upon the very bedrock of the knowledge of thy character. Wilt thou so give life and vitality to our thoughts and purposes and words and deeds that we may daily live out the gospel that we profess.

Bless this time of worship. Bless the homes of all who are assembled here. Bless our individual lives with their constant requirements for decisions, with moral control and spiritual stimulus. Grant that all may find the true meaning of their life in that which links them to thee.

We pray for all who are sick, that thou wilt give them the restoration of health and strength by the touch of thy Spirit. Wilt thou bless all who are in anxiety and give them that inner peace that enables them to deal courageously with life's difficulties. Wilt thou abide in our hearts, in our purposes, in our deeds and make good use of us in thy holy kingdom. For we pray in Jesus' name.—Lowell M. Atkinson

LECTIONARY MESSAGE

Topic: Establishing Priorities
TEXT: Mark 1:29–39

It is much easier to distinguish between the bad and the good than it is to distinguish between the good, the better, and the best. Most of us are satisfied if we are doing the good and do not worry unduly about the better and the best. Jesus helped us to see that there is a best which summons us.

I. An act of compassion. It was the beginning of his ministry as Mark relates it. He had called some followers and on the Sabbath day they had attended the synagogue in Capernaum. He healed a demoniac and the countryside became alive with reports about this new teacher. From the synagogue they went to the house of Simon and Andrew. Now, away from the synagogue and the crowd, he found time for a personal ministry. It was the Sabbath and Jesus had healed in the synagogue, but there was as yet no conflict as to Sabbath observance.

The mother of a friend was ill. They had seen the healing in the synagogue and they told him that Peter's mother-in-law was in bed with a fever. There was no publicity to be gained, no wide scale impressions to be made. He simply ministered to her need and healed her. In turn she ministered to them. He did a good deed. What could be nobler than this compassionate act?

II. The claim of fame. It doesn't take very long for the report of compassion to get out. Everyone admires compassion—especially if it is accompanied by deeds of mercy. He must have remained in Peter's house that day. It was the Sabbath, and they waited until after the Sabbath ended at sunset to bring their burdens of the sick to him. It was legal after sunset.

So he moved, or was moved, to a public ministry. They learned where the healer was staying and they came to him. It seemed to Mark or his informant that the whole city had come to be healed. They were all gathered together at the door. He healed them. Out of compassion and not out of any ambition to be honored he healed them. He even demanded silence of the healed demoniacs lest they stir up the crowds. Perhaps this ministry was a better use of his time and ability than merely staying in the house all day after one healing there. There is nothing wrong with a claim to fame if it is well deserved for a healing ministry. What could be finer than this well-deserved fame?

III. "To this end." Without any reflection on those who like to sleep late, let it be clear: he arose a great while before day. Was he anxious to get away from the crowds? At least he left the city and the crowds. There is no indication that he had exhausted his opportunities for healing there. He left the disciples and their pride in his healing ministry. "Wait until tomorrow—he'll heal you tomorrow." He went to a deserted place and prayed. Now there's a time and place for prayer . . . but when so many needed him . . .

He left mankind for God. Not even his disciples understood his desertion. They "pursued" him, and the word implies a hostile intent—they tracked him down and claimed his time and his talents as their own . . . everyone's looking for you. Surely he had made a bad move. He could not be restrained by one city or by one group.

"Let us go elsewhere," he said, "for to this end I came forth." And he went through all of Galilee preaching and casting out demons. What could be better than to accomplish God's will? Freedom to recognize and to respond to human need . . . is this the greatest priority of ministry?—J. Estill Jones

SUNDAY: FEBRUARY THIRTEENTH

SERVICE OF WORSHIP

Sermon: To Keep a True Lent

TEXT: Joel 2:12–13

The mightiest themes of the Christian religion confront us in Lent and Easter and challenge our minds to make these life-transforming truths available to our people. This is a time for greatness, not our greatness, but the greatness of the Gospel. We turn to the Bible to seek afresh the mighty meanings of Lent, Calvary and Easter.

I. The keynote of the Lenten season is found in the Old Testament reading for Ash Wednesday. "Therefore also now, saith the Lord, turn ye even to me with all your heart, and with fasting, and with weeping, and with mourning. And rend your heart, and not your garments, and turn unto the Lord your God; for he is gracious and merciful, slow to anger, and of great kindness, and repenteth him of the evil" (Joel 2:12–13). Lent calls us back to God. For most of us this means a turning from our self-concern to a new experience of looking to God. Thus the Book of Joel is both mirror and window. When we look in the mirror and see our moral and spiritual wrongness, we know well our need of penitence. Hence the call to fasting, weeping, and mourning. When we look through the wonderful window of faith, we see the gracious character of our God: "For he is gracious and merciful, slow to anger, and of great kindness." Look to yourself; look to God! This is to enter into the deeper meaning of Lent.

In the seventeenth century, Robert Herrick interpreted this truth in his poem, "To Keep a True Lent."

Is this a fast, to keep
The larder leane?
And cleane
From fat of veales, and sheep?

Is it to quit the dish
of flesh, yet still
To fill
The platter high with fish?

Is it to fast an houre,
Or rag'd to go
Or show
A down-cast look, and sowre?

No: 'tis a fast, to dole
Thy sheaf of wheat,
And meat,
Unto the hungry soule.

It is to fast from strife,
From old debate,
And hate;
To circumsize thy life.

To shew a heart grief-rent;
To sterve thy sin,
Not bin;
And that's to keep thy Lent.

II. The words, "To sterve thy sin, not bin," bring us to the central meaning of the Lenten season, first given in Joel: "Rend your heart, and not your garments."

(a) The Gospel reading for Ash Wednesday likewise gives judgment on the insincerity that substitutes the outward appearance of piety for the inner sorrow for our sin. Not what men see but what God sees in us is the important matter. "But thou, when thou fastest, anoint thy head and wash thy face; that thou appear not to men to fast, but unto thy Father which is in secret; and thy Father, which seeth in secret, shall reward thee openly" (Matt. 6:17–18). How we look to man is not so important as how we look to God!

We may well pause on Jesus' words, "when thou fastest," for few of us fast. Yet Jesus said "when," not "if." And fasting works. It quickens us to new sensi-tiveness. It brings us in line with the example of Jesus. The fact is that we are awash in money, surfeited with affluence, overfed and overweight, to the detriment of our true life. It is time to reconsider the relevance of fasting to the spiritual life. "Moreover," says Jesus, "when ye fast, be not, as the hypocrites, of a sad countenance" (Matt. 6:16). Let the joy shine through. Don't look dismal.

A layman in a British church was assigned to meet an incoming guest preacher at the train station. Upon seeing a sour-visaged man in dark clothes, he stepped forward and said, "You must be the Reverend Mr. Smith." "No, I'm not," returned the sour-looking man. "I'm not a clergyman. I'm not even interested in religion. It's my indigestion that makes me look like this!" We have been warned, "Be not . . . of a sad countenance."

(b) The Epistle for Ash Wednesday points up our most serious modern problem—the quest for meaning. Only God can give life a meaning worthy of a man. St. Paul calls us to a life of purposeful living, with goals to strive for, self-discipline, training, and the temperance that insists on nothing too much. "So run, that ye may obtain," "So fight I, not as one that beateth the air" (1 Cor. 9:24–26). Lent is a time to shape up!

Ezekiel chapter 33 reminds us that the deepest truth about our life is our power to choose. "If he turn"—the words confront us with life's supreme challenge. We are made by God and made for God. There is hope for the wicked "if he turn." There is tragedy for the righteous "if he turn." The wicked who turn to God "shall surely live." The righteous who turn from their righteousness to commit sin shall die. Here is the challenge of Lent: will we use our freedom to turn to God and live, or to turn from God and die? True repentance is the key that unlocks the dungeon door of despair and turns us toward God with new hope and eagerness to live for him.

How Jesus endeavoured to help men make the right turning! The rich man wanting eternal life ran eagerly to Jesus. He was a man who had everything, yet

Jesus' word to him was, "You lack." He had so much, and Jesus "beholding him, loved him," but the great turning was too much for him "and he was sad at that saying and went away grieved, for he had great possessions" (Mark 10:22). How we need to look beyond what we have to what we lack! The disciples were astonished that so well-to-do a person should not be accepted as a disciple, and that Jesus should declare it easier for a camel to go through the eye of a needle than for a rich man to enter into the kingdom of God. "Who then can be saved?" they exclaimed. But Jesus was thinking of the power in the human heart to turn to God, whose amazing grace is waiting for all that turn to him. "With men it is impossible, but not with God, for with God all things are possible" (Mark 10:27).

III. The two weeks before Easter direct our thoughts and worship to the Passion of our Lord. The poignant question of the boy Isaac may well set the stage: "Where is the lamb?" (Gen. 22:7). On Calvary we find the answer—Jesus Christ, the Lamb of God. St. Paul wrote with awe of the mighty self-emptying of the Son of God who gave himself that he might save others. He "made himself of no reputation . . . and became obedient unto death, even the death on the cross." So the vision of Isaiah of a Suffering Servant who accomplished God's purpose through pain found fulfillment in the Christ who died to save. "He was wounded for our transgressions . . . and with his stripes we are healed" (Isa. 52:5).

Beyond Calvary the sky is bright with the glory of Easter. The triumphant joy of Easter is the key to the Christian interpretation of life. Faith marched on victory ground. Easter created the Christian church. "And we declare unto you glad tidings, how that the promise which was made unto the fathers, God hath fulfilled the same unto us their children, in that he hath raised up Jesus again" (Acts 13:32–33).

Be sure of this: if we seek Jesus, we shall not find him in the place of death. "He is risen; he is not here" (Mark 16:6). How big is your faith? Is it big enough for Easter? St. Paul calls us to lift our sights to grasp the eternal dimensions of our faith: "If in this life only we have hope in Christ, we are of all men most miserable . . . But now is Christ risen . . . !" (1 Cor. 15:19). Christ is our champion. He has won the victory. He asks us not to be faithless, but believing. And the life-transforming promise is for all who believe—"in Christ shall all be made alive!" (1 Cor. 15:22).—Lowell M. Atkinson

Illustrations

THE VANQUISHING OF EVIL.   Whatever the truth about the devil, the Church stands secure against the devil and all his hosts if she stands in "God in Christ." Her concern is with the wiles of the devil, not with his ancestry. Her task is to keep her gaze firmly fixed on Christ. An interesting commentary on this comes to us from early Christian literature in the second and third centuries, when converts were being made in large numbers from a world where demons were everywhere believed in and feared, and where the devil was a figure dreaded and respected. Over and over again, almost with monotonous reiteration, these converts are enjoined no longer to fear the devil. Christians are actually described as those who no longer fear the devil. They have renounced him in more senses than one; they have put him out of their minds.—William Robinson

THE ANATOMY OF STUPIDITY.   In the year 1890, a fairly wealthy Hungarian lawyer left an estate of some size. He stipulated in his will that whichever of his relatives would provide the best answers to three questions would inherit all his wealth. The three questions were: What is eternal and yet finite? Why do men need money? Why do people carry on lawsuits? For fifty-five years, litigation, bickering, and even violence developed among the four or five dozen claimants to the fortune of the deceased until at last, shortly after the ending of World War I, the estate was virtually wiped out by the economic tidal wave of the Great

Depression, and no one received a single penny.—Charles P. Robshaw

Sermon Suggestions

BLESSED SIMPLICITY. TEXT: 2 Kgs. 5:1–14. (1) *The Story*: Naaman is healed of his leprosy when he obeys the word of God through his prophet. (2) *The Meaning*: God's requirements of us may be exasperatingly simple, but nonetheless necessary. (3) *The Application*: a. Faith in Jesus Christ is simple, but it has vast implications. b. Love of neighbor is simple, but it, too, has many applications.

THE AIM OF SELF-DISCIPLINE. TEXT: 1 Cor. 9:24–27. (1) There is a prize to win. (2) The prize may be forfeited by self-indulgence. (3) The prize may be won by strict, even painful, self-discipline.

Worship Aids

CALL TO WORSHIP. "He that dwelleth in the secret place of the Most High shall abide under the shadow of the Almighty. I will say of the Lord, he is my refuge and my fortress: my God, in him will I trust" (Ps. 91:1–2).

INVOCATION. Enter our worship, O Lord, with fresh winds of the Spirit, pour across our parched souls with living water and renew us after your will to ever faithfully worship and wait.—E. Lee Phillips

OFFERTORY SENTENCE. "The earth is the Lord's, and the fullness thereof; the world, and they that dwell therein" (Ps. 24:1).

OFFERTORY PRAYER. Gracious Lord, we acknowledge your ownership of all the earth and everything and everyone in it. What we confess with our lips may we prove with our deeds. Through him who gave his all for our salvation.

PRAYER. O Lord, we turn again to thee marveling at thy patience. Each time we turn we bring thee the same disappointments, the same sins, the same promises. Too many times we have plied thee with prayer on prayer, without earnest and honest effort to put our house in order, to labor at the foundations, and to practice with diligence the elementary drudgery of training our souls to be spiritually competent. Forgive us, Lord, for words uttered without serious intention, words that mean nothing at all, words that make us forget how deeply we need thee. Help us now to turn again to thee with every real hunger of our self that we may learn of thy love, through Christ our Lord.—Samuel H. Miller

LECTIONARY MESSAGE

Topic: A Tough Touch

TEXT: Mark 1:40–45

We are accustomed to describe a too-generous person as a soft touch. It may be somewhat derogatory. We may despise a person who does not have the ability to say "no." In the process, however, the soft touch may prove to be quite costly to the toucher. This was the case with Jesus whose "soft" touch proved to be a "tough" touch. It looked like a typical day. He had become famous for his healings. Every kind of needy person approached him. Some had faith.

I. What kind of faith? A leper drew near and knelt before him. He had faith in the widespread report of Jesus' healing. He had faith in the ability of Jesus to heal him. He had some doubt as to the willingness of Jesus to heal him. Is God good as well as powerful? Up to this time the reports of healing had not included a leper . . . unclean spirits were cast out, a feverish woman was healed, many who had diverse diseases were made well . . . but no leper has been mentioned so far.

Yet the statement was clearly one of faith: "If you will, you can make me clean." Jesus rewarded that faith, though strangely expressed. The leper doubted Jesus' good will, not his ability to heal. Jesus, being a soft touch, was moved with compassion and touched him. Jesus touched a leper! The leper was immediately made clean. The leper's faith confronted Jesus' compassion and cleansing resulted. But Jesus had touched a leper—tough!

II. What kind of obedience? Jesus strictly charged him. It may better be translated, Jesus sternly charged him. It was a clear command. Say nothing to any man; show yourself to the priest; make an offering for your cleansing. It could hardly have been clearer. God does not mince words when he gives a command. There were good reasons for the three mandates. Leprosy was a serious disease and it was a dread disease. Do not forget that Jesus had touched a leper.

And how did he obey? He did not obey. His disobedience was almost as clear as the commands. He went out from Jesus' presence and began to tell everyone he met. Such a testimony under different circumstances might be admirable, but under these circumstances it was deplorable. There must be some contexts in which the good news is not good.

There is no indication that the cleansed leper even went to the priest with an offering. He may have, but the disobedience to the first command was so clear that Mark does not add other details. It is interesting however that no word of appreciation is recorded to Jesus. That failure in itself marked the encounter as a "tough touch."

III. Unclean! It was a tough touch. By touching the leper and having the report spread abroad, Jesus had himself become unclean. He could no longer enter the city, and only "after some days" (Mark 2:1) did he return to Capernaum. The crowds continued even as his popularity increased, but legally he was unclean.

Did Jesus sense this possibility when he healed the man? Certainly he knew of the laws concerning leprosy. He touched him anyhow. "The Wounded Healer" suffered rejection by the law of his own people, and he had acted out of compassion. Do our attempts at helping ever prove to be a tough touch—even when they mark us as a soft touch? Should we move compassionately anyhow? What is God's will in the matter? Do you get the feeling that God's love overflowed from Jesus and that because of who he was he couldn't do anything but heal the man—soft touch or tough touch?—J. Estill Jones

SUNDAY: FEBRUARY TWENTIETH

SERVICE OF WORSHIP

Sermon: Things Need Not Be as They Are

TEXT: John 8:12

There are more prophets of gloom in the world than there are prophets of hope. If some visitor from another planet were to come to us, he, too, would see our hurried life, our outer tensions, and our inner conflicts. He would see much gaiety in our time but little buoyancy; he would observe our pleasures but find little happiness; and he would leave us with the thought that we are overwhelmed by the present.

This was evidently the impression Jesus gained as he looked upon the people of his own time. They were irritated by foreign oppression. They lived in the midst of confusion and uncertainty, and they resented it. They were without purpose and direction. But it was not necessary that people should have been like that then, and it is not necessary that we are like that today. What Jesus said to his own generation he would surely say to us: "I am the light of the world: he that followeth me shall not walk in the darkness, but shall have the light of life." He always felt that way about people. They need not walk in the darkness; they could always walk in the light—if they wanted to.

I. We have a concern about the state of the world. We salve our conscience by saying that things could be a great deal worse. Of course, they could be.

(a) We might have had four wars instead of three in our time. We might be completely governed by a bureaucracy instead of hanging on the fringes of our freedom. We might have placed our teachers and spiritual leaders into complete servitude instead of merely disrupting our sense of values and creating a world wherein we reward those who teach our children with the least and those who please our fancies with the most. Yes, things might be worse, but they are bad enough, and it need not be so.

(b) We are equally concerned about ourselves. We live in physical comfort, but we are spiritually and morally uncomfortable. We rarely speak with any finality about truth or virtue. We no longer know what values are valid in our changing world. We are troubled by the fact that the comforts and luxuries science has brought us do not minister to our inner well-being.

Of course, matters might be worse than they are. We might be more neurotic than we seem to be. We might be more fiendish in the prosecution of war than we prove ourselves to be. We might derive less joy from our families than we do. But things are bad enough, and they need not be so.

(c) As one talks with men and women here and there on a score of different problems, one is soon overwhelmed by the frightening realization that most of us have great convictions on small issues and small convictions on great issues. Now, of course, matters might be worse than they are. We might have no convictions on any issues; that would be worse. But things are bad enough, and they need not be so.

II. So Jesus comes unto our battered world and says, as he did long ago, "He that followeth me shall not walk in the darkness, but shall have the light of life." We do not have to walk in the darkness. Things need not be as they are.

(a) How often must we be told that man does not live by bread alone? Have we no eyes? Are our minds impenetrable? Are our souls so rigid that they cannot absorb anything life teaches? Do we remember nothing from our history books? Do we not know that we are not the first materialistically inclined generation? Do we not know that there were others before us and the way they went? They went to destruction.

(b) How many wars must we fight before we learn that in the end war will completely destroy us? How many homes must be broken up before we learn that a house is not a home? How often must we be told that when a people loses its moral foundations it is on the way to ruin and death? Are we so incredibly arrogant that we believe that we are history's fair-haired child and that what happened to generations before us will never happen to us? Are we, of all the generations in history, the only one which can successfully defy the moral laws of God and of nature?

III. If things are what they are, it is because we have left God out of our affairs. This is the final and most significant word to be said. To many a cynical soul this might appear as pious phrasing, but deep in our hearts we know that it is sheer realism. If we had not left God out of our affairs, the world would not be what it is today; we would not be frightened of what is to come, and the present would not overwhelm us. If we had drawn God into our thoughts, we would not find ourselves in a state of constant tension and apprehension.

(a) When do we include God in our everyday affairs? Life is made up of everyday occurrences. Days pass upon days without anything significant happening to us. But that is life, and in the midst of this sort of life we find our joys, our sorrows, our successes, and our failures. Well, when do we include God in our concerns?

(b) If we look at our lives with regrets, then let us think of these words of Jesus: "He that followeth me shall not walk in the darkness, but shall have the light of life." The present need not overwhelm us and the future must not frighten us. The present can be good; the future will be good. It can be different. It can be different with us if we will have it so. Not that we shall be free from trials or tribulations; not that there will be no sighs or tears; not that we shall walk without burdens; not that we shall not ask and wonder. But at least we shall know the way, and we shall know this: that all things can be different when

God comes into our lives.—Arnold H. Lowe

Illustrations

LIFE'S SURPRISES.   I recall, as a boy, one man who lived on one of the most thickly settled streets on the East Side of New York City. We children coming and going from school would ofttimes see him. He was a little old man with a gray, straggly beard, who dealt in coal and ice. He had his place of business in a dark basement underneath a huge tenement. In winter he sold coal and in summer he sold ice. He would sell coal by the bucketload and would carry these buckets up three and four flights of stairs. In the summer, he would buy large cakes of ice, cut them into smaller cakes, and carry them up five, six flights of stairs to his customers. He was always bent under a load. We called him "Humpback," though he was really not humpbacked. This little man with the gray, straggly beard, "Jacob the Humpback," died quietly like all humble folks, as he had lived. A few years ago I learned that one of his sons, because of the labors of "Jacob the Humpback," had become a professor of mathematics in a large university, and another had become a surgeon. I suddenly asked myself, "Little man, how big were you?"—Abba Hillel Silver

WHAT IS LACKING.   These benefits of science help us to get more quickly from one place to another; they aid us in accomplishing our purpose with greater ease and dexterity; they free us from the burdens of manual labor; they guide us into a deeper knowledge of the universe in which we live; they put us on the road to innumerable conquests over handicaps and disease. But they do not make us more secure in our sense of right and wrong; they do not quicken our judgments or our conscience; they do not give us more serenity.—Arnold H. Lowe

Sermon Suggestions

THE SIGN OF THE RAINBOW.   TEXT: Gen. 9:8–17. (1) That God has made a universal convenant through Noah's three sons, ancestors of all nations, verse 9. (2) The God has made an ecological covenant, "with every living creature," verse 10. (3) That God has designated a permanent reminder of his mercy in the earlier token of his wrath.

THREE REDEMPTIVE PARADOXES.   TEXT: 1 Pet. 3:18–22. (1) Christ the righteous suffered for the unrighteous. (2) Christ was put to death in the flesh but made alive in the spirit. (3) In the time of Noah, water destroyed, but now in baptism it is a symbol of salvation.

Worship Aids

CALL TO WORSHIP.   "Oh that men would praise the Lord for his goodness, and for his wonderful works to the children of men! For he satisfieth the longing soul, and filleth the hungry soul with goodness" (Ps. 107:8–9 KJV).

INVOCATION.   Lord, we are rushed and tethered and busy about many things. Calm us as we come to worship. Adjust us to the climate of holiness. Still us in the sanctuary of mercy. Then fill us with a vision of heaven and fit us for earth because we sought and found that alone which satisfies: the Lord our God.—E. Lee Phillips

OFFERTORY SENTENCE.   "For every beast of the forest is mine, and the cattle upon a thousand hills" (Ps. 50:10).

OFFERTORY PRAYER.   We are thine, O God. Thou has created us. Thou hast redeemed us. Thou hast given us the power to gain the fruits of our labors. And now we bring as offerings of gratitude and love only what is already truly thine.

PRAYER.   O Father, your mercies have been ever of old, but they are new every morning and present in every watch of the night. Out of your mercies we know the blessing of a new day—the joy of this place—the encouragement of the family of faith. Experiencing your mercy today and in our every yesterday, we find ourselves singing with the psalmist: "Surely goodness and mercy shall follow us all the days of our lives . . ."

Your great mercy toward us is calling us to be merciful toward all others. In our life together may we be merciful—loving and thoughtful, forgiving and encouraging—that we may call each other out to that fulfillment that you have ordained in your creative love toward each of us as a person. In this Lenten season may we hear your call in Christ challenging us to that maturity that was in him "who when he was reviled, reviled not again; when he suffered he did not threaten," but trusted you as Father who judge all persons justly. In him, O Father, we see ourselves not only as we are but as the persons we can become, for in him is the fullness of your truth and your grace.

We pray for grace for ourselves and for each other: Where there is any hurt among us we pray for your healing; where illness and anxiety for loved ones who are ill seem almost more than we can bear, we pray that we may be strengthened and encouraged that we may be there for those who need us; when circumstances would victimize us, we pray that we may be victors through that victory that is your promise in Christ.

We pray for truth and justice—understanding and compassion—for all peoples and nations. There are so many thoughtless hurts, because we are at cross-purposes with you and hence at cross-purposes with ourselves and with one another. Free us from fear of others by living in fear of you. Through him who is your perfect love to cast out all fear.—John Thompson

LECTIONARY MESSAGE

Topic: Human and Divine

Text: Mark 1:9–15

The Gospel of Mark has been noted for its emphasis on the human nature of Jesus. The opening chapter of the Gospel makes the point that in Jesus there is a combining of his humanity and deity. There is an emphasis both on Jesus joining with the crowds of Judea and Jerusalem (1:5) who went out to be baptized by John and the distinctiveness of Jesus in that "when he came up out of the water" (1:10) the heavens opened and God addressed him directly. The opening experience of his public life casts him with "all men" and yet sets him apart as different from all. Human and divine are joined in him. This emphasis is especially important for the first Sunday in Lent.

I. Dual nature defined. His uniqueness is attested by the voice of God. John had foretold of the "mightier" One. He had spoken of how worthy the coming one would be and how he would baptize with the Spirit. Now the open heavens, the descending Spirit, and the voice from heaven all attest to the significance of this One.

It is impossible to miss that God has selected him for a special mission. The anointing of Jesus is graphically portrayed. The words echo that God has chosen him and set him apart for a specific task.

To be identified as the "beloved" or "only" son speaks of the unique relationship, but it also foreshadows the unique role. Only he is uniquely related to God but, also, only he can fulfill the unique role of saving the world. He, and only he, has the qualities that will make his suffering acceptable for destroying the bonds of sin that beset and bind all humankind.

The unique relationship foreshadows the divinely appointed task which would lead to the singular conclusion, the Cross.

The temptation experience continues the dual experience of both the similarity to all other persons and the uniqueness of Jesus. In being tempted, Jesus faced the common experience of all humanity. Being "with the wild beasts" (v. 13) seems to stress the carnal aspects of his temptation. In this he again was like all others. But his unique quality is also present in that angels ministered to him.

II. Victory of the Divine. A dual quality for the passage is again emphasized at the arrest of John the Baptist. In the simple presentation and seeming implication that human power has triumphed is contrasted the announcement of Jesus that "the Kingdom of God is at hand" (v. 15). Those who heard must have wondered how both the triumph of human power and the presence of God could be demonstrated in the events (see 1:14–20). Yet, Jesus challenged them to see that God does work even in the face of apparent defeat. The telling of these events by the Gospel writer already foreshadows the attitude that will be required in facing the circumstances of the Crucifixion and the seeming defeat of the purposes of God in the life of Christ.—Arthur L. Walker

SUNDAY: FEBRUARY TWENTY-SEVENTH

SERVICE OF WORSHIP

Sermon: Why People Do Bad Things in the Name of God

TEXT: Luke 22:47–53

Life is certainly not easy in the waning years of the twentieth century. Every day I watch the television screen and read the newspaper and am unable to escape the fact that people often do very bad things in the name of religion.

I constantly ask myself how is it possible for people to be so convinced of the rightness of their causes that they justify murder, torture, and the mass destruction of homes, businesses, and governments. How can the ideas of any one human being be so important that they make us so angry at others? How can I become so loyal to a teacher of right living—or a government leader—that I decide to do hurtful things to those who respect a different teacher or leader? And what if we both claim that we are following the same God, the same teachings, and yet we disagree with each other so violently that we do each other harm?

I sincerely believe that this is one of the most important questions we can ask: why do some people often do such bad things in the name of God?

Let me offer three insights which have been helpful to me as I have wrestled with this question particularly in the past few days.

I. First, right religious belief will usually result in right religious behavior.

(a) Generally speaking, religion is the result of a person's efforts to discover his or her place in the world. That means that, in one way or another, most people are religious. Even those people are religious who never mention the name of God or who hold no traditional beliefs or practices such as prayer or worship. A person who has a sense of "the way things are" and the way things ought to be in the world is, in a general sense, a religious person.

(b) This is precisely where the basic difference between the Christian faith and all other religions becomes most clear. The Christian faith is not the result of man's efforts to discover his place in the world. Rather, the Christian faith represents man's authentic response to God's revelation of his purpose and plan for his creation.

That response begins with belief—belief centered in and focused upon Jesus Christ. Christians believe that Jesus represents the fullest revelation ever given of God's nature.

(c) But, it is important to understand that the Christian faith is not merely a matter of believing. Authentic Christian faith is expressed in authentic Christ-like behavior. It's in the way a person chooses to live his or her life that you most easily detect what that person believes about life in general and the part he or she plays in it. It's in the daily, tangible actions of life that you are able to comprehend most fully the authenticity of a person's faith.

(d) The text recalls the night when Jesus was arrested—handed over to his enemies by a defector from his own ranks. What made Judas' betrayal most repugnant, however, is the way he carried it out: disguising his treason with a kiss, a

sign of affection. One of Jesus' other
disciples—no doubt, one who genuinely
loved him—drew a sword and actually
wielded it in defense of his Lord.

What was the difference between what
Judas did and how this other disciple re-
acted? An enemy had come with a kiss
and a friend had come with a sword. But
the actions of both were acts of betrayal
because neither reflected a life controlled
by the grace of God.

II. The second insight related to why
people do bad things in the name of God
is this: God has always had a peculiar and
particular fondness for sinners.

(a) Most of us tend to look on the
bright side of things and believe the best
about people. For the most part, we believe that people are so much more than
they seem to be and that, given the
chance, they will usually rise above their
weaknesses and handicaps. They will always overcome their selfish tendencies
and destructive temptations.

We also tend to believe that God has a
particular fondness for good people—
religious people, like us. However, the
Bible reveals just the opposite about God.
If we believe what the scriptures tell us,
then we must conclude that God especially loves the sinner.

(b) Once when some religious people—
Pharisees and teachers—questioned Jesus
about the company he kept, he responded: "It is not the healthy who need
a doctor, but the sick. I have not come to
call the righteous, but the sinners to repentance" (Luke 5:31). On another occasion, he told Zaccheus that "the Son of
Man came to seek and to save what was
lost" (Luke 19:10).

What that means is that the material
with which God chooses to do his work is
flawed material. The people whom he
chooses as his partners in grace are people who do sinful, bad things by nature.
He chooses them because he loves
them—not because of their sin,
certainly—but in spite of it.

(c) Too many religions leave us the way
they find us because they fail to come to
terms with our sinful nature. The Gospel
of Jesus Christ, however, tells us that we
are sinners. But it also tells us that God

loves the sinner too much to leave him in
his sin. The Gospel tells us that God has
committed all his assets to rescuing the
sinner.

III. That brings me to the third insight: spiritual transformation usually
takes a while. It seldom occurs immediately.

(a) When I struggle with an issue like
the one before us now—why people do
bad things in the name of God—it always
makes me uneasy. The reason is that I
realize that I am not only passing judgment on others and the world in which I
live, but I am also forced to admit that
there are some of the same tendencies
within me. I really am judging myself
also.

I know that I am often guilty of harsh
feelings, impatient words, and unkind
acts against a person who deprives me of
something I desperately want.

(b) But there is something else I know
that is perhaps even more important. I
know that I am not what I should be.
Ever. I know that there is a gap between
what ought to be and what is. It's easy for
me to see that when I look at the world,
at others, at some of you. But it is also an
inescapable fact of existence that it is true
about me.

(c) People do not immediately cease
doing bad things by virtue of their being
"religious"—not even because they become Christians. The failure of most religions is that people are deluded into believing that they are better than they
really are—that the gap has been
bridged. The Christian faith, however,
never allows you to lose sight of who you
are, where you are, how far you need to
go, who it is that will go with you all the
way, and by whose power you will ultimately be changed into the person God
wants you to be.

(d) God knows I need to be changed.
He knows that we all do! God knows our
world desperately needs to be changed.
And he promises that he will do it. But
his way is through the cross of Jesus
Christ, not through brutal acts of terror-
ism. His call is to holy living, not holy
war. His invitation is to discipleship, not
senseless fanaticism.

He promises that "If any man is in Christ, he is a new creation; the old has gone, the new has come!" (2 Cor. 5:17). God knows that's what we need most right now!—Gary C. Redding

Illustrations

"TOXIC RELIGION." You remember the mass suicide of more than 900 followers of a cult leader named Jim Jones, don't you? In the name of God, he ordered them to drink poison, and they blindly followed him to their death. Then there was one of those occasional, sensational stories in the newspaper about an eighty-five-year-old woman in Buena Vista, California, who was stabbed several times by her live-in nurse during an argument over religion.—Gary C. Redding

CONCERN FOR ALL PEOPLE. I was preaching revival services in the jack pines of Minnesota. We were hiking down the firebreak trails, stopping at each little cabin to invite the folks to attend. When I asked about one particular road, I was told that only one house was on it, right at the end of the trail. I was told that the old hermit who lived there would probably be the last person in the world to be interested in coming to church.

When you are a seventeen-year-old evangelist out to save the world, you are not deterred by such pessimistic assumptions. The grizzled old man who answered my knock, even as the folks had said, assured me God wasn't interested in him and he sure wasn't interested in God.

I challenged him that if I could prove God was interested in him, would he be interested in God. He told me that he just might be. Then I asked him to read 2 Peter 3:3–9. When he had finished reading, he looked up with tears in his eyes and replied, "First time I ever knowed God cared about mountain men the likes of me."—Walter M. Fox

Sermon Suggestions

GOD'S COVENANT WITH YOU. TEXT: Gen. 17:1–7, 15–16. You and I are not Abram, but we too can have an agreement with God. (1) God initiates the covenant. (2) God imposes certain requirements: a., to live in God's presence. b., to be blameless. (3) God promises a gracious outcome.

THE SPIRIT AT WORK IN US. TEXT: Rom. 8:13–25. (1) Conquers our lower nature (verse 13). (2) Leads us to filial freedom (verses 14–16). (3) Promises our ultimate redemption (verses 22–25).

Worship Aids

CALL TO WORSHIP. "Jesus answered and said unto him, If a man loves me, he will keep my words; and my Father will love him, and we will come unto him, and make our abode with him" (John 14:23).

INVOCATION. Today, our Father, increase our love for thee, that we may know more of thy infilling presence and in turn share in a greater way with the world the Good News of thy salvation.

OFFERTORY SENTENCE. "The silver is mine, and the gold is mine, saith the Lord of hosts" (Hag. 2:8).

OFFERTORY PRAYER. O Lord, receive our offering this day, and our pledge anew to be good stewards, faithful witnesses, and a people of prayer.—E. Lee Phillips

PRAYER. Lord, as we come to you we are aware that we live in a world that is yet in the making. Mystery lies all about us. Truth seems to come by bits and pieces and after much struggle. We ask for your light to lead us as we journey along. We ask that you be with those who are set aside as leaders that they may guide us in the ways of peace. Deliver them from personal ambition and from the desire for exaltation and power, that they may be guided by justice and righteousness rather than folly and misfortune.

Bless those who keep the wheels of life turning and are never recognized for their efforts. Thank you for the steady work they do, for the endless days they labor, and for the great good they do for those who walk a more exciting pathway.

Bless those who instruct the mind, who teach at all levels of learning. Thank you for their dedication and their sacrifices that better prepare us to deal with the issues of life as they arise all along our lifeway.

Bless those who challenge us by demanding the best that we have to give. Thank you that they make us stretch our efforts and many times our faith in order to meet their challenge.

Bless those who make us more aware of your presence in our midst. Thank you that they are among us to instruct us in your ways, to show us by their example the higher way of life and to enable us to experience steady growth in grace and Christlikeness.

Open for us the windows of heaven and let us see, if but for a fleeting moment, the wonder of the working of your Spirit moving among us and calling us to you. For this we pray in Jesus' name . . .

—Henry Fields

LECTIONARY MESSAGE

Topic: Peter and James and John . . . and Jesus

TEXT: Mark 9:2–9

The first prediction of the Passion is recorded in Mark 8:31. Jesus spoke the saying openly and Simon Peter rebuked him . . . this will never happen to you! Jesus deplored Peter's rebuke and rebuked him in turn: Satan! The Transfiguration was designed to prepare the disciples for the inevitable sufferings of Jesus. So, six days after the prediction of the Passion Jesus took Peter and James and John with him to the mountain. Why not all of the disciples?

I. He was transfigured before them. His garments became glistening white, and Mark adds the detail (from Peter): no fuller or cleaner or laundry could make them so white. He was shining so brightly as to be unapproachable. His appearance was overwhelming.

Were they beginning to understand the prediction of the Passion and the de-

mands of discipleship? There is no such indication. Was Jesus becoming more than a good fishing buddy? How does Jesus appear to you in various situations?

II. He talked with Elijah and Moses. We have come to identify Elijah as the ideal, courageous, clearly speaking prophet. He represents all of the prophets. We have come to identify Moses as the miracle-working, masterful leader, law-giver. He represented all of the Law that day.

Sometimes we forget that both Elijah and Moses experienced death in a manner designed by God. Elijah was borne aloft in a fiery chariot. Moses was buried by God in the land of Moab, and no one knows where. This suggests at least that God is to be close at hand in the suffering of his Son. It is Luke who tells us the subject of their conversation: the Exodus. The word means departure aside from its historical reference. It refers to death—the Exodus or departure which Jesus was about to accomplish in Jerusalem. What could Elijah and Moses tell Jesus about death?

III. Peter made a proposal. Peter was most apt to make a proposal. It was not evil, but not practically good either. Let's stay here. We can worship. We can rejoice. Let's preserve the inspiration of the moment. The result, and Peter may never have thought of it, would be to ignore the needs of others. As it turned out, Jesus was desperately needed by a father and his son in the valley.

But then Peter was scared out of his wits. He did not understand the prediction of the Passion and he did not understand what was happening to his friend Jesus.

IV. He talked with Peter and James and John. The cloud overshadowed their fear and embarrassment. The voice acclaimed Jesus as God's Son. They were not to be anxious about Elijah and Moses. They were to hear Jesus only. Jesus dealt patiently with their misunderstanding. He understood their reluctance to accept his suffering and death. He knew that they would like to preserve his presence and his power.

As they came down the mountain he counseled silence. They were not ready to tell of their experience. They did not yet understand it. Until they understood the meaning of his suffering they were to be silent. Until after the Cross and the Resurrection they were to remain silent.

They could not understand the glory of the Transfiguration until they experienced both defeat and triumph.

And we too must experience the Cross and the Resurrection before we can understand the transfigured glory of God's Son.—J. Estill Jones

SUNDAY: MARCH SIXTH

SERVICE OF WORSHIP

Sermon: The Parable of the Tares Among the Wheat

Text: Matt. 13:24–30, 36–43

When we considered the parable of the mustard seed, it may have appeared at first glance that here we were going to be presented with an optimistic prognosis of the development of Christianity. After we read this parable we can hardly slip into the misconception of a "happy ending" for church history. For this parable speaks of a dark menace, a mysterious power that is everywhere at work—and not only out there among the dubious excrescences of civilization, but also in the innermost sanctuary itself. In this very moment in which the Word of God sounds from the pulpit that sinister power is also sowing its toxic seed among the furrows. Where theologians sit poring over the scriptures that dark power sows between the lines the seeds of man's own thinking, causing the wisdom of the Greeks to triumph over the foolishness of the Cross and spreading the grave clothes of human, all too human thoughts upon the open Easter grave and turning the mighty acts of God into the humbug of idle self-assertion.

I. Now, depressing as these intimations of Jesus may be, they may also reassure us, for at least they accord with our own experience.

(a) We have only to look at life with open eyes to see this strange ambiguity: There are no fields or gardens in this world where only grain or flowers grow; the weeds are always there too. And when we declare somewhat resignedly, "There is nothing perfect in this world," this is only a somewhat trite expression of this experience.

(b) We have this experience even outside the church of Jesus. We need only think of technical science to demonstrate this. There is such a thing as progress in technical science. We have penetrated deeper into the mysteries of nature and are able to coax from it energies undreamed of by former generations. But since, with all this progress, man has remained the same, has not changed, his increasing power over creation is paralleled by the increasingly cruel and murderous power which he uses against himself and his fellows.

(c) And now this parable shows us that this same mysterious twilight hangs over the church of Christ and that here too another figure, spectral and shadowy, a demonic double, follows the divine sower, scattering seeds of negation and destruction. For example, there is that Word of God, formulated by Paul, which says that where sin abounds grace abounds all the more (Rom. 5:20). But strangely enough, "overnight" even this greatest of the gifts of God is poisoned. We turn it into a "pretext for evil" (1 Pet. 5:20). That is, we say to ourselves: Well, if we are always in right with God anyhow, a little more or a little less dirt on our conscience doesn't matter. A few side trips more or less into the far country don't matter to us, for, after all, God is not really angry and nothing really bad can happen to us in the end anyhow. So we turn this costly grace, for which Jesus shed his blood, into cheap, marked-down merchandise.

II. It is very strange how everything—even the greatest thing that Jesus gives us—mysteriously spoils, decays, and is delivered over to ambiguity when that dark power gets its fingers on it. Beneath these fingers it is not only the wheat field that is sown with weeds; the grace of God itself becomes a cadaver and our Father's royal declaration of emancipation is turned into wastepaper.

(a) Thus the weeds are always mixed with the divine seed. On the one hand, God is concerned that his gospel should give a man some inner support. But no sooner is God there than others too are approaching him. Overnight somebody comes to him and whispers something, plants something in his years. And so they turn Christianity into a political ideology, something to hold the body politic together, opium for the people.

Always during the night that dark figure has gone through God's fields, and the next morning something altogether different comes up. Alongside of the Word of God something else grows up high. From a distance it looks very much like the Word, just as the weeds look like real grain from afar. But when one looks a bit closer one finds that what is left of the divine words is nothing but empty Christian words in which there is no fruit. There is the word "grace," and it is only a religious term for "nonchalance." There is the word "Christianity," but instead of containing the seed of eternity it represents nothing more than sterile hypocrisy. People think the purpose of the gospel is only to make people better, more serious, more respectable, when its real concern is rather that death may be conquered, that we may be delivered from fear and find a new security.

(b) And what is true about the content of the message is true also of the people who have gathered around it. There is Judas in the midst of the apostles, here are real disciples alongside of merely nominal church members, here are martyrs and apostates, orthodoxists and heretics, people with halos and sham saints, Pharisees and harlots, all mixed together. How in the world can we ever distinguish between them? How can we refrain from crying out: Get rid of the weeds! or even: This Christianity is a dreadful mess!

III. What really happened during that mysterious night the parable speaks of?

(a) The man who sowed the good seed went home and laid himself down to sleep. What happens next—the outcome of his sowing, the effect of the Word— this is no longer under his control.

At first nothing happens that can be seen. But one morning he is bewildered to discover that overnight and altogether unnoticed something terrible has happened and there ensues a lively argument with his servants which is replete with expressions of amazement and dismay.

(b) How many a father, how many a mother has had the same experience? They have reared their child carefully, surrounded him with a good clean atmosphere, cherished him with love, and prayed with him and for him at his cradle at night. And, despite all this, something else begins to grow. Strange things happen in him. They see stirrings and impulses in him that they do not want to see at all. Another influence comes beaming in from an altogether different quarter and they can do nothing about it.

(c) What should be done? We understand the angry reaction of the servants, who want to go out immediately and rip out the weeds, even though, from a farmer's point of view, this is almost impossible. Nor does the Lord permit this. Rather, he says, "Let both grow together until the harvest. You can't change things. Leave the decision, leave the separation of the weeds from the wheat to the judgment day of God. "This is not your affair. God will take this thing in hand in his good time."

IV. What is it that causes our Lord, so strangely, it seems, to stifle the holy zeal of his people and to say to them, "Hands off! You cannot change the field of the world as it is anyhow"?

(a) If I am not mistaken, he had three reasons for this. First, he is saying: Please do not think that you can exterminate the evil in the world by your activity and your own personal exertions. After all, that evil is within you yourselves. This is not some human resistance that you must break down; rather it is the power of the great adversary which is at work in what is happening and intervening here. You are not fighting against "flesh and blood," but against the secret ruler of this world.

At this point human power is of no use whatsoever. "If your own power were of any use," Jesus is saying to us, "then I would not have had to die for you, then a moral appeal would have been enough. Therefore, judge not, but rather think of your own vulnerability! As for the rest, wait for the surprises of the last judgment. Until then let God's sun shine on the just and the unjust. Let God's clouds drop their rain on the good and the evil!"

(b) Second, the householder in the parable rejects any forcible intervention on the part of the servants for the same reason that Jesus forbade his disciples to call down fire from heaven to consume the hostile Samaritans (Luke 9:52 ff.). On that occasion he cried out in anger to his people, "You do not know what manner of spirit you are of; for the Son of man came not to destroy men's lives but to save them." We would therefore be spoiling God's plan of salvation if we were to organize a great "Operation Throw-them-out" if we were to cast out of the temple the hangers-on, the hypocrites, the "borderliners," and all the other wobblers in Christendom, in order to keep a small elite of saints.

For this would mean that we would rob these people of the chance at least to hear the Word and take it to heart. This would be to slam the door of the Father's house in their faces—and we would become a sect. But the very reason why Jesus died was to open the Father's house to everybody, including the superficial, the indifferent, the mockers, and revilers.

(c) Third, the householder in the parable explicitly points out that the servants are completely incapable of carrying out any proper separation of grain and weeds, which they look so much alike, and therefore in their zeal for weeding out the tares they would also root out the wheat. Here we come up against a point which is by no means a simple one for the interpreter. The problem is this: All of them, the householder as well as the servants, see that tares have actually been sown. So the fact is that they can distinguish between them. And yet the householder says, "Do not rip out the weeds too soon; otherwise you will destroy the real fruit along with them." And this means that they cannot distinguish, after all.

Who is not reminded here of Jesus' saying: "Judge not, that you be not judged"? We ought rather to pray for imperiled souls—and also for our own souls, which are so beset by the spirit of care and judgment and self-righteousness. We ought to let God give us the long patience that serenely and confidently awaits the last day and its surprises.

V. The last judgment is full of surprises. The separation of sheep and goats, of wheats and weeds will be made in a way completely different from that which we permit ourselves to imagine. For God is more merciful than we, more strict than we, and more knowing than we. And, in every case, God is greater than our hearts. But one thing is certain and that is that Jesus the King will come with his sickle and crown. Then our sickles will fall and all the false and illegal crowns will drop from men's heads. Then all will be changed and everything will be different, utterly different. But one thing will remain: love, the love in which we have believed and hoped and endured, the love which never let us forget that God can find and bring home and set at his table even the blasphemers, the erring, the deceivers, and the deceived.

May he give us the grace of the long view and the calmness to live confidently in the name of his victory—until one day he shall say to us and to those for whom we have interceded: "Well done, good and faithful servant; enter into the joy of your master."—Helmut Thielicke

Illustrations

TAKING A SECOND LOOK.   You know, every time I think I have God, or life, pretty well figured out and I start rummaging through the Bible, then zap!

Some new shaft of light shatters my neat little God-package or life-package. My cozy figuring out is undercut or deflated, and I've got to take a fresh look at the whole business again. Of course, if this didn't happen the Bible would have no authority for us. It would not convey a word from the beyond at all; it would simply be a dull, commonplace book, handy to have around to confirm me in my prejudices and partial understandings. For if this Bible is in any sense a Word of God, then by its very nature it has to startle and surprise, shake us up. It just won't let me spell life, or God, with the letters of my alphabet.—Edmund Steimle

PROTESTING TOO MUCH. This is the tragedy of all social reformers and moralists; they want to root out vice, drinking, smoking, free love. And as they set out in grim earnest on their virtuous crusades these good people are quite oblivious of the fact that (to speak with Goethe's Faust) the devil has hung himself about their necks. Why is it that as a rule we find it so hard to endure these do-gooders and reformers? Why do they make us feel so uncomfortable? Because we sense something Pharisaic and superior in them, because the very vice upon which they are making a frontal attack is at the same time in their own hearts, like a partisan army fighting in their rear.—Helmut Thielicke

Sermon Suggestions

INDICATIVE AND IMPERATIVE. TEXT: Exod. 20:1–17. (1) God is gracious and merciful toward his people, despite their unworthiness, verses 1–3. (2) God requires of those redeemed people an ethical response worthy of what they have received, verses 4–17.

THE HEART OF THE GOSPEL. TEXT: 1 Cor. 1:18–25. (1) What it is not: it is not what one would expect. a., It defies the canons of power. b., It defies the canons of wisdom. c., It does not depend on human eloquence (see 1:17). (2) What it is: it is "the message about the cross". a., The

cross demonstrates a different kind of power, confirmed in Christ's Resurrection. b., The cross manifests a different kind of wisdom revealed by the Spirit (see 2:14–16).

Worship Aids

CALL TO WORSHIP. "The hour cometh, and now is, when the true worshipers shall worship the Father in spirit and in truth; for the Father seeketh such to worship him" (John 4:23).

INVOCATION. Lord, as we meet we know we are met. As we pray our prayers take different forms. As we listen we sense the will and working of God in new ways. Lord, do new things in us today as we worship and wait.—E. Lee Phillips

OFFERTORY SENTENCE. "Seek ye first the Kingdom of God and his righteousness, and all these things shall be added unto you" (Matt. 6:33).

OFFERTORY PRAYER. Our Father, we have trouble establishing our priorities in life. Help us to know what really counts in the end, so that we may give our hearts to matters of first importance. Let no earthly love stand between us and our doing what life is all about. In the name of him who loved us, lived for us, and died for us.

PRAYER. O God of joy and gladness, you have placed us in the midst of a world in which each of us may find mountain-top experiences of relationship. You have blessed our homes with the cries and coos of infants, the giggles and gregariousness of children, and the gentleness and grandeur of parents in loving relationships. You have given us a glimpse of who you are, as we have loved and been loved as husband and wife.

We have seen the dark side of life as well, dear God, as relationships have not turned out to be what we had hoped. Some of us have lost loved ones to disease before dreams were fulfilled. Some watched as children chose pathways that we could not walk with them. Some have experienced abuse in relationships fed by self-gratification rather than grace.

In the spirit of hope, we come to you in search of those positive paths of life that will enable us to live in celebrated joy and winsome gladness. Grant unto us the peace of mind that comes with knowing there are some aspects of life that will remain unchanged, that there are circumstances and events that will call us forth with conviction to change, and that wisdom will be found in discerning the difference between the two.

Enable us, then, to make a difference in the place where we live. Grant us the maturity that will allow our children to grow and become individual members of your family, expressing the uniqueness you have placed within them. Grant us the love that will bring wholeness to relationships as we each seek the good of the other. Drive away the dark despair of death by the assurance that each of us has a room in your heavenly home.

Set us, then, upon the journey of life with the certainty that in all things you work for good in those who love you. Bring joy and gladness upon us so that our lives might reflect who and what you are and we might become your blessing in the place where we live. Through Jesus Christ, our Lord.—Robert F. Langwig

LECTIONARY MESSAGE

Topic: Temples

TEXT: John 2:13–22

Temples were built as the dwelling place of deities. They became places of worship by virtue of the deity's presence. But ancient temples were not built for the comfort of the worshipers—padded pews, air conditioning, central heat, etc. The Temple in Jerusalem was reasonably new after having been under construction for forty-six years. At the Passover season the Temple was a busy place. Jesus considered the Temple to be his Father's house. Earlier the child had lingered in the Temple "in the things of my Father" (Luke 2:49). Now he visited the Temple and registered disappointment at what he saw.

I. A desecrated Temple. There was little room for God. Some of his worshipers found little room. The paraphernalia for sacrifice was necessary. Was it necessary in the Temple itself? True—it was more convenient for a Galilean to purchase an ox in Jerusalem for the sacrifice than to drive one from Galilee to Jerusalem. True—it was more convenient to change Roman coins into acceptable Jewish coinage than to go to a bank for the transaction. But human greed dictated such excesses that the Temple no longer resembled either a dwelling place for God or a place of worship.

In all probability the trading took place in the court of the Gentiles. It was the only place where they could worship and now they were effectively excluded from it. It is Mark who adds the striking phrase, "for all the nations." "My house shall be called a house of prayer for all the nations." Where would we have worshiped in Jerusalem's Temple? Did they and other Jews resent this mercantile intrusion? Does a neighbor's dog pen adjacent to your house cause resentment?

II. A dedicated Temple. Only John includes the detail of the scourge of cords. Jesus appears angry in this Gospel and this justifiable divine wrath served to cleanse the Temple. There is an element of human courage present, too. He did not simply step into the Temple courts and shout "get out." He intentionally prepared to dedicate the Temple. He made a scourge of cords, whether to use on the livestock or the traders we do not know.

He drove out the animals. He poured out the money of the tradesmen. What profits must have resulted from their piety! He overthrew their tables. The prescribed furniture in the Temple was sparse. He forced the dove-dealers out. And doves were the symbols of peace. He rebuked them all for having made the dwelling place of God a merchandise mart.

III. A new Temple. "What do you mean?" "By what authority have you done this?" "Who gave you the right?" "Don't worry," he said, "Destroy this Temple and in three days I will raise it up." The Jewish leadership did not understand that he spoke of his body. A different Greek word, *naos*, is used in verse 19. It is distinguished from *hieron* as the sanctuary, the place made holy by God's dwelling. *Hieron* may well refer to all of the Temple complex. Beyond sacrifices there would be new life. Beyond the Resurrection there would be new understanding.

The Temple reached its zenith in sacrifices. Beyond his sacrifice the new Temple would continue as a dwelling place for God. And so it did, and so it does, for we are members of his body. Only after the resurrection did they understand. That's true for us as well. — J. Estill Jones

SUNDAY: MARCH THIRTEENTH

SERVICE OF WORSHIP

Sermon: Learning How to Believe

TEXT: John 4:46–53

Here is the story of a man who learned to believe. God might use John's little story to help us learn how to believe. Is it possible that we think that we have no such need? We may protest that we have been believers for a long time.

But we may think too that if we did not need faith at all, then we would know what life really is, what it means to be truly human. That would interest us much more than a God whom we never quite know. However, if we are really sincere about that, if we actually live and refuse just to vegetate, then we have to ask ourselves whether we can actually live without meeting him who gives this life its ultimate meaning and its profoundest justification.

We now come to our text: Here is an important man, secure, looking forward to a pension. Yet for him it is one of those times when a man cannot just go on marking time but has to live on the alert. Here, for instance, is a child at the point of death, and one has to think about him day and night; one must try to find some way to save him; one must keep in mind others who are hard-pressed trying to care for him. One must give comfort and help and at the same time play through to the end the drama of life oneself.

I. Life does not just run by itself. Every morning, and hour by hour, one has to attempt to meet life in the right way and to avoid mistakes. Often in times of suffering and need we live much more alertly and intensely.

(a) For the man in our story it is, of course, the time of heavy burden. During this time he dares something. He dares to pray. He dares to expect help, not merely from what he does, but from Jesus. As yet, he knows very little about Jesus. He is no believer in the sense that he is convinced that Jesus is the Son of God or anything like that. But he dares very earnestly to count on him. Why he does so remains a mystery.

(b) The true beginning of such a story is forever a mystery. When we are able really to pray for the first time, we may pray very unsurely and perhaps stumble again and again, for we will not be content to go on just repeating what others have taught us. So, in spite of misgivings and mistakes, it is an incredible, inexplicable gift. But I am persuaded that this gift is available to us much more often than we are aware, for we are preoccupied elsewhere when the opportunity comes, and those times when our heart could learn to pray just pass by.

II. The man in our story is still childlike enough to admit that he now needs God and comes for that very reason. He does not know exactly who Jesus is, but he tells Jesus clearly and distinctly what is in his heart and that he expects him to do something for him.

(a) "Jesus therefore said to him, 'Unless you see signs and wonders you will not believe.'" The first thing the official learns is that prayer does not help. He learns that God is not a vending machine into which a man can insert a prayer instead of a dime and get an answer to prayer instead of a chocolate bar. If we pray in such a manner that we insist on seeing "signs and wonders," if we determine to compel God more or less with our praying to carry out our purposes and give him the alternative either of helping us or of no longer being taken seriously, then God will stand aloof. For that would be magic, not greater faith.

(b) The person who prays earnestly is precisely the person who encounters the hidden, incomprehensible God. This God brings us into need and temptation, for God's will is often so different from ours that we endure long, agonizing hours before it finally dawns on us what God intends to do with us. The hard No of Jesus, which the man had to hear before he heard anything else, may last days, weeks, or months. It lasts until we can pray from the depths of our hearts in such a way that we do not demand the kind of "sign and wonder" that would please us; it lasts until we are willing to meet God and take everything on his terms.

(c) "The official said to him, 'Sir, come down before my child dies.'" The splendid thing about this man is that he does not give up; he simply asks again when Jesus would have said nothing. He does not take Jesus to task because Jesus does not give him immediately what he wants. He does not say, "That proves it again—there is no God. I've just been chattering into thin air." He keeps on asking and says the same thing over again. He just stays where he is and refuses to be driven off.

III. And now comes the most difficult thing of all: "Jesus said to him, 'Go, your son will live.' The man believed the word that Jesus spoke to him and went his way." This man has nothing to go on but a word. We do not put much stock in words. In our experience, words too often have been nothing but words. Theologians have sometimes contributed to our disappointment at this point.

(a) The man in our story bore in mind that enormous power is often embedded in a word spoken with authority. The text tells us that he began to believe. Faith is something that begins to grow. We reach a very significant turning point when once we dare take the word that Jesus speaks to us so seriously that we begin to live by it. With only a word to go on, the official walks or rides back fifteen miles.

(b) However, his faith does not end there. "As he was going down, his servants met him and told him that his son was living. So he asked them the hour when he began to mend, and they said to him, 'Yesterday at the seventh hour the fever left him.' The father knew that was the hour when Jesus had said to him, 'Your son will live'; and he himself believed, and all his household."

IV. So the man is permitted to discover God. God really happens. I am well aware that many children die in spite of their fathers' prayers. But I also know that if we venture with God we actually learn to know him. For us it can be every bit as wonderful as it was in this story.

(a) The experience can assume widely different forms. Paul once wrote that the deepest experience of God he had known came when the Lord Jesus refused to grant his petition but said to him that God's power was nearest in his weakness—and said it in such a way that he learned to believe it.

(b) Once again, our text tells us that the man came to believe. But what was the highest, the ultimate occasion of faith? When the man went toward home solely on the basis of the word of Jesus? The text does not say that. The highest occasion is the experience of the living God. His faith has increased so much that he gives light to others, and all of his household are drawn into faith with him. The entire New Testament is aware of this goal of faith. It speaks again and again of its consummation in the resurrection of the dead, in the kingdom of God.

V. So a man dares to make a petition simply because he is in serious trouble. He keeps at it even though it seems that nothing at all may come of it and that Jesus has nothing to say to his problem. He dares to rely on the word, although for the next stretch of the road he has nothing but a word. At the end of this stretch of the road he is permitted to learn that God is real and that the word is true. And he is permitted to radiate enough of his experience to make it possible for others associated with him to be received into this faith. So that is the way God wants to go with us all at this very moment. And he is already on the way with us.—Eduard Schweizer

Illustrations

FORGIVENESS AND ASSURANCE. While the Word accepts and sustains us, there is nevertheless no fusion of God's being with ours, no identification of the godly nature with human nature. The Word accepts us and bears us in that he forgives sin and keeps us in the commandments of God. The relationship of the Word to us is one of providing forgiveness and assurance along the pathways of our lives.—Dietrich Bonhoeffer

EXPERIENCING GOD. I have had experiences in my own life that seem to be totally alien to an experience of God. Yet they turn out to be substantial experiences—real, authentic experiences—of God.

A nurse told me about a young man who was struck down by severe infantile paralysis and could breathe only with the aid of an artificial lung. After four years he was completely embittered and defeated. The miracle of God happened to him when he was able to say "yes" to what he had to live with. Inwardly he was totally free from that moment.—Eduard Schweizer

Sermon Suggestions

WHEN SICKNESS COMES. TEXT: Ps. 107:1–3, 17–22. (1) It may be nobody's fault. (2) It may be the result of our "sinful ways" (verse 17). (3) In any case, it is time to cry to the Lord (verse 19). (4) Healing is an occasion for thanksgiving (verses 20–22).

JOURNEY FROM SIN TO SERVICE. TEXT: Eph. 2:1–10. (1) Our condemnation—sinful, guilty, and on the way to ruin. (2) Our frustration—unable to save ourselves. (3) Our salvation—the undeserved favor of God received through faith. (4) Our vocation—good works as our way of life.

Worship Aids

CALL TO WORSHIP. "Rend your heart, and not your garments, and turn unto the Lord your God: for he is gracious and merciful, slow to anger, and of great kindness, and repenteth him of the evil" (Joel 2:13).

INVOCATION. Hear us, Lord, as we sing and pray and repent. Deal with our sin, our hopes, our searching after the things of God, and fill us with the expectant hope that faith brings.

OFFERTORY SENTENCE. "Unto whomsoever much is given, of him shall be much required; and to whom men have committed much, of him they will ask the more" (Luke 12:48).

OFFERTORY PRAYER. Lord, redeem with our gifts where new life is needed; restore with our gifts where new hope is needed; revive with our gifts where love is needed; that the gifts of a few may bless many as the gift of One blesses all, even Christ, our Savior.—E. Lee Phillips

PRAYER. Lord, you called Matthew from the tax tables and fishermen from their nets to come and follow you. Grant us the grace to accept you as our Savior and follow you as our Master.

You welcomed the Apostle Peter's confession of faith when he declared you to be the Christ, the Son of the living God. Grant that we may enter into a saving knowledge of you as the eternal Christ and our Savior.

You welcomed the inquiry of the Greeks, the faith of a Roman centurion, and the thanks of a grateful Samaritan. Grant us the grace to rise above prejudice for those of a different race or creed that our personal relationships may be in harmony with your love for all human-kind.

Lord, you welcomed the support of the disciples who stood by you in your trials. Grant us the wisdom to make the right decisions at the parting of the ways and give us the courage to pursue right as you give us the ability to see right. You commanded your apostles James and John to fling away ambition and become as little children. This morning deliver us from unseemly ambition and grant us the grace of humility.

You declared yourself to Thomas as "the way, the truth and the life." Lead us along the path that we should go and bring us to the Father's house in peace, we pray.

Then, Lord, you sent forth seventy disciples through the cities and towns of Galilee to prepare for your coming. Use us as ambassadors of good tidings as we make our way through the towns and villages of our day in the Galilee where we daily walk. You have said that you will judge people at the last according to their faith and service to the world in your name as ministry is given to the sick, the imprisoned, the poor, the hungry, and the dispossessed. Give us the grace to serve the needy in your name, to spend and be spent in the ministry of compassion, reconciliation, and caring for the least, the last, and the lost. This prayer we make in your powerful name.—Henry Fields

LECTIONARY MESSAGE

Topic: Loving the Light and Eternal Life

TEXT: John 3:14–21

We're so well-acquainted with our text that we no longer really see it. Our familiarity breeds spiritual blindness. The famous verse 16 is the chief example. It is "the gospel in a nutshell"—or to put the matter more formally, in the words of Alvah Hovey, "an epitome of the whole gospel." The entire mission of Jesus from its origin in God's love, through its climax in Christ's death and Resurrection, to its goal in eternal life is capsuled in one much memorized verse.

So, let's pretend to be like Nicodemus—a first-time hearer of Jesus' discourse. Nicodemus has been engaged in a searching dialogue with Jesus about being "born again" and "born from above." Now that dialogue—and Nicodemus along with it—fades into the background. The spotlight then focuses upon Jesus alone.

I. Lifting up the serpent (vv. 14–15). Jesus recalls the story from Numbers 21:4–9. To stop the plague of poisonous serpents, following the Lord's instructions, "Moses made a serpent of bronze, and put it upon a pole; and whenever a serpent bit someone, that person would look at the serpent of bronze and live" (Num. 21:9, NRSV).

The Hebrew word (*nes*) used for that standard-bearing pole literally refers to a miraculous sign. So, John sees the miracles of Jesus (the Christ lifted up on the cross) as signs (Greek *semeia*) which point to the true identity of Jesus. Persons who see the signs and spiritually understand the works and words of Jesus will be led to eternal life. Nicodemus is one of those seekers who are led to encounter Christ because of the miraculous signs Jesus performed (3:2).

II. Loving the world (vv. 16–18). At the foundation of the Christian faith is not world-denial, but divine love for the world. Christians may at times be commanded not to love the evil "things in the world" (1 John 2:15), but they are always to express God's love to the people in the world. God not only loves the disciples—the children of the light—but the whole of humanity—"all the children of the world."

The result of God's supreme and universal love is expressed in two great themes of the life of Jesus. First, Jesus is given to humanity in his birth. This is the teaching of Incarnation, "the Word became flesh and lived among us" (John 1:14). Second, Jesus is given to humanity through his death. This is the doctrine of atonement, "he was wounded for our transgressions, crushed for our iniquities" (Isa. 53:5). Jesus is the suffering Son of God. All who believe in Jesus Christ—

God incarnate in suffering love—will receive the gift of eternal life.

John emphasizes God's positive purpose for the world in the gift of Jesus (v. 17). God loves the world and sends the Son to save it, not to condemn it. Christian proclamation which does not stress salvation through God's love in Jesus Christ is false gospel because it distorts or evades the intention of God. The reality of humanity's unbelief, however, is not ignored. Verse 18 points to the self-created condemnation of "those who do not believe." As Hovey observes, unbelief is not "the only sin," but it is "the reason why, as a matter of fact (humanity) is still condemned for sin of whatever kind." Christian proclamation which does not acknowledge the condemnation of unbelief is false gospel because it ignores the reality of sin.

III. Living in the light (vv. 19–21). The powerful imagery of light illumines the truth of Jesus' teachings in this discourse. We see the judgment (Greek *krisis*) of God as the sad accompaniment to the coming of light into the world. We have the choice of either drawing near to the light or separating ourselves from it. Fear of exposure by the light of truth drives people away from the light.

This dark side is the *result* of our rejection of God; it is not an expression of the purpose of God. As John Marsh explains, "The perishing of the unbeliever is not a punishment for unbelief inflicted by a ruthless God; it is the self-determined end of the person who does not believe."

If we choose the darkness over the light, then we will experience condemnation, rather than the saving purpose of God. We will live in self-chosen separation from "the light of the knowledge of the glory of God in the face of Jesus Christ" (2 Cor. 4:6). What a tragic irony that God's light of salvation has been refracted by human rejection into the dark night of judgment.

Verses 20 and 21 present us with two ways. The people who follow each way are polar opposites. Along one way are those who "hate the light," fearing its exposure of their evil deeds. On the other are those who "come to the light," which will reveal that they "do what is true." The choice is ours.

Living in the light means committing our lives to doing the truth. When we do the truth and come to the light, it will reveal that our "deeds have been done in God"—empowered and sustained by God's grace.—Charles J. Scalise

SUNDAY: MARCH TWENTIETH

SERVICE OF WORSHIP

Sermon: The Suffering Question

TEXT: John 18:1–11

There hung, for as long as I remember, a special painting in the little brick church where I grew up. The picture was a very good reproduction of Johann Heinrich Hoffman's "Christ in Gethsemane."

In that painting, Jesus knelt in the garden. His hands were folded before him on the rock in prayer. If you looked very closely, in the distance you could make out the dim figures of the sleeping disciples. Further back, in the darkness, you could almost see the gates of the city of Jerusalem. It was night. The only light in the painting shone from above. The light illuminated the face of Jesus.

The garden portrayed so clearly in that painting is not as carefully defined in John's Gospel. John 18 begins the Passion narrative by saying: "When Jesus had spoken these words, he went forth with his disciples across the Kidron valley, where there was a garden, which he and his disciples entered" (v. 1).

A great many events are compressed into one paragraph. Judas led the soldiers to arrest Jesus. Simon Peter, in anger and defiance, pulled out his sword and lopped off the ear of one enemy. Jesus strongly rebuked his disciple.

I. In this turbulent setting, Jesus asked the suffering question of Simon Peter:

"Put your sword into its sheath; shall I not drink the cup which the Father has given me?" (v. 11). Only here does John use the word cup. Mark employs the word on several occasions to speak of Christ's suffering. This "cup" represented many things: Christ's pain, his agony at facing God's will of the cross. The "cup" was the facing of his own death.

(a) Simon Peter had not understood at all. In an act of great courage, he had drawn his sword to protect his Lord. Simon would have spared his Lord that "cup."

(b) Most of us do not want to face the suffering question either. We do not welcome suffering. We are more comfortable with growth, success, and acceptance.

(c) Yet the picture of Christ in the garden remains. Gethsemane is at the heart of the story. Without that "cup" filled with suffering, pain, and death, there would have been no gospel.

II. The tools of Christ's trade reversed all the values the world holds important. The weapons of his warfare were never carnal. He chose the foolish things to confound the mighty. One day it would be a towel and a basin; another day it would be prayers and forgiveness. On another occasion it would be turning the other cheek and walking a second mile. There, at the end, he took a "cup" and drank all the hurt and pain the world could offer. The next two chapters of John's Gospel define more clearly the suffering question.

III. My own pilgrimage with the suffering of Jesus continued several years ago when I was invited back to that little church where I had grown up. It was an anniversary occasion, and they had invited people who had been members through the years to come back for that special day. As I prepared for that occasion, I remembered the painting that hung over the pulpit and the choir all my growing-up years. I had not thought of that picture in twenty years. But it all came back—the picture of Jesus in the garden. As I stood to preach, I looked out on a sea of faces, and the memories washed over me. I talked to them that day about how we had lived all our lives while Jesus knelt in the garden.

(a) I told them that once upon a time there had come One who knelt in a garden and prayed for the likes of us—One who took a "cup," terrible and bitter, and drank it all for us. And I told them that if he could endure and discover and find something redemptive in his journey, we could find it, too.

(b) That morning, my old neighbors from down the street were there to see if I could preach. My mother had told me they both were dying of cancer. Halfway back, on my right there was the sweetest woman I have ever known: a widow with diabetes. After the service she came by to say that she could not see me, but she heard every word. She sat with her youngest, a seventeen-year-old boy on crutches.

Two rows back from the back sat my old high school buddy, fat and bald as a billiard ball. Beside him sat his wife, beautiful as the day we graduated but flawed with a fever that left her motor functions awry.

On the front row was my neighbor. We had lived side by side, and I had played with her only son. She could not even hold a song book—the arthritis was so bad. She sat there blinking back the tears, for she had lost her only son—my age—five years before with a heart ailment. We had all gathered to listen again to the old, old story. Jesus knelt in the garden and prayed for us all. And he took a "cup" and drank it for the suffering of us all.

IV. No wonder, through the years, that little cotton-mill congregation kept that picture of Jesus in the garden high above their pulpit. It was a reminder that in it all—the good and the bad, the dark and the sunny—God identifies, God suffers, and God cares. This is the suffering question. It takes us all in. And, in the taking, it changes us one and all. For those who come to terms with this question bear, believe, hope, and endure it all—not as the defeated—but more than conquerors.—Roger Lovette

Illustrations

THE WAY LIFE IS. I once read about a man who shortly before World War II believed that a global conflict was coming. He decided to find a place he could be safe whatever happened. He studied the map of the world and chose one of the most remote and least populated islands on the globe. He moved there. The island turned out to be Guadalcanal, the scene of one of the bloodiest battles in human history.—Ernest A. Fitzgerald

LIKE THE EAGLE. E. Stanley Jones somewhere describes an eagle flying high among the mountain crags. Suddenly a quick storm descends, and it seems for the moment that its fury will dash him to death against the cliffs. But the eagle faces the storm, tilts his wings at a proper angle, and slowly the fury that might have crushed him begins to drive him upward—until at last he rises above the storm. The very power that would have destroyed him became the power by which he reached a new serenity high above the fury below. Faith in God is the tilting of the wings of the soul. The sorrows of life are the raging storm. Slowly the soul rises until it moves in a richness and peace never before known. And, strangely enough, the circumstance that causes its rise is one that normally would have crushed its spirit.—Jack Finegan

Sermon Suggestions

THE HEART OF THE MATTER. TEXT: Jer. 31:31–34. When God finally has his way with us: (1) It will not be the result of formal acceptance of an external code, too easily violated. (2) It will be the result of an inner consent, difficult to resist. (3) It will assure complete forgiveness of sins.

THE PRIESTHOOD OF JESUS CHRIST. TEXT: Heb. 5:5–10. (1) Appointed by God, not by human authority. (2) Not temporary like Levitical priesthood, but eternal. (3) Not without struggle, but through submission to God's will and the cross.

Worship Aids

CALL TO WORSHIP. "The sacrifices of God are a broken spirit; a broken and a contrite heart, O God, thou wilt not despise" (Ps. 51:17).

INVOCATION. Lord, though we gather for inspiration and fellowship, direction and instruction, we come first of all to praise and adore the Lord our God. Praise God from whom all blessings flow, praise the Lord forevermore!—E. Lee Phillips

OFFERTORY SENTENCE. "It is required in stewards, that a man be found faithful" (1 Cor. 4:2).

OFFERTORY PRAYER. Father, may we learn to trust more and more in your kind providence and care for us all and may our submission to your will be revealed in the deep devotion expressed through these gifts we offer today in Christ's name.—Henry Fields

PRAYER. Call us to your side, O Christ, even when following you is difficult. Your courage makes us strong. We would be near you in any trouble rather than without you in any peace. We remember and are thankful for what you did in those last days of your earthly life. We are thankful that your humility made kingship an instrument of thankful service, for your brave defiance that made courage visible, your tears of sorrow and love that were shed as you looked upon the troubled and needy and unconcerned of Jerusalem, your forgiveness of your enemies, thus showing us how to forgive, your thoughtfulness for those near and dear to you, your strong trust in God's love even when his face was hidden from you and you felt so utterly forsaken. How we thank you that you let us know once and for all that cruel death cannot conquer, and that in God's hands it is only an open door to life glorious and free from the pressing cares of this present age. With that grand truth we can stand in the face of circumstances that would otherwise crush us, and we can continue our appointed journey across the trail of life.

Because we know that you love each of us with love that is unending, we bring before you the cares and concerns of our hearts. Those who have suffered the earthly loss of loved ones come this morning with dry eyes but weeping hearts, Father, and in this sacred hour they are seeking some assurance for themselves, some understanding for life, some courage to walk on in their loneliness. By your infinite grace, still their troubled souls, calm their turbulent fears, undergird their courageous efforts with your infinite strength and bring them to new meaning in life, new faith in living and renewed love for you.

Those with troubled lives and confused relationships come this morning in their confusion seeking some strong guidance in their hard situations. Enable them to find light in their darkness, hope in their hopelessness, and meaning in their present existence. Out of their turmoil may there come the brightness of joyful days, the wonder of renewed faith, and the delight of stronger, renewed relationships when the present storms are stilled and past.

Those dealing with degrading temptations come this morning to find strength to resist evil and courage to follow good. Only you can bring into their lives the might of forgiveness, the power of high purpose, and the strong sense of noble dedication to your calling that is needed to fortify their wavering spirits.

Through all that we do here this morning let your name be glorified and magnified as we worship together for strength and guidance, praise and thanksgiving in the mighty name of Jesus Christ our Lord and Savior.—Henry Fields

LECTIONARY MESSAGE

Topic: The Cost of Discipleship
TEXT: John 12:20–33

A modern Christian martyr was the author of a book which bore the title, "The Cost of Discipleship." Dietrich Bonhoeffer, sacrificed to the cruel tyranny of Adolf Hitler, already knew a great deal about his subject, but was finally to experience the full cost. His witness, underscored by his final faithfulness, rings out loud and clear.

In the last public discourse recorded by John, Jesus spoke of the cost of following God's will. Four principles may be deduced from the discourse.

I. Life through death. It was a moment which might have been marked by high elation. A group of Greeks who had come to Jerusalem for the Passover celebration asked to see Jesus. The raising of Lazarus had vastly increased the popularity of Jesus. Preliminary description indicates that he may have been protected from the crowds by well-intentioned followers: the Greeks asked Philip, Philip asked Andrew, together they asked Jesus.

"Except a grain of wheat fall into the earth and die . . ." It is a natural truth: This is the way a seed sprouts. It loses its identifiable life and then comes really alive. It is a supernatural truth, soon to be verified by Jesus' own death and its consequences. His was to be a life unbounded. National and racial ties would disappear in his new life . . . and so for his followers. This life would be a life abundant. Had he not promised, "I have come that they might have life and have it abundantly" (John 10:10)? This new life was to be for his followers a life incarnate. Paul was to write clearly, "Not I but Christ lives in me" (Gal. 2:20).

II. Gain through loss. Life is a gamble, a calculated risk. Count the cost. Paul commended Epaphroditus (Phil. 2:30) for risking his life. Jesus in his temptation experience took a calculated risk:

The devil said, "Here's the easy way to satisfy your physical appetite." Jesus replied that to choose God's way is better. He always gave of himself to others.

The devil said, "Here's the easy way to win a following." Jesus replied that to choose God's way is better. He never dealt superficially with people.

The devil said, "Here's the way to gain a kingdom." Jesus replied that to choose God's way is better. One gains a kingdom by losing one's self.

III. Honor through service. It's the natural attitude of the disciple to his master. Jesus related a story of the judgment in which he described the "inasmuch as" service to be the basis of judgment. It is more than an instantaneous decision. It is to be a life of service.

From Martha Berry to Mother Teresa we may take our example. From Clarence Jordan to Jimmy Carter we may take our example. The Berry Schools, the world ministry to the poverty-stricken, the Koinonia Farm to the Habitat for Humanity we may take our example.

There is no other way to be his disciple . . . "If any man serve me, him will the Father honor."

IV. Victory through defeat. This was his Gethsemane in this Gospel. He was on the winning side—beyond the defeat of the cross. The disciple is on God's side, the winning side. This was God's promise: "I have both glorified it and will glorify it again."

But the crowd thought that it had thundered!—J. Estill Jones

SUNDAY: MARCH TWENTY-SEVENTH

SERVICE OF WORSHIP

Sermon: The Palm Sunday Sermon

When Jesus rode into Jerusalem on the Sunday before the Passover, the city went wild with excitement.

We can see why. For one thing, the city was in a state of hypertension at that particular time, both religiously and politically. The pious were swelling with religious zeal as the pilgrims poured into the city to keep the great national festival of the Passover. The nationals were preparing for a revolution which, incidentally, began just about thirty years after this event. The collaborators were playing the game with Rome as well as they could, trying to keep one foot in each world. The hierarchy were trying their best to protect the beloved establishment, to save it from destruction. The Romans were steering a steady, relentless course of law and order.

Into that tense situation, with the friction so great that you can feel it if you have any imagination at all, went Jesus in a way not calculated to calm things down. He was a young man in the prime of life, riding on an ass (a donkey, we would say), a beast of burden, reminding every good Jew what one of the prophets had said: Your king will come to you, meek, humble, gentle, riding upon an ass. And the crowd along the way hailed him as their king.

That would be enough to excite any city, particularly at such a time. If it happened in an American city today, he would probably be either mobbed, or murdered, or ridiculed; or simply ignored. In Jerusalem, however, the people asked a question. Do you remember what the question was? They asked, Who is he? Who is this who has come into our city in such a way, implying so many things? Who is he?

I. The fact is that no one really knew who he was, not even his closest friends, and you can't blame them too much. For one thing, he would never tell them. They were looking and waiting for the one they called Messiah, God's Man, who would get them out of the mess they were in, straighten them out, and put them on the up-and-up again.

(a) A few wondered whether this carpenter might not be that Man. There was just enough about him to make him seem a possible candidate for the high office. John the Baptist was in prison, but he sent representatives to ask whether he was that Man, but he never gave them a direct answer. He knew, I suppose, that you can't tell anyone anything unless he already knows it. I realize that there are exceptions to that, but when it gets to one of the great things in life, you can't tell it to anyone unless he already knows it, or in some way has an inkling of it.

(b) So that is one reason why he didn't tell them. Also, he knew that his idea of the Messiah and theirs were as far apart as day and night. They were looking for a Messiah who would put them back in power. His idea of the Messiah was a person who would put them into service, put them to use. See how different that is. He wasn't thinking at all of the Messiah who would restore the national grandeur of the nation. He was thinking of a Messiah who would take the seeds of redemptive suffering that had been sown among his people and scatter them to the four winds of the world.

(c) Another reason why they never knew exactly who he was was that they were baffled by the contradictory things he said. He said, for instance, that the peacemakers are happy because they are the children of God; and in almost the next breath he said, I am come not to bring peace, but a sword! He said, I am come not to destroy the law, but to fulfill it; and the next day he encouraged his disciples to break the law, to work on the Sabbath day, to eat without observing the ceremonial laws about washing their hands. He told one man that if he wanted to have life that amounted to anything, one of the things he had to do was to honor his father and mother. In almost the next breath he said, I have come to set a man against his father and a daughter against her mother.

(d) What he did was even more contradictory, and what he did, he did on this very day. He rode into the city in such a way that it suggested to every good Jew the idea of royalty. They couldn't miss it. They could accept him on that basis or not, but they couldn't miss the intention of it; and yet not a hand was lifted against him. There was no violence, no troops were called out, not even the police. There must have been something unusual about him, because he had the people in the palm of his hand, and if he had wanted to ride to victory on the backs of the people, he could have. But he didn't. He did not take the city by storm.

Yet on that day he went into the open porches of the Temple and drove out the people who were conducting business there; and it wasn't secular business, it was church business! He was protesting against the idea that in this open place, the one place open to Gentiles by the way, men conducted a business partly for their own profit. It was a place for worship, and anything that distracted from the worship of God was out of place.

He was angry, and, in one way, this was so out of character. You can see how it affected the people. But thank God he had the capacity for righteous indignation, and on occasion he showed it. Yet it is no wonder that they weren't quite sure who he was.

Truth is seldom simple. It may be simple in its essential being, but as we comprehend it, it is not simple. It is far too complex to be put in any single sentence. Truth, as we comprehend it, has at least two sides, and the one side often seems to contradict the other. That's another reason why they were never quite sure who he was.

(e) And to top it all, they were not endowed with an overactive imagination. Even his closest friends, we might as well admit it, were not exceptionally smart or perceptive. They often came close to the point and then missed it completely.

They were always drawn to him, but they didn't always know quite why. By and large, I would say, people are like that. Most people prefer black and white to varying degrees of gray, and it is hard for some to appreciate that every man, including himself and myself, is a mixture of each. Even our heroes may have a dash of badness in their blood, if only to save them from being bland.

Those who knew him best didn't really know who Jesus was. We can't blame them too much. He was too subtle for most of them to grasp, and fresh light, don't forget, is always blinding.

II. Now to turn to those gathered here now, what can we say to this question, Who is he? We think we know who he is. We say so every Sunday. We say that he is Jesus Christ, his only Son, our Lord and Master. We say that he is our Saviour, that for our sins and our salvation he came down from heaven and became man.

(a) At our best, we mean what we say, but there are times when we say to ourselves, Who is this strange man, so out of his element in this technological, distraught twentieth century? Who is he, so far out of his natural environment of thought and behavior, and yet in some ways so much a part of it? We can see him even in the revolt against conventions, machines, and materialism.

(b) What do you say? Do you say anything like this? This is what I often say; at least, it is a part of what I say: "I know who you are, but what I feel I cannot always find words to express. The ancient words of the Bible and the Creed are a great help. But sometimes I must reach after words of my own. Through you and in you I meet God. Once I see God in you I see him everywhere. You make God real to me; you personify him.

"Most of the time I am sure that I know who you are; but not always. If I were too sure, I would be sure that I was wrong. But I will follow you wherever you go, as well as I can; and when I fall behind, as I often have, and often will in the future, I know that you will come and pick me up. In some strange way, you are the king, like no other king; my friend, my master, and my king."—Theodore Parker Ferris

Illustrations

GOD INVOLVING HIMSELF. Those who find comfort and reassurance in the cult of astrology these days, some inscrutable plan held in the stars and their constellations, can have it! It's like some implacable fate, some unmoved god who pulls the strings so that things happen. And what you and I feel doesn't really matter. We are puppets at the end of his strings. I don't know about you but I prefer Jonathan Edwards' God who cried after the fall of Adam and Eve in the garden. I prefer Hosea's God who struggles within himself with love and anger as love wins out in the end: "I am God and not man." I prefer the God Jesus ached and died for, Abba, the child's name for

father—with all the tenderness and compassion and involvement in the lives of his children which that name suggests.—Edmund Steimle

EXPERIENCING IS BELIEVING. Suppose I told you that the Bach B Minor Mass is one of the great moments in musical history. If you had never heard it, had never known anything about it, I could tell you that a thousand times and it would mean absolutely nothing except that there were people who thought it. Not until you heard it could you take in what I said.

Or, if I said to you, Florence is one of the most fascinating cities in the world, you could hear it, you could take it as a fact that I believed it, but you could not really take it in until you felt it yourself, until you had been there and had seen it, or at least until you wanted to see it.

Sermon Suggestions

THE LIFE AND FORTUNES OF GOD'S SERVANT. TEXT: Isa. 50:4–9a. (1) God's servant is taught by God. (2) God's servant shares God's teaching for the comfort of God's people. (3) God's servant is faithful to his task, even in the worst of conditions. (4) God's servant expects God's vindication.

DESTRUCTIVE COMPETITIVENESS AND ITS REMEDY. TEXT: Phil. 2:5–11. (1) The example—Jesus Christ. (2) The means—self-denial. (3) The reward—God's approval.

Worship Aids

CALL TO WORSHIP. "I acknowledge my transgressions; and my sin is ever before me" (Ps. 51:3).

INVOCATION. We come to thee, our Father, confessing our sins. We could not hide our misdeeds from thee if we would. Yet we come with the confident expectation of thy forgiveness and cleansing. May we listen for the word or hold ourselves in readiness for some movement of thy Spirit that will purge us of those transgressions that have hindered our fruitful fellowship with thee.

OFFERTORY SENTENCE.   "Each one, as a good manager of God's different gifts, must use for the good of others the special gift he has received from God" (1 Pet. 4:10 TEV).

OFFERTORY PRAYER.   Lord of providence, let our generosity reflect our hearts and our lives reveal the glory of a God of love.—E. Lee Phillips

PRAYER.   O Father, as we live out this Holy Week made so unholy by the machinations of all of us that crucify Christ again and again and put him to an open shame—make us sensitive to our involvement in the agony of this world—our blood-guiltiness—that can only be cleansed through your redeeming grace at the cross. Humble us to pray:

Nothing in my hand I bring,
Simply to thy cross I cling.

As through your grace we are called to be instruments of reconciliation, may we not turn from the agony of love when it comes to us in the shape of a cross. May we be so in tune with your love-purpose that we may be courageous to pray in our Gethsemane: "Not my will but yours be done." With the Master, may we consecrate ourselves for the sake of others—those near and those far away. We pray for all peoples struggling for the freedom and dignity you have claimed for them in Christ. Teach our nation—our leaders and us as citizens—the paradoxical nature of the truth that he who is intent on saving his life shall lose it, but he who gives his life for the sake of others shall find it.

Grant to those among us broken in mind, body, or spirit, the wholeness of your holiness; to those who are lonely, bereft of loved one or friend, the consciousness of your loving presence; to the stranger within our gates, a sense of at-homeness with your people.

May the highest aspiration for your church be confirmed in and through us, that indeed "the kingdoms of this world may become the kingdom of our Lord and his Christ" who is present among us as your Word to every generation.—John Thompson

LECTIONARY MESSAGE

Topic: Witnesses

TEXT: Mark 15:1–39 (40–47)

All of the ministry of Jesus had been leading up to the cross. Indeed Mark writes (Mark 3:6) that the Pharisees and the Herodians decided to destroy him early in his ministry. The conflict between Jesus and the religious leaders continued without letup. A number of persons witnessed his suffering with varying reactions. All of them were witnesses.

I. There was Pilate the politician. From his position of supposed authority he looked down on Jesus. Was he not the Roman governor? Pilate marveled that Jesus did not defend himself. The chief priests accused him of many things. Jesus did not reply. Pilate was not comfortable. He knew Jewish religious leadership. He also knew that the leadership with the crowds could send an uncomplimentary report to Rome.

He attempted a compromise: let me release Jesus to you—this is our custom. That way the crowds might have accepted his guilt and his release and Pilate would not have to make a judgment. As it turned out Pilate satisfied the vocal majority and delivered Jesus to be crucified. Later the fickle crowd was to turn against Pilate. Such is the life of the politician.

II. There was Simon the Cyrenian. He was an innocent bystander. He had come from the country at the wrong time. Roman custom required that he serve the wishes of the soldiers. He was not a voluntary witness but he was a witness. His sons are named, probably both known to the Christian community. Perhaps one of them, Rufus, became active in the church (Rom. 16:13). Simon bore the cross for Jesus. How do you suppose he described the events of that day?

III. There was the nameless centurion. Call him what you will. He had been placed in charge of the execution, not a pretty sight. He had opinions about Pilate and the Jewish leadership. He had an opinion about Jesus. How much did he know? He had seen the superscription, the king of the Jews. This probably did not put the fear of the Lord in him! But he saw the mocking and he saw the suffering and he saw the dignity with which Jesus bore up under it. The centurion did his duty. In the process he saw Jesus for who he was. He heard him call upon God. He saw him die. Surprisingly he confessed Jesus to be God's Son. Could not the crowds see this? Could not the religious leadership see this? Was it left for a Roman centurion to make the confession?

IV. There were women the watchers. They watched from afar. The curious cruel crowds were clustered up close. They knew more about him than the crowds. They had ministered to him—many women who followed him from Galilee to Jerusalem.

You wonder in Mark's account where the disciples were. Were only the women watching? Perhaps that's the story Simon Peter related to John Mark. They were witnesses to his death and were to become witnesses to his Resurrection.

V. Joseph the Jew. There are some of us who are glad that a leading Jew was a witness to the Crucifixion. Joseph was a respected Jewish leader. Luke describes him as "a good and righteous man; he had not consented to their counsel and deed" (Lk. 23:51). He anticipated the kingdom of God. He boldly asked for the body of Jesus. Pilate granted his request. With Nicodemus (Jn. 19:39) he tenderly cared for the body.

The chapter closes with the simple statement that Mary Magdalene and Mary the mother of Jesus saw where he was buried.

Witnesses all . . . How would they bear witness? "You are my witnesses . . ."— J. Estill Jones

SUNDAY: APRIL THIRD (EASTER)

SERVICE OF WORSHIP

Sermon: You Will Live Also

TEXT: John 14:19, "Because I live, you will live also."

My dear brothers and sisters, *I live.* Jesus Christ has said that, and now he is saying to us again: "I live."

Let me recall another of his sayings which may help to explain these two short words. "Where two or three are gathered in my name, there I am in the midst of them." We are gathered here in his name, and hence not in our own. Not because we enjoy dealing with him, but because he is pleased to deal with us. Not because we are for him, but because he is for us. Not because we have earned the right of his companionship, but because he has paid the highest price for our companionship with him. He sealed it when he came into the world, calling out: "Come to me, all who labour and are heavy-laden, and I will give you rest."

Not only did he express this invitation and promise in words; he validated it through the mighty act of his entire life and death. Through this call and this act he has created a fellowship on earth, where at all times and in all places he is the Lord, the shepherd, and the teacher. He has gathered us into his fold right here and now. Because this is so, he is in our midst even here and now, testifying to the truth: "I live." He is not in the tomb; he is risen, as we have heard it read from the Gospel. He himself tells us to forget about everything else and to stick firmly to this fact: "I live."

I. Clearly, if he says "I live," he says something more, something else and better than if I, or one of you for that matter, said it. What indeed is our life compared to his? True, our life is at stake. It is significant that the affirmation "I live" is immediately followed by another "and you will live also." Hence when Jesus says "I live," he speaks about the redemption of our life, of its freedom and holiness, its righteousness and glory. Yet if we are to understand the affirmation about ourselves, we first must be attentive to the all-inclusive affirmation about him. "I live"—a life very different from yours, not at all to be compared with it.

(a) *I live.* As Jesus Christ's own statement this means: "I live as true man *my divine life.*" We must take this quite seriously and literally. I live the life of the eternal and almighty God who has created heaven and earth and is the source and fullness of life. What does this mean? Perhaps that I live this divine life of abundance intent on laying hold on it, keeping it and enjoying it for myself, as a rich man likes to lay hold on his possessions, keep them and enjoy them? Or that I offer it as a most peculiar and most precious treasure for your admiration at a distance? Or maybe that I hand out occasional alms from its bounty? No, my brothers and sisters, this is not the life of God, not the life of him who, in time and eternity, refuses to be for himself and by himself but wills to be and is *our* God, sharing with us all the riches of his life.

(b) *I live.* When spoken by Jesus this means: "I live my divine life *for you.* I live it fully by loving you. Without you I do not care to be the Son of God or to enjoy my divine life. I live it fully by pouring it out. Without reticence or reservation I give it away for you. I live my divine life by taking your place, the place that is allotted to you. I become what you are (not just some of you, but all of you), a prisoner, a convict, sentenced to death. This I do, by the power of my divine life spent for you, that the darkness and perplexity, the sorrow, anxiety and despair, the sin and guilt of your petty, wicked and miserable life may be canceled out, and your own death may once and for all be extinguished and annihilated. In this giving of myself, in this saving power I live my life, my divine life."

(c) *I live.* Asserted by Jesus Christ this means: "I live *my human life* as the true Son of God. It is indeed the life of a weak, of a solitary, of a tempted man dying in shame, like you, totally like you. How so? Perhaps I reserve the better

part for myself after all? Or perhaps I rebel against my human existence in misery, or try hard to put up with it in mute and fierce defiance? No, definitely not so. In so doing I would not really want to be like you, your neighbor, your brother, the neighbor and brother of the most needy. I would desert and betray you. I would refuse to be the one who lives from God's mercy alone. I would deny my sincere desire to be true man, let alone to be God's child."

(d) *I live.* This affirmation by Jesus means: "I live my human life without opposition or resistance *as your own,* such as life is. I live it in acceptance of the fact that all folly and wickedness, all anxiety and despair, your own and that of the world, are laid upon my shoulders. I live it by carrying this burden in obedience to God who has laid it upon me, and thereby I lift it from you. I convert, renew, and baptize in my person your human life in all its aspects, transforming your perdition into redemption, your sin into righteousness, your death into life. This I do so that you may be born again in me to new beings who, in hope, give God glory and stop seeking their own. This I do so that you may grow in me into men with whom God is well pleased. Lifting it up for your sake, I live my life, my human life, my life as your own."

Therefore: "*I live* only to pour out my divine life in your service and to lift up my human life in the service of God." This is the Christ who appeared to his followers on Easter morning. This is the Christ who is in our midst here and now, proclaiming: "I live." The subsequent affirmation concerning ourselves is contained in this primary affirmation by Jesus about himself.

II. (a) *You will live also.* In our German Bibles this statement reads: "And you shall live also." Yet the significant fact to remember is precisely not an obligation we are invited or urged to fulfill, so that we may, or may not, live. We are not merely given a chance; nor is an offer made to us. "You will live also" is a promise. It is an announcement referring to the future, to our future. "You will live also" succeeds the present of, and our presence in, the "I live" like two succeeds one, B succeeds A, the thunder succeeds the lightning. He who comprehends the "I live" will right away comprehend the "You will live also." You are a people whose future issues from my life and hence does not lie in your sin and guilt, but in true righteousness and holiness. Not in sadness, but in joy, not in captivity, but in freedom, not in death, but in life. From your present participation in my life, you may anticipate *this* and no other future.

(b) Let me explain further what is at stake for us when we have heard both, "I live" and, immediately following, "You will live also."

It is now all-important for us to cling to this truth that *he*, Jesus Christ, in *his* life, is our present. Not our past is our present. Not the great darkness casting its shadows out of yesterday into today. Not what we rightly or wrongly hold against ourselves and probably against others as well. Not the world with its accusations and we with our counter-accusations. Not even the well-deserved divine wrath against us, let alone our grumbling against God, or our secret thought that there might be no God after all. Therefore, not we ourselves, as we are today or think we are, make up our present. He, Jesus Christ, his life is our present: his divine life poured out for us, and his human life, our life, lifted up in him. This is what counts. This is what is true and valid. From this point on we may continue our journey into the future. And this is the future which grows out of this present: *You will live also.*

It is now all-important for us to accept his gifts for the journey, to be equipped and nourished by him. My brothers and sisters, none of us can help himself, can create life from within himself, or acquire anything by himself. Whatever man wishes to seize bears the mark of sin and death. But there is really no need for us to seize anything. We may simply receive what is already laid out for us. Everything is prepared for us all. Whatever had been in disorder has been put to order. We only need to accept the already established order. We only need to see

what is spread out before our eyes and to hear what is said with unmistakable clarity. We only need to open and stretch out our hands instead of ever again hiding them in our pockets and clenching our fists. We only need to open our mouth and eat and drink, instead of setting our teeth, as we used to do when we were children. We only need to walk forward instead of going backwards in the manner of fools.

It is vitally important for us to let grow the tiny root of confidence, of earnestness, of joy, which seeks ground in our hearts and minds, in our thoughts and intentions and opinions—perhaps this very Easter morning. It is truly impossible that Jesus Christ proclaims: "I live," without the answer arising from somewhere within us: "Yes, you live, and because you live, I shall live also, I may and I can and I want to live! I for whom you, true God, became a true man—I for whom you died and rose again—I for whom you accomplished all and everything needed in time and eternity!"

It is all-important now that not one among us consider himself excluded, either too great or too insignificant or too godless. It is all important that each one of us consider himself included, a partaker of God's mercy in the life of our Lord as revealed in his Resurrection from the dead on Easter morning. It is all-important that we believe humbly yet courageously that we are those born again in him to a living hope: *You will live also.*—Karl Barth

Illustrations

THE ACID TEST OF LOVE.   Here is the acid test of genuine love: its ability to forgive; and here, the wisdom of the Christian marriage vow is seen in its inclusion of a promise "to bear with each other's infirmities and weaknesses." Here also is the gospel itself, which declares that "while we were yet sinners, Christ died for us" (Rom. 5:8), the ungodly, the fickle, the rebellious.—Charles P. Robshaw

THE SIGN. The Lord's Supper is quite simply the sign of what we have said: Jesus Christ is in our midst, he, the man in whom God himself has poured out his life for our sake and in whom our life is lifted up to God. Holy Communion is the sign that Jesus Christ is our beginning and we may rise up and walk into the future where we shall live. The Lord himself gives us strength, food, and drink for our journey, from one bread and from one cup, because he is One, he the One for us all.—Karl Barth

Sermon Suggestions

THE BOTTOM LINE OF THE GOSPEL. TEXT: Acts 10:34–43, esp. verse 43, NRSV. (1) Jesus Christ is the fulfillment of God's redemptive plan testified to by the Old Testament prophets. (2) Jesus Christ is the object of faith in God's gracious purpose. (3) Everyone, of whatever nation, who believes in him receives forgiveness of sins through his name.

IS THE GOSPEL YOUR GOOD NEWS? TEXT: 1 Cor. 15:1–11. (1) What is the gospel? verses 3–4. (2) What does this good news mean to you? a., Presumably you have received it. b., Presumably you are standing firm in it. c., Presumably you are being saved—in a continuing experience of it. (3) What is the alternative? a., No sense of forgiveness, verse 15:17. b., No assurance about life beyond death, verse 15:19.

Worship Aids

CALL TO WORSHIP. "Ye seek Jesus of Nazareth, which was crucified; he is risen." "The Lord is risen indeed." (Mark 16:6; Luke 24:34)

INVOCATION. Thou hast conquered, O living Christ, and thou hast brought life and light into our dark world and into the dark places of our personal lives. Continue to shine upon us today, and banish the lingering shadows of guilt and fear and unbelief that may still haunt our hearts.

OFFERTORY SENTENCE. "Jesus sat over against the treasury, and beheld how the people cast money into the treasury" (Mark 12:41).

OFFERTORY PRAYER. Lord of creation, thou hast made the desert rejoice and blossom as the rose; the thirsty land has brought forth springs of water. Bless our poverty-stricken lives with new life, new gifts, and new generosity. May we find, in the little that we think we have, the true riches of possibility. Amplify like the loaves and fishes what we now bring to thee.

PRAYER. Almighty God, thou hast brought again from the dead our Lord Jesus Christ, and we believe that mighty works can be done in our lives today. Raise us from our despair by a boundless hope. Raise us from our guilt by an unfaltering trust in thy forgiving mercy. Raise us from our fears by a new measure of courage. Raise us from our lethargy and inactivity by a growing love and concern for others. Help us to see that no circumstance in life is beyond improving, that no duty is beyond our doing, and that no impossibility is beyond thy power or will to change either the situation or us.

LECTIONARY MESSAGE

Topic: A Growing Faith
    TEXT: John 20:1–18
    I first noticed it on Maundy Thursday. It appeared on a bulletin board in front of a church on a city corner. Stark and concise it read, "They have taken away my Lord." Undoubtedly it was the sermon announcement for Easter Sunday morning. I thought about it and realized that it was true in our culture. They (or we) have certainly taken away the Lord. They have taken him to the funeral home—his presence is appreciated there. They have taken him to the hospital—sick people are encouraged by his presence. They have taken him to the wedding—bride and groom bask in his blessing. They have taken him to the church—worshipers come there to meet

him and departing leave him beyond. It's a current cry.

I. Despair at loss. Mary Magdalene came to the tomb early on Sunday morning. The stone was rolled away. It was enough that she had suffered the grievous loss through the death of Jesus. Her anxiety level rose perceptibly as she realized what the stone's removal signified. The stone had offered security for the body of Jesus. It was safe from wild beasts and human marauders. Now with the stone removed she suspected the worst. The cries for his Crucifixion, the sound of the crowd's mocking— drummed in her ears. She ran to tell two disciples.

II. Hope beyond hope. Peter and the other disciple (whose name we do not know) wasted no time. They immediately ran to the tomb. Strange that they had not anticipated her visit with one of their own! Now what were their thoughts? Did they have any hope? Had they not witnessed the finality of his death and burial?

Peter entered the tomb first, though he had followed the other disciple. What did he expect to find? He found the linen cloths of burial lying there and the napkin that was on his head rolled up in a place by itself. Put yourself into his place—how would you react? The other disciple entered the tomb and believed. What did he believe or who did he believe? Did Peter not believe? Was the hope of the other disciple moving toward faith? Is hope so closely related to faith?

And at this point the account is disappointing—they went to their own home.

III. Waiting and weeping. Had Mary followed them back to the tomb? Could she have stayed away? Was she there while they entered the tomb? They went back to their home. She stood outside weeping. A neat dialogue followed. She determined by looking that there were two persons in the tomb. "Woman, why are you weeping?" they asked. "They have taken away my Lord, and I don't know where they have laid him," she replied—was this the immediate source of grief—a missing body?

"Woman, whom do you seek?" asked Jesus. She, blinded by grief, did not know him. "Sir, tell me where you have laid him." "Mary!" he spoke briefly. "Teacher," she echoed briefly. It was enough—her waiting and weeping were rewarded by a challenge to faith. His words clinched it: "Go, tell."

IV. "I have seen the Lord." And she did. This was her clear witness. She told the disciples. Her faith had matured to the point of witnessing. "I saw him." Peter and the other disciple might have seen him if they had waited around. "I talked with him." There was no doubt in her mind. Her confession marked the maturity of her faith.

It is a clear Easter confession: I have seen the Lord. "The Lord is risen." And the others were soon to join in, "He is risen indeed."—J. Estill Jones

SUNDAY: APRIL TENTH

SERVICE OF WORSHIP

Sermon: Look for the Blessing

TEXT: Psalm 118:24

I. A tried and tested spiritual exercise practiced by many Christians is to begin each new day with a repetition of the psalmist's words, the words which say, "This is the day that the Lord has made; let us rejoice and be glad in it." Regardless of the weather or the circumstances of the world or any other condition, the discipline of repeating that refrain gives energy and optimism to those who say it. Here is an answer to discouragement, to anxiety, to negative feelings and fears.

Somewhere it has been said that having nothing to carry is life's heaviest burden. Having nothing to do is life's hardest work. Having nothing to look forward to is life's darkest picture. To all of that emptiness the testimony of the psalmist offers a fulfilling response. Finding ourselves able to say, "This is the day that the Lord has made; let us rejoice and be glad in it," lifts us out of bleakness and futility. It gives us a reason for looking upward and beyond limiting and troubling concerns.

What this psalm verse says to me as I recite it is this: "Look, John, look for the blessing. Each day, look for the particular blessing that God is waiting to bestow." Reading or saying these simple words about the day God has made suggests strongly to me that unique things are in store if I am alert to them. If I rejoice and delight in the hours at hand, I shall discover at least one blessing, and probably many more than that as the day goes by. God is in the midst of the minutes opening before me; when God's presence is acknowledged by me, good things cannot help but lie ahead. Problems, even crises may arise as well, but my affirmation through the psalm verse is that God is there and God's blessings ultimately will prevail.

Look for the blessing! That is the message behind the saying that God is the maker of our days. "What immense joy for us," one scripture translation explains. Not by accident, this passage from the 118th Psalm is sung on Easter Day in many liturgical churches. The glorious blessings of Resurrection and life eternal are heralded on Easter Sunday, a day God indeed has made, and made memorable for all of us.

II. Look for the blessing! Jesus spoke about seeking and finding; his lesson is recorded in these words: "Ask, and it will be given you; search, and you will find; knock, and the door will be opened for you." Perseverance in looking for the blessings of each new day will be honored, according to this promise of Jesus. I like the story of that child whose eyes were intently focused upon the sidewalk as she and her mother walked together. "Whatever are you looking for?" asked the mother. "For something to find," answered the child. "Something to find" for the Christian, that "something" is the blessing which God stands ready to reveal. As the scriptures remind us, such blessings are "new every morning." The exact reference from the Old Testament reads like this: "The steadfast love of the Lord never ceases, his mercies never come to an end; they are new every morning; great is God's faithfulness." So it is that we are to look for the blessing, whatever it may be.

Lest that sound unrealistic, given the burdens and trials of our lives, I suggest we attend to the amusing experience of Molly Picon. In the Jewish community Molly Picon was known as one of the brightest lights of the Yiddish stage. As an actress she traveled a lot, spending nights in cramped hotel rooms with others in her acting company. One night, after many nights of such inconvenience, Picon overheard some of the performers griping about their living conditions. She listened for awhile, then interrupted them. "I never complain about such things," Molly Picon told them. "My grandmother brought up eleven children in four rooms." "How did she manage that?" they asked: Picon smiled and replied, "She took in boarders!"

She turned a burden into a blessing, is one way of saying it. People like Molly Picon's grandmother, as well as the actress herself, looked beyond the complication immediately at hand and found something else to celebrate. That may be our necessity, too, when a day dawns that seems filled with more problems than possibilities. The practiced observer still will look for the blessing, perhaps saying, in the words of a black spiritual, "I don't want to move the mountain, Lord; just give me grace to climb."

III. "This is the day that the Lord has made; let us rejoice and be glad in it." If we speak those words as our first waking thought, we give ourselves a framework in which to place all of the day's activities and events. We create order out of the jumble of experiences which come our way. We reverse the question that sometimes confronts us, the question about "Why did this have to happen?" to, "What am I going to do about this so that it will become a creative instead of a disabling experience?" Repeating that psalm verse enables us to look for the blessing which abides beneath the rush and tumble of outward circumstances.

(a) I cannot repeat that verse, however, without being aware of its inclusive emphasis. Notice that the psalmist says, "Let *us* rejoice and be glad" in the day that God has given. Using the plural pronoun, saying "us" instead of "me," suggests two things: (1) First, God bestows blessings freely and widely, not exclusively or privately. Jesus made this point by his comment that God makes the sun rise "on the evil and on the good, and sends rain on the righteous and on the unrighteousness." Blessings are to be found in abundance, and in actuality we are to help each other find them. "Let *us* rejoice," said the psalmist, enlarging the arena of perception—not limiting it to just my vision or just yours.

(2) The second implication of this plural pronoun is that we can be a blessing ourselves. Not only are we to assist one another in recognizing the gifts of God in each new day; we can offer ourselves to the people around us, giving gifts of friendship and caring, encouragement and help. An old gospel song has us sing, "Make me a blessing, to someone today." If, on the one hand we are to look for the blessing, on the other hand we are to *be* a blessing, insofar as that is possible for us. In other words, we have the privilege of helping others to rejoice and be glad, sharing these important feelings beyond ourselves.

(b) At day's beginning, the Bible verse which I hope we have committed to memory becomes our guide. One translation of it says, "This is the day of the Lord's victory; let us be happy, let us celebrate!" Once more there is that emphasis upon God's jurisdiction over each day, followed by each believer's enthusiastic response. Out of that context I am saying that we are to look for the blessing, or the many blessings that God will impart. We are to claim God's gifts; moreover, we are to point others to them and we are to share them widely. Finally, at day's end, it becomes us to review those blessings. Reflecting upon the hours God has granted us and all of the good things which have been part of those hours becomes our way to conclude the day which the Lord has made. Having looked for blessings and having found them, we then can appreciate their power to displace hurt and negativity and any other demoralizing thing. It at once is evident to us that God's grace is more than sufficient. God's provision for our need is greater than we can ask or think.

I offer as a new and lasting imperative for life this simple counsel: Look for the blessing. Such blessing will be discovered when each and every day is received from God as a product of divine handiwork, a gift worthy of glad acceptance. Through all of this I would also have us keep in mind the statement of Italian author Ugo Batti. It was he who wrote, "To believe in God is to know that all the rules are fair and that there will be wonderful surprises." Look for the blessing. Look for the wonderful surprises.—John H. Townsend

Illustrations

THINGS MADE NEW. The speech of God makes things new! The decisive speech of Yahweh is to be uttered again by the preacher. Each time it is uttered, the community again has a chance for new life. This speech of salvation declares and enacts Yahweh's sovereignty. It declares and enacts Yahweh's sovereignty over situations that seem out of control. This speech assures that Yahweh does indeed govern even when situations are experienced as chaos, exile, enslavement, and death. The center has wobbled, it has not seemed to hold. But it will and it does hold wherever Yahweh comes in faithful power.—Walter Brueggemann

ANSWERED PRAYER. "In my distress I called upon the Lord, and cried unto my God: he heard my voice out of his temple, and my cry came before him, even into his ears" (Ps. 18:6). A column by Ann Landers caught my eye. It was called, *When Life Depends on a Stroke of Luck.* I know that Landers does not write the captions—an editorial job. I would have called the piece *Answered Prayer.*

A California woman in a Glendale restaurant almost choked while eating lunch. She could not exhale—a condition that lasted a minute and a half. A man rushed from across the room and gave her a sharp blow across the back. She said, "It was like a miracle. Almost instantly I was OK." She said that she had been praying and he was the answer to her prayer. She simply said, "Thank you, sir—you saved my life." The man left the restaurant.

A waitress came over to the woman who had been stricken and said, "That man has had lunch here every Wednesday for the last 11 years. Today is Thursday."

Was this simply a matter of blind luck? It was God's miracle.—Harold E. Dye

Sermon Suggestions

WHEN THE SPIRIT PREVAILS.   TEXT: Acts 4:32–35. (1) Believers experience a profound unity. (2) Believers experience an extraordinary impulse of generosity and sharing. (3) Believers reflect a living witness to the Resurrection.

BELIEVERS AND THE PROBLEM OF SIN. TEXT: 1 John 1:1–2:2. (1) In principle, true Christians do not sin—deliberately, as a lifestyle. (2) In fact, true Christians do sin—committing sin by neglect and act. (3) However, sincere and striving Christians who confess their sins: a., can trust their Savior not to abandon them; b., can be assured of forgiveness; c., can begin again, clean and courageous.

Worship Aids

CALL TO WORSHIP.   "To the Lord our God belong mercies and forgiveness, though we have rebelled against him; neither have we obeyed the voice of the Lord our God, to walk in his laws, which he set before us by his servants the prophets" (Dan. 9:9–10).

INVOCATION.   O Lord of the open tomb, give to our worship today a depth born of sacrifice and a hope born of Resurrection that we may grow in the grace of Christ our Lord.—E. Lee Phillips

OFFERTORY SENTENCE.   "And the children of Israel brought a willing sacrifice unto the Lord, every man and woman, whose heart made them willing to bring for all manner of work, which the Lord had commanded to be made by the hand of Moses" (Exod. 35:29).

OFFERTORY PRAYER.   O Lord of the open tomb, open us to the power of the Resurrection that as we give our gifts today they may be used to proclaim the gospel of triumph over sin and death.—E. Lee Phillips

PRAYER.   "Wait for the Lord; take courage, be strong; wait for the Lord." What does it mean to wait upon you—you who are holy and eternal?

It is surely to wait in reverence—acknowledging who you are and realizing who we are. But, yet, we can come in confidence, for we are not grovelling slaves but your sons and daughters. We have been adopted into your family, the household of faith, not because of our merit, but because of your grace—your unmerited love. The spirit that we have received is not a spirit of slavery leading us back into a life of fear, but the spirit that makes us your children.

To wait on you is to be silent until all our strivings cease. It is to be still—how still—to know that you are God. It is to be still, that above the clamoring of self-will we may hear the still, small voice of your will.

To wait upon you is to trust—trust utterly. It is to let go and let you be God. But how difficult this is for us. We are all the time playing God. We come, even now, in our anxious activism thinking that we have to beat upon the door, or even knock it down to get your attention—when actually the door is always open; we but need to walk through it. As we turn toward home, you are running down the road to meet us with outstretched arms and a kiss to greet us.—John Thompson

LECTIONARY MESSAGE

Topic: Proofs of the Resurrection

TEXT: John 20:19–31

Those who have experienced a great loss may be able to understand some of the sense of defeat experienced by the disciples. Their loss was multiplied. They had lost their friend and teacher. They had seen the apparent victory of his and their enemies. Their hope for the establishment of the Kingdom of God and the nation Israel was destroyed. The prospects for the future were dismal.

I. Jesus appeared to the disciples. Into this utter despair, behind locked doors, among huddled, frightened disciples, Jesus appeared. His first words, "Peace to you." They may well have thought, "How can this be?" All seemed to be lost.

John repeated the greeting two other times. The repetition seems to have significance. There was reason to hope, even if only defeat was apparent. Jesus is present, even though they have seen him crucified and buried, and he announces peace in their midst.

It may be that he was reminding them of his words earlier in the upper room. There he had told of a special revelation of himself that the rest of the world would not have. He had not only told them of his "own peace" given to them, he also had told them not to be afraid (John 14:27, RSV). They had forgotten what he had said, and they were afraid!

II. Jesus showed his hands and side. The disciples were present when Jesus was nailed to the cross and his side was pierced. To see his hands and his side become proof of his identity. He was the same one they had seen suffer. These were also reminders that though the world may do its worst, he was still with them and had not been overwhelmed by all that had transpired. His victory over the circumstances he had faced was adequate for him to claim peace for them and to challenge them to overcome all enemies and the distress they were facing.

The resurrected Lord not only gave the basis for courage, he gave them a task. They are to be the continuation of the ministry he was sent to perform. The challenge of his victory is the source of strength which they may expect in fulfilling the task he called them to do.

III. Jesus appeared when Thomas was present. Thomas had already proven himself a skeptic (14:5). His response to the report of the appearance of Jesus was an expected one. The passage of time since his earlier appearance seemed to confirm the skepticism.

Repetition of the greeting, "Peace to you" may well emphasize that there was reason for hope even for the skeptic and in the despair they felt. Their resurrected Lord was reason enough for hope. He would also be the foundation for the hope of the whole Christian church.

Jesus also challenged the faith of all who believe without having seen the physically resurrected Christ. It is as though he anticipates the times yet to come when believers will fall into the despair of the disciples.—Arthur L. Walker

SUNDAY: APRIL SEVENTEENTH

SERVICE OF WORSHIP

Sermon: On Moving Mountains

TEXT: Matt. 17:14–21

I am fairly well convinced that many of us who come to church come with wavering faith, with serious doubts, with our trust in the God who stands behind Jesus all but drained dry, if not simply vanished. I frequently think of us here as a congregation of individuals who come with flickering faith and exhausted hopes, eager to be among those whom we believe to stand on firm foundations, their presence an encouragement to our own sputtering faith . . . and vice versa; what they believe to our firm foundation, grit and courage for their waning faith.

I. Did you know that? Your presence here, even with a nearly evaporated and meager faith, offers confidence and encouragement to the evaporated and meager faith of the person next to you, in front of you, in the pew across the aisle? They think you've got it all together and as a result, they are strengthened and assured. You see, we are greater in this room than the sum of all our parts. We sing, we pray, we commit ourselves to things together we might have a hard time doing by ourselves. Indeed, perhaps together we can even generate faith the size of a mustard seed—the smallest of all seeds—faith, Jesus said to a frazzled and frustrated bunch of disciples, that was enough to move mountains.

(a) Faith enough to move mountains. Mountains! What kind of mountains? Jesus is not talking about magic removals. He does not pretend prayer can push Mount Washington into the Atlantic Ocean or Mount McKinley into the Gulf of Alaska. But he is saying that faith the size of a mustard seed can move the mountains blocking the horizons of our hopes, shadowing the light and beauty of love, limiting and bounding the scope of our lives. He is saying that faith the size of a mustard seed can make the improbable possible, indeed, can make what looks impossible to be a vital and radiant present reality. He is saying that faith can stand up to and move, indeed remove, the things that trap us, the stuff that scares the daylights out of us, the things that test and erode our confidence in the love we feebly trust is at the heart of the universe.

(b) Faith, you say? Faith in what or whom? What must I risk? What must I trust? What leap must I take? Here it is, friends: the faith that removes mountains in our lives is the faith that says, finally, "Nothing—nothing—can cut us off from the God whom we see in the face, the activity, the grace, the love and cross of Jesus Christ."

II. If anything could separate us from the love of God, we would see it at the cross where the worst life can do to us, indeed, what appears to be the ultimate separation, a miserable death, plays itself out. But what, in faith, do we see at the cross? Not separation from God, but in faith we see the unflagging, indefatigable love of God for us and for our welfare alive and at work right through the worst life can do to us.

(a) I want to insist this morning that faith in the love of God we know in Christ Jesus—faith just the size of a mustard seed—can ground us in power and release to the point where the improbable becomes probable, the impossible becomes possible, our fondest and deepest hopes result finally in a miracle—yes, where faith the size of a mustard seed can move a mountain from here to there.

(b) The mountain of shame and self-rejection, for instance. That's right, self-rejection! One of the great difficulties of our time resides inside ourselves where we are ashamed of our selves. It is not what I do that is not good, it is me who is no good. Somehow we hear the voices or the threat of voices either whispering or screaming at us: "You're a failure; you're ugly; you're worthless; you're flawed." Our every move and prayer is to prove to God, ourselves, and others that we are worth something.

(c) For heaven's sake, time out! Hold it! Wait a minute! Hear this: You are loved! You are loved!! Amid everything in your life that says "NO," and I know there is a ton of junk, the gospel says—and this is why it is gospel—you are loved! You are not out there hanging onto dear life all by yourself. We call the news of Jesus Christ good because amid all the bad news eating us up and beating us down someone stoops to join us in our crisis, embraces us in our pilgrimage through the dark night of the soul, reaches for our hand as we traverse the thin ice over what feels like 70,000 fathoms of water.

III. Lord knows we do not always feel that trust in the love of God. We do not always believe that. Our faith in the love of God for each of us is most of the time a small fraction of a mustard seed, or we believe the gospel true for everybody else but ourselves.

(a) Talk about a mustard seed of faith removing a mountain! Just that much faith—a mustard seed's worth—in the abiding love of God for each of us and our welfare, would remove a huge mountain of self-rejection; it would allow us to rest easy in the all-embracing arms of the everlasting God of our savior, Jesus Christ. It would release us from having to prove ourselves worthwhile to our parents, our colleagues, our having to prove ourselves worthwhile to our parents, our colleagues, our children, our boss, our subordinates, our minister, the folk at church—whoever. We would truly know the meaning of grace—grace—love encircling and undergirding us without our having to make any deals, any bargains, any promises. What a faith! What a release! What freedom that is for each and all of us!

(b) And do you know what else happens in this grace and freedom? Just as we know release, so we are enabled to release others. Just as we know freedom finally in the love of God, so would we bring freedom to others in our certainty of God's love for them. Do you see, we participate ourselves in the delivery of the divine love. We become channels ourselves of the One who loves us without strings. Talk about moving mountains!

Faith, the size of a mustard seed, in the steadfast, enduring, tenacious love of God: Jesus isn't kidding, it is faith enough to move mountains.—James W. Crawford

Illustrations

MEANING IN BAPTISM. When Martin Luther's faith itself ran up against a brick wall he had to write on a blackboard simply the words, "I have been baptized!"—a simple declarative sentence affirming God's love for him while the devil broke loose and his life seemed a wreck.—James W. Crawford.

OVERFLOWING FAITH. It has been a great part of my life to see people brought into the Christian faith who then begin to bring others into it. They are not superhuman salesmen, but ordinary men and women, students, working people, businessmen, housewives. They have pushed off from the shore of safety and convention, and launched out into the deep of experiencing faith in action and

then drawing others into it. There is no way to tell people how to do this. If you are full of it yourself, it will overflow, as good nature and good humor will.—Sam Shoemaker

Sermon Suggestions

MOMENTOUS CHOICES. TEXT: Acts 3:12–19, especially verses 14–15. (1) *Situation*: We have been given the freedom and responsibility of choice. (2) *Complication*: We often choose—perhaps in ignorance—in the direction of hurt and even ruin. (3) *Resolution*: God is infinitely resourceful, overturning or overruling for good our worst designs.

ON BEING MISUNDERSTOOD. TEXT: 1 John 3:1–7. (1) God is transforming us. (2) God does this sanctifying work through our expectation of ultimately being like Christ. (3) No wonder the world sometimes does not understand us and in some cases rejects us!

Worship Aids

CALL TO WORSHIP. "Let us praise God for his glorious grace, for the free gift he gave us in his dear Son! For by the death of Christ we are set free, that is, our sins are forgiven. How great is the grace of God, which he gave to us in such large measure" (Eph. 1:7–8a TEV).

INVOCATION. Lord, help us to meet you here today, to recognize the holy in the common, the transcendent in the ordinary, and the truth when it is spoken.—E. Lee Phillips

OFFERTORY SENTENCE. "Will a man rob God? Yet ye have robbed me. But ye say, Wherein have we robbed thee? In tithes and offerings" (Mal. 3:8).

OFFERTORY PRAYER. Thanks be to thee, our Lord Jesus Christ, for all the benefits which thou hast given us, for all the pains and insults which thou hast borne for us. O merciful Redeemer, Friend, and Brother, may we know thee more clearly, love thee more dearly, and follow thee more nearly.—St. Richard of Chichester

PRAYER. As the spring rains refresh the dry and thirsty earth so does your Word as a fountain spring forth into everlasting life renewing our jaded spirits. For teaching and preaching that brings new perspective to old stories that challenge with a living Word and calls to new life—the life of the Spirit—we praise you. How we thank you for fresh bread when there are so many who are put off with the stale, dry crusts of an orthodoxy, a literalism that kills. We sense now that he who turns water into wine, the ordinary into the festive, the mundane into sacrament is here among us ready with some miracle of the Spirit according to our need. He who draws life from the depths and satisfies with that drink that is drink indeed stands among us as the Messiah who is come to one and all. For the gift of metaphor in the Word becoming flesh that can take the common prose of our every day and transform it into the rhythm and beauty of poetry, we are indeed grateful.

What a fellowship, what a joy divine to experience the blessedness of your church in this time and place—the caring, the sharing which your giving in Christ inspires. We pray for one another as brothers and sisters in the family of faith. Where faith staggers under burdens that are difficult to bear, we pray not for lesser tasks but for faith equal to our tasks. With the Master, we pray that we may be strong for the sake of others. May we be sensitive to opportunities for conversation that can mediate and celebrate your grace—the good news that the gift of life is here for all. To be there—all there—for someone else according to his or her need is the engagement to which you are calling us.

In this day of unprecedented opportunity may we have the courage and good will to converse with enemies as well as friends, that the power of your grace given for the healing of the nations may hasten the day of world community.

We pray through him who is your word declared and deeded from the beginning and is present now teaching us to pray with all peoples: *The Lord's Prayer*—John Thompson

LECTIONARY MESSAGE

Topic: Why Do You Doubt?

TEXT: Luke 24:36b–48

The Gospels anticipate that believers, at times, will have questions and that doubts will arise for all. Some would offer a religious experience which never encounters doubt. The result may be a loss of all hope and even of religion itself.

The truth of the Resurrection is so far beyond ordinary experience that one needs to examine its evidences. The proof of Jesus' identity and corporeal existence (24:39–42) encourages that one acknowledge doubts and find ways to overcome these.

The value of having all the Gospels is demonstrated in moving from one to the other in seeking an understanding of the Resurrection. The earlier consideration of the Resurrection in this series of sermons was taken from the Gospel of John. That writer placed an emphasis on the repetition of appearances and the pronouncement of peace. In turning to the Gospel of Luke the continued value of repetition is demonstrated.

I. The gift of peace overcomes doubts. Experience gives the awareness that all persons lose important parts of life with the passage of time. The greatest temptation is to assume that such losses are restricted to one's own experience.

(a) The loss of peace. The followers of Jesus had lost their hope and the promise of the relationship they had with him. All who lose hope and the relationship with him have lost the peace he brings.

(b) The restoration of peace. This passage teaches that both hope and promise come from trusting in Jesus. Peace is the result of trusting him even when all human experience argues otherwise. The gift of peace is not the result of proof, it is the result of acceptance of his continued concern and power in life.

II. The gift of power withstands doubts. Power is more often sought by individuals than even great wealth.

(a) The purpose of power. The followers of Jesus were promised the power to change the world. In the midst of their experience with the result of their contact with the raw political and human power, they were no doubt disappointed with the results of power. The power he promised was related to the great religious heritage they had known (24:44–45). The power that he promised brought hope and expectation.

(b) The nature of true power. True power is not involved in controlling others but in enabling them to reach their potential and achieve the purpose of God for them. The disappointment of the disciples with the evidence of the abuses of power was answered by his picture of what his power can accomplish in the life of the world.

III. The result of their experience. Jesus promised that they would see the result of all that he offered.

(a) The answer to doubt. The preaching of repentance and forgiveness would be the ultimate answer to their doubts.

(b) The proof of his promise. The faith which they would demonstrate would be the basis for the victory he promised. When this victory came they would see it as the evidence that his promise had been fulfilled.—Arthur L. Walker

SUNDAY: APRIL TWENTY-FOURTH

SERVICE OF WORSHIP

Sermon: When Faith Meets Magic

TEXT: 1 Sam. 17:31–40, 48–50; Acts 8:9–24

Faith as the Bible describes it looks like courage. It's not believing a lot of things, it's trusting one thing. It's not holding onto doctrines so much as it is letting go of fears. It's not so much a matter of reciting creeds, but doing deeds, especially difficult deeds, deeds beyond your strength. That's why faith, when you see it, looks like courage.

I. The story of David and Goliath is the perfect paradigm for biblical understanding of faith.

(a) It is there as a model of what faith ought to look like. David, just a youth, wanders into the adult world saying that he can defeat the giant that has filled everybody else with fear. David, whose only work experience had been shepherding, answered that in protecting the sheep he was called upon to kill wild animals, and reckoned that fighting Goliath would be no more difficult than fighting a bear.

(b) That seems terribly naive. That's the way biblical faith often appears to the world. The most common criticism you hear of religious answers to the world's problems is that they are naive. That's why Saul, this worldly man, says to David, "You haven't even seen this Goliath. What makes you think you can defeat him?"

But Saul is out of alternatives. His men refuse to fight, and Saul himself is not about to do it, so he says to David, "Let's see how you look in my armor." It must have been humorous to see David trying to get into Saul's armor. Saul is a great big man, David is still a boy.

(c) David doesn't put his faith in armaments, but in God. "The Lord who delivered me in the past will deliver me again." So he removes the armor, goes out to meet the giant with what he is used to, just a slingshot and five smooth stones, saying to Goliath when he meets him on the battlefield, "You come to me with a sword, and a spear, and a javelin, but I come to you in the name of the Lord of hosts." Whereupon David slew Goliath with just one stone. Often it took four or five stones to slay a bear or a lion, but only one stone to slay this giant that everyone was afraid of.

(d) This story is so simple. It's all there. Faith is the courage to go out and meet the giants in your life. Faith trusts in God alone. Stories like this one are common in the Bible, especially in the Old Testament. Not only does David go up against the Philistine, but Moses goes up against the Pharaoh and all his army, and Elijah goes up against Jezebel and all the priests of Baal. All of them are small, insignificant, powerless, unarmed people going up against the great powers of the world.

II. But there are some in the New Testament as well, and our lesson from the Book of the Acts of the Apostles is one of them.

(a) Simon Magus. Just the name itself is intimidating. Simon Magus, "the power of God which is called great." No wonder all of Samaria was amazed, and also fearful, I would think, because he looms in this story as such a powerful man, a giant like Goliath.

(b) Into Simon Magus' land comes Philip, the apostle. Philip, like David, is a shepherd of sorts. He's a pastor, a follower of Jesus, a preacher. He comes into that land preaching the good news of Jesus Christ. You notice in the story there are no adjectives to describe Philip, no "Philip the Great," or "Philip the Magnificent," just old Philip, the preacher.

Philip is just a poor preacher. There are no adjectives in this text like Magus, spelled with a capital M. Philip comes to Samaria, in other words, not in strength, but in weakness. He comes like David before Goliath.

(c) There's an interesting footnote in this story. It seems that Philip, who had converted Simon, hadn't been doing the baptisms quite right. Evidently Philip stumbled along in this as he did everything else.

The complaint was that he was not following the water baptism with the anointing, the laying on of hands, the blessing of the Holy Spirit.

The headquarters in Jerusalem had to send two first-string preachers, Peter and John, to Samaria to straighten out this terrible omission of not anointing with the Holy Spirit. So they go around "laying on hands" on everybody, saying, "Receive the Holy Spirit, receive the Holy Spirit, receive the Holy Spirit."

Simon saw all of this, thought it was some kind of magic. So he took Peter and John aside, "Look, you show me how to do that and I'll make you rich." And Peter, shocked at this display of raw ambition, rebukes Simon Magus with the words, "Your silver will perish with you, because you thought you could obtain the gift of God with money." That scene, incidentally, is the origin of the word "simony," which means trying to buy high office, or power, or influence with money.

III. The story is not about simony, but about the contest between faith and magic. Magic is speaking words that will change the world out there. Faith is trusting the word that will change me, inside here. And the point of this story is that that word, the Word of God, the gospel, is stronger than any magic in this world. Even when the word is spoken by a poor preacher, even when that preacher can't get it right. Even if he can't get anything right, even the sacraments. It's stronger than that preacher. It is stronger than anything else in the world.

(a) Evidently when Christianity went outside the boundaries of Israel into the gentile world it immediately confronted those who expected Christianity to be something like magic, something that would allow you to manipulate the world out there so that things would the way you want them to be. Magic is simply the manipulation of the powers that be to get what you want. Magic tries to change things out there.

(b) I confess, I want to believe in magic, because I want to believe that the problem is out there. The problem is not here, it's out there. I also want to believe in magic because I'm tired of struggling, and working hard. I want my life to be easy. I want to believe in magic because I want to be in control. I want to believe in magic because I am insecure about the future, and I want to secure it any way I can. I want to remove the uncertainty in my life so I will know exactly what is going to happen.

IV. That's magic. That's believing that the words I say will control things out there. I'm sure that that's what Philip was up against when he went into Samaria. People were confusing Christianity with magic. They assumed there was some simple formula for gaining this power, some steps we can follow, some rules that we can learn, some words that we can say over and over, maybe a little money. Money can work miracles, you know. That's magic. Magic is the attempt to get God to work for us. Faith is letting God work through us.

(a) Here comes Philip. He is like David. He is just a kid, vocationally speaking. He's armed only with the gospel. Philip didn't do it very well. There were others who could do it better. Once they had to send some people from Jerusalem to do it better. He made mistakes, but that didn't matter, because he went there in faith, expecting God is going to use me. And God did. And Simon Magus was amazed. He thought, it must be magic. It's the only explanation. But it wasn't. It is what happens when you stop trying to use God for your purposes and let God use you for God's purposes.

(b) Miracles are what happens to you when the gospel reminds you who you really are. Jesus didn't work magic. The Temptation story in the Gospels is there to say Jesus did not work magic. He rejected that. Jesus simply spoke words that freed the person from bondage. Words like, "You are forgiven," and "God loves you," "You are a child of God." Faith means trust those words. If you do, when you go out unarmed to face the things that are most difficult in your life, it will look like courage.—Mark Trotter

Illustrations

IN OUR HANDS.   One of the happiest birthdays of my life was my tenth. About that time in school we had begun to study geography and for the first time the world began to appear to me as a whole, with different people living in different lands in different ways. Living in countries that were shown in beautiful, vivid colors on the marvelous globe that we had in our classroom. That year as my birthday approached, my father and mother asked what I would like to have for my birthday, and there was only one thing that I wanted—a globe like the one we had in school. I didn't think I was really going to get it. It just seemed too beautiful, perfect, and expensive.

I'll never forget that birthday. There was the box, and I opened it . . . and there before me was the globe of the world. What a thrill it was to look at it, to see that perfect globe and to hold it in my hands. The whole earth! I will never forget that experience. In that moment, consciously and deliberately, my mother and father placed the world in my hands.

You say, "But wait a minute, I thought we used to sing, 'He's got the whole world in his hands.' I thought the world was in God's hands." Yes, it is ultimately. But the message of the Bible is that within history, God has turned the world over to us. That's what the story of the Garden of Eden is about: That God made this fantastic universe, and then gave us as human beings the responsibility of caring for the earth.—David James Randolph

IN CONTROL!   When I was a child I was taught to say prayers at night before I went to bed. I believed that if I didn't do that, something terrible would happen the next day. Old Simon Magus would have been proud of me, because I thought the next day was up to me. So if I didn't say my prayers, and if I didn't say them right, then something terrible would happen. I could control the next day, in other words, if I said the right words. I will admit that I am still that way when I get into an airplane. It's my practice, when the plane starts down the runway for takeoff, to start reciting the Lord's Prayer, and to keep saying it until we are aloft. It takes two-and-a-half Lord's Prayers to get a 727 off the ground.—Mark Trotter

Sermon Suggestions

NO OTHER NAME.   TEXT: Acts 4:5–12, especially verse 12. Why such a sweeping, exclusive testimony? (1) Because Jesus Christ and the Father are one. (2) Because Christ reaches out in love to all of God's people, regardless of gender, race, or nation. (3) Because Christ brings salvation to expression with undeniable evidence. (4) Because Christ's salvation is personally experienced in its transforming power, as in the case of Simon Peter.

WHENEVER OUR HEARTS CONDEMN US. TEXT: 1 John 3:16–24, RSV. (1) We can take comfort in the "God who knows everything." (2) We should be challenged by Christ's commandment that we love one another. (3) Then we will be able to go on to a new confidence before God and expectation of answered prayer.

Worship Aids

CALL TO WORSHIP.　"This is the day which the Lord hath made; we will rejoice and be glad in it" (Ps. 118:24).

INVOCATION.　Lord, you have given us a joyous day in which to celebrate the presence of love—your love, which we see shining in the faces of others who lift our hopes and enable our dreams. We come to thank you for the special gift you share with us in allowing us the opportunity to enter each others' lives. All of this, in a world full of beauty, causes us to kneel in awe. Thank you, Lord, for being with us where we are, through Jesus Christ, our Lord.—Robert F. Langwig

OFFERTORY SENTENCE.　"Whoever shares with others should do it generously" (Rom. 12:8 TEV).

OFFERTORY PRAYER.　Lord, lift some spirit, alleviate some sorrow, comfort some soul, and save many through this small offering made large through your grace, sealed by your Spirit.—E. Lee Phillips

PRAYER.　From the waters of our baptism, O Father, you have called us to be and become. You call us to love not only with all our heart and all our soul but with all our mind. Forgive us when we check our brains at the front door of the sanctuary as we enter and clamor to be lulled to sleep by time-worn cliches and harmless shibboleths that have lost all their edge, when it is a living and active Word "sharper than any double-edged sword" to which you keep calling us. You challenge us to think your thoughts— to do your deeds. In this place we are reminded that your thoughts are not our thoughts and your ways are not our ways but as the heavens are higher than the earth, so are your ways higher than our ways and your thoughts than our thoughts.

When in your Word in Christ you challenge us to stretch our minds and to enlarge our hearts to embrace enemy as well as friend, may we not turn away in disappointment, or even disgust. When we fail your love in Christ, we fail our brother and sister, and when we fail to be brotherly and sisterly, we fail you as Father, for the way we treat others is the way we treat you.

What an awesome responsibility to be spiritual mentors to others whether to our children, grandchildren, or others with whom our lives are set. We are called to free others to be and become but how often we seek to make them but carbon copies or rubber stamps of ourselves because we are not free. Your grace is as a tale from a far country but not a personal experience. Cleanse us and we shall be clean, heal us and we shall be whole, free us with your truth and we shall be free indeed. As the parched earth is refreshed with the spring rains so may our minds and hearts be renewed by the showering of your Spirit upon us.

O Father, we pray for those who teach among us, those who lead the praise of your house, those who minister and administer, those who challenge us to world mission—all those who keep the pressure of your Spirit upon us that we fail not man nor thee.

We would embrace in your love those persons among us—family, fellow members and friends—who suffer brokenness of mind, body or spirit—heal in your infinite wisdom, love, and mercy. For any in the valley of the shadow we pray the hopefulness of the light of an eternal day.—John Thompson

LECTIONARY MESSAGE

Topic: The Breadth of the Shepherd's Love

TEXT: John 10:11–18

The love of the Good Shepherd for his sheep is clearly shown in his promise in verse 16, "Other sheep I have, which are not of this fold: them also I must bring, and they shall hear my voice; and there shall be one fold, and one shepherd."

I. The inclusiveness of Christ's love is what got him killed and made him eternally the Savior of all who come to him in faith. The recognition between Christ and the Father is a natural deep truth of their mutually divine being; the recognition between Christ the Good Shepherd and those who are his is likewise a natural bond formed by mutual affinity. It is a soul-based acknowledgment, not a mind-generated or logically induced compulsion.

It is the Good Shepherd's willingness to shepherd "strange" sheep that will finally make of us all one fold. Many are the declarations in the Scriptures of the unity of the Kingdom of God and of the Church of Jesus Christ. This is one of the most beautiful and appealing of all those promises—"There shall be one fold and one shepherd." It is beautiful and appealing to the sheep who recognize the true shepherd—hateful and galling to those who jealously guard their false claims to exclusivity in the fold.

Love descends in the form of the Spirit, and we all know that the Spirit of God, like the wind of earth, "bloweth where it listeth." The spirit of the love of the Good Shepherd is abundant, infinitely more plentiful than one nation, race, tribe, clan, or family of humanity can require—or contain.

II. This recognition by all of humanity, not just those born into a certain ethnic or political division, that the Good Shepherd has a place for us is the saving truth of our lives and eternities. It is a truth which God revealed many times to those who were part of his specially appointed people. In Isaiah 56:8 we read, "The Lord God which gathereth the outcasts of Israel saith, 'Yet will I gather others to him, beside those that are gathered unto him.'" The preceding verses in that chapter establish the truth—the son of an attached foreigner cannot say he is left out; the eunuchs that keep the Sabbath and adopt the covenant are assured of a place and a name better than those of sons and daughters—"Their burnt offerings and their sacrifices shall be accepted upon mine altar."

Each one of the sheep must hear the shepherd's voice. Therein lies the recognition. In the cacophonous plenum about us, one voice speaks with the loving care and commandment which appealingly draws from our hearts the response of ready obedience and the allegiance which springs from trust. We cannot wander so far into any lonely wilderness of the soul that the Good Shepherd's call cannot penetrate our isolation and restore our belonging once again in his community. We must listen if we are to know him. And if we hear him and come to him, no matter what fold we come from nor how far we have gone astray, he receives us; and, laying down his life, he keeps us safe forever.—John R. Rodman

SUNDAY: MAY FIRST

SERVICE OF WORSHIP

Sermon: God's Own People

TEXT: 1 Peter 2:4–10

1 Peter 2:4–10 reminds us that there is something special about Christians. We are "a holy nation, God's own people." Wonderful things have happened because of God's touch upon our lives. We are let loose in the world to "declare the wonderful deeds of him who called you out of darkness into his marvelous light." Spirit-filled Christians are the happiest people on earth. The coming of God into our lives has made the great difference. "Once you were not people but now you

are God's people; once you had not received mercy but now you have received mercy." The word that describes the special quality of the Christian is "holy." We are a holy people set apart to give glory to God and to tell the great things he has done.

I. Leviticus 19:1–2 lifts God's standard to which men of faith must repair. "You shall be holy: for I the Lord your God am holy." Our God is a God of moral character, and we are to become like him. Unique among the religions of the world is the character of our God, whose goodness and strength are in the service of his love. In the service of the Holy God, our lives take on special dignity and meaning. We need never think poorly of ourselves, for our body is "a temple of the Holy Spirit" (1 Cor. 6:19). When St. Paul preached to the Corinthians in the Bema of Corinth, he stood between two heathen temples—the temple of Aphrodite on the Acro-Corinth and the temple of Apollo near the sea. Heathen temples honored the desires of the flesh. The temple of Aphrodite had a thousand sacred prostitutes. St. Paul preached a radically new idea of the body. "Do you not know that you are God's temple and that God's Spirit dwells in you? . . . God's temple is holy, and that temple you are" (1 Cor. 3:16–17). Our human life takes on new dignity and glory as we see God's purpose of holiness for our lives. We are called of God to a life that is special. It is the life of holiness—likeness to God. "So glorify God in your body" (1 Cor. 6:20).

II. The call to holiness is a challenge not only to individual believers, but also to the Church, "God's own people." The Church is called of God, and in God's call to holiness is the promise of renewal. We need this strong sense of purpose, for we cannot help others if we are unsure about our own state. The need of the Church is to believe in what it is doing, for it is called of God and in doing his will it finds its strength. The Church is called out of the world to constitute a colony of heaven on earth. The Church is in the world, but not of the world, for it has a special mission from God. In the rhythm of withdrawal to be with God and return to serve men, the Church finds the dynamic of its true life. Owing all to God, it is a fellowship of the forgiven—those who rejoice in newness of life because they have known the touch of God's grace. The fellowship of the forgiven becomes the fellowship of the forgiving. As we receive God's love, so we share it with others in witness and in deed. So the Church becomes a channel through which the holy love of God flows with transforming power into the places of need and hurt in the world.

Only God gives goals worthy of a man. The Church looks to God for its marching orders, its mission to link men to God. The Holy Spirit created the Christian Church at Pentecost, the initial release of a spiritual vitality that transformed disenchanted disciples into flaming apostles on that memorable occasion, and has never lost that power.

The Bible message of our call to holiness makes us think long thoughts about the Church today. Is it a form or a force? Does it have the form of godliness without the power thereof? Is it a thermostat that sets the moral and spiritual temperature, or merely a thermometer that records it? Our deep need is to seek out the central meanings of our faith and discover in personal experience the mighty hope and transforming power that God gives to all who look to him in faith. The coming of the loving God into the heart of man touches our life with an eternal splendor that the world can neither give nor take from us. It is the glory of the Church to bear witness to this newness of life that only God can give, and to bear the name "God's own people."

III. Mark 1:4–11 tells the surprising story of the baptism of Jesus. Why should the Son of God be baptized? John the Baptist raised the question when Jesus came to him to be baptized. "John would have prevented him, saying, 'I need to be baptized by you, and do you come to me'" (Matt. 3:14). Jesus simply said, "Let it be so now: for thus it is fitting for us to fulfill all righteousness" and walked with John into the Jordan and was baptized.

In going to John to be baptized, Jesus was identifying himself with John's call to a humbling of self under God in penitence and change of heart. Baptism under John was a symbol of repentance and a resolve to enter a new life cleansed of the sins of the old. John was the greatest preacher of righteousness in his time and Jesus chose to be identified with John's preaching of the moral character of God and the human hope of a new life of character made possible by repentance and the touch of God. Jesus might have identified himself with the zealots and becoming a revolutionary. He might have joined the Essenes, withdrawing from normal life to find holiness, and entering an ascetic community, like the nearby Qumran, famous today for the Dead Sea Scrolls. Rather he went to this strong, active prophet of God who proclaimed God's righteousness as the life-transforming hope of man. In the humility of baptism, Jesus witnessed to the world that his life was totally dedicated to God's moral standards and to God's holy will. As Son of man, he humbled himself as he earnestly willed that all men should do, giving our loyalty to the highest and looking to God for our true life.

God was pleased with Jesus' humility. The heavenly voice said, "Thou art my beloved Son, in whom I am well pleased." God's blessing is always given to man's humility. And when Jesus humbled himself under the hand of John in baptism, he heard God's words of happy approval. Jesus had made full surrender to God in this experience of baptism, and descending in humility, he ascended as God lifted him up with words of loving acceptance. What kind of words are we permitting God to speak to us? Only words of judgment on slack or recalcitrant disciples? Only words that seek to whip life into a flagging will, weary in well-doing? Have we ever heard God say "with thee I am well pleased"? The glory of the dedicated life is the knowledge of God's loving acceptance, and the joy of purposeful living as his colleagues in doing his work in the world.—Lowell M. Atkinson

Illustrations

HOW YOU ARE REMADE.   Christianity begins with *being*, not with doing, with life and not with action. If you have the life of a plant, you will bloom like a plant; if you have the life of a monkey, you will act like a monkey. If you have the life of a man, you will do the things a man does, but if you have the life of Christ in you, you will act like a Christian. You are like your parents because you partake of their nature; you are like God if you partake of his Nature.—Fulton J. Sheen

ARE YOU LOOKING FOR GOD?   There is that neighborhood tailor I once knew. One day, shortly after the end of World War II, I was in his shop and he stopped me as I was leaving and said in his thick accent, "Mr. Steimle, I have a problem. As you know, I am a Jew and my wife, she is a Christian. Her brother was a violent Nazi. When we were in Germany he hated me and did nothing to help us. He was glad to get rid of us when we came over here. But now he is in a prison camp and he has written us asking us to send him some food. My wife, she says no. We send him nothing. But I say yes. We should send him something. What do you think, Mr. Steimle?" I don't know how you would have felt. I felt humble and ashamed. Ashamed for his Christian wife, of course, but more ashamed of myself that I had not been prepared to hear the voice of God on the lips of a pleasant neighborhood tailor.—Edmund Steimle

Sermon Suggestions

THE STORY OF A CONVERSION.   TEXT: Acts 8:26–40. (1) A willing witness. (2) An interested prospect. (3) A scriptural opening. (4) A simple proclamation. (5) A full commitment. (See Isa. 56:3–5; cf. Deut. 23:1).

BECAUSE GOD LOVED US FIRST.   TEXT: 1 John 4:7–21, REB, especially verse 19. (1) We love God. (2) We love our fellow Christians.

Worship Aids

CALL TO WORSHIP.   "Grace to you, and peace, from God our Father, and from the Lord Jesus Christ" (Phil. 1:2).

INVOCATION.   Lord, so fill us with a vision of the holy that we may become more like the children God intends us to be through Christ, our Lord.—E. Lee Phillips

OFFERTORY SENTENCE.   "If you are eager to give, God will accept your gift on the basis of what you have to give, not on what you don't have" (2 Cor. 8:12 TEV).

OFFERTORY PRAYER.   Lord, we lift our hearts in prayer as we give these gifts of money, that one joined with the other might produce much good fruit of the Spirit, saving and edifying many souls.—E. Lee Phillips

PRAYER.   Eternal Spirit, thy servants seek thee not so much to secure what they desire as to open their hearts to the gifts which thou desirest to bestow. Through another week we have imposed imperious wishes on the world to get our will and we confess before thee the evil and unwisdom of our craving. Give thou to us not what we would ask but what thou wouldst bestow.

We seek easy and fortunate circumstance while thou hast in thine hand courage with which to face ill fortune and win a shining victory against hardship and adversity. Lord, give thy gifts to us—thy will, not ours, be done—courage, let it be, that we may prove ourselves the sons of God and heirs with Christ in overcoming the world.

We seek from thee happiness and like children would stand with open hands to receive life's pleasures, while thou hast a task to give us which will call us out of ourselves and claim all that we are for thee. A task, then, let it be, O God, according to thy wisdom! Give us a duty which will dignify our days that we may join the honorable company of thy true servants who, called of God, have found their vocation and have done it well. We would seek thy sanctuary, not to present our unwise wishes, but to put ourselves at thy disposal. Release thy power in us. Reveal thy wisdom through us, and grant that in and for and because of us thy will may be done.—Harry Emerson Fosdick

LECTIONARY MESSAGE

Topic: The Secret of Christian Fruitfulness

TEXT: John 15:1–8

Jesus and the disciples stayed long in the upper room. Jesus washed the disciples' feet after supper and sat down again to comfort them in the face of his near departure from them, assuring them of his closeness to them. Judas left; Jesus gave the New Commandment (hence Maundy Thursday) and assured them of their eternal home and of the companion for their remaining days. Then Jesus led them out of the room. It seems safe to assume that the inspiration for our textual words came from the appearance of a grape arbor as they emerged from the building; or, as Jesus thought of the Jews, it might have come from their representation as a vine on current coins.

I. The purpose for the vine and its branches is the production of fruit. The vital union of branch and vine is the means through which the life of the vine breaks forth into bud and fruit. The fruit bears the seed which may give life to new vines. The emphasis is not only on feeding the living, but also on spreading the life of the true vine to other needy people.

Verses 2 and 8 emphasize the glory God receives from the fruit believers bear for him. In verse 8 Jesus also adds the promise that if we demonstrate the grace which God provides for us in his Son, we shall truly be his disciples. The verb translated "be" may also be translated "become," from the root connected with origin, creation, and growth. Christians are always "becoming," always growing and developing.

II. Abiding in the vine is the source of comfort, strength, vigor, and fruitfulness. Jesus' sustaining power flows through the believer. We know the need of abiding, as branches, in him as the vine. A branch receives nutrient, food, prepared for assimilation. As Jesus' followers, we receive the food of the word, the refreshing streams of living water, by his spirit. As long as we "abide in the vine," we have it as part of our nature, not to be sought and found, incapable of being lost, naturally a part of our lives. But there is a warning here to the one who allows anything to sever the close connection between the believer and Jesus. Detached Christians are dead to Christ. Our fellowship in the Church is a life-or-death matter.

III. The "cleaning" or pruning of fruitful branches and the disposal of fruitless ones are the work of the vinedresser, the husbandman, who Jesus says is his Father.

(a) The amputation of the fruitless vine is a regular part of cultivation. One thinks nothing of this severance—it is merely disposal of waste to allow precious room and nutrients for the fruitful branches. Verses 2 and 6 state this truth

and enlarge on it. Here again, the abiding in Jesus is the secret. One who does not is "cast forth as a branch," and hence becomes a form without life, soon shrivels, and eventually disintegrates.

(b) The pruning of the fruitful branch is a simplifying of form to fulfill purpose more efficiently, to allow growth to multiply branches, to conserve the vital power for fruit, rather than allow it to go into wood alone.

(c) It is hard to realize that God looks on our lives as means to his ends, rather than as ends in themselves. It is God's purpose for us to live fruitful lives, lives that bring glory to him. We are protected, nourished, cared for, and—pruned. We have to realize that it is only in our lives that Jesus can be seen in the world. We need to keep our connection strong; our faith, taught by him and perfected by him, active; our hopes, our motives, and our needs centered on him; and then we shall receive all the life we need, all the holy energy of Christ necessary for us to be his disciples.—John R. Rodman

SUNDAY: MAY EIGHTH (MOTHER'S DAY)

SERVICE OF WORSHIP

Sermon: A Good Word for the Mother-in-Law

TEXT: Ruth 1:6–18

Counselors agree that three problems commonly surface in the early years of marriage: finances, sexual adjustment, and in-law relationships.

The individual bearing the lion's share of criticism in the latter area is the mother-in-law. One wit noted that while the mother rocks the cradle, the mother-in-law rocks the boat.

How tragic that a relationship intended to be an enrichment to marriage often is castigated.

I've found it helpful to talk about in-law adjustment in premarital sessions. I assure couples that when they become

parents, they'll better understand why in-laws often feel compelled to act for the well-being of their child. We always feel responsible for our children. Understanding this can help us be more tolerant.

Those planning to be married should also remember that they become someone's in-law. We receive a larger family at marriage. Such an acquisition is a wonderful gift which we should cherish. The relationships we inherit must also be nurtured. We should employ the finest interpersonal skills possible within our family structure. Our witness begins here.

I. The Book of Ruth speaks a good word for a mother-in-law, Naomi. The Book of Ruth is a charming story. Macartney says Franklin read it to fashionable company in Europe. His audiences always were delighted with the tale.

They also were surprised to learn it was a biblical story.[1]

Naomi and her husband, Elimelech, left Israel for Moab during a time of famine. The word "sojourn" (RSV)[2] in verse 2 indicates their intention was to remain only a short time. Unforeseen events, however, caused their sojourn to be lengthened.

In the land of plenty, Elimelech died. His sons disobeyed the law of Israel by taking foreign wives. After 10 years both sons also died. Naomi selected a nickname (see Ruth 1:20): Naomi means "joy" or "pleasant," but she saw her life more as "Mara," or "bitterness."

Naomi decided to go home. She encouraged her daughters-in-law to remain in Moab and remarry. The levirate marriage provision in the Canaanite lands stipulated that the male next-of-kin would marry a childless widow. Children were important, for they provided "social security" for aged parents.

Orpah remained in Moab, but Ruth refused to leave her mother-in-law. Her beautiful words rank among the best-known in the scripture (see Ruth 1:16–17).

II. Naomi, a mother-in-law, lived a worthy example in several respects:

(a) *An example in her witness.* Even in a foreign land Naomi testified of her God. When Ruth committed herself to Naomi's God, she didn't use the general Canaanite name, *Elohim,* but the particular Jewish name, *Yahweh* (see Ruth 1:17). No doubt she had heard Naomi talk about Yahweh, his people, and his promises.

One's home may be the most difficult of mission fields. We often fail to be as kind and loving inside our home as we are outside. Naomi lived and taught her faith in the home. This is where our Christian witness begins.

(b) *An example in concern.* Naomi wanted her daughters-in-law to be well-cared for. Though it broke her heart, she encouraged Orpah and Ruth to remain in Moab where they could more readily find domestic stability. Naomi later refused to cling selfishly to Ruth but encouraged her in her relationship with Boaz (see Ruth 3:1–5).

H. G. Wells said of Napoleon: "He stood at last for nothing but himself." What a tragedy! The highest level of concern is for another's well-being, not for one's self-interest. Jesus demonstrated this kind of sacrificial love on the cross. Paul reminded us to incorporate this caliber of love in our lives. Godly love is unselfish; it "seeketh not her own" (1 Cor. 13:5).

(c) *An example in healthy relationship.* Naomi sought a healthy relationship with her daughters-in-law. She dropped the "in-law" and called them "my daughters" (Ruth 1:11). Later Ruth and Boaz had a son. The neighbors reported, "There is a son born to Naomi" (Ruth 4:17). Her acquaintances must have seen Naomi's big heart and realized her grandson would be treated as her own son.

In response to an oft-asked question about whether marriages are made in heaven, J. Allan Petersen wrote, "I do not know whether your marriage was made in heaven but I do know that all the maintenance work is done on earth."[3] Naomi did a good maintenance job. She worked hard to be a supportive mother-in-law. Her family relationships were exemplary.

In-law relationships can be satisfying when we purpose to love our extended family just as we do our nuclear family. This should be the goal of every Christian in his or her family life.

The story of Ruth has a happy ending. Naomi's grandson, Obed, became the father of Jesse. Jesse's son, David, became the greatest of Israel's kings and a forerunner to Jesus Christ, the Messiah.

[1]Clarence Edward Macartney, *Great Women of the Bible* (Grand Rapids: Baker Book House, 1977), 10.
[2]From the *Revised Standard Version of the Bible,* copyrighted 1946, 1952, 1971, 1973.

[3]J. Allen Peterson, *The Myth of the Greener Grass* (Wheaton: Tyndale House, 1983), 67.

Naomi was a good mother-in-law, and her faith had long-lasting results.— Michael Brooks

Illustrations

MOTHERS-IN-LAW. Are you old enough to remember some of the thousands of Burma Shave highway signs that once dotted America's countryside? Here's how one of them read:

You'll love your wife
You'll love your paw
You'll even love
Your mother-in-law
If you use Burma Shave!

Mothers-in-law don't deserve all the kidding they get. But this simple jingle touches on a basic theme in family life: the cohesive power of love that holds us together, whatever comes.—Robert J. Hastings

ALL SHE HAD. When Betty Morris of Bay City, Texas, retired after 31 years of missionary service in Lebanon, Jordan, and Africa, she reminisced about her commitment. She said she argued as hard as she could, both to herself and to God. She prayed, "Lord, you don't want me; I don't know how to do anything. I'm not a nurse, I'm not a doctor, I'm not a teacher; I don't even know how to type, and I don't know how to sing or play the piano. Call somebody else."

But in the end she went! She traded her fear of change for security in God's will. She probably felt like the widow who had only a handful of meal and a cup of oil. But God multiplied what each had to offer. God is still using the multiplication table to achieve his purposes!—Robert J. Hastings

Sermon Suggestions

THE HOLY SPIRIT AT WORK. TEXT: Acts 10:44–48. (1) The Holy Spirit attends the Word of God. (2) The Holy Spirit transcends human barriers.

THE CHRISTIAN LIFE EXPLAINED. TEXT: 1 John 5:1–6. (1) By our spiritual birth.

(2) By our love for our spiritual family. (3) By our victorious faith.

Worship Aids

CALL TO WORSHIP. "Behold, I stand at the door, and knock: if any man hear my voice and open the door, I will come in to him, and will sup with him, and he with me" (Rev. 3:20).

INVOCATION. O Christ, we open our hearts individually to you; we open the heart of our fellowship of believers to you; and we would open the hearts of men and women everywhere to you. Grant that the intimacy of our communion with you may deepen our finest motives to serve you both here and wherever we go in this world.

OFFERTORY SENTENCE. "Give unto the Lord the glory due unto his name: bring an offering, and come into his courts" (Ps. 96:8).

OFFERTORY PRAYER. Gracious Father, we have opened our mouths and thou hast filled them with good things. Now open our hearts to others, we pray, that we may help bring fulfillment to their hopes and prayers. Bless these offerings and direct their use, so that nothing be wasted.

PRAYER. Almighty God, who ordained the family for the welfare and happiness of humankind, we give thanks for that mighty gift which has nurtured us all in some form, even though not always perfect forms. We thank you for the nest of our incubation and for the fledgling years until we become strong enough to try our own wings.

Today we give special thanks for the mothers of the home and for the positive lessons we learned under their tutelage. Thanks be to you for the ones who showed us your love in action on a daily basis and led us to understand the mysteries of faith, many times unaware that such was even being done. Thank you for teaching through these avenues that love is patient and kind—not judgmental, but forgiving. Thank you for letting us learn that it is better to believe in good rather than gloat over evil and that there is in us the power to persevere through good times and difficult, in sickness and in health for short times or long.

In this family of faith we pray for those this morning who suffer brokenness and ask for the generative powers of your amazing grace to make them whole again. For those passing through the valley of the shadow of death, seeing human finiteness, we ask the strength of your everlasting arms. For families going through the pain of hostilities and struggle we pray that the Prince of Peace will be crowned in their lives that solution to hostilities may be found.

Strongly warm our hearts now, we pray, in this worship hour. Call your children to you and may conviction lead to commitment as we linger in your presence now for a little while, we pray in Jesus' name . . . —Henry Fields

LECTIONARY MESSAGE

Topic: The Love of Christ and His Friends

TEXT: John 15:9–17

The love of God is the force that has bound Jesus to the Father, and now it binds us to Jesus forever. As Jesus takes his nature and thus his duty of affection from God, our nature and our affection are to come from him. When we conform ourselves to Jesus Christ in faith, loving his truth, his being enfolds us in a transforming, even a transfiguring, world of caring devotion. The result is an incomprehensible transport of joy, even to us who know its source in the powerful contradiction of logic, that we could love as he has loved. This is the core of our Christian living—that all our joy henceforth springs from being like him in our love.

I. It is an *obedient* love that Jesus communicates to all his disciples. Jesus has kept his Father's commandments and remains in his Father's love. We, he says, shall remain in his love by keeping his commandments. The love enables the obedience. The love ennobles the obedience. The love animates the obedience. The life of joyous love is the life of devoted obedience. Just as water makes what it touches wet, so Christ's love makes its recipients obedient, by its nature. That is the eternal source of their joy, that they stand in the same relationship to him as he to his Father.

II. It is a *self-giving* love. Thus it is the greatest possible love. Can anyone say he loves if he is not willing to give his all? What a mockery of married love they make who write prenuptial agreements that limit the amount of giving in the exchange of love. There can be no such limits in our love to Christ, as there is no limit in his love to us. There is no possibility of greater love than to give life for the loved one. How can there be less in return for such a devotion? This is not doting; this is donating. This love of God we share is the giving that means we are among the living.

III. It is an *understanding* love. Jesus says that he has revealed to his disciples everything that he has heard from his Father, so that we can have a knowledge of his plan for us and our lives. He reveals the Father's truth to us because we have become his friends by receiving his love and obeying his commandment to love one another. As also in 13:35, the mutual love of believers is the evidence of our belonging to Jesus. When we understand the truth as Jesus reveals it, the truth of redemption, our lives redeemed by the great love that led him to die for us, we cannot fail to love him and live for him, not as slaves but as friends, animated by belonging to his purpose.

IV. It is a *fruitful, life-giving* love that is shared by Jesus with us and by us with our world. We are chosen, by what ineffable selection we can only accept. We are ordained by him for the bearing of spiritual fruit (see Gal. 5:22, 23) and the reproduction of the life we have. His appointment is our commission for the service of his purposes. We no longer need fumble for fruitless pastime or occupation. We have been claimed for the cause of loving life in order to perpetuate that life of lasting blessing. Jesus has reverted to the figure of the vine and branches to show the indwelling force that will enable us in our work for fulfilling his commandment. We are not without infinite resources for his purpose. His Father will meet our needs according to his purpose.

Can love be commanded? In return for his love, our love is his to command. Love is promised in marriage, and we can fulfill Jesus' urgent entreaty by the surrender of our will to his command.—John R. Rodman

SUNDAY: MAY FIFTEENTH

SERVICE OF WORSHIP

Sermon: When the Well Runs Dry

TEXT: John 4:10

All of us come to the inevitable time when life is difficult. At such times we cease to live from the deep. Discouragement takes hold upon us; our judgments are impaired; our self-esteem is in the balance. The well has run dry and there seems to be no refreshment for us.

What are we to do then? In the fourth chapter of John, Jesus has something to say about it. He clearly intimates that to those who will yield themselves to him he will bring something which in the end will be like a living fountain of waters—a fountain which shall never run dry. How wonderful it would be to find such a fountain. Would not you and I readily turn to it and would we not gladly fill our cup and drink of it as though it were the very nectar of life?

I. Let me try in simple language to show what this unfathomable well can be to us. For one thing, when the well runs dry and the resources for living seem to have failed us, we can move out of ourselves into the larger things of life.

(a) So the psalmist, hemmed in, feeling himself forgotten and lost in a terrible loneliness, cried out, "When I consider thy heavens, the work of thy fingers, the moon and the stars, which thou hast ordained; What is man, that thou art mindful of him?" Back of the span of the firmament there lies an endless mind, and back of the greatness of music and art and literature there lies a generous creativeness.

(b) So one would like to say to people who find themselves in difficult times, "Move out into the largeness of things."

It is always so in a man's experience. When the world grows small and the fence is built close in, let him move out and consider the great things. It is only greatness that can fully tax a man's soul. Let him be taxed. Let him be called and challenged.

II. When life becomes difficult and the well runs dry, when we have nothing now by which to live, let us remember that life is not so much a road to happiness as a road to opportunity.

(a) Whatever difficulties we may encounter and whatever frustrations come our way, it is almost always because we feel that we have been cheated out of happiness. Happiness is not something that we find at the end of the road. Happiness is something which we fashion within ourselves. Happiness is fashioned out of some deep inner satisfaction, out of our own self-respect and our own integrity and the knowledge that we have done well.

(b) Happiness is not life's gift to us. Opportunity is. Happiness is our gift to life. Once we find that life is a road to opportunity and that spiritual achievements are still before for us, everything about us can be or become the anvil upon which we beat out lasting things.

III. When the well runs dry and living becomes difficult, let us consider how others before us have lived. How often we exclaim, "No one can possibly understand what I am going through." But that is sheer folly. Others have suffered like we have suffered, and others do understand what we go through.

(a) The road on which we walk is not a lonely road. Others have walked on it. In our own need and scarcity of soul it is good to look at them. In our moments of shallow thinking we divide all mankind into two classes: the happy and the unhappy. The happy are those who are fortunate. They have all of life's possessions; they have the fulfillment of their desires; they have the satisfaction of their wants; they have success. The unhappy are those who are forgotten by this world. They are the poor; they are the physically handicapped; they are the unsuccessful.

(b) But how utterly unreal such a division of mankind is. It defies all truth and all experience. The Apostle Paul was not fortunate. He was poor. He hardly knew from one day to another where his livelihood would come from. But he was radiantly victorious and he was happy. Our Lord Jesus was not fortunate. Tragedy was his constant companion. His followers were few. His antagonists were many. The road was strewn with thorns and the cross became inevitable. He was not fortunate, but he was radiantly victorious and happy.

(c) There is something redeeming about looking at other men who also followed upon this road and found their well running dry. Looking at them we can say with the author of the Letter to the Hebrews: "Therefore let us also, seeing we are compassed about with so great a cloud of witnesses, lay aside every weight, and the sin which doth so easily beset us, and let us run with patience the race that is set before us."

IV. When the well runs dry and living becomes difficult, let us contemplate Jesus. It is strange how Jesus comes to life in one's quiet thinking. It is strange how one hears him say, "Now is my soul troubled; and what shall I say? Father, save me from this hour. But for this cause came I unto this hour." Everything within us that is real and virile and spiritually strenuous takes shape and lifts us up. It is strange when one contemplates him how one remembers that he found himself in practically every circumstance in which we find ourselves, for we read that he was tempted in every way, even as we are.

V. When the well runs dry and living

becomes difficult, let us grow silent that we may hear God speak to us.

(a) In those moments of life when we are aggravated and when the taste upon our lips is a bitter one and everything about life seems to be twisted, we talk. We state our case, we plead our cause. We speak of all the injustices and the wrongs we had to endure.

(b) So long as we thus talk and speak, there is no hope for us. The well stays dry. Then, happily, into this dire monologue which only darkens our days, God comes and he speaks: "Be still, and know that I am God." All the world falls away. And once again the well flows.

(c) Well, how is it with us? Do we ever grow still long enough to hear God? We cannot live greatly, we cannot give to others, we cannot stay on the road until we hear that voice, for in the end the voice will still speak and then it is that we will hear him say, "Come unto me, all ye that labor and are heavy laden, and I will give you rest."—Arnold H. Lowe

Illustrations

VICTORY.　　George Matheson—the man who gave us the great hymn, "O Love That Wilt Not Let Me Go"—was not fortunate. He went blind at an early age. The woman whom he loved most had torn his life in two. But he was radiantly victorious and happy. Beethoven was not fortunate. At what seemed to be the very summit of his career, he became stone deaf. He plunged into the deep of despair. He thought he was losing his mind. And then he rose out of the deep and said, "I will take life by the throat," and wrote more brilliantly than he had ever written before. He was not fortunate, but he was radiantly victorious.—Arnold H. Lowe

JOY.　　Unlike happiness, which is based on circumstances, joy is based on God's promises.—Jay E. Adams

Sermon Suggestions

THE WORK GOES ON.　　TEXT: Acts 1:15–17, 21–26. (1) Judas Iscariot forfeited his ministry with the apostles. (2) Despite disappointment, the apostles in faith and with prayer chose a replacement to become with them a witness to the Resurrection. (3) However, God exceeded their expectations in commissioning Paul, who "worked harder than any of them" (1 Cor. 15:8–10, NRSV).

THAT YOU MAY KNOW. TEXT: 1 John 5:9–13. (1) God gives those who truly believe in his Son assurance of eternal life. (2) This assurance is confirmed by a life that demonstrates union with Jesus Christ in word and deed.

Worship Aids

CALL TO WORSHIP. "Holy, holy, holy, is the Lord of hosts: the whole earth is full of his glory" (Isa. 6:3).

INVOCATION. O Lord of the ascended Christ, who hears and awaits the saints, incline your ear to us as we worship, and lift us by faith to respond in gratitude and commitment.—E. Lee Phillips

OFFERTORY SENTENCE. "Honor the Lord with thy substance, and with the first fruits of all thine increase" (Prov. 3:9).

OFFERTORY PRAYER. Loving Father, thou dost care for all living things. Not even a falling sparrow escapes thy notice. Help us in the giving of our gifts to become extensions of thy love, especially to thy creatures made in thy image. May the gifts we bring minister to their deepest needs.

PRAYER. Dear Heavenly Father, we come to thee this morning to thank thee for thy many blessings, and for the privilege of coming into thy house to renew our love and faith to thee and to our friends and to continue to pray for thy guidance. Give us, we pray, the mind to seek greater use for the power and ability with which thou hast endowed us. No matter how rough the road may be, keep us ever mindful that if we just reach out in faith, thou wilt lead us in the path of peace and love.

Father, we thank thee for all of those with whom we share the mystery and wonder of thy kingdom in this place. May we seek to be an encouragement to one another in the hearing and doing of your Word. We are grateful for those in other times and places—parents, family, Sunday school teachers, ministers, youth counselors—who through much love, patience, and understanding led us to the Gospel, thy saving Word in Christ. To be stewards of this Word in these tumultuous times, in any time, is a high calling, but we would not ask for a lesser task, but for a faith equal to our task.

That we may be faithful to our task, cause us to realize that the world does not exist for the sake of the Church but the Church for the world. As your people we are responsible for the world. Thou hast commissioned us to be the light of the world and the salt of the earth. May we so walk in the light as to lead others to him who is the "light of life," and may we so live as to savor the life of the communities in which we share with thy peace and joy.

We pray for all of those who share responsibilities of leadership. To leaders of nations, grant the wisdom, faith, and courage to choose ways of reconciliation that alone can lead to your peace. Committed to peace-making we shall know thy blessing upon our efforts rather than thy judgment that falls upon profligate ways.

Thy word in Christ present in the beginning teaches us to pray as one people, saying: "Our Father . . ."—John Thompson, with acknowledgements to Sophia Bombar

LECTIONARY MESSAGE

Topic: In the World But Not of the World

TEXT: John 17:6–19

I. In our passage, verses 11 and 15 need to be taken together. They are Jesus' words of petition to the Father to keep from evil the ones he had given to Jesus. Their situation is critical, because the place where they must live their lives is the place where they must perform their ministry. They are in the world specifically to live for Jesus, but now, in his absence, no longer do they have the consoling and comforting, the counsel and the confidence he has been giving them in person. He is gone, is no longer in the world, but they remain among men and women. So Jesus prays the Father, "Preserve them in thy name which thou gavest me."

II. As many neophyte believers have discovered, to go the way of the world among their peers would present hardly any difficulty. The difficulty appears because they no longer "belong" to the world, and it soon begins to treat them as misfits. For that reason they must be one together, as Jesus and the Father are one. The constant consciousness of the godly knowledge Jesus had given them of the Father would keep them united. They must be "kept" in his name.

Jesus prayed for his Father to keep his own from the evil in the world. Whether we translate it "from the evil" or "from the evil one," we know that he meant to keep us free from all evil, in any form, from whatever source, as long as we live. That is what it means to be kept by God through his name. The holiness of God's name has been sacred since the day that Moses brought down from the mountain the commandment not to take it in vain. One who prays through the name of Jesus calls upon the holiness imparted to us in the world as long as we bear that holy name. The anger of the world could be escaped by our removal, but Jesus specifically denies that petition. Holiness is purposeful, not passive but active. The world is its scene, its arena.

III. Both of us know that the sources of evil are in the human heart, that within ourselves there are sufficient voices of evil that it is to no purpose to isolate ourselves from those about us. We need the keeping power of the communion of the saints, created holy by the word of truth, and speaking it with voices of tender love, to keep us from the evil to which we ourselves are otherwise liable.

There is evil in the world, calling to believers to join in. But Jesus' prayer resounds. "As thou hast sent me, even so send I them into the world. And for their sakes I sanctify myself, that they also might be sanctified through the truth." We are to join with each other and become God's intrusion, God's invasion, God's intervention, an extraordinary mission in the world, for its redemption. The hope is that the world in which we live will associate with us, be close to us, hear our thoughts, and catch our spirit, just as the apostle who relates this to us caught the spirit of our Lord. Then it may be touched by the spirit of God, and thereby also be made holy.

The mysterious operation of truth as it sanctifies God's people is not to be overly analyzed, but is to be appreciated, to be partaken of. Only by this shall we become fit to be in the world but not of it. —John R. Rodman

SUNDAY: MAY TWENTY-SECOND (PENTECOST)

SERVICE OF WORSHIP

Sermon: On Being Pentecostal

Text: Acts 2:2–21

Pentecost is a noun. It is a good noun, strong and clear, confident of its identity, able to stand up in any room and say what it is. That's what nouns are; that's what nouns do. If you want definitions, nouns can give you definitions. *Pentecost*: An early harvest festival celebrated in the ancient Near East, among many peoples, including the Jews. *Pentecost*: An early harvest festival transformed into a celebration of the revelation of the law given at Sinai. *Pentecost*: The birthday of the church. *Pentecost*: A festival celebrated fifty days after Easter or, in Judaism, seven weeks and one day after Passover. *Pentecost*: The last day of the liturgical year and the beginning of ordinary time. *Pentecost*: The last Sunday of Easter. Pentecost is a noun: clear-eyed, level-gazed, certain of its identity.

But when you make Pentecost into an adjective, it grows anxious, nervous, and uncertain, standing first on one foot, then on the other. It wants to be a good adjective, as it runs around looking for a noun to modify, but doesn't know which noun and doesn't know what we are talking about. The adjective is "Pentecostal." We don't admit we don't know; we use the word and assume we know.

"Did you know that my roommate is Pentecostal?" she asked.

"Really?" ("Really?" is a way of responding as though you understand.)

"Well, I know, at least I've heard, that she's Pentecostal, but she's doing well in her classes."

"Really?"

"How is your church doing?"

"Well, I'm not sure. I've only been there a year, and we have a fairly heavy Pentecostal element."

"Really?"

"Our church is growing. On Sunday morning, we have a regular, formal, traditional service, but on Sunday evening some have a Pentecostal service."

"Really?"

What are we talking about?

A few years ago, when I was on the West Coast to speak at a seminary, just before the first lecture, one of the students stood up and said, "Before you speak, I need to know if you are Pentecostal." The room grew silent. I don't know where the dean was! The student quizzed me in front of everybody. I was taken aback, and so I said, "Do you mean do I belong to the Pentecostal Church?" He said, "No, I mean are you Pentecostal?" I said, "Are you asking me if I am charismatic?" He said, "I am asking you if you are Pentecostal." I said, "Do you want to know if I speak in tongues?" He said, "I want to know if you are Pentecostal." I said, "I don't know what your question is." He said, "Obviously, you are not Pentecostal." He left.

What are we talking about?

In spite of the fact that the church doesn't know what the adjective means, the church insists that the word remain in our vocabulary as an adjective. The church is unwilling for the word simply to be a noun, to represent a date, a place, an event in the history of the church, refuses for it to be simply a memory, an item, something back there somewhere. The church insists the word is an adjective; it describes the church. The word, then, is "Pentecostal."

Now this word has been embarrassing sometimes, because different groups in the church have, with sincere motives in most cases, I am sure, sought to implement that term by saying, "Let us reproduce, let us imitate the events and experiences of Acts 2." In other words, the way to be Pentecostal is to reproduce the first Pentecost. Now that's embarrassing and tragic, because one cannot actually imitate an event from another time and place. Events that are meaningful are geared to the time and place and people and needs and circumstance in which they occur, and to take that uncritically to another time and place and people is confusing and fruitless, however sincere the motive. Sometimes it has been embarrassing because some have tried, again quite sincerely, to manufacture the enthusiasm and achievement of the Pentecost which Luke describes. But one does not manufacture enthusiasm and achievement. You know and I know, we all know that Pentecost was a gift of God. It was not generated by those present, neither leaders nor observers. It was at the initiative of the Holy Spirit that there was a Pentecost.

In spite of these misguided efforts, the church still insists that somehow "Pentecostal" is an appropriate adjective for describing the church. In the renewal of its life and witness, especially in times of faltering evangelism, the church seeks to reclaim, to recover that quality, perhaps reading, praying, asking, thinking, reflecting again on Pentecost. Perhaps that day will not be just a memory, but also a hope, something that will occur again. And that's what I'd like for us to do; think again about Acts 2 and Pentecost.

After a rather chaste and brief—surprisingly brief—description of the unusual, extraordinary phenomena of that day when the believers were all gathered together, Luke provides a rather detailed presentation of the audience. The crowd is very large. Jews have come from every nation under heaven. In addition, there are converts to Judaism and other visitors. From every nation they have come, and they have come to Jerusalem! And they have come for the festival that celebrates the revelation of God to Israel. Now that, too, is very important, because no festivals or celebrations live very long if they are nothing but recollections of the past. What keeps them alive is that in the bosom of every good memory lives some hope that maybe it will all be true again. And so they come—with a yearning, with a seeking, with an asking—to Jerusalem.

Do you not find it striking that Luke describes the listeners before he presents the preacher or the sermon? Luke starts the story at the ear of the listener, not at the mouth of the preacher. Luke begins with the appetite and then gives the bread. He does not take the bread and throw it at the heads of the people in the audience. He does proceed as if to say, "First of all, this is what is to be said; now let's figure some clever strategies by which we can get them to hear it." In fact, there is no sermon until the people say, "What does this mean?" There is no call to be Christians until the people say, "What does this mean?" There is no call to be Christians until the people say, "What must we do?" Let's think about what it means to begin with the listeners. We are talking about timing. We are talking about appropriateness. How often has the door been closed to the gospel because of someone's poor timing or inappropriate comments, even about Jesus Christ? Luke begins with the listener, with listening to the listener. The world is full of good speeches that failed because they were given at the wrong time to the wrong people.

Notice also that Luke says this audience is made up of folk from every nation under heaven. He gives a partial list of the known nations of that time. "Every nation under heaven" consisted primarily of the world around the Mediterranean, including sub-nations and islands in the sea. Asia is represented. Europe is represented, North Africa is represented, and peoples from those places are all present on the occasion of the first presentation of the gospel of God concerning the dead and risen Christ.

Now what does that mean? Obviously, the first thought is that the gospel is universal, it's for everybody in the world, and that is true, stated not only by Luke but by all the writers in the New Testament. To the Jews first, but also to the Greeks, says Paul. To every creature, says Matthew. From Jerusalem to Judea to Samaria, and to the ends of the earth, says Luke. We know that the gospel is for the whole universe, but what is vital in this story is that these nations—all nations of the earth—are present when the gospel begins. Think what this means! All nations of the earth are not just the destination of the gospel; they are the point of origin of the gospel. Where did it all start? And the Asians said, "With us." Where did it all start? The Europeans said, "With us. We were there when it started." The Africans said, "We were there when it started." From every nation under heaven, the people said, "We were there when it started."

To understand Luke's Pentecost it is necessary to understand that the gospel doesn't just go to the ends of the earth; the ends of the earth are present from the very first day. There is no second-hand, third-hand or fourth-hand faith. There is no church or nation that can say, "It belonged to us and now we are going to give it to you through our benevolence, evangelism, and mission work." No, no, no! Our listeners rise up and say, "We were there that same opening day you were there." For any church that would be Pentecostal, Pentecost removes all ground for any sense of triumphalism, for that ugly sense of arrogance and superiority that takes over the church sometimes simply because we get the notion that the salvation of other people in the world depends upon our behavior. Luke says it started in all the world at the same time. Now you can take that literally, symbolically, figuratively, or whatever, but his point is very clear. And if we miss it in Luke, we can get the figures from 475 Riverside Drive. The information that comes to me indicates that when China was closed to the United States and to the West in 1959 there were six hundred thousand Protestant Christians and about one million Roman Catholic Christians in China. When China was reopened to America and to the West twenty years later, in 1979, there were more than three million Protestant Christians and more than three million Catholic Christians, and we weren't over there doing the converting. How did that happen? Pentecost says that the beginning point as well as the destination of the gospel is the whole world.

Luke says that in this audience the people heard each in his or her own tongue. This is admittedly a complex expression, difficult to understand. What does it mean? Does it mean that we are to make sure that we translate the Christian faith into every language and dialect and idiom of the world so that everybody can hear in his or her own tongue? Of course, it means that anything less is disobedience. But in Luke's description, the reference is not to the duty of the evangelist, but to the condition of the listener. The listener heard in his or her own language. Luke is referring to the capacity of the listener to hear the gospel. Now this is a tedious subject.

Over fifty years ago in Germany there was a running debate between Karl Barth and Emil Brunner over what was called "the point of contact." What is the "point of contact" of the gospel upon the ear of an unbeliever? Professor Barth said, "There is no point of contact. The image of God in the listener has been totally erased by sin." He said to his students, "Don't prepare introductions to your sermons. What are you trying to do, get them interested? Don't get involved in the idolatry of preaching, trying to be interesting. Just present the gospel. God prepares the ear, God gives the message; trust totally in God for all of it; that's it." Professor Brunner said, "No, no, no, no . . . . There is something very important in the way you craft the sermon. Many a

preacher will, on account of what is said, go to heaven, but on account of how it is said, go to hell. We have responsibility for attracting listeners and for being clear because there is some capacity in the listener, however you may describe it, to hear the gospel." Later Paul Tillich rephrased the issue and responded to it with his method of correlation between the life questions asked by a culture and the responses given by the Christian faith. The assumption is that anyone who can ask an ultimate question is also capable of hearing an answer. Rudolf Bultmann shifted the meaning of "contact" between message and hearer. "Let's not talk of point of tact; let's talk of point of conflict. There is disturbance and resistance whenever the gospel is preached, because sinful persons encounter the power and the grace of God." Whether you call it contact or conflict, *something* occurs because the listener is not totally dead spiritually. Luke has no term for it. He doesn't refer to natural theology nor to the listener's "image of God." He doesn't say there is in everyone a faint recollection of Eden, nor does he have a term like "prevenient grace." What Luke says is, "People who listen to the gospel for the first time can hear it; people who hear the gospel for the first time *recognize* it."

You would expect such a view when Luke is describing the movement of the gospel among the Jews in Jerusalem. When Peter preaches in Jerusalem, he can say to his audience, "Jesus' way of life you all know. You know the prophets, you know the writings." Of course they knew and could *recognize* in Jesus some of their own tradition. But when the gospel moved out beyond the reach of Moses and the Law and the Prophets, beyond any knowledge of the Bible or of the life of Jesus Christ, what did the preacher say? When the preachers arrived in Lystra (Acts 14), they faced an audience that didn't know Moses or Jesus or scripture. To them the preachers said, "Listen, folk, we come to you as people of a common nature, created from a common God, the beneficiaries of a common providence to talk to you about a God who has never been without witness in the world, seeing that God gives to everyone everywhere goodness and rain and fruitful seasons and makes glad the human heart." Please do not misunderstand: the preachers are not saying, "What you already know is all we came to say." They came to preach Jesus Christ, but in doing so they said, "What we came to preach to you about redemption concerns the same God you know through creation. There is a continuity with what you already have discerned."

When Paul arrived in Athens, Greece (Acts 17), he stood on the Areopagus, looked around and said, "This unknown God of yours is the subject of my sermon." Of course he could not make Old Testament references or refer to Jesus' life. Paul simply said, "There is one God who created all of us, a God who gave us life in appointed places and times for us to live. This is a God who created every one of us with a certain reaching, longing, seeking in our hearts. This is a God who has stirred even your own poets to say, 'In God we live and move and have our being.' This is a God who stirred even your own philosophers to say, 'We are all the offspring of God.'" And so he continued his message.

Point of *conflict*, point of *contact*, I don't know. I do know that Luke began the story of the church insisting that there was something in the listener that recognized the truth of the gospel, call it what we will.

Now I do not mean this as some kind of preacher ploy on the part of Luke or on my own part. Not at all. It may sound that way: "Ah, this is really beautiful; match up the appetite with the food and say, 'How symmetrically it worked out.'" That is not what Luke is doing, nor am I. It is not a case of putting a magnet in every human breast in order to say, "Notice how people are attracted to the gospel." What Luke is saying and what I am saying is exactly what the whole world knows: there is a hunger for what the gospel offers. Even the systems of tyranny in the world are but perversions of this same longing, seeking capacity of the human spirit. When Adolf Hitler sold his

program to the German people, he didn't sell prisons and ovens and genocide. You know what he sold? He spoke of a way to peace and joy, of every home a quiet place, of children happy and well. Did Germany want that? Of course! Then came the means, the painful, necessary steps. Holocaust! I do not seek to excuse anyone, but rather to say the German people didn't vote for the Holocaust. They voted for something for which people everywhere search, search, search.

When Karl Marx sold the Russian people on a system of communism, he didn't sell them on the idea, "Let's get rid of forty million Ukrainians; let's put microphones in every public building; let's suspect, watch, imprison, exile." He didn't sell that. What he sold was, "From each according to ability, to each according to need, so that all may. . . ." "So that all may"; what a wonderful thing! The most terrible systems of the human race are distortions of a longing for peace, quiet, love. The depths to which people sink are but another register of the heights to which they are capable of rising, because God has never been without witness in the world. Never. anywhere. That is why upon hearing the gospel for the first time, listeners experience déjà vu; they have a sense of familiarity when offered a new experience.

Actually it does not really matter whether one is an old liberal who says, "I think the image of God is still there in all of us." It does not really matter if one is Barthian and says, "'Twas grace that taught my heart to fear, and grace my fear relieved." It does not matter whether one prefers Tillich's or Bultmann's construction of the human situation. Nor does it matter whether one thinks of the human spirit as having a *memory* of Eden or a *hope* of Eden. Rather, Luke's word for us is simply this: "Do you want to be Pentecostal in a good, healthy, lively, renewing sense? Do you want the church to be Pentecostal? Then spend some thoughtful, careful, prayerful, listening time—listening to the listeners, in their concrete, historical circumstances." And if we listen to the listeners, carefully, prayerfully, thoughtfully, then we will notice, and will stand among them and say, "I think I speak for every person here, Parthians, Medes, Elamites, Europeans, Asians, Americans, Chinese, Africans, South Americans . . . I think I speak for every person here when I ask, 'Show us God and we'll be satisfied.'"— Fred B. Craddock

Illustrations

LIVES CHANGED.   I once wrote an Easter play in Africa. Staging it was a big task. Easter has a lot of drama in it, lots of soldiers. It was very hard to keep the Africans from clowning around as soldiers. I wrote a one-hour play. It took three hours to do it. That's because in Africa everybody ad-libs, no matter what you write. But if you walk 20 miles to see a play, you don't want it to be over in an hour anyway! They knew the audience would be too big for the church, so they built a stage outside. Estimates were that there were 1,000 sitting on the grass and standing around. I wasn't too happy with the way things started. There was a lot of clowning around and a lot of laughter. I thought, "This is not Christian education! This is comedy!" So I gnashed my teeth and watched the thing unfold. Finally the fellow who was playing Simon of Cyrene stood alone and sang, "Were You There When They Crucified My Lord?" The disciples were hiding up on the stage. The women walked by carrying (on their heads) the perfumes and oils to anoint Jesus' body. They went down a steep path to the river, because he was supposed to be buried in a tomb over at the edge of the river. We could hear them calling back. "What did you do with him?" Women in Africa have strong voices—they yell at each other across the fields! We could hear them, "What did you do with his body?" "Where is he?" "Who took him?" "He's our Lord." Then a woman said, "He's alive, like he said!" We saw the bottles bouncing as they came back up the path at a run. Now we had Christian education! They came up shouting, "He is risen as he said!" They were supposed to go tell the disciples. They went right past the stage, and left the disciples sitting there! I was up on the truck bed saying, "O, grief." They started into the crowd, saying to people, one at a time, "We can't find him! He's alive." "He's alive! He arose from the dead as he said!" They got to the back of the audience and they didn't know what to do next. I didn't know what they should do next either! It wasn't my play any more. The African pastor went down in front and stood there with the befuddled disciples. He knew this could turn into an evangelistic meeting. He said to the people, "If you never knew before today that he is alive and can live in your heart, come down and talk to us." Amazed, I watched them go forward to have their lives changed by the Spirit of God. I have thought about that scene many times. I decided that those women forgot they were pretending—it was so real! They believed it with such power, that they went out and changed lives. That's what it looks like to be filled by the Spirit of God. Are you filled with the Spirit? —Janey Smith

GUIDANCE.   We can never predict how the Holy Spirit will guide us.

One Sunday morning I had arrived early for Sunday school in order to prepare snacks for the college students with whom I worked. To get from the church kitchen to the building where our department met, I had to go outside to the sidewalk that ran in front of the auditorium. As I neared the street, I saw an Oriental man briskly walking down the other side. I thought he might be Japanese. Usually I do not call across the street to a perfect stranger, but I felt led to do so that morning. I greeted him in the Japanese language. I had been a missionary in Japan for 17 years before family health problems forced us to return to the United States.

The man was startled to hear a foreigner speak Japanese and stopped to talk with me. I learned that he was doing graduate study in education at a nearby university. He never had been to a Christian church, but since coming to the United States he had become curious about Christianity.

That morning I introduced him to the woman who worked with a class for internationals in our church. He attended the class regularly, considered our church people his friends, and eventually became a Christian. His family joined him in the United States for a short time. When they returned to Okinawa, Japan, they continued as active church members and witnesses for Christ.

I have no doubt the Holy Spirit prompted me to ignore the rules of polite behavior and yell across the street to this stranger.—Ernest L. Holloway, Jr.

Sermon Suggestions

LESSONS FROM A PROPHET'S VISION. TEXT: Ezek. 37:1–14. (1) God has a hopeful word for the most unpromising situation, verses 1–6. (2) God makes good on his promises, verses 7–14.

HELP OF THE HELPLESS. TEXT: Rom. 8:22–27. (1) God gives us patience through hope, even despite the most formidable conditions. (2) God himself refines our imperfect prayers, and his Spirit within us prays beyond our weakness and lack of understanding.

Worship Aids

CALL TO WORSHIP. "Ye shall receive power, after that the Holy Ghost is come upon you: and ye shall be witnesses unto me both in Jerusalem, and in all Judaea, and in Samaria, and unto the uttermost part of the earth" (Acts 1:8).

INVOCATION. Creator God, the signs of life touch us in ways that we sometimes fail to recognize and appreciate. But we are grateful for the life with which you have surrounded us ... the amazing rhythm of the seasons, with their unique beauties; the friendships which often free us to enhance our personalities and which touch us with caring support; the families whose enjoyments, arguments, challenges, and frustrations teach us the meanings of acceptance and growth; the church, in whose communion we may discover a vitality of faith, a commitment to serve, a joy to celebrate. Renew us, Creator of Life, to share with you the adventure of re-creation, with Jesus Christ, our Lord.—Robert F. Langwig

OFFERTORY SENTENCE. "Offer the right sacrifices to the Lord, and put your trust in him" (Ps. 4:5 TEV).

OFFERTORY PRAYER. Teach us, good Lord, to serve thee as thou deservest: to give and not to count the cost; to fight and not to heed the wounds; to toil and not to seek for rest; to labor and not to ask for any reward, save that of knowing that we do thy will.—St. Ignatius of Loyola

PRAYER. Almighty God, who sent the promised power of the Holy Spirit to fill disciples with willing faith: we confess that we have held back the force of your Spirit among us; that we have been slow to serve you, and reluctant to spread the good news of your love. God, have mercy on us. Forgive our divisions, and by your Spirit draw us together. Fill us with flaming desire to do your will, and be a faithful people; for the sake of your son, our Lord, Jesus Christ.—The Worshipbook.

LECTIONARY MESSAGE

Topic: The Spirit of Pentecost

TEXT: John 15:26–27, 16:4b–15

The Holy Spirit is the subject of much conversation and speculation. Jesus spoke openly and clearly about the Holy Spirit. On this Pentecost Sunday we search the identity of the Spirit. Who is he? How is he related to the world? What does he do? He is variously described, depending partly on the translation assigned to the Greek word, Paraclete. Literally the word means "called alongside." We understand the Holy Spirit to stand alongside us in our witnessing and in our worrisome problems.

The term is also translated "Comforter," as one on whom we can depend in grief and anxiety. We may cry on his shoulder. Sometimes the translation "Advocate" is used, indicating a legal relationship of protection. He becomes our defender against those who would harm us. Often the translation "Helper" is given, a broad term suggesting many activities on the part of the Spirit.

The variety of translations for the same Greek work indicates an understanding of his person and work in many different situations. I like the figure of the football coach who is required by the rules to stay off the field during play, but calls from the sidelines—words of rebuke, of encouragement, of information. In a sense he is calling alongside. This is something of the activity of the Holy Spirit, though he can't be kept from the field!

I. He is God in our midst. The followers of Jesus might well have felt like orphans when their Master/Teacher departed. Jesus promised that the Holy Spirit would proceed from the Father at the will of the Son. Even as Jesus came forth from the Father, so the Spirit was to come forth from the Father.

When he comes he will witness to Jesus. The faithful preaching of the disciples, the preservation of the story in both oral and written form bear evidence of the Spirit's witness. His witness is consistent with the ministry of Jesus—his deeds and his words. He will so sharpen the witness of Jesus' followers that they will be effective both in stirring support and opposition. "Greater things than these will you do because I go to the Father."

As Jesus was "the Word become flesh" so the Holy Spirit in truth assumes our flesh in the continuation of the Incarnation. God has not left us alone. He is in our midst.

II. His presence reproves the world. Jesus is described (John 3:17ff) as carefully separating himself from a judging position. God did not send his Son to judge the world. Yet his presence became the judgment of the world—"he that believeth not has been judged already." Against the backdrop of his ministry, Crucifixion, and Resurrection the Holy Spirit reproves the world.

He will reprove the world for the sin of not believing the Son. He will reprove the world of righteousness in the vindication which was clear in the Resurrection. He will reprove the world of judgment in the ultimate defeat of sin. Thus the Holy Spirit becomes our advocate in a legal sense, heaping up the evidence on our behalf . . . and on behalf of God's Son.

III. He guides into all truth. Jesus had said clearly of himself, "I am the truth." Now the Holy Spirit will not set himself apart from or contrary to that absolute truth. He will confirm the truth of Jesus' ministry and set it in the context of world history. The Holy Spirit, the Spirit of truth, will be closely aligned with the truth about Jesus. Thus Father, Son, and Holy Spirit are all loyal to the truth.

But it is more than a passive existence. The Holy Spirit will actively guide the believer into all truth. There is no discrepancy in the threefold witness.

And when the Holy Spirit made his presence manifest at the Feast of Pentecost Simon Peter was empowered to speak the truth about Jesus. Witnessing is the spirit of Pentecost. The Holy Spirit is the Spirit of Pentecost.—J. Estill Jones

SUNDAY: MAY TWENTY-NINTH

SERVICE OF WORSHIP

Sermon: Creative Insecurity

TEXT: Acts 9:15, 16

We are told that the new kind of person who is just now making his appearance in history—post-Christian, post-individual, post-moral man, as he is called—finds it very hard to believe that there is a God; though if one were to judge from the plays and novels that he writes, with all their anguish of rebellion, the bitter emptiness which comes of being utterly without purpose, when the mask is off and the chips are down he finds it even harder to believe that there isn't.

But none of that is really hard. What is really hard is to find that every time you open the Bible you have to reckon with another kind of believing altogether: the kind that will never allow you to manage your own life any more. It isn't so much a question of "believing" or "not believing": in the Bible you run the risk of meeting him. You run the risk of finding out that he isn't at all the kind of God who will stay out there somewhere and let you look at him, or talk about him. He's forever coming, and at his own convenience, not ours. He's forever choosing, and for some purpose he has in mind: it may not jibe with ours in the least.

Take the story of Paul's conversion, there on the road to Damascus. What God had in mind for him certainly didn't jibe with what he had in mind for himself. Something familiar, something which seemed solid and secure, was finished; he was snatched away from it. Something which looked like nothing at all that was solid, something which looked like the last word in insecurity, had begun; he was headed for it. From something, to something: that's our cue. It's how the lines run for us as well, these lines of God's direction.

I. From what comes first.

(a) Did it ever actually strike across your mind with some little anxiety that Paul wasn't converted from an evil life, but from a good life; not from impiety, but from piety; not from irreligion, but from religion? Everything inside of him had been swept and garnished, not to stay starched and ironed, for years.

Yet something was wrong. He doesn't seem to have had any overwhelming sense of sin. It wasn't his conscience that bothered him. It wasn't the boredom which comes of having nothing to do.

All the way along he had been trying to manufacture his own stockpile of seemly behavior and righteous living; and that's tiresome business. For what other reason does Christianity turn out so often to be so dreadfully dull? You have seen what a universal phenomenon student riots have become during the last quarter of a century. How do you account for it? It's partly because the culture of which they are a part has lost its enthusiasm. I should hate to think that we now have to say the same thing of Christianity—when in fact it's a drama far more exciting than any other the human mind has ever conceived. You may call Jesus anything you like, but you cannot call him dull. It was because his enemies couldn't tame him that they had to crucify him. It's his friends who have decked him out in pastel shades and made a gentleman of him—chiefly perhaps by wanting of him no more than some sense of security, which in the end, we have to admit, almost inevitably turns out to be so insecure that even a bad cold can upset it.

(b) Under such circumstances, what we like to think of as our religion can do nothing for us but hand us over to the tyranny of some good which is always just out of reach; but we have to go on clutching for it, like a drowning man, to keep our heads above water. Only to find ourselves at last, like Paul, desperately far away from the Kingdom of God precisely when we think we are safely and squarely in the middle of it, and quite well, thank you. We have grown used to the pride which we have learned to call humility, and are quite content to mistake our sober satisfaction with what we are for three hallelujahs and the sound of a great amen.

Maybe you are saying to yourself right now, "Well, thank God, I am not like that." In which case, instead of thanking God, you must allow me to thank you. You have helped me to make my point. That's what the Pharisee said in the temple. And it's more than self-righteousness. What frightens me is that it's blasphemy.

(c) There is no way at all of striking a bargain with God and holding him to it: doing this and doing that, so as to make these lives of ours shipshape, then expecting a smooth passage in return. Dickering is out. And by the same token tinkering is out too, on whatever scale, big or little. Nobody has a right to be cynical about what is sometimes spoken of as returning to religion. But if much of it adds up to nothing more than being afraid "for looking after those things which are coming on the earth"; and so, not knowing what to do, attempting to get in under what the Bible tells us to do, on the off chance of being able somehow to arrange matters a shade more in our favor—then God pity us! And I doubt that he will have any means of showing it. An acid comment on all such tomfoolery was made by a recent cartoonist. Some well-dressed fellow had just passed the sign which reads "Prepare to meet thy God" and was standing now in front of the mirror on a cigarette vending machine, taking off his hat, brushing his hair, and straightening his tie.

(d) Why then can't we come to terms with what we can't dodge? It isn't safe to believe in the God of the Bible. Indeed it isn't safe to live! Security at its peak is little more than sterility. Only insecurity has some chance of being creative. If your life is dull, you haven't been taking any chances. If it's uninteresting, you've made it so. And you are not likely to help things much by acquiring a few added "interests" in the shape of luncheons and lectures and book clubs. Life doesn't want to be safe. It doesn't want to absorb something. It wants to create something. It wants to breast some slope. It wants to be gallant. Insecurity is its heritage.

II. But at that point we've got to add something. And this is the second thing I wanted to say. Paul was not only converted from; he was at the same time converted to. To what?

(a) Don't let the word conversion upset you. It doesn't necessarily have to do with becoming either a saint or a Christian. It has to do very simply with turning around, which is a maneuver we engage in, I dare say, pretty much every day we live. Everything that through the centuries had made God and kept him God had broken into the world again in Jesus Christ, and Paul had to right-about-face from one kind of belief to another kind entirely. He was tossed bodily out of the security of what God had done into the insecurity of what God was doing; and he found it to be the insecurity of a manifold and unreckoning grace!

You'll not be given a blueprint of what needs doing. Paul didn't get one either. He said, "Lord, what wilt thou have me to do?" And the Lord said, "It shall be told thee what thou must do." All you can count on is that it will be no craven thing: it will be a brave thing, something that will take more than you have in your own right, something God wants to get done, something he has in mind now. Make no mistake about that. To say as much about him is to say no more than you have to say if you say anything about him at all.

(b) He was well aware of the absurdity of it in his case; he was bewildered by it, baffled every time he tried to figure out the reason for it. Paul knew how much, and knew it better than anybody else. But he knew that this unreckoning grace which had beckoned to him wanted out, and it wanted out where he was. Nothing mattered but that. He knew he couldn't manage by himself. Who can? But he knew enough about the past, and had already plunged deeply enough into the present, to know how God works. He understood that whatever salvation there was, God had wrought it; but that didn't let him off. You couldn't think that if you had even the foggiest notion of what the love of God does when it gets hold of a man. It turns Sinai into Calvary, and as surely as there is nothing you can do, so surely there is nothing which at God's word you won't do!

(c) And there was something more that Paul knew. He didn't have any special privileges now. Not any longer. He used to have, as a Jew, or thought he had; and he had done his best by strict obedience to hold on to them. The gospel had stripped him of them. That he knew. But he never let the obedience go. For all his vaunted freedom, he lived the Law; but he lived it as love. And that made all the difference. Once he had had to read all the others out, sinners and Gentiles alike; under the eyes of Christ he had to read them in, every one of them. The boundaries of God's Kingdom were not his to tamper with any more. God could alter them, he couldn't. And God would alter them if any of the elect began to figure they were the elite!

(d) But there was still more. And this Paul did not know. There was the "how great things he must suffer for my name's sake." Are we willing now, in the shadow of the cross, to listen to that? Paul found out. And I have more than just a twinge of conscience when I say it. It hasn't been given many of us. We have only to face the disciplines of life. Sometimes they are hard, yes. We have to face its uncertainties and its insecurities, the devotion that's without any safeguard; death, when it comes to us, or to some one we love. Shall we resent them? Can't we manage, with all we have, to bear redemptively what we shall have to bear in any case? The greatest joys the world has ever known have come that way out of its sorrows. It's the grace of God, that incredible, gallant thing, that wants out; and it wants out where we are!—Paul Scherer

Illustrations

WALLS.   Joel Gregory described the ruins of a magnificent castle in Ireland, the ancient home of the Castlereagh family.

For a long period this elegant mansion was unoccupied and thus fell into disrepair. One reason was that when local peasants needed to repair a road or build a chimney, they scavenged stones from the castle. The finely cut stones of the castle were there for the taking at little work and expense.

One day Lord Londonderry, an heir to the castle, came to inspect it. He was shocked at the vandalism.

Londonderry gave orders to erect a wall six feet high to keep trespassers out. He then went on his way.

When he returned three or four years later, he was shocked more than ever, for workmen had wrecked the entire castle to get rock to build the security wall. He now owned a magnificent wall, but no castle!—Robert J. Hastings

THE CALL OF COMPASSION.   I sat with a group of ministers who were talking about the missionary enterprise of the Church in so-called foreign lands, and about the extent to which our support of it had fallen off here at home. Everybody was exhorting everybody else. And everybody, it seemed to me, was incredibly mistaken about the why and the wherefore of the whole undertaking. We had to save these people. They were lost. We had to pluck them like brands from the burning. And nobody said what I am sure has to be said, that we've got to quit fooling around with labels. Jesus mixed them up so thoroughly that they are of no use to us. Who are the saved? You can hide from God himself behind that label. Who are the lost? Everybody who thinks he isn't! Leave the labels to God. We've got to go and do simply because the compassion which holds out its arms to us in Christ won't let us sit on the front porch and rock ourselves to death. If that isn't it, we'd better resign from the entire project, at home and abroad. We go because that's what the grace of God has chosen us to do.—Paul Scherer

Sermon Suggestions

SPEAKING FOR GOD IN A TIME OF CRISIS. TEXT: Isa. 6:1–8. (1) The greatness of God becomes acutely evident in a time of human limitation, verses 1–3. (2) Contrast of human character with God's character follows and leads to confession and repentance, verses 4–5. (3) God himself forgives and prepares a mere mortal to live worthily before him and to speak for him, verses 6–8.

NO LONGER SLAVES.   TEXT: Rom. 8:12– 17. (1) Our motivation—the Spirit of God, not slavish fear. (2) Our assurance—the joyous recognition of our loving Father, Abba. (3) Our vocation— suffering with our crucified and risen Lord. (4) Our reward—sharing the riches of Christ's own glory.

Worship Aids

CALL TO WORSHIP.   "Out of my distress I called on the Lord; the Lord answered me and set me free" (Ps. 118:5 RSV).

INVOCATION.   Gracious Lord, whose Holy Spirit fell in power to spread the gospel, stir in us today that we may be filled to speak to others as in Christ Jesus we have been spoken to and changed forever.—E. Lee Phillips

OFFERTORY SENTENCE. "Lay not up for yourselves treasures upon earth, where moth and rust doth corrupt, and where thieves break through and steal; but lay up for yourselves treasures in heaven, where neither moth nor rust doth corrupt, and where thieves do not break through nor steal: for where your treasure is, there will your heart be also" (Matt. 6:19–21).

OFFERTORY PRAYER. Lord, we are grateful to have this offering to give. We know that in your power it can accomplish more than we can see or comprehend, and for that we humbly pray. —E. Lee Phillips

PRAYER. Eternal Father, thy children, who have wandered far from thee, return once more to stand in reverence before thy face. From the superficiality of life, where so much that we see is cheap and so much that we touch is tinsel, we return once more to find in thee stability and depth and strength. From our lack of resource to meet the difficulties that besiege us and the temptations that assail us, we return to thee to find resource, reserve, and power. From the restlessness of life, its feverish haste and hectic ways, we return to thee to feel around our restlessness thy rest. From the harshness of life, its unkind ways and ungentle thoughts, from the vindictiveness of men and the harbored grudges that often make our own hearts bitter, we come to thee again to learn good will.

O God, welcome us, we beseech thee, granting us the priceless treasure of thy Spirit's presence. May souls that have been sore buffeted, that have fallen on discouragement and have lost hope, find power and comfort, fortitude and peace in thy sanctuary!

Make this day a sacrament of memory. Bring to our minds those recollections that shall cleanse and encourage, inspire and empower our hearts. We remember our homes. For the rich heritage that has come from them to us, for the sustaining traditions handed down from faithful homes to faithful sons and daughters, for the nurture and admonition of the Lord that we discovered in the tireless love of our families, we bless thy name.

We remember before thee those whom the world calls dead but who are not dead but alive. Bring them close about us on this day of reminiscence. Let those that have walked with us in times past be real to us that we may be inspired by the companionship of the world unseen and eternal.

We thank thee for the memories of our churches. For their faults and failures we seek thy pardon, but for all the grace and goodness in them, for the ways they have channeled to our hearts faith in Christ and love of Christlike values, blessed be thy name. Give us vision and dedication in our day to be more worthy of the saints and apostles, the prophets and martyrs who have borne a good witness to the gospel, and have served their generation according to thy will before they fell on sleep.

We thank thee for our national heritage. For all that is unworthy there, for our selfishness, our pride of wealth, our vanity in prosperity, our forgetfulness that righteousness and liberty must be paid for by sacrifice in every generation, forgive us, O Lord. In these days when evil hands soil the sacred things for which our fathers died, when righteousness is forgotten in high places, when crime betrays the nation and the moral level of our living sinks, forgive us, good Lord. But for all that is noble and right, for all that is excellent and of good report, for contributions made to freedom, to democracy, to righteousness, blessed be thy name.

O God, our Father, who, amid all the vast concerns of the universe and of the nations, never dost forget the individual, cross thou the inner thresholds of our hearts this day. Thou knowest the anxieties there. Sickness is in our homes and we are solicitous as we remember before thee those whom we love better than we love ourselves. Temptations are in our hearts because of which we are burdened before thee. We face problems that perplex us, tasks for which we feel unequal. Our inner lives are battlefields where faith and fear, confidence and doubt, contend for the victory. We see within our lives failures that only thy mercy can pardon, and possibilities of good that only thy grace can bring to fulfillment. See thou the unspoken prayers which no tongue can utter for this varied congregation. Upon every secret aspiration send thy help. For every need send thy supply. We ask it in the name of Christ.—Harry Emerson Fosdick

LECTIONARY MESSAGE

Topic: Inquiring Minds Want to Know

TEXT: John 3:1–17

There are three kinds of people in the world. There are those who wish to do something but for some reason never get around to it, those who are afraid to do anything different, and those who step out, take a chance, and do something unexpected.

Disciples are a lot like the latter. One can think of the rich young ruler who wanted life eternal but who never got around to real commitment. And the image of the Pharisees who were afraid to step outside their laws and customs easily comes to mind. But then there is Nicodemus, a man who decided to color outside the lines of his tradition, a man who was not afraid to do something different; to go by night to a private audience with Jesus and to test if this unconventional rabbi had anything to say to one whose life had been so completely given to keeping the law. What he learned forever changed his expectations and direction in life.

I. First, Nicodemus learned that stepping out on faith means a total re-orientation of life. Jesus was not flattered by Nicodemus' accommodating remarks about the signs and wonders that even the common among them understood came from God. Scarcely did he get the words out of his mouth when Jesus took the conversation in an entirely new direction, "Nicodemus, you must be born again." Jesus' words pierced to the heart of Nicodemus. His life-long search that had been characterized by futile attempts at being righteous never expected such a requirement as Jesus set forth. For all his theological training, Nicodemus apparently did not understand the implications. How could one who is old start life all over? It was simple however. And it was not based on physical change. It was a change from within. Instead of being the architect of his own righteousness Nicodemus would have to re-orient his life to follow one who appeared to others to be only a poor carpenter. Salvation comes in a way we would never expect. It comes not by our tendency to manipulate or fashion it, but by grace from God who chose to live among us and to give his life as a ransom for our sins. For Nicodemus this was a radical break with all that he had learned before of righteousness and salvation. And for us today, re-orienting life to follow the Savior will require abandonment of self-constructs of righteousness and demand reliance upon Jesus who alone can conform us to the image of God.

II. Nicodemus also had to learn that God's power to change our lives is not limited to what we see and know in the physical world. For one who lived by a set of pragmatic rules, seeing with spiritual eyes was immeasurably difficult. And so it is for us today. We want proof. Proof that something works.

Very few of us are trusting enough to question that which is untried in our experience. And yet, that is exactly what is required in trusting God. Nicodemus was no doubt unsure about stepping away from the solid ground of his pragmatic faith and onto the thin ice of trust in the words of an unlearned teacher. Even Jesus had related to Nicodemus that being born anew would be like experiencing the wind: it could not be tied down, measured out, handled, or seen. The wind will blow where it wills. For one who lives by the Spirit, life will be like the wind; unpredictable, yet free to blow in directions not yet known or anticipated.

The power of God to re-define lives, to put a new spirit within, is as mysterious as the wind, yet just as powerful. Those born of God are not content to restrict God to the natural order of things and to predictability, but they are confident of God's creative presence—as confident as those who see the wind's presence in the rustle of the leaves.

III. For Nicodemus, and for all who would be born again, the discussion about the kingdom of God and righteousness inevitably leads to Jesus himself. Jesus says plainly that we speak about what we know and have seen. Jesus has seen the Father and has been with the Father. Who better to tell us what the Father requires than one who came down from heaven? What a shocking thought for Nicodemus to entertain. How could this one talking in the dead of night be one with the God of the universe? Do we believe it today?

For some today, Jesus is a good teacher still, only an important figure of ancient history. But for those of us who live by faith he is the one who has shown us the Father in ways we could never have discerned through earthly eyes or human striving. Suddenly Nicodemus realized that he would have to place all his hopes on the one called Jesus. So also must we.

IV. Finally, John comments on the discourse between Nicodemus and Jesus by showing that the conversation between the two of them was not applicable only to Nicodemus but to all who would believe. However, a word of warning is hidden within. This is God's last word to us. And that word is His divine Son. It is a word of salvation for those who will believe. Sin can drive us into an everlasting night of despair. But the good news of the gospel for Nicodemus and for us is that Jesus is the light of the world.—Ronald W. Johnson

SUNDAY: JUNE FIFTH

SERVICE OF WORSHIP

Sermon: Friends and Strangers

TEXT: Heb. 13:1–2

I've noticed that people are not as willing to open their door to strangers as once they were. Some people discovered that it's not always so wonderful to be on the giving end of hospitality.

And that's what brings us to the biblical text for today: "Do not neglect to show hospitality to strangers, for by doing that some entertained angels without knowing it" (v. 2).

I. Abraham and Sarah are the unnamed people recalled by this verse. One day they opened their door to three strangers and got the surprise of their life! (Genesis 18)

(a) You and I tend to offer hospitality to only a limited number of people—persons whom we already know, mostly relatives and a few close friends. But, in Abraham's time, hospitality was extended to whomever needed it—strangers and acquaintances alike. In fact, in its original form, "hospitality" combines two separate words—one meaning friend and the other meaning stranger. So, from the beginning of its usage, hospitality has carried with it the idea of making friends out of strangers.

(b) Abraham and Sarah were the quintessence of the gracious host and hostess. He made sure the guests were comfortable—offering facilities where they could clean up from their journey and rest under the refreshing shade of a nearby tree. She went far beyond her husband's understated offer of a morsel of bread and prepared instead a lavish and generous meal—including calf-meat, truly a rare luxury at that time. He stood by their table in hospitable concern, making sure that every need was met.

(c) The point the author of Hebrews made in recalling that bit of ancient, biblical history was to remind his readers of an important truth: when you open your door to a stranger, you may well be opening your door to God. Actually, it's also reminiscent of the words of Jesus in his parable of the final judgment. "I was a stranger and you welcomed me" is a clear reference to hospitality (Matt. 25:35). And in terms of that parable, giving and withholding hospitality when you are in a position to offer it is a decisive indication of the presence or absence of real spirituality in your life—or, in your home.

II. Throughout history, people have often opened their doors to God. And that's wonderful. But I warn you: when you invite God in, you don't know how you're likely to be surprised.

(a) Apparently, there were some Christians early on who were about to miss the blessings of this divine intrusion. This section of the letter to the Hebrews was aimed directly at them. We know from the history of the Christian faith that there were some who wanted to put a fence around the gospel and announce that it was "For Jews Only!" They would gladly have nailed a placard on the door of the church that read, "Gentiles Keep Out!"—and felt when they had done it, that they had done a good day's work.

(b) But the Bible will have nothing to do with that kind of faith. There had come to New Testament Christians a blinding vision that the grace of God in Jesus Christ is all inclusive. There could never be any going back on that vision. And so, to those good Christians who were fiddling with the church keys and thinking of locking the doors to keep out certain people, the gospel says, "Don't do it! Don't you dare even try it! Don't even think about it! Learn instead how to love and live with each other!"

III. Can you imagine how the early church would have fared without hospitality? When Jesus sent out the Twelve and the Seventy, he expected them to be received hospitably (Matt. 10:9ff; Luke 10:4). In fact, he regarded the refusal of a warm and gracious reception as tantamount to an outright rejection of their message.

(a) Not only did the missionaries and Christian businessmen need hospitality, local churches also required it. For the first 200 years of the Christian faith, there was no such thing as a church building. Homes were pressed into use as places where worship, discipleship, and fellowship were centered.

(b) From its beginning, the Christian faith was represented by people with open doors. In fact, the Apostle Peter reminded Christians that no one who has a permanent shelter over his head can complain of not having at least one gift of the Holy Spirit (1 Peter 4:9). He believed that when God gives us a home, he has presented us with a gift which he wants us to invest in building the kingdom of God: a home which we can welcome both friends and strangers.—Gary C. Redding

Illustrations

WHY DO I HAVE TO BE ME? Alas, we do envy our neighbors. We do ask, "Why do I have to be me?" "Why was I born in a humble village of the windswept plains of Kansas, a portion of the globe barren of historical significance, instead of on a famous country estate in Virginia?" "Why was I given an ugly nose instead of the features of the campus Apollo or Hollywood hero?" "Why, supposing that I am known as a handsome cavalier, did whoever hurled me into the world not give me brains as well? Or, conversely, supposing that I do have a scholar's gifted mind, why am I awkward at a dance and a Sad Sack at a party?"—Theodore O. Wedel

CHRISTIAN HOSPITALITY. Several years ago, in another pastorate, I received a letter. A portion of it read:

When my wife and I moved here three years ago, we felt we needed to make contact with a local church. We hoped to make new friends. When we went to church, we heard good sermons on which you spent a great deal of time and trouble and which always gave us something to think about. But our hope that we would make REAL contact with our fellow Christians in the same pew came to nothing. We often left church as lonely as we were when we came in.

Can you imagine how long a church will survive unless it learns the lessons of Christian hospitality?—Gary C. Redding

Sermon Suggestions

GETTING WHAT YOU WANT AND NOT LIKING IT. TEXT: 1 Sam. 8:4–11 (12–15), 16–20 (11:14–15), especially 8:18–19. (1) We humans are full of desires that are attracted to the lifestyles of others—people we admire or envy. (2) Even the most reasonable advice will not deter those determined to get what they want. (3) We will have to live with the consequences of our folly.

WHY WE DO NOT LOSE HEART. TEXT: 2 Cor. 4:13–5:1. (1) Basically because God raised Jesus from the dead, which assures us of our own resurrection into his presence. (2) Also, because our inner nature is being renewed daily. (3) Moreover, because God is preparing an eternal home for us.

Worship Aids

CALL TO WORSHIP. "He that hath an ear, let him hear what the Spirit saith unto the churches" (Rev. 2:29).

INVOCATION. Speak now to us, O God. Tell us again of thy loving judgment, which ferrets out the wrong in our lives, to make life better and happier for us all. Tell us again of thy judging love, which brings to life again the dying embers of neglected faith, to give new purpose and drive to our futile wanderings. And may we carefully listen as thou dost speak to us.

OFFERTORY SENTENCE. "Bring ye all the tithes into the storehouse, that there may be meat in mine house, and prove me now herewith, saith the Lord of hosts, if I will not open you the windows of heaven, and pour you out a blessing, that there shall not be room enough to receive it" (Mal. 3:10).

OFFERTORY PRAYER. It is just a small portion of our personal blessing from

you, Father. We offer it in faith and ask that you guide it to your highest use for humankind.—Henry Fields

PRAYER. Gracious God, we come here to find ourselves: it is so easy to get lost in the labyrinth of this world. We are your children by your grace—in creation, in redemption, in sustenance day by day. When we are in good health and enjoying prosperity, how grasping, possessive, and selfish we can be—forgetting the gifts of life. We do not acknowledge and confess that in you we live and move and have our being. Your daily providence we so often take for granted rather than receive with gratitude. How often, too, your grace has kept us from destroying ourselves. "If you should keep a record of our sins, Lord, who could stand?" We praise you, O God, that yours is a steadfast love and that with you there is plenteous pardon.

In Christ the fullness of your grace is present. In receiving your grace in him—the revolution begins—life is never the same again—a new day dawns. No longer do we seek laboriously to be worthy or to earn our redemption but in faith we receive the new life that is here to which before we have been blind. In your graciousness towards us we discover a grace by which we can be gracious toward all others.

How we need your grace, that there may be community among the nations and that all people may live in peace and brotherhood and sisterhood rather than in fear and hostility and the tragedy of war. How you have shed your grace upon us as a nation. May we not fail our calling to be gracious in bringing reconciliation and peace to the troubled areas where we have been partners in perpetrating and perpetuating hostilities and supplying implements of death. We pray for your church: For our church, "Grant us wisdom, grant us courage that we fail not man nor Thee."

Wash us, O Father, and we shall be clean; heal us and we shall be whole through him who is your Word of grace.—John Thompson

LECTIONARY MESSAGE

Topic: Friends and Foes

TEXT: Mark 3:20–35

Jesus had successfully begun his ministry. He could hardly shake the multitudes who followed him. Both before and after he called the Twelve the multitude was thronging in. They threatened his privacy. They even interfered with his eating schedule. Would you call them friends or foes?

I. A threat. The multitude constituted a threat to Jesus' ministry and his own well-being. He had once before (1:35) left them behind for a night of prayer—much to the consternation of his close followers. So, when his "friends" heard of the multitude they concluded that Jesus needed their help. They loved him so much that they were willing to terminate his ministry—"to lay hold on him."

Earlier he had avoided the multitudes. Now the multitude appeared to control him. His friends thought that he was mentally unbalanced—"he is beside himself." Were they friends? It is not always easy to distinguish between friends and foes.

II. A charge. He cast out demons. He healed those possessed by unclean spirits. The scribes following from Jerusalem could not understand it. The most pitiable conditions, the most misunderstood forces, the most dangerous challenge to the powers of good were the evil spirits which seized upon persons. Jesus had successfully cast them out.

It was the province of the scribes to explain such phenomena. They concluded simply, "He has Beelzebub." They further determined that in league with the prince of demons he cast out demons.

Certainly they were foes. But how like the charge of his friends, "He is beside himself." Jesus himself charged them with blasphemy against the Holy Spirit, the ultimate sin. They could not even distinguish between good and evil—between friend and foe.

III. A parable. It was time for a parable, a simple story that would help his followers understand the situation. "How can Satan cast out Satan?" Either the unclean spirit was not Satanic or Jesus had not cast him out or Jesus was not in league with Satan. If Satan's house is divided it is doomed.

Either Satan is powerless against the Spirit of God or Satan is powerless in his self-division. In either event Satan is powerless in the presence of Jesus. To suppose otherwise is to blaspheme against the Holy Spirit. If one is so bound up in the possession of prejudice against the good that he can no longer tell the difference between good and evil he is beyond the reach of God's forgiveness. He is certainly a foe.

IV. A fellowship. His family came calling him. They appear to be the same as the "friends" of verse 21. They could not see him because of the multitude. He is certainly beside himself, they reaffirmed. When told that his family sought him, he said a strange thing: Why, this is my family gathered here!. . . A fellowship beyond family.

Were they family? Were these friends? Or were these foes? Here there was a fellowship beyond friends, beyond foes. What determines friendship with Jesus? Doing God's will! This determines one's friends and foes. Doing God's will—the great determinator.—J. Estill Jones

SUNDAY: JUNE TWELFTH

SERVICE OF WORSHIP

Sermon: What Is Your Life?

TEXT: James 4:13–17

Do you remember the story of the fellow who one day approached Jesus and asked, "Good Teacher, what must I do to inherit eternal life?" That's a ponderous question, isn't it?

What is the meaning and purpose of your life? That's a very important question, too, isn't it? Certainly neither as ponderous nor as critical as that other question, yet vitally important nonetheless! I'm sure some of you are wondering why I've brought these two questions together.

Because, you see, they are—by nature of their shared interest—related. Raise one, and you'll soon discover that you've awakened the other as well.

Somewhere in and around 45–50 A.D., James wrote an epistle to his church at Jerusalem. In this letter, James discusses everything from the substance of faith to the content of compassionate and Christ-inspired works. His overall concern is with the development of Christian character. His desire is that the members of his church grow in every Christ-like grace.

And along the way, as most preachers are wont to do, he touches on some subjects that don't sit well with some folk. But, that's just the wonder of the way our God chooses to dispense his grace—isn't it?

God sent his Word when he inspired James to pen these powerful words: "Now listen, you who say, 'Today or tomorrow we will go to this or that city, spend a year or so, carry on business and make money.' Why, you do not even know what will happen tomorrow. What is your life? You are a mist that appears for a little while and then vanishes. Instead, you ought to say, 'If it is the Lord's will, we will live and do this or that.' As it is, you boast or brag. All such boasting is evil."

Now remember, the church at Jerusalem was predominantly Jewish. And the Jews were the great commercialists of the ancient world. In many ways that same world encouraged the development of Jewish trade and commerce. It was, in fact, considered a compliment to the ever expanding Roman Empire.

New cities of commerce were being founded all the time. And, like today, the founders welcomed those who would provide a profitable economic enterprise with more jobs and capital gain.

(a) Do you begin to see what James is doing? He creates the image of some saintly entrepreneur looking over a map of the Roman Empire. Suddenly this guy flicks his finger to some dot on the map, and says: "Now there's a city with commercial success written all over it! I'll hop on over there, spend a year or so making my connections, haul in the big bucks, and come home that much more ahead of the game."

And James—who is anything but a Wall Street whiz-kid!—calls people on the carpet for having such an attitude. He assures us that it is unbecoming the saints to have such wild notions of what constitutes real security!

(b) He wants to remind us that no one has the right to make such confident plans for the future. And in particular when the "confidence" is placed in anything less than Christ—and God as Creator. Are you familiar with the cliche? It says—with tongue in cheek—"we may propose, but then only God can dispose!" It is simply another way of telling us to take God's lordship over our lives—seriously!

James is saying that planning is not the problem. Confidence, trust, faith are! Human life is as fleeting as a morning mist.

II. But you know already that your life is fragile and subject to each and every form of sickness? Surely we have—each of us and all of us—learned that human life is seriously limited. We haven't the power to select our natural parents—and we haven't the authority to dismiss our own death!

(a) And James admonishes Christians to stare, without flinching and in faith, straight into the steely eyes of life's limitations. He wants us to receive an important word: This uncertainty of human life is not a cause for either caution or fear.

It is, however, the sole reason to realize our complete dependence on God. In other words, when we come to acknowledge the limitations of life, we've arrived, not at the point of fear—but rather, at the place of faith!

(b) Is it any wonder, then, that Christians are often found singing: "This is my Father's world: Why should my heart be sad? The Lord is King, let heaven ring!

God reigns; let the earth be glad." This, James tells us, is the true Christian way!

III. We are not to be terrorized into fear, nor paralyzed into inaction by the uncertainty of the future. Instead, faith empowers us to commit the future, and all of our tentative plans, into the hands of our gracious God. And yet, he admonishes us to remember that even "the best laid plans" may not be within God's purposes for his people.

(a) For the Christian it's only and always by the "illuminating power of a faith centered upon Christ (that life) finds its focus, its foundation, its framework, and its final goal." And that, you understand, provides the answer to the more poignant question: "What must I do to inherit eternal life?"

(b) This morning, James is here to remind us that no one will ever love us more deeply, more deliberately, or with such unfailing devotion as our God! And in Christ Jesus, God has revealed that he doesn't merely "wish (us) well." But rather, in grace beyond all belief, God extends to each of us the gift of eternal life in his coming Kingdom.

With such knowledge as this, and with faith in such a loving Father, we begin to see that "life is a boundless privilege."—Albert J. D. Walsh

Illustrations

INNER BRACES.   While in high school I worked for two summers as a carpenter's helper. I worked on the framing crew. We built the foundations and the inner shell around which the house was constructed.

Although you couldn't see my work from the outside after the house was complete, I knew my contribution was vital. Without the inner skeleton, the outer covering would have nothing for support. The inner shell braced the house against wind and storm.

Without God's strength in our inner lives we cannot stand up to the trials and troubles of life. But by God's Spirit, which lives in us as our interior fortification, we endure all difficulties.—Gary Parker

WHO HOLDS TOMORROW?   In the Book of Proverbs, chapter twenty-seven, you'll find some very helpful advice to nurture your faith: "Do not boast about tomorrow, for you do not know what a day may bring."

Even the pagan philosopher, Seneca, had enough sense to see and then to say: "How foolish it is for a man to make plans for his life, when not even tomorrow is in his control." Or again, and even more graphically: "No man has such rich friends that he can promise himself tomorrow."—Albert J. D. Walsh

Sermon Suggestions

GOD'S CHOICE.   TEXT: 1 Sam. 15:34–16:13. (1) *The Story:* God's choice of David. (2) *The Meaning:* God's ways defy human canons, verse 9b. (3) *The Application:* Do not be surprised if God calls you or me or anyone else he pleases.

NEWNESS.   TEXT: 2 Cor. 5:6–10 (11–13), 14–17. (1) A new way of walking, verses 7–8. (2) A new aim in life and death, verses 9–10, 14–15. (3) A new creation, verses 16–17.

Worship Aids

CALL TO WORSHIP.   "Since then we have a great high priest who has passed through the heavens, Jesus, the Son of God, let us hold fast our confession. For we have not a high priest who is unable to sympathize with our weaknesses, but one who in every respect has been tempted as we are, yet without sin. Let us then with confidence draw near to the throne of grace, that we may receive mercy and find grace to help in time of need" (Heb. 4:14–16 [RSV]).

INVOCATION.   O God, we come to thee with boldness this day, not because we are worthy, but because thou hast assured us that we may come, that mercy is available, and that our needs will be met. Give us a fresh vision of our Savior, our great high priest, who sympathizes with all our weaknesses and has power to strengthen us at our most vulnerable points.

OFFERTORY SENTENCE. "Every good gift and every perfect gift is from above, and cometh down from the Father of lights, with whom is no variableness, neither shadow or turning" (Jas. 1:17).

OFFERTORY PRAYER. Lord, our Creator, who can take a mustard seed and build a great tree; take this small offering and accomplish mighty deeds with it for Jesus' sake.—E. Lee Phillips

PRAYER. Voice of the Call, Guide for the Journey, our steps have taken us throughout this city, our state, and nation this week past; yet, now all our paths have brought us back to this time and place, O God. Weary and spent from the toil, we come into your glad presence asking in our own way the question asked of Jeremiah: Is there any word from the Lord?

For those battling threatening diseases of the body, is there any word from the Lord? For those wounded in spirit, struggling hard not to give up, is there any word from the Lord? For those whose vocation, integrity, and service to you are being questioned, even attacked, is there any word from the Lord? For those shaken and defeated by the brutal events in our community, of beatings, murder, shooting of mate and then self; in face of all these senseless events, is there any word from the Lord?

Revealing God, unlike for Jeremiah, you have spoken your best and living word in Jesus Christ, our Savior and Lord. And though we believe not in easy answers and simple explanations in face of much evil and deep mystery, we do know and are called to remember that: Jesus is the Good Shepherd for the shadows and not knowing times in our lives.

Jesus is the truth for our highest calling and best knowing. Jesus is the Way for our paths and steps, the Light in our darkness. Jesus is Life and Resurrection for our now and forever. We give thanks for the Word from God.

God of truth, our moment to decide has come, for we are in the strife of truth with falsehood. Cleanse us with the truth that burns like fire and free us to be a bold friend to truth.—William M. Johnson

LECTIONARY MESSAGE

Topic: A Growing Kingdom

TEXT: Mark 4:26–34

Why did Jesus teach in parables? Was it because the interesting little stories proved popular? Was it because the parables would be more easily remembered? Was it because other popular teachers used parables? Was it because he could make a point more clearly? Was it because a parable demanded a response from the hearers? Or was it a mixture of these reasons?

The parable of the sower or the Parable of the Soils introduced Jesus' extensive use of the parabolic method of teaching. When this emphasis on the responsibility of listening was made he began to talk about the kingdom of God. In a series of parables, perhaps two, perhaps three, he spoke of the kingdom.

I. "The kingdom of God is like . . ." We can talk about it today against the background of his teaching. But how did the concept seize his hearers? Did they hearken back to the pre-Saul days when Samuel rebuked the people for wanting a king and thus rejecting the rule of God? Did they remember David and long for a military force that would guarantee their independence? Did they look at other nations and note how their kingdoms had been swallowed up by Roman legionnaires?

We can compare it to life as we know it. Even the term "kingdom" calls to mind historical entities but few contemporary governments. Indeed we no longer think in geographical or even governmental terms. "The earth is the Lord's . . ." How then shall we set boundaries for his kingdom? It is here that we favor the translation of *basileia* as sovereignty . . . the sovereignty of God. We are not annexed into that kingdom. We are not subjugated by superior force. We accept that sovereignty by faith. We pledge our love and loyalty in response to God's grace.

II. The kingdom of God grows of itself. Here is the first parable. Few of us understand the mystery of growth in a seed. We may have placed a bean seed on a wet blotter to note the phenomenon—but with minimum understanding. It is true—the seed grows of itself. The planter plants and then the sleeper sleeps, and the seed grows. There is no pressure applied to make the seed swell and burst into life. Life is inherent.

It grows all the way to God's harvest, and perhaps the concept of the harvest comprises a separate parable. Yet it is still of God—for he reaps the harvest. Conditions of growth may be improved by the farmer, but growth and maturity remain within the confines of the seed. There is movement, there is growth, in the kingdom of God, but it is God's doing, not ours. Thus it is probably improper for us to speak of "building the kingdom of God." It is God who is growing it! He is extending his sovereignty into the hearts of his subjects.

III. The kingdom of God grows to encompass all kinds of folks. We emphasize the infinitesimal smallness of the mustard seed, and small it is. So the kingdom which Jesus preached seemed small indeed, apart from the greatness of God. We look ahead to the mature plant, greater than all the herbs—and so it grows in Israel.

Its size and stability offers a resting place for all kinds of birds. Jesus emphasized not only its size, but its universal appeal . . . sparrows and hawks, robins and eagles. It is symbolic of his unlimited ministry. To all kinds of folks the sovereignty of God offers refuge.

And with many such parables he spoke . . . as much as they could understand. Privately he explained . . . and explains.—J. Estill Jones

SUNDAY: JUNE NINETEENTH

SERVICE OF WORSHIP

Sermon: Will Our Children Have Faith?

Text: Deut. 6:4–9

Most of us are very much interested in learning how to help our children have faith in God and how to help them grow in their faith. For some of us, making sure our children have faith is a real, heartfelt need!

It's also a desire rooted deeply in biblical faith. At the end of their four decades of frustrating wandering in the desert, Moses spoke to the Israelites about what life would be like in the Promised Land. They were about to be scattered throughout the land. They would be confronted with and impacted by people whose values, lifestyles, and faith were altogether different from their own. It was essential that they devise a strategy for surviving—and thriving—as the people of God in a hostile environment.

Ancient and contemporary Jews refer to Deut. 6:4–5 as the Shema. It comprises the most important scriptural command they ever learn. It's repeated at the beginning of each new day by those who seriously long to live a godly life.

Ever since Moses first spoke those words, parents who want their children to have a vibrant, living faith in God have followed this command. Let me show you three principles based upon this passage that will help you help your children to have faith.

I. The first is the principle of experience (v. 6). Did you notice Moses' first concern? Before parents can reasonably hope that their children will have faith, they must first model their faith. It must be ". . . upon your (own) heart," Moses said, "before your children will ever try it out for themselves."

(a) Children watch their parents. They are extremely perceptive and they quickly recognize whether there is a connection between their parent's faith and the way they live. Unfortunately, the failure of many Christian parents to effectively model their faith leads some children to reject Christianity, albeit a distorted version because they have never been exposed to the real thing.

(b) Thomas Aquinas once told some students, "Preach Christ everywhere you go. And if necessary, use words." That's a pretty good word for parents, also. Still, I don't think any of us are ever as good as our words imply that we are. On the other hand, the Christ we so feebly struggle to love, serve, and incarnate is so much more than others can see in the way we live from day to day. I suppose that our children always expect more of us than we can actually deliver—in almost every aspect of life. But when it comes to our Christian faith, there will never be any excuse for our own children concluding that we are phonies and that we never meant business with God.

II. The second guideline toward helping our children have faith is the principle of exposure (v. 7a). The King James Version uses the two words, "teach diligently," while the New International Version translates the Hebrew as "impress." The literal meaning is "to say something twice" or "to repeat."

(a) The Hebrew word originally referred to the sharpening of a blade or a tool by rubbing it repeatedly against the whetstone. The word evolved in its meaning: first, from the act of sharpening, then to a piercing action, and finally, to the process of teaching. The basic idea of this verse then, is that by repeating the

teachings of the Law over and again, parents will eventually drive it home in the hearts and minds of their children like a piercing weapon.

(b) To this day, Jews celebrate the ancient Feasts of Passover and Hanukkah—in their homes and synagogues, recalling every year the divine intervention of God in their history. Christians regularly observe the ordinances of baptism and the Lord's Supper, and celebrate the seasons of Advent and Christmas, Lent and Easter. It's our way of telling the story of our salvation over and again and thereby keeping our faith alive!

Unfortunately, most contemporary celebrations of the Christian faith are largely confined to the church. Consequently, relatively little is done in our homes which is intended to keep our faith alive.

(c) Believe me, I know how Christian parents worry about "pushing" their children to make a profession of faith! But the solution is not to do nothing at all! Christian parents, listen! We pound into our kids' heads the necessity of making good grades and the urgency of getting a good college education. We repeatedly talk to our kids about responsible social and sexual behavior. We prod them toward success in everything they do. We spare no expense to make them pretty, poised, popular, positive, and prepared to face the world—and apparently, we do it all with little or no reference to God and the Christian faith. Tell me, parents: what have you done to prepare your children to face God and eternity?

III. The third way to help your children have faith is the principle of encouragement (vs. 7b–9). Everything a Christian parent does in the home should be directed toward encouraging their child's personal salvation through Jesus Christ.

(a) I believe that we have recently entered a new era in the Christian faith. For many years, a church could expect its own children to declare their own personal faith in Jesus. Things have changed drastically, however, in the last fifteen years!

Christian parents have assumed a new posture. For the most part, they expose their children to only mild doses of the Christian faith and religion. For fear of being accused of using undue influence, many parents give virtually no encouragement to their own children's declaration of personal faith in Jesus Christ. "It's up to the kids to decide if they want to be a Christian," more and more parents tell their ministers. "There are so many options available to them today. We'll just wait and let them decide."

(b) There may be a variety of ways to earn respectability, a reputation, and a reward. There may even be a whole host of religious options from which a person may be free to choose. But I tell you on the authority of God's Word, there is only one way to God—and that is through his Son, Jesus Christ. To allow for any other way is wrong and deadly! Your children will never become Christians by mere exposure to the Christian faith—either in mild or large doses! Neither is it enough to give your kids "a little taste" of what the Christian life is all about—by enrolling them in Sunday school and Vacation Bible School, and making sure that they attend "most of the time." By its very nature, the Christian faith demands conversion. And by virtue of your position as the most influential person in their life, you owe it to your children to see to it that they are presented with the claims of Jesus Christ upon their life! In other words, you have a responsibility to encourage them—and to influence them—to make Jesus their personal Savior and Lord.

Will our children have faith? Will your children have faith? In large measure, that depends entirely upon YOU! You tell me: If it's left entirely up to you, what's the answer to the question?

Illustrations

TROUBLE.   While we cannot understand all trouble and while it is perfectly normal for us to turn against it, this fact is incontrovertible: there is no progress without it. A father was showing his son a path up a mountain. "But, Dad," the boy said, "that's not a path, that's just a bunch of rocks and boulders." The paths to the summits are inevitably troublesome.—Gaston Foote

REASONS FOR REJECTING THE FAITH. Several years ago, more than eighteen hundred participants at a national youth conference in Washington, D.C., took part in a survey. At the end of the questionnaire, twelve reasons why children raised in Christian homes might possibly reject the Christian faith were listed. Participants were asked to indicate which of those reasons—or others not listed—would most likely lead a teenager to reject his or her faith. Three of the top five responses related to the influence of non-Christian friends. The remaining two of the leading five responses related to the breakdown of Christian influence. "Hypocrites in the church" was the second most frequently response. The fifth most frequently registered was "poor Christian role models in my home."—Gary C. Redding

Sermon Suggestions

FOR THOSE WISE IN THEIR OWN EYES. TEXT: Job. 38:1–11. (1) An accusation, verse 2. (2) A challenge, verse 3. (3) Some searching questions, verses, 4–11.

WITH HEART WIDE OPEN.   TEXT: 2 Cor. 6:1–13. (1) In our service to Christ and his gospel, we may be grossly misunderstood. (2) Nevertheless, even where we are most open to criticism, God may be at work for good. (3) Our unrelenting goodwill will challenge the resistance of critics and may bring a positive response sooner or later.

Worship Aids

CALL TO WORSHIP.   "This is how we know what love is: Christ gave his life for us. We too, then, ought to give our lives for our brothers! If a rich person sees his brother in need, yet closes his heart against his brother, how can he claim that he loves God? My children, our love should not be just words and talk; it must

be true love, which shows itself in action"
(1 John 3:16–18 [TEV]).

INVOCATION.   O divine love, help us
today to rise to the challenge of the needs
of the world, and to do it by making new
commitments, followed by faithful service to you and to every soul for whom
Christ died. Make us strong in your
strength.

OFFERTORY SENTENCE.   "They gave according to their means, as I can testify,
and beyond their means, of their own
free will" (2 Cor. 8:3 [TEV]).

OFFERTORY PRAYER.   God of grace,
God of glory, help us understand that we
are recipients of thy mercy. What we are,
thy grace has made us. What we have,
they providence has given us. And now,
do they gracious work also in others,
through the gifts we bring.

PRAYER.   Eternal Spirit, thou dwellest
in light unapproachable, beyond the
power of our thought to comprehend or
our imagination to portray. Yet thou art
revealed to us in the order of the world
we live in, in the truth our minds discover, in the inward presence of thy
Spirit, and above all in Christ, thy Son.
With reverent hearts we worship thee.

We would bring our fragmentary lives
into the presence of thy wholeness. We
would bring our transient thoughts into
the light of thine eternity. We would
bring our restless spirits into the calm
strength of thine everlasting purpose.

See what complaints we have brought
into thy sanctuary against the circumstances that have fretted us, against the
human friends who have failed us,
against the enemies who have wronged
us, and even against the justice of thine
order that has hurt us. Teach us, nevertheless, we beseech thee, to search our
own lives, to see that each man is his own
destiny, that each soul is its own heaven
and its own hell. Send us back into our
own souls to find there by thy grace,
peace and power, and adequacy to conquer life. May we be victors and not
victims.—Harry Emerson Fosdick

LECTIONARY MESSAGE

Topic: After the Storm

TEXT: Mark 4:35–41

A French saying phrases it neatly: "To
suffer passes. To *have* suffered never
passes." All of us are familiar with suffering. Sometimes it seems overwhelming. Sometimes it appears endless. We
survivors know. Are there lessons to be
learned from suffering? No one of us
would be so foolish as to induce suffering
as an educational experiment, but is
there educational value?

I. Storms occur. They were frequent
on the Sea of Galilee. Even today a squall
may trouble tourists if not natives. No
one ought to be surprised. So much of
Jesus' ministry developed around the Sea
of Galilee—and with fishermen—and
with boats. He must have enjoyed the
brisk winds, the tossing waves—an occasional storm. At least he left the crowd.

He was always leaving the crowd. We
modern ministers seek a crowd. Jesus
sought to escape a crowd. They went to
the other side of the sea. Why can't we
stay put? Why do we have to move?
Things are going great here. You have a
successful ministry here in your own
country. Why bother with that crowd on
the other side? They are suspect. They
are not thoroughbreds. They don't keep
the Law. The disciples must have felt
something like that.

A furious storm came up. It may have
exaggerated the storm the disciples experienced with Jesus' strange behavior. The
wind was strong and the waves were high
and the boat was filling with water. Now
the fishermen aboard had endured many
storms on the Sea. Was this one so much
more severe as to frighten them? Or
were they upset anyhow? How were they
accustomed to dealing with the inevitable
storms?

II. Jesus is present. We believe that he
is, but we are still terrified. The disciples
had heard him teach and they had witnessed his miraculous powers. Their attitude was different from that of the
daredevil who feels reckless confidence
in the Lord's presence. He was there in
the boat with them. True—he was not

dressed for the occasion: they took him as he was in the boat.

And while the storm was raging fiercely, he slept soundly . . . in the stern on a cushion. That's normal for a person who has been quite busy and isn't worried about the weather. A child is not apt to be terrified if a present parent is calm. Why should not the fishermen have taken their cue from Jesus? He cared for them. He cared if they drowned. They were not sure about his concern. They appear to have been more confident about his power. Is it a repeat of the leper's plea in 1:40?

At last they awoke him. They were not certain how much help he might be, but they wanted to be sure that he knew what was happening. There is an element of faith in their action.

III. Storms yield to Jesus' presence. Make no mistake about it: there are different ways in which the danger of a storm may be abated. The truth is that he exercises authority over them. He is present, concerned, and awake. And he is able. They must have felt more secure just to know that he was awake.

There is no evidence that he shouted down the winds and the waves. There is no evidence that he conjured up a magical trick. He spoke calmly, "Peace . . . be still." And the storm ceased.

Did he at the same time relieve the storm at the center of their experience? Or did his action challenge the faith of the disciples? They were yet afraid . . . afraid in a different way. They once sought his presence. Now they were fearful of his presence.

"Even the winds and the waves obey him!" How about disease? Is it obedient? How about demons? Are they obedient? The storm was over for the present. The encounter with the demoniacs on the opposite shore would stir up another storm.

Storms must occur. Jesus is present and concerned and powerful. Why are we afraid? Do we learn nothing during the storm for use after the storm? —J. Estill Jones

SUNDAY: JUNE TWENTY-SIXTH

SERVICE OF WORSHIP

Sermon: Biblical Authority

TEXT: 2 Tim. 3:16–17

The book just lies there. Maybe it is on a back dusty shelf. Maybe it is in a place of honor, gathering dust on a coffee table. Maybe you keep it on your bedside table for emergencies like you keep the flashlight in the drawer. But the book just lies there.

The book, of course, is your Bible. It is the book that we as Christians claim to be the divinely inspired Word of God, but as long as it lies there, unopened and unused, it is no more than any other book, a lifeless collection of pages, no more useful than a corpse.

I. But open the book and we assert as Christians that something truly wonderful happens. We believe that when an honest seeker opens the Bible that God himself speaks. Not just that God once spoke in some ancient time and place and men wrote down what he said, but that God actually speaks today to our time and our personal situations.

(a) Open the Bible with a little child and let God show her for the first time how he created the world. Let him tell her about Noah and his big boat, about David fighting off the lions and the bears and the giant, about Jonah being swallowed by a big fish. Then let him tell her about his Son Jesus and all the weird people he hung around with like Zacchaeus and John the Baptist and Peter the Fisherman. Then, as God lets his own story of love and redemption unfold, let him tell her about how Jesus loved her so much that he died for her. Let God tell her the story in his own words, and while you are opening up this marvelous story for her, you hear it again as if you were hearing it for the first time.

(b) Or open up the Bible with someone who has never darkened the doors of the church. He may find all the pages and the small print and the strange names foreboding at first, but don't let that deter him. Start him off in the book of John and I can guarantee you that somewhere there God will show him someone who is very much like himself. It may be that God will lead him to identify with the Samaritan woman or with the man born blind or with the woman caught in the act of adultery. Somewhere through all this, as the covers are opened and the pages are turned, salvation can come to your friend, because God has spoken a fresh and a new Word through the Bible directly to this person.

(c) Open up the Bible with a person who is confused, facing perplexing issues and feeling that he has no way of solving them. Allow God to show him that there is no situation that he could possibly face that God has not already dealt with a thousand times in the lives of other people.

If God could show Moses how to deal with cantankerous people, Joseph how to deal with the jealousies of his brothers and the cunning wiles of a rejected seductress, Paul and Silas how to sing, even in prison, then he can help him to deal with the depression and disappointment that are part and parcel of all human life.

II. And while you are at it—opening up the Bible for the children and the lost and the confused—open up the Bible for yourself. It is so easy for us as Christians to talk about the Bible without ever letting God speak through it to us. But he still can.

(a) It might happen something like this. Right now the things that you have to do are so many and the hours to do them so few that you don't know what to do. You have struggled all week and now the only feeling you have is an overwhelming fatigue, a tiredness that will not let you go. But then you turn to God's word and he says to you: "I am your shepherd, you shall not want. I will make you to lie down in green pastures; I will lead you beside still waters. I will restore your soul." Or in the words of Jesus, you may hear this invitation: "Come unto me, all who labor and are heavy-laden and I will give you rest" (Matt. 11:28).

(b) Or it might happen something like this. You have just found out that the physical condition that you thought was going to be merely an ongoing annoyance has turned into an immediate crisis. And in the midst of your shock and sadness, through his Word, God says this to you: "I am your refuge and strength, a very present help in trouble. Be still and know that I am God" (Ps. 46:1, 10).

(c) Or it could happen like this: You are facing some of the most difficult ethical decisions of your life and everyone is telling you what to do. In the midst of the roar of other voices, you hear this clear word from the Lord: "I am your hiding place. I will preserve you from trouble. I will compass you about with songs of deliverance. I will instruct you and teach you in the way that you shall go. I will guide you with my eye" (Ps. 32:7, 8).

(d) It might even happen that on this particular day in your life you have no pressing needs. You simply recognize that life comes from God and you want to thank him for it, and so he gives you the words even for that: "Make a joyful noise unto the Lord, all ye lands. Serve the Lord with gladness, come before his presence with singing. Know ye that the Lord, he is God. It is he that hath made us and not we ourselves. We are his people and the sheep of his pasture. Enter into his gates with thanksgiving and into his courts with praise. Be thankful unto him and bless his name. For the Lord is good. His mercy is everlasting and his truth endureth to all generations" (Ps. 100).

III. Through all of these words of scripture God can continue to speak to each one of us today, if we will only let him. If you ask what authority we stand under we certainly say that we stand under the authority of Jesus Christ, but we believe that his will for us is found as he speaks to us through the Bible. But it does no good for us to shout those beliefs and then leave our Bibles closed and unused.

So go back and find your Bible. Get it down off the shelf or out of the bedside drawer. If you don't have one, take the one from the pew rack. But open it up and read it, and let God speak to you. —James M. King

Illustrations

SOMETHING TO STEER BY.   To think religiously is to steer by the starry heavens and the shining sun. Far from known shores on the oceans of life we have the eternal signs of the faithfulness of God to direct us. Faith, hope, and love abide, for they are heavenly stars, dependable in their courses. Those who love mercy because they do rightly know how to walk humbly with their God. By day the sun shines, lighting our course. We can steer safely by the sun, proceeding forward toward the goal of our lives. Eyes for the daylight recognize in the Son of God's love the sun for life's steering. To fix one's attention on life's direction in the light of the sun of truth is man's supreme wisdom. Religion becomes real, for the light shows the right direction.—Nels F.S. Ferre

COMMITMENT.   There is the story about Britain's royal yacht. The captain was carrying Prince Charles and Princess Diana, sailing along on the ocean at night. Suddenly the captain saw lights approaching. He sent an urgent signal, "Please alter course!" A message came back, "You alter course!" The angered captain replied, "This is John Jones, captain of the royal yacht. The Prince and Princess are on board. In the name of and by the authority of the queen, YOU CHANGE COURSE!" An answer came back, "This is Fred Smith, and I have been keeper of this lighthouse for 22 years, and I CAN'T CHANGE COURSE."—Richard Lee Spindle

Sermon Suggestions

GOD AND THE LAST ENEMY.   TEXT: Wisd. of Sol. 1:13–15, 2:23–24. (1) God's purpose for us is life and immortality. (2) This purpose, however, may be thwarted by: a., The words and deeds of the ungodly. b., The work of the devil.

HOW TO BE GOOD STEWARDS OF OUR FINANCIAL RESOURCES.   TEXT: 2 Cor. 8:7– 15. (1) Strive to excel in this as well as in other areas of Christian experience. (2) Remember the generous act of our Lord Jesus Christ. (3) In any case, try to strike a fair balance in terms of the generosity of others; in terms of your abundance and others' need.

Worship Aids

CALL TO WORSHIP.   "How beautiful upon the mountains are the feet of him that bringeth good tidings, that publisheth peace; that bringeth good tidings of good, that publisheth salvation; that saith unto Zion, thy God reigneth" (Isa. 52:7).

INVOCATION.   Mighty God, your kingdom has come in Jesus of Nazareth, and grows among us day by day. Send us into the world to preach good news, so that men may believe, be rescued from sin, and become your faithful people; through Jesus Christ our Savior.—*The Worshipbook*

OFFERTORY SENTENCE.   "For ye know the grace of our Lord Jesus Christ, that, though he was rich, yet for your sakes he became poor, that ye through his poverty might be rich" (2 Cor. 8:9).

OFFERTORY PRAYER.   Out of full hearts and grateful lives we bring these offerings today. We know, Father, that you can do without them, but we cannot do without giving them. Work through them for your glory among people everywhere, we pray in Jesus' name.—Henry Fields

PRAYER.   Thou ever-blessed and eternal God, we thank thee for the revelation which thou hast made of thyself, far down through ranks of being. Thou hast been pleased to reach unto us. Not below us shines the light of truth and knowledge. We, brought up, at last have met the light in our sphere. We are taught of thee and of ourselves. We are pointed to the bright and blessed immortality beyond. All our sorrows are assuaged by its promises. All our joys are quickened in its glory. But thou, O God! by thy living presence, by thy sympathy, by thy helpfulness, by the inspiration of the Divine Spirit, dost chiefly help; for it is what we receive, it is what thou dost help us to do, and not what we work out by our own thought, nor what nature inspires, that makes us strong, and wise, and rich. We rejoice in thy Fatherhood. We rejoice in the benignity of thy government. Nature is full of thunders and threats; and the law, everywhere, under our feet, and in our bodies, and in the world which we inhabit, pursues every transgressor. The law of the soul, and the law of the mind, and the law of the flesh, work together for perpetual punishment; and we are under perpetual condemnation. But already, and all the time, from thee comes the blessed word, "I have found a ransom." From thee is remission and help. Thou dost set us free from the penalties which we are incurring from day to day. For thou knowest that what nature could do thou canst; that what nature will not do thou wilt. And thou art healing, and wilt heal, by that which thou art in thyself. By thy soul upon our soul; by the medicine of thy thought upon our distempered thought; by thy love upon our imperfect and impure love, thou wilt heal us.—Henry Ward Beecher

LECTIONARY MESSAGE

Topic: The Other Side

Text: Mark 5:21–43

We have a saying, the grass is greener on the other side of the fence. Of course it is probably not true—it looks greener, that's all. My recent grass planting looks better from a distance, but up close there are bare spots and wild strawberries and dandelions. Now Jesus crossed the sea, back to more familiar territory. The second crossing was more peaceful than the first. He had stilled the storm. And he had healed the Gerasene demoniac—a different kind of storm.

Now he and his disciples returned to peaceful Galilee, to beautiful Galilee. Almost immediately it seemed a multitude gathered. They had felt deserted. They welcomed him back. Two stories of healing stood out to the one telling the story. There may have been more. The needs were so great that one story overlaps the other, thus interrupting its telling.

I. A father's daughter. Fathers and daughters have a special relationship. The father's name has been preserved, Jairus. His plea was simple. Before the multitude he confessed his need of the healer. His daughter was at the point of death. Would Jesus come and touch her so that she might live? He followed the father and a great multitude followed him. How strikingly different from the plea for help on the other side ... "What have I to do with you ...?" (5:7)

II. A suffering woman. She had suffered and was yet suffering. She suffered physically and had suffered for twelve years. (Note that time span!) She suffered at the hands of many physicians. She had spent all that she had on doctors and was none the better. In truth, she was growing worse. She had heard about Jesus healing many. Was there a chance for her?

She joined the multitude and touched him. It was a touch of faith ... If I but touch his garments I shall be made whole. Immediately she was healed—she felt it in her body. Perhaps she sought to get out of the crowd and enjoy good health. But Jesus, sensitive to human need, knew that healing had gone out from him and stopped, "Who touched me?" The disciples, ever practical, reminded him of the crowded conditions ... Everyone touched you!

He spotted her and she came to him, telling him the story of her long suffering, of the disappointing doctors, of her simple faith. "Daughter," he said. Was it not another daughter at the end of the journey, a daughter who suffered? It is a loving term from a sensitive healer. "Your faith has made you whole."

"Go in peace." No more storms. No more anxiety. No more disappointment.

No more plague. After twelve years she was free from her scourge.

III. A grieving father. Events tumbled into one another, so busy was this side of the sea. Messengers came from the house of Jairus: your daughter is dead. Why do you trouble the Teacher? We can almost feel the heartbreak . . . if that woman had not delayed his progress, he might have healed my daughter. Now it's all over.

"But Jesus. . . ." It's a simple phrase. Yet it transforms the scene from one of hopelessness to one of hope. Jesus spoke to the father's need. . . . Don't be afraid; only be believing. They came to his home. The multitude probably followed. The mourning process was already begun—loud, tumultuous, weeping, wailing. What a welcome for the father! It was Jesus who turned their lament into laughter—of scorn: she is not dead, only sleeping.

He left the multitude and the mourners. With the family and his disciples he went in where the daughter lay. What hope had the father? What faith had the father?

IV. He touched her. And he spoke to her, "Arise." In faith she stood up and walked. Whose faith? The daughter's? The father's? Jesus'? "Only believe," Jesus had challenged. He certainly believed now. The daughter was twelve years old. The woman had suffered with the flow of blood for twelve years. Coincidence? I don't know. Both daughters were healed. Both experienced a touch of faith.

There are opportunities of ministry on both sides—of the sea, of the street, of the fence. A simple touch and simple faith and compassion may well effect healing. There are persons everywhere dying for a little bit of love.—J. Estill Jones

SUNDAY: JULY THIRD

SERVICE OF WORSHIP

Sermon: Don't Wait for Agreement

TEXT: Amos 3:3

I. Good relationships depend less upon the parties involved agreeing with one another than upon their accepting one another. If that were not true, a lot of marriages would never last very long, a great many friendships would never develop, and most churches would splinter.

As a matter of fact, the reason so many marriages, friendships, and churches are in trouble today is partly because people do not recognize the difference between agreement and acceptance. As far as I know, the only community where no disagreement exists is a cemetery. Wherever there is life there is difference. That is a large part of what makes our being human so wonderful a privilege. Humankind is a choice maker. When we choose this, we choose against that. Why should we insist that those close to us should elect or be compelled to make the same choices we have made?

I submit that much of our anxiety is caused by the neurotic need to have others agree with us. So there are some marriages in which—according to reports about them—there has never been a disagreement. How frightfully limiting, and how incredibly dull! What that really means is that one partner has ceased being a partner and become a flunky who is present only in body.

Have you ever wanted to be friends with someone who made it plain that the only way he/she would have you for a friend is that you never disagree with him/her? That kind of friendship soon becomes an intolerable burden, does it not? There is no acceptance in it. It is a one-way street.

Sometimes pastors are terribly threatened by disagreement. I heard of a pastor who would present a program to his church staff and then say, "Everybody who agrees with this proposal say, 'Aye.' All who disagree, say 'I resign.'" I suspect that it was said in jest, but there are plenty of situations in which that kind of conformity is required. If the pastor interprets all expressions of disagreement as acts of disloyalty to God and himself (he ought to be able to tell the difference between God and himself, but sometimes appears unable to do so), the church is in bad trouble.

The dynamics of every healthy community include, I am certain, lively disagreement. It is the "loyal opposition," and it is needed to keep us from getting too comfortable with our narrow and marred visions. To presume that others may need us to correct them but that we don't need them to correct us is to assign ourselves an omniscience which belongs only to God.

II. A verse in the Book of Amos speaks to me powerfully about this. The prophet is illustrating the inevitability of God's judgment upon evil, and he does so by citing a half dozen well-known proverbs. A proverb is a brief, pithy summary of a chunk of human experience.

The first of these maxims used by Amos says:

Do two walk together unless they have made an appointment? (3:3)

If you meet your neighbor for an early morning brisk walk, it will only be by appointment. Oh, you might once in a while run into him or her, but if you walk together every morning or three times a week, or on Mondays, it will be because you have planned to do so, and each has made the necessary arrangement of his/her schedule to see that it happens.

Now, the King James Version reading of this proverb can be misleading. It has the prophet ask, "Can two walk together, except they be agreed?" The problem here is not so much in the translation as in the meaning assigned to the words. "Except they be agreed" meant simply that they had made an appointment. It did not mean, as it has so often been interpreted, "You can't fellowship with somebody with whom you disagree."

I have heard that interpretation in sermons all my life. It made me uncomfortable even before I knew why. It just didn't sound like Christ. Then, lo and behold, one day I discovered that Amos did not say that at all. He did not even

imply that. He would have deplored the notion it suggests. What he said is that people do not find common ground by accident. They work to find it. They make appointments with one another. They know that relationship happens only where there is some kind of continuing commitment to the process of relationship.

I am deeply troubled by what appears to me to be a serious drift in this society away from the principles of "management by appointment" and toward a rigid totalitarian view of "management by agreement." It is the kind of mentality which fixes another with a flinty look and says coldly, "If you don't agree with us, get out." "If you don't like it here, go somewhere else." "America—love it or leave it!" What ever happened to loving America and wanting to make it a more equitable and just nation?

When people get threatened, their willingness to tolerate disagreement narrows. The more we feel insecure, the less we are willing to allow for those who have a different view from our own. Just now the pressure for agreement rather than commitment to mutual acceptance is the prevailing current in the stream of much of American religious and political life. It bodes ill for the health of the body.
—L. D. Johnson

Illustrations

THE INCLUSIVE SOLUTION.   Two young children [are] playing together and wanting to play different games. The girl said, "Let's play next-door neighbors." "I want to play pirates," the boy replied. "Okay," said the girl, "then you can be the pirate that lives next door."—Sharon Parks

STRONG FAMILIES.   Nick Stinnett, who is chairman of the Human Development and Family Department at the University of Nebraska, decided to study strong families and determine what were their common strengths. Here are some of the important things he found in almost every solid family:

· *A high degree of religious orientation.* Not all belonged to an organized church, but nearly all considered themselves highly religious.

· *Appreciation.* Family members gave one another compliments and sincere psychic "strokes."

· *Time together.* In all areas of their lives, meals, work, recreation, the family members structured their schedules to spend time together.

Many families grow apart not because they are poorly matched or because their purposes in life are in conflict; they grow apart simply because they do not take the time to build intimacy. As André Maurois has said, "Marriage is an edifice that must be rebuilt every day."—Alan Loy McGinnis

Sermon Suggestions

WHAT IS A PROPHET? TEXT: Ezek. 2:1–5. (1) *Identity:* A prophet is an ordinary mortal. (2) *Inspiration:* But such a person is one into whom the Spirit has entered. (3) *Intent:* A true prophet: a., Speaks only what God directs; b., Speaks faithfully regardless of the response.

APPROPRIATE MODESTY. TEXT: 2 Cor. 12:2–6. (1) *Then:* Paul had an unusual spiritual experience that he was reluctant to exploit. (2) *Always:* Some intimate experiences with God may be too personal and special to be displayed when the result is self-serving. (3) *Now:* a., God answers prayer, but not in order to glorify us. b., God calls into service, but not in order to make us the focus of praise.

Worship Aids

CALL TO WORSHIP. "If we say that we have no sin, we deceive ourselves, and the truth is not in us. If we confess our sins, he is faithful and just to forgive us our sins, and to cleanse us from all unrighteousness" (1 John 1:8–9).

INVOCATION. Show us, O God, what we have not yet seen, reveal to us what we have not yet understood, use us as we have never been used before because we paused to pray and wait and worship in openness and trust.—E. Lee Phillips

OFFERTORY SENTENCE. "It is written, he that had gathered much had nothing over; and he that had gathered little had no lack" (2 Cor. 8:15).

OFFERTORY PRAYER. O Lord of our lives, as our material blessings multiply, grant that the grace of giving may be increased. May we sustain no spiritual loss because of an abundance of material goods, nor may we fail of thy grace when the fig tree does not blossom, and no fruit shall be in the vines. At all times and in all conditions may we be thy faithful stewards.

PRAYER. O Father, for the gift of your Word that creates church and sacrament, we give you thanks. That your Word present from the beginning is a Word of grace—love, forgiveness, reconciliation creating community, we praise you. That in this community of faith we are privileged to live and celebrate your Word together, we are grateful.

May we be careful how we hear, for your Word is never heard on the periphery but only at the center of one's being. Let us be discerning lest our words pose as your Word.

We praise you for the new birth of freedom that pervades people and nations. In celebrating the privilege of freedom may we with others not lose sight of its challenge to be responsible before you and all others. What do you require of us but to do justice, to love in all relationships, and to walk humbly before you. In struggles for freedom in this hemisphere may we no longer deny the freedom to others that we demand for ourselves.

In Christ we are free—free indeed—free to love. As your eternal Word he is among us not only teaching us to pray but empowering us to live.—John Thompson

LECTIONARY MESSAGE

Topic: Are You Listening?

TEXT: Mark 4:1–13

An effective preacher of a past generation frequently injected the question in his sermons, are you listening? He was doing more than ensuring their attention. He was emphasizing that listening is an act of the will. Listening is more than the mere perception of sound. On one occasion God spoke to Jesus and part of the crowd said, It thunders. Persons respond differently to the same sound and to the same message. Jesus told a parable about a sower and seed and soils. It was, in a sense, a cover parable introducing this manner of teaching. Understanding parables calls for a certain quality of listening.

I. You may listen without a response. The same sower scattered the same seed. Only the soils were different. Indifferent hearing makes it possible for any message to get through or be ignored. There is so much competition for response that we often do not even hear the message. It is as if birds follow the grass seeder along the pathways and gobble the seed before the soil has a chance at it. The sower is good, the seed is good, but the soil does not respond.

II. You may listen with mere enthusiasm. Ours is an age of enthusiasm . . . radio, television, and ball games. A great deal of expense and energy is devoted to training cheering squads for college and professional football, but a football game has rarely been won by cheerleaders. There are those who listen to the message as cheerleaders . . . beautiful, eloquent, interesting, entertaining. These lack depth and respond both quickly and in shallowness.

It is not a question of insincerity, only a lack of depth. When the first warm breeze of criticism or opposition blows, the heat is too much. It has no root to sustain the response. It withers away. It

responds quickly and dies quickly because it has no root.

III. You may listen to too many sounds. Silence is golden and rare. Ours is an age of sound. We magnify sound so that it becomes almost unbearable. The loss of hearing is frequently attributed to too much noise. Distinguishing sounds is an art, developed with maturity. Spin a radio or television dial. Sit in a room filled with conversation. Unless you will to zero in on a particular sound, you will not understand.

It is as if grass seed, struggling to live, was choked out by dandelions and plantain weeds. The seed is good. The sower is the same, but the soil is filled with other seeds. Even if the good seed grows it can never mature into fruit-bearing. But the seed is not responsible. It's the soil. It's the hearer.

IV. You may listen with commitment. There is a bright side to the parable. There is a bright side to preaching. The same sower, the same seed, may fall into receptive soil. The hearer listens with a will to understand and responds in commitment. Fruit bearing is inevitable, whether the harvest of the Spirit . . . love, joy, peace . . . or reproduction in effective witnessing.

Are you listening? It's a parable of listening. "Hearken," he said. And the conclusion of the parable: "Who hath ears to hear, he is to listen." It's an act of will. It's a matter of grace, the mystery of grace. "To you is given the mystery . . . but unto them that are outside . . ." The question of acceptance or rejection is ages old. "Who hath ears to hear, he is to listen."—J. Estill Jones

SUNDAY: JULY TENTH

SERVICE OF WORSHIP

Sermon: When Life Reaches Its Depths

TEXT: Psalm 42

There are days when our lives do go down into the depths. To be sure, life

happily has not only depths but shallows, not only profundities but gaieties. We could not endure life without that. Our thought this morning concerns our most serious moods, but this other side of our nature is important, too—the superficial, if you will, the light-hearted, cheerful, and merry.

The psalmist's experience had run out into the depths in trouble, and remembering the thundering cataracts that pour down in springtime from the melting snows of Mount Hermon, and roar, and echo, and answer one another in the gorges beneath, he used that similitude to describe his experience. "Deep," he said, "calleth unto deep at the noise of thy waterfalls." Every serious life has that experience, where the profundities within ask for an answering profundity. No longer do the shallows suffice. Life within faces some profound abyss of experience, and the deep asks for an answering deep. So when deep calls unto deep and the deep replies, we face the essential experience of religion.

I. This explains the deathless hold that religious faith has upon the human spirit.

(a) There is no God, says irreligion, no divine purpose in life, no goodness beyond our human goodness, no high source for our existence, and no destiny at last except a universal ash heap. Nevertheless, while irreligion thus takes all depth of meaning out of the universe, it leaves man still with the deep in him—depths of trouble, of love, of moral need, of ethical devotion, of spiritual insight—the same old profound experiences that man's nature has known throughout its history. But in irreligion when these deeps within call for a responsive depth, only the shallows are there to answer.

(b) To see how true it is, and how indispensable a matter Christian faith is standing for, consider those hours when life does move out into its depths. For example, in trouble. A man, let us say, has had a smooth and easy life where tragedy has been like a rumor from a far country, but one day a knock comes on his door and tragedy steps in. That experience always adds a new dimension to life, and it is the dimension of depth. When the psalmist says, "Out of the depths have I cried unto thee, O Lord," we know what he means. He is in trouble.

(c) Each of us has a date with this experience, and when it arrives the psalm-ist's words come true: "Deep calleth unto deep." When death takes those we love, when children slip through our arms, when war breaks and catastrophe crashes down and life tumbles in, then out of the depths the soul cries for answering depths. In such an hour how shallow irreligion is!

(d) In Christian faith, however, the deep in us is not thus answered by the shallows. For when our profundities call out for an answering profundity, Christian faith says, God is there; his eternal purpose comprehends all life; this world is a place for the growing of souls, and in that process adversity is as indispensable as joy; all supreme spirits have come up out of great tribulations; there is power available to enable one to win that victory. So, deep calleth unto deep!

II. Carry our thoughts further now and see that in another area life runs out into its depths—not only in trouble but in love.

(a) Wherever love is strong and beautiful life reaches its depths. Anyone, for example, who has had a great mother has had one of the unfathomable experiences. Strange how powerfully it keeps its hold long after the mother herself has passed into the invisible! Strange how a man fights his battles out and wins such victories as he is able, and grows old, older far than his mother was when she died, but still feels that to her he owes the major part of everything that he has done. Others might fail him, but she never; others might doubt his possibilities, but she rose on them like the sun and fell on them like the rain, in her encouragement.

(b) Now, over against this deep of true love put a summary statement of irreligion by one of its brilliant contemporary devotees: "Living," he says, "is merely a physiological process with only a physiological meaning." How can one believe that? Then the deep of love in man is solitary—nothing at the heart of reality to answer it; it came from nowhere and is going nowhither; it is an accident; when it cries out for the deep there is no deep to respond. That is the tragedy of irreligion.

(c) Christian faith does fight an indispensable battle for man's depths. For Christian faith says, Love is real, the divinest reality in the universe; "God is love," "Now abideth faith, hope, love, . . . and the greatest of these is love." That, I am sure, is the only philosophy that can ultimately sustain man's greatness. Alas for souls in whom this deep goes unanswered by any corresponding deep, until at the last they are tempted even to deny the deep within themselves!

III. Carry our thought further now by noting that life runs out into its depth not simply in trouble and in love but in moral need.

(a) A man can hardly go into a room without leaving traces of himself. He leaves fingerprints all over. He leaves fibers from his clothes and hairs from his head. Always where he goes he leaves something of himself behind. Man discovers that he does that morally. He leaves his moral fingerprints on everything he touches. He cannot go into a room without leaving his traces. And in hours of penitence he understands what the converted sinner in Masefield's poem meant when he said, "The harm I done by being me."

(b) In such hours of penitence and moral need how utterly shallow irreligion is! Picture a man in real moral need, the deep crying out for the deep, and nothing there to answer him except a vast indifference! Christian faith is fighting a battle for man's profound experiences, and to everyone here today in moral need it offers no fast indifference as an answer, but forgiveness, a second chance, the possibility of a fresh beginning, reinstatement, an inner spiritual power potent enough to enable you to win the victory. So, when in the far country the prodigal comes to himself and says, "I will arise and go to my father," there is not a vast indifference at the other end of the journey, but a father where deep can call unto deep.

IV. Take a further step and note that life runs out into its depths not only in trouble, love, and moral need, but in the very opposite of moral need—profound sacrificial ethical devotion.

(a) When a man honestly cares about doing right, when he is profoundly in earnest about setting his compass to the true pole, he wants to know that there is a true pole there to be true to. He cannot be content with subjective feeling only; he wants an objective right to be dedicated to. When a man has sacrificial devotion to give, he wants a real God to give it to.

(b) When Jesus in Gethsemane said, "Not my will, but thine, be done," that was a deep experience. But picture Jesus going into Gethsemane and finding there awaiting him nothing but what irreligion can offer—a vast indifference! How different his story would have been! When one has a great ethical devotion to give, he wants a great God to give it to.

(c) So the Christian faith is fighting a battle for what we see and feel in our hours of deep trouble, deep love, deep moral need, deep ethical devotion, and profound spiritual insight. And if someone says, But life is not all such serious business, I say, No, but it is the deep sea that supports the dancing waves upon the surface; it is the profundities that sustain the superficialities and make them lovely; and if a man tries to live only in the shallows, with no deeps answering his deep, then the nemesis is that some day his shallows will grow intolerably wearisome.

V. Note, now, the conclusion of the matter. Throughout this sermon we have been starting with the profundities in ourselves, and saying that they are answered by profundities in God. Suppose, however, that someone asks, What makes you think that these profundities in God that Christian faith believes in are really there? I would say in answer, Where did the profundities in ourselves come from? How did they get here? If fish have fins, it is because the water was there first. If birds have wings, it is because air was there first. If we have eyes, it is because the sun was there first. All the functions of living beings are but responses to something objective in the universe. Always the universe was there first, and our powers and capacities are but our answer to it. How can one suppose that the deeps in the human spirit are the only exceptions to this universal law? In a world where lungs argue the priority of air, where eyes argue the priority of light, where the esthetic instincts in man argue the priority of beauty, where scientific curiosity in man argues the priority of truth, how can it be that the deepest things in man—great fortitude, great love, great moral want, great devotion, deep insight—argue the priority of nothing? It is preposterous.

The deeper truth is that God came first, and all that is fine, true, and beautiful in us is but our partial response to him. As the New Testament says, "We love him, because he first loved us." So today may the deep in the Eternal call unto the deep in us, and may there be indeed in our spirit a depth to answer it.—Harry Emerson Fosdick

Illustrations

"HONEST TO GOD." Where is one to go when the bottom drops out? What is one to say if the doctor has just hinted that you better enjoy this Christmas because it will probably be your last, or you have been told that your own child has drowned on a camping trip, or the pain killer which used to have minimal effect now doesn't seem to help at all? What is appropriate to say to God at a time like that? Should you thank God for being so nice to you? We Christians do have a problem knowing how to express negative feelings, or even knowing if it is legitimate for us to do so. We are surprised and fascinated by the character of Tevye in *Fiddler on the Roof* because he dares to say things to God that we may have thought about but quickly suppressed.—Daniel J. Simundson

ON DOING ONE'S BEST. In answer to friends quoting certain critics, Abraham Lincoln said, "I do the very best I know how—the very best I can; and I mean to keep doing so until the end. If the end brings me out all right, what is said against me won't amount to anything. If the end brings me out wrong, ten angels swearing I was right would make no difference."

Sermon Suggestions

OF PEOPLE AND PROPHETS. TEXT: Amos 7:7–15. (1) An exacting standard for God's people, verses 7–9. (2) A vital qualification for God's prophet, verses 10–15, especially verse 15b.

WE ARE CHOSEN. TEXT: Eph. 1:3–14, NRSV. (1) When—"Before the foundation of the world." (2) How—"in Christ." (3) Why—"to be holy and blameless before him in love." (4) Who—"us (Jews)"; "you (Gentiles) also."

Worship Aids

CALL TO WORSHIP. "Lord, who shall abide in thy tabernacle? who shall dwell in thy holy hill? He that walketh uprightly, and worketh righteousness, and speaketh the truth in his heart" (Ps. 15:1–2).

INVOCATION. Lord, give us genuineness of compassion and depth of courage as we absorb every aspect of this service of worship for our blessed Savior's sake.—E. Lee Phillips

OFFERTORY SENTENCE. "He which soweth sparingly shall reap also sparingly; and he which soweth bountifully shall reap also bountifully" (2 Cor. 9:6).

OFFERTORY PRAYER. O God, you did not spare your own Son, but gave him up for us all. Your daily mercies are beyond our counting. May our joyous giving reflect something of the prodigality of your giving.

PRAYER. O thou great Father of us all, we rejoice that at last we know thee. All our soul within us is glad because we need no longer cringe before thee as slaves of holy fear, seeking to appease thine anger by sacrifice and self-inflicted pain, but may come like little children, trustful and happy, to the God of love. Thou art the only true Father, and all the tender beauty of our human love is the reflected radiance of thy loving kindness, like the moonlight from the sunlight, and testifies to the eternal passion that kindled it.

Grant us growth of spiritual vision, that with the passing years, we may enter into the fullness of this our faith. Since thou art our Father, may we not hide our sins from thee, but overcome them by the stern comfort of thy presence. By this knowledge, uphold us in our sorrows and make us patient even amid the unsolved mysteries of the years. Reveal to us the larger goodness and love that speak through the unbending laws of thy world. Through this faith, make us the willing equals of all thy other children.

As thou art ever pouring out thy life in sacrificial father-love, may we accept the eternal law of the cross and give ourselves to thee and to all men. We praise thee for Jesus Christ, whose life has revealed to us this faith and law, and we rejoice that he has become the first born among many brethren. Grant that in us, too, the faith in thy fatherhood may shine through all our life with such persuasive beauty that some who still creep in the dusk of fear may stand erect as free sons of God, and that others who now through unbelief are living as orphans in an empty world may stretch out their hands and find thee near. — Walter Rauschenbusch

LECTIONARY MESSAGE

Topic: The Ghost of a Prophet

TEXT: Mark 6:14–29

A good ghost story captivates an audience. Several recent film productions have made good use of the popular theme. Ghost fantasies, like science fiction fantasies, make for high book sales. This is not a recent development. Ancient writers and storytellers took advantage of superstitious readers and listeners. We are not surprised then to read of King Herod's superstition. In his own mind he was confronted by a ghost — the ghost of John the Baptist. He had heard reports of Jesus' ministry and decided that Jesus was the ghost of the prophet. He had good reason to be frightened.

I. John had rebuked Herod publicly. In a period of political pressures and in an area of potential revolt John had rebuked the king for his marriage to Herodias. Herod was never popular with his Jewish subjects, ruling by the power of Rome. He had used his powerful position to take Herodias from his brother Philip who was her husband. Strict Jews would have found religious precedents violated. Others would have seen the injustice of the action.

In an area dangerously near the rule of Aretas, Arab offended by the divorce of Herod's first wife, John had denounced the union of Herod and Herodias.

II. Herod had arrested John. The charge might have been treason or simply disrespect for the king. It is probable that Herodias instigated the arrest and imprisonment. She would have liked to kill him herself. All of these recent developments plagued Herod's memory. John was certainly not a criminal, dangerous to the people. He was certainly not a vile or lewd person: he was a Nazarite from birth. Why then had he been arrested? "For the sake of Herodias."

III. Herodias hated John. She could have killed him in her anger, but she could not persuade Herod to execute him. We can imagine the sort of pressure she put on the king to get rid of the pestilent fellow. She must have nagged interminably. She must have enlisted all her friends at court in her campaign against John. Like Joseph of old, John was the victim of an enraged wife.

But the more Herodias railed against John, the more Herod seemed fascinated by his prophet prisoner ... "he heard him gladly." Then her opportunity came.

IV. Herod had John executed. At the oft-described party the daughter of Herodias danced. It was quite a birthday celebration for Herod. John was not invited! All of the important people were present. All congratulated the king. And the daughter danced. She was so enthusiastically acclaimed that the king was magnanimous. Anything you want, he said, even to half of my kingdom!

She went to her mother for counsel. Perhaps it was with some disappointment that she heard her mother's request for the head of the prophet. There must have been less gory gifts in the king's treasury. Nevertheless, she made the request and the king felt a new sort of pressure. He had made the rash promise before his friends; he must keep it. Executioners were dispatched to the dungeon and brought the head of John to the banquet hall. Herod must have remembered the tragedy in great detail.

V. He is a prophet. This is what they said about Jesus. He is *the* prophet,

Herod thought about the reports of Jesus. A new kind of pressure now forced Herod into superstition. Others might think of him as Elijah come back to life, but the king was sure that Jesus was the ghost of the prophet John . . . "John whom I beheaded, he is risen."

It is so easy to succumb to superstition—against the background of misdeeds, against the foreground of multiple pressures. Here was not the ghost of John, but the spirit of prophecy. Let us then give up any fragments of superstition about ghosts. Jesus was and is a living reality . . . "God was in Christ, reconciling the world unto himself."—J. Estill Jones

SUNDAY: JULY SEVENTEENTH

SERVICE OF WORSHIP

Sermon: Hope Unashamed

TEXT: Romans 5:1–5

Every few years a different religious idea pops up, and it would seem that we almost wear it out talking about it. Hope, as an essential ingredient of the Christian faith, has never completely dropped out of our vocabulary, though it has been sometimes ignored.

In the magnificent thirteenth chapter of 1 Corinthians, the Apostle Paul mentions hope, along with faith and love, as one of the abiding realities: "So faith, hope, love abide, these three; but the greatest of these is love" (1 Cor. 13:13, RSV). The symbol that has long stood before the United States Naval Academy chapel, in Annapolis, is an anchor which also bears the form of a cross. This anchor with the cross is the abiding symbol of hope.

Do we need hope in these days? Since we talk so much about it, it must be especially necessary. We need hope because of our everyday discouragements and vexations and frustrations. When life becomes cluttered, hope offers a way through. Also, occasional crises arise, such as illness, persecution, failure, mar-

ital difficulty, and bereavement. Hope enables us to survive these seismic tremors at the foundations of our existence. But it is the inevitably of death which all of us face that offers the most sweeping challenge of all. Without hope, a pall hangs over the sweetness of every infant, the beauty of every flower, and the grace of every virtue. Therefore, let us examine this shining word that God has thrust among us in the midst of darkness, defeat, and death.

I want to say three simple things. First, hope is ours. Second, hope is hard-won. And third, hope is reliable.

I. First of all, then, the apostle tells us that hope is ours: "We rejoice in our hope of sharing the glory of God" (Rom. 5:2, RSV). Now there are different levels of hope. When we use the word, we can mean different things.

(a) One kind of hope may be only wishful thinking. Charles Dickens's Mr. Macawber is a man who lives impecuniously, hoping that his luck will improve tomorrow. In and out of debtor's prison for nonpayment of his bills, he keeps hoping that his ship will come in, that tomorrow will be better than today. The main problem is that he never undergirds any of his hopes with honest toil.

For him hope is a substitute for work. The American humorist Josh Billings once said, "I never knew a man who lived on hope but what spent his old age at somebody else's expense." If the world's leaders keep hoping that problems created by the population explosion in certain parts of the world will go away and yet do nothing significant about it, then we are headed for disaster. If we continue to pollute the air and water, hoping that everything will be all right, and do nothing significant to correct the problem, then, again, we are headed for disaster. If we continue to waste our natural resources as if they were inexhaustible, hoping that there will always be enough to meet our human needs, then, once again, disaster awaits us.

(b) Another kind of hope is reasonable expectation. A man is injured in an automobile accident. The family is filled with anxiety about his recovery. He receives the best medical attention, and after a consultation among the doctors, one of them says to the family, "You have every reason to hope for the best." Their experience with similar cases makes it possible for them to offer hope, for there is reasonable expectation of recovery.

(c) However, the hope the apostle speaks of is certainly more than wishful thinking, more even than reasonable expectation: it is confident assurance. Assurance of what? Assurance of sharing the glory of God. That is, through our faith in Jesus Christ, we have the confident assurance that we will partake in God's triumph over sin and death. When a preacher was asked why the Christians in the black churches have always been so joyful in their worship, even when things were going very badly for them everywhere else, he said, "We rejoice in what we are going to have." Indeed, regardless of what is happening around us, regardless of our discouragements, our crises, and the grim fact of death itself, we can rejoice—not because of our troubles, but because of what we are going to have. We can enjoy the confident assurance that we shall share the glory of God. This glorious assurance is ours for the taking.

II. Now let us go a step further. The apostle also tells us that hope is hard-won: "Suffering produces endurance, and endurance produces character and character produces hope" (Rom. 5:3–4, RSV).

Hope at its best lies at the end of a long road.

(a) Hope at its best begins in suffering. If one suffers, hope may seem and actually be far, far away. But for Anton Boisen, hope began in a mental hospital where he was a patient. For Dostoevsky, the Russian novelist, hope began as he stood before a firing squad for execution and received a last minute reprieve. For Ernest Gordon, chaplain at Princeton University, hope began in the filth, stench, and death of a Japanese concentration camp during World War II, where, as a prisoner and an agnostic, a new window on life was opened up for him. In still other kinds of suffering, hope for many persons has had its first frail beginnings. Hope followed hard on the heels of failure, of illness, and of discouragement.

(b) On the way to hope, suffering produces endurance. When an athlete is training for the *big* game, it is suffering that produces the endurance necessary for the real performance. Sometimes he may think his lungs will burst and he will almost scream from the agony of his training, but it is this very suffering that produces the endurance necessary to win when the actual contest takes place. Suffering is bearable if it has meaning, if it looks forward to something, if it has a goal. Suffering is transformed by meaning. My maternal grandmother was an invalid for several years. She never complained, but in answer to a question, she said, "I suffer death every minute." Once she said to me, "I don't know why I have to suffer as I do, but I believe I'll understand sometime." Suffering actually produced a triumphant endurance that lasted through those years.

(c) Endurance produces character and brings God's approval. As you endure, your value system changes. Little by little, you learn what is important in life and what is unimportant, what is worth striving for and what is empty of meaning; you learn why what God expects of you and plans for you is more important than what you had planned for yourself. In other words, what you work for and what you expect gradually come into line with what God wills for you. It is little wonder, then, that the poet Keats, wrote: "The world is the vale of soul-making." God must look at the souls of men and women who have endured all kinds of sufferings and achieved unusual depths of character and integrity, and say, as he said after he had created the world and man, "It is good . . . it is very good."

God's approval creates hope. When one is sure that God has accepted him, that God has affirmed him, that God has said *yes* to him, he has reason to hope. "We belong to God" was Israel's conviction. In all of the nation's shifting fortunes, Israel believed that God was on her side. Even when God opposed the nation, even when God brought the nation into defeat in battle and exile, Israel never ceased to hope, to have the radiant assurance that all of this was the work of God, creating a marvelous future. Of course, the people often doubted and complained. Their prophets remonstrated with God, like Tevye, in *Fiddler on the Roof*, who asked the Lord why he couldn't choose someone else once in a while.

If you know that God is on your side, though he sometimes may punish you, you never have to give up hoping. You may even sing in the words of the Broadway musical, *South Pacific,* "I can't get it out of my heart."

III. And now a final step. The apostle tells us that hope is reliable: "And hope does not disappoint us, because God's love has been poured into our hearts through the Holy Spirit which has been given to us" (Rom. 5:5, rsv).

(a) This hope of which the apostle speaks is reliable because it rests on God alone. True hope is not built on our intelligence, our performance, our character, or our connections. Our wisdom, our works, our goodness, and our friends at some point fall short of the glory of God. Though we are created in the image of God, our humanity is forever showing through and in one way or another dishonoring God and bringing shame to ourselves. The future in which God is leading us can never be built on the foundations of human achievement. God has to work with sin and failure and defeat and death. It was William Manson who said, "The only God the New Testament knows is the God of the Resurrection." And just as our character apart from the grace of God cannot determine the Christian's hope, neither can outward circumstances decide the questions of the Christian's hope. "For I am sure," wrote the Apostle Paul, "that neither death, nor life, nor angels, nor principalities, nor things present, nor things to come, nor powers, nor height, nor depth, nor anything else in all creation, will be able to separate us from the love of God in Christ Jesus our Lord" (Rom. 8:38–39, rsv).

(b) This hope is reliable, also, because it is certified by the Holy Spirit within us. Samuel Johnson, the English author, was once asked by a woman, "How does one know when he has sinned?" Johnson replied, "A man knows when he has sinned, and that's that!" So it is with the presence of the Holy Spirit within us, creating hope. A man knows when the Holy Spirit is in his heart and life, and that's that! The Holy Spirit, of course, does not make us infallible, does not guarantee that we shall never be discouraged, does not make us perfect beings. But even while we enjoy the knowledge that the Holy Spirit is in us, he is transforming us, making us into new and different and better persons. Assurance, confident assurance, and transformation of our lives go together. If a man claims to have the Holy Spirit within him and yet it makes no difference in how he thinks and lives and behaves toward other people, then his hope is false. "God's love has been poured into our hearts through the Holy Spirit which has been given to us." God loves us, and we love others. "We know that we have passed out of death into life, because we love the brethren" (1 John 3:14, rsv).

This hope can enable you and me to face life today undaunted. The ultimate enemy, death, cannot destroy our confident assurance that God will create "new heavens and a new earth." The crises that again and again burst rudely into our lives, such as failure in marriage, in business, or in health—these cannot destroy the bright confidence that God is doing great things in our lives even in the hour of our suffering. And certainly the little difficulties and vexations of everyday living are not too much for God, and what God has promised will make all of them more bearable, and actually shame us for our preoccupation with trivialities while God is offering his glory to us.

Accept the suffering of the present moment. Don't regard as the sign of God's rejection of you the pain that he lets you feel. Rather, look at it as a token of his acceptance. "For whom the Lord loveth he chasteneth, and scourgeth every son whom he receiveth" (Heb. 12:6). As theologian Karl Barth put it, "The gate at which all hope seems lost is the place at which it is continually renewed."—James W. Cox

Illustrations

UNDERSTANDING. I preached with vigor against the racist attitudes I heard in my first little church. Later, my sermons became tempered as I really got to know these people. I was still against racism and thought it an offense against the gospel. But I came to admit that many of my racial attitudes had been conditioned by my education, my family, and my experiences—privileges that had been denied most members of my congregation. Many of their attitudes were due to simple ignorance or lack of exposure to others. Their racism was still a sin, but at least it was a more understandable sin and my lack of racism seemed less a virtue than a mere circumstance of fate.—William H. Willimon

PERMEATED. In a celebrated passage Arthur Gossip tells how he noticed in the Hebrides that you never get away from the sea. Inland it thrusts arms at you, at every turn you see its grayness or glitter; the tang and the roaring of its breakers come to nostril and ear. The ocean has soaked into the people's very soul, so that even in their music one can hear the sobbing and the cluck and the gurgling ripple of great waters. Christians, the common day can so be permeated with the scents and sounds and mysteries of a God who walks beside us.—Frederick B. Speakman

A KEY TO COMFORT. When John Bright lost his lovely young wife, his friend Richard Cobden came to comfort him in his blinding grief. Cobden told Bright about the thousands of British homes which were in the shadow of hunger because of the Corn Laws, and challenged the brilliant statesman to go out and help relieve the suffering. In going forth to lift the burdens of others, John Bright found solace in his own sorrow.—Ralph W. Sockman

Sermon Suggestions

OF SHEEP AND SHEPHERDS. TEXT: Jer. 23:1–6. (1) *The historical situation:* The rulers of God's people failed God and the people and invited God's displeasure. (2) *A relevant application:* Those who presume to lead and protect God's people a., must do their work on the basis of God's will; b., or will see their efforts come to naught (see 1 Cor. 3).

CHRISTIAN UNITY. TEXT: Eph. 2:11–22. (1) It is the goal of God. (2) It is possible because of the cross of Christ. (3) It is realized by participation "in one Spirit" (verse 18).

Worship Aids

CALL TO WORSHIP. "Delight thyself also in the Lord; and he shall give thee the desires of thine heart. Commit thy way unto the Lord; trust also in him; and he shall bring it to pass" (Ps. 37:4–5).

INVOCATION. O God, humble our hearts before thee, that we may truly know thee; soften our hearts toward thee, that we may gladly obey thee; lift up our hearts in thy joy, that we may exalt thee.

OFFERTORY SENTENCE. "Every man according as he purposeth in his heart, so let him give; not grudgingly, or of necessity: for God loveth a cheerful giver" (2 Cor. 9:7).

OFFERTORY PRAYER. Lord, may what we give and what we keep, what we own and what we desire to own, be conformed to your holy will, our strength and our Redeemer.—E. Lee Phillips

PRAYER. Somehow, amid all the noise and hurry of life, may we find you, Father. We get so busy with small deeds and limited activities that we neglect the larger matters of life, like faith development, in-depth learning of things of the spirit, or meaningful understanding of the use of the adversities of life for our growth and development. We need to find you, for we cannot handle the many intrusions which disturb us without divine insight and help. In our more sane moments we know that it is not you who have abandoned us, rather it is we who have turned from following after you. So this morning, Father, show us how to find you in power and love, peace and purpose.

Indeed we find ourselves facing some new realities, many of which we would not have chosen for ourselves. In the power of your Spirit may we be reinforced in our knowledge that we do not have to be victims of the struggles of life, but can be victors in spite of them. Call us to the cross that we might understand this truth more clearly. Remind us of the victory of life Jesus wrenched from the agony of death. In the light of that truth give us the poise of faith when life for us becomes difficult and threatening.

We pray this morning that the good work you have begun in us as a congregation may continue and grow that we might truly be a light shining as on a hill, giving hope to all who are tossed on the storm-driven oceans of life. Make of us a haven of salvation, an instrument of redemption and a vessel of hope for all who come our way. May healing come in the marketplace, in homes, in legislative halls, and among nations as we more closely attend to your Word and follow your leadership in the days and months before us.

Now in eagerness we wait for you to do with us and among us whatever is your good pleasure, in Christ's name.—Henry Fields

LECTIONARY MESSAGE

Topic: Jesus, the Real Miracle

TEXT: Mark 6:30–44, 53–56

Unless we can believe in miracles, we cannot believe in a personal God. The reason is quite simple. A God remote and uninvolved in the world would not have any reason to demonstrate his presence in the world or concern for it. And thus, we would never know him.

But a personal God, one who desires the kind of relationship that our Father desires with his children, transcends the laws of the universe he has so carefully constructed and leaves miracles in his wake as he visits mankind. Because God is superior to the universe as he has created it, we call it a miracle to see him do things that we cannot understand through our limited world view. In this we are like the disciples.

Here in Mark 6 the apostles had just returned, having been sent out by Jesus and had themselves done many wondrous deeds as authorized by their Lord. But upon relating to Jesus all that they had done, no doubt with amazement and excitement, they apparently did not realize the implications of these deeds. Their faith fell short upon seeing the huge crowds and upon hearing Jesus as he instructed them to feed the crowds. They failed to use their earlier experiences as a basis for faith and expectation of other miracles from their Lord. For Jesus again patiently demonstrated to them the presence of God as he gathered the crowds and broke the bread and fish till all were filled. In this demonstration the disciples learned important things about Jesus and miracles.

I. First, they learned that Jesus was not limited by their inability to provide. When Jesus told them to feed the crowds they replied to Jesus, "Shall we go and buy two hundred denarii worth of bread, and give it to them to eat?" They had probably never seen two hundred denarii. Certainly they did not carry that much money. How could they possibly feed such a crowd on their meager savings? They had apparently forgotten that they had just come back from preaching where they cast out many demons and anointed with oil many that were sick and healed them, all done upon the authority of the one who just told them to feed the crowds.

No doubt Jesus sighed within himself. One can almost hear Jesus echo the words of Moses, "Step back and see the salvation of the Lord." How many times do we have to be shown God's power in our lives and his ability to transcend every situation we face? Our faith seems so small. Are there miracles we fail to see?

II. Second, while the apostles were no doubt amazed to watch the fish and loaves multiply, for Jesus this miracle was not unusual. He knew the Father so intimately that there was never a doubt in his mind that the compassion he felt for the crowds' wanderings and hunger could be met by all the resources of heaven.

He was able to diagnose the ills of people, whether they were straining to touch the hem of his garment for healing or huddled in large gatherings hoping for a taste of bread or a glimpse of him. Jesus wanted to demonstrate to the apostles very clearly that their reliance had to shift away from their resources to those of the Father. To live in the miraculous as Jesus did demands that we shift our eyes away from our agenda to his.

III. Lastly, Mark seems to be quietly saying underneath all the miracles recorded in his book that the real miracle is Jesus himself. The Bible is the record of God's miraculous work leading up to the greatest miracle of all: Christ's coming as a babe in a manger, his sinless life, his atoning death, and his triumphant Resurrection.

Here in Mark is an example of the miraculous events taking place all around Jesus as demonstration of Emmanuel. Jesus lived and taught in the midst of criticism from religious leaders and skeptics. His own disciples had to be shown repeatedly miracle after miracle and told over and over again that his kingdom was a spiritual one, of heaven. But he endured patiently and let those around him see it clearly as he broke loaves and fish and healed those who touched him. And we are the recipients of Mark's record and testimony of these wondrous events, all of which proclaim that the greatest miracle is Jesus. —Ronald W. Johnson

SUNDAY: JULY TWENTY-FOURTH

SERVICE OF WORSHIP

Sermon: Faith's Foundations: The Centrality of Christ

TEXT: John 14:1

This chapter of the Bible is a favorite of church members, and even those whose church-going is confined to an occasional funeral service have heard it many times. Which of us doesn't respond in moments of stress to the simple and satisfying beauty of the words: "Let not your heart be troubled"?

But suppose you had never heard those words? I think what would strike you is not so much the comforting sound of "Let not your heart be troubled" as the astonishing words that follow: "You believe in God, believe also in me." For in that little word "also" lies the unique claim of the Christian religion. This is where Christianity parts company with all other religions. Moses doesn't say this. Mohammed doesn't say this. "Believe also in me." The trust, the confidence, the awareness, the worship that are due to

God alone are to be given to him. And if we want to ask the natural question "why?" the answer is given later in the chapter in the simple but dazzling words: "He who has seen me has seen the Father."

I. So we met the Christian claim head-on this morning. I have no desire to explain it away. The Church has not endured for two thousand years with the message "You believe in God, and Jesus was a very good man." Its slogan was "Jesus is Lord," and that remains our central creed.

(a) "You believe in God, believe also in me." These words imply what is known as the "divinity of Christ." I know from experience that this is the one point at which many sincere seekers for a faith to live by are held back from membership in the Christian Church. I have more respect for such inquirers than for those who mumble the orthodoxies of the faith without real conviction, or enjoy singing hymns of praise to the Lord Jesus simply because they like the tune. There are, of course, loyal church members who still have trouble with this belief. Don't we all, when it comes to putting it into words? But they, like me, are content to say that we are a group of people who are seeking to understand more fully what is meant by saying that "Jesus Christ is our Lord and Savior." And I invite those who are feeling the tug of Christ on their hearts and minds to listen to him—and not to those who want to ram some dogma down their throats.

(b) From what I hear from those who are bothered by the phrase "Jesus is Lord," they don't want to unite with any community that claims to know the whole truth and damns all other religions as false. There is a natural reluctance to commit oneself to any belief that seems to consign other religions to outer darkness. Not long ago there was a kind of religious imperialism in the churches of the Western world that, in the name of Christ, dismissed even the most saintly adherent of another faith as a godless infidel. There are some who think that this is still the attitude of the Church in its world-mission today. There has, in fact,

been a sea-change. Those who represent us of the historic churches in other parts of the world approach other religions with deep respect. They don't think of themselves as thrusting our religion on others but simply, like the first missionaries of the Church, as bearing witness to Christ as the Savior of all, the Light of the World.

(c) What some do not understand is that it is possible to hold fast to the centrality of Christ as lord of all, and to desire to share our discovery of him, without any arrogance or denigration of other faiths. What threatens our churches today is not that old religious imperialism, but rather the loss of nerve, the loss of conviction, the false ecumenism that seeks to eliminate all that is distinctively Christian in order to arrive at a goulash religion with no real convictions at all.

II. "You believe in God," says Christ, "believe also in me." Belief in God can mean everything or almost nothing. The Christian is one who says: "I know whom I have believed"—and it is the God who reaches us in Christ.

(a) I believe that Christ is my Lord and my God because I find that from the very beginning my thoughts of God were thoughts about Jesus, my picture of God was a picture of Jesus. Ask anyone who claims to believe in God what his God is like, in this part of the world, and you get an answer that is based on what we know of Jesus. Apart from him what evidence have we, for instance, that God is love? There is plenty in the world to disprove that proposition. Why do we believe that God can be so near us that we can speak to him as children to a parent? Isn't it because Jesus has taught us to say: "Our Father"?

(b) I would say to anyone who worries about the doctrine of the deity of Christ something like this: "Forget the theological or philosophical arguments. While you worry about these Christ has already come to meet you. He has come in the image of God you have accepted in your mind. He has come in those moments when you realized that the God you turn to is offering the very gifts that Jesus offered, according to the records— forgiveness of your sins, spiritual power for your daily life, and the conviction that you are destined for something more than life that ceases when the curtain drops.

III. Yes, God reveals himself everywhere as the Light that shines in the darkness. Yes, God has made known to all his will for his human family. Yes, God has spoken through many holy men and women and especially through those inspired writers, the Hebrew prophets. As the epistle to the Hebrews says: "When in former times God spoke to our forefathers, he spoke in fragmentary and varied fashion through the prophets. But in this final age he has spoken to us in his Son." There is the news that shook the world.

(a) Thus Christ lights up for us all that we seek to know of God. Once he breaks through to us we cannot call him anything but Lord—which was the divine name in the Old Testament so holy that it was literally unspeakable. Now that supreme and distant Lord has the warmth and reality of Jesus Christ. For the Christian there are not two Gods. When we say "The Lord is my Shepherd," it is Jesus we are thinking of. When we hear Job cry out through his agony: "Oh, that I knew where I might find him," and then find the courage to say: "He knoweth the way I take; when he hath tried me I shall come forth as gold," that "he" for us is the Jesus who suffers for us and with us. And when we read: "All we like sheep have gone astray; we have turned every one to his own way, and the Lord hath laid on him the iniquity of us all" it is the cross of Christ that rises up behind these words.

(b) In our world, with its relentless machinery of discovery, we all long for the human touch. And in our religious jungle our longing is the same. What the Christian gospel offers is exactly that— the human touch of Christians who care. And why do we care? Because at the center of our religion is nothing other than the human touch of God. And his name is Jesus Christ.

Illustrations

FAITH UNDER FIRE.   There is suffering in the world. We have answers that help, but they are partial. Faith, after all, is not faith any more if it is certainty. We believe, and yet we do not. We lament, and yet we hope. We die, and yet we live. God has sent us words to help us understand and endure our sufferings. He has sent us his Son so that we may know what kind of a God he is and so that we may find it easier to believe, even in the midst of suffering. In times of trial, we, like our biblical ancestors, may wish for more. But what he has given us is enough.

"My grace is sufficient for you, for my power is made perfect in weakness" (2 Cor. 12:9).—Daniel J. Simundson

FRUIT BEARING.   When I was a boy, we had a huge fig tree beside our back porch. Its trunk was big and strong. Its foliage provided a dense canopy that shaded the porch. Best of all, its branches were covered with figs. In time, however, the branches of taller trees spread over it and cut off the light from the sun. The foliage became less dense with each passing year. The limbs became weak and broke off. Within a few years, the tree stopped bearing fruit. It became a stunted shrub, and then it died. Just like our old fig tree, Christians derive their strength and life-giving power to produce fruit from an external source. Without the constant giving of that source, the plant and the Christian cannot bear fruit.—Harry L. Poe

Sermon Suggestions

A SINNER COVERS HIS TRACKS.   TEXT: 2 Sam. 11:1–15. (1) The temptation, verses 1–3. (2) The sin, verses 4–5. (3) The attempted cover-up, verses 6–15. (4) The bottom line, verse 27b.

AN APOSTOLIC INTERCESSION FOR US. TEXT: Eph. 3:14–21. (1) That we may have inner strength. (2) That we may experience the indwelling presence of Christ. (3) That we may know "the fullness of God" in comprehending the dimensions of the love of Christ.

Worship Aids

CALL TO WORSHIP. "Whatsoever things are true, whatsoever things are honest, whatsoever things are pure, whatsoever things are lovely, whatsoever things are of good report; if there be any virtue, and if there be any praise, think on these things" (Phil. 4:8).

INVOCATION. Father, we have gathered in this sacred place at this holy hour to worship you. Around all that we do we have erected a ritual designed to enable us to withdraw from the demands of life and concentrate on the things of God. May our preparation be a channel whereby we encounter your living Spirit. May our praise be a vessel pouring out our joy from the depths of our souls. May our listening be attuned to hear some mighty redeeming and guiding word from you. May our commitment rest on the sure foundation of experienced faith. O Father, lead us through this sacred hour that when we come to its end we will know that we have been in the very presence of Almightiness, even as did those disciples whom Jesus taught to pray: (Lord's Prayer). —Henry Fields

OFFERTORY SENTENCE. "God is able to give you more than you need, so that you will always have all you need for yourselves and more than enough for every good cause" (2 Cor. 9:8 [TEV]).

OFFERTORY PRAYER. Gracious Lord, thou hast given us all things to enjoy, to share with others, and to make us better and more useful servants of thine. Now deepen our love, open our hands, and help us to know the joy of a cheerful giver.

PRAYER. O God who watches over the destiny of men and of nations, may we bring to these momentous, exciting times that sense of destiny that we have been born to the kingdom for such a time as this—"that we fail not man nor thee." It seems that sometimes the things for which we pray we have difficulty in receiving, or believing in, when they are offered or given: "We believe, help our nonbelief!"

We should know from the history of your people Israel that when those who claim your name fail to give leadership to your world purpose, you raise up leaders from the most unlikely places. That one man—a foreigner—in the face of the mistrust of some and the skepticism of many should turn the tide from war to peace in a few short years is almost more than some of us can grasp. The dawning of the new day is too blinding for eyes that have become so accustomed to living in the darkness of hostility, mistrust, doubt. Is it that we are too small—too parochial, too sectarian, too nationalistic to catch the vision that you dream for all peoples? This is no time for timid reaction but for bold response. Forgive us our slowness of heart to believe when your love and grace goes out to all others whoever the others may be.

We praise you for your Word of forgiveness and reconciliation so faithfully and insightfully proclaimed on this occasion. As the ecclesia, the called out ones, the Church, we are entrusted with the gospel of reconciliation and pray for a renewed sense of mission that through this congregation we may go into all the world and all the worlds of persons as the Master has commissioned us. May we realize that a faith that is not shared is soon lost.

For this household of faith where your love, your forgiveness, are so real, we praise you. May we embrace in the strength of your love those among us who are ill, those facing the loneliness of bereavement, those made anxious with difficult decisions. May all of us through an increase of faith discover those unfailing resources of your spirit by which we may live to your glory through him who for the joy that was set before him endured the cross despising the shame, and as our risen Lord is among us now.—John Thompson

LECTIONARY MESSAGE

Topic: Bread and Water

TEXT: John 6:1–21

The miracles of Jesus provide a model for ministry. Although only a few Christians are called to ministry as a vocation, all Christians are called to ministry as Christian service. Although even fewer Christians are called to a miracle-working ministry, all Christians are to model their ministries after the Master.

I. Providing the bread (vv. 1–15). Jesus' feeding of the five thousand is the only miracle performed by our Lord which is described in all four gospels. Just as this story was important to the evangelists as a picture of Christ's ministry, so this miracle should be important to us as a paradigm for our ministries.

(a) Seeing the need: Jesus' question (vv. 1–6, especially v. 5). Like Moses of old, in v. 3 we see Jesus "seated, as on a new Sinai, with his disciples around him" (R.H. Lightfoot). Jesus takes the initiative. His question in v. 5 not only identifies the need of the people for food, but points to the major obstacles which prevents "business as usual" from meeting the need.

Jesus' question recalls Moses' cry in the wilderness, "Where am I to get meat to give to all this people?" (Num. 11:13a NRSV). The great difference, however, is that Jesus already "knew what he was going to do" (v. 6). John tells us that Jesus is testing Philip. Jesus wants to discover if his disciples, personified by Philip, really know who he is.

(b) Organizing the response: Jesus' action (vv. 7–11, especially v. 11). Philip fails the test. He does not understand the true identity of Jesus, but instead v. 7 shows that Philip "deals with the Lord's question solely at the economic level" (Lightfoot).

In contrast, Andrew's concerns (vv. 8–9) are not economic, but pragmatic: "Here is something to eat, but with these small resources how can even Jesus meet the needs of the multitude?"

Barley loaves (v. 9) are "the bread of the poor" (George Beasley-Murray). Readers of the gospel who were steeped in the Old Testament might recall the story of Elisha miraculously feeding a hundred men with twenty barley loaves (2 Kings 4:42–44).

Jesus performs this miracle not only to meet the people's needs but as a sign of who he is. Likewise, our ministries should not just meet needs, but also should be signs of our identity as followers of Christ. Jesus' action has a fourfold pattern: he takes the loaves, gives thanks, distributes them, and then gathers up the fragments. This protocol strikingly resembles the actions of the Lord's Supper. Ministry and symbol are united in a common pattern.

(c) Picking up the pieces: Jesus' direction (vv. 12–15, especially v. 12). The need to "gather up the fragments left over" (v. 12) is characteristic of any significant ministry. In Jesus' miracle there were many pieces. Each of the twelve baskets was "a large, heavy basket" (Greek *kophinos*—Bauer, Arndt, and Gingrich).

Jesus is aware of the dangers of political reactions to his ministry. The people (v. 14) identify Jesus with Moses' prophecy in Deuteronomy 18:15, "The Lord your God will raise up for you a prophet like me from among your own people; you shall heed such a prophet." As Beasley-Murray observes, "The step from a prophet like Moses (v. 14), the first Redeemer and worker of miracles, to a Messianic deliverer [v. 15] was a short one for contemporary enthusiasts in Israel to make."

II. Passing over the sea (vv. 16–21). How does ministry in the name of Jesus overcome fear? John focuses this miracle story upon Christ's assuring revelation of himself in verse 20: "It is I [Greek *ego eimi*]; do not be afraid." (This foreshadows the other "I am" declarations of Jesus in vv. 35, 41, 48, 51, and throughout John's Gospel.)

The disciples were afraid. (This is the only place in the Gospel of John where we see the disciples' fear in relation to Jesus.) Like so many people today, they were without Jesus on a rough sea in the dark, with a strong wind blowing (vv. 17–18).

They were terrified that the figure of Jesus might be an apparition or a ghost. But they were reassured, in the midst of the storm, by hearing Christ's voice. So, the chapter moves from "the Lord's works" to "the Lord's words" (Lightfoot). May our ministries today enable those in fear to hear the reassuring voice of Jesus.—Charles J. Scalise

SUNDAY: JULY THIRTY-FIRST

SERVICE OF WORSHIP

Sermon: The Kingdom of God is Predicated Upon Human Relationships

TEXT: Luke 16:19–31

Our Gospel this morning is that familiar story between Dives and Lazarus. It is very difficult for us to listen to Jesus. It was even more difficult for the disciples in that day and age to hear Jesus, because he was taking a very familiar story and telling it in a very different way.

It was a familiar story to all those who surrounded Jesus. They knew the story, but the story they knew was that those who have a good life here will be deprived in the life after death, and those who are tormented and deprived in this life will live sumptuously in the afterlife. When we listen to Jesus tell the story as the people knew it and then move on and give it a very different meaning, we *listen.*

I. What Jesus does is take the obvious and ask us to look beyond it.

(a) What Jesus is attempting to show us in this story is the relationship between Dives and Lazarus. When I insulate myself from those around me, there is a great chasm created between me and the promises of God. Jesus is describing the kingdom of God, and the kingdom of God is predicated upon human relationships. That is God's treasure. And that is the point of Jesus telling this story.

(b) Psychologically, we, like Dives of old, are frightened, so we clothe ourselves in all the trappings of separation. Jesus is addressing, in this parable, the problem that we all experience: the temptation to somehow separate ourselves from the agonies that surround us. It is at once a very exciting age that you and I are privileged to share and a very demanding age, demanding because we all must deal with the stranger in ourselves and the stranger in our society.

II. Do you believe in resurrection? Most people do in all cultural settings and religious traditions, in one fashion or another.

(a) Our text says that Abraham replied to Dives that he had Moses and the prophets to listen to during his lifetime, but Dives, not satisfied with that, wanted to live in a two-dimensional cardboard universe wherein somehow, dramatically, miraculously, one would rise from the dead. Then presumably the brothers of Dives would not have to deal with the day to day, hour to hour struggle of becomingness. They would not have to wrestle with the promises of God and the problems of our civilization.

(b) You and I know we do not have to walk within a block in the city of Boston to see many examples of Lazarus. But the divine secret that our Lord sets before us this morning is that I can only bring my life to fruition and discover God's resurrection in my life, in my soul, when I first find it in another. The kingdom of God is predicated upon human relationships.

III. In his parable, our Lord said to his disciples of all time, when you and I bring our gift to the altar of God, and there remember that our brother or sister has ought against us, we need go to them and be reconciled before we bring our gift to God.

When we seek confidence, fulfillment, resurrection in life, we hear the Lord Christ say to us, open your life where you truly live to the secrets and promises of God, and go forth in humanity to discover God's resurrection, God's hope, God's compassion in another.—Spencer M. Rice

Illustrations

OUTREACH. The church has been called a glacier at times because it seems too slow-moving, is often cold to human needs, and picks up all it can along the way in a self-serving way.

Even if there is only a grain of truth to such a criticism, we must recognize that when glaciers finally reach the sea they usually break up into hundreds and thousands of icebergs that move toward the open water, latching on to the swiftest current passing by. And they melt—both by the direct rays of the sun, and indirectly by the sun-warmed water.

In other words, the coldest church may still be a missionizing church, for when it sends its icy members into the mainstream of life, their hearts will be warmed by human needs around them, and in being melted by the sun of righteousness, they will add to the world's betterment by the total giving of themselves as Christ's witnesses.

Such a church, it should be observed, can never call its iceberg flock together again, for such a church could never be the same glacier as before.—Richard Andersen

REBIRTH. The ideal marriage is not merely a union to which children are born. It is a union in which husband and wife are reborn—reborn into the world of united interests, of shared joys, of vastly multiplied appreciations, of infinitely tender experiences. Husbands and wives who have lived long and happily together, who have climbed the steep ascent of success or walked through the valley of the shadow of adversity, who have come to rely more and more upon each other as the swift seasons roll—what do they say life was before they met and joined their hearts? Many of them would say with all sincerity and without a trace of sentimentality, "That single life wasn't living."—Ralph W. Sockman.

Sermon Suggestions

A SINNER FACES HIS SIN.   TEXT: 2 Sam. 12:13–22:26. (1) *Situation:* David com-

mitted adultery with Bathsheba. (2) *Complication:* David's attempts to cover up his sin failed. David got deeper and deeper into sin. (3) *Resolution:* Though David could not undo his wrongs, God graciously confronted David through his prophet Nathan and brought David to repentance.

UNITY AND DIVERSITY.   TEXT: Eph. 4:1–16. (1) A plea for unity, verses 1–3. (2) The argument for unity, verses 4–6. (3) The means of unity, verses 7–13. (4) The achievement of unity, verses 14–16.

Worship Aids

CALL TO WORSHIP.   "Know therefore that the Lord thy God, he is God, the faithful God, which keepeth covenant and mercy with them that love him and keep his commandments to a thousand generations" (Deut. 7:9).

INVOCATION.   Enter our hearts, O Lord, as only you can, as only you are meant to, as only a Creator can do for the created, and make us all your own.— E. Lee Phillips

OFFERTORY SENTENCE.   "God, who supplies seed for the sower and bread to eat, will also supply you with all the seed you need and will make it grow and produce a rich harvest from your generosity" (2 Cor. 9:10).

OFFERTORY PRAYER.   We could not be here today, our Father, if thou hadst not given us our daily bread. As thou hast provided for our needs through thy manifold mercies, now make us instruments of that same providence that others' needs may also be met.

PRAYER.   We praise thee, O God, for our friends, the doctors and nurses, who seek the healing of our bodies. We bless thee for their gentleness and patience, for their knowledge and skill. We remember the hours of our suffering when they brought relief, and the days of our fear and anguish at the bedsides of our dear ones when they came as ministers of

God to save the lives thou hadst given. May we reward their fidelity and devotion by our loving gratitude, and do thou uphold them by the satisfaction of work well done.

We rejoice in the tireless daring with which some are now tracking the great slayers of mankind by the white light of science. Grant that under their teaching we may grapple with the sins which have ever dealt death to the race, and that we may so order the life of our communities that none may be doomed to an untimely death for lack of the simple gifts which thou hast given in abundance.—Walter Rauschenbusch

LECTIONARY MESSAGE

Topic: Bread Across the Water

Text: John 6:24–35

Once people know that you are serving a free lunch, they will always be at your door. Church soup kitchens are not known for complaining of a lack of clientele! When ministries successfully meet physical needs, they soon struggle with how to keep from being overwhelmed by the demand.

I. The bread of miracles (vv. 24–27) After feeding the five thousand, Jesus wisely moves on to Capernaum. The people, however, find themselves hungry again for some of that miraculous bread. They commandeer some boats and come "looking for Jesus" (v. 24).

Although the multitude is "looking for Jesus," they are really only seeking their own self-fulfillment. This is one of those points at which a crowd of modern church-goers has more in common with a crowd of Galilean peasants than we like to admit.

The crowd has missed the deeper meaning of Jesus' miracle of feeding. They only saw the bread, but missed the reality to which it pointed. Their focus upon material things causes them to miss the spiritual significance of Jesus' sign. So, Jesus' reply in verse 26 is emphatic ("very truly I tell you") and sharp ("because you ate your fill of the loaves"). Jesus is not naive about the true motivation of his popular following. Unlike many religious leaders, he is not afraid to jeopardize his standing with the crowd by telling them the truth.

Jesus urges his followers to work for spiritual food (v. 27). By faith they can do the work of God (cf. v. 29). Jesus teaches that we should not center our lives upon perishable food, but upon the food which "endures for eternal life" (v. 27).

Using a similar image, the book of Isaiah had called Israel to the word of God: "Ho, everyone who thirsts, come to the waters; and you that have no money, come, buy, and eat! Come, buy wine and milk without money and without price" (Isa. 55:1 NRSV; cf. also 49:10a). God's grace is a priceless spiritual gift, which cannot be purchased or manipulated.

In his remarkable dialogue with the woman at the well, Jesus promises his gift of living water: "those who drink of the water that I give them will never be thirsty" (John 4:13).

II. The bread of life (vv. 28–35) The crowd, of course, wants to know how "to perform the works of God" (v. 28), so that they can get some more of that miraculous food. Jesus does not respond with a spiritual "how to" manual (e.g., "Ten Easy Steps to the Bread of Miracles"). He instead discusses the necessity of faith to do the work of God (v. 29). Faith itself is the greatest work, which underlies all true action by the followers of Jesus. Without faith our works mean nothing, but our faith does not exist without works that embody it. Jesus calls his disciples to a work of faith, which shapes their daily lives.

In response, the people clamor for Jesus to do another work—like the ancient miracle of manna (vv. 30–31). The rabbis interpreted passages like Exod. 16:4, "I am going to rain bread from heaven to you," to mean that the Messiah would bring manna from heaven. So, the crowd is challenging Jesus, "If you're the Messiah, do the sign we expect, and bring down manna from heaven." They don't want just barley bread and fishes (vv. 9–11); they want manna—the "wonder bread" from heaven!

But Jesus knows that manna is a spiritual sign, not just a physical food. God provides it, not Moses. Manna is "a parable of the real food God gives" (John Marsh). The Incarnation—not physical bread—is the long-awaited manna from heaven of the prophecy.

Yet the crowd continues to misunderstand Jesus (one of John's favorite ways to set the stage for Jesus' self-revelation). The people just want this bread of miracles all the time (v. 34).

Then Jesus plainly declares to them that he is the Bread of Life (v. 35; cf. v.

48). The title means that Jesus is "the bread that gives life" (R. E. Brown). Like bread, Jesus is necessary for life. Coming to Jesus is not like eating some spiritual dessert; it is like being sustained by the main course. Jesus himself is the Messiah who incarnates the Bread of Life.

We are spiritually fed by the presence of Christ. So, when people come to our ministries looking for a free lunch, will we serve them the Bread of Life?—Charles J. Scalise

SUNDAY: AUGUST SEVENTH

SERVICE OF WORSHIP

Sermon: Death Is More Friend than Foe

TEXT: Romans 8:31–37

I want to talk about death, but not because I am feeling morbid, sad, or even old. "Old" to me is when you get into your rocking chair and have trouble getting it started. "Old" is when you get winded playing checkers. "Old" is when the only glint in your eye comes from the sun hitting your trifocals just right. No, I want to talk of death because it is good, from time to time, to contemplate the end towards which, with irreversible steps, we all walk.

Let us take as a text three words of Paul found in 1 Corinthians 13:8, "Love never ends." Love feels just like that, doesn't it? Love feels like it's forever. And because love refuses to be imprisoned by time, when someone we love dies, grief renders everything unreal. But when unbearable grief becomes bearable sorrow, we can profitably meditate on certain truths about death.

I. In the first place, death is not the enemy we generally make it out to be. Consider only the alternative, life without death. Life without death would be interminable—literally, figuratively. We'd take days just to get out of bed, weeks to decide what to do next. Students would never graduate, and faculty meetings, deacon meetings, and all kinds of other meetings would go on for months.

Chances are, we'd be as bored as the ancient Greek gods and up to their same silly tricks. Death cannot be the enemy if it is death that brings us to life. You see what I'm after: just as without leave-taking, there can be no arrival; just as without a growing old, there can be no growing up; just as without tears, no laughter; so without death, there could be no living. So let us pause to thank, with brief thanksgiving, our Creator who so organized things that "all mortal flesh is as the grass" (Prov. 40:6).

Death enhances not only our individual life, but our common life as well. Death *is* the great equalizer—not because death makes us equal, but because death mocks our pretensions at being anything else. In the face of death, all differences of race and class and nationality become known for the trivial things they ultimately are. I love the old Moravian cemeteries, which house no pyramids to the ego, all tombstones being flat; and when Mrs. Schmidt dies, her final resting place is next to the person who died just before her in the community. What a wonderful thing it would be if the structure of Moravian cemeteries could also influence our communal life!

I recently learned something else about death, something quite wonderful and unexpected. In Arthur Miller's play *After the Fall*, one of the characters cries out, "Good God, why is betrayal the only truth that sticks?" That's a truth that most of us know well! What I hadn't known was that death has a way with grievances, a way quite wonderfully described in a sonnet of John Greenleaf Whittier's called "Forgiveness":

My heart was heavy, for its trust had been
Abused, its kindness answered with foul wrong:
So, turning gloomily from my fellow men,
One summer Sabbath-day, I strolled among
The green mounds of the village burial place;
Where pondering how all human love and hate
Find one sad level, and how, soon or late,
Wronged and wrongdoer, each with meekened face,
And cold hands folded over a still heart,
Pass the green threshold of our common grave,
Whither all footsteps tend, whence none depart,
Awed for myself and pitying my race,
Our common sorrow, like a mighty wave
Swept all my pride away, and trembling, I forgave.

When my son was killed in January 1983, sorrow "like a mighty wave, swept all my pride away," and I realized that as never before, I was able to forgive someone who had hurt me deeply. It made me see how, in one more way, the death of someone we love can change us, not from what we were, so much as toward what we essentially are—loving, forgiving people.

II. Which leads to the next point: what are we to say when someone dies too soon, of an accident, of cancer, of AIDS? One thing we must never say is that it is the will of God. No one knows that for sure, so let no one pretend he or she does. Why would it be the will of God that a particular person die young, while the rest of us live on? What we *can* say are St. Paul's words, "Love never ends"; because as St. Paul also says, "I am per-

suaded that neither death nor life . . . can separate us from the love of God" (Rom. 8:38). In other words, the abyss of love is deeper than the abyss of death. That means our own loves—pale reflections of God's love—are right to reject death. And we can say more: The seers and saints, those most attentive to God's presence in this word, have always claimed that the best lies ahead. Bach entitled one of his greatest arias, "Komm, susser Tod" (Come Sweet Death) and an American slave saw "a band of angels coming for to carry me home."

Of course, life after death can no more be proved than disproved. "For nothing worth proving can be proven, nor yet disproven" as Tennyson said. As a child in a womb cannot conceive of life with air and light—the very stuff of our existence—so it is hard for us to conceive of any other life without the sustaining forces to which we are accustomed. But consider this: if we are essentially spirit, not flesh, if what is substantial is intangible, if we are spirits that have bodies and not the other way around; then it makes sense that just as musicians can abandon their instruments to find others elsewhere, so at death our spirits can leave our bodies and find other forms in which to make new music.

III. And one more thought: Love is its own reward. For its inspiration, love does not depend on the pay it receives, which is why, out of hand, we have to reject all notions of heaven as pie in the sky by and by—deferred gratification. (I hate the way some evangelists try to overcome my selfishness by appealing to my selfish motives!) But the fact of the matter is, love does have a reward. Just as the proper benefits of education are the opportunities of continuing education, so the rewards of loving are to become yet more vulnerable, more tender, more caring. It is also a fact that human life aspires beyond its grasp. As God led Moses to the mountaintop, so life leads us to a place where we can view a land that is promised but never reached. To me, it is hard to believe that a loving God would create loving creatures who aspire to be yet more loving, and then finish them off before their aspirations are complete. There must be something more.

But again, we don't know the circumstances. We know only who, not what, is beyond the grave. This side of the grave, we are like the Swiss child asked by a traveler, "Where is Kandesteg?" The child answered, "I cannot tell you where Kandesteg is, but there is the road." We are on the road to heaven if today we walk with God. Eternal life is not a possession conferred at death, it is a present endowment. We live it now, and continue it through death.

Death is not the enemy. If death enhances both our individual and common life, and if death is no threat to our relationship with God, then death is more friend than foe. The good news is, "Whether we live or whether we die, we are the Lord's" (Rom. 14:8).—William Sloane Coffin

Illustrations

ACTIVE LIFE. I have known so many people, especially men, who fall into despair when their "active lives" end at retirement. They withdraw from the work they have been doing, and it is as if they had withdrawn their hands from a pool of water: The water closes up as if their hands had never been there. True despair is the failure to learn before we die that the water eventually closes up over everything, that we never manage to leave the indelible marks of our dreams. But once we learn that, and once the gifts of life are acknowledged, we can proceed to be makers in new and more hopeful ways.—Parker J. Palmer

IN THE DEATH CAMP. Another time we were at work in a trench. The dawn was grey around us; grey was the sky above; grey the snow in the pale light of dawn; grey the rags in which my fellow prisoners were clad, and grey their faces. I was again conversing silently with my wife, or perhaps I was struggling to find the reason for my sufferings, my slow dying. In a last violent protest against the hopelessness of imminent death, I sensed my spirit piercing through the enveloping gloom. I felt it transcend that hopeless, meaningless world, and from somewhere I heard a victorious "Yes" in answer to my question of the existence of an ultimate purpose. At that moment a light was lit in a distant farmhouse, which stood on the horizon as if painted there, in the midst of the miserable grey of a dawning morning in Bavaria. "Et lux in tenebris lucet"—and the light shineth in the darkness.—Victor Frankl

Sermon Suggestions

A FATHER'S RELENTLESS LOVE. TEXT: 2 Sam. 18:5–9, 15, 31–33. (1) Absolom's treachery. (2) David's charity. (3) David's grief.

IMITATORS OF GOD. TEXT: Eph. 4:25–5:2. (1) The right attitude: a., Negatively—putting away all that hinders; b., Positively—embracing all that heals. (2) The effective motivation: God's forgiveness in Christ of us.

Worship Aids

CALL TO WORSHIP. "Ye shall know the truth, and the truth shall make you free" (John 8:32).

INVOCATION. God, this could be the day when some truth may dawn upon us with a brighter and surer light. Open our minds and hearts to be ready to hear the old, old story with its timely message for each of us. Through him who is the Light of the World.

OFFERTORY SENTENCE. "The rendering of this service not only supplies the wants of the saints but also overflows in many thanksgivings to God" (2 Cor. 9:12 [RSV]).

OFFERTORY PRAYER. O Lord, may these gifts we bring go forth in quietness and strength to do thy work in the world, in the sanctuary and in the slums; in the healing of body, mind, and spirit; in the proclamation of the gospel at home and abroad.

PRAYER. Standing on the precipice of unknown tomorrows, we turn our thoughts and eyes upward to you, Father, seeking guidance for the journey we are called upon to make into the future. In our weakness give us strength, in our fear give us courage, in our frailties grant us stability as we begin our onward march. We know that you have revealed yourself to us in Jesus Christ. We have set out on a path to follow him. Grant that no obscuring cloud of doubt or faithlessness may turn us aside from the journey we have started in company with him. May we truly find the treasures of your grace that await us as we make our way along with the Lord of life into the unknown.—Henry Fields

LECTIONARY MESSAGE

Topic: Bread from Heaven

TEXT: John 6:35, 41–51

We spend so much of our lives focused upon and worried about material things. Whether it is bread to eat or "bread" of the financial sort, there seems to be so little time and energy to be concerned about the Bread of Life—the bread from heaven that gives eternal life. As John Marsh explains, ". . . real 'bread from heaven' is not matter dropping from the sky, but the incarnation of the Son of God."

I. Heavenly origin (vv. 35, 41–42). Jesus declares that he is the Bread of Life. Believing in Christ and coming to him cannot be separated (v. 35b, cf. vv. 64–65), for they belong together in one faith experience. The consequence of this new relationship with Jesus is that the basics of physical life—hunger and thirst—are seen in a new perspective. Our own physical hunger and thirst will seem unimportant compared to our fulfilling experience of eternal life. What really matters—the "bread" of our lives— becomes redefined in light of our encounter with Jesus.

The complaining of "the Jews" (v. 41) recalls the murmuring of Israel in the wilderness during the Exodus (Exod. 16:2–3). As George Beasley-Murray comments, "the grumbling against the message of Jesus is a rejection of Jesus himself." We are not dealing here with honest doubt or confusion regarding the origin of Jesus, but with skeptical unbelief.

The familiarity of these Galilean Jews with the hometown background of Jesus offers a plausible rationale for their unbelieving complaints (v. 42). Like Nathaniel, an earlier skeptic who became a disciple, they are doubtful whether anything of heavenly "good" can "come out of Nazareth" (1:46). The Jews doubt Jesus' divine origin because they know his parents or at least think they know of them. (Ironically, Jesus is not really "the son of Joseph" (v. 42) but the Son of God.) It is not Jesus' claim to be like bread, but his claim to be "bread *from heaven*" that is the object of complaint. The people are grumbling about Jesus' assertion of his heavenly origin.

II. Divine mission (vv. 43–46). Jesus directly challenges the complaints (v. 43). He describes his mission from God and points to the promise of the Resurrection (vv. 44ff). God the Father draws us near to Jesus, through whom we will be raised from death to life. As the book of Isaiah proclaims, "Incline your ear and come to me; listen, so that you may live" (Isa. 55:3a NRSV).

Jesus supports his response to the skeptical complainers by freely quoting a text from the prophets. He is probably referring to Isaiah 54:13, "All your children shall be taught by the Lord,. . ." (cf. also Jer. 31:34). Then Jesus describes his relationship with God the Father (v. 46) in a way which reminds us of his role as the *logos*—the true mediator between God and humanity (John 1:1–18; cf. 3:13).

III. Eternal life (vv. 47–51). Jesus contends that the real bread from heaven is not the manna that descended from heaven upon ancient Israel, but the living bread from heaven that gives eternal life. The manna which the people want Jesus to provide (cf. vv. 31ff) is just perishable food. Furthermore, the ancestors of the Jews who ate it perished as well (v. 49).

In contrast, the Bread of Life transforms death. Although physical death is not eliminated, it becomes a stage on the way to life beyond. Jesus, the living bread from heaven, brings eternal life (v. 51). The followers of Jesus are encouraged to eat the bread from heaven and thus experience eternal life.

John's focus upon the Word which became flesh in the Incarnation (1:14) and upon the physical death of Jesus on the cross (especially 19:32–35) shapes the gospel's view of the bread as flesh, both in verse 51 and throughout the next section.

The bread from heaven challenges our earth-bound, materialistic perspective and redefines the "bread" of our lives. It calls us to come to the incarnate one "who is from God" and "has seen the Father" (v. 46). It promises that, if we believe, we will not die, but will have eternal life. — Charles J. Scalise

SUNDAY: AUGUST FOURTEENTH

SERVICE OF WORSHIP

Sermon: The Hound of Heaven

TEXT: Psalm 139:7–12

When I was a boy most farmers had several dogs. Francis Thompson, an English Catholic poet, described God as a hound who pursues man in his poem, "The Hound of Heaven."

God knows our scent, and we are not hard to track. The increasing legalization of gambling, laws providing for abortion on demand, a high divorce rate, expressions of racial prejudice in which we slay our enemies rather than our enmities, a steady stream of homeless people in our streets, the easy access to drugs, and the rampant desecration of the Lord's Day are signs of our escape route.

As the hound of heaven, God is relentless in his pursuit. We try every trick in the book to throw God off the track. We lead him through every moral briar patch in our asphalt jungle. We doubleback. We become devious. We vote God "Man of the Year" and pay tribute to him in assorted currencies. We rationalize our sins. We resort to the theological trimming of God down to our size. We change our addresses.

God is never thrown off the trail. God looks in every corner: Eden, Egypt, Exile, everywhere. God is a retriever. He wants to bring us back. He wants to be our *go'el,* our redeemer, our heavenly kinsman who will emancipate us from spiritual slavery.

As the hound of heaven, God runs close to his quarry. We may follow "afar off," but God stays close to his prey. He crowds us. We can hear him breathing. We hear his whispers. When we are caught, there occurs a close encounter of a godly kind.

I. In describing God as the hound of heaven who knows our scent, we are expressing the message of Psalm 139:7–12. This entire psalm describes God as inescapable. Man is a besieged city. God has us surrounded.

(a) God is inescapable because of his habitat. Heaven, the uttermost parts of the sea, light, or darkness can be God's dwelling place. He rides upon a cherub and makes the darkness his canopy (Ps. 18:10).

(b) God is inescapable because of his habitat. God is also inescapable because of his holy love. The two greatest words in the Bible with which to describe God are the words "holy" and "love." God knows our downsitting and our uprising. God knows our thoughts (see Ps. 139:2). Still he loves us. God's love is spontaneous, sacrificial, self-giving, value creating.

(c) He is inescapable, further, because of his heart searching. Psalm 139 begins with the words, "O Lord, thou hast searched me . . ." The psalm ends with the prayer, "Search me, O God, and know my heart . . ." (v. 23). God has sworn out a search warrant for man, and he signed it with his blood.

II. For God's search to mean what it should, there must be some mutual seeking. This is the problem. Many use every resource to escape from God and not to be found by him. As I read Psalm 139, I do not pick up the impression that the psalmist wants to escape, but he certainly considers the possibility. Many today consider the possibility, and they work overtime to make the possibility a reality.

(a) Have you ever wanted to get away from it all? Have you ever wanted to close the door and never look back? Have you ever run, even from God? I suspect that every one of us at some time has at least dreamed of that tropical island where all is sunshine and comfort with no responsibilities, no deadlines, no problems, and no burdens to bear. Who of us at some time has not run from God?

(b) Some run from God by using our noisy world to drown out the voice of God. The noise of industry, the jets overhead, the television in the house, the roar of the crowd, the chatter of daily commerce, the non-stop conversation of some motormouth people are used as mufflers for the "still, small voice." Somehow, somewhere, however, that soft, penetrating, persistent voice is going to get through to us.

(c) Men run from God in many ways, but the message of Psalm 139 is that God is inescapable. When the psalmist wrote Psalm 139, he was on a high peak of inspiration. This psalm is the overflow of a life lived in intimate fellowship with God. Dr. A. F. Kirkpatrick says of this psalm, "The consciousness of the intimate personal relation between God and man which is characteristic of the whole Psalter reaches its climax here."

III. Psalm 139 mentions some obvious results of God and man tracking each other.

(a) One is praise. Verse 14 reads, "I will give thanks to thee; for I am fearfully and wonderfully made." Being found by God, we should sing "O for a thousand tongues to sing my great redeemer's praise."

The French word for "praise" is *preiser* which means "to prize." When we praise God, we prize God. When we praise God, we "press toward the goal for the prize of the upward call of God in Christ Jesus."

It has been well said that the doxology is a life to be lived as well as a song to be sung.

(b) Another result of finding God is joy. In verse 17 the psalmist declares, "How precious also are thy thoughts to me, O God!" *Webster's Dictionary* defines "joy" as "gladness, delight, or the expectation of good." Those qualities characterize our personalities when we find the Lord. The Hebrew language uses thirteen different words for "joy" or "rejoice." Four of the words mean shouting, singing, dancing, or clapping. Galatians 5:22 tells us that joy is one of the fruits of the Spirit-filled life. First Peter 1:8 describes Christians rejoicing with "joy inexpressible and full of glory."

(c) A result of our spiritual rendezvous with God is submission to the leading of God. Psalm 139 closes with the prayer, "And lead me in the everlasting way." God does lead. He is not standing still. The footprint of the obedient sheep really is found within the larger footprint of the shepherd. Too frequently, we respond to God with words from an old commercial, "Please, I want to do it myself."

The word "submit" comes from two Latin words, *sub* (under) and *mittere* (to send). To submit is to be sent under, to be sent under orders, to yield one's will. It means we become pliable clay in the hands of the master potter. It means, as Dr. John R. Sampey preached, that we should "give Christ all the keys."—William C. Lacy

Illustrations

ADDICTION AND GRACE.   After twenty years of listening to the yearnings of people's hearts, I am convinced that all human beings have an inborn desire for God. Whether we are consciously religious or not, this desire is our deepest longing and our most precious treasure. It gives us meaning. Some of us have repressed this desire, burying it beneath so many other interests that we are completely unaware of it. Or we may experience it in different ways—as a longing for wholeness, completion, or fulfillment.

Regardless of how we describe it, it is a longing for love. It is a hunger to love, to be loved, and to move closer to the source of love. This yearning is the essence of the human spirit; it is the origin of our highest hopes and most noble dreams.—Gerald G. May

A SUMMARY OF CHRISTIAN THEOLOGY. Robert Coles, professor of psychiatry and medical humanities at Harvard University, reported these words of a twelve-year-old boy in one of Coles' discussions with children about Christian salvation: "You know, I guess the Lord and us, we're all in this together: us hoping to be saved, and him wanting to save us." Coles commented: "So much complex Christian theology worked into such a disarmingly simple, folksy summary!"

Sermon Suggestions

ON PRAYING FOR THE RIGHT THING. TEXT: 1 Kings 2:10–12; 3:3–14. (1) Solomon's prayer for wisdom. (2) God's answer (see Matt. 6:33).

LIVING SMART. TEXT: Eph. 5:15–20. Biblical wisdom goes beyond conventional wisdom, yet it is prudent and sometimes profitable to: (1) Use your days in doing God's will, rather than in succumbing to the spirit of the ages; (2) Find your "highs," not in chemical stimulants, but rather by experiencing the Spirit in all circumstances.

Worship Aids

CALL TO WORSHIP. "I will praise thee with my whole heart: before the gods will I sing praise unto thee. I will worship toward thy holy temple, and praise thy name for thy loving kindness and for thy truth: for thou hast magnified thy word above all thy name" (Ps. 138:1–2).

INVOCATION. O Thou who dost neither slumber nor sleep, but keepest a watchful eye over thy creation, sustaining it by thy power and might, grant that we may join thee more heartily today in what thou seekest to do through us. May thy service in the sanctuary continue in our service outside. To that end help us to worship thee in spirit and in truth.

OFFERTORY SENTENCE. "My God shall supply all your need according to his riches in glory by Christ Jesus" (Phil. 4:19).

OFFERTORY PRAYER. Lord, reveal to us the needs of others about us as we bring our own needs before you this day, that by bearing one another's burdens we may fulfill the law of Christ and find the deeper meanings of love.—E. Lee Phillips

PRAYER. We, who would invoke your presence, O living God, are as the blind, for you are always present in the eternity of your love. In you "we live and move and have our being." You are always faithful. We are the faithless, the wanderer to the far country. How we need to pray that we may be all here—to love you with all our mind, heart, and person. As the prophet assures: "Those who seek you with all their heart shall surely find you," and as the Master promises, blessed are the pure in heart, those who concentrate, those who are of a single mind, those who are committed, for they shall see you.

Whatever our circumstance this morning, our need is a renewed vision of your glory in Christ. May we hear your call in him: "Awake you who are asleep and Christ shall give you light—life." Morning has broken. The new day has dawned. The kingdom is. Christ as the great physician unstops our ears and opens our eyes to hear the cry of the weakest and to see the furthest away, the adversary, as your child, our brother or sister.

Open our eyes to those persons with whom our lives are set for whom we have responsibility, that no one else has. Sometimes those closest in proximity are as aliens in our lack of concern, sensitivity, love.

Open our eyes to see the many persons who labor daily in our behalf that we may have nourishing food, good clothes, comfortable housing, ready transportation, instantaneous communication. We praise you for the diversity of gifts complimenting one another, contributing to the fullness of the life we enjoy.

Grant to us the eyes of faith—the insight of your Word—challenging the easy securities by which we so often choose to live, calling us to a faith for insecurity, to live on the growing edge, to live as a pilgrim looking for that city whose builder and maker you are.

We pray for all peoples, that together we may see the new thing you are doing in our day and have the faith, the courage, the love to follow this vision wherever it leads.

Heal the brokenness among us— whether of the heart, the mind, the spirit, the body—that we may glorify you as we live by your grace in Christ, who is here among us as your eternal Word teaching us to pray and live with all peoples.—John Thompson

LECTIONARY MESSAGE

Topic: Bread as Flesh

TEXT: John 6:51–58

Why is the Lord's Supper spiritual communion rather than pagan cannibalism? After all, Jesus said that we eat his flesh and drink his blood. So, isn't Christianity just a refined form of paganism?

Jesus is teaching in the synagogue at Capernaum (v. 59). He plainly asserts the literalness of his sacrifice for us. The focus shifts from the Father's role in giving salvation to the Son's role as the one who brings salvation through his death.

These verses point to the Lord's Supper more explicitly than any other portion of the Fourth Gospel. Historically they have unfortunately been the source of more division than unity in the body of Christ. Perhaps preachers and teachers of the gospel today can lead us beyond distinctive denominational interpretations of these verses to discover the spiritual oneness we share in the flesh and blood of our Lord.

I. The literal impossibility (vv. 51–52). Unlike the other three gospels, John contains no explicit account of the Last Supper. So, New Testament scholars like Raymond E. Brown think that verse 51 preserves John's report of Jesus' words of institution of the Lord's Supper: "the bread that I will give for the life of the world is my flesh."

John may have specifically chosen the term "flesh," rather than "body," because of the early church's struggle with the Docetists, who wanted to spiritualize away the physical nature of Christ's suffering and sacrifice.

In any case, the Jews vigorously dispute Jesus' teaching (v. 52). The Greek word (*Emachonto*) literally describes a "fight." Even today different groups of Christians trace their divisions to conflicting answers to the question which the Jews were disputing: "How can this man give us his flesh to eat" (NRSV).

II. The spiritual reality (vv. 53–58). Behind the literal impossibility of Jesus' words lies the spiritual reality to which they point. If Christians are ever going to move beyond their routinization of the Lord's Supper in worship and their tragic misuse of the Supper as a denominational battle zone, they must rediscover the unity and power of the spiritual reality that lies in Christ's physical death and spiritual presence.

(a) The physical death of Jesus. The images of eating the flesh of the Son of Man and drinking his blood dramatically concentrate the believers' relationship with Jesus. We symbolically participate in Christ's suffering and death. As George Beasley-Murray describes this development in Jesus' teaching, "Coming and believing [v. 35] are replaced by eating and drinking [v. 53]." The images remind us that, unlike manna, the "bread that came down from heaven" (v. 51) is costly. The price of eternal life is the sacrificial death of Jesus.

During the late Middle Ages and the Reformation of the sixteenth century, verses 53–55 were at the center of Christian controversies regarding receiving the Lord's Supper "in both kinds" (i.e., laity receiving both the bread and the cup during Communion). The use of any part of the Lord's Supper to promote clerical elitism or social division among

SUNDAY: AUGUST TWENTY-FIRST 153

the body of Christ is sinful. We need to remind ourselves that it is the *Lord's* Table, not the church's.

(b) The spiritual presence of Christ. Those who have eternal life will abide in Jesus. Receiving in faith the elements of the Lord's Supper expresses the close communion Christ's disciples share with their Lord. Spiritually understood, we "eat [Christ's] flesh and drink [Christ's] blood" (vv. 54, 56). We share in the life of God when we partake of the Supper (v. 57). As the Son lives in the Father, so Christians live in

Christ the Son and thus in God the Father. The unity of the Father and the Son models the communion that should exist between Christ and his disciples. So, "a mutual indwelling is set up between the believer and [the] Lord" (R. H. Lightfoot), which enables the Christian to glimpse a little of the "ultimate *koinonia* . . . between the Father and the Son" (Beasley-Murray).

As we eat the flesh of the living bread, may we sense the great unity of God calling us beyond the little kingdoms of this world.—Charles J. Scalise

SUNDAY: AUGUST TWENTY-FIRST

SERVICE OF WORSHIP

Sermon: Who Is Wise?

TEXT: James 3:13–18

I. "Who is wise and understanding among you?" James is concerned about finding the wise. Bertrand Russell, a British philosopher who died in 1970 and who made his reputation exploring the relationship of pure mathematics and logic and received the 1950 Nobel prize for literature, was more upset because he could not find in the New Testament a single word in praise of intelligence. In Dr. Russell's eyes it was a serious failure. How could any book which was concerned with truth not have a single word in praise of intellectual ability? In fact, according to the Concordance of the Revised Standard Version the word "intelligence" is used only six times in the whole Bible: three times in Exodus, twice in Proverbs, and once in Acts.

Wisdom. Intelligence. Many people have become concerned and troubled by the strong anti-intellectual attitude and thrust of many portions of the Christian community. Often the Christian faith is made simply a matter of feelings, about loving the Lord without any expectation that the mind will be a part of that. The Christian faith is just a matter of believing, and believing has nothing to do with understanding—so forget the questions and the intellectual seeking!

Douglas John Hall, a Christian teacher at McGill University, even goes so far as to suggest that throughout its long history, Christianity has not required of its followers that they should think the faith. The historical events when Constantine conquered the Roman Empire in the name of Christianity created a situation where lots of people became Christian merely by being a part of the political, social, and cultural community. Thinking about the faith was purely optional. Dr. Hall claims we have to admit that for countless Christians through nearly 15 centuries the Christian religion has been not only an "unthought" affair but the Christian faith has been an aid to thought repression, a tranquilizing agent to assist people to pass through this vale of tears with a minimum of original reflection, thought or decisions upon the whole mystery of life, death, and faith.

II. Yet here is James asking, "Who is wise and understanding?" In fact the Bible has a lot to say about wisdom. Bertrand Russell is right about intelligence, but not because the Christian faith does not care about the mind's involvement in the faith. The scriptures are concerned about wisdom, because the scriptures know that intelligence is no road to salvation. The higher the I.Q. simply means the smarter the crook. The Bible knows that those who have a very high I.Q. are tempted to pride and arrogance. There is a vast difference between those who can answer every question on "Jeopardy" and those who have an immense amount of common sense. The higher the I.Q. means the more information that can be retained and recalled, but it says nothing about the kind of information that will be retained or what is done with it. The Christian faith sees intelligence as another of God's good and glorious gifts. Those who have high intellectual abilities have an awesome responsibility. They have much, and of them much will be expected. But the biblical story is much more concerned about the gift of wisdom and understanding—about having eyes and being able to see what is happening, about having ears, and being able to listen and know what is being said. The Bible has a great deal of praise and appreciation for wisdom and understanding. Who is wise and understanding? In the Bible it is wisdom more than intelligence that is to be sought. There is a vast difference. Intelligence is the ability to retain and to recall information. Wisdom is the ability to make sense out of the confusion of facts. Wisdom is the understanding of what is happening because of the information.

The Bible praises those who are wise, those who have wisdom, those who have had a glimpse of the way that life is put together, those who have sorted through all of the pieces of life and who have found a pattern in those pieces. Life is so much a doing of a puzzle with all the thousands of pieces and not having the picture on the box top. Wisdom is the vision of the picture. But wisdom and faith still have to travel together, because even where there is a suggestion, a clue as to the whole picture, that has to be accepted by faith, for there are others as well who think they have the keys to understanding how life works.

III. All you have to do is to turn on the television late Sunday night and there are channel after channel of gurus who have bought television time to tell you that they have discovered the ingredients which make life work. They know the secrets of how life is constructed, how to obtain power, how to achieve success,

how to be happy in life. They have found the solution. If you listen to them, if you follow them, if you pay them a small fee, they will share this wisdom with you!

Or if you prefer you can be like Sancho Panza, the wise sidekick of Don Quixote, and find your solutions to life in the proverbs and sayings of tradition. "Money makes the world go round." "Walk softly but carry a big stick." "The way to a man's heart is through his stomach." There have been many different pictures of reality provided by many different wisdom traditions.

One of the great new developments in the last twenty or thirty years is our living in a one-world culture—the capitalist culture. This means that there are not alternative wisdom traditions to choose from. The capitalist culture is one explanation of how life works, and with the collapse of state socialism in eastern Europe, a whole dimension of another wisdom interpretation has collapsed. If you think about the understanding of the human being in the capitalist culture, human beings are reduced to being just consumers, spenders. In the capitalist wisdom about life, human beings are just economic agents whose interest ought to be in making money and acquiring material items. In the capitalist view there is no need or use to be neighbors, friends, or family—or to share. In fact sharing reduces the amount of consuming, and so is bad! The capitalist culture sees the meaning of life as production and consumption. All other aspects of life— dreaming, creating, poetry, fishing, anything we do without the purpose of selling or exploiting it for a profit—are unnecessary or unimportant.

IV. So, at the moment the conflict is between the capitalistic wisdom and the presentation of wisdom in scripture. That is why James is concerned as we are about the wise and understanding. The Bible offers a view of life. The Bible shares a form of wisdom. The Bible defines wisdom and seeks to share with us its vision of reality, so that we too may be wise. The Bible says that the beginning of wisdom is the fear of the Lord. If you seriously want to understand reality and to live in harmony with the powers and forces that govern this world, then you have to begin with the awe-filled recognition that we are not alone, that we are not masters of this creation, that we did not make ourselves, that we do not keep ourselves, and that we are not the sole decision-makers for our future. The fear of the Lord is that trembling acknowledgement that as one walks into a dark room there may be someone else in the room. Another's will is present in our life as we make our decisions, the holy will of God making choices and decisions. As we intend actions, the intention and purposes of God that affect our intentions and will are present.

The Bible knows that the fear of the Lord is the beginning of wisdom, for it involves the recognition that God who is involved with us does not always act the way we think the Almighty ought to act. The Bible story is one long story of a God who keeps surprising his people. He continues acting in ways of grace and mercy that keep shattering the expectation of judgment and punishment. The fear of the Lord is God's surprise, for God does not act or move or be as we have been led to believe that God should behave. God startles Moses in a bush. God makes Sarah laugh with his promise of a son. God catches Mary off guard by his request to use her. God embarrasses the Roman guards and Jewish authorities when they cannot keep Jesus' body in the tomb. God gives visions and plants dreams that keep breaking open the future and making it possible for life to start over and for life to have the possibility of being more abundant.

The wisdom of the Bible is that life has its beginning in God, that this God is still involved with creation—he made us and still cares about us; God is still at work to bring us to place he intends for us, and yet grants us a place, a role, a responsibility for our participation and our decisions.

Wisdom is supposed to help us understand how life works. We do not want to waste our lives on things that do not matter. We all want to make a contribution to life. We want to be a part of the things

that will endure. We seek wisdom to help us sort out those things that will last. The wise know what really matters in life. It has most often been called the chapter on love, but it is really the summary of the wisdom of the Bible. St. Paul says, "Let me wise you up a little. Let me tell you about the things in this world that last. This is the essence of the Christian wisdom, and we know this because we have seen it lived out in the life, death, Resurrection of Jesus Christ. "So faith, hope, love abide, these three, but the greatest of these is love." At the center of this creation is God who loves and who has made this world and all who are in it, so that faith, hope, and love endure. Oh, sometimes they take a beating, but they survive. When we live, act, do, and be with faith, hope, and charity, we build on a foundation that will not be destroyed and will not fail. Living in such wisdom brings, James observes, a sense of peace, gentleness, reason, mercy, and good fruits without insincerity.

The wisdom of the Bible keeps offering this understanding of life. It is a different understanding of life and human beings. The Christian lives by the wisdom that we are creatures of the living, loving God and when we live by faith, with hope, in love we live in harmony and joy with each other and with God.—Rick Brand

Illustrations

CONTINUING EDUCATION.   Some years ago a doctor said to his minister, "Why should I go to church? I learned the Ten Commandments and a lot of Bible stories when I was a boy. Why do I need to go and hear all that stuff again?" Suppose he adopted the same attitude in his practice of surgery. Suppose he read no professional journals, attended no clinics, studied no books because he once went to medical school. We would not care to have such a backwoods surgeon operate on our backbone.—Ralph W. Sockman

SELF.   Mark Rutherford said, in blunt terms, that "the mind and heart of the average churchgoer need to be shifted from what is *self* to what is *not* self." To effect that shift is a matter of self-discipline, something one has to learn to do. It is a matter of getting God, and all that God stands for, in the place that is too often and too naturally occupied by one's self.—Willard L. Sperry

Sermon Suggestions

TWO WORTHY PETITIONS.   TEXT: 1 Kings 8:(1, 6, 10–11), 22–30, 41–43. (1) That God hear the cries of his people in their need, especially for forgiveness. (2) That God hear the prayers of foreigners and thus spread abroad the knowledge and worship of God.

CHRISTIAN   WARFARE.   TEXT: Eph. 6:10–20. (1) Our struggle, verse 12. (2) Our defense, verses 10–11, 13–16. (3) Our offense, verse 17. (4) Our sustenance, verses 18–20.

Worship Aids

CALL TO WORSHIP.   "Lord, I have loved the habitation of thy house, and the place where thine honour dwelleth" (Ps. 26:8).

INVOCATION.   We come in all our diversity and needs, Lord, searching, hoping, praying, seeking again the light and love that drew us here in other days, that makes us long for the courts of our God and there find home.—E. Lee Phillips

OFFERTORY SENTENCE.   "Bear ye one another's burdens, and so fulfill the law of Christ" (Gal. 6:2).

OFFERTORY PRAYER.   Lord God, some of us struggle to bring these tithes and offerings. Know our hearts. Give us joy in what we give today because it will tell others about Jesus.—E. Lee Phillips

PRAYER.   O Infinite Source of life and health and joy! the very thought of thee is so wonderful that in this thought we would rest and be still. Thou art Beauty and Grace and Truth and Power. Thou art the light of every heart that sees thee, the life of every soul that loves thee, the strength of every mind that seeks thee. From our narrow and bounded world we would pass into thy greater world. From our petty and miserable selves we would escape to thee, to find in thee the power and the freedom of a larger life. It is our joy that we can never go beyond thy reach; that even were we to take the wings of the morning, and fly unto the uttermost parts of the earth, or were we to make our bed in hell, there should we find signs of thy presence and thy power. Wherever we may go thou art with us, for thou art in us as well as without us. We recognize thee in all the deeper experiences of the soul. When the conscience utters its warning voice, when the heart is tender and we forgive those who have wronged us in word or deed, when we feel ourselves upborne above time and place, and know ourselves citizens of thy everlasting Kingdom, we realize, O Lord, that these things, while they are in us, are not of us. They are thine, the work of thy Spirit brooding upon our souls.—Samuel McComb

LECTIONARY MESSAGE

Topic: Bread as Words
TEXT: John 6:59–69
We are surrounded and bombarded with words. Words are used to sell, to seduce, to proclaim, to punish, to deduce, to deceive. Words create the social reality in which we live. In our age many words promise life and love, but few deliver. Christians claim that the words of Jesus are the true bread that gives eternal life.

I. Words of offense (vv. 59–61) At the end of the sixth chapter of John, the focus shifts again. Now, instead of bread as flesh in the Lord's Supper, the gospel speaks of the life-giving words of Jesus.

Jesus' teaching is so difficult that John uses a word meaning "hard" or "harsh" (Greek *skleros*) to describe it. For Jews in the time of Jesus the scandal of drinking any blood—let alone the human blood of Jesus—is tremendous. One of the few prohibitions that the Jerusalem council of the primitive church insists on laying upon Gentile believers is that they "abstain . . . from blood" (Acts 15:20, 29).

So, when Jesus asserts that, "Those who eat my flesh and drink my blood have eternal life" (v. 54), the people decide that the time has come for a parting of the ways (v. 66). Even though this miracle-working rabbi from Nazareth could feed them with barley loaves and fish (vv. 1–15), his flaunting of the Torah and of Jewish sensibilities will certainly bring him to no good end.

II. Words of Spirit and life (vv. 62–65). Jesus responds to his disciples' complaint by creating more offense. In verse 62 Jesus asks a "what if" question which indirectly foretells his Resurrection. Just as the descent of the Son of Man from heaven created offense, so the ascent of the Son of Man back to heaven will increase that offense. In Jesus' earlier words to Nicodemus, "No one has ascended into heaven except the one who descended from heaven, the Son of Man" (3:13).

The Incarnation and Resurrection of Jesus are the two great stumbling blocks of the faith—both to Jews at the time of Jesus and to most unbelievers today. In addition, as R. H. Lightfoot comments, these verses teach the truth of the adage "no cross, no crown."

Yet, despite the offense, the ascended Son of Man gives life. As verse 63 proclaims, Jesus' words "are spirit and life." If the words of Jesus are spiritually discerned and appropriated, they will bring life.

Jesus contrasts his offensive, life-giving words with the familiar words of the flesh, which bring death. We cannot gain spiritual life on our own—"the flesh is useless." Eternal life comes only through faith in the words of Jesus.

Jesus' divine foreknowledge means that he is not surprised by the offense, disbelief, and even betrayal of his disciples (v. 64). Rather Jesus' knowledge reflects his relationship to God the Father (v. 65) and is an expression of the preexistence of Christ (v. 62).

III. Words of eternal life (vv. 66–69). With the last verses of this chapter Jesus' Galilean ministry draws to a quiet close. It would not be judged "a successful ministry" by the standards of many in the church today.

In one chapter we see the extremes of the fickle, popular mind. In verse 15 the people wanted to "take [Jesus] by force to make him king"; now many of the same disciples "turned back and no longer went about with him" (v. 66). We are reminded of the contrast between the Hosanna-shouting crowd in Jerusalem on Palm Sunday (12:12–13) and the "Crucify him" mob on the Day of Preparation for Passover (19:14). Jesus is not a triumphant political Messiah, but a Messiah whose "own people did not accept him" (1:11).

The disbelief and abandonment of Jesus by the crowd contrast with the faith of the Twelve (vv. 67ff). Yet, ironically even one of the Twelve will prove to be a traitor. There is no easy line between "saints" and "sinners." No disciple should take his or her own spiritual situation for granted.

Peter's confession (vv. 68–69) recalls his famous response in Matthew 16:16. As the "Holy One of God," Jesus has been consecrated by the Father and sent on a mission into the sinful world (cf. 10:36). Christ the Messiah belongs to God and dies to bring us back to God.

Like Peter and the Twelve, we must all confront the question, "to whom can we go" for the words of eternal life? Christ, God's eternal Word, is the Bread of Life, in whose words we can find eternal life.—Charles J. Scalise

SUNDAY: AUGUST TWENTY-EIGHTH

SERVICE OF WORSHIP

Sermon: The Power of a Praying Church

TEXT: Acts 4:23–31

Acts 4 is an account of a church at prayer. What wonderful things happened! An earthquake shook the building. Christians were filled with the Holy Spirit. Boldly they began to witness. There was unity in the church. The church had great power, and grace was upon every member of the congregation.

Have you ever seen God's power released in and through a church—a local assembly of his people? If so, that church must have been a praying church, for the power of God operates through a praying church.

I. In a praying church there is a continuous desire to pray.

(a) A praying church recognizes the supreme importance of prayer, and always desires to pray. Peter and John went up to the Temple to pray. Later Peter and John were in prison, and while they were there the church prayed. When Peter and John were set free from prison, they immediately hastened to join the church meeting to let them know what happened to them (Acts 4:23).

When the Christians heard their report, what did they do? "They heard . . . they lifted up their voice to God with one accord" (Acts 4:24). This church recognized the supreme importance of prayer.

(b) We must recognize the supreme importance of prayer. All of us must have a continuous desire to pray. We need to be like J. Hudson Taylor who stated: "The sun has never risen upon China without finding me at prayer. In forty years I saw 700 missionaries and 1,000 native workers in China."

II. In a praying church the eyes of faith and expectancy are toward God.

(a) "Lord, thou are God, which hast made heaven, and earth, and the sea, and all that in them is: . . . For to do whatsoever thy hand and thy counsel determined before to be done" (4:24, 28).

In the beginning there was only God. He created the heavens and the earth. The universe is sustained in him. Whatever God determines to be done will be done. He knows tomorrow's headlines and what will happen a day, a year, a century, and a millennium from now. He is the sovereign God. Jesus said, "All power is given unto me in heaven and in earth" (Matt. 28:18).

(b) We are told that when the disciples prayed, they quoted from the Old Testament Scriptures, and they reminded themselves of all that God had promised to do and all that he had already done. In verses 26 and 27, they recognized their dependence on God to reveal himself to them. God had revealed himself to them through the prophets and the kings such as David. Do you know God? Has God revealed himself to you? He will as you read his Word, open your heart to his Spirit, and pray. Jesus said if anyone wills to do his will, "He shall know of the doctrine" (John 7:17).

(c) As these Christians prayed they said, "Lord, behold their threatenings" (Acts 4:29). These Jerusalem Christians were not looking at their problems, but they were looking at the power of Almighty God. They were not thinking about the possibility that Peter and John might be returned to prison; they lifted up their voice to God. They waited on him. They expected God to do something.

III. In a praying church there is a desire to evangelize.

(a) Verse 29 is the most challenging verse in this scripture. "Now, Lord, . . . grant unto thy servants, that with all boldness they may speak thy word." As these disciples praised God who had brought the release of Peter and John, the burden of their prayer did not become a plea that he would now keep them safe. They pleaded to the Lord that he would enable them to go on proclaiming the gospel with greater courage.

(b) It is relatively easy for some of us to stand before a group and tell them that

Jesus saves. It seems to be more difficult to speak to one person and witness to that person about Christ. Yet many souls are won to Christ, one-on-one, as we speak to our family, our neighbors, and our friends about Jesus.

(c) In a praying church there will be burdened hearts, burdened soul-winners, burdened sowers, and burdened reapers. Members will have a passion for souls and an earnest longing to make Christ known. The psalmist recorded the promise, "He that goeth forth and weepeth, bearing precious seed, shall doubtless come again with rejoicing, bringing his sheaves with him" (126:6).

IV. In a praying church there is grace in the lives of God's people. Luke told us that "great grace was upon them all" (Acts 4:33). The word *grace* here could be exchanged for the word Christlikeness. These people had the Spirit of Jesus Christ because they imitated the prayer life of the Savior.

(a) First, God gave them the grace of unity. The Bible tells us that they had one heart and one soul (Acts 4:32). Because they prayed, they experienced the unity of the Spirit and the bond of peace (Eph. 4:3).

(b) Second, there was the grace of renunciation. The church members were unselfish. They were willing to share their possessions. "Neither said any of them that ought of the things which he possessed was his own; but they had all things common" (Acts 4:32). What a marvelous inflowing and outflowing there was of the love of Christ!

(c) Third, there was the grace of liberality. There is a great need for Christians to be generous in their giving through the church. The Jerusalem church "had all things common" (Acts 4:32). In fact, Luke went on to report: "Neither was there any among them that lacked: for as many as were possessors of land or houses sold them, and brought the prices of the things that were sold, and laid them down at the apostles' feet: and distribution was made unto every man according as he had need" (Acts 4:34–35).

V. We live in a dry and desolate place, a world where souls are desperately in need of the water of life. Since we as believers have found that water in Christ, we have an obligation to share it with those who are dying of spiritual thirst. The cry should be ringing out from our lips, "Water! Water!" This invitation should be sounded everywhere: "Ho, everyone that thirsteth, come ye to the waters" (Isa. 55:1). To do so is more than a solemn responsibility—it is an absolute necessity.—Ralph M. Smith

Illustrations

NEGLECT OF PRAYER.   Unfortunately, many Christians pray like anorexics eat! Some anorexics eat nothing at all, to speak of, and starve themselves. Christians deny themselves the nurture and power necessary to produce the fruit of Christ's character when they neglect prayer, the greatest privilege a Christian enjoys. A Christian who neglects the privilege of prayer is as self-destructive as a person who refuses to eat. By his atoning death, Christ opened the access to God and became our high priest making constant intercession for us.—Harry L. Poe

GOD IN EVERYDAY LIFE.   My message to the people of today is simple. We must love one another as God loves each one of us. To be able to love, we need a clean heart. Prayer is what gives us a clean heart. The fruit of prayer is a deepening of faith and the fruit of faith is love. The fruit of love is service, which is compassion in action.—Mother Teresa

Sermon Suggestions

WHAT TO DO WITH THE WORD OF GOD. TEXT: Deut. 4:1–2, 6–9. (1) Don't try to make it easier to do by adding to it or taking away from it. (2) Let the outsiders see your faith at its best and desire what you have. (3) Teach faithfully what you have experienced, for the blessing of those who come after you.

DOING THE WORD.   TEXT: Jas. 1:17–27. (1) Break with your wicked past. (2) Give way to the saving gospel. (3) Let your religion find expression in all practical aspects of life.

Worship Aids

CALL TO WORSHIP. "We are laborers together with God: ye are God's husbandry, ye are God's building. According to the grace of God which is given unto me, as a wise master-builder, I have laid the foundation, and another buildest thereon. But let every man take heed how he buildeth thereupon. For other foundation can no man lay than that is laid, which is Jesus Christ" (1 Cor. 3:9–11).

INVOCATION. Lord, open us this day to new vistas of praise, new visions of service, and new depths of commitment because we have sought and found the will of God.—E. Lee Phillips

OFFERTORY SENTENCE. "Blessed be the God and Father of our Lord Jesus Christ, who hath blessed us with all spiritual blessings in heavenly places in Christ" (Eph. 1:3).

OFFERTORY PRAYER. Generous Lord, through whom we enjoy so much, multiply the work of the church through these offerings and build the unvanquishable kingdom of God as never before.— E. Lee Phillips

PRAYER. O thou who are the source of all life and the light of all seeing: through the Word so urgently and clearly spoken in this hour may we have the insight to see that none are so blind as those who refuse to see. How many of us who think we see are blinded by the scales of self-righteousness, of tradition, of prejudice, of familiarity. How skillfully the Master diagnosed our astigmatism—intent on removing the speck from our brother's eye with a plank in our own. O thou giver of all sight, grant us the insight to see that our affliction is not just blind spots but we do not see anything really until we see all things through the lens of grace. How adroitly grace brings all of life into focus. We are able to see our bigotries, our prejudices, our preoccupations, for what they really are—and just how blind we have been.

We praise thee, O Father, for opening our eyes by grace to grace. We see this world anew in all of its pristine beauty as the gift of thy love and grace. We gain insight to see ourselves as stewards of its life and resources. With our eyes wide open we know that no one lives or dies unto himself or herself. We are all a part of the bundle of life. We are one family, and we had better start living that way. May we see all others through the compassionate eyes of the Master.

Through him who is present in all of life as the fullness of thy grace, taking the dimness of our soul away as he opens our eyes to the universal and teaches us to pray with all peoples: "Our Father . . ."— John Thompson

LECTIONARY MESSAGE

Topic: The Letter of the Law

TEXT: Mark 7:1–8, 14–15, 21–23

It's hard for some people to accept a gift, especially if that gift is given freely, no special occasion. For whatever reason they cannot bring themselves to receive unmerited favor into their lives. Sometimes these persons will reject the gift, perhaps out of embarrassment and leave the giver of the gift with feelings of hurt. For them, receiving a gift is possible only because they have done some good deed, and thus they expect to be rewarded. They feel they must earn what they receive—pay for all they have. Only then does a gift become something worth having.

So it is for many in terms of salvation. Some people cannot understand how God could offer the gift of salvation to those who would simply receive it. After all, they have to work for everything else they have in life, why not for salvation?

Here in Mark 7 Jesus rebukes the Pharisees and scribes for the legalism and hypocrisy of their religion. They have honored their traditions instead of their heavenly Father. Instead of receiving salvation from God, they are content to construct their own righteousness. But it is a shallow righteousness and will not stand the testing of grace.

I. Grace cannot be earned. When we work we expect to be paid. A day's work yields a day's pay. That is a concept understood by every person who has hired someone to do a task or who has been employed by another. And when we work we expect little else than our pay.

It is not required of the employer to heap praise on us when we complete a job. If we are paid for the task, that in reality is enough, and all most people expect. While it is nice for our employer to say, "Well done," it is not a requirement. If, on the other hand we are lazy in the job, we may not be paid, and may be released from employment.

But grace is different. It comes to those who can never possibly earn it no matter how well the job is done or how poorly it is done. It cannot be bought, sold, or bartered. Grace is unmerited favor, freely given.

II. Grace helps us to look to someone else. There are times when we cannot help ourselves. Literally. We come upon problems that are impossible for us to solve. We turn to others for help. The Bible is very clear that we cannot save ourselves, earn our way into heaven. In this matter we are helpless. God's grace in our lives causes us to look to him and to understand that he alone is capable of doing for us what we cannot do for ourselves. It is as if we are people drowning, thrashing about in the water, unable to save ourselves. And suddenly we catch a glimpse of one on the shore with a rope ready to toss it to us. Our eyes fix on him, our voices cry out to cast the rope, and we reach to grasp it. And forever we are in debt to the one who stood on the shore and tossed the rope. Grace causes us to look to God who reaches his hand to us in the midst of our dying.

III. Grace brings joy. When that one who has felt death's icy grip is suddenly rescued, there is joy. He will embrace his savior and forever be in his debt. For the Christian there is a sense of joy, joy in knowing that Jesus has saved us and not because of our efforts but according to God's grace. No one understands joy like a person rescued from perishing.

The Pharisees kept the law. But they knew no joy. Instead, their hearts grew cold, judgmental, and angry when they saw others being liberated and saved from their sins. Such is the plight of those who would reject grace. Their hearts yield only evil. But for the one who would receive grace, joy abounds. And their heart yields the fruit of the Spirit: of love, joy, peace, patience, kindness, and eternal life.—Ronald W. Johnson

SUNDAY: SEPTEMBER FOURTH

SERVICE OF WORSHIP

Sermon: Finding Your Niche and Being Happier In It

TEXT: Colossians 3:22–25

Recent data indicates that as many as 80 percent of working Americans feel some degree of unhappiness or frustration in their work.

I just don't believe that this is the way God intends it to be. It's a tragedy when people work—including Christians—feel miserable and trapped in the jobs they hold and the work they do. Imagine investing a minimum of 8 hours every day, 5 days a week, for 48 or 50 weeks a year—that's 80,000 hours over 40 years or so, more time than you will spend with your family and friends or in the worship of God combined—time doing something that you really don't care for! That's a waste of life! There's got to be a better way. When the early Christian slaves complained that they had a slave-driver for a boss, they were telling the truth—literally. When they griped about never having any time for themselves, you could believe them. When they said that they felt trapped in a dead-end job and that there was nothing else they could do except what they were doing at the moment, they were right on the money. When they said that they felt as though their jobs or bosses owned them, you knew intuitively that in fact they did.

Imagine, if you can, living under those conditions. Imagine trying to be a Christian in those circumstances. Yet, that's what the Apostle Paul encouraged them to do.

I. First, the work you do in no way diminishes your individual worth to God.

(a) Our work is either skilled or unskilled, menial and manual, blue collar or white collar, essential or non-essential, high tech and high powered, behind the scenes or highly visible. In such a world it's easy to conclude that real heroes are those few towering and distinguished individuals who shape a community's life or who are able to dramatically change the course of history. It's difficult to imagine that we might ever become people of significance and influence.

But, did you notice how the Apostle Paul counters that presumption? In verse 22, he writes in almost an imperative tone: "Slaves. . . ." It is as if to say, "Don't stand over there in the corner—hiding, cowering, hoping no one will notice you. You cannot hide from God. Step out here. I have something to say to you also." It was his way of building their sense of self-worth and importance.

(b) In a remarkable passage in 1 Corinthians, Paul re-cast all jobs in light of the Christian calling. He wrote: "Were you a slave when you were called (to be a Christian)? Don't let it trouble you—although if you can gain your freedom, do so" (7:21). It was as if he were writing: "Were you working as a night watchman when you became a Christian? No big deal! If you get a chance to change jobs, to improve yourself or your position, go ahead and go for it. But don't worry so much about changing jobs that you lose sight of your Christian vocation. You don't have to do something else for a living before you can begin to serve the Lord or honor him through your work."

(c) You see, God himself is a worker who is as deeply involved in his work as you are yours. His responsibilities include providing food and clothing and meeting a wide range of needs. His work includes health care, farming, and government. And believe it or not, he has chosen you to be his junior partner in getting his work done. All that he asks is that you remember that he is your boss!

II. The second thing to note is this: How you do what you do for a living does matter to God.

(a) The Apostle Paul wrote: "Whatever you do, work at it with all your heart, as working for the Lord, not for men. . . ." (v. 23). His words constituted an urgent caution to the slaves to guard their attitude.

It remains a compelling word for working Christians. If you work under difficult conditions, or are miserable in your job, personally dissatisfied and unfulfilled at your work, stressed out, or unhappy in your relationships with your co-workers, you must continually guard your attitude!

The one thing all of us can change is our attitude and our response to what we are facing. You can't make an angry, self-centered boss as thoughtful, caring and fair as Jesus. You can work on your attitude toward him, however. You can learn to be content under all circumstances and in all conditions. You may not be able to pursue any career you want. However, you can learn to bring real dignity, integrity, and significance to whatever it is that you do!

(b) It should never be said of Christians that they are half-hearted, careless, tardy, irresponsible, whiny, or negligent in their work. No matter what your circumstances or working conditions, behavior like that embarrasses God. Christian workers should epitomize qualities like self-discipline, perseverance, and initiative. They should be self-motivated, prompt, organized, and industrious. Whatever they do should be marked by the very highest quality.

(c) You and I hold within ourselves the key to finding our niche and being happier in it. It doesn't require every one else's transformation—nor a complete change in our working environment. But it does require a change in us! One of the most profound truths in God's Word is that positive change can be initiated through the difficult experiences of life.

III. Underlying everything else the Apostle Paul wrote to the slaves in Colossae is the third fundamental principle: YOU matter more to God than anything else in his entire creation! Your value to him is not connected to what you do, nor to how much you produce or earn. Your value to him is not in any way connected to your credentials nor to your work experience. Your value to God lies entirely in the fact that you are—that you exist—that he made you and he has never lost interest in you, nor has he ever stopped loving you from the moment you became a gleam in his eye!

Will you come to him now and allow him to give you the overhaul you need? Someone once said that trying to fulfill all your dreams without him is like skydiving without a parachute. If you do it, you are going to get hurt.—Gary C. Redding

Illustrations

BAD NEWS-GOOD NEWS.   Life is like the mail. Some days it is really unpleasant: bills, notices, an unhappy letter from a friend. It can be disappointing and discouraging.

Even the *Christian* life is like that. There are bills in it, notices and unhappy letters from friends—but each becomes a meaningful challenge, a great opportunity, a chance to share in God's concern for mankind.—Richard Andersen

THANKFUL.   Let me end with a remark made to me a few years ago by one of Harvard's most distinguished professors, Arthur Edwin Kennelly. He was nearly blind; his wife was dying of a painful disease in an upper room of the home where I had called to see him. I tried to say something intimate about this world which was closing in around that home. He brushed all that aside, and as I parted from him he said, "We ought to be profoundly thankful for having been allowed to live at so great a time as this." In his blindness and with pain all about him and sorrow awaiting him he was singing the Lord's song in a strange land.—Willard L. Sperry

Sermon Suggestions

THOSE WHO ARE TRULY RICH.   TEXT: Prov. 22:1–2, 8–9, 22–23. (1) They value a good name above money. (2) They share generously such blessings as they do have. (3) They recognize God's involvement in the fortunes and misfortunes of the poor and the afflicted.

TWO NECESSARY RELIGIOUS PRINCIPLES. TEXT: Jas. 2:10 (11–13), 14–17. (1) The decision to keep God's law or to his will is not a matter of selection but of commitment. (2) Faith in God is not a matter of pity and professions but of action.

Worship Aids

CALL TO WORSHIP.

Leader: Create in me a clean heart, O God,

People: and put a new and right spirit within me.

Leader: O Lord, open thou my lips,

People: and my mouth shall show forth thy praise.

INVOCATION.   We would enter into your gates with thanksgiving and into your courts with praise, O God, for all of your goodness to us and to all peoples. We praise you for today—fresh with the sparkling dew, bright with the splendor of the morning sun, and alive with all the livingness of your perennial Spirit. For this opportunity to celebrate your Word spoken through the prophets in times past and in these latter days through your only Son, we are grateful. Through love and faith and trust may we be open to hear and enabled to do. Praise be to you: Father, Son, and Holy Spirit.

What then shall we say? If God is for us, who can be against us? He who spared not his own Son but delivered him up for us all shall he not with him freely give us all things? The "all things" includes the forgiveness of our sins through God's amazing grace in Christ. In his forgiveness may we hear the call to a new beginning. Glory be to God!—John Thompson

OFFERTORY SENTENCE.   "Let him who is taught the word share all good things with him who teaches" (Gal. 6:6 [RSV]).

OFFERTORY PRAYER. Our Father, we would honor thee in honoring those who serve in thy name. By our tithes and offerings we support and strengthen the work of our pastors, our missionaries, our denominational workers, our local church staff, and others worthily employed in thy kingdom. Help us to support and strengthen them also by our prayers and goodwill, knowing that man does not live by bread alone, but first by every word that proceeds from thy mouth and then by the good words that proceed from our mouths.

PRAYER. Bless the Lord, O my soul; and all that is within me, bless his holy name! We praise you, O Father, for daily bread: for the good earth out of which our sustenance comes—for the fertile fields, the pregnant seed, the sun and rain—we praise you for work: for strength for our tasks, for machines which lighten our work, for the fruit which crowns our labor.

We thank you, too, for those who have faithfully planted the seed of your Word in our lives, who have carefully watered the newly planted seed, and cultivated the soil, that your loving purpose might be expressed in and through us.

We praise you for the glory of this mountaintop experience in worship; through realization of your amazing grace in Christ, our lives are strangely transformed.

O Father, may we not leave the glory that we have experienced here but carry it forth into the valley of human need that bread, and the Bread of Life, may be lovingly and generously shared.

Help us to see our work as a sacrament that "Whatever we do in word or in deed, may be done in the name of the Lord Jesus."

To pray "Our Father" as we so often do may we realize how intimately we are bound together in a common bundle of life—that "no one lives and no one dies unto himself." What an amazing network of production, finance, and commerce nurtures and sustains our daily lives! On this occasion we would pray for all of those to whom we are indebted for life-giving services, that we all too often take for granted.

We pray for members and friends where health is precarious. We pray for those ill, and members of their families who so faithfully and lovingly care. For those of us passing through the valley of the shadow of death, we pray the light of your presence.

For those students, our children and grandchildren, who have entered into new opportunities of education, we pray a wise investment of this year. May those who are their teachers, professors, counselors see their vocation as a high calling, not only to impart knowledge, but to mediate life.

For those in positions of political authority, we pray such discernment of your Word and commitment to your purpose that "justice may roll down like waters and righteousness as an ever flowing stream."

And now, O God, grant to each of us such responsiveness to your Word that the good work you have begun in us may be perfected to your honor and glory, through him who teaches us to pray together: [The Lord's Prayer].—John Thompson

LECTIONARY MESSAGE

Topic: To Be Set Free

TEXT: Mark 7:24–37

The entire text of Mark 7 needs to be read to get a better picture of verses 24–37. Mark sets the stories of the Syrophoenician woman and the deaf man in contrast with the legalism and racial prejudice that existed in that day between Jew and Gentile.

These stories exemplify faith in its pristine form. The Syrophoenician woman bursts into the scene brushing aside the barriers of race. She is a desperate woman. She expects Jesus to bring healing to her daughter because he is from God and she senses that he will be merciful. The deaf man cannot help himself. He is in as much need for Jesus as any Jew. But what stands out here is the symbolism of the stories. For those who are prejudiced are deaf to God and their speech becomes an impediment to a gospel witness. Thus we learn some important things from these two stories.

I. Faith in God demands that we keep our eyes on him. One can almost imagine that the woman who burst in upon this scene had one thing on her mind, healing for her daughter. She was not threatened by the presence of those outside her race. She looked intently at Jesus as she approached him. She was determined. She would not be put off. So it is with us. There is much to distract us today. Many voices cry for our attention. But those who would know God must keep their eyes fixed on Jesus. Discipleship is not easy. It requires our total attention upon the author of our faith in the midst of a world racked with prejudice and hatred.

II. The gospel establishes no barriers for those who wish to respond to God's call upon their lives. It is not the keeping of any law or tradition or racial superiority that makes us accessible to God. He desires fellowship with all people and reaches out to us. Mark seems to record these stories in chapter seven to focus attention away from human efforts and human prejudice and upon the life of Jesus which was the perfect paradigm of God's love for all people.

III. The heart is what God examines. The Syrophoenician woman paid no attention to what others thought of her. She responded to Jesus because in him she recognized one who could help. Her motive was pure. It was love for her daughter, and she was willing to risk all for that. God looks at the heart. What are we willing to risk for God? What is our motive to serving him? When we are discouraged, what happens to our faith?

IV. No matter what the barrier, the gospel can transcend it. Here in Mark's day it was prejudice and the law, among other things, that served as barriers in the minds of the early believers to the spread of the gospel. One only has to remember the story in Acts 10 to witness the impact of prejudice upon Peter's life and his surprise that Gentiles could receive the Holy Spirit as he did. Today prejudice still takes on racial forms. The law still tries to rear its head in the traditions of our churches. We must ask ourselves if we are willing to let the gospel transcend barriers in our lives, in our churches. If we are willing, it will always do so. And we, like Peter, will marvel at the pouring out of the Spirit on the Gentiles of our day.—Ronald W. Johnson

SUNDAY: SEPTEMBER ELEVENTH

SERVICE OF WORSHIP

Sermon: Saintly Steps and Tears

TEXT: Psalm 119:129–36

Whenever I read from the Book of Psalms, I find—almost everywhere—an echo of my own soul's voice. There they all are, collected in one book. My complaints, struggles, joys, sorrows, confessions, anxious expectations. The prayers of pleading and petition, of promise and peace. I know them. I've even voiced them.

It makes you wonder, doesn't it? Where would we be if not for the Psalms? How would we have survived those onslaughts of oppressive guilt, had we not been able to pray: "Be gracious to me, O Lord, for I am languishing; O Lord, heal me, for my bones are shaking with terror"?

This Lord loves us so deeply, so deliberately, and so completely—that he would not have us face life's hardships and troubling heartaches without a Word. A prayerful Word.

A Word of comfort and challenge and encouragement. A Word arising from the human heart and the heart of humanity—but blessed with a holy inspiration and a divine benediction. A Word to speak for us, with us, within us, and about us.

A Word we can hear and lay hold of, and claim for our faith. It's the only Word which to hear means to heal! As the psalmist speaks, we receive this Word. And as the psalmist prays, his prayer echoes the voice of each and every saintly soul.

Life is just that way. Filled with ambiguity, incongruities, circumstances beyond our control. And being a member of God's covenant community will never shield us from the mystifying and merciless experiences of life.

(a) But being a member of God's covenant community does mean to be gifted with a voice.

A voice which first took form in that community of faith we have come to know as Israel. Their history tells all—doesn't it? In fact, so does the name of "Israel" itself. Do you recall it's literal meaning?

(b) "Israel" means "the one who strives with God!" I suppose you could say that Israel's history is a succession of saintly steps and tears. Faithfulness, sin, repentance, renewal. Saintly steps and tears. And at least to some degree Israel's history is the history of each of us and all of us.

"The one who strives with God" is you and me! And the struggle of sainthood is the sum and substance of the Psalms. Faithfulness, sin, repentance, renewal. Saintly steps and tears.

II. Psalm 119 speaks directly to the burdens and blessings of sainthood. Each major section of the psalm begins with a letter of the Hebrew alphabet. Quite simply this means that—when it comes to addressing the dimensions of sainthood—the psalm covers everything from A to Z!

(a) This psalm concerns itself with creation, with covenant loyalty, with confession of sin, with the Lord's compassion, and with the confirmation of the saints. With faithfulness, and sin, and repentance, and renewal. Saintly steps and tears.

(b) Candidly the psalmist confesses that, unaided, he'll never cope or remain committed, constant, steady. He fears that his steps will falter—at best! Sainthood is a struggle. So, in his distress he prays not only for deliverance, but also for deeper insight into the Lord's will for his life. A will revealed in God's Word.

III. Where does the psalmist turn for strength and spiritual fortitude in the dry and barren places of devotion? When his knees begin to buckle, and his faith falters, where does he turn? What is the source of light illuminating his soul, now darkened by distressful circumstances?

(a) He proclaims God's Word as the torch for a darkened path. God's Word is the only light to guide his life—come wind, come stormy weather. And so, his determination to deepen his devotional living becomes all the stronger as his soul is nurtured and sustained by God's Word.

(b) So often this frail human life of ours is threatened and weakened. Perhaps we begin to crave that fullness of life which forms the heartbeat of the psalmist's own desire as well.

Then, like the psalmist, we remember, don't we? Only God can keep us steady, strong, and straight. Our surest ground is found in God's Word. The psalmist prays: "Revive me according to your Word." Or again, "Strengthen me according to your word." And as he reflects on those times when misfortune—or misery—has knocked him to his knees, he recalls the source of his only consolation and courage: "This is my comfort in distress," he prays, "that your promise gives me life."

IV. In verse 92 the psalmist prays: "If your (Word) had not been my delight, I would have perished in my misery." And I've no doubt but that the psalmist's misery encompasses much of the stabbing pain and arduous struggles you and I must face.

(a) Some scars are nothing less than the markings of sainthood! And those who have been brought through affliction know, only too well, that when all the other props have been kicked away—there is God! Only God! Always God! Coming to them in their distress and to deliver. And coming clearly in his Word and through the power of prayer.

(b) God's Word is the only real source of genuine sustenance. It is God's channel of true life! When struggles make our steps unsteady, we can always anchor ourselves to the Word of God. God has promised his presence and peace and power to be with us, within us, for us. And God's priceless Word keeps us strong, and straight, and steady on our feet of faith.

(c) C. S. Lewis once said that "our leisure, even our play, is a matter of serious concern. There is no neutral ground in the universe: every square inch, every split second, is claimed by God—and counterclaimed by Satan."

I'd imagine that's exactly why sainthood can be—and often is—such a struggle. Whatever is claimed by God is counterclaimed by Satan. And in order to be sustained, what we need is a spiritual strength from beyond ourselves. Which, of course, is exactly why the psalmist's prayer must also become our prayer:

Keep my steps steady
according to your promise . . .
and never let iniquity
have dominion over me.

Amen and Amen!—Albert J. D. Walsh

Illustrations

COURAGE. Toward the end of his long life, during which he had suffered much and thought intently, Josiah Royce found no little help in a magazine story he had read years earlier. It was a tale of a circle of timid persons gathered around one man who through much hardship had learned to be courageous.

Don't you see [he says to them] what ails your point of view? You want absolute security. And security—why, it's just the one thing a human being can't have, the thing that's the damnation of him if he gets it. To demand it just disintegrates a man. The main thing is to take the road fearlessly, to have courage to live one's life. Courage, that is the great word. Courage is security. There is no other kind. You have a right to trust the future. Myself, I believe there is some One to trust it to.—Willard L. Sperry

PRAYER OUR REFUGE. The story is told that Abraham Lincoln, during a particularly troubling time in his presidency, re-

quested that his Cabinet members join him in prayer. Apparently one of the Cabinet officers thought the suggestion childish and silly. And Lincoln is said to have responded: "I have been driven many times to my knees by the overwhelming conviction that I had nowhere else to go!"—Albert J. D. Walsh

Sermon Suggestions

THE VOICE OF THE PROPHETESS. TEXT: Prov. 1:20–33, NRSV. (1) Good counsel is offered, verses 20–23. (2) Good counsel is ignored, verses 24–27. (3) Irreversible consequences follow, verses 28–32. (4) However, those who listen to good counsel "will be secure," verse 33.

TEACHERS—WATCH OUT! TEXT: Jas. 3:1–12. (1) To be a teacher of religion is an awesome responsibility. (2) The problem is that what the teacher says may not be motivated by high motives, either in content or manner. (3) As a result, the teaching effort may be counterproductive, even destructive.

Worship Aids

CALL TO WORSHIP. "Worship the Lord in holy array; tremble before him, all the earth!" (Ps. 96:9 [RSV]).

INVOCATION. O God, our loving Father, teach us today what to be thankful for, even if at the present moment our problems, our pain, or our need might lead us to believe that we have no cause for thanksgiving. Let thy Spirit open our eyes to thy unfailing goodness.

OFFERTORY SENTENCE. "Upon the first day of the week let every one of you lay by him in store, as God hath prospered him" (1 Cor. 16:2).

OFFERTORY PRAYER. Lord, as we give, help us to remember from whom all blessings flow and share those blessings with others because we care.—E. Lee Phillips

PRAYER. O Lord! thou hast made promises to all that put their trust in thee, that thou wouldst renew their strength. Be gracious, and fulfill thy promises to many today. Cleanse those whose hearts have come up hither laden with trouble. Comfort those that are as shrubs, when rains have fallen, every leaf weeping. Shake them, that every leaf may cast off its tears, and that only refreshment may come from the down-sweeping storm upon them.

We beseech of thee that those who are cast about, and tried, and know not which way to go, may yet, though there may not be open before them the way of outward prosperity, have an anchor ground in thee. May they no longer be strangers. May they be children brought home to the Lord Jesus Christ.

Comfort any that are feeble. Be with any that are sick, and console them. And if long patience is required, in thy providence, for long-continued infirmities of sin, grant that they may have that patience, and that it may have its perfect work. Prepare for death those who are to depart, and prepare for life those who are passing from sickness to health. And grant that none of these outward things, none of the dealings of God, through nature, with the flesh, may separate between the soul and thee. May men not murmur nor complain. May they not look at the narrowness of their lot here, for whom is reserved the blessings of their Father's house. And grant that none may envy others, and pine at the prosperity of men round about them. May they be content to stand where the dear Lord has put them, and fulfill the office that he needs some one to fulfill. May none proudly swell, and ask why he should suffer. Shall the disciple be greater than his Lord? If thou didst go down to the lowest and the least, and didst cheerfully walk the bottom way, to the very ignominy of death, shall any refuse to follow thee—thou pure and spotless, they stained with sin; thou bearing others' trouble, they bearing their own transgressions?

Rebuke pride. Rebuke every unreasonable and wicked disposition of our hearts. And grant, O Lord our God! that we may be grateful every day and content every day; that we may become meek, and gentle, and hopeful and truthful, and loving, knowing that the time cannot be far away, but that the gate is already ajar, and is soon to be opened. It is opened for one and another, and they fly thither from the winter storm, and are safe. For others still it will be opened, and for us. And may we not be discontented. Already come within sight of it, almost within sound of the joys behind the gate, grant that we may be content. Oh, let us not cast away now, vilely, our hope or our confidence; and may we lean more heavily than ever upon thee, for all the earth cannot burden the omnipotence of thine arm. Thou that bearest up the universe—may we lean upon thee wholly. May we cast our burdens and our cares upon thee, and walk careless, since God cares for us.

Bless us, we beseech of thee, in the further services of the day. Remember the Sabbath-schools under the charge of this church. Remember the superintendents, the officers, the teachers, and the children. And we pray that the dissemination of the truth may be perpetually a life-giving work. Accept our thanks for the great good already done. The fields that open are almost beyond employment; and grant that more and more may be stirred up to give their time and wisdom and hearts' treasure for those that are needy.

And we pray that thy kingdom may come everywhere, and that thy will may be done throughout all the earth. And to thy name shall be the praise, Father, Son and Spirit.—Henry Ward Beecher

LECTIONARY MESSAGE

Topic: Say It Isn't So

TEXT: Mark 8:27–38

Here the disciples are confronted with three very difficult teachings. We can glean insights from them for our lives today.

I. The problem of sensationalism. Jesus seems to play down all attempts of others to make a celebrity of him. In earlier chapters in Mark, Jesus tries to escape notoriety, but the crowds always recognize him and press him. Here, alone with the disciples, Jesus asks them to tell him what others are saying. Peter's confession stands apart from all the sensational reports. But Jesus tells them to not tell anyone. The question is why? No doubt Peter's confession thrilled Jesus. Why not let others know it?

The answer seems to lie in the next series of teachings that came from Jesus. He seems to want to prepare them for a life, not in the spotlight of religious celebrity, but of sufferings beyond their wildest imaginations. Mark seems sensitive to the high cost of discipleship. Those today who serve God understand that to be on the Lord's side against Satan is not a life of ease.

II. Sufferings will come. One can almost hear the gasps, then silence as the disciples try to understand what Jesus has just told them. He must die, and not quickly. He must be rejected, suffer, and then be killed. Only then can he complete his mission. Peter did what we all want to do. We want to keep our Lord from harm. We want the easy way, for him and for us. For some it is easy to leave houses and lands and kindred and to hear Jesus say to us, "It will all be restored." But we don't like to hear what Mark adds to Jesus' words in Mark 10:30: "with persecutions." Persecutions are never easy. But they remind us of the high cost of our redemption.

III. And then there is self-denial. "If any man would come after me, let him deny himself. . . ." For most, this does not come easy. Most know denial of self in rather simplistic ways. But it is the rare person who pays the price of self-denial like that seen in the lives of the disciples after the Resurrection. The temptation to remain in our comfort zones of religious satisfaction keeps the majority of Christians from ever knowing the fellowship of his sufferings. Perhaps here is where we need to examine our lives, and to ask ourselves, What price have I paid for my faith in Christ? To live in our modern wicked and adulterous generation and never to suffer for Christ should cause us to examine our lives. Maybe it can be said that if we never suffer for Christ, we are also not living for him.—Ronald W. Johnson

SUNDAY: SEPTEMBER EIGHTEENTH

SERVICE OF WORSHIP

Sermon: The Fire that Burns

TEXT: Matthew 5:21–26

Anger is like a fire. It can warm and stimulate, but it can also consume and destroy. Disciplined and controlled, anger is a valuable friend; neglected and unrestrained, it is a devastating enemy. No man can toy with it without getting his fingers burned.

I. The early Hebrews observed that when a man was angry his nose swelled and his nostrils trembled. If a man became angry, they said "his nose burned." Long since, men have discovered that anger not only burns the nostrils but the heart and the head and the hand as well. In the Bible, the expression "to be angry" carries a variety of meanings such as "to snort," "to smoke," "to burn," "to be filled with fury," and "to be full of bile." A bad temper is like a fire that burns.

(a) Anger, like all natural emotions, is neither good nor bad in itself; it depends on the use made of it. Anger is a two-edged sword. It can be a virtue as well as a vice. We can destroy ourselves and others with it or let it move us to wage war against evil, oppression, and injustice. The great reform movements of history were led by men who were righteously indignant. Had Martin Luther's temper been as even and sweet as that of Erasmus, the world might still be waiting for the Reformation. Luther is reported to have said, "When I am angry, I preach well and pray better."

(b) Anger is not always the opposite of love; sometimes it is love's clearest expression. Anger has been called "the sinew of the soul." It can give love courage. A weakness of our generation is the lack of righteous indignation in the face of present evils. Perhaps our greatest tragedy is not the strident clamor of bad people but the appalling silence of good people. Too few are angry enough to speak out.

Anger, properly motivated, rightly directed, and carefully controlled, can be an asset; but our basic immaturity, our self-centeredness, our human weaknesses make it a very dangerous possession. Righteous anger must be restrained by the spirit of Christ, or it will degenerate into personal hatred.

(c) Anger is wrong when it proceeds from an evil origin. Provoked by hypersensitivity, an excess of self-feeling, or a lack of self-control, it is both dangerous and sinful. Unrestrained, it is an emotionally immature response, the petty reaction of a peeved child, the childish outburst of a self-centered man.

Anger is evil when it produces evil. So often it merely generates more anger, separates rather than unites, mutilates and does not heal, degrades and does not uplift. Ungoverned anger confuses judgment and damages personality. Many ills of mankind result from self-mutilation, and anger more often than not is self-mutilating. It turns upon itself.

II. It is surprising how much the Bible has to say about anger. In Proverbs we read: "He that is slow to anger is better than the mighty; and he that ruleth his spirit than he that taketh a city" (16:32).

(a) However, the teachings of Christ probe the very heart of the problem. Nowhere is the deity of Christ more apparent than in the sheer excellence of his moral and ethical teachings. He came, he said, not to destroy but to fulfill. It is interesting to note how he fulfills the Old Testament law. He made it inner stead of outer, stressing the motive in the heart instead of the external deed. He transformed religion from a series of negative prohibitions to a positive relationship. He emphasized the person instead of the abstract, the spiritual instead of the material.

(b) Jesus had no "thou shalt nots," but the nearest he came to one was his warning against uncontrolled anger in Matthew 5:21–26. The King James Version has the words "angry with his brother without a cause." Our Lord's standards are stern and uncompromising. To yield to ungoverned passion is to give place to the devil. To be angry is to be in danger of the judgment.

(c) To Christ's teachings we must add those of the apostles. Paul warned the Ephesians, "Be ye angry, and sin not; let not the sun go down upon your wrath; neither give place to the devil. . . . Let all bitterness, and wrath, and anger, and clamour, and evil speaking, be put away from you, with all malice: And be ye kind one to another, tenderhearted, forgiving one another, even as God for Christ's sake hath forgiven you" (Eph. 4:26–27, 31–32).

III. A frank admission of what causes anger is a step in controlling. One must come to see that anger is a symptom of immaturity and often motivated by insecurity, weakness, fear, and hatred.

(a) An honest evaluation of my own weakness is a mark of maturity and helps me take myself less seriously. It does not mean despising, belittling, or depreciating myself. Rather it means learning to love myself in Christ, which is really the prelude to loving my neighbor in Christ. When a man truly loves God and himself, excessive and prolonged anger against his neighbor becomes impossible.

(b) It is ultimately through the love of God in Jesus Christ that men come to harness the fire that burns, to conquer the wild horse of anger. It is in the power of a redeemed life that men find the resources for victory. It is in the presence of the king that we discern the pattern and the power of the kingdom.—Luther Joe Thompson

Illustrations

BALANCED EMOTIONS.   When we lose our tempers or our balance, we have lost our ability to control ourselves. We have let go the mechanism by which we exercise sovereignty over ourselves and become like a machine without a driver.

When someone tells us to keep our tempers or hold our tempers, what are they saying? They are urging us to hold on to our balance, not to fly off on a tangent, and to control ourselves.

To temper something involves reducing its intensity by the addition of something else. When we make iced tea, we put three bags in a small tea pot and let the tea steep. But the brew is too intense to drink like it is. It has to be diluted or tempered by the addition of cold water. Even though we set out to make tea, when it becomes too intense it ceases to be good. The tea becomes overpowering when the balance with water is not right. Just like tea, the emotions that play a part in our health and happiness can become bitter and overpowering when one grows out of balance with the rest.—Harry L. Poe

CONTROL IS POSSIBLE. Lafontaine, chaplain of the Prussian army, once preached an earnest sermon on the sin and folly of yielding to a hasty temper. The next day a major of the regiment accosted him, saying, "Well, sir! I think you made use of the prerogative of your office to annoy me with some very sharp hits yesterday."

"I had no intention of being personal or sharp," replied the chaplain.

The following Sunday, Lafontaine preached on self-deception and the vain excuses men are accustomed to make. "Why," said he, "a man will declare it is impossible to control his temper, when he very well knows that were the same provocation to happen in the presence of his sovereign, he not only could, but he would control himself entirely. And yet he dares to say that the continual presence of the King of kings imposes upon him neither restraint nor fear."

The next day the preacher again met the officer, who said humbly: "You were right yesterday, chaplain. Hereafter, whenever you see me in danger of falling, remind me of the king!"—Luther Joe Thompson

Sermon Suggestions

PRAISE FOR A CAPABLE WIFE. TEXT: Prov. 31:10–31. What are her qualities? (1) Trustworthiness. (2) Industriousness. (3) Generosity. (4) Foresightedness. (5) Reverence.

TEACHERS—STAY ON GUARD! TEXT: Jas. 3:13–4:3, 7–8a. (1) You can be victimized by envy and selfish ambition. (2) You can be victorious through prayer and submission to God.

Worship Aids

CALL TO WORSHIP. "Thanks be to God, which giveth us the victory through our Lord Jesus Christ" (1 Cor. 15:57).

INVOCATION. Today we meet to worship in the assurance that in our Lord Jesus Christ, we are victorious both in this world and in the world to come. May the joy of this assurance radiate in our prayers, in our hymns, and in all our spoken and wordless acts.

OFFERTORY SENTENCE. "Whatsoever ye do in word or deed, do all in the name of the Lord Jesus, giving thanks to God and the Father by him" (Col. 3:17).

OFFERTORY PRAYER. Lord, because what we give represents what we believe, help us to give generously and live gratefully as did our Savior who died for his beliefs about us.—E. Lee Phillips

PRAYER. O God, creator of the universe and our Father, thy greatness overwhelms us. We press to the outer limits of human knowledge, and at last we stand before thee alone. Before the mountains were brought forth, or ever thou hadst formed the earth and the world, even from everlasting to everlasting, thou art God. We profess to know nothing of thee but that which thou hast revealed. We trace thy works in the things thou hast made and stand amazed before thy wisdom and thy power. We see in the manifold acts of thy providence, especially in the gift of thy Son, our Lord and Savior, thy righteousness and thy loving kindness. Yet thou hast hidden so much from our sight and hast challenged our hearts with so many mysteries, that we must walk by faith and not by sight. When we cannot understand, help us to trust. When we cannot feel, help us to go on believing. And grant that our wilderness wanderings may at last be rewarded with new strength of character and greater ability to bless others with the very graces that we ourselves have received from thee.

LECTIONARY MESSAGE

Topic: But They Did Not Understand

TEXT: Mark 9:30–37

Over the past few years a number of books have appeared with the title, "All You Wanted to Know About __ and Were Afraid to Ask." You can fill in the blank with a multitude of subjects. We human beings are an interesting lot. When we don't understand something we are often afraid to ask for a further explanation. We may be afraid to ask because it might mean we would have to change in light of the new understanding. We may be afraid to ask because it might expose our ignorance and bring embarrassment. We might be afraid to ask because there is a certain fear of the unknown.

It is obvious from this passage in Mark that the disciples did not understand. And they were afraid to ask Jesus for a further explanation.

I. They did not understand the Passion-Resurrection prediction. Even though Jesus is still in the safety of the north country, he has turned his eyes toward Jerusalem and his imminent death. There is no longer an option; he must leave behind him a group of disciples who have his message written on their hearts. The teaching intensifies in private, but the results are still the same. They do not understand.

Jesus' first prediction of the Passion-Resurrection had come earlier with Peter (8:27–33) but ended in Peter's misunderstanding and the severe rebuke by Jesus.

Now a second prediction (9:31) brings the conviction of nonperception of the disciples. Mark explains, "But they did not understand the saying, and they did not understand the saying, and they were afraid to ask him." There is always the danger that their lack of perception and then fearful inhibitions will reinforce one another and lock them into ignorance.

Are we so different? Even twenty centuries later we still have difficulty in accepting the full implication of the Christian message. In our post-Resurrection era we know the gospel story and we sense the joy that would come in accepting it, but we often find ourselves falling short of giving it our full commitment and shaping our lives around it. We still don't understand.

II. They did not understand the nature of greatness. The sense of misunderstanding is reinforced in verses 32–35. Mark continues to accentuate the inability of the disciples to comprehend the nature of discipleship. Jesus had just made his second pronouncement concerning his impending suffering, death, and Resurrection but their concern soon passed from Jesus to themselves. Who among them was the greatest was the topic of discussion as they continued on their journey.

This preoccupation with their own greatness provided Jesus with another teaching opportunity. He sat down in rabbinic fashion and made a strong pronouncement. "If any one would be first, he must be last of all and servant of all." For their own power and prestige they wanted a Messiah of power. Jesus rebuked their misunderstanding by calling them to a discipleship of servanthood. There is no place in the kingdom of hierarchical authority. Authority comes only through servanthood. They misunderstood.

III. They did not understand the need to help the helpless. Jesus continues his teaching. Taking a child in his arms he makes another pronouncement. "Whoever receives one such child in my name receives me; and whoever receives me, receives not me but him who sent me."

The illustration reinforces his earlier emphasis on servanthood.

One could make a strong argument that this passage relates to the treatment of children, but there is more. The child represents all who are helpless and in need. Jesus' followers must be willing to give themselves to the helpless even though those folk will be unable to repay that kindness. Our attitudes toward a small, helpless child should be our attitude toward the helpless and hopeless people of the world. In some miraculous way we meet God in the lives of the simple, humble, ordinary folk as we minister to them. The disciples didn't understand and I'm not sure we do.

Conclusion: It was a hot afternoon when I sat down on a New York park bench beside a bag lady. I was astonished that she had on four dresses on such a sweltering day. We exchanged a few passing remarks about the birds and then I offered to buy her something to eat. "Just a hot dog. That's all I want." As she ate, I found out that she had been a telephone operator in New York for years, but lost her job to technology. Unable to get a job at her age she took to the streets, which had been her home for five years. We talked for maybe a half hour and then I offered a parting remark. "I want you to know I love you and that Jesus loves you." Brushing her hair back, she sat up straight and with a tear trickling down her cheek, she whispered, "You don't know how long it's been since anyone said that to me." For a moment I knew God had joined us on that park bench.

"Whoever receives one such child in my name receives me; and whoever receives me, receives not me but him who sent me."

The disciples misunderstood and far too often so do we.—John P. Dever

SUNDAY: SEPTEMBER TWENTY-FIFTH

SERVICE OF WORSHIP

Sermon: A Knock at the Door

TEXT: Revelation 3:20

Here is a word from Charles Lamb to which everyone will respond and say: "That is absolutely true."

Not many sounds in life, and I include all urban and rural sounds, exceed in interest a knock at the door.

We all know from our own experience that it is true. Sometimes it has been tragically true. Under totalitarian rule, in Germany and in Italy and in Russia, an unexpected knock at the door has often meant the swift coming of the secret police, and imprisonment and death. To multitudes of helpless people, that knock has been the very crack of doom. Someone has said with graphic truth that the mark of a free country is that, when you hear a noise in the hall, or a knock at the door, you know it is the milkman, and not the Gestapo!

One of the most impressive scenes in all the plays of Shakespeare is the knocking at the gate in Macbeth, after the murder has been committed. It sounds like the coming of doom. It is. It dramatizes the breaking in of conscience and consequences, the breaking in of the eternal into time.

This observation of Charles Lamb's throws a light on the word of Jesus: "Behold, I stand at the door and knock." Nothing in life approaches in importance Christ's knock on our door.

I. *Christ knocks at the door of life when it unfolds,* when one looks out on the years and considers life's possibilities. He says, "Let me in. Let me be a part of your life, your guide, your friend, your master." That is the great red-letter day of your life, when one answers that knock and says: "Come in, Lord."

II. *Christ knocks at our door with opportunity.* He knocks to call us out of our little rooms into wide fields of service. "The Master is come and calleth for Thee." When he knocks, with his summons to be a fellow workman with God, do not hang up the sign "Busy," or "Not at home."

III. *Christ knocks at the doors of grief.* He comes into dark rooms as well as into brightly lighted ones. We read in the Gospel of John: "And Jesus came, the doors being shut." Often doors of grief are tightly shut, so tight that there seems to be no chance of there ever being any sunlight again. If we will open, he will come in, even to the darkest gloom, and we can hear him say, convincingly: "Be of good cheer. I am the resurrection and the life."—Halford E. Luccock

Illustrations

VOCATION.   It comes from the Latin *vocare,* to call, and means the work one is called to by God.

There are all different kinds of voices calling you to all different kinds of work, and the problem is to find out which is the voice of God rather than of society, say, or the superego, or self-interest.

By and large a good rule for finding out is this. The kind of work God usually calls you to is the kind of work (a) that you need most to do and (b) that the world most needs to have done. If you really get a kick out of your work, you've presumably met requirement (a), but if your work is writing TV deodorant commercials, the chances are you've missed requirement (b). On the other hand, if your work is being a doctor in a leper colony, you have probably met requirement (b), but if most of the time you're bored and depressed by it, the chances are you have not only bypassed (a) but probably aren't helping your patients much either.

Neither the hair shirt nor the soft berth will do. The place God calls you to is the place where your deep gladness and the world's deep hunger meet.—Frederick Buechner

SUBSTITUTE GODS.   Where the true God is not known, persons turn to substitute gods, to idols. Devotion to the gods of success, pleasure, intellectualism, politics—even religion, good though it is—is nevertheless idolatry. A young man

graduates from the university full of vision for his future. He gives himself to his job, imagining that it will fulfill the cry of his soul for meaning. It does, briefly. But once he has achieved his goal, the old haunting cry returns. The idol of success does not satisfy permanently.—Ben Campbell Johnson

Sermon Suggestions

SHARING LEADERSHIP.   TEXT: Num. 11:4–6, 10–16, 24–29. (1) The people's discontent. (2) Moses' frustration and complaint. (3) The Lord's solution.

THE USES OF PRAYER.   TEXT: Jas. 5:13–20, NRSV. (1) For relief from oppression. (2) For recovery from illness. (3) For spiritual support through mutual intercession. (4) For restoration of those who wander from the truth.

Worship Aids

CALL TO WORSHIP.   "Blessed is the man that trusteth in the Lord, and whose hope the Lord is" (Jer. 17:7).

INVOCATION.   We come into your presence, Father, keenly aware of our need for your forgiveness and guidance. Along the way of this past week we all have sinned and come short of your glory for us. We have all ignored the opportunities of service which have presented themselves at our door. We have not loved our neighbor as we have ourselves and with that sinner in the Temple on that long ago day we can simply cry out, "Lord, be merciful to me the sinner." In this sacred hour call us unto you and do with us what is needed that we might become more able followers as we move from this sanctuary to meet the world.—Henry Fields

OFFERTORY SENTENCE.   "I will freely sacrifice unto thee: I will praise thy name, O Lord, for it is good."

OFFERTORY PRAYER.   We wandered far, O Lord, but you came near. You delivered us in our time of trouble. You have given us good things to enjoy, which we do not deserve. Now we praise you, not only with our tongues, but also with our gifts. Bless and use these offerings that your presence may be brought near to others in their need.

PRAYER. O God, we rejoice that today no burden of work will be upon us and that our body and soul are free to rest. We thank thee that of old this day was hallowed by thee for all who toil, and that from generation to generation the weary sons of men have found it a shelter and a breathing space. We pray for thy peace on all our brothers and sisters who are glad to cease from labor and to enjoy the comfort of their home and the companionship of those whom they love. Forbid that the pressure of covetousness or thoughtless love of pleasure rob any who are worn of their divine right of rest. Grant us wisdom and self-control that our pleasures may not be follies, lest our leisure drain us more than our work. Teach us that in the mystic unity of our nature our body cannot rest unless our soul has repose, that so we may walk this day in thy presence in tranquility of spirit, taking each joy as thy gift, and on the morrow return to our labor refreshed and content.—Walter Rauschenbusch

LECTIONARY MESSAGE

Topic: Jesus Forbids Exclusive Christianity

TEXT: Mark 9:38–50

Almost from the beginning Christianity has had fissures within it. Paul's Letter to the Corinthians is about fractures in the church in Corinth. Groups with exclusive claims were already gathering around various leaders. Centuries have come and gone and the divisions have multiplied. Catholic, Orthodox, Protestant! Baptist, Methodist, Episcopalian! Fundamentalist, Neo-Orthodox, Liberal! All had and have their exclusive claims. "Teacher, we saw a man . . . , and we forbade him, because he was not following us."

I. Disciples—He was not following "us." A charismatic prophet had appeared who called on the name of Jesus but did not belong to the apostolic group. This situation occurred often in the early church and the early Christian literature gave various solutions. Note, however, that the problem is not that the prophet was not following Jesus, the problem was that he was not following the Twelve. He had not joined their group. He is not following "us" (the established leadership).

There has always been a homogeneous principle that operates within groups. We want to be with people who think like us, dress like us, smell like us, worship like us, etc. We want to be with "our kind of people." All of us understand this, but when this homogeneous principle operates to the exclusion of others who call upon the name of Jesus, Jesus has something to say about it.

II. Jesus—Do not forbid him. Jesus' answer to the disciples is categorical. "Do not forbid him." Then he dismisses their exclusiveness with three "for-sayings." These three statements seem to establish a rather large inclusive umbrella for Christendom. Who is included?

1. Those who do mighty works in Jesus' name.

2. Those who are not against Jesus' followers are for them. (Interesting concept!)

3. Those who give a cup of water to someone because they bear the name of Christ.

Once the early church began to create doctrines to explain its beliefs, these broader concepts seem to have been forsaken. Doctrine always provides an "us" and "them." Divisions resulted.

My own denomination has been embroiled in controversy for over a decade. In kinder moments the "us" and "them" are conservatives and moderates. But in the trenches they are fundamentalists and liberals and the exclusion principle is prominent. Doctrinal differences are great and a division may eventually take place, but someone needs to remind us that the bonds in Christ are much greater than our differences.

Doctrinal differences throughout Christendom tend to divide us and we need to remind ourselves that we have strong bonds in Christ Jesus. Up and down the theological spectrum we have one important thing in common. Jesus came and walked among us, died on Calvary, was buried, and arose the third day. This was the message of Paul as he established churches in Achaia and Macedonia. It was the message of the gospel writers. It has been the essential message of the church throughout the ages. Whether the emphasis is on the blood spilled, or a life given, or the old rugged cross, the message is the same. Whether it is preached in a one-room church in rural Alabama, where the funeral fans are being waved vigorously, the wasps are buzzing around the preacher's head and a gospel quartet is singing "On the Jericho Road"; or it is being preached in a county seat town in Missouri with a semi-formal service, an air-conditioned sanctuary, an educated preacher, and the choir singing an arrangement of "Amazing Grace"; or it is being preached in the mega-churches of Texas with their 200-voice choirs, 5,000-seat auditoriums, evangelistic preachers, and television ministries; or it is being preached in the stately churches of New England with their stained glass sanctuaries, formal services, robed ministers, and trained choirs offering anthems to God, the basic message is the same—the Son of God came, lived among us, died, was buried, and arose the third day. And that message binds all of us.

"If they are not against us, then they are for us."—John P. Dever

SUNDAY: OCTOBER SECOND

SERVICE OF WORSHIP

Sermon: Understanding the Supper— Knowing Its Names

TEXT: 2 Cor. 11:23–26

Do you understand the meaning of the Lord's Supper? Unfortunately there is a lot of misunderstanding about it. Down through the years argument over this particular celebration has been a bone of contention between religious groups. It has led to furious debate and fractured fellowships. It's a tragedy that what God intended to be a reminder of what we have in common has often been a reminder of what separates us.

I. It is known as the Lord's Supper.

(a) This is the name that I prefer and use more than any other. I like it because it reminds us, for one thing, that is the *Lord's* Supper. He is the one who brought this into being. It was on the night in the upper room, after they had eaten the Passover meal that celebrated their deliverance from slavery in Egypt, that Jesus added this part: He took the bread, he took the cup, and he said, "Do this in remembrance of me." This supper was not the creation of any church. It was not the idea of any man or denomination. The supper was created by Christ for every one of us. He is the one who started it. He is the one who offered the invitation to it.

(b) The Lord's Supper is also a symbol of what he has done for us. He said, "Do this in remembrance of me." That's a key phrase in our understanding of the supper. He set this apart to aid our memory because it would be easy to forget, with all that goes on in life, just exactly what the heart of the gospel is about. The supper is to remind us of what Christ did. It is a symbol, a sign-post, something that prods our imagination, and causes us to think of another reality. These elements are symbols: bread that symbolizes his body broken on the cross; the cup that symbolizes his blood shed for us on the cross. They are symbols that point to the Resurrection of Christ and his Crucifixion. It reminds us that God loves us so much that he was willing to die on our behalf to give us love that we didn't deserve, forgiveness that we desperately need, and a hope of eternal life that we must have.

II. It is called Eucharist.

(a) That is a strange word to us. It's how our Catholic friends describe their celebration of the Supper. It's a good word. The word means "to give thanks." To celebrate this Supper is an act of thanksgiving to God for what he has done.

Surely this is what we ought to be doing, too, as we remember all that Christ has done for us. We ought to be filled with the spirit of thanksgiving and joy when we participate. It is a way of thanking God, for he has saved us from our sins, and our lostness.

(b) When we cut ourselves off from God we feel frustrated, miserable, and empty inside. No matter what we do to numb the emptiness inside of us, it won't happen because we're cut off from the one we need to be at home with. What Christ has done is to remove all of the barriers that keep us from going home, all the barriers that keep us from being at one with our heavenly parent. Every one of us can go home again. Christ has made it possible. There's no one who needs to be cut off from God because Christ has taken care of our rebellion and the consequences of it. If we want to go home to God, we can.

To remember that ought to cause us to offer praise to God, to offer thanks. That's what we do by our participation in this. We're thanking God for his willingness to offer us a chance to be his children again.

III. It is called Communion.

(a) The Communion service is often what we call it, and that word means "to experience another," "to have a close union with another." When we commune with nature, we experience nature. When we commune with a friend, we experience friendship. When we commune with God, we experience God. We do not remember and celebrate what a dead person did. We celebrate a living presence. Because Christ rose from the dead, he is alive, and the hope of our celebration is that we will experience the presence of God in a new way inside of us.

(b) The scripture tells us that where two or three are gathered, he is with us (Matt. 18:20). We are two or three; therefore, the presence of God is indeed with us in this experience of worship. The hope of our worship is that we will experience in our lives that this is really Christ here, really Christ speaking to us through bread and cup.

IV. It is called sacrament.

(a) That word scares us, but it ought not to because it's a good word. Sacrament means "oath of allegiance." Its original meaning had to do with the oath that a Roman soldier swore at the beginning of his military service. He swore that he would serve the emperor to the death. Every now and then throughout his career, the soldier would be asked to renew his sacrament, his oath of allegiance, his pledge of loyalty.

In this Supper, we remember Christ's sacrament to us. He pledged his loyalty to us to the death. He pledged to God that he would do whatever was needed to bring us a chance at salvation. He kept that pledge, all the way through to the death and beyond.

(b) When we remember all that, hopefully we will renew our sacrament, our pledge of allegiance, our oath of loyalty. We made them, didn't we? When we became a Christian, we were full of all sorts of promises and pledges. We were going to be this, and we were going to do that. Sometimes in the rush and busyness of life we forget the promises we've made. But we can renew them! The experience of celebrating this Supper is supposed to do that for us. As we participate, remember, give thanks, and open ourselves up to his presence, hopefully the result of it will be that we will renew the pledges, the commitments, and the loyalties that we offered him. We will do what we said we would do: serve him to the end.

V. So we come to celebrate this Lord's Supper. He invites us to do that, to remember his sacrifice on our behalf. We celebrate this Eucharist, by giving thanks to God for doing what he did for us. We celebrate this Communion, as we open ourselves up to the living presence of Christ who is here even now. We celebrate this sacrament, as we renew our pledge of loyalty, devotion, and commitment to this Christ who committed himself so to us.—Hugh Litchfield

Illustrations

NECESSARY HABITS. My grandmother used to remark, when she heard that someone was ill, "They have been neglecting their habits." By this she meant that their lives had been chaotic and disordered, to the detriment of their wellbeing. Many today do not feel the presence of God, are not motivated toward any responsibility for their neighbor, sense no claim upon their lives, because they have been "neglecting their habits."

"I don't want to go to Sunday school today," declared our six-year-old.

"Why?" we asked.

"Because they never do anything new there," was his reply. "It's always, 'Jesus, Jesus, Jesus.'"—William H. Willimon

RENEWING OUR VOWS. Sometimes a couple comes and wants to renew their vows of marriage. They made them at the beginning. However, sometimes a promise made at the beginning of marriage gets broken or forgotten, so some will come and say, "We need to renew our vows." So we enter a sanctuary and go through the vows, and they speak them to one another again, renewing their commitment to keep the promises of love. In the same sense, when we participate in this Supper, it is our way of renewing our promises of commitment, our promises of love that we have made to him.—Hugh Litchfield

Sermon Suggestions

THE BAD AND THE GOOD. TEXT: Job. 1:1, 2:1–10. (1) The most blameless person may be severely tested. (2) The most severely tested person still receives good from God.

THE WORK OF CHRIST. TEXT: Heb. 1:1–4; 2:5–12, NRSV. (1) Through his Son, God "created the worlds." (2) Christ reflects God's glory. (3) Christ "sustains all things" through his word. (4) Christ sits enthroned in majesty and authority, having suffered the death of the cross and "made purification for sins."

Worship Aids

CALL TO WORSHIP. "The Spirit and the bride say, Come. And let him that heareth say, Come. And let him that is athirst come. And whosoever will, let him take the water of life freely" (Rev. 22:17).

INVOCATION. O God, breathe upon us with thy Spirit and inspire us to worship thee with all our heart, so that we may be energized to serve thee with all our strength.

OFFERTORY SENTENCE. "Verily, verily I say unto you, he that believeth on me, the works that I do shall he do also; and greater works than these shall he do; because I go unto my Father. And whatsoever ye shall ask in my name, that will I do, that the Father may be glorified in the Son" (John 14:12, 13).

OFFERTORY PRAYER. Lord, make of our stewardship this day a force that seeks to grapple with the demands of the faith and give a clear and telling witness of Christ Jesus in a world of need.—E. Lee Phillips

PRAYER. Father, what privilege to be among your people to celebrate Word and sacrament together. In this special place surrounded by the symbols of the faith we are reminded of your mighty deeds of grace for our salvation. Your Word of grace spoken from the beginning brings order out of chaos. In your Word conclusively declared in Christ in these latter days we discover that order for life on this planet that you have ordained from creation. From the earliest disciples, those who make this discovery enthusiastically confess: Christ is Lord.

With crumbling walls and old orders giving way to new, how we need to live life with great expectancy for "eye has not seen, nor ear heard, neither has entered into mind of man what you have prepared for those who love you." Let us not be so unimaginative—so laggard in thought, so slow to believe—that we cannot share the exultation of these days. Let us exult in the insight of the prophet, so boldly apparent in these changing times, when you put it in his mind to declare: "It is not by might, nor by power, but by my Spirit," says the Lord. Never has the weakness of power to bring order out of chaos been more evident in the history of humankind than today. When we are being prodded by cataclysmic events to "beat swords into plowshares and spears into pruning hooks" grant us the faith, a vision, courage to lead the way. Grant to us imaginative and courageous leadership that we may be freed from the shackles of the military-industrial complex, that our rich resources may be invested in tools for life rather than implements of death.

Forgive us for being a part of the problem rather than a part of the solution in pursuing a foreign policy that puts nationalistic interests before the needs of weak countries and little people. For those who have committed their lives to be your instruments in bringing reconciliation to troubled areas, we pray. We pray for the people who have suffered and are suffering and rejoice in their victories of faith, and courage, and hope. We pray for your gift of Shalom and that right soon.

As a family of faith we are very conscious of needs among us. For those broken in health we pray the wholeness of your healing. For those of us lonely in bereavement, we pray the companionship of the Good Shepherd to strengthen and encourage. Bless us now as Christ leads us to pray together: "Our Father . . ."—John Thompson

LECTIONARY MESSAGE

Topic: Jesus' Teaching About Marriage

TEXT: Mark 10:2–16

Setting: Jesus is continuing his move toward Jerusalem and once again the crowds gathered around the Lord. As he teaches them, the Pharisees approach with a question that is currently a part of the scribal debate. "Is it lawful for a man to divorce his wife?" Matthew 19:3 adds "for any cause" which is probably a more accurate statement of the question.

The debate centered on the teaching of Moses recorded in Deuteronomy 24:1: "When a man takes a wife and marries her, if then she finds no favor in his eyes because he has found some indecency in her, and he writes her a bill of divorce . . ." What was this "indecency"? The school of Shammai interpreted it in the strictest manner. This indecency consisted of adultery and nothing else. The school of Hillel gave a very loose interpretation. "Indecency" could be anything from being a poor cook to adultery.

The more liberal view had made divorce a common practice among the Jews of Jesus' day. Family life was threatened, and the wife had been reduced to common chattel. Although she could not divorce her husband for any cause, he could at the slightest whim divorce her and cast her out into the world.

Jesus takes this opportunity to give a very significant teaching about the family and marriage. There is also a strong affirmation of women as persons equal with men in the sight of God.

I. Marriage is God's divine plan. Jesus requested that they quote the law, and in doing so they gave him an opportunity to turn their question upon them. "Moses allowed" this bill of divorce because of the hardness of their hearts. In adopting this as their starting point they implied that God approved of divorce. In fact this pronouncement of Moses stood as a divine judgment on humanity's refusal to abide by God's true will for them.

"From the beginning" God had instituted marriage as his divine plan. There was a goodness in God's design in creation and God did not approve of the rupture in human relations that divorce entailed. In a moment Jesus had shifted their attention from divorce to marriage.

The teaching here parallels other New Testament teachings of Jesus. Human and spiritual values are to be set above the law. The law of divorce brought cruelty and violated the commandment of God and the purpose of marriage. His reply is a logical extension of the "you have heard, but I say to you" passage in the Sermon on the Mount.

II. Marriage is to be permanent. No matter how one tries to explain it or skirt around it, the teaching is plain. The man and woman are to become as one flesh in a permanent relationship. Jesus makes this plain in his answer to the Pharisees and in his further explanation to the disciples. This was the point of reference from the beginning and is to be the point of reference today.

Jesus moved the question from law to grace. Marriage was God's gracious gift to humankind. It was to be responded to in gratitude. The church has no choice but to hold up the ideal of the permanency of marriage as the creative principle of God. Our sexual and psychical needs can best be met and sustained in a life-long union sustained by commitment to God's divine plan.

The church began to make concessions early. The exception clause in Matthew 5:32 may or may not have been added by the church. Paul adds his own concession in 1 Corinthians 7:13. They and we know that some marriages fail and become a mockery of the divine intention. But human failures should not be taken as an opportunity to accommodate the values set forth by Jesus. For those approaching marriage the idea should still be there. Marriages cannot be entered as though they were on a thirty-day trial basis. Permanence is a part of their essential nature.

But we live in a less than perfect world, and we are less than perfect people, and we often make a mess of our lives and our marriages. Divorce may be the only solution to an unredeemable situation. Divorce is not the unpardonable sin. But it is a sign we have not reached the ideal that God holds for us. What then? Well, that is what the New Testament is all about. We have fallen short of the glory of God. Confession still brings forgiveness.—John P. Dever

SUNDAY: OCTOBER NINTH

SERVICE OF WORSHIP

Sermon: The Danger of Going to Church

TEXT: Isaiah 1:12; Luke 4:24–30

Ministers commonly talk about churchgoing, but what they usually say about it is that we ought to go to church. Today I confront myself and you with something else in the Bible about churchgoing which troubles me—its scathing disapproval of churchgoers.

Read the first chapter of Isaiah, where in the Temple, crowded with worshipers, the prophet hears God indignantly saying to the throng: "Who hath required this at your hand, to trample my courts?" So that is what churchgoing can degenerate into—Temple trampling!

Jesus himself pictured a Pharisee going up to the Temple to pray. That is a pious practice which we have had urged on us from our youth up. But, says Jesus, that man stood in the Temple and prayed with himself, saying, "Lord, I thank thee, that I am not as the rest of men." One of the most sarcastic things Jesus ever said about anybody was about people who, as he put it, "love to stand and pray in the synagogues." Especially recall that Sabbath when Jesus spoke to the crowded sanctuary in Nazareth about interracial goodwill, about God's grace caring for Syrians and Sidonians just as much as for Jews. All the churchgoers that day, we read, "rose up, and cast him forth out of the city." You see what I am getting at. According to the Bible, some of God's worst trouble has been with churchgoers.

I. To begin with, it is easy to see how church attendance can become trivial and futile.

(a) Of all the millions who attend church in this country, for example, how many are merely spectators? So they go to a football game, but they do not themselves play ball; they watch other play. So they go to the theater, but do not themselves act; they watch others act. So they come to church and watch the ministers and the choir worship in the chancel, and comment on how well or ill they do it. They are spectators, not participants. Nothing vital, renewing, transforming, happens inside them. What a pity!

(b) Or think of all the people to whom church attendance is only a pious formality. One of religion's most dangerous aspects is that it makes sacred everything it touches, so that all sorts of externals can become invested with hallowed meaning, until outwardly to observe them is mistaken for genuine religion. Nowhere is this substitution of ritual observance for vitality more obvious than in some churchgoers.

(c) Here in this church today, with the great tradition of the Christian heritage around us, with Christ's way of life exalted above the sordid level of our vulgar world, with God calling us to lift up our eyes unto the hills from whence cometh our help, we are all within reach of wealth for our souls, which can make us resourceful, secure, confident, dedicated, strong. Don't miss it! Don't give God occasion to say to anyone here: "Who hath required this at your hand, to trample my courts?"

II. Now let us come to grips with two vital aspects of churchgoing which we are all in danger of missing.

(a) First, coming to church can issue in renewed, sustained, dedicated personal character. It can make an ethical difference in our daily living.

Today there is a popular movement afoot in our churches which loses sight of this deep ethical meaning in public worship. I refer to the obsession of many of our new churchgoers with peace of mind and nothing else. To be sure, peace of mind is a basic spiritual need, and in this upset generation many of these new churchgoers are rightly seeking in the Christian faith the cure of their anxieties and fears. The trouble is that to some of these new churchgoers peace of mind becomes an end in itself. The church to them is simply a place of escape, an island of safety, a pillow to lie down on, an ivory tower. All they want of it is inner tranquillity—period! Tranquillity alone does not make a Christian. Too many churchgoers use religion as a sedative. Friends, if Christ were in this pulpit today, speaking to us as he did in the sanctuary at Nazareth, would that be sedative? My word!

If someone here deeply needs inner serenity, I hope that something in this service may minister to this want, saying, like Christ himself: "Peace I leave with you; my peace I give unto you." But Christian worship means more than peace; it is not a lullaby, but a challenge to character. I want some ethical consequences from our worship here today.

(b) There is a second area, however, where we confront, I suspect, the Bible's most disturbing difficulty with churchgoers. Churchgoing can make people littleminded, bigoted, sectarian, confirming and sharpening their prejudices and fanaticisms.

That was the trouble in the Nazareth synagogue that day when Jesus came back to his hometown. He knew those people. He had grown up with them. They went up to the synagogue every Sabbath, and came down more narrowminded and prejudiced than they had been before. Jesus was speaking to their real condition when he preached that day a universal God. He appealed to their own great traditions—many widows in Israel, but Elijah was sent to a widow of Sidon, many lepers in Israel but Elisha healed Naaman the Syrian. Could they not see what their own great tradition taught—what the prophet Malachi meant when he cried, "Have we not all one father? hath not one God created us?" But they would have none of it. They threw him out. They wanted their churchgoing to confirm their prejudices. Well, look at our American churches today and see how all too commonly that kind of churchgoing is being reduplicated here.

This is what Jesus was thinking of when later he told the story of the Good Samaritan. We think that story beautiful. I never get over my amazement at people who think that parable beautiful. Those who first heard it did not think that. They were horrified at it. For, who was it that passed by on the other side and refused to help the wounded man? The priest and the Levite. Where were they going? Down from the Temple in Jerusalem. They had been to church, but of what going to church ought to mean, they had not the faintest idea. It was a Samaritan, who never went to their church, whom they despised as a heretic from an outlawed race, who really understood what the worship of God means. Make no mistake about it, our Lord could be very severe on churchgoers.

(c) One of our outstanding American ministers, Howard Thurman, once talked with Gandhi and asked him, "What is the greatest enemy that Jesus Christ has in India?" and Gandhi answered in one word. "Christianity," he said. That sounds dreadful, but, before we brush it off, think about it! Doesn't Christ face some of the worst enemies of his gospel in bigoted, prejudiced, narrow-minded, small-spirited Christianity? Isn't he still saying to us in the church, "Not every one that saith unto me Lord, Lord . . . but he that doeth the will of my Father who is in heaven"?

III. This morning I am trying to tempt you. I know that every Sunday we pray, "Lead us not into temptation," but today, if I can possibly manage it, that is precisely where I should like to lead every one of us—into temptation. For it is not alone the seductions of evil which tempt us. No! In our better hours, which ought to come when we worship God together, goodness is tempting too, and decency, and unselfishness, and magnanimity. To do justly, to love mercy, and to walk humbly with our God—that in our better hours can be alluring, tempting, challenging, too. When Jesus said to the fishermen of Galilee, "Follow me," he was tempting them. And still the Master is the most tireless tempter of our race, generation after generation appealing to us in our personal lives and our societies to follow him.

God alone knows what youth may be here this morning, facing now, like Isaiah, a call divine which would make history if he should surrender to it. Jesus was only twelve years old when he went up to the Temple, but something happened there which mankind never can forget. He came to a great conviction there. "Wist ye not that I must be about my Father's business?" That kind of experience could happen here this morning.

Ah, Lord! What kind of churchgoer am I?—Harry Emerson Fosdick

Illustrations

FORMATIVE IMAGES.   Robert Lifton has written that "human existence itself can be understood as a quest for vitalizing images." Not only to the study of religion, but to every discipline, academic department, and professional school, the young adult comes seeking vitalizing, fitting, and "right images" by which to name self, world, and "God." The young adult has a unique capacity to receive images that can form the vision and fire the passion of a generation to heal and transform a world.—Sharon Parks

CHANGED.   Don't be a mere Temple-trampler this morning! Robert Louis Stevenson's description of what happened to him can be true of you: "I came about like a well-handled ship. There stood at the wheel that unknown steersman whom we call God." That is what coming to church this morning can mean to someone here.—Harry Emerson Fosdick

Sermon Suggestions

WHEN YOU CANNOT FIND GOD.   TEXT: Job. 23:1–9, 16–17. (1) It may be a time of bitterness. (2) It may be a time of frustration. (3) It may be a time of terror. (4) But coming to terms with Jesus Christ is the answer (see John 14:1–14).

WITH JESUS AS HIGH PRIEST.   TEXT: Heb. 4:12–16. (1) Our real self exposed, verses 12–13. (2) Our deepest need provided for, verses 14–16.

Worship Aids

CALL TO WORSHIP.   "They that wait upon the Lord shall renew their strength; they shall mount up with wings as eagles; they shall run, and not be weary; and they shall walk, and not faint" (Isa. 40:31).

INVOCATION. Open us in this hour of worship, Lord, to receive what you have wanted to give us for so long and would never want us to be without.—E. Lee Phillips

OFFERTORY SENTENCE. "As ye abound in everything, in faith, and utterance, and knowledge, and in all diligence, and in your love to us, see that ye abound in this grace also" (2 Cor. 8:7).

OFFERTORY PRAYER. We confess, O God, that sometimes our giving is the last important problem to solve in our Christian life. Help us to grow in this grace as we grow in all others.

PRAYER. Father, we can think long thoughts of you, but we cannot comprehend you fully. We can utter words of praise to you, but we cannot fully behold you. We can seek to know your will, but we cannot totally grasp it in every measure. So we stand in awe of you even as we worship you. To you we bring our stumbling praise and broken prayers. Somehow we ask that you hear the utterance of our hearts and build in our souls a sanctuary where we are humbled by your mighty presence. Let us hear with clarity the words of direction with our lives as we walk the road opened before us.

As we travel along, open our ears to hear the cries of suffering which arise from people amid the pains of life. Open our hearts to the struggles which burden folks as they wrestle with weighty issues of life.

Open our hands to lift the fallen who without assistance will never rise again. Open our mouths to speak words of salvation and encouragement to those who walk in darkness and seek light and life which only Christ can give. Open our eyes to see the movement of your spirit as transformation takes place in so many areas of life.

Give us the wisdom to know how to care, after the fashion of Christ. Give us the compassion to embrace those who are in need of the health-giving care which only Christ can bring. Give us the courage to act in faith so that joy may abound and lives may be made whole and hope may be born among people everywhere.

Pray, Father, meet us in your power, lead us into your peace. Guide us in service to others and enable us to make this world a better place for all to live as we seek to love and follow you through Christ our Lord.—Henry Fields

LECTIONARY MESSAGE

Topic: Inheriting Eternal Life
TEXT: Mark 10:17–31
Introduction: Mark uses this section of his Gospel to emphasize what it means to be a disciple of Jesus. The small group of evangelists are once again on the road moving toward Jerusalem, and the teaching continues. Evidently Jesus had just finished a rather convincing discourse on the kingdom of God when a man in the crowd ran up to him, fell on his knees, and with a great deal of emotion asked, "Good Teacher, what must I do to inherit eternal life?" For twenty centuries people have asked the same question, so the first century answer continues to have great importance for us.

I. What must I do? Jesus' first response is not exactly what one would expect. He seems to "throw cold water" on the man's enthusiasm by criticizing his use of "Good Teacher." "No one is good but God alone." Was he rejecting the conventional flattery? Was he simply moving the man away from his emotion so he could deal more rationally with the questions to come? Whatever the reason, one should not take it as a theological dogma for the denial of Jesus' divinity.

When Jesus queried the man about the commandments, he enthusiastically responded that he had observed these from his youth. With a loving affirmation, Jesus then asked him to do one more thing: ". . . Go, sell what you have, and give it to the poor, and you will have treasure in heaven; and come, follow me." Jesus hit him with five imperatives: go, sell, give, come, follow. For this man discipleship meant the disposal of his wealth because it stood between him and God. He found the demand too great so he turned away. This is the only account in Mark where someone turns down the invitation to come and follow.

There is a serious problem with this passage and it centers around the word "do." "What must I do to inherit eternal life?" If nothing followed this verse, one could conclude as the Jews had concluded in interpreting the law, that salvation can be earned by good works. This is one of the greatest fallacies in religion and ethics. Eternal life is not a reward for "doing."

II. Is "doing" enough? Jesus gives an emphatic "No!" Turning to the disciples, Jesus says, "How hard it will be for those who have riches to enter the kingdom of God." The disciples were amazed. The rabbis had taught for years that prosperity was the sign of God's favor. Surely this was a sign of goodness.

Jesus knew that material things tend to draw a person's attention to this world, and soon things and persons are valued in terms of price or financial worth. But there is a more important lesson here and it comes when the disciples ask, "Then who can be saved?" And Jesus replies, "With men it is impossible, but not with God; for all things are possible with God."

Discipleship demands our obedience and following the leadership of God's Spirit, but no matter what we do, it is not enough to attain eternal life. That life belongs to God, and we can receive it only as a gift from God. Jesus' words to the rich man might have led us to a works-salvation, but his teaching to the disciples makes it clear that salvation involves gift and demand. The two exit together in paradox.

III. Who can be saved? The whole event brings some consternation to the disciples, and Peter in his accustomed manner speaks for the group. "Lord, we have left everything to follow you, and now you say that's not enough." They still don't quite understand, and Jesus reassures them once again: The reward for those who follow me for the sake of the gospel will be great, both in this time and in the age to come. He doesn't say it here, but this seems to be an elaboration of an early pronouncement: "Whoever loses his life for my sake and the gospel's will save it."

Who can enter into the kingdom of God? Those who follow out of love and commitment. Those who love God because he first loved them. Those who follow not to be first among their peers, but to be servant of all. Discipleship is tough, and it may even bring persecution, but when it springs from one's relationship to God it is accompanied by eternal life—life in the kingdom of God. But still that life is the gift of God.—John P. Dever

SUNDAY: OCTOBER SIXTEENTH

SERVICE OF WORSHIP

Sermon: Healing the Pain of our Past

TEXT: John 8:2–11

The scene is the Temple in Jerusalem early in the morning. Already a crowd had gathered around Jesus when the Pharisees arrived with this woman. "Teacher," they said to Jesus, "this woman was caught in the act of adultery. In the Law Moses commanded us to stone such women. Now what do you say?" (vv. 4–5).

It was a trap. If Jesus said kill her, he violated the law of Rome. If he said set her free, he seemed to be violating the law of Moses. What did Jesus do? He made no direct response at first. Rather he bent down and began to write with his finger in the dirt.

I believe that Jesus was writing something. We don't know what it was. I wish that John had recorded what he wrote.

But I would like to suggest some things that Jesus may have written. He may have written any of these because they are true to his nature and true to the story.

I. Does she have a name? Much of the problem of religion in Jesus' day is that it had forgotten people as persons. Anytime religion sets out after sin without loving the sinner, it becomes judgmental. (a) This woman had sinned. No doubt about that. She had committed adultery, and Jesus told her to go and sin no more. But nowhere in the story do we have the slightest hint that her accusers ever saw her as a person. She was simply someone to be caught and used to try to trap Jesus.

(b) Does she have a name? The only name that I have ever heard her called is "the woman taken in adultery." But we all have a name, and we all have dreams and desires for life. We are persons created by God, children of God by creation waiting to become his special children through Christ.

c) We are more than just the sum of our sins. We are not just adulterers or whatever our sin may be. We are persons, and Christ treated her with a beautiful blend of compassion and challenge: "Then neither do I condemn you . . . Go now and leave your life of sin" (v. 11).

II. Don't you have anything better to do? The Gospel of John tells us that this whole drama was played out at the break of day. Apparently, the enemies of Jesus had been out at least most of the night trying to find some sin. It's almost funny to imagine these religious leaders moving around in the shadows of the night ready to pounce on the first available sin.

(a) Don't you have anything better to do? Is the business of religion to expose sin? In a way, the answer is yes. Everything is not relative and all's not right with the world. Our nation faces moral chaos with the collapse of vital values. The church is called to speak powerfully to the things that degrade, demoralize, and devastate the lives of people.

(b) But we are not just against things! We are for the gospel of Jesus Christ which is the good news. That is what is missing in the way that the Pharisees dealt with this woman. No grace, no mercy, no hope, no forgiveness, and no good news. She sinned. Let's stone her! That's the end of the story.

(c) But that's not the end of the story for Jesus. He knew that along with the bad news, "we have failed," comes the best news, "we can be forgiven." That's the message of the cross. When I look at the cross, I see the shame of my sin, but I also see, as John Bunyan said, "Grace abounding."

III. Some have said that instead of saying anything in particular, Jesus might have written in the sand different sins that people commit. Adultery, self-righteousness, hatred, jealousy—one by one. He wrote the sins in the sand. And one by one the accusers of the woman slipped through the crowd and were left to ponder the question, "Which of us is without sin?"

(a) In his writings, Frederick Buechner has reminded us of the power of words. Home—that word elicits a multitude of images. Love, family, death, divorce—words have the power to bless or to bite. Take the word sin. In many ways that word has lost its power among us. Maybe we need a new word, but the problem is finding a word to replace it. Our great problem is that we have learned to talk about sin in general but never be confronted or convicted by our own sins.

(b) Faith that loses its humility becomes harsh and judgmental. Humility is keeping before me my own failings and my need to depend upon God. It's reminding myself that when I preach I am a sinner saved forever but strengthened each moment by the power of God. To people who wanted to throw stones, our Lord held up a mirror. And if we dare to look at ourselves, we will see someone who struggles with his or her own sins.

IV. The past is over. Go and claim your future. Jesus may very well have written something like this. It's consistent with the text. Jesus forgave her past when he said, "Neither do I condemn you." But if Jesus wrote something like, "the past is over; go and claim your future," it's not just consistent with the text but more importantly it's consistent with all of Jesus' ministry.

(a) He came to tell us about a Father who calls us by his grace through faith to a forgiven and fulfilled life. Jesus can liberate us from the stain and pain of our past and then liberate us to a life worth living.

(b) But did the woman in the story accept the offer of Jesus? We don't know. She had some options. She might have gone back to her old life of adultery. That was the way she knew, and some of us find it more comfortable to stay with things simply as they are. We know to do better, but it does take courage to change.

(c) My hope and prayer are that this woman in the story went home forgiven, fulfilled, and forever changed. But it was her decision, just as it is up to each of us to say yes or no to the invitation of Christ.

So I want to ask you. Is it yes? Or is it no? How we answer will make all the difference in our lives.—Charles B. Bugg

Illustrations

BEYOND NEGATIVES. I have always enjoyed the remark of the little English girl who asked her overstrict nurse wistfully, "If I'm extra good in heaven, may I have some little devils in for tea now and then?" She had sensed so young what the years cushion us into forgetting that there is something dreadfully lacking in any approach to life which has no other word but "No, no, no" for life's valid instinct is to enjoy itself.—Frederick B. Speakman

FELLOW PILGRIMS. About once a month some patient at the psychiatric clinic where I work will, with a gesture of exasperation, say. "How can you listen to such depressing stories all day long? Don't you get disgusted with all these sick, messed-up people?"

I never know just how to answer, for those I counsel usually become cherished friends, and I'm uncomfortable to have them referred to—even by themselves—with disdain. I do not see them as "sick,"

but as fellow pilgrims who have many of the same struggles I have and who perhaps will gain some clarity as we look at their situations together. Not only do they honor me with their friendship, they continue to teach me about the human soul. And as we talk together about the inner recesses of their lives, I gain some insight into my own.—Alan Loy McGinnis

Sermon Suggestions

WHEN GOD QUESTIONS US. TEXT: Job 38:1–7 (34–41). (1) First, we question God: It is almost inevitable. We are human. (2) Next, God questions us: it is "meet, right, and proper" for him to do so. He is Lord and Creator. (3) Then, we stand in the presence of mystery, and the ultimate questions belong to God.

JESUS, OUR HIGH PRIEST. TEXT: Heb. 5:1–10, NRSV. (1) "He became the source of eternal salvation" for us, (2) Through the fervent prayers, (3) And through his "reverent submission," which made him the perfect Savior "through what he suffered."

Worship Aids

CALL TO WORSHIP. "Stand fast therefore in the liberty wherewith Christ hath made us free" (Gal. 5:1).

INVOCATION. O Lord, our God, you have called us to be your people, a people to bring honor and glory to your holy name. You have put us forth into the world as your witnesses. Strengthen us now by your Spirit in our inner selves that we may be and become that special people who call others also to praise and serve you.

OFFERTORY SENTENCE. "He that hath a bountiful eye shall be blessed; for he giveth of his bread to the poor" (Prov. 22:9).

OFFERTORY PRAYER. God of grace, take this offering and use it mightily from here to mission fields far distant, all close to the heart of God.—E. Lee Phillips

PRAYER. O Lord, our God, our Father in Jesus Christ thy Son, our brother! We give thee thanks that everything is as we have attempted to say and to hear it once more today. We are sorry to have so often been blind and deaf to the light and the meaning of thy word. We are sorry for all the perversion of our life, resulting from this obstinacy. We know very well that without thee we go astray, time and again. We ask thee for thy Holy Spirit to touch us, to awaken us, to make us attentive, humble, and courageous.

This we ask not only each one for himself, but each one for all others, for the inmates of this house and all prisoners throughout the world, for the sick in body and soul, for the destitute and the refugees, for all those whose grief and needs are hidden from us, though not from thee. We ask this also for our families, for all parents, teachers, and children, for government and court officials, for the preachers and missionaries of thy gospel.

Help them and help us all to bear what must be borne, but also to think, to speak and to do what is right, above all to believe, to love and to hope according to the measure thou wilt give to them and to us. ["Our Father . . ."]—Karl Barth, a prayer offered in the prison in Basel, Switzerland, where Barth preached regularly.

LECTIONARY MESSAGE

Topic: Rank and Power vs. Service and Servanthood

TEXT: Mark 10:35–45

One always hesitates to give credence to a philosophical argument by an atheistic cynic, but Nietzsche's prophecy that the "will to power" would fill the twentieth century vacuum of values seems to have held true. It is true on the corporate level of business and national and world politics. It is also true on the personal, individual level as people try to shed all restraints and attain autonomy.

As I write these words, there are seventy-two days left before the 1992 presidential election. The drive for that power position has already brought out the worst in both parties. The price of power looms so great that any price will be paid to win. While many basic values such as family and education are being proclaimed, some even more basic values such as truth and integrity are being tossed out the window. Our desire to control our own destiny and to impose our will on others still is very basic to our human or, should I say, sinful nature.

I. Rank and power. James and John had been a part of the inner circle of disciples. It is obvious that Jesus had noticed their leadership abilities and wanted to make sure they were prepared to take over after his death. Whether it was the result of this special treatment or their somewhat privileged background as the sons of a successful fisherman, or their human "will to power," these young men were ambitious. When it was all over and Jesus had triumphed, they wanted to be the chief ministers of state. In their world, power and position were synonymous.

Things haven't changed much in the latter part of the twentieth century. Power is still connected with position or money, and money controls position. If this were simply true of the secular world, one might understand better. But it is also prevalent in the church. Like James and John we often seek the glory and power of the kingdom. Power and position within the ranks of the church are prizes often sought by ministers and laity.

Church conventions rival political conventions. Would-be power brokers prowl the halls to get certain persons elected to positions of power knowing they will reap their reward with an appointment or at least input into future decisions. Although it takes a different form, the local church is often plagued by those who seek power and positions that will get their name in the limelight.

James and John misunderstood greatness and so do we. Jesus had much to say to them and to us.

II. Service and servanthood. First, Jesus insisted that they didn't know what they were asking. Great tribulation and suffering lay ahead. Would they be able to drink his cup of sorrow or be baptized with his baptism of fire? Their quickness to respond indicates that they had not really pondered the challenge of Jesus. Their own "will to power" had blinded them to the real intent of Jesus.

Second, Jesus pointed them to a new approach to attain greatness. Very few persons in the first century (or the twentieth) would have associated the words service and servant with the term greatness. This was the role of a slave. But Jesus said, "Whoever would be great among you must be your servant, and whoever would be first among you must be slave of all." This was what Jesus was called to do, and it was what he was calling them to do. Paul understood this when he wrote: "Have this mind among yourselves, which you have in Christ Jesus, who, though he was in the form of God, . . . emptied himself, taking the form of a servant" (Phil. 2:5–7).

This is Jesus' call to us in the church today. We are still expected to be a community of servants. This seems to defy everything we are taught from childhood. Don't let anyone take advantage of you. Stand up for your rights. Individualism and self-centeredness are a part of our culture. Jesus says you do not accomplish greatness by elevating yourself over others. Greatness comes when we become servants of all.

Conclusions: Charles "Chuck" Colson had risen to the heights of power in the Nixon administration. He fell to the depths of despair and frustration during the Watergate incident. He wrote in *Life Sentence:* "All my life I labored for success, wealth, acceptance, and power. The more I obtained, the less I discovered I had. Surrendering everything in absolute brokenness, however, was the beginning of finding the identity and purpose for which I had battled so hard. In giving my life to Christ, I had found it." He discovered his servant role as minister to those in prison.

Maybe Jesus is saying to James and John, "See fellows, that's what I was talking about."—John P. Dever

SUNDAY: OCTOBER TWENTY-THIRD

SERVICE OF WORSHIP

Sermon: Mercy Mediated Through Jesus

TEXT: Hebrews 4:14–16

From what I can gather, the epistle to the Hebrews was written to a people struggling with pain and perplexity. Read the letter; you'll see for yourself. And frankly, it matters very little the exact nature of their discomfort and distress.

What does matter is their apparent request for some word to lift their failing faith; some certainty upon which to anchor their sinking souls; some promise to keep their legs steady and spirits strong; some presence greater than their deepest grief!

I. It is so common to feel completely alone in our misery, isn't it? That hospital room can take on the dimensions of a dungeon when some deadly disease has you flat on your back. That living room will look like a dark and desperate place if your spouse or child or parent will never again come through that door.

(a) Here's the question: Who really cares? Is there someone—anyone—we can be assured truly understands?

The author of the Letter to the Hebrews wrote that—in and throughout all their struggles and sufferings—his people need not despair. But, rather than point to some power within human potential, he proclaimed Christ, the "great high priest."

(b) How could it not comfort us to hear this truth about the crucified and exalted

Christ? Jesus knew, intimately, of those life experiences which so often strain our spirits to the breaking point.

And he knew of those human pains which, if left unconquered, will eventually lead only to doubt, despair, and a deadly form of discouragement, which can cause one to disown the Christian confession. Then the soul is left to wander in the wastelands of self-pity and a hopeless preoccupation with its own darkness and distress. But there's another way, you know.

II. Were you aware that when the author of Hebrews speaks of "mercy," he means, first and foremost, the forbearance of God? In other words, God forever stands behind his promise to be with us and for us, despite our petty foolishness and failures in faith. You know how that goes, don't you?

(a) God's heart simply overflows with tender compassion for creature and creation. And mercy is the pity which places the Lord's love smack-dab at the center of every human weakness, misery, and helpless heartache we could ever possibly have.

(b) The Letter to the Hebrews proclaims our God as one who possesses a generous and kindly disposition. And it also suggests that "mercy" has to do with God's sympathy for our deepest, darkest struggles within this life. Because, as John Calvin once said, "Christ has put on our feelings along with our flesh."

(c) Perhaps we'll never understand why we suffer so many senseless pains in this life. But shouldn't it somehow remove such sufferings from the realm of meaningless affliction if we know that Christ bears them with us and within us? Isn't it a comfort to know that Christ, above and beyond all others, cares continuously?

(d) In essence, Hebrews tells us that there's nothing in human existence—or the entire realm of creation, for that matter—that we, in Christ, cannot see through to triumph!

III. But let's remember this: The primary thing is neither the physical distress, nor the mental turmoil—much less, the spiritual anguish we sometimes suffer. No! The primary issue is the inner

response which the soul and spirit make to these outward influences. And that's why the author of Hebrews would encourage us to "approach the throne of grace with boldness."

(a) He's talking about prayer, isn't he? And we must be careful. In our misery, we may well become powerless. But we should never become prayerless! I've seen that happen to some of the most saintly souls. They suffer some incurable disease, or some unyielding sorrow—and then they begin to doubt both the purpose and power of prayer. The depth of their misery makes them wonder if God pays attention to even the weakest word.

And yet, when properly understood, prayer isn't so much about the power of words—as it is the placement of our hearts!

With prayer we can place every confusion, fear, frustration, and pain which plagues our hearts before the presence, and therefore, in the power of God.

(b) Prayer, even stammering, stuttering, stumbling prayer, will bring our pain into the presence of the God who welcomes us, and the Christ who truly understands and comforts us.

Christ knows how we feel whenever hardships bear down on our lives. And he does "because he himself was tested by what he suffered," and so, "he is able to help those who are being tested." Now, what do you think? Shouldn't the assurance of Christ's sympathy encourage and sustain us when things go from bad to worse?

"Since, then, we have a great high priest who has passed through the heavens, Jesus, the Son of God, let us hold fast to our confession. For we do not have a high priest who is unable to sympathize with our weaknesses, but one who in every respect has been tested as we are, yet without sin."

IV. Jesus Christ has once and for all taken our human needs to his heart. This, beyond doubt, was a significant feature of his Passion. And although Jesus did all of this once and for all, he did not do it once only!

(a) Because, we confess, Jesus Christ has been raised from the dead! Or, in the language of the Letter to the Hebrews, Jesus has "passed through the heavens." So now the exalted Christ takes all human need to heart "with undiminished severity!"

(b) In Hebrews, Christ guarantees a merciful and boundless compassion. With that, he gives the despairing Christian—or the entire congregation—the confidence to trust that he is ever near with mercy to soothe our hearts, compassion to console our fears, and the power to see that, by his grace, we soon prevail.

"Let us therefore approach the throne of grace with boldness, so that we may receive mercy and find grace to help in time of need!"—Albert J. D. Walsh

Illustrations

ADDICTION AND GRACE. Addiction cannot be defeated by the human will acting on its own, nor by the human will opting out and turning everything over to divine will. Instead, the power of grace flows most fully when human will chooses to act in harmony with divine will. In practical terms, this means staying in a situation, being willing to confront it as it is, remaining responsible for the choices one makes in response to it, but at the same time turning to God's grace, protection, and guidance as the ground for one's choices and behavior. It is the difference between testing God by avoiding one's own responsibilities and trusting God as one acts responsibly.—Gerald G. May

CONFIDENCE. I'll call her Esther. She knew neither fortune nor fame. She was a very common and careful woman. Simple and straightforward. There came the time in her life when the cancer couldn't be contained. And, as her pastor, I witnessed her waste away to mere skin and bones.

Now this woman had nothing and she had no one. Each time I would visit Esther, I'd ask if anyone had visited, written, or called. And her response was always the same. She'd hang her head and whisper, "No." Wouldn't you expect such

a woman to sooner or later become bitter and broken? Broken, that is more by disinterest, neglect, and loneliness than by the disease.

But not Esther. She continued to display such a strong and noble character. And she would often glow with a confidence that simply defies description. Then, on the day of her death, I held her hand as she struggled to say: "I've all that I need. I've the mercy of my Lord Jesus. I've got Christ's mercy—He remembers me—there's nothing more!"—Albert J. D. Walsh

Sermon Suggestions

JOB'S FINAL WISDOM. TEXT: Job 42:1–6, 10–17. (1) God's purpose cannot be thwarted. (2) We talk when we should be listening. (3) Only through experience do we truly know God. (4) The proper response to these truths is to repent in humility.

A PRIEST FOREVER. TEXT: Heb. 7:23–28. (1) Christ lives forever to plead our case. (2) Christ died once for all as a sacrifice for our sins.

Worship Aids

CALL TO WORSHIP. "The Lord by wisdom hath founded the earth; by understanding hath he established the heavens. By his knowledge the depth are broken up, and the clouds drop down the dew" (Prov. 3:19, 20).

INVOCATION. O God, we would escape from ourselves this hour, from our little and partial selves, from our mean and selfish selves. We would escape from our fragmentary and broken selves into thy greatness. Teach us once again the everlasting mystery that only as we lose ourselves in something higher than ourselves can we find ourselves.—Harry Emerson Fosdick

OFFERTORY SENTENCE. "I have shewed you all things, how that so laboring ye ought to support the weak, and to remember the words of the Lord Jesus, how he said, It is more blessed to give than to receive" (Acts 20:35).

OFFERTORY PRAYER. Lord, grant to our giving sustenance, to our intent holiness, and to the result the glory due your name.—E. Lee Phillips

PRAYER. Father, we know that you are able to give light which will make it possible for us to see in the darkness through which we so often have to walk. We know that you give life which causes us to rejoice amid the gloom of despair. We know that you give peace which brings quietness to our troubled spirits.

We know that most of the darkness and despair and unrest which we encounter are of our own making. We get busy seeking those treasures which moth and rust corrupt and satisfying our self-centered drives and do not take the time to engage in those enterprises which will glorify your name and bring good to everyone. So we come asking forgiveness for our lack of sensitivity to your truth and the following of your leadership as we walk through each day. Arrest us this morning with some word fitly spoken, some thought rightly placed, some visions timely delivered, so that we can begin the walk along the road that will lead us to where you would have us be and allow us to do the deeds you have called us to do. O Father, deliver us from continuing to center all our energies on our demands, so that we can follow your commands.

And before you this morning we also bring the many sufferers of our congregation, community, country, and continents. Our feeble efforts seem so small beside the massive pains of others. This morning be with those who care for the wounded, those who wait through hours of anxiety, and those who endure afflictions. Somehow in the murkiness of disease and pain, make your powerful presence known as you come with healing in your wings to minister to the sufferers. Now we commit the hour to you even as we commit ourselves to your care and keeping.—Henry Fields

LECTIONARY MESSAGE

Topic: Voices from Jericho—Voices from San Francisco

TEXT: Mark 10:46–52

Introduction: New Testament Jericho was one of the magnificent building projects of Herod the Great. The architecture and layout of the city rivaled Pompeii, but Jericho was constructed on a more expansive site. Pools, parks, sunken gardens, and villas dotted the landscape, and magnificent homes and buildings were located close to the stream that ran through the city. The balmy winter climate made it a perfect winter capital for Herod.

Jericho was a city of wealth and a city of beggars. Luxury and poverty coexisted in the confines of this Judean city. There were wealthy tax collectors such as Zacchaeus who lived in the finest homes in the city—homes that compared with the best in Pompeii. There were street people like blind Bartimaeus who eked out a living by appealing to the pity or religious guilt of the upper class. Not so different from the cities of America.

I. A voice from the outcasts. One can only imagine the near mob scene that accompanied Jesus as he left Jericho that day. His visit with Zacchaeus had brought him instant celebrity status. There in the crowd, being pushed and shoved, was a perennial beggar. This was his street corner and now the mob was destroying his business. He too had heard of this prophet from Nazareth and surely he could count on Jesus for a few coins and just maybe he would perform one of his miracles on him. What had promised to be a good day was being threatened by the surging procession.

"Jesus, Son of David, have mercy on me!" came the cry from the dirty, smelly street beggar. Again and again with strained voice, "Jesus, Son of David, have mercy on me!"

My wife and I have just returned from San Francisco. What a magnificent city. Beautiful architecture, scenic wonders, exciting blend of ethnic cultures, gourmet food, enticing shops are just a few phrases that one could use to describe the West Coast wonder. But the scenes that linger in our minds are those we saw on the streets of San Francisco. In the midst of wealth, poverty abounded. A woman with two children and a sign, "We are hungry." A weather-beaten woman clutching her beautiful begger can as she screeched out a song of despair. A man in a wheelchair who never left his corner, day or night—you can imagine the rest. A blind beggar—I wonder if his name was Bartimaeus?—asking for any extra change. The voices of the poor and the outcasts still cry out in San Francisco and in Chicago and in New York and in. . . . The list is infinite.

II. A voice from the establishment. "Shut up you miserable wretch. Jesus may speak any moment. We don't want to miss a word. Someone call the authorities and get this howling dog removed." The clean, recently-bathed establishment types were embarrassed that these smelly beggars would try to use this opportunity to get a few more coins. This Bartimaeus was a particular nuisance. "At the very next city senate meeting I'm going to propose an ordinance to ban these people from the streets of downtown Jericho." This must have crossed the mind of more than one local leader.

How to deal with this group of outcasts has plagued the establishment for centuries. Do you put them in institutions? Do you solve the problem with soup lines? Do you ignore them and hope they will go away? They are a pain! They congregate in the cities and exasperate the overburdened police department. They hurt the tourist trade. Why don't they just shut up and go away?

III. A different voice. "Jesus stopped and said, 'Call him.'" Startled that his efforts had been rewarded, Bartimaeus decided to go for it all. "Master, let me receive my sight. Make me whole again." And Jesus responded, "Go your way; your faith has made you well." And the scripture says he received his sight.

There is no way I can imagine the joy that surged through that man's soul that day. I won't even try. But what I can do is imagine the astonishment of the crowd when Jesus stopped and called for the beggar and healed him. Eating with Zaccheus was one thing. Healing this worthless wretch was another. I wonder if they learned anything that day. Maybe I should ask if we who are alive twenty centuries later have learned anything from the actions of Jesus.

Jesus saw Bartimaeus as a person of worth—a person with potential. Jesus taught us that people are more important than things. People are more important than buildings. People are more important than expensive clothes. People are more important than gourmet food. People are more important than. . . . I guess we haven't learned yet!—John P. Dever

SUNDAY: OCTOBER THIRTIETH

SERVICE OF WORSHIP

Sermon: Extraordinary Living for Ordinary People

Text: Romans 1:1

Enthusiastic sinners often become lazy saints, but such was not the case with Paul. He went all out no matter what he did. When he was bad, he was very, very bad: the chief of sinners, he called himself (see 1 Tim. 1:15). When he was good, he was extraordinarily good: "not a whit behind the very chiefest apostles" (2 Cor. 11:5, 12:11), he claimed. Second only to Jesus, Paul easily ranks as the most extraordinary person in the history of Christianity. He is living proof extraordinary living is available for ordinary people. What made his such an extraordinary life? Perhaps unwittingly the apostle set out his secret in the text. From it, ordinary people can learn what extraordinary living demands.

I. *Surrender.* The apostle enjoyed the prized privilege of being a free-born Roman citizen and further rejoiced in the freedom of the sons of God, but he delighted in calling himself "a servant of

Christ Jesus!" Actually this word, *doulos*, indicated the lowest kind of slave.[1] A *doulos* had no choice in any matter. He worked without pay, praise, or time off and owed his master unquestioning obedience, even to the point of breaking the law or giving up his life. In short, a *doulos* belonged to his master.

In this same spirit Paul served Christ. He had made that kind of surrender on the road to Damascus when he knelt in the dust and whispered, "Lord!" From that day Paul was Christ's man. He was at his disposal and under his command. He was the slave of Christ to be sent or to stay, used or laid aside in jail, whatever the Master pleased. Absolute surrender to the Lord Jesus made Paul's life extraordinary.

Ordinary people who want to live extraordinary lives must begin with full surrender to Christ. They must take Jesus not as partner, copilot, or "good buddy," but as Master. Aiming to do the Lord's will, nothing more, nothing less, and nothing else, will make any life extraordinary.

II. *Service*. In the New Testament an "apostle" was a fully authorized representative.[2] Paul stood as a proxy for Christ, in the place of Christ, and with the personal authority of Christ. Paul's words and deeds in the name of Christ were as much the words and deeds of Christ as if Christ himself had done them.

If it is important that Paul was an apostle, it is even more important for the present purpose to see how he got to be one. This was not a role he took for himself. Neither was it given him by the Jerusalem congregation. He had received a divine call to this work. Yet Paul would have admitted quickly that other believers had received a divine call to some other kind of service.

In a Roman household the master assigned some slaves to cut grass and tend gardens, others to keep records and teach children, and still others to clean house and cook. Not all slaves did the same job. That principle holds in the household of God. The Lord has a purpose for each of his servants. He called Paul an apostle. He called some lawyers and nurses. He called others teachers and farmers and still others secretaries and homemakers. The way to extraordinary living lies in hearing and heeding God's call, no matter what it is. Finding and fulfilling God's purpose will change any person's life from ordinary to extraordinary.

III. *Separation*. Some people focus on things Christians need to be "separated from." This is a valid emphasis. However, Paul put separation into a positive form, "separated unto the gospel." This phrase meant that Paul had dedicated himself wholeheartedly to Christ and his gospel.[3] The person so separated rarely has to worry about giving up things. He will find that many things give him up. Few boys make a conscious decision to give up playing marbles. But when tough football and tender girls claim their attention and time, marbles give them up. Many things, some of them perfectly fine things, give up the person whose all-consuming passion for Christ and the gospel leaves him no time for them.

An ordinary person who devotes himself to Christ has little time for life's less important things. He will find his life most extraordinary.

An old tale is told about a wild goose who happened by a barnyard and gathered all the tame farm geese around him. "You do not have to waddle around in this muck and mire," he honked. "You can soar on winds and travel to parts unknown. Break out of the ordinary and come fly with me!" he urged. The tame geese listened attentively and applauded

[1] R. Tuente, "Slave," *New International Dictionary of New Testament Theology*, ed. Colin Brown (Grand Rapids, MI: Zondervan, 1986), 593.
[2] Karl Heinrich Rengstorf, "Apostolos," *Theological Dictionary of the New Testament*, ed. Gerhard Kittel (Grand Rapids, MI: William B. Eerdmans Publishing Co., 1964), 398–447.

[3] John Murray, *Epistle to the Romans* (Grand Rapids: William B. Eerdmans Publishing Co., 1965), 3.

his message. "What a wonderful thing," they cried, but they turned and waddled back to their grain trough, leaving the wild goose to fly on alone.

Paul has given positive proof that extraordinary living is possible for ordinary people. What will you do? Listen politely and then go back to ordinary living? Or rise to fly with him?—Cecil Taylor

Illustrations

WHAT WE OWE.   We owe God faith, said Luther, not works. We owe our neighbors good works. Only by trusting God are we enabled to love the neighbor selflessly. You get good works from good people. You don't seek apples from a thorn bush, Luther noted. Christian ethics arise out of Christian faith. That is why Paul, in his letters to young churches, lists his ethical injunctions after his theological affirmations. First he talks about God, then with a transitional "therefore" or "because," he talks about the implications of God's behavior for our behavior. Paul believes that our actions flow from our being.—William H. Willimon

SOMETHING MORE THAN FAITHFULNESS. Sometimes in a pastoral counseling situation a man or woman will say to me, "I have never been unfaithful to my spouse." This is one good and important building block, but it is not enough of a foundation to build a warm and nourishing home. The question I want to ask such a person is this: "But what have you done positively to grow in your faithfulness together?"

It is not enough to stand before God and humanity and say, "I have never murdered anyone." This negative achievement is commendable but hardly adequate to satisfy the grand intention of God's law. Have you "loved your neighbor as yourself" (Lev. 19:18)? Have you "proved neighbor to the man who fell among the robbers" (Luke 10)? In the same way the family needs more than mere faithfulness to fulfill the mandate's intention, but it does need faithfulness!—Earl Palmer

Sermon Suggestions

HEAR, O ISRAEL—AND EVERYONE ELSE! TEXT: Deut. 6:1–9. (1) The commandment, verse 5. (2) The reason, verse 4. (3) The method, verses 6–9 (cf. John 14:15).

THE WAY OF HAPPINESS.   TEXT: Ps. 119:1–8. (1) It is the way of seeking the Lord, verse 2. (2) It is the way of obedience, verses 1, 2a, 3, 4. (3) It is the way of prayer for steadfastness, verses 6–7. (4) It is the way of praise, verse 7. (5) It is the way of commitment, verse 8.

Worship Aids

CALL TO WORSHIP.   "If ye then be risen with Christ, seek those things which are above, where Christ sitteth on the right hand of God" (Col. 3:1).

INVOCATION.   Almighty God, our Father, who brought again from the dead our Lord Jesus Christ, help us to live the lives of those who have been raised with him to walk in newness of life. Give us high aspirations in all things and lift our thoughts above everything that would keep us from fulfilling thy purpose for us.

OFFERTORY SENTENCE.   "Whatsoever ye do, do it heartily, as to the Lord, and not unto men; knowing that of the Lord ye shall receive the reward of the inheritance; for ye serve the Lord Christ" (Col. 3:23, 24).

OFFERTORY PRAYER.   Father, make us aware that every kingdom on this earth, even yours, can only survive as money is made available to carry out its purposes. We haven't done too well in supporting yours. Help us to see the need to do better, even today, we pray in Jesus' name.—Henry Fields

PRAYER.   For the gift of this day to celebrate the Reformed tradition of which we are heirs, we praise you! For the renewal which came to the Church in an earlier generation and which keeps coming in every generation as men and women through faith discover and rediscover your Word strangely alive by the power of your indwelling Spirit, we are grateful. Let us not forget or neglect that we have inherited a revolution—a continuing revolution—old things are passed away, behold all things are becoming new. That the Reformers discerned our true relationship to you and to one another, that we are as priests before you and that we are priests to one another, is occasion for much rejoicing. For this amazing access, that the finite can have audience with the Infinite as a child speaks to his or her father is of your grace. That the ground is level at the foot of the cross and that the way to your presence is equally open to every person, we are glad. It is your grace that saves us from ourselves and our pride. We no longer need to plummet ourselves in straining after good works, but through faith receive your mighty deeds for our salvation in Christ. Here is the light that no darkness can ever put out, the light of your love and grace that perseveres through every dark night of the soul.

How difficult sometimes, O Father, to discern your love when life-threatening crises come crashing into our lives. In the face of such vicissitudes increase our faith to hear your Word spoken through Christ at the cross: "I will never leave you or forsake you." That we are kept by a love that does not let us go in life or in death is the mystery of your perennial presence.

As this Reformation Sunday reminds us of our high calling to be priests before you and to one another may we be all here for you and for all others. So many times you knock at the door and nobody is home and others knock and turn away disappointedly. May your words spoken in another context, verily speak to us this morning: "Except your brother be with you, you shall not see my face." The way we treat others is the way we treat you. To hear your Word in Christ, to follow him, means nothing unless we are as he was, a person for others. To enter into the mystery of intercessory prayer is to affirm and celebrate the mystery of your

grace in using the human instrument, us, in the fulfillment of your love purpose.— John Thompson

LECTIONARY MESSAGE

Tropic: The Main Thing

TEXT: Mark 12:28–34

After being attacked by the chief priests and scribes, the Pharisees and the Sadducees, Jesus probably just wanted to go home. But here, at the end of the day, came an honest question from a curious lawyer. What did Jesus think was the most important command in the Law?

Other rabbis gave summaries, and most of them stressed the same sorts of things Jesus did. When Jesus was done, this lawyer who was not part of Jesus' crowd could find nothing wrong with his answer. It was not noteworthy, then, because it was a radical or original answer. What Jesus said came from the very heart of Judaism, and Christians and Muslims could agree with it as well. So why is this, the most important commandment, so special?

I. Love God with all you are—that's the first and most important commandment. The one God who made all things, who made you as well, commands your absolute and utter devotion and loyalty. Nothing you do will matter as much as whether you can take your ambitions, emotions, commitments, and thoughts and dedicate them to God. That's what love in this context means, you understand. Love, not as a warm feeling, but as constant giving, constant obedience, constant bowing in God's direction.

But I can't do that. I can't even keep all my ambitions straight to give them to God. Every time I think I know what I want with my life, some desire I didn't even know I had surfaces, and makes me wish for greener pastures. And emotions? Some days I do better than others, but after all these years I still yell at the referees on the basketball court. Thoughts? Forget about it. Turn the page, and listen to part two of Jesus' summary.

II. Love your neighbor as yourself. The Age of Me has taught us that to love others, it is necessary to love ourselves. We cannot give to others if we constantly beat ourselves up over our failures. That is true; but it seems that all the self-help we've lavished on ourselves over the past decades really has not improved our neighbor-love all that much. Jesus' emphasis was on love as something we do for someone else who needs it—Zacchaeus needed a friend, Jairus needed his little girl's life, and so forth. Can any human being really do as much for someone else as he or she does for himself or herself? Can we really spend as much time meeting another's needs as we spend meeting our own?

Love God with all that you are, and love your neighbor as yourself. It is ridiculously simple; it does not even have twelve steps to it. It is a recognized truth of at least three great world faiths, so that it is not even unique. But it is agonizingly hard to bring off. If you make this summary your life's goal, you will spend your life trying to reach it.—Richard B. Vinson

SUNDAY: NOVEMBER SIXTH

SERVICE OF WORSHIP

Sermon: The Cutting Edge of Christian Life

TEXT: Hebrews 4:12–13

At some point in time we've all made poor choices, and we've also witnessed, in others, the painful consequences of our own careless behaviors. None of it reflects well on our characters. So, we simply pack it away. We hide it somewhere in the darkest corners of our hearts.

Believe it or not, this human propensity for keeping things hidden in the heart has been around for a long time. So long, in fact, that the very first occurrence is recorded in the Book of Genesis. I'm certain you remember the story, don't you?

Adam and Eve had fallen from grace, in the lame desire to grab more than their fair share of freedom. Some folk are never satisfied to be "in the image of God"; they must "be like God"—answerable to no outside authority!

Anyhow, subsequent to their sin, the story reads: "They heard the sound of the Lord God walking in the garden at the time of the evening breeze, and the man and his wife hid themselves from the presence of the Lord God among the trees of the garden." They hid behind some trees?

Sometimes we try to conceal our personal sins, by taking shelter on a Sunday morning, behind the corporate prayer of confession. Maybe we hide behind the self-righteous conviction that our sins are seldom as significant as those of another, or others. Then again, perhaps we avoid having to confess anything of any real significance by burying ourselves in a busy schedule.

Stay clear of God—and you'll be better able to cover up your guilt. We make every effort to conceal that which ultimately can't be hidden.

Which is exactly what was said in the letter to the Hebrews. Do you remember? "Indeed," the letter reads, "the word of God is living and active, sharper than any two-edged sword, piercing until it divides soul from spirit, joints from marrow; it is able to judge the thoughts and intentions of the heart. And before (God) no creature is hidden, but all are naked and laid bare to the eyes of the one to whom we must render an account."

I. "The word of God is living and active, sharper than any two-edged sword." When I read those words I no longer wonder just why it is that so many have abandoned the regular reading of scripture. We all know it's true, don't we.

(a) God's word is much more than a mere historical record of past events, isn't it? Just open your Bible, and each time you do, you run the risk of being confronted by your Creator! That's why we're mistaken if we suppose that we can take scripture lightly—as though it were nothing more than fine literature. When in fact, the Spirit of the living God breathes between each and every line!

(b) God searches out all human hearts, speaks to each of us and all of us through his Word—today. Today God renews his appeal, extends his extraordinary promises, and repeats his warnings against wandering far from his will. As someone has said, "to step out of God's will is to step into nothing."

(c) This Word of God not only lives—it works! It's an effective Word, and a relevant Word as well. It's like a sharp sword, cutting its way through this entanglement of resistance stuck away in the human heart. God's living Word goes right to the core of our character, scrutinizes our most sinful self, and eventually uncovers all of those ugly things which are first conceived—and then concealed—in the heart.

II. In his letter to the church at Rome, the Apostle Paul speaks to the very same reality when he writes: "I am not ashamed of the gospel; it is the power of God for salvation to everyone who has faith . . . For in it the righteousness of God is revealed through faith for faith."

(a) In other words, the gospel—as Living Word—is God's effective way of working for human salvation. As someone once said, "God has purposes and performs particular actions—(and he) is a concrete, choosing, commanding, prohibiting, God." And from this God, the human heart hasn't the slightest chance of hiding with any lasting success!

(b) Have you noticed how God's Word will reach down deep into the recesses of our hungering hearts? Have you seen how God searches out our lives—looking into those dark, desperate corners in which we attempt to hide our most hideous thoughts and most thoughtless deeds?

(c) Have you listened as God spoke with a still small voice, speaking to the far reaches of your soul? Have you heard God speaking to you in those places where, because of this world's bewildering and preoccupying noises, no other voice could easily be heard? And have you felt God's voice cutting away at the cancer of sin in your life? Well, have you?

III. God's Word drives deep into our hearts and souls, because God is compelled by a compassion that won't relent until it rids us of everything and anything that prevents us from more fully becoming his people. That's the length of God's love. In fact, it was C. S. Lewis who also said that, "it costs God nothing, so far as we know, to create nice things; but to convert rebellious wills cost him crucifixion!"

(a) Christianity is a life in which we continue—moment by moment—day by day—to submit to the authority of our Savior. Not merely here or there, but everywhere we willingly expose our hearts and souls to the cutting edge of God's Word. In this Christian life "we realize that everything which really needs to be done in our souls, can be done only by God," through the Spirit of our Savior.

(b) Have we personally believed the gospel? Are we willing to freely, and faithfully, bare our souls before the Savior? Do we trust the incredible tenderness and love of this Lord?

(c) And maybe even now someone out there will say: "But I've sinned today. See all my weakness, my broken resolutions, my shame. I want so much to be and become a more faithful follower—a more committed Christian. But I've been a miserable failure. How can I ever come and bare my sickened soul before God?"

IV. There's the gospel, remember? You can come, and you must come because God has already provided the Way!

(a) And that Way is through God's living Word, Jesus Christ. The Letter to the Hebrews praises Christ as "our great high priest." A priest who, himself, once tasted the pain of our very own struggles with temptation. A priest who knows, intimately, the weaknesses of his wounded people. A priest who holds out the promise that he will "neither leave (us) nor forsake (us)." And through this Word, God bids us—"Come!"

(b) Believe me, we needn't come cringing either. In Christ we can come and stand openly before the mercy seat of this gracious God. And we can do so because his love is unconditional. This God knows all, sees all, and loves us still. But perhaps the greatest wonder of his sharp and unrelenting love, is that it wounds us in order to finally and forever heal us!— Albert J. D. Walsh

Illustrations

CONSCIENCE. To say that a person performs certain acts and abstains from others because he fears God's punishment would be to travesty the experience of most religious people, whose consciences have more to do with love than with fear. An inclusive path of life is adopted that requires discipline, charity, reverence, all experienced as lively obligations by a religious person. If we encounter in a personality fear of divine punishment as the sole sanction for right doing, we can be sure we are dealing with a childish conscience, with a case of arrested development.—Gordon W. Allport

HYPOCRISY EXORCISED. The reformer, John Calvin, has rightfully earned the reputation of being a "caustic Christian." Seldom are his observations less than razor-sharp. And when he discusses the surgical characteristics of God's Word, his remarks are no less cutting.

In his commentary on Hebrews, he writes: "Hypocrisy, which has wondrous and infinitely tortuous dens in the human heart, must be beaten out. We must not be gently scratched, but we must be deeply wounded, so that we are laid low by the sense of eternal death and learn to die to ourselves." You see, with God's Word—and only with God's Word—there's a kind of "killing that makes alive."—Albert J.D. Walsh

Sermon Suggestions

UNFAILING RESOURCES. TEXT: 1 Kings 17:8–16. (1) *The story:* A widow provided for the prophet's needs from her meager resources and was blessed by God's provision for her and her son. (2) *The meaning:* God cares for the needs of those who do his will and live by faith. (3) *The application:* a., We should not shrink from doing God's will when faced with hard-

ships. b., We can count on God's presence and blessings when we obey him (cf. Matt. 4:4 and 6:25–33).

THE COMING OF CHRIST. TEXT: Heb. 9:24–28, NRSV. (1) The first time—to deal with sin by his sacrifice on the cross. (2) The second time—to save those who are eagerly waiting for him.

Worship Aids

CALL TO WORSHIP. "Lift up your hands in the sanctuary, and bless the Lord. The Lord that made heaven and earth bless thee out of Zion" (Ps. 134:2–3).

INVOCATION. Almighty God, cause us to scale new heights in our understanding of the Christian life today and leave us not the same.—E. Lee Phillips

OFFERTORY SENTENCE. "Unto whomsoever much is given, of him shall be much required: and to whom men have committed much, of him they will ask the more" (Luke 12:48).

OFFERTORY PRAYER. Grant us to be as generous with thee and with others, as thou hast been with us. We do thank thee for all thy blessings and for the privilege of faithful stewardship.

PRAYER (for new members): Father, we thank you for the Church and for the churches. For those churches which in previous times and other places have challenged us to Christian discipleship and awakened us to eternal life, we are grateful. We praise you for those ministers, parents, Sunday school teachers, youth counselors, friends who through their faithful witness to the gospel have shared the good news with us not only in word but in deed. For this congregation which in this time and place now becomes our spiritual home, we praise you. As we share the worship, the fellowship, the ministry of this congregation, together may we grow toward the maturity that is Christ. On this occasion may a renewed sense of mission infect all of us that we may truly be the Church in all the world and in all the worlds of persons. Through him who loved the Church and gave himself for it.—John Thompson

LECTIONARY MESSAGE

Topic: Give Till It Hurts
TEXT: Mark 12:38–44

I. This story slips up on us. It begins honestly enough: the poor widow's poverty contrasted with others' wealth makes an easy moral. What counts in giving is the sacrifice. She gave lavishly, without restraint, as did the woman who poured out the perfume on Jesus' head. She gave sacrificially, as did the disciples when they first began to follow Jesus. They were not wealthy, either, but they left their homes and businesses, their families and employees. They followed Jesus sacrificially, abandoning their previous lives.

She, too, gives her whole life, all she had to live on. Is this really necessary? Mark thinks so. In his day, becoming a Christian might have been more than a life-changing choice. For many early believers, following Jesus was a life-ending choice. Mark would have his readers know that, and make the choice with their eyes open.

In our day, becoming a real Christian will end our lives as normal Americans. We will no longer unthinkingly accumulate clothes, cars, gadgets, summer homes, boats, vacations to Europe, etc. Our own consumption will not be the center of our universe. If we become real Christians instead of normal Americans, we will abandon, as much as we can, the materialism that fastens onto us from

birth with its leech's mouth and sucks our commitment to God right out of us. If we become real Christians, we will give ourselves to God, and our lives will never again be normal.

II. So far, so good; that is a good story with a powerful message. But the story slips up on us. We are to give to God. But how do we do that? Usually we give to God's messengers or to God's institutions. But beware, says Jesus.

(a) On the one hand, you have the smooth messengers of verses 38–40. They can pray some mighty fine prayers; they are in the front rows at all important meetings; everybody thinks they are fine, godly folk. Watch out for them: they eat up widows' homes. They consume the offerings of God's folk, spending them on clothes, cars, gadgets, summer homes, boats, vacations to Europe (or maybe the Holy Land), etc. Watch out for them, says Jesus.

(b) And beware the institutions, too. The widow threw her two mites into one of the collection boxes in the Temple. She did it sincerely and sacrificially. But Jesus had already attacked the Temple by this point, and was about to predict its destruction in his next words—hardly the place for a wise believer to sink her life's savings. Religious institutions, particularly religious bureaucracies, can also swallow widows' houses in a single gulp.

Give till it hurts? Yes, especially in our luxurious, no-pain culture. But give to God, and not to slick scribes or greedy institutions. Go find a poor widow who has just lost her last two coins, and make sure she doesn't starve in the shadow of God's people.—Richard B. Vinson

SUNDAY: NOVEMBER THIRTEENTH

SERVICE OF WORSHIP

Sermon: Her Whole Living
TEXT: Mark 12:38, 43, 44

I. These seemingly unrelated vignettes of proud scribes and a humble widow are inexplicably linked in Mark's Gospel. My

re-reading of this passage brought to mind one of the first stories I can remember being told. It was about a fabulously wealthy Texan (of such stereotypes are stories made) who decided that when the day came he would be buried in his car. The day came. An astonished little boy watched from a distance as a huge crane lowered the car and owner into the ground.

It was a dream car, a "Rolls-Cadillac-Benz" gold plated and silver filled. No doubt with four on the floor . . . four on the column . . . and two in the glove box. The boy, overcome with this ten-speed splendor, cried out, "*Now, man, that's living!*" What he really saw were the trappings of life, even fine living, but they covered a stark reality: *the man inside was dead.*

II. In this same chapter, we read the account of a scribe who was vibrant, alive, seeking. The scribes pictured in the first story in today's passage are certainly not seeking truth. They had it all. They seemed, in terms of their culture, to have achieved what we seek in ours . . . things worth living for: prominence, respect, money. Now that's living.

One of the goals of living soon adopted by the developing child is prominence. We want to stand out, be recognized, make our mark. The cultural symbols of this prominence may change but the need is cross-cultural. I remember learning in a high school sociology class that status is how people rate us. It is really learned in the hallways and playgrounds. In the scribe's culture, an inferior never spoke first to a superior. The scribes were greeted (give "salutation") first. They had the best seats in the congregation in front of the Ark of the Covenant. Also the best seats at banquets. To be in the "in group," given preferential treatment, fawned over, now that is living!

For some of us, that is a bit too obvious, even crass. Our goal for living is much more honorable; we want to be well-respected by our peers and perceived as wise and learned. That was what the robe symbolized for the scribe. It was a sign that the wearer did not do manual labor. He was to be revered as a person who did not have to get his long robe tangled up in common work. He had earned the respect of the community. That's living! But do we wear our robes well, do we begin to take our learning, wisdom, and ourselves too seriously?

Maybe the most honest folks are those who clearly admit their goal is to make money. Millard Fuller, the founder of Habitat for Humanity, can remember when he set himself the goal of becoming a millionaire while in his 30s and he did it! But acquiring the trappings of living did not satisfy him. He raises money for a very different purpose now. Money is not an evil, it is not an unmentionable from the pulpit. But how is that money acquired and used? It was said of the scribes that they devoured widow's houses. They used the defenseless for their own gains. Is that living?

III. This description of the scribes is linked to the story which follows by the catchword "widow." But I believe it is more than that. Mark has an eye for contrast . . . here contrasting two different ways of living. For it is said of this widow that she gave HER WHOLE LIVING. A woman probably with no prominence, little formal learning, and two thin coins, offers her whole living to God through the very human organization of the Temple (read church). Would not our young friend watching this exclaim, "That is suicide, man, that's dying."

Yet, Jesus chose this widow and her actions as the standard of Christian giving and stewardship. One of the benefits of this season is that we can examine our own standards for the use of our time, talent, and money. In the latter (our emphasis *this* Sunday) have we moved past a tithe of our income? Have we moved to five percent through the church and five percent to other charities? These are helpful gauges, but there is one standard: Our Creator and Redeemer deserves nothing less than our *whole living.* That turns it around and allows us to ask not how much we give but how much we keep back.

Jesus, as he sat across the Temple treasury, could see the streams of people going about the business of giving their tithes and offerings. There were thirteen coffers looking like inverted trumpets in the outer courtyard of the Temple. Some were for the needs of the Temple in its worship and service of God; others were for food for the destitute and clothing for the poor. In passing, would it be wrong to suggest a need as churches and individuals to give our two leptas or coins to both of these needs? There should be balance in our giving.

IV. But the main point of Jesus noticing these two small coins over the din of weightier donations is that the woman did not hold one back. This is significant. It is significant because Jesus is concerned not with an offering of money, but the offering of a life. She gave, according to this translation, "her whole living." That's the way Jesus counts an offering. The little girl was given two quarters, one to go in the offering and the other to buy a candy bar (it's an old story). When she came home eating her candy bar, she explained to her mother that she dropped her money on the way to Sunday school and God's quarter fell down the storm drain. A quarter is a small item after all. How much smaller are two almost worthless coins, lepta? Yet, they became the standard of real giving around the world. Her offering was all of her living, all of her life. What she received from God was more than can be measured.

V. This very brief story makes a good conclusion of Jesus' public ministry. Is it an accident that this story of a widow who gave her all provides the transition to the story of the Passion where Jesus gives himself for us? The events of this week remind us again that "life is too short to be small." It is in Christ's dying for us that we are able to die, to turn over concern for ourselves, and be born to a new life with God and others. The real question of Christian stewardship is, Can we offer any less than our whole living? The lives that turn out to be small are the ones that give only what they don't need. I don't know about you, but I don't want a small life. T. S. Eliot's Prufrock says, "I have measured out my life with coffee spoons." What a sad epitaph! The *New York Times* writer, William Raspberry, often asks audiences to write their own obituary. He asks, "Based on your plan and priorities to date, what will be your lead?" He gave some examples, "He earned $65,000 a year and managed to shelter virtually all of it." "She had a really nice house and drove a BMW...."

Now think of this poor widow woman. It is said of her, She gave her whole living. Her epitaph is a living one for she points to the Christ who gave himself for us, she has pointed the way to giving that is truly large.—Gary D. Stratman

Illustrations

COMMITMENT.   Halford E. Luccock used to chuckle at the denominational hymnal which had the hymn #364, "Jesus Demands My All," with an asterisk after it. The asterisk referred to the bottom of the page where this note occurred: "For an easier version, see #365."—C. Neil Strait

LOVE DEMONSTRATED.   Love needs to be demonstrated, to find expression in gifts, both personal and ritual gifts. Many people look down upon our common traditions, politeness, gallantry, things which they call hollow and formalistic make-believe. But let no one fool you: there is deep meaning in such customs. They are intended to please, and in pleasing others to afford a real pleasure in living to the person who is acting.—Paul Tournier

IF I CAN STOP ONE HEART FROM BREAKING.

If I can stop one heart from breaking,
I shall not live in vain;
If I can ease one life the aching,
Or cool one pain,
Or help one fainting robin
Unto his nest again,
I shall not live in vain.—Emily Dickinson

Sermon Suggestions

THE TABLES TURNED.   TEXT: 1 Sam. 1:4–20 (2:1–10). (1) Hannah's sorrow, verses 4–8. (2) Hannah's prayer, verses 9–18. (3) Hannah's victory, verses 19–20. (4) Hannah's song, 2:1–10.

HOW TO GO THROUGH GOD'S OPEN DOOR. TEXT: Heb. 10:11–14 (15–18), 19–25, NRSV. (1) "In full assurance of faith." (2)

With unwavering hope. (3) With practical mutual love.

Worship Aids

CALL TO WORSHIP.   "Awake, awake, put on thy strength, O Zion" (Isa. 52:1).

INVOCATION.   Eternal God, our heavenly Father, you have given us every reason to rejoice. You have forgiven us of our sins through our Lord Jesus Christ. You have strengthened us in times of temptation. You have led us in marvelous ways all the days of our lives. Help us now to cast aside our fears, confess our unacknowledged sins, look to you for guidance, and praise you with all that is within us. For the sake of your glorious name.

OFFERTORY SENTENCE.   "Give, and it shall be given unto you; good measure, pressed down, and shaken together, and running over. . . . For with the same measure that ye mete withal it shall be measured to you again" (Luke 6:38).

OFFERTORY PRAYER.   Lord, through these tithes and offerings extend the light of Christ Jesus into every needy heart, saving to the uttermost all who believe.—E. Lee Phillips

PRAYER.   O God, we who are bound together in the tender ties of love, pray thee for a day of unclouded love. May no passing irritation rob us of our joy in one another. Forgive us if we have often been keen to see the human failings, and slow to feel the preciousness of those who are still the dearest comfort of our life. May there be no sharp words that wound and scar, and no rift that may grow into estrangement. Suffer us not to grieve those whom thou hast sent to us as the sweet ministers of love. May our eyes not be so holden by selfishness that we know thine angels only when they spread their wings to return to thee.—Walter Rauschenbusch

LECTIONARY MESSAGE

Topic: Don't Be Led Astray

TEXT: Mark 13:1–8

I went into the labor room with my wife for the birth of our first son, armed with a thermos of coffee and a crossword puzzle. The nurse thought the coffee was a good idea, but she laughed at the puzzle; later, as things progressed, I found out why. I was prepared to be there a while, but unprepared for how hard it might be.

I. Jesus tried his best to wake the Twelve up a little. He pounced on an innocent remark—"Isn't that a beautiful building?"—with a cold prediction: "It will be destroyed piece by piece." This was the Temple, mind you, the central institution of God's people, a holy spot of prayer and sacrifice. It will all come crashing down, said Jesus.

Not only that, but you people will be plagued with all sorts of hard times. False saviors will pop up, leading people astray. False sightings of the real Jesus will multiply. There will be turbulent times: physical disasters, earthquakes, and famines; and political disasters, rebellions, and wars. You people, said Jesus, will go through it all. But don't be led astray. You will think it is the end of the world, but don't be fooled. This is just the beginning of a long night of labor pains. The first ones may hurt, but just wait until you've been there a while.

II. Notice two points of focus here.

(a) Think first about the words Jesus is saying. Crashes, upheavals, tragedy—Jesus is saying that this is the stuff of history. These things will happen, and they will happen to you. You disciples, don't look to be spared these things because you are God's people. Don't look to be rescued out of your disasters by some miracle. Maybe you will be spared or rescued, but don't bank on it. Some women endure only a short labor. But if that's what you are counting on when you come up to that moment, your resolve may fail. Don't count on a miraculous rescue. Instead, make up your minds that you may be there a while, and keep your faith strong.

I read this, and think of our brothers and sisters in Rome under Nero, who faced the wild animals and the torches for their faith. How they must have longed for Christ to come! How they must have wished for a miracle to save their lives, or the lives of their families! But the world went on, and their faith held in the face of disaster, and the church was born. Don't count on a short labor and a rescue; steel your faith for the long haul.

(b) Second focus: Look at the audience for these words of Jesus. If you took wagers at this point in Mark's text, no one would bet on the disciples making it through even one earthquake or rumor of war. These guys have shown very little stamina or perceptiveness. They don't understand Jesus and they are afraid to commit to his message of the cross. But Jesus addresses them as if they have a chance to succeed.

This is grace, the obverse of faith. This is God saying, "I know who you are. I know exactly how weak you think you are, but I know you are stronger than you realize. And you will not have to face the disaster alone. In the moment of crisis, listen for the voice of the Spirit. You must endure, but not without help."

Dreams will fail, disasters will come, and they will come to the best of us. If we follow Christ we will find ourselves up against some wall, wondering if we can make it. Beware, he says, I have warned you ahead of time, so don't let the hard times catch you napping. Steel your faith to face the hardest times. And listen in your hearts for the Spirit's help, because you will not be alone.—Richard B. Vinson

SUNDAY: NOVEMBER TWENTIETH

SERVICE OF WORSHIP

Sermon: Saying Thank You

TEXT: Luke 19:1–10

I. There are people in our community who live in houses that are architectural showplaces. The lawns are immaculately manicured and professionally landscaped. The furnishings have been carefully chosen from the best shops and perfectly arranged by a professional decorator. The rooms are spacious, with vaulted ceilings and open expanses that would hold a large crowd of people. If these people were ever to hold a party, however, the only people who would show up would be business associates and employees who came out of a sense of obligation. While these families who live in these huge, opulent houses may appear to have all the material possessions that anyone could desire, they have few, if any, true friends.

There are people in our community who can easily afford to wear the latest fashions all the time. Their clothes are tailored for a perfect fit. They have an outfit for every imaginable occasion and could wear a different one every day of the month if they chose. Their clothes, if worn by a professional model, could grace the cover of any fashion magazine. However, some of these people are so aware of their own physical unattractiveness that their tonsorial splendor brings them no pleasure. They think that no matter how fashionably they are dressed people will still look at them and think that they are ugly and no amount of window-dressing is going to change that.

There are people in our community who are not comfortable in public gatherings. It has nothing to do with an innate fear of people or phobia about wide-open spaces. It has to do with the judgmental stares and condescending looks that they feel from people on the street. You see, these are people who have committed rather messy, very public sins. These are people whose names have been in the paper or, at the very least, have been the hot topic on the gossip grapevine and everywhere they go they think that people must be looking down their noses at them. Perhaps once they enjoyed being the center of attention, but now they avoid all publicity and one thing that you can almost guarantee about these people is that the last place they will be seen is inside the church.

II. And all of these people—the rich but unpopular, the well-clothed but physically unattractive, the publicly scorned and judged—have someone with whom they can identify in Zaccaheus. Here was a man who could buy just about anything he wanted, but the way in which he earned his money made him so unpopular that no one would have anything to do with him. He could afford to have all of his robes imported and tailor-made, but his lack of height made him feel inconsequential. His business of collecting taxes forced him into the public eye, but the fact that everyone knew that the way he made so much money was by overassessing the value of their goods made it uncomfortable for him to move around town. In short, here was a man for whom everything he had—his career, his possessions, his status in the government—brought him no satisfaction.

Now perhaps I am reading too much into this story. All Luke tells us is that he was rich, short, and treated with contempt by the crowd. Maybe he had learned to deal with these problems. Maybe he had settled into a comfortable life in a big house and he had made peace with himself, reconciling himself to the fact that his life was not perfect, but being rich beat the daylights out of being poor.

But if he were at peace with himself, then why would he go to such lengths to see Jesus? Idle curiosity would not account for a grown man acting like a little kid, climbing up a tree, his robes hitched up over his knees, clinging desperately to a branch. Here was clearly a man who recognized that life was not all it should be and that the answer to his dissatisfaction had to be found in something other than his house and his clothes and his bank account. Here was a man who had to find out if Jesus was the answer.

The crowd is certainly not going to help him in his quest. They could hardly have been expected to part in order to let a puny, hated tax collector get close to the front where he could see Jesus pass by.

No more than you and I could be expected to seek out the people in the big houses whose possessions we secretly covet and ask them to come to church.

No more than we could be expected to stop on the street and talk to an insecure person who dresses in the style to which we would like to become accustomed but who seems to be sad and alone.

No more than we could be expected to be seen in the company of someone whose life has been touched by scandal or crime. Our fear, of course, is that anyone who sees us will believe that we have become like them instead of hoping that they have become like us.

III. No, it isn't likely that you and I as upstanding members of the church of Christ are going to make it any easier for sinners to come to Jesus. Our attitude of separation from the world, our judgmental spirit when it comes to those whose sins are more visible than our own, our disdain for people who have more than we have ourselves—these things are going to prevent us from bringing people to the Lord who can give them forgiveness and peace.

And yet, some of them make it to Jesus just the same. Some, like Zacchaeus, throw caution and appearance to the wind and climb the sycamore trees. They read their Bibles and they find a Lord who loves and forgives all. They hear his invitation to come down and join the party and they take him at his word. Just as Zacchaeus saw Jesus look up and call him by name, they understand that he is interested in them personally and really does want to have a relationship with them. And it is to this free, open, and unbelievably loving invitation that they respond.

And when this happens do you and I rejoice in it? Maybe, but not likely. Luke tells us that when Jesus told Zacchaeus that he was going to eat lunch at his house that day, the crowd murmured. They said that "he has gone to be the guest of a man who is a sinner" (v. 7, RSV). In other words, as far as they were concerned the jury was still out. They would wait to see if Zacchaeus made this radical transformation that he was talking about. Maybe after a few years of being on probation, if he was still walking the straight and narrow, they would believe that he really had turned over a new leaf. But in the meantime they weren't going to have anything to do with him.

And that is a real shame. It isn't a shame because it had any effect on Zacchaeus. All he seemed to see that day was the loving face of Jesus. He seemed oblivious to the crowd and to their attitude. But it was a shame that they couldn't learn from Zacchaeus's response to the forgiveness of Jesus. Zacchaeus knew how to say thank you. He knew that his gratitude to Jesus would not be expressed simply by saying how grateful he was that he had all of those things that he had. His gratitude would best be expressed by using those things to help others. He didn't promise to give back what he had taken and to give half of everything he owned to the poor in order to get Jesus to like him or to approve of him. He did it because of what Jesus had already done for him just by coming into his life. This wasn't just another scam that Zacchaeus was pulling off. This was a genuine response of thankfulness.

IV. And at this time of the year when we are supposed to be expressing our thankfulness, perhaps you and I can learn from Zacchaeus as well. I am afraid that most of us express our gratitude with a sense of nervousness. We pause to thank God for all the material things that he has given us, first of all because those are the things that we believe are important, and secondly, because we are afraid that if we don't say thank you often enough that God might take them away from us.

But Zacchaeus has figured it out; he's learned the lesson. He knows that all those things he has aren't worth a hill of beans when compared to what he has found through his relationship with Jesus Christ. And so he is willing to give all of them up and live off just what he needs to show Christ how grateful he is.—James M. King

Illustrations

GRATITUDE.   Earl Nightingale commented, one time, about a defective IBM ribbon. As he took it out of the typewriter, the thought occurred to him, that of all the IBM ribbons he had used, this was the only defective one! Rather than focus on the negative—the defective ribbon—he thought of all the positive times he had used an IBM ribbon and taken it for granted.—C. Neil Strait

FAITH WITHOUT WORKS.   One critic said he had gone to many churches and heard the preacher say, "Don't try to impress God with your works" or "Don't attempt to please God with your merits" or "Don't try to keep the rules and regulations and thus win your way." He looked around at nearly slumbering collections of utterly casual Christians and wondered, "Who's trying?"—Martin Marty

Sermon Suggestions

THE NIGHT VISIONS OF DANIEL.   TEXT: Dan. 7:9–10, 13–14, NRSV. (1) The Ancient One: God sits in judgment upon his enemies. (2) The "one like a human being": This figure progresses from the Jewish remnant to the archangel Michael to the Messiah. a., He does the will of the Ancient One; b., He is given universal dominion; c., His lordship is everlasting.

THE FAITHFUL WITNESS.   TEXT: Rev. 1:4b–8, NRSV. (1) He loves us—continually. (2) He freed us from our sins—once for all in his sacrificial death. (3) He appointed us "a royal house of priests" (G. B. Caird)—through whom he can mediate his redemption to the world.

Worship Aids

CALL TO WORSHIP.   "Honor the Lord with thy substance, and with the first fruits of all thine increase; so shall thy barns be filled with plenty, and thy presses shall burst out with new wine" (Prov. 3:9, 10).

INVOCATION. We have been blessed, O God, beyond all that we could ask or think. Beyond all material things, we have been enriched in the more important matters of the spirit. We would pray for our daily bread, but realizing that we do not live by bread alone, we would pray that we might receive thine own self—known, loved, and obeyed—for what thou art: God of love and grace.

OFFERTORY SENTENCE. "Walk in love, as Christ also hath loved us, and hath given himself for us an offering and a sacrifice to God for a sweet-smelling savor" (Eph. 5:2).

OFFERTORY PRAYER. Around us is beauty, Lord, beside us is bounty, within us is gratitude; accept our praise for this time of harvest that the blessings of this season may lead to a richness of soul that will never die.—E. Lee Phillips

PRAYER. O God, we thank thee for life, and all the beauty and the wonder of it, for the people that we have known and loved, and for the rare opportunities that we have had to enter into the deeper things of life. Forgive, O God, our triviality, and overlook our foolish ways. Help us to deepen and cultivate our understanding of primary things, things that come first, and then give us the will and the grace to make this nation strong that it may endure and that it may not go the way of others into exile and oblivion.—Theodore Parker Ferris

LECTIONARY MESSAGE

Topic: Forced to Choose
TEXT: John 18:33–37

I. Let us imagine this scene as a conversation between a believer and a nonbeliever. This is John's genius, to approach evangelism by illustration. He draws pictures of disciples responding with whole-hearted faith, of Nicodemus almost getting there but not quite, and of the Samaritan woman going all the way from non-faith to faith. Pilate's moment under the lamp is unpleasant for him. He wants to avoid the choice, and offers several attempts to wriggle away. Jesus presses him, and makes him choose.

II. "Are you the King of the Jews?" Pilate asks, out of the blue, because in John's account the chief priests have made no specific charge. He is the tough-minded realist here. No mush about spiritual kingdoms for him. Either Jesus has territory and an army to defend it, or he is nothing important. In his modern incarnation, Pilate says that unless Christianity can make my business or family run better or perhaps cure my cancer, then it is not worth the effort.

Jesus, of course, was not buying it. "Why ask that question? Did somebody put you up to it? Do you, Pilate, really believe that nothing intangible has value?"

III. "I am not a Jew, am I?" Here is the "cultured despiser" of the faith, the sophisticate who sneers at spiritual questions. Pilate's spirit lives on in a woman who told me that she thought too much to be a Christian. "Quite right," I said, "best to leave it to brainless slugs like me." But Jesus was kinder than I was. He told Pilate that his mission was to take the covers off truth. Is there any person with a grain of curiosity who could resist at least looking at what he claimed to unveil? Maybe you don't believe he can pull it off, but surely it is worth a look.

"What is truth?" So much depends on the tone of his voice and the way he held his head. Was he curious, cynical, confused? I think—uncharitably—lazy. I hear the voice of the theological couch potato here, who turns up the volume on the TV to drive out any thoughts of destiny or responsibility. To this, Jesus had no response.

IV. In the end, though, Pilate had to decide. He tried to pass his job on to the crowd, but they backed him into his judge's chair and would not let him leave until he sentenced Jesus to death. He was forced to choose, and so must we all. Then we who have chosen for Christ get to stand where he stood, and talk to our own Pilates. Listen well to your master, and do as he did. Don't be cowed by them. Answer sweetly, but bravely, and remember that not even Jesus was able to reach all of them.—Richard B. Vinson

SUNDAY: NOVEMBER TWENTY-SEVENTH

SERVICE OF WORSHIP

Sermon: Was Jesus God?

TEXT: John 10:22–38

Throughout the Christian era there has existed a struggle among theologians as to the nature of Jesus Christ. Was he God? Was he man? Or was he the God-Man or God in human form? The purpose of this message is to show that Jesus did indeed declare his oneness with God the Father.

I. Demand for Identity (John 10:22–24)

Following the Feast of Tabernacles Jesus left Jerusalem for a ministry in Judea. Almost three months separate verses 21 and 22. Luke 10:1–13:21 records this ministry.

(a) Jesus was walking on Solomon's Porch, a covered, colonnaded area running the full length of the Temple area on the eastern side. It was at this time that the Jewish religious leaders, literally, suddenly formed a circle about Jesus (v. 24). Doing so, they made a demand. "How long does thou make us to doubt? If thou be the Christ, tell us plainly." Literally they said, "Until when do you lift up our souls." They were still fretting over their verbal defeat during the Feast of Tabernacles. He had held them in suspense.

(b) Jesus had deliberately avoided using the term "Christ" in public. The Jewish idea was that of a political-military figure. He would lead a revolt, throw off the Roman yoke, and establish his kingdom in which—with him—the Jews would rule the world. Jesus avoided use of "Son of David" for the same reason.

(c) If only he would say, "I am the Christ," they could charge him before Pilate as a threat to Roman supremacy. It was now only a few months before Jesus' death. His popularity with the people was great. So the rulers were desperate for grounds on which to charge Jesus.

Jesus had called himself the Son of God. But his favorite term of self-designation was "Son of man." It had messianic connotations but without the political-military aspect. But, as always, he refused to be drawn into their trap.

II. Jesus' Identity of Himself (John 10:25–33)

To "If thou be the Christ, tell us plainly," he did not say yes or no. Instead, he replied in his own way and time. What he said left no doubt that he was the Christ. But he did not simply say yes. Indeed, he said far more.

(a) Jesus began by reminding them that he had told them previously who he was, but they refused to believe him. Furthermore, his works done in his Father's name had not evoked their faith (vv. 25–26a).

Then Jesus reopened the matter of his being the Good Shepherd, about which they had debated during his visit three months previously (John 10:7–18). They had not believed in him because they were not his sheep. "My sheep hear my voice, and I know them, and they follow me" (v. 27).

(b) Then Jesus made a tremendous statement: "I give unto them eternal life; and they shall never perish, neither shall any man pluck [snatch] them out of my hand. My Father, which gave them me, is greater than all; and no man is able to pluck them out of my Father's hand" (vv. 28–29).

Here is one of the great passages on the security of the believer. And it came from Jesus himself! Literally Jesus said, "Most certainly, no one of my sheep will go to hell." "Neither" renders a strong negative. So again, "Most certainly, no one snatches them out of my hand." Furthermore, his Father is greater than all, and literally, "Nothing [man, devil, or thing] is powerful [enough] to snatch them out of my Father's hand."

(c) Then Jesus gave his plain answer to the Pharisees' question, "I and my Father are one" (v. 30). Jesus mentioned himself first because the question concerned his identity. Note that he still did not use the word Christ. But he said more. He asserted his identity and equality with the

Father. In plain words Jesus claimed to be God in flesh (see John 1:1, 14).

To the Jews, this was blatant blasphemy, punishable by death by stoning (v. 31). There were no stones on Solomon's Porch, but so enraged were these Jewish leaders that they went after stones. Jesus asked for which of his good works were they planning to stone him (v. 32).

"The Jews answered him, saying, For a good work we stone thee not, but for blasphemy; and because that thou, being a man, makest thyself God" (v. 33). In John 5:18 the charge was "making himself equal with God." But here it is "being a man, makest thyself God." Some modern theologians may miss the point. But those theologians on the spot did not miss it. Definitely, Jesus called himself God!

III. Proof of Jesus' Deity (John 10:34–38)

Jesus was in dire peril. The Jewish rulers had murder in their eyes. Since his first visit to Jerusalem in his public ministry, the Jewish leaders had opposed him. Immediately following this incident he left Jerusalem, not to return until his time had come (vv. 39–42). However, before departing, he justified his claim to deity.

(a) Jesus first appealed to the scriptures. Assuming that these Jews were Pharisees, this was the ultimate in authority. He quoted from Psalm 82:6 where unjust judges were called "gods." If this be true, he asked, why then did they propose to stone him for blasphemy because he claimed to be God? (vv. 35–36). Because, as they would agree, "the scripture cannot be broken." These judges were unjust. But Jesus is the One "whom the Father hath sanctified [set apart for God's service], and sent into the world." Of course, these Jews would deny this claim.

(b) So Jesus cited his works as evidence that this was true (vv. 37–38). "If I do not the works of my Father, believe me not. But if I do, though ye believe not me, believe the works: that ye may know, and believe, that the Father is in me, and I in him."

IV. So we return to our question: Was Jesus God? He certainly and emphatically declared that he was. Either he was an extreme fanatic and guilty of the worst of blasphemies or else he was who he said he was/is. History gives a resounding yes to the latter.

(a) There is yet one more question to answer, and no one but you can answer it. Who is Jesus to you? The Bible presents him as God's virgin-born Son, God himself in flesh for human redemption. History declares him to be the greatest person who ever lived. He is the supreme teacher and perfect example in doing God's will. All of these are important beyond the ability of human language to express.

(b) What is your personal relationship to him? In the final analysis, for you that is the supreme question. How you answer it determines the quality of life you live on this earth and in the ever-unfolding eternity beyond. I pray that you will receive him as your Lord and Savior. For anything less than this is to deny him. Your acceptance or denial of him has eternal consequences! —Herschel H. Hobbs

Illustrations

GOD'S SECRET. We should honor great men, saintly men are noble examples for us, but no great or saintly man can reveal God's mystery to us and bind us with God; no man can take away our guilt and make us certain of the completion of life in eternal life. This God alone can do, and he does just that in Jesus Christ, who for that reason is not merely a great man, but the Son of God. How does it happen that God comes to us as man? I do not know, I do not even know how it happens that something becomes alive, that a man is born. That is God's secret as Creator. How much more the Incarnation of God remains his secret. But what I can know, and what I can rejoice in every day as a Christian is that God bestows his love upon me in his Son, and that he will give it to all who believe in him, the Son of God. —Emil Brunner

INCARNATED. Jesus is unique because he alone of all mankind of whom we have any external evidence or internal experience was truly normal. He was *the* Son of man, *the* Son of God, the Proper man, who lived in a relation to God and his fellow men in which we are all called to live but fail to live. This doesn't mean that he had everything or was everything (you mention it, he had it), but that here was a man who uniquely embodied the relationship with God for which man was created. In this man, God was reflected, as John puts it, in a simile from family life, as in an only son of his father—he who had seen him had seen the Father. Or as Paul puts it, he was the image of the invisible God, the perfect reproduction as opposed to the distorting mirror, of his fullness, his glory.—John A. T. Robinson

Sermon Suggestions

"IN THOSE DAYS." TEXT: Jer. 33:14–16. (1) God will fulfill his promise of a Messiah, verses 14–15a. (2) This Messiah will bring justice and righteousness to the society.

PRAYER IN TWO DIRECTIONS. TEXT: 1 Thess. 3:9–13. (1) Prayer of thanks, verse 9. (2) Prayer of concern for others: a., for completion of faith, verse 10; b., for increase of love, verse 12; c., for confirmation in holiness, verse 13.

Worship Aids

CALL TO WORSHIP. "Then the seventh angel blew his trumpet, and there were loud voices in heaven, saying, "The power to rule over the world belongs now to our Lord and his Messiah, and he will rule forever and ever!" (Rev. 11:15 [TEV]).

INVOCATION. Lord, do something mighty in us today that will give perspective to all else we do because the God of everywhere is become the God of everything that matters to us through our Lord Jesus Christ.

OFFERTORY SENTENCE. "Offer unto God thanksgiving; and pay thy vows unto the Most High" (Ps. 50:14).

OFFERTORY PRAYER. Saving Lord, we pray this offering may be used to save and nurture many souls in need of God.—E. Lee Phillips

PRAYER. For all the things for which we have never given thanks to thee, O Lord, we humbly bow our hearts. For common things of earth which sustain our bodies in health and strength, though we pay scant attention to them, we give thee thanks. For far-off things in the ages past or in lands distant from us which enlarge our heritage and expand our horizon, we give thee thanks. For invisible things of heaven and earth which sweeten life with beauty and grace, we give thee thanks. For things of the spirit which disclose to us the beauty of thy holiness and sanctify the passing time with eternal meaning, we give thee thanks. For things bought with a great price, given to us without cost, by which we are deepened and heightened to the measure of Christ our Lord, we give thee thanks. Though there be no end to thy gifts, help us to number them as they are revealed to us day by day.—Samuel H. Miller

LECTIONARY MESSAGE

Topic: Transformed and Transformers
TEXT: Luke 21:25–36

Well, if you are reading this, then Jesus did not come back on October 28, 1992, as predicted by a pamphlet I got in the mail. How hard would it hit you to believe that Jesus was coming on a certain date and for that not to take place? To judge from Christian history, sometimes that hits like a sledgehammer. I know a former Christian, present atheist, who lost faith when he put the Christian expectation of Jesus' return together with Jesus' nearly 2,000-year delay and concluded that someone was lying.

For Luke, this was not an academic issue. His sources said, "This generation will not pass until Jesus returns," but it had and he hadn't. His sources hinted that when the Temple fell, so would the world, but that great building had been in ruins for years when Luke wrote. Some folks' faith went by the boards—what would Luke say about it?

I. For one thing, his Gospel stresses more the presence or the dawning of the age to come. Future time has invaded present time, said Luke: "The Reign of God is in your midst," says the Lukan Jesus. Luke's first witnesses to the Resurrection do not recognize Jesus when they stand next to him, but only when they break the bread together; that's the way Luke's church members would have known Jesus, too. In Luke, you don't have to wait until the end of time to begin to be transformed and a transformer.

II. But Luke does not drop the future entirely. "They will see the Son of Man coming. . . . It will come upon all who live on the face of the whole earth." The present, transformed by the future, is moving toward a happy ending. Move with us, says Luke. Cast off the baggage you picked up from the old age and pray that you'll have the strength to hold out all the way to the future. Be apart of the process of transformation.

III. Can we jaundiced moderns believe in a happy ending? We ridicule the believers who, staking their faith on Jesus coming at one time and place, sit and wait for their salvation. "Pie in the sky," we say. But if we lose our hope that the future can be better than the present, we too may "faint from fear and foreboding," paralyzed into inactivity by the complexity of the problems we face. Look up—wake up—God's reign has begun in our midst. God's power will transform this tiny seed into a giant tree, with or without us. Let us then be transformed and transformers.—Richard B. Vinson

SUNDAY: DECEMBER FOURTH

SERVICE OF WORSHIP

Sermon: The Royalty of a Life

TEXT: Matthew 1:15–16

You'd be bored to tears if I read through the whole of the genealogy with which St. Matthew's Gospel begins. But suppose your *own* name was in the list! Or the name of someone you knew! . . . I was looking through some old genealogies a few weeks ago belonging to the seventeenth century. And there I discovered names of four or five families known to me quite well. Do you think those tables were boring after that? They were one of the most interesting sections of the book! . . . and that is how it was with the genealogy at the beginning of St. Matthew's Gospel. The Jews for whom it was written *raced* their eyes down it. So *this* is who Jesus was! These were his ancestors! You can see it for yourself in his family tree—"The book of the genealogy of Jesus Christ the son of David, the son of Abraham"—St. Matthew was committing no blunder in style when thus he began.

I. But what does this genealogy mean?

It means first of all that Jesus was a Jew. Do not let anyone attempt to rationalize that fact away. It cannot be done. Jesus belonged to that portion of Jewry which returned from exile and probably became the Ashkenazim of Europe, the people who have produced Einstein, Trotsky, Freud, and Marx.

But this isn't all. It means that when God became incarnate in this world, he did not assume human flesh in the abstract; he became part of a family, a family with a family tree, a family with blood biologists could catalogue, a family with a history historians could trace. There may be advantages in such membership of a family. Glory can be inherited—but so can dishonor. Family membership cuts two ways. So that when God entered this world he entered in such a fashion as to experience our problem—the family problem. The problem of *illustrious* relations; the problem of disgraceful relations, the problem of the skeleton in the cupboard; the problem of mediocrity.

James Stalkner in his book *Imago Christi* pictures the doorbell ringing one night and on going out you see a stranger on the doorstep, a stranger from a strange land. You know nothing of him. He is outside the circle of your interests. He is 10,000 miles away from your spirit. But suppose he says, "Don't you know me? I'm your brother." What happens? In one step he journeys 10,000 miles. You and he are connected by an indissoluble bond; and the bond may be a golden clasp, or it may be an iron clamp burning and corroding your skin.

This is the institution called the family that God entered when he took our flesh. And remember, not merely in theory, but also in practice. Jesus' brothers did not believe in him. From John, chapter 7, we can sense the animosity in the Nazareth home. And before that day, and since that day, in Judea and in Central London, upright men and women have had to endure an endless petty persecution at home worse than public opposition. *That* is what God assumed when he assumed our flesh. It has its own message this morning to any troubled at home. Christ knows what you feel, the poignancy of some family relationships, he felt it himself.

II. ". . . and Eleazar begat Matthan; and Matthan begat Jacob; and Jacob begat Joseph the husband of Mary, of whom was born Jesus, who is called Christ." What else does this dull-looking genealogy mean? It means that when Christ entered our world, he entered a family in circumstances calling for a defense.

You see it isn't an ordinary family tree in Matthew chapter 1. Four women's names occur in it. That is unusual. And more than that, the life of each woman mentioned was not without some sort of suspicion. There was Bathsheba. You all know about her! And Tamar's reputation was similar. And Rahab is bluntly called in scripture "a harlot." And the fourth woman, though virtuous, wasn't even a Jewess at all, but a Moabite. Her name was Ruth. All these four women are listed as ancestresses of Jesus! Their names are *dragged* in. Why? Because when Matthew was writing his Gospel he was facing Jewish opposition. Opposition

which persisted in pointing the finger of scorn at the mystery surrounding Jesus' birth—"Who was his father?" And Matthew, unable to deny the strangeness of Jesus' birth, ran his finger over the long story of Hebrew history crying, "God has overruled before, God has overruled appearances before. What about Tamar! What about Bathsheba! What about Rahab! What about Ruth!"

"Judge not the Lord by feeble sense, but trust him for his grace."

God is righteous; and if so the manner of the child's birth was righteous whatever the strangeness. He was no bastard, as some Jews would have men think. And the measure of our shock when such words are used is the measure of the sordidness Christ willingly entered to come and rescue this our world.

Once more I examine this genealogy: ". . .and Eleazar begat Matthan; and Matthan begat Jacob; and Jacob begat Joseph the husband of Mary, of whom [feminine!] was born Jesus, who is called Christ."

It is an artificially constructed genealogy. There are three groups of fourteen generations, though the number is achieved in the third group only by repeating a name. No doubt the arrangement is to aid the memory. But more than this, it is to show that kingship achieved in David and lost in Jechoniah was recovered in Jesus.

III. What does this mean? It means that out of the complications of a family network, out of birth circumstances apparently compromising, Jesus achieved kingship. Not a kingship of this world. Not a throne on Zion's hill. But a royalty of life surpassing any that any man has seen before or since. But it is God's royalty, God's regal saintliness.

Is this challenging? It is meant to be challenging. Where we fail and excuse ourselves by pointing to our limitations of home, environment, and opposition, Jesus did not fail. He exhibited the kingly life amidst all the tensions of a family network. And when on the Ascension Mount he gave the apostles the royal commission to be his witnesses, beginning at Jerusalem (their home city), he was but commanding what he himself had achieved—a royal life in a family in a village.

Am I addressing myself this morning to someone worn with troubles at home? Am I addressing myself to someone beset by family problems: a marriage breaking up, a marriage broken up—some disgrace, some scandal, some skeleton? It would be a strange congregation if nothing here were known of such troubles as these. To live these days is to touch these problems. And at this point we are sensitive. That of which we should be proud is that of which we may be ashamed. And you ask me, perhaps with no expectancy in your voice, What has the Christian religion to say to such a situation as mine? My friend, it has this to say—and it will surprise you—Christ entered it. That is the Gospel according to St. Matthew. Christ entered it. I haven't invented the idea. You can see it for yourself by turning to the first page of St. Matthew's Gospel. The Gospel begins amid the heartbreaks and splendours of a family tree. That is where Jesus began to achieve our rescue. From the place where you are; from the place where I am. That is the Gospel according to St. Matthew. And the remarkable fact is, it can best be appreciated by the man looking out from a broken home. All of which cries aloud—doesn't it?—that no one need feel forsaken after this. God knows. God understands. And his grace is free for you, whatever your need, whatever your problem.—D. W. Cleverley Ford

Illustrations

GOD'S CARE.   The word in the scripture that we often translate as "rainbow" is really the Hebrew word for "bow" or an archer's war bow. God now promises Noah, "See, I've set my war bow in the heavens. I'm not going to fight with you anymore. I'm not against you, but all for you."—C. Neil Strait

APPREHENDED.   On a college campus a student who had flung off the restraints of his home and school training and was headed for moral disaster, when reasoned with to stop, said bluntly: "I feel that I ought, but I don't want to." And for a while he didn't. Subsequently, he managed to get himself in hand to redeem his college standing. And when asked what had happened, he remarked: "I just had to quit: something out of my Christian training rose up and grabbed me." He was unconsciously repeating the apostle's metaphor: "I was *apprehended* of Christ Jesus."—Henry Sloane Coffin

Sermon Suggestions

"THE DAY OF HIS COMING."   TEXT: Mal. 3:1–4, NRSV. (1) It is a day of judgment: a., For God's enemies; b., For God's own people. (2) Yet it is a day of salvation.

WHAT MAKES AN APOSTLE—OR PASTOR!—HAPPY.   TEXT: Phil. 1:3–11. (1) Fellow Christians who share in the gospel. (2) Who show promise of faithfulness to the end. (3) Who have determined affection for their spiritual mentor. (4) Who will have brought forth the harvest of righteousness for the glory and praise of God.

Worship Aids

CALL TO WORSHIP.   "Repent ye: for the kingdom of heaven is at hand" (Matt. 3:2).

INVOCATION.   Stir in our hearts this day, O Lord, stir and revive us, stir and inspire us, stir and use us for your great glory.—E. Lee Phillips

OFFERTORY SENTENCE.   "Greater love hath no man than this, that a man lay down his life for his friends" (John 15:13).

OFFERTORY PRAYER.   Your love, O God, transforms us when we permit you to have your will and way in our lives. We are forever in your debt, and it is our joy to share our means and our love in your name.

PRAYER. O Lord, thou leadest us again this year to the light, the joy, and the festivity of Christmas, the day when thy love is manifest in the greatest event of all. For thou so loved the world that thou gavest thine only begotten Son that whosoever believeth in him shall not perish, but have everlasting life.

What gift may we bring to thee? There is so much darkness in our human relationships and in our own hearts! So much confused thinking, so much coldness and resistance, so much folly and hatred! So many things which are displeasing in thy sight and separate us from each other, which are of no help to us! So much that is directly opposed to the glad tidings of Christmas!

What canst thou do with these our gifts? What with such people as we all are? And yet it is nothing else than these miserable gifts, together with ourselves, that thou expectest at Christmas. Thou wilt lift the burden from us and give us Jesus our Savior instead, and with him a new heaven and a new earth, new hearts and a new mind, new clarity and new hope for us and all mankind.

Be with us as we prepare ourselves . . . to receive him as thy gift! Grant that we speak and listen and pray rightly, in truly grateful wonder at what thou didst plan, what thou hast already decided and done for all of us.—Karl Barth

LECTIONARY MESSAGE

Topic: Prophecy

TEXT: Luke 3:1–6

I. The oracle sits on a tripod stool, inhaling smoke from hemp burning on the fire in front of her. Soon she begins to sway and then to babble. The priest nearby takes account of every syllable, and from it all renders . . . prophecy! A pilgrim wants to know his destiny, and for a fee, the system will deliver. "You will meet a delphic end," or perhaps, "sow your seed while you may, eat your bread while you can, for your way will not be long."

Prophecy! It is the stuff of snaggle-toothed, wild-haired men and women, whose sight of this world has gone dim and whose second sight has come clear. It is the territory of tarot cards, oija boards, seances, and channelers. It is old as the hills, because all people have felt it was necessary. Necessary, because the beyond is hidden from us, obscure and murky, and even when it is revealed by the oracle it comes in a riddle. We know the oracles and prophets may be charlatans, and that their riddles may be so vague that one can never judge them true or false. But we long to know what our destiny is, and so we consult our horoscopes, we call our psychics, we read the self-help books that predict what we will do next. And we hope that we can control our future a little better as a result.

II. Contrast that with this. Notice Luke's careful, almost pedantic references to historical figures. Emperor, procurator, tetrarch, high priest—there is no mystery there, only real people at a real time. Then there is the prophet, the oracle, the vessel chosen to give the message. He does not sit in a cave to wait for his customers. He goes to them and offers their destiny to them for free.

(a) God is coming! The great power of the beyond, enigmatic and mysterious, is building a superhighway to your back yard. And when God is here, humanity will no longer need oracles, for the Divine will be visible to all. Better than that: God comes in peace. Your destiny is salvation, if you will but turn from your wickedness and embrace the forgiveness God holds out.

(b) We celebrate the Advent of God's new era. There is always a freshness to the season for me, but no mysteries. Long ago, the gospel was shouted to the world as a general announcement. No more riddles, no more secret messages, no more hidden meanings. Good news, people, your destiny is crystal clear, and it is good. God has built the highway, and it comes all the way to your hidden, dark, murky world. Open your hearts to the good news. Reach out for your destiny, and live in the new era—Richard B. Vinson

SUNDAY: DECEMBER ELEVENTH

SERVICE OF WORSHIP

Sermon: Can There Be Peace on Earth?

TEXT: Luke 2:8–14; John 14:27

Two thousand years ago an angelic chorus heralded the birth of Jesus with the words, "Peace on earth, good will to all upon whom God's favor rests." Peace on earth! What beautiful words from an angelic choir!

Where is peace on earth? Where can we find it? Those angelic words did not stop the bombs that were dropped on Pearl Harbor. Nor did they stop the bombs the United States Air Force dropped on Nagasaki and Hiroshima. Nor did these words stop persons from being put in concentration camps in Germany in World War II or others from being imprisoned, terrorized or brutalized in Vietnam, Iraq or in other parts of the world. Where is this peace on earth? What could these words possibly mean in a world in which war has continued before and since the birth of Jesus? Let's pause for a few moments and see if we can understand what they mean.

I. In the time of Jesus there existed what was called Pax Romana, the Roman peace. The Roman Empire claimed that its reign had brought peace to the world.

(a) But what kind of peace was it? It was a peace built on terror, militarism, force, and intimidation by the power of the Roman army. They had a peace of subjection. Few, in my judgment, would call that peace today. The fact that people wanted so much to throw off the yoke of Rome indicates that it was only an imposed "peace."

(b) Isn't it ironical, though, that many even today think that real peace can exist only under some kind of military regime? Real peace cannot be imposed. Too quickly we get caught up in the wartrap mentality which declares that military might is the answer to the problems of peace in the world. The possibility of war today is more frightening than ever. The nuclear bombs that could be dropped today are a thousand times more powerful than the two bombs that were dropped during the Second World War on Japan. At that time 214,000 people were killed by two bombs. Think of it, 214,000! Yet, our bombs today are a thousand times worse. There will be no winners in a nuclear war.

II. Christians, on the other hand, preach and follow One who is called the Prince of Peace. His way is Pax Christi, the peace of Christ. Jesus spoke to his disciples in that upper room, knowing that the cross was looming before him and that his death was certain. "Peace I leave with you. My peace I give unto you. Not as the world gives, give I unto you. Let not your hearts be troubled, neither let them be afraid."

(a) The peace which Christ offers is different from what the world offers. The peace that Christ offers us is not merely a cabin in the mountains or a little peaceful ocean cottage away from all the troubles and noise of the world. As nice as those may be, that is not the kind of peace that Jesus Christ offers. Jesus' peace was drawn from his union with his Father. Jesus was living in the Father's will, and the will of the Father was in him. As we are drawn into Christ and his spirit into us, we have inward peace that is different from the world's peace.

(b) The peace of Christ is a peace that no one can snatch away. Jesus gives us a peace that is internal. That is the real peace he gives us. This is not merely a peace of mind so we have some inner calm. It is an internal peace that comes from the presence of God. Jesus had this kind of peace as he faced his own death. He had such a vital union with God that it gave him the strength to face whatever came.

(c) But the peace from Christ is also relational. Genuine peace is expressed in how we relate one with the other. The peace of Christ is not just some kind of sweet peace of mind. The peace of Christ enables me to relate effectively with other people. Peace will cause me to build bridges of understanding and compassion. I will try to restore broken relationships and to bring about reconciliation. III. But Jesus instructs us to be persons who wage peace. Why is it we can wage war so much better than we can wage peace? Robert E. Lee once said, "It is well that war is so terrible, or we should grow too fond of it." (a) We must remember the horrors of war and wage peace. Just as a garden cannot really produce any kind of crop if we do not remove the weeds that are there, so in our own lives we need to weed out hatred, bigotry, animosity, fear, misunderstanding and learn to sow gentleness, love, compassion, hope, kindness, and understanding. We need to work to wage peace with all of our strength and effort. Jesus called us to be peacemakers, not just pray or teach about peace. (b) Why do you think the angelic song has been hushed? Has it been hushed because of the greed, arrogance, selfishness, and pride of men and women? Has it been silenced by the apathy, complacency, abundance, selfishness, self-satisfaction of so many? I don't know. But . . . wait . . . I still hear faint whispers of the angelic song. I hear it as a few coins and bills are dropped in the Salvation Army kettle. I hear it as young people volunteer to serve in the Peace Corps or at some mission point in the world. I hear it as someone goes to work to help the underprivileged and the homeless in our society. I hear a whisper of that song when a kind word is extended to a person who is hurting. (c) O God, we want to hear the angels' song again. We want real peace within our own hearts, with our relationships toward others, and within our world. Help us, O God, to learn how to be peacemakers as we follow the Prince of Peace, whose birth we celebrate in this Christmas season. Amen.—William Powell Tuck

Illustrations

STORMS AND MORE STORMS. For several years my family and I lived in Slidell, Louisiana, a small town across Lake Pont-chatrain from New Orleans. While we were living there the area was struck by several devastating hurricanes with winds in excess of 120 miles an hour. I shall never forget the howling winds which shook our house as though a giant force had its grip on it, and the pounding rain which beat down upon the house like watery hammers with a ceaseless rhythm, and the awful feeling within of whether or not the house could continue to withstand such pressures upon it. Then, suddenly and unexpectedly, although I had read about it, and heard about it, a great calm engulfed the area, and the storm ceased. The sun came out, the birds began to sing again, and all seemed peaceful and quiet. Here, to my amazement, was the calm at the center of the hurricane. Later the other side of the hurricane hit with all of its force, and I was keenly aware that the storm was not yet over.—William Powell Tuck

DECEPTIVE CLEVERNESS. We must look to the ends of life and not be deceived by short views of the means employed. Recall how many Americans at first admired the efficiency of Mussolini as he brought order out of chaos in Italy. We failed to look far enough to see the fascist objectives toward which Mussolini was heading. Or remember how many good church people were thrown off their guard against Hitler at the beginning because he did not drink or smoke and was a celibate. We failed to see that he was fanatically dedicated to principles which were headed in the wrong direction. It was his very dedication and discipline which made him so dangerous when wrongly directed. We Christians ought to remember that the old-fashioned traditional theology never pictured Satan as a drunken derelict, but as a clever, smooth, well-organized individual.—Ralph W. Sockman

Sermon Suggestions

WHEN GOD AT LAST HAS HIS WAY. TEXT: Zech. 3:14–20. (1) His people will be secure from fear. (2) It will be a time of rejoicing. (3) The oppressors will be dealt with. (4) God's people will enjoy universal respect.

WHY REJOICE? TEXT: Phil. 4:4–7, NRSV. (1) The Lord is near. (2) We can pray to God about all our needs. (3) God's peace will guard our hearts and our minds.

Worship Aids

CALL TO WORSHIP. "The voice of him that crieth in the wilderness, Prepare ye the way of the Lord, make straight in the desert a highway for our God" (Isa. 40:3).

INVOCATION. O God, prepare our hearts for the great things you would do within and among us today. Prepare our lives for the great things you would do for others through us. We await your help.

OFFERTORY SENTENCE. "Every one of us shall give account of himself to God" (Rom. 14:12).

OFFERTORY PRAYER. Merciful Father, you open springs in the desert and give good things to us when we least expect them. Grant us now one gift more: the grace of cheerful giving, even when personal circumstances make our stewardship difficult.

PRAYER. Lord, as we look back over the days just past, we marvel at your mercies. You have blessed us with your presence. You have heartened us with new opportunities. You have strengthened us with the gift of friends. You have helped us turn aside from many temptations. You have assured us of your forgiveness as we have confessed our sins to you and as we have made amends for wrongs done to others.

Show us how to be grateful and how to live out our gratitude. Help us to bring your presence near someone estranged from you, to open new doors for someone deeply discouraged, to share with someone the warmth of our Christian love, to bolster the moral courage of someone sorely tested, to assure someone that you truly will forgive all manner of sin. May we herald your coming with salvation.

LECTIONARY MESSAGE

Topic: Guess Who's Coming?

TEXT: Luke 3:7–18

I. Guess who's coming? John the Baptist, that leather-throated, locust-eating, bullhorn-voiced prophet of God, thought he knew. "You think I'm somebody? You just wait until Messiah comes. I baptize you with water; he'll baptize you with fire and the Spirit. I preach to you about your sins, but he's coming with his axe in his hand, ready to cut down all the dead wood in Israel. You'd better repent, and be quick about it!"

But who came? Jesus came, and after John saw Jesus in action, he was bitterly disappointed. John, after all, had stood up in Herod Antipas' face and had told him he was a wicked man, unfit to rule over any of God's people, and Herod put him in jail for it. What did Jesus do? He healed sick people, he fed hungry people, and he stayed away from Herod. Finally John sent his disciples to ask, "Have I made a mistake? Are you really the Messiah?"

II. Have you ever seen a child open a brightly wrapped Christmas package and find that inside are socks or underwear? Or have you ever met a man or a woman who thought they were marrying the world's only perfect spouse, only to find that she snored and that he picked his teeth at dinner? What were we expecting?

We wait for Christmas every year, and we celebrate the birth of the Savior. What are we expecting? Maybe, like John, we expect a prophet or a king who will clean up the mess in the world, a law and order candidate. Maybe, like some preachers we hear, we expect a cosmic Santa, ready to make all true believers rich and healthy, if only we have been good enough. Maybe by now, after so many Christmases have come and gone, we expect nothing at all except socks wrapped in bright paper, bills to pay after the first of the year, and a little vague disappointment after it's all over.

III. What we get, every year, whether we expect him or not, is Jesus. The promise of the text is that he comes to us. But he comes to us as he came to the people in the text, and that means that we may be as surprised as they were. Like Martin the cobbler in the old Christmas story, we must be ready to see Jesus in whatever form he presents himself. Being Christians may not make us rich, or comfortable, or better-adjusted. It may not keep us from grief or mental anguish. It will, on the other hand, put us into contact with God, in ways that we may not be able to anticipate ahead of time. This Christmas, let us look for God's presence in our lives, and rejoice wherever we find it.—Richard B. Vinson

SUNDAY: DECEMBER EIGHTEENTH

SERVICE OF WORSHIP

Sermon: Because God Is Our Friend

TEXT: Matthew 1:23; Romans 8:31

I. It means first that God, the very king of the universe, is with us in darkness, in loneliness, in the prison houses of our sin. This is the meaning of Christmas, that God has entered the world to save. Emmanuel is one of the names given to Jesus; it means "God with us." For large numbers of people this has become a lost meaning of Christmas.

(a) The real meaning of Christmas, about which the angels sang and for which the star shone, has been overlaid with centuries of sentimental varnish and commercial dust until millions see in Christmas only the sweet story of a baby in a manger for whom we are moved to pity, or the occasion for an organized, commercialized, vulgarized carnival of gaudy splendor.

(b) But if this were all, what have we on December 26? Nothing to put hope in fainting hearts. Nothing to lift the load from bending backs. But if God can shine through the accumulated varnish of Christmas to give the light of his glory in the face of Jesus Christ with the promise, "I am with you and your friend," then hope will be ours.

(c) The Christmas angels ought to be a vivid reminder of God's guardian angels that do not forsake us, whether at Bethlehem, or in the wilderness, or at Gethsemane. Because God is our friend he does give us angel voices that do not fail. They were with Christ in his temptation—"Then the devil left him, and behold, angels came and ministered to him." They were with the Master in the Garden of Gethsemane—"And there appeared to him an angel from heaven, strengthening him."

(d) Some person to whom I speak now faces a great hour of temptation just ahead. In every man's or woman's armor is some Achilles' heel, some vulnerable weakness which exposes him or her to frightful consequences. You know all too well what it is with you. But the Christmas gift of the gospel is this, that when in some wilderness of temptation an urge stronger than your power to resist takes you by the arm and leads you out under the fierce heat of some enticing waywardness, there comes the voice of one who loves you saying, "Fear not, my love is holding you fast."

Surely someone close to us now is not far from the valley of the shadow of death. When someone you love goes on through that valley you need not be afraid. Your faith will see you through, a voice saying, "Let not your heart be troubled. I am the Lord of life and of death. I am with you and those you love, on this side and on the other." Because God is our friend, these are the Christmas angels that do not "go away from us into heaven."

II. In the second place the Christmas gift of the gospel means that God has given each of us a divine identity. Parents know how children learning things by hearing sometimes come out with amazing repetitions of what they thought they heard.

(a) Do we not spend most of our lives inconspicuously keeping caught up by routine, nobodies so far as fame and position are concerned? A wife going about the affairs of a home into which but a handful of people come from one year's end to the next. A man working in office, shop, or laboratory, of importance only by the measure of what he produces. But if God is our friend, he does know our names. Everybody is somebody, child of God. The humblest life takes on divine identity. God is present at the lowliest birth. God shares the loneliest life with every man who sits in darkness. Life means something when God shares it. On the birth certificate signed at Bethlehem was your name, along with that of Jesus, son of Joseph of Nazareth.

(b) One of the deepest theological meanings of Christmas is that the child Jesus is born as a twin to every child so that he will not be lonely, ever! No child ought to be lonely in our world after the birth of Bethlehem for God is "born again" in each new birth. All childhood is sanctified. If God is our friend, then it lays upon us the divine imperative to see in every child's face the face of the Christ child, and in every human face the face of the Master. Woe to that man who by any negligence keeps a child from knowing that God is his friend!

III. Yet once more, Christmas means that God has come into the world to bring us out of the prison houses which we make for ourselves and for each other.

(a) Long before Jesus, the prophet of the exile spoke of the Lord's Anointed in these terms: "I will give thee a light to the Gentiles, to bring out the prisoners from the dungeon, and them that sit in darkness out of the prison house." And Jesus began his own ministry with the proclamation, "He sent me to proclaim release to the captives." This is the very heart and soul of the gospel.

(b) This was the truth and the gift of the gospel. Our names were on the lips of the angels, proclaiming our release from the prison house of evil and death. For one was born in Bethlehem who could set me free, give me a new stature, a new love, a forgiveness for my sin, and a reconciliation with God. Good tidings of great joy which shall be to all people. That is the gift of Christmas.—Robert E. Luccock

Illustrations

INCARNATION. The Sunday school teacher announced to her class that they were going to talk about God. One little boy had a look of disgust on his face as he said, "I don't want to talk about God. He won't come out and show himself." This really happened. I don't mean just that a boy actually said it, though that is true. I mean that in Christ God DID come out and show himself.—David W. Richardson

FADE IN, FADE OUT. In New York's Hayden Planetarium a special Christmas holiday show was enhanced by an added feature. A giant lollipop tree was projected onto the planetarium dome, surrounded by a horizon filled with brilliantly colored toys which came to life and cavorted to the tune of "Jingle Bells." At the climax a huge figure of Santa Claus faded out in a snowstorm, and the Star of Bethlehem broke through into a sky that reproduced exactly the Palestine sky on the night of the nativity. The designer of this show may not realize that he dramatically staged the supreme Christmas message our world needs to understand: the recovery of the lost meaning of Christmas. This is not said in any criticism of Santa Claus; the effect must have delighted the hearts of all children who saw it, without doing any violence to their love of Bethlehem. But for adults it is a tragic loss to substitute "Jingle Bells" for "Hark! the Herald Angels Sing," and a lollipop tree for the manger of Bethlehem. The instinct is right to fade out these things in the light of the Christmas star. It is about God's incarnation that the angels sang—God with us.—Robert E. Luccock

Sermon Suggestions

THE IDEAL RULER. TEXT: Mic. 5:2–5a, NRSV. (1) What he does for his people will be "in the strength of the Lord." (2) He will enable his people to "live secure." (3) His reign will be characterized by peace.

"THE SPIRIT OF GRACE." TEXT: Heb. 10:5–10, especially verse 10, NRSV. (1) Our status: "sanctified." (2) The means: "the offering of the body of Jesus Christ once for all." (3) The reason: "by God's will."

Worship Aids

CALL TO WORSHIP. "I heard a great voice out of heaven saying, 'Behold, the tabernacle of God is with men, and he will dwell with them, and they shall be his people, and God himself shall be with them, and be their God'" (Rev. 21:3).

INVOCATION. Most Holy Father, meet us in this sacred place this morning we pray. We come together before you from all walks and conditions of life needing assurance that life can change, that power is available and that you can supply our every need. Teach us to trust you that we may trust one another, to love you that we may love others aright and to follow you that we may lead all people in the paths of righteousness and truth. Before you this morning we bow in reverent waiting that your spirit may minister to us, inspiring us to praise your name a-right all the day long and into the tomorrows. For this we pray in the name of Christ Jesus our Lord.—Henry Fields

OFFERTORY SENTENCE. "As every man hath received the gift, even so minister the same one to another, as good stewards of the manifold grace of God" (1 Pet. 4:10).

OFFERTORY PRAYER. "Lord, you have given differing gifts to us all. There are many ways we can do each other good. Let none of us despise our own modest means of blessing. And help us to see that these fruits of our labors, which now we bring, are one important means by which we can serve you and minister to one another.

PRAYER. O God, our God, in time before time you made ready the Creation. Your Spirit, your wisdom, your love, issued forth and brooded over the deep, bringing to birth heaven and earth, winds and waters, sun and moon and stars; growing things, both plants and animals, and finally humankind. You made us in your image, male and female, to love and care for the earth and its creatures as you love and care for us, your children. When the time was full, when all things were ready, you sent forth your only Son to redeem us from our waywardness and recall us to our true estate—to be sons and daughters of the Most High. For all your goodness to us and to all peoples, we worship and adore you.—John Thompson

LECTIONARY MESSAGE

Topic: Christmas Musical
TEXT: Luke 1:39–45 (46–55)

This scene in Luke has always reminded me of a movie musical, where the characters break into song at certain points. Elizabeth, filled with the Spirit, prophesies about Mary, and Mary responds with a song. To Luke's readers, it would have been an old familiar tune, a lot like the song Hannah, Samuel's mother, sang when she found she would be pregnant in her old age. Let's stage this scene:

I. The first shot is a close-up of Mary: "My soul magnifies the Lord." She looks happy and sings a lively tune, celebrating the best thing that has ever happened to her. After all, what nice Palestinian girl wouldn't relish the idea of having a baby conceived out of wedlock by someone other than her fiance? Why is she so happy?

Let Thomas Merton answer that one. We have a choice, he said, to be real or unreal, to put on a mask or to wear the face God created for us. But we can only be ourselves in one way, and that is God's way. "The secret of my full identity is hidden in him. He alone can make me who I am, or rather who I will be when at last I fully begin to be" [New Seeds of Contemplation, 33]. Mary has been touched by her destiny, and now even though she knows life may be more difficult and more dangerous, she also knows she will be happier doing what God intended. For that reason, she can sing.

II. The second shot is a wide-angle shot, drawing back the focus so that we can see the whole room where Mary is, with the members of Elizabeth's household gathered around. "His mercy is great on those who fear him," she sings. "He has shown strength with his arm, he has scattered the proud, he has lifted up the poor." God's reign has begun. Now God's poor people, like the ones in the camera shot with her, will begin to get an even break for once in their lives.

Wouldn't it be wonderful if the birth of a baby could really do all that? It seems unlikely—something that could happen only in a movie musical. But think about this: In the year 1809, President James Madison began his term of office. The United States signed a trade agreement with the British which was repealed later the same year. Napoleon was carving up Europe and monopolizing most of the world's attention. And in a log cabin in a very rural part of the United States a baby boy was born to a fairly poor, uneducated family—Abraham Lincoln. If his mother had sung about how he would shape the future of the planet, no one would have believed her, either.

III. Think about how the first two shots are connected. Mary first had to agree to be the obedient servant of God's will. Then Jesus himself had to accept the role laid out for him in her song, the champion of the poor. That is why the last shot is a split-screen shot. In the last part of Mary's song, she sings about how her baby's birth will bring good news to Israel, "according to the promise God made to Abraham and to his descendants." In this last shot, one part of the screen shows her singing those words, while the other part shows Christ being crucified. Tragically, the good news was offered but rejected.

Mary's song ends, and the action moves on towards the birth in the manger that we know so well. But her song has touched us. She tells us that if we want to be happy, we must give ourselves to as much of God's will for us as we know. She tells us that if we do this, we can never be certain how important the results will be—it might change the world. But she tells us that if we don't, the results will be tragic for us. Sing her song, take up your task, celebrate your calling and help change the world!— Richard B. Vinson

SUNDAY: DECEMBER TWENTY-FIFTH (CHRISTMAS)

SERVICE OF WORSHIP

Sermon: Only God Can Make a Christmas

TEXT: Isaiah 7:10–14

What God promises, he performs! That is the glorious truth at the heart of the Christmas story. Isaiah 7:10–14 gives God's wonderful promise, "Behold, a young woman shall conceive and bear a son, and shall call his name Immanuel" (v. 14). God lifts a banner of hope for a desperate world. Something good is going to happen! God's supreme blessing is yet to come, and to this sure hope men of faith could cling.

For there was no Christmas then, only the long ages of waiting, the hardships of a difficult life only lightened by the expectancy of faith. Only God could make a Christmas, for Christmas was God's coming among us, to do for man what man could not do for himself. The age-long waiting for the Messiah was rewarded at last by the coming of Christmas. "Immanuel" to Isaiah was the name that enshrined his forward-looking faith—"with us-God." Matthew 1:23 joyously lifts up this ancient prophecy. The Babe of Bethlehem is the hope of the ages, God with man, as Savior. "You shall call his name, Jesus, for he will save his people from their sins" (Matt. 1:21).

I. The message of the angel came to Joseph in a dream, God's dream that wakes us. Joseph had been troubled in mind because Mary was with child, but God spoke through his angel in a dream, and the dream awakened Joseph to faith and obedience. "When Joseph woke from sleep, he did as the angel of the Lord commanded him . . ." (Matt. 1:24). For God was in action; his Holy Spirit is at the center of the Christmas story—"That which is conceived in her is of the Holy Spirit." When questions throng and answers tarry, we take the way of trust and obedience until God's leading brings us into the light. So Joseph obeyed, taking Mary for his wife; but he "knew her not until she had borne a son; and he called his name Jesus" (Matt. 1:25).

II. The thrilling spirit of expectancy fills the first chapter of Luke, which is the story of two pregnancies. The dramatic story of Elizabeth's unexpected conceiving in advanced years, and the birth of St. John the Baptizer, illustrates the expectancy of faith and its fulfillment through the mighty working of the Spirit of God. The "Benedictus" (Luke 1:68–80) is an exuberant song of joy in the God who fulfills what he promises:

Blessed be the Lord God of Israel for he has visited and redeemed his people . . . to perform the mercy promised to our fathers.

The Annunciation to Mary gives the glad news that God is giving a Savior to his people. The salutation of the angel, "The Lord is with you," proves puzzling to Mary. The angel tells her to put aside her fears, for she shall be the mother of Jesus, "the Son of the Most High." Mary asks, "How can this be, since I have no husband?" She is perplexed at the strangeness of her role in God's purpose, yet open to God's leading. When the angel announces that the child will be called the Son of God, and that the Holy Spirit would come upon her, she probably was still perplexed, but not disobedient. With beautiful simplicity of faith, she pledged her obedience to the will of God, "Behold I am the handmaid of the Lord; let it be

to me according to your word" (Luke 1:38). As I stood in the Church of the Annunciation in Nazareth recently, reflecting on these words, I felt they were a superlative expression of readiness to obey, being willing to be willing, an inspiration to us all to place ourselves in God's hands with total humility and complete confidence. God can do wonderful things, if we but believe. "With God nothing will be impossible" (Luke 1:37).

When Mary visited Elizabeth, it was a time of rejoicing in the Lord. Elizabeth "was filled with the Holy Spirit" and cried, "Blessed is she that believed that there would be a fulfillment of what was spoken to her from the Lord" (Luke 1:45). This joyous rhythm of faith and fulfillment is at the heart of the Christmas story. God brings his greatest blessings to man, and man's part is to look to God in faith and expectancy. For those without faith, it is winter without Christmas. Only God can make a Christmas, and only faith can receive it. The whole mood of the Christmas story is joy in the Incarnation, breaking through the fears and perplexities of God's people. If we stop looking at our fears, and focus on the face of God, we shall see in our Heavenly Father that love and goodness and strength that make all our human fears and perplexities unimportant.

III. John 1:1–14 proclaims the fact that fulfills God's promise. "And the Word became flesh and dwelt among us . . . ." How these mighty words have thrilled mankind! For this is the fact of Christmas that fulfills the faith of Christmas. The hopes and fears of all the years, the quivering expectations of God's people, the forward look of faith for prolonged generations, all come to glorious and satisfying fulfillment in the fact of Christmas—"the Word became flesh and dwelt among us." Isaiah's "Immanuel" has come to live the life of a man, God with us in human form, "full of grace and truth," revealing to us the wonderful capabilities of our humanity, that can incarnate the Living God! This is God's Christmas gift to mankind, the answer to the ages of waiting, the fulfillment of the promise of a Savior, the reward of expectancy and hope. This is the Christmas fact that fulfills the Christmas faith!

IV. It is only the touch of God that gives Christmas its true joy. Only God can make a Christmas. His Incarnation is the fact that makes the mighty foundation of our faith, thrilling us to the depths of our spirits with the joyous truth that God cared so much he would not leave us lost, that he personally came to save and deliver in the magnificent ministry of Jesus the Savior that began on that first Christmas when hope was born.

The message of the Word made flesh is good news that heartens us with confidence and joy, gratitude and love. God's blessings abound in the Christmas story, but only those who believe can receive them. There are many people who seek to make merry at Christmas, only to find there is no mirth without belief in the Savior's birth. Without the Christmas meaning at the center of our joy, our holiday becomes a hollow-day. But when the Christmas message takes possession of our mind and spirit, our hearts will sing as we welcome our Savior and king. The Christmas song is the exultation of the spirit in the joyous sense of God's gift. The reason for our mirth is Jesus' birth. The thought of God's mighty deed kindles a glorious faith in us that enables us to move out of the shadows of sorrow and despair into the place where God's light falls upon us. The thought that God cares that much and wills for us only what is good is the central meaning of the Incarnation and the glorious truth that transforms Christmas from an observance to an experience, from a tradition to a time of praise and rejoicing in Jesus born to be our Savior, the fulfillment forever of the promises of God.—Lowell M. Atkinson

Illustrations

NOT WHAT, BUT WHOM. Christmas means this at least: a personality has come into the world concerning whom millions believe that he is the answer. Even Paul never said, I know what I have believed. The mystery of life so deep, the confusion of the world so great, he sometimes did not know what he believed. What Paul said went deeper: "I know him whom I have believed." That is Christianity! I wish I could persuade someone here who never has accepted it, to accept it now. I am not inviting you to sign a theological creed on the dotted line. I am not inviting you to join a sectarian denomination, and subscribe to its peculiarities. I am inviting you to see Christ, his revelation of God, his basic principles, his way of life, his spirit and quality, and so seeing him to say, He is the answer! Cannot we see whither the contrary answers are plunging the whole world now? He is the answer! That is the everlasting truth!—Harry Emerson Fosdick

A REAL CHRISTMAS. I read of a girl who was writing of her Christmas. When she was eight years old her father had died and there wasn't much money in the home and the mother had to work. Christmas came and they just didn't have many presents. The other kids had bikes and wagons and big toys. She and her sister just had a little rubber doll; the boy had a toy car. Both gifts cost less than a dollar apiece. She remembered the depression, and the feeling of sadness and emptiness she felt. It seemed that she was left out. Someone had forgotten her.

But in between her eighth and ninth year, a Mrs. Brown came into their lives and loved them and cared for them and ministered to them. That next Christmas, there was a station wagon full of toys and bikes, and they knew what Christmas was about in the sense of receiving love and joy. "That Christmas," she said, "I remember going in to my mother and saying with tears rolling down my cheeks, 'Mother, Christmas is for real.'"—Hugh Litchfield

Sermon Suggestions

WHEN GOD'S ZEAL IS AT WORK. TEXT: Isa. 9:2-7. (1) His people will know a new, bright day, verses 2-5. (2) This blessing will come through the offices of the Christ: a., His authority; b., His functions. (3) His peace will last forever.

BECAUSE THE GRACE OF GOD HAS APPEARED.   TEXT: Titus 2:11–14. (1) Salvation is made available to all. (2) Disciplined lives follow the experience of this salvation. (3) We wait in hope for the blessing of the glorious final appearing of Jesus Christ.

Worship Aids

CALL TO WORSHIP.   "The angel said unto them, Fear not: for behold, I bring you good tidings of great joy, which shall be to all people. For unto you is born this day in the city of David a Savior, which is Christ the Lord" (Luke 2:10–11).

INVOCATION.   O Lord, of the infant Jesus, through whom all prophecy was fulfilled and all hope abides to this day; open us this Christmas Sunday to the depths of Incarnation and the joys of salvation, as we herald again our newborn king.

OFFERTORY SENTENCE.   "When they were come into the house, they saw the young child with Mary his mother, and fell down, and worshiped him; and when they had opened their treasures, they presented unto him gifts: gold, and frankincense, and myrrh" (Matt. 2:11)

OFFERTORY PRAYER.   Lord, Most Holy, accept our Christmas offering, as we who are recipients of the Bethlehem birth and a Calvary hope, come to thee through our faithful advocate, King Jesus.— E. Lee Phillips

PRAYER.   The years may come and the years may go. Centuries pass and time dims away. But still the wonder of the years and centuries is Christ.

Again, on this particular day we bow at the manger and worship in simplicity and in truth. Again our eyes are filled with wonder and our hearts are at peace. We stand with those far wiser than ourselves and lay our gifts before the Christ child.

In all humility we promise him obedience as we journey on across the years.

We thank you, Father, for the quiet of Bethlehem which comes to us in the midst of our busy days. We thank you for the simplicity of the ancient year which bids our present complexity and confusion to cease. We thank you for the new light that shines upon our path, for without it all would be gloom and darkness. For sadness turned to gladness, for sorrow turned to joy, for burdens lifted, for weakness overcome, for guilt assuaged and sin forgiven our hearts are ever thankful. That all your grace was one day given to us in a baby at Bethlehem is more than we can comprehend. We can grasp such truth only by faith. That he should live and die and live again forever in our midst is indeed mindboggling. But such is our peace, such is our rejoicing.

This morning we pray for the Child's coming again and that all hearts may be ready to receive him. May all barriers to his coming be broken down. May a star shine again to lead kings and empires to his feet. May the song of angels stir all us humble and common folk to journey again to Bethlehem and see this thing which has come to pass which the Lord has made known unto us. This morning may we indeed come and adore him, Christ the Lord!—Henry Fields

LECTIONARY MESSAGE

Topic: The Sign

TEXT: Luke 2:1–14

Signs point beyond themselves. Sometimes they do it quite literally, like the arrows that tell us to turn left or right to get to a place. Sometimes they do it more figuratively, like advertisements that first draw us to themselves and then to the product we're supposed to buy. Sometimes they are unintentional landmarks, as in "turn right when you get to the billboard with the potato chips, and you'll be almost to my house."

I. Jesus' birth is called a sign in Luke 2:12, meaning that it pointed to something beyond itself. To what? On the simplest level, the angels just meant to tell the shepherds how to recognize the right infant. "He'll be the one wrapped in linen cloth, lying in the feed trough." The cloth was pretty standard fare for infants, but the manger was a definite give-away.

What if the sign had been a halo around his head? or a robe of pure gold? or the fact that the infant could greet them by name when they got there? The only thing that made the infant Jesus unusual that night was perhaps the level of poverty of his parents. Too poor and too unimportant to command a room, too unconnected to stay with family, they were in the barn and he was in the manger. Christmas is a sign to us that Christ knows about being needy. He was human, and human on an underprivileged level. He knows about those things, and he cares.

II. No one could tell at the time, but the manger was also a sign about the life Christ would lead. It is as if his entrance helped to set the tone for the rest of his ministry. In *The Sting*, Paul Newman's first presentation to the camera is lying crumpled up on the floor between a bed and a wall, his nose squished against the baseboard, snoring. Talk about an entrance setting a mood!

Now, if I had been writing the script for Christ's entrance, it might have had more red carpet and trumpets. The angel army was a nice touch, but it was wasted on those poor scared shepherds. Why not tell the folks in the palace as well, instead of just the peasants out in the fields? But, then, that's the way Jesus led his life. He ate with the sinners. He hung around with the tax collectors, those thieving skunks. He touched lepers on purpose, for God's sake!

III. What are our signs of Christmas? An overdecorated tree piled 'round with presents. Mountains of homemade cookies and sweets. Santa Claus, who uses his omnipotence, omniscience, and omnipresence to bring toys to children in proportion to their parents' economic status. A more appropriate sign to us at Christmas would be a homeless family taking shelter under a bridge. Christmas was not meant to make us feel secure and sentimental in our affluence; it was meant to show us where God's priorities lie and to indicate where God's Savior would be spending his time. Let us get our bearings again by the sign of Jesus' birth.—Richard B. Vinson

SECTION III.
Messages for Communion Services

SERMON SUGGESTIONS

Topic: The Suffering Servant

TEXT: Isaiah 53

Isaiah 53 is one of four Servant Songs found in this prophecy. The others are found in Isa. 41:1–4; 49:1–6; and 59:4–9. Each of these songs refers to the "servant of Yahweh."

Who was the Suffering Servant described in Isaiah 53? Obviously, the nation of Israel filled that role to some degree. Some have suggested the servant of the Lord was a king like either Hezekiah or Uzziah or a prophet like Jeremiah or even Isaiah himself. No satisfactory answer to that question is found until we move to the New Testament and look at Jesus Christ. Jesus is the Suffering Servant who died for the sins of the world. That is the way the New Testament writers understood this passage in Isaiah. Of the twelve verses in Isaiah 53, only one does not appear in the New Testament. For the New Testament writers, Isaiah 53 was a reference to Jesus Christ.

When you accept this approach, suddenly the passage explodes with meaning. Isaiah is painting a portrait of the suffering of our Savior.

I. *Visible suffering.* The suffering of Jesus, both his physical and his spiritual suffering, marked his body. Isaiah describes this in Isa. 52:14.

Reference is also made in the New Testament to the effect of Jesus' suffering on his body. Once, near his death, when Je-sus was about thirty years of age, some of the Jews referred to him by saying, "You are not yet fifty years old" (John 8:57). Evidently, the suffering through which Jesus went gave him the appearance of premature age. Jesus was visibly marked by his suffering.

II. *Valiant suffering.* Because of the suffering of the Savior, some thought he was being punished by God (see Isa. 53:4). However, the unanimous testimony of the New Testament is that Jesus knew no sin. The New Testament writers talk about the glory of Jesus' life (see John 1:14), the wisdom of his life (see 1 Cor. 1:24), the unsearchable riches in him (see Eph. 3:8), and the fullness of God in him (see Col. 1:19). But no biblical writer ever makes reference to Jesus' sin, for he knew no sin. Therefore, he did not deserve the punishment of God. Yet he valiantly bore it.

III. *Voluntary suffering.* Isa. 53:7 declares that when suffering came, the servant of the Lord did not open his mouth. Such silent submission was not traditional among the Hebrews. We read in the Old Testament of the complaints of Jeremiah, the laments of Habakkuk, and the bold queries of Job. Yet Jesus didn't open his mouth.

Why? Jesus did not suffer for us on the cross because he had to. He did it because he chose to. His suffering was voluntary.

In John 10:18, Jesus said about his life, "No one has taken it away from me, but I lay it down on my own initiative."

Jesus did not stay on the cross because of the hostile crowd or the power of the Roman officials or the nails which pierced his flesh. Jesus stayed on the cross because of his love for mankind. He died voluntarily for the sins of the world.

IV. *Vicarious suffering.* Vicarious means that one person who does not have to, for the sake of those who do deserve it, takes upon himself the burden of their need. Isa. 53:5–6 clearly describes the vicarious nature of Jesus' suffering. Jesus died for "our transgressions" and "our iniquities."

Paul describes the marvelous transaction that took place on Calvary in 2 Cor. 5:21: "He made him who knew no sin to be sin on our behalf, that we might become the righteousness of God in him." Jesus' suffering was vicarious. It was for us.

V. *Victorious suffering.* The suffering of the Savior brought justification and forgiveness to those who received his gift of life. The cross was not the final word. The Resurrection was. The victorious outcome of the death of Christ is clearly depicted in Isa. 53:11.

We often become discouraged about the cause of Christ. So little seems to have been accomplished. So few are being reached. Evil seems to be winning the day.

We need to remember that discouragement is not the final answer. The current success of the evil that we see all about us is not the final answer. The cross is the final answer. In his suffering on the cross, Jesus won the victory, a victory which is available to each one of us today.—Brian Harbour

Topic: The Lord's Presence—and Seeming Absence

Text: Job 23:1–10

In Shakespeare's play *Hamlet*, Hamlet's uncle killed his father, the king of Denmark, and married his mother, the queen. Hamlet was bent on avenging this crime. One day he came upon his uncle, the guilt-ridden king, alone—at his prayers. However, Hamlet refused to take advantage of the situation and kill his uncle. Hamlet was afraid that if he killed him while he was praying, the uncle might go to heaven. That was not the destination Hamlet had in mind for his father's murderer.

The king complained privately, "My words fly up, my thoughts remain below: / Words without thoughts never to heaven go."

There are times when the heavens appear to be brass to us. Our prayers cannot seem to get through. This experience is called, in the words of St. John of the Cross, "the dark night of the soul." God's absence is experienced by saintly people at times.

I. *The seeming absence of God.* At times our prayer requests are denied. This may be because what we ask is not really best for us. Or it may not be in God's will for us. Or the timing may be off, and God must answer, "Not yet" or "Not now." When our petitions are not granted, the Father may have something far better in store for us. A friend once remarked, "God does not give us what we ask. He gives better than we ask."

Job felt abandoned by God. He cried out, "Oh, that I knew where I might find him!" These are "my autumn days," he moaned. Job's anguish was real. He cried out at the silence of God, but the Almighty refused to answer his pleas for relief from his suffering. Job felt he had been abandoned by God—*absconditus.* The Lord appeared to be far away.

Faith's greatest test comes when our prayers go unanswered. All our requests appear to be met with stony silence. This can be an awful experience indeed.

Moses prayed to enter the Promised Land. It was the goal of his life. Reaching the Promised Land was the obsession of his forty-year ministry, yet it was not to be. He died on Mount Nebo, within sight of the land.

Paul "besought the Lord" three times that his thorn in the flesh might be removed (2 Cor. 12:8). It was an impediment to his mission work, but the apostle's earnest request was denied. He was assured that God's grace was sufficient for him.

Jesus prayed repeatedly in Gethsemane that "the cup" might pass without his having to drink it. No one wants to die at thirty-three. Jesus shrank from suffering and death on the cross. Still he prayed, "Nevertheless not my will, but thine, be done" (Luke 22:42).

Why do we on occasion seem to experience the absence of God? Why are our prayers not always answered? At times we pray incorrectly—in the wrong spirit or not in accordance with God's will. We may pray from a sinful heart. There are unrepented sins or dark resentments in our lives. We may pray selfishly. There are times when we are stubborn or arrogantly insist on our will being done.

We may experience the absence of God because we look for him in the wrong way. Martin Luther sought the Lord for years, but he was trying to earn his salvation. Only when Luther saw salvation as being by grace alone did God find Luther. The silence or seeming absence of God is a dreadful experience.

II. *The Lord's Supper celebrates the presence of God.* "Then you will call upon me and come and pray to me, and I will hear you. You will seek me and find me; when you seek me with all your heart, I will be found by you, says the Lord" (Jer. 29:12–14). Clyde T. Francisco called this the most beautiful passage in Scripture. Remember that the prophet Elijah realized God's presence not in the storm, earthquake, or fire. God became real to him in a "still, small voice" (1 Kings 19:12). Jesus reminded us to "ask, and it will be given you; seek, and you will find; knock, and it will be opened to you" (Matt. 7:7).

Jesus taught that God seeks us. This is one of the lofty insights of Scripture. In one passage, Luke 15, the Master told three parables about a lost sheep, a lost coin, and lost sons. All three stories depict God as one who seeks those who are lost. If Plato taught that God is found through reason and Buddha taught that we find God in contemplation, the Bible teaches that God discloses himself. He finds us.

The Lord's Supper is an opportunity to realize God's presence through worship. The Supper is characterized by powerful symbols. They are reminders of the high cost of our salvation—Christ's body and life's blood given on our behalf. The risen Christ is present with us in our worship. He promised that whenever we gather in his name, he is in our midst.

As we wait to receive the broken bread, let us confess our sins to God. Then as we wait to receive the fruit of the vine, let us thank God for the assurance of his pardon. We can appropriate divine forgiveness by repentance and faith. "Your sins are forgiven," Jesus said (Matt. 9:2). "Go, and do not continue in sin" (see John 5:14; 8:11).

When we encounter God, he turns our question marks into exclamation marks of praise. He can make the crooked straight. Job exulted, "When he has tried me, I shall come forth as God" (v. 10).

The absence of God can be real—and so can his presence, here at his table.—Alton H. McEachern

Topic: Jesus, Saviour
Text: Matt. 1:21

It is familiar fact that Hebrew names were commonly significant—a natural and pleasing custom. This being no longer a usage with us, we often give names of great and good men who have lived in other days. Sometimes heroes of fiction. This, too, is beautiful. Names often make an impression upon those who bear them. So with many who have borne the names of warriors, orators, sometimes of preachers, and other good men. But names have often been falsified, and more often, there are those who dishonor some renowned and venerable name which has been given to them. These things are not wholly unimportant. And especially might we observe that one name, not individual, but of a party, is often borne in vain—the name *Christian*. Truly it is many times "a word and nothing more."

But the name here directed to be given was not in vain. The word *Jesus* means "Savior". And truly did he become a Savior. He is Jesus Christ, the Savior anointed—he ever lives to save. In the reasons assigned for giving him this name, there are taught great and glorious truths. Let us attend to them.

I. *He shall save.* Emphatic in the original.

(a) He, and not we ourselves, save us. We could not have accomplished the work. And it is not a joint affair, by the union of his merit and ours. He alone saves.

(b) He is the Savior and not our faith in him. Danger of exalting faith into an agency and giving it credit for our salvation, while it is but a relation to him. Faith ought not to be regarded as a meritorious work, "paying part of our debt." Such an expression is most unfortunate. He is the author of eternal salvation. Let us not think there is merit in ordinances nor in exercises, but Jesus is the Savior. Let us look to him, receive him, submit to him, make him our all and in all.

(c) He is to be seen, not as exalted, but as humbled—not as living a life of splendor, but as dying a death of shame. The expectations of his earthly friends were to be disappointed; his cherished, even strengthening hopes to be blasted, but when the sword of acutest suffering was piercing his soul, *then* would he be accomplishing his great work, *thus* becoming the author of salvation. Jesus Christ, and him crucified—the climax of his life, the center of his work.

Of his death alone did he appoint a memorial—not of his miracles, not of his brief hour of seeming earthly triumph, but his disciples in all ages must meet and eat bread and drink wine to "show forth the Lord's death." Yes, it is our dying Lord that is the Savior—yet not *dead* for he rose again, he burst the bars of death, he is alive forevermore.

He then shall save. In his own discourses we observe what with reverence may be called a sublime and holy egotism. Fitly does he speak of himself, for he is the Lord and with beginning and end, author and finisher. In him be our trust, to him the glory—yea, his beloved name shall be in the chorus of the everlasting song.

II. *He shall save his people.* No longer in a national sense, as the Jews would have supposed. "He gave himself for us, that he might redeem us from all iniquity, and purify, etc., a peculiar people," etc.

All that receive him, that believe in his name become his people—"power to become the sons of God." What an honor, what a happiness, to be of the people of Jesus! The Queen of Sheba thought that Solomon's servants were blessed. How much more are they happy who belong to the people of God, heirs apparent to thrones and crowns in heaven, joint heirs with Jesus Christ, and already blessed with angels as ministering spirits. So angels as they come on their missions of love, with what interest may we suppose them to gaze on those here and there whom they know to be heirs of salvation. They are sadly few, yet found in every rank and condition—in kings' palaces and wandering in the wilderness; rich like Abraham or poor like him whom the angels bore to Abraham's bosom; learned and ignorant, master and servant—yea, now in every quarter of the globe with their diverse languages and customs, etc., yet they love Jesus and serve him. They are his people, greatly blessed now and to be greatly exalted hereafter.

Who of you would not be of his people? Then come to Jesus; turn, quickly now, unto the Lord, receive Christ as your Savior.

III. *From their sins.*

(a) From the penalty of their sins. It is well to reflect upon and seek to realize the awful truth that we deserve to die, to suffer eternal damnation. Suppose we should reflect upon it, each for himself. "I have sinned against God—I know I have." Excuse and extenuate as I may, I know I am a sinner. I deserve to suffer the penalty—to be consigned forever to the damnation of hell. I do not have remorse, etc. And then positive punishment—something as bad as an undying worm and quenchless fire. And I cannot cease to sin—and if I could, what shall make amends for my past sin? Ah, yes, my friends, we all deserve to perish—but Jesus! he died to save us from perdition. Let us flee to him.

(b) From the dominion of sin. Ye shall die in your sins, a most terrible doom. It were a very inadequate salvation merely to be delivered from positive punishment and be left sinful. If we have right ideas of sin, we must greatly desire to be saved from our sins. And this Jesus came to accomplish. (1) If we love him, we have new motives to resist our sinful tendencies. (2) Jesus has procured for them that believe in him the special indwelling of the Holy Spirit the Sanctifier. For his gracious influences we may pray and hope to become more and more holy—to gain more and more the mastery over our sinful dispositions, till the hour of death shall be the hour of perfect deliverance, and we enter upon an eternal existence of sinlessness, of purity. That, that will be heaven.—John A. Broadus

Topic: Three Events

Thomas Wolfe, whose too early death was so deeply regretted, left a book, "You Can't Go Home Again," one chapter of which was in the form of a letter to a friend about religious faith, that of his friend and his own.

It was entitled "Ecclesiastes," after the Bible book of that name. He did not accept the "hopeful fatalism" of the book as final, but when he stated his own credo so passionately it remained rather vague.

Hear now these gritty words from Ecclesiastes: "All things come alike to all: there is one event to the righteous and to the wicked"—meaning death, which he tells us we share with the animals.

Look now at the three crosses standing stark on "the Place of the Skull," on the first Good Friday. There three men were dying, three different men meeting the same muddy end, good and bad alike.

The nails were the same; the downward drag of the body, the blood, the cramp, the buzzing flies, the blistering sun the same. At the end the merciful cloud of death, hiding the hideous scene, was the same.

But was it the same to all three? Outwardly, yes. Inwardly, no. Each met the same end in a different way, making it a different thing. "There is one event," yes; but from the inside there were three events.

One man met his death in anger, railing at fate, mocking life, cursing Christ to his face—hopeless and as hard as nails. One was softened, subdued, touched by the majesty of Jesus—a penitent at prayer.

Jesus met the same bitter, brutal death, no item of agony spared—but his prayer for his enemies and for all blind souls hallows the earth and haunts our race to this day like a divine benediction.

Nay, more: he took death, so terrifying to mankind, and made of it a tool, a key, wherewith he unlocked unknown revelations and redemptions. He did not defy death, he conquered it—leaving it behind, outsped.

Did one event come alike to all? Yes, certainly; but each one dealt with it in a different way, making three events. In a way beyond our knowing, Jesus made the darkness of death "the master light of all our seeing."

Not fatalism, but faith, has the last word—opens a door to the light on the other side of life.—Joseph Fort Newton

Topic: The Church in Your House

TEXTS: Rom. 16:5; 1 Cor. 16:19; Philemon 2

House-churches in the New Testament have been likened to modern cottage prayer meetings or weekly Bible study groups that meet in homes. The analogy is helpful, though the church is more than either. A church in the house brings together two institutions that are indispensable for human happiness and welfare. Each has its unique functions, but in the purpose of God they are allies, charged with the spiritual and moral well-being of humanity.

The church in the house practices forgiveness and acceptance of persons. There was a church in the home of Philemon (Philemon 2). Philemon was a wealthy Christian who owed his spiritual life to Paul's witness. Onesimus, slave of Philemon, had run away from his owner and gone to Rome. There he had met Paul and through him found freedom in Christ.

The apostle's personal letter to Philemon contained a plea that he receive Onesimus back into the household, "no longer as a slave, but . . . a beloved brother . . . both in the flesh and in the Lord" (v. 16). Under Roman law, a master had unlimited power over a slave. A thief and a runaway like Onesimus could have been punished by death. Paul acted as a mediator working to bring about reconciliation, restitution, and forgiveness. Onesimus must return to his master; Philemon must show brotherly love and forgiveness. The church in Philemon's house would then gain a new member. Forgiving love would create a new situation as it always does.

Within the family, love and forgiveness form the proper environment for the development of members. Indeed, these qualities are indispensable due to the personality differences and conflict situations typical of most homes. Husbands and wives often run afoul of each other; parents and children have clashes; children fuss and fight among themselves. The small battles can develop into sharp conflicts, leading to open breaks. Maturity and patience are tested in most households.

Forgiveness sometimes requires one to forsake "rights" if the wrongdoer is to be restored to his or her place within the family. Philemon had to set aside his rights as a master in order to receive Onesimus back into his home. Onesimus, in turn, could not allow his newfound freedom in Christ to override his sense of responsibility toward his earthly master. Because they both had experienced God's love and forgiveness, they were able to love and forgive each other. Forgiveness removes barriers that keep persons apart. It ends the war and ushers in peace.

Forgiveness and love lead to the acceptance of persons. Not only Philemon and his family, but the church in his house accepted a runaway slave as a brother. Any household or church may contain members whose self-righteous, pharisaical spirit causes them to turn away from the repentant prodigal. The refusal or the inability to forgive others, however, reflects upon one's ability to receive forgiveness (Matt. 6:15; 18:35). Where the forgiving spirit is present, families can resolve differences and consolidate interests. Love leads us to respect persons, accepting them as unique beings of worth, and enables us to handle conflicts when they arise.

Every home can be a church, for the church is a fellowship where Christ dwells. Those New Testament Christians who made up the house churches remind us that home and church are allies. Both are God-given institutions. Both are committed to the spiritual welfare of persons. They share similar goals and experience similar joys. Halford Luccock has well said that "the Christian home has been the church's secret weapon in God's Holy War against evil."

Is there a church in your house, dear friend?—Nolan P. Howington

Topic: The Resurrected Lord Along Our Dusty Ways

TEXT: Luke 24:13–43

On Easter, Jesus overtook two of his disciples going to Emmaus, a small town seven miles west of Jerusalem. They were so caught up in their grief and sorrow that they were not aware of his presence. Jesus spoke to them, but they made no immediate response. "They stood still, looking sad" (v. 17).

Jesus asked them what they were talking about. They were surprised. How could anyone have been in Jerusalem for the last few days and not know what everyone was talking about? So one of his disciples, Cleopas, asked: "Are you the only visitor to Jerusalem who does not know the things that have happened there in these days?" (v. 18). A prophet, Jesus of Nazareth, who had caught the imagination of the nation, had been put to death with two criminals just north of the city along one of the main highways. The place was so cosmopolitan that they wrote his accusation in three languages: Hebrew, Latin, and Greek.

Jesus talked of how the Scriptures were being fulfilled in his death and Resurrection. It was he to whom the great drama of Scripture had been moving.

Time passed fast as they engaged in such exciting conversation. Sundown found them at the entrance of the village. It seemed obvious that Jesus was going on, but at their insistence he went in to have supper with them. They asked him to say grace, and as he did they recognized him. There was something so familiar in the way he broke the bread, blessed it, and passed it. And with the recognition, he vanished out of their sight.

I. *Recognized at a table.* Who the stranger was remained a complete mystery until the Emmaus travelers asked him to say grace. The grace was probably one they had heard all their lives: "Praised be Thou, O Lord, our God, King of the universe, who brings forth bread and food from the ground." There was something different in the way he said it. They recognized him, and he vanished out of their sight.

The table was as important in that day as it is today. At the table they remembered they were not disembodied spirits. They had bodies that became tired, grew hungry, and needed food. The reality of hunger and bread bound them with humanity everywhere.

Not only are physical needs met at the table but social ones as well. It is so much better when we eat together than when we eat alone. When we sit at a common table, whether with friends or strangers, our relationships are changed. We are never the same again.

The origins of terms are interesting. Sometimes they will uncover basic and pertinent meanings long forgotten. For example, the term *companion* comes from *companis,* which means "with bread." One of the best places for friendship and companionship is the dinner table.

The dinner table for Jesus was a place of social acceptance and reconciliation. The fact that he ate with publicans and sinners spoke more effectively than anything he could have said. The dinner table was the place where the last barrier to social acceptance was broken down.

The dinner table was a place of religious significance. No matter how hard you had worked for the meal on the table, when you traced the bread to its ultimate source you came upon the open hands of God. The dinner table, therefore, was a place for prayer and thanksgiving.

It has always been a fact of great interest to me that when Jesus gave the church two ordinances, one of them was a meal: the Lord's Supper. The church down the centuries has variously interpreted that Supper, but all have agreed that Christ meets us there as nowhere else.

II. *Burning hearts.* After the supper where Christ had blessed the bread and then vanished out of their sight, they began to say to each other, "Did not our hearts burn within us while he talked to us on the road, while he opened to us the scriptures?" (v. 32).

Burning hearts remind us of something that psalmist said: "My heart became hot within me. / As I mused, the fire burned; / then I spoke with my tongue" (Ps. 39:3). The words reflect the experience of Jeremiah: "There is in my heart as it were a burning fire / shut up in my bones, / and I am weary with holding it in, / and I cannot" (Jer. :9).

There should be a total response to God's Word. The mind should say: "It is credible. I believe it." The heart should say, "I feel its truth and exult in it." The will should say: "I will clothe it in flesh and blood. I will live it."—Chevis H. Horne

Illustrations for Communion

COMMUNION SERVICE.   When friends in Scotland wrote to James Chalmers in the New Hebrides, asking if there was anything he would like them to send, he replied: "Send a communion set." At that time there was no church where he was, not even a convert; but he knew that there would be.—Charles L. Wallis

LOYALTY.   Long ago a Cavalier soldier had sold much of his property and given a great deal of his money to the Royalist cause. Then he was killed in a battle against the Roundheads. His friends paid tribute to his memory in these words: "He served King Charles with a constant, dangerous and expensive loyalty." It is to the same type of self-denying service that we are called, though for a king and cause greater by far. Freely we have received, freely we must give, not grudgingly or of necessity, for God loves a hilarious giver.—Robert James McCracken

TILL HE COMES.   In the very moment a man and woman are joined together, we speak of their parting. People are married "till death do us part." So in our communion service we speak not only of its continuance but also of its discontinuance. We keep the Lord's Supper "till he comes."—Robert C. Shannon

ANY TIME.   In Hiroshima, Japan, the town chimes ring every day at 8:16 A.M. Why such an odd time? Because it was precisely at 8:16 A.M. on August 6, 1945, that the atomic bomb struck that city and killed seventy-eight thousand people. We like to meet on Good Friday from noon until 3 P.M., matching the hours of darkness when Jesus hung on the cross.

But we are in a different time zone, and the hour is not the same. It doesn't matter. Our best time for remembering Christ's death is not regulated by clock or calendar. It is when the table of memory is set before us and we eat and drink in his honor . . . and in his presence.—Robert C. Shannon

ANY PLACE.   When a national news magazine in the United States did a story on Jerusalem, its reporter interviewed a man at the Western Wall, a man with prayer book and prayer shawl. "This is where the Presence resides," he said. "This is where he will always be. Forever!" We believe that God is omnipresent; that neither he nor Christ can be said to reside in any one place. We are equally certain that in every place where Communion is truly observed Christ keeps his promise and eats and drinks with us.—Robert C. Shannon

SECTION IV.
Messages for Funeral Services

SERMON SUGGESTIONS

Topic: The God of Comfort

TEXT: 2 Cor. 1:3–7

"Life is completely fair; it breaks everybody's heart." To the breaking of hearts Paul offers his God: "The God of all comfort who comforts us in all our afflictions, so that we may be able to comfort those who are in any afflictions, with the comfort with which we ourselves are comforted by God" (1:3–4). Paul offers this God and Jesus Christ, the One whose broken heart has become the gateway to life.

Ministry begins in suffering. The grace of God is poured from broken heart to broken heart. Unbroken hearts are quite unusable for ministry; they are like shiny pottery vessels with no openings either to receive or to give the healing balms of God. For the desolation of hearts only God's consolation will finally do, a consolation brought by Christ and his servants.

Ten times in five verses we see the word *comfort*. Do you get an idea of its importance? The New Testament word is *paraklesis*. You may remember that word from some other place: Jesus talking of God sending us another Paraclete, another like *him* (John 14:16ff.). *Paraclete* literally means "one called (*klesis*) alongside (*para*)." Wayne Oates says that God's presence comes in two forms: as *over-againstness* (the Holy Other meeting you face-to-face) and as *alongsideness* (God coming to walk by your side as friend).

Jesus was the supreme Paraclete of God, alongsideness made flesh, God's Son who came to earth and walked beside us as friend.

But this friendship was a suffering friendship. Jesus was the "Suffering Servant" envisioned by the prophet, a man of sorrows and acquainted with grief, one who bore our sins and bore them away, the one whom we would despise and reject but by whose stripes we find our healing.

It is his broken heart that becomes our passage to the grace of God. He is the Christ of sorrow and comfort. I love the way H. C. G. Moule expanded on this climactic moment from Bunyan's *The Pilgrim's Progress*. Christ is the Man at the Gate:

"Here is a poor burthened sinner," said the Pilgrim; "I would know, Sir, if you are willing to let me in."
(And we would say with the pilgrim) "Here are stricken and broken hearts; we have heard, Sir, that your heart was once broken, and has stood open ever since, and that its great rift is turned into a gate by which men go in and find peace. We would know if you are willing to let us in."
"I am willing with all my heart," said the Man; and with that he opened the gate.

The broken heart of the Son of man has become the open gate to eternal life. It has also been the occasion of our calling into the ministry of Jesus Christ, the ministry which is not for professionals only but of the whole people of God.—H. Stephen Shoemaker

Topic: Now is the Time

The beauty and calm which, we trust, shall dwell within our souls toward the evening and close of our day are not to be won in the evening itself but are to be gathered in through all the hours and days of our life. We must not look for peace, for order and beauty in our life toward the end, if today and now and always we are not setting ourselves against the riotous elements of our nature. If we hope to have in the evening of our life the beauty of holiness, the comfort of a quiet mind, the outlook of an untormented spirit, now is the day to seek them, now is the day to sound that note through every region of our life—through body, soul, and spirit.

It is this which makes the passing of time a serious thing. It is not merely that time is passing. It is, I think, rather this: that from the point of view of the culture of our souls, time is opportunity. In other words, there is a season for everything, and once the season is past for doing a particular thing or acquiring a particular grace, we are almost helpless. There is, for example, the season of youth, in which for the most part we are called upon to be severe with ourselves, in short to resist. In the later seasons of our life we are called upon, for the most part, to endure rather than to resist. Or we might say that in youth we are asked to practice virtue; later on to yield to grace. Of course, it is never quite sound to divide the seasons of our life in that way or in any way. But it is admitted by all who are in earnest that there are certain temptations and weaknesses which threaten us peculiarly at certain times, and that it is then and not afterward that these must be dealt with and transformed. Youth has its own dangers and excesses; so has middle life and so doubtless has old age—and it is in the actual besetting hour, i.e., it is all along the line, that the good fight has to be waged. There is a time for doing things, and though in God's mercy any one of us may

have such preeminent grace given to him that he may recover ground, still if we have been unfaithful in some true matter of life we have no right to escape a certain sense of loss, a certain sorrow of regret at the end.

Whoever would be a good man one day must be a good man now. Justice is done. In the matter of character and destiny, we shall all get what, in our true and innermost soul, we were always looking for. To faithful souls there will surely come in the evening a time of true peace, with the light coming in from the west. As at the touch of death the autumn leaf yields up its secret, hiding no longer the golden glory which was always there—the beauty drawn from spring and summer, from sun and moon and stars—surely we may believe that it shall not be otherwise in the world of human souls.

Even here and already, we may have seen the holy thing take place, a wonderful light beginning to come into the face of one who in some private matter has fought the good fight in some last trench of faith. And, not to draw upon the firm promise of our Lord that so indeed it will be, surely it is what we should look for from the Eternal Justice, that here in part, but in the other world in all perfection, the fruits of all holy living, the reward of every faithful deed, the beauty that came from every personal sacrifice, shall survive and shall clothe in glory those whose due it is.

But let us make it very plain to ourselves that it is in these actual days and in our own circumstances that we must win any beauty, any peace of mind, any happy outlook toward our final destiny—such as we surely would desire to have in the evening of our life and at its close. Let us make it plain that at the end we shall appear simply as we are; that what we are in secret will be made manifest, as though it were proclaimed from housetops. Let us see to it that we are seeking now those things of the spirit which we would not be without at the end. If, for example, there is any habit in our life which we feel one day must cease; if there is anything in our behavior, in our temper of mind which we ourselves mean shall be changed; if there is anything which we are keeping back from God, which nevertheless we know will one day trouble us; well, now is the time; now is all we have.—John A. Hutton

Topic: Yes, God Can

Text: John 19:26–27

One of the great concerns of the dying is for the ones who are going to be left behind. Jesus set the pace in showing us how to die. He wanted to see that the family's needs were adequately met.

That might mean different things for different people. Providing adequate insurance coverage for our loved ones is perhaps the most common way we try to meet that need. Seeing to it that the household is on a sound financial base is so important. Many families have suffered in other ways after their grief experience due to the mess they found themselves in financially.

Obviously, the intensive care unit of the hospital is not the best place for accomplishing this goal. Since we're all in the process of dying, that is, since we are all moving toward that appointment, the time to start preparing for the family's future is now. When you are dying, it will be helpful for you not to have to worry about this matter.

There are other family needs one might want to meet. I have been present when a dying person has called the family members into the room. I have heard them talking to their loved ones about dreams and wishes. I have heard them ask for forgiveness where they have done wrong to someone. I've seen the tears, heard the prayers, watched the embraces, and felt the power of human emotion in times of reconciliation.

The dying one must always recognize that his or her departure from this life will leave an empty place for others. Someone will feel the pain and anxiety. Someone will wonder about what to do. How beautiful it can be when the dying one, like our Lord, looks out for the interests of the living and does everything possible to care for the needs of others.

We might also note that when Jesus turned to John and asked that he care for his mother, it was a way of turning to the network of friends we have and seeking help from them. John was honored to be so recognized by the dying Lord. Many times our friends are more than glad to do the extra thing that will give us comfort and give our loved ones necessary help.

We need our friends in the time of suffering and death.

Grief is harder when there is no established network of supporting friends who can give intimate support in times of sorrow. Each of us needs a group of quality relationships, rather than exclusive dependence on only one or two people.

That's also where a good church family enters the picture. The fellowship of the church and the strength one derives from the people of faith is invaluable to the dying and their loved ones.—Jerry Hayner

Topic: God Is Over All

Charlotte Brontë, at a time when sorrow was added to sorrow, wrote to her closest friend. Her sister Emily was dead; Anne was ill of the same incurable disease. Her brother Branwell had died of drink.

Such was the setting of the brave, wise, dry-eyed letter in which she said, "I avoid looking forward or backward and try to keep looking upward. This is no time to regret, dread or weep. God is over all."

Today our plight is much the same. If we look backward, we are depressed; if we look forward, we are confused and terrified. It is time to look upward—aye, to be lifted above the cloud-shadows.

"Watchman, what of the night?" the prophet Isaiah was asked. "The morning cometh, and also the night; if ye would inquire, return later," he replied. Elsewhere he added, "Neither fear ye their fear, nor be afraid."

In other words, if there is a rhythm of light and shadow in history, as in nature, it is the way and will of God. Above all things we must avoid the infection and panic of fear, which blinds us and betrays us.

"When shall we be relieved at least of 'great events' and 'great men,' and allowed to return to our peaceful little daily lives with their simple, healthy joys?" a woman asks. Not for many years, perhaps not in our lifetime.

No one can see, even dimly, the shape of things to be. The picture is too confusing, the factors too bewildering. But it is no time to doubt, much less to despair and sink into cynicism: "God is over all."

Surely he is a blind soul who does not see that a divine purpose and plan are being worked out in our human world. Until man is wise enough to see that plan and humble enough to follow it there will be upheaval and disaster.

Many surprises await us. Things will happen with startling suddenness; changes will be radical. We are entering another age, the cycle has come full circle; it is another era. Let us be unafraid, "God is over all."

Only a great faith will be equal to a great future—faith which is both a gift of God and a law of the soul. According to our faith and forgiveness so it will be unto us and to those "who after us remain," as Dante added.

"Behold I make all things new" was a great Bible word, when the world was falling to pieces, to be remade after another pattern. Only a creative faith is equal to days such as these—days of the right hand of God.—Joseph Fort Newton

Topic: The Sympathy of Christ

There are two systems at work—one which is supervising the events of human life with reference to their final reward in heaven and another in which we are seeking to gather out of each day the harvest that belongs to that day. We are legislating for time and for eternity. We have our condition meet for our character. We work for the sake of joy—God for the sake of purity; we for abundance—he for moral nobleness. These two administrations are constantly coming into conflict of jurisdiction. One or the other must have superiority. The secret of more than half our trouble in life is that we are attempting to shape our life for the world, and God, who loves us, is attempting to overrule that bad enginery, and to shape our life for the glory of the eternal world. And so much of suffering I see in life I sympathize with—and I do not! When an organ is at concert pitch, everything else has got to come up to it—and the instrument is generally at concert pitch. Some note by and by falls away; and then, when the stop is drawn and the scale is played, every time that note comes in, it wails. Why? Because all the other notes are against it, you would think. So they are, when a note is out of tune. Once having a string of a violin below pitch, and all the three other strings are fighting it. Let one note of a piano be out of tune, and all the rest of the piano is at enmity with it. If one pipe of an organ is out of tune, all the rest of the organ is against it. That note wails and wails, and all the other notes are sweet sounding. By and by, the hand of the tuner begins to bring it up; and up and up it goes, crying and whining; but the moment it touches the concert pitch, it falls in, and there is no longer any conflict of one note with the other. The moment it comes into harmony, there is no longer any "wolfing" of vibrations, no longer any turmoil. It is in tune. And the sorrows and troubles of this world are but just discordant wails that men make when God takes them and attempts to bring them up into harmony by bringing them to concert pitch.

Now, I am sorry for suffering; but I am heartily glad that God is willing to make men suffer. I am glad to see men whose pride does not satisfy them. I am glad to see men whose selfishness does not make them happy. I am hurt when I see too much joy with sensuousness; but I rejoice when I see men vexed and plagued—men who are following the bent of their lower nature.

"I," says the psalmist, "was envious at the foolish, when I saw the prosperity of the wicked." "Their eyes stand out with fatness; they have more than heart could wish." "Pride compasseth them about as with a chain." God did not care for them, it would seem. He cast them off. They were reprobates. But as for him, he washed his hands in innocence. And yet the waters of affliction rolled over him; and he moaned and pined. Why not?

God was dealing with him as with a son. But at last he found out the meaning of these things. When "I went into the sanctuary, then I understood their end." Oh! what slippery places they stood on. As for himself, he goes off into that sweet descant in which he declares that God shall be his portion in time and in eternity. One of the noblest and sweetest of the psalms I think is that. And I see that very psalm enacted every day. Men in trouble; men whom God is loving; men that oftentimes think they are set apart for mischief—such men God is blessing and helping.

Dear Christian brethren, I bring to your memory a Savior who is in sympathy and in blessed relations with you. Fall not into that weak and poor way of thinking of the sympathy of Christ as if it were merely showering sunlight on you. God makes his sun to rise on the good and on the evil alike. This came to my mind when I came out into the sunlight this morning, and I said to myself, "Yes, there are the crickets, there are the mice, there are the bugs, there are the worms, there are creeping things innumerable; and the sun does not know how to make any difference between these things and men. It makes no discriminations. It shines on me, and it shines on everything else just as much." But when my God looks on me, I hope he makes a difference. I hope, when he administers toward me and the brute, it is not all the same. I want to feel that he is pressing down the bad and lifting up the good in me. And if it hurts, only let me know what the hurt means, and I am willing to bear it. If it is only God, let him take anything and everything. Empty my crib; empty my cradle; wring my heart; shut me up; do anything—Lord, God, love me, and then do anything! But give me all the world and all that can shake down as from some tree of paradise on my head, and if all I am to have is what I can pick up here, and pick up on the ground at that, Lord, thou dost not love me!

To be loved of God; to be nurtured here; to be disciplined; to be taught; to be prepared for the heavenly estate, and then go home to be present with the Lord forever—that is joy unspeakable, as it shall be full of glory.

May God give us this better portion, and so may Christ's sympathy make us better men.—Henry Ward Beecher

Topic: Learning from a Teacher
Text: 1 Cor. 13:9–12
There is a time to be born and a time to die. This is a fact of life that we all know and all must face. Our faith helps us to face this truth. The message of Easter should still be heard. "Death is swallowed up in victory." How can this be? How can death be a victory? The risen Lord has made it a victory for all who believe in him. Death has been swallowed up in victory because death does not have the final word. God does! And God in Christ has promised, "Because I believe you shall live also."

There is more to life than what we see in this world. That is a statement of faith, and when it is accepted, then that faith informs our response to death.

Today we remember a dedicated teacher, and as such, he would want us to learn from this event. As a teacher, he had a special gift that affected his work and his contact with students and colleagues alike. His special gift was that he was a very positive person. He was positive about life and about living and about people.

What lessons then can we learn? They will be different for each person here because each one of us has had a different relationship with our remembered friend.

The sudden death of a person, like our friend, who has been involved with so many people causes us all to remember, once again, the importance of showing appreciation for what others do at the time we are the recipient of their helpfulness. If you did express appreciation for his dedication and leadership, fine. Life has taught you well. If not, if you are saying to yourself: "I wish I had . . . ," then learn today and remember to say those much needed "thank you's" of life.

Many of you were his coworkers or were involved in his special programs, which brings us to another important son for life. He was a person you could count on.

As a Christian, he often thought more about what was good for someone else than what was best for himself. He did more than his share in any venture. Perhaps he did too much; but that is not for us to say, for each person will live life as they see it. But what we need to see when we look at life together is to make sure that our own contributions to cooperative work is not just to let Bill or George or whoever do it all.

When people work together for the common good, then those workers each need to shoulder their share of the responsibility. That was his way of working. If you so live that you help others, then you are following his example. If your pattern of life has been to pass up your share of the work, then learn from this day and learn to help lighten the burden of your fellow travelers through life, for that was the pattern we have seen in this dedicated teacher.

What comfort can we seek in this hour of bereavement? He had plans, which did not come to be. There were major events, soon to come forth in his life, that were to be happy times. All that is changed now. Is there any possible comfort to be found in this moment? In faith, we say that death is a type of second birth. We leave this world we know for greater knowing. We set aside the outer shell that we call the body so that the true person within, the unique personality, can be set free for its new life with God.

One of the things we need to do at a time like this is to not limit our concepts of that "greater knowing." Can you imagine Christopher Columbus discovering this new world and saying to his men, "I see here a place from where people will cross the ocean in half a day. I see a world where people will talk with one another from their own home to any other place in the world. They will be thousands of miles apart, but they will carry on a conversation as though they were in the same room. I see a country where people will fly from here and stand on the moon." The great discoverer of this country had no idea what would happen

here. Yet we know, for we are here, and we have seen it, and we have lived it. Is it so far afield then for us to think that in God's new world there will be wonders beyond what we have seen here? One of the causes of our sadness is to think of our friend as missing those special events still to come. . . . Let us not limit God and his love. It may well be that provisions are made for this husband, father, and grandfather to see and rejoice. We are like the explorers of old. We have no idea of the potential and grandeur of that new world. Therefore, that new life can be pictured as a time of new opportunities and new challenges, a time for continued growth and service. In that new life, our friend and loved one will face new challenges and will have new opportunities for continued growth and service. That is what gave meaning to his life in this world. That is the way he lived in this life.

Has it all been for nought? Let us believe in the fuller life offered in our resurrected Lord. We grieve for our loss, but in faith we can rejoice in his gain. So take up his torch for living life to the fullest and pass that light on to others as you live out your days. Remember him and offer your own private prayer of gratitude for him. Remember him and learn from him and look forward to your new life with him; when the time comes for us to leave this world we know for greater knowing.—Kenneth Mortonson

Illustrations for Funeral Services

BY ROBERT C. SHANNON

FOR YOUNG AND OLD.   These words were inscribed on a tombstone in England: "Reader, who e'er thou art, let the sight of this tomb imprint in the mind that young and old without distinction leave this world and therefore fail not to secure the next."

THE REAL THING.   Some call death paying the debt of nature, but Spurgeon said it is more like taking in a paper note and getting gold in exchange. American paper money used to be a silver certificate that could truly be exchanged for silver. That is no longer the case, but the illustration holds true. When we die, we exchange the paper for the real thing.

IMMORTALITY. McCullough wrote, "How irrational it would be to think of the Parthenon standing for thousands of years and the Phidians living a paltry three score years and ten; of Handel's Messiah existing but not Handel; of da Vinci's Last Supper continuing but gone forever; of Michelangelo's Moses remaining but Michelangelo forever dust!"

A MATTER OF DEATH AND LIFE. When there is a real emergency, we often say that it is a matter of life and death. Christians know, however, that our time on earth is just the opposite: a time of death and life! We are not dying people in the land of the living. We are living people in the land of the dying.

WALKING WITH GOD. The last song Mario Lanza ever sang was "I'll Walk with God." He recorded it for the movie version of *The Student Prince.* Just afterward he became ill and died. What a great way to end one's life declaring, "I'll walk with God"!

SECTION V.
Lenten and Easter Preaching

SERMON SUGGESTIONS

Topic: The Inner Circle

TEXT: Mark 14:32–35

There are some who accuse Jesus of being a loner. After all, he often went into the hills to pray . . . all alone (Matt. 14:23). We read of no one accompanying him to the Jordan when he was to be baptized by John, and certainly he was alone when Satan tried to lure him into his evil power in that tempting wilderness struggle (Matt. 3:13–21). We may cite other instances, but for the most part Jesus was a very social person; not at all a loner!

He enjoyed children (Mark 10:14). Repeatedly, he doted on them singling them out as worthy examples (Matt. 18:2–5). He loved adults, young and old. We know that from the way he called to life and healed young people, as well as those who were more mature in their years. He attended a wedding party at Cana (John 2:1–11). He feasted at banquets at the home of Lazarus, Mary, and Martha, as well as Simon the Leper, Zacchaeus the tax collector of Jericho, and Simon the Pharisee, to mention a few. In Jerusalem, he joined in celebrating Passover several times, which is a religious event in a social context, and attended other festivals there. We know he appeared at least at two, possibly three, funerals. Although his brothers and sisters misunderstood him initially, one became an apostle and the author of a biblical letter, James. He always looked after his mother, right to the last breath on the cross.

Throughout his earthly sojourn, Jesus was involved with people. Sometimes it was one-on-one. At other times, it involved huge throngs. Yet those with whom he spent most of his earthly ministry became his closest associates. These colleagues comprise what we know to be the twelve disciples, but this body was divided into two smaller groups: what many scholars call "the inner circle" and "the outer circle." Much as a church council is divided between the officers and the general members, the disciples were in two groups yet united as a whole. Jesus loved them all . . . yet he was more closely associated with three than the rest. They were more than an executive committee, but those with whom he shared some of the most significant moments of his life, such as the prayer time at Gethsemane before his betrayal, the Transfiguration on that high mountain (Matt. 17:1), the raising of Jairus's daughter (Mark 5:37), and that day in Holy Week when he spoke of signs of the end as they looked upon the Temple from the Mount of Olives (Mark 13:3). At that time, an additional disciple was present—Andrew, Simon Peter's brother.

For the most part it was a threesome. They were Peter, James, and John. What a mighty executive committee they were . . . while being full of frailties and foibles as well. All three were fishermen, residents of Capernaum, and deeply in-

240

volved in their business partnership (Luke 5:10).

It's anyone's guess why Jesus chose these three to be his closest colleagues. Scripture gives us some strong hints about their weaknesses as well as some clear indications of their strengths. Yet opposed to the remaining disciples, why were these three in the select "inner circle"?

I'm not sure that anyone can readily answer that question. I do know, however, that two of the three became monumental leaders in evangelizing the world, while the third became the first martyr among the apostles. Jesus saw something in these men that we may miss, but we can never miss the fact that they were his most intimate friends.

And they were not that different from many of us, whether we examine their gifts or their courage. Surely they were not as well educated as most of us . . . except they spent three years under the personal tutelage of the Master, and therein they have the academic superiority. Somehow they caught not only the message of the gospel but its importance for the world, and they did not fail to share it. Peter, we're told, provided his witness as the basis for Mark's Gospel. John wrote his own. Both Peter and John wrote epistles that are included in the New Testament, and John contributed the Book of Revelation.

Sought by Jesus, they acceded. Taught by the Lord, they conceded. Wrought by the Spirit, they proceeded to turn the world upside-down for Christ. They were the "inner circle" in *The Personalities of the Passion*.

I. Literally, they were sought by Jesus. Andrew, Simon Peter's brother, was a follower of John the Baptist (John 1:40). He heard Jesus preach and was so enthralled that he brought his brother to meet the Lord. It was Jesus, however, who called them to ministry to be his disciples and follow him. To the three fishermen of the inner circle, he said, "Do not be afraid; from now on you will be catching people" (Luke 4:11). In the next verse, Luke tells us, "When they had brought their boats to shore, they left everything and followed him." There was an immediate, positive response to the Lord.

It was early morning on the crystal waters of the Galilean lake. A crowd had assembled around the rabbi Jesus, so that they were pressing upon him, unintentionally pushing him into the surf. They were eager to hear God's Word. Jesus, rather than stand in the water, climbed into Simon Peter's boat and asked him to pull away from the shore a little distance. He had a "moat" to keep the people back far enough so he could successfully teach the whole crowd. Afterward, the Lord instructed Peter to set sail and lower his nets for a catch. The big fisherman had labored all night with his partners, but he couldn't refuse the Lord. "If you say so, I will let down the nets," and he did.

The result was the great haul of fish. But it was more than that. Jesus learned several things in that brief encounter.

First, he knew Peter was interested in his message. He listened eagerly. He did not hesitate to let Jesus use his boat either as a floating pulpit. He did not protest pushing the boat away from the shore a few feet. Peter had a cooperative spirit.

Second, Jesus discovered that, as weary as Peter, James, and John must have been from fishing all night, they were not reluctant to try it again . . . at his word.

Third, when Peter saw the large catch, he humbled himself before Jesus, saying, "Go away from me, Lord, for I am a sinful man!" Jesus knew Simon's humility . . . and more. He knew that this diamond-in-the-rough would one day gleam as a jewel. It was true of James and John also, the sons of Zebedee, Peter's partners. All three could be blustering boasters, but deep down they were humble, faithful men.

Jesus sought them, and they acceded. One of the Greek words translated as "called" really means "selected" (Luke 6:13). William Barclay teaches us that "it implies deliberate choice and selection" on the part of Jesus.[1]

[1]William Barclay, *The Mind of Jesus* (New York: Harper & Row, 1976), 63.

Jesus is still seeking and selecting disciples today. He is still calling us to follow him. He welcomes you to listen, but he invites you to fish with him as the twelve once did . . . and especially the inner three. He sought them—weaknesses and all—and they were caught by his love. Are you?

II. As he sought them, so he taught them, and they conceded that the messianic promises were fulfilled in him.

James and John gained the nickname "Sons of Thunder" for their sibling bickering (Mark 3:17). Jesus gave it to them, and in that name is an indictment about their temperament, as well as a bit of the Lord's good-natured humor. One of the things they quibbled over was the right to sit on either side of Jesus in his heavenly glory (Mark 10:37). Matthew gives a little different twist to the story and says it was James and John's mother who requested the honors (Matt. 20:20–28). Granted it was audacious to the point of being ludicrous—whether done by an opportunistic Jewish mother or two enterprising young go-getters—yet it demonstrated something about James and John . . . and their mother, perhaps. They had been successfully taught. They knew Jesus to be truly the Messiah and wanted to be eternally close to him.

Peter, too, made that confession, but in a far more obvious and humble way. It was at Caesarea Philippi that he announced unashamedly, "You are the Messiah, the Son of the living God," in answer to Jesus' question, "Who do you say that I am?" (Matt. 16:16,15).

In the three years they traveled the countryside with Jesus, Peter, James, and John, as the inner circle, were taught the holiest subjects of the universe, and they yielded to his teaching. It was not always easy to apply those ideas in the real world. As you know, Peter denied Jesus not once but three times. It is one of the most documented facts in the New Testament (Matt. 26:69–75; Mark 14:66–72; Luke 22:54–62; John 18:15–27). Both Peter and James fled the Crucifixion in fright, holing up in the upper room. Only John stayed at the foot of the cross, together with his own mother, as well as the Lord's. To him Jesus gave the supreme honor of caring for his mother Mary (John 19:25–27). Despite their frailties, Jesus taught these men—especially these three—in such a way that they not only accepted the gospel, but became its chief proponents.

Tradition teaches us Peter went as far as Rome sharing the good news. We know John dwelled in Ephesus and was exiled on the Island of Patmos just off shore. Thus we know he went as far west as the Aegean Sea to preach the good news. Some believe that James went as far as Spain to share his witness before he was martyred in Jerusalem on a return trip, but there is little evidence to support that tradition. We know from Acts 12:1–2, that James "was killed with a sword" by the order of King Herod Agrippa between A.D. 42 and 44. A cathedral in Jerusalem commemorates his martyrdom and is the seat of the Armenian Orthodox church there.

Writes Dr. Barclay, "Jesus chose his staff with wisdom. He chose men who had learned the lessons of life not in an academy or in a seminary but in the business of living. He chose men whom life had already molded for his purposes. He chose them, first to be with him, then to be sent out as his ambassadors to men."[2]

If we cannot be Peter, James, and John and be included in that inner circle who were not only taught with the remaining nine disciples and, as the Lord's most intimate friends, saw some very special events in Jesus' life, we can let Jesus teach us through his Word today. The Bible is a living book that gives new life to everyone who not only studies it but believes it.

This is the way you can still be taught by Jesus and accede to his Word and be included in that inner group. It's a way of being his friend today.

III. Finally, the three were sought and acceded to his call; they were taught and conceded that Jesus is Lord. Peter, James, and John were wrought by the Spirit and proceeded to share the good news.

[2]Ibid., 65.

It is the late Archbishop Fulton Sheen who sums up the Lord's purposes for the twelve but particularly these three: "They were to be the 'light of the world,' the 'salt of the earth,' and the 'city that cannot be hid.' He bade rather insignificant men to take an almost cosmic view of their mission, for on them would he build his kingdom. These chosen lights were to cast their rays over the rest of humanity, in all nations."[3]

At the tail end of John's Gospel, the youngest member of the disciples, the "one Jesus loved," writes about an incident after the Resurrection and before the Ascension (John 21). Jesus made breakfast for the eleven on the shores of the Sea of Galilee. He gave them bread and fish in a fashion that was not unlike Holy Communion. As they finished eating, Jesus asked Peter three questions. They were essentially the same. "Do you love me?" he asked twice, after first asking, "Do you love me more than these?" Peter assured him that he did.

"Feed my lambs," instructed Jesus the first time.

"Tend my sheep," he said the second time.

And finally Jesus told Peter, "Feed my sheep."

Then Jesus told Peter about his impending martyrdom. Peter was curious. "What about him?" he asked, pointing to John who was following them as they spoke. Jesus did not disclose by what death John was to die, but there is the strong implication that John was not to die an unnatural death. Even in the Lord's last hours on earth, he had special words for two of the inner circle.

Between Jesus' instructions for Peter to feed and tend his lambs and sheep, and the deaths that would inevitably come, Peter and John—and I think James, too—knew how to proceed.

They had been wrought as iron in a forge. They could stand the intense heat of persecution that would come. They would be able to withstand the chill winds of indifference and rejection, as well as the rains of disappointment that could rust them to oblivion if they did not proceed. You see, Jesus wrought them into the shape of a manger so that lambs and sheep could be fed good news. Before death came, they had work to do . . . and a mission to fulfill: feeding and tending the Lord's flock.

Here was the leadership of the Twelve, the executive committee of Jesus' board for the new church! They were not to sit on thrones and issue commands, deciding policy and approving expense vouchers, they were to feed and tend. They were not to legislate rules and pontificate about higher positions. They were to feed and tend. They were not to develop organizational charts and invent catchy programs for capturing the Roman Empire for Christ. They were to feed and tend, to nurture and encourage, to move naturally and easily from one neighbor to the next in a spirit of love that would disarm the haughty and cause the sinful to surrender to Jesus and become winners with him.

That's still the role of the inner circle of any congregation, of the church at large, as well as its various jurisdictions. It is to proceed with the Gospel by feeding and tending the little lambs as well as the more mature sheep.

Jesus trusted those he sought, taught, and wrought to be the witnesses this world requires. It's the same today. You and I are the Peters, the Jameses, and the Johns of this era. We are still part of his plan.

How about it? In this season of Lent, in this much larger calendar of life, will you carry Christ's message to all the world . . . at least to your little world?

Jesus says to us, "Feed my lambs and sheep and tend them both." You see, he makes us part of the "inner circle" now. Are you willing to be that kind of friend to him? —Richard Andersen

Topic: Servants

TEXT: Matt. 20:20–28

I. I have always been particularly intrigued by two of the disciples of Jesus, James and John, because they remind me

[3]Fulton J. Sheen, *Life of Christ* (New York: McGraw-Hill, 1958), 110.

so much of myself. Earlier in Matthew's Gospel we find them getting angry at a village of Samaritans for rejecting Jesus. They asked Jesus for permission to call down fire from heaven to destroy the no-good unbelievers. And I find myself resonating with that sentiment every time I try to do my best to share the gospel of Jesus Christ with someone and they turn a deaf ear. (Why can't they just see what perfect sense I am making?) This week we find them engaged in a scheme to beat out their fellow disciples for the best seats in the house when Jesus sets up his kingdom, and, as much as I hate to admit it, that also sounds like something that I would do.

Have you ever worked late at the office even though you were all caught up on your work, just because you knew that your boss would come by and find your light on?

Have you ever arrived early for a dinner party so that you could arrange to be seated next to someone who could give your career a boost?

Have you ever campaigned for an office in your service club because it was a good way to get your name known and to make business contacts?

Have you ever dated—or married—the boss's daughter or son because that was the surest trip to employment security?

If you have ever done any of these things you have a lot in common with James and John. After all, they were just trying to get ahead. When the other disciples heard that the two of them had sent their mother to beg Jesus for the places of honor, they were indignant, but I have an idea that the only thing that made them mad was that they hadn't thought of it first.

II. We might argue that it is one thing to try to get ahead in the business world but that the sin of James and John was in applying the same techniques to God's work. It would be nice if we could separate the way we do things at work and the way we are at church, but we can't.

There are people who join one church rather than another because they are more likely to make business contacts there.

There are people who accept jobs within the church on the basis of maximum exposure and minimum sacrifice and work.

There are people who choose their friends within the fellowship on the basis of the other person's overall popularity and prestige.

And so if we can identify with the sons of Zebedee in our business dealings, we are likely to identify with them in our church life as well. We find ourselves with James and John, eagerly peering from behind the back of their mother, waiting to hear what Jesus is going to say. And what he says catches us completely off-guard.

III. Instead of getting mad and telling them that they don't have any business asking a question like that, Jesus says, "You have no idea what it is that you are asking." Well, they thought they knew exactly what they were asking. They were asking to be important; they were asking to be powerful; they were asking to be somebodies instead of the nameless nobodies that they had been all of their lives. So Jesus presses them further: "Are you able to drink the cup that I am going to drink?" In other words, are you willing to pay the price that it takes to be the greatest in my kingdom?

The two brothers shoot back without thinking, "Yes, Lord, we are able. We will do anything you ask." At that moment I am sure that they were completely sincere. They really did think that they could do anything that Jesus asked. Don't we?

Don't we think we can do anything Jesus asks us to do because he is not going to ask us to do anything that is beyond our strengths or talents?

Don't we think that we can share the gospel with anyone to whom God sends us because we know that he would never send us to anyone with whom we did not get along?

Don't we think that we could accept any job in the church that we feel God is leading us to because we know he would never give us a job that we wouldn't enjoy?

But what if he did? What if he did all

of those things that we don't expect him to do, like asking us to do hard jobs or sending us to people that we don't like and that don't like us or giving us responsibilities that we don't enjoy? Then would we still be able to say, "Lord, we are able to do anything that you ask"? Many of us would not be so eager to answer under those circumstances.

IV. Then Jesus added the real clincher. Basically he told them that they were going about it in the wrong way. He said, "Whoever would be great among you must be your servant, and whoever would be first among you must be your slave." This was almost more than the disciples could bear to hear. Here James and John had come, asking for the privilege of lording it over the others, and they find that if they really want to be great in God's sight they will have to sink to the lowest position in society, that of a slave. And if you think that was an unpopular notion then, it is even more unpopular now.

It is simply not in our natures to enjoy being the one who serves instead of the ones being served. Yet this is what Jesus taught his disciples over and over again. In the Sermon on the Mount he included a complete portrait of a servant in the section known as the Beatitudes. The true servant is to be humble, compassionate, gentle, just, merciful, and authentic. He is to dedicate all of his life to serving his fellow human beings.

Just how different this way of life is from the way we follow in this world is illustrated by J. B. Phillips's reversal of these same Beatitudes:

· Happy are the "pushers": for they get on in the world.
· Happy are the hard-boiled: for they never let life hurt them.
· Happy are they who complain: for they get their own way in the end.
· Happy are the blasé: for they never worry over their sins.
· Happy are the slave-drivers: for they get results.
· Happy are the knowledgeable men of the world: for they know their way around.
· Happy are the troublemakers: for they make people take notice of them.

We must come to grips with the fact that most of us believe all this, and the role of the servant is not one with which we are very comfortable. And yet, time and time again, that is what Jesus called us to be simply because that is what he was himself.

V. There is an old legend in the Talmud that might be the beginning of our understanding of what it means to be a servant.

Rabbi Yoshua ben Levi came upon Elijah the prophet while he was standing at the entrance of Rabbi Simeron ben Yohai's cave. He asked Elijah, "When will the Messiah come?" Elijah replied, "Go and ask him yourself."

"Where is he?"

"Sitting at the gates of the city."

"How shall I know him?"

"He is sitting among the poor covered with wounds. The others unbind all their wounds at the same time and then bind them up again. But he unbinds one at a time and binds it up again, saying to himself, 'Perhaps I shall be needed: if so I must be ready so as not to delay for a moment.'"

At best all of us are nothing more than wounded healers. One of the aspects of Lent is the recognition that we are all sinners in need of repentance and that if we are truly to be God's servants we must recognize that we are nothing more than that, sinners saved by the grace of God.

VI. Even if we accept that truth, we still envision our servanthood as something dramatic and impressive. We see ourselves as the subject of movies about our brave adventures in saving mankind. Realistically, that is not likely to be our lives, and yet we do what we can.

A Scottish minister of a previous generation recounted a dream to his congregation. He dreamed he had died and came to the Pearly Gates. To his dismay, he was denied entrance until he presented his credentials. Proudly, the pastor articulate the number of sermons preached and the prominent pulpits occupied. But St. Peter said no one had heard them in heaven. The discouraged servant enumerated his community involvements. He was told they were not recorded. Sorrowfully, the pastor turned to leave, when Peter said, "Stay a moment and tell me, are you the man who fed the sparrows?"

"Yes," the Scotsman replied, "but what has that to do with it?"

"Come in," said St. Peter, "the master of the sparrows wants to thank you."

Here is the pertinent though often overlooked point: Great and prominent positions indicate skill and capacity, but small services indicate the true depth of one's servanthood.

VII. But we still come back to Jesus' original question: "Are you able to drink the cup of which I drink?" Are we able to make the kind of sacrifice that Jesus made? The disciples had assumed that when Jesus came into his glory he would sit on the tall, stately throne of a king. Instead, when he was glorified by God, his throne was a cross, and the ones who had the choicest spots on his right and his left were two thieves who had to die with him.

Are we willing to die for our Savior? If we are honest with ourselves, we must say that in our own strength we are not. However, we might take heart from knowing what happened to one of his original disciples. James, one of the two who wanted a place of honor in the kingdom, got his wish. He was the first of the twelve to be killed rather than renounce his faith. If Jesus can take someone as obtuse, as self-centered, and as misunderstanding as that and make him one of his first martyrs, I have an idea he can do some great things through us as well. —James M. King

Topic: The Fool on the Hill

TEXT: 1 Cor. 1:22–25

I. The world and all that is in it are the Lord's . . . who dares to approach the Lord on his holy hill? The God of the universe . . . Immortal, Invisible, God only wise—Now that is a God we can believe in. What is much more difficult to believe (maybe impossible) is that this God had anything to do with the grim spectacle we call the Crucifixion. Richard Jeffries in his novel described a young boy viewing a picture of Christ on the cross: "The crucifixion hurt his feelings very much, the cruel nails, the unfeeling spear, he looked at the picture a long time and then turned the page saying, 'If God had been there, he would not have let them do it.'" Wouldn't we react much the same way to that weak, helpless figure pinioned to a crude instrument of execution? What makes it more obscene is that he was a believer in an all-powerful God. He described this God as a loving Father who would unashamedly *run* to meet his estranged son; he was one who knew and cared for even a worthless sparrow. It is just this God who seems to be missing in this dark scene of the cross, for if he had been there surely he would have saved this pathetic man abandoned on a lonely hill. Even the early opponents of Christianity reviled this scene most of all. Celsus saw Jesus as "unhelped by his Father, and unable to help himself." We, like Celsus, are prone to reject this kind of God and his Christ.

We, like the Jews that Paul referred to, literally demand signs of God's power and majesty. As the hymn phrases it, "A God of might and miracles, 'tis written in the sky." Paul knew only too well the demand for proof that God was the God who moved mountains, caused the sun to stand still. Surely if Jesus was God's Messiah, he would show his power and step down from the cross. Isn't there a part of you and me that demands God to prove himself and come to our aid in just the way we think he should? It is our "if . . . then" clause that is seldom talked about in church. *If* you heal my daughter, make my wife more attentive, bail us out of financial difficulty, *then* I'll worship you, tithe, work for social change, share the gospel. The next step is to say (not aloud), "If you are not God on my terms, don't look for any obedience or sacrifice from me." Even if God does "come through" and deliver the healing, the intervention we pray for, how long does this evidence of his power convince us? Frederick Buechner, the novelist-preacher, has said that Jesus "galvanized thousands with his miracles ... feeding a whole ball park with his five loaves and two fish, but like Chinese food, the miracles didn't stick to their ribs ...." The power of miracles wasn't enough then; is it now?

II. How then shall we know God, if miracles and signs are not enough to bridge the gap? One answer is that we will be *seekers* who seek after the highest wisdom that will enlighten and enable our lives. There is nothing more commendable than being a seeker after truth. But whose wisdom are we seeking? Do we seek the divine wisdom or Logos, or the wisdom of this age, the shrewdness and cunning to "make it"? Aren't we something like the Corinthians who seemed to beat a path to the latest "great teacher" who appeared on the horizon? An early description of some of the prevailing Corinthian wisdom of the second century was "enlightened selfishness." Enlightened selfishness. Aren't we speaking about the kind of wisdom that sells books and motivates people? We learn as children to play "king of the hill," and we are taught that we should never give up the game. Grab the highest ledge on the hill and you can be prepared to throw off those who might pass you by. Not so? Look at the spate of books on "how to look out for number 1" or "how to win through intimidation." Seminars abound on power and success.

What concerns me most about this "wisdom of the present age" is the way we in the church have often bought the philosophy uncritically. What happens then is an effort to create God in our image. The immortal, invisible, wise God is clothed in hand-me-downs of our current wisdom. So now Christians are marketing and selling the God who "wants us to prosper." We christen our own values of power and success with Christian symbols and words. Soon we have the model of the successful Christian who plays the game by the going rules but is careful to give God credit for the winning. We wonder why conventional Christianity has lost its vitality.

III. Sooner or later we must face up to the fact that we cannot create God in our image—*his ways are not our ways.* None of

us here dare approach his holy hill on our own merits; demanding miraculous or rational proof will not apprehend him. No, instead our text tells us that God does literally the *foolish thing,* becoming vulnerable, risking all on the power of sacrificial love. That risk has brought God's Christ the image of fall guy, buffoon, clown, fool. And by the standards of conventional wisdom he was a fool. Taking him seriously demanded the foolishness and weakness of the cross. Willing to be rejected and called the fool on the hill, Jesus displayed the power and wisdom of God that draws all men and women to himself.

The church may find a more popular, pleasant message, but if we neglect the cross, we lose our identity as the people of God. Theologian Jürgen Moltman says, "A Christianity that does not measure its theology and practice by the cross loses its identity and becomes confused with the surrounding world; it becomes a chameleon which can no longer be distinguished from the tree in which it sits."

If you're afraid of appearing *foolish,* don't get mixed up with Christianity. For Jesus was the one on the eve of his final suffering and death who foolishly claimed, "I have overcome the world." What kind of wisdom is that? It is the wisdom of God that seems so foolish in ears that are attuned to enlightened selfishness. The wisdom of sacrificial (*agape*) love just doesn't make sense, but it does make a difference ... *the difference.* Don't be offended at the crucified Christ, the fool on the hill, for the foolish thing of God is wiser than human wisdom. —Gary D. Stratman

Topic: The Fourth Word: "Why Hast Thou Forsaken Me?"

Text: Matt. 27:45–46, kjv

I. Christ was dying. The Light was dying, and there was darkness.

Darkness which hung over the land like a funeral pall. And there was another darkness, too: a deeper and lonelier darkness, which enshrouded the soul of our Savior as he hung there dying.

Something in us recoils from the notion of Christ abandoned by his heavenly

Father. Is he not the very Son of God, himself divine? How can God abandon God?

Moreover, speaking of this very moment, speaking about his Crucifixion in John 8:28 and 29, this same Jesus had so confidently and solemnly declared, "When you lift up the Son of man, then you will realize that I AM"—"I AM," the proper name of God, revealed to Moses at the burning bush when asked to identify himself. "When you lift up the Son of man [Christ] on the cross, you will recognize my divine nature." And how he *is* lifted up ... and he says that God has forsaken him?

There is more. In that same place in St. John's Gospel, chapter 8, verse 29, Jesus adds, "The one who has sent me—surely the sender is the Father—the one who sent me is with me. He has not left me alone, because I always do what is pleasing to him." And how, now that he is doing his Father's will, even unto death on a cross, his Father is not pleased? And consequently turns aside, abandons his Beloved Son? How can we ever hope to understand this?

II. There is, of course, an easy answer. There's always an easy answer. In this case, it is Psalm 22, a psalm which is clearly prophetic of the suffering and the triumph of the Messiah. This psalm begins with the words "My God, why hast thou forsaken me?" And it is this psalm, then, that Christ was praying. Christ was praying aloud. Christ was calling attention to the fulfillment of this scriptural prophecy, which foresees so many details of the Gospels' Crucifixion story:

- verse 8: All who see me scoff at me; they mock me with parted lips, they wag their heads.
- verse 9: "He relied on the Lord, let him deliver him! Let him rescue him, if he loves him!"
- verse 15: All my bones are racked, my heart has become like wax melting away in my bosom.
- verse 16: My throat is dried up like baked clay, my tongue cleaves to my jaws.
- verse 17: They have pierced my hands and my feet, they look on and gloat over me.
- verse 19: They divide my garments among them, and for my vesture they cast lots.

Is this an explanation? A full and satisfying explanation of this fourth word from the cross? The dying Christ is praying? Teacher par excellence to the very end, he is still instructing his followers on the meaning of the Scriptures, pointing out how that scripture is fulfilled in him?

It's a good explanation, particularly if we read the psalm whole. If we see how the plaint of the sufferer in the psalm gives way to a paean of joyous exultation which evokes for us the triumph of the Messiah and his Resurrection.

"He did not turn his face away from the wretched man in his misery, but when he cried out to him, he heard him" (Ps. 22:25).

"To him my soul shall live, my descendants shall serve him. Let the coming generation be told of the Lord, that they may proclaim to a people yet to be born the justice he has shown" (vv. 30–32).

And yet, though all this is true and unimpeachable, it is also a bit too easy, too facile. It stays on the surface, which does not make it totally wrong, since the surface is a part of the reality. But by the same token, it does not get to the bottom of things. And so we are in danger of missing something important. Two important considerations, in fact: one about Christ and one about us.

One about Christ. What was it like for him? What was he like? Obviously, knowing Christ—really knowing him—is of supreme importance for our religion, for our spiritual life, for our eternal life. "This is life eternal," Christ says in John 17:3, "that they might know thee the only true God, and Jesus Christ whom thou hast sent."

Just as obviously, we can never really fully understand what it was like to be both divine and human, completely the one and completely the other, at the very same time. We hardly understand our own humanity, and we are so often at a loss to understand the humanity of others, even of those who are closest to us. Then how can we pretend to comprehend fully a man who is also the Son of God? All we can do is to bow before the mystery of this divine and human being who can somehow be abandoned or forsaken by God the Father. And if he was not, then the very first verse of messianic Psalm 22 was not being fulfilled. And yet our supposition is that everything in Psalm 22 was happening to Christ on the cross, not only the mocking and the scoffing and the piercing of hands and feet, the thirst and the dividing of his garments, but also the feeling that God had let him down, abandoned him to his enemies, forsaken him when most he needed help and protection.

It would seem, then, that he who became like us in all things but sin (Heb. 4:15) became like us in this, too: that he could feel the darkness, the loneliness, the troubling suspicion that even God has let us down.

And this is where the lesson comes through for each of us. "All those who travel, soon or late, must enter in that Garden Gate; must kneel alone in darkness there, and grapple with some fierce despair."

Christ the Man, really man, really human, came to share our lot. Came to drink of the bitter cup which is the portion that falls to so many human beings. Something that seems, in a way, to be a necessary part of the human experience, of being human at all. Now, Christ was human—beautifully, breathtakingly human. We can never claim that he had it too easy. That he didn't really know what it was like to live our limited existence. To feel alone in the dark sometimes, and helpless and friendless and literally God-forsaken. To feel that everyone has let us down—even our heavenly Father.

III. Someday, for all of us—and for some of us sooner than others—the darkness will begin to close in around us. It will be time for us to pass through the dark valley and the shadow of death, to reach the light and joy of our Father's kingdom. There we shall know the festive table and the brimming cup, the goodness and kindness that will enfold us forever. Afterward comes the light. But first come the shadow and the gloom and the darkness.

Can we be surprised, can we complain, knowing that the Lord himself had to pass this way? Can we perhaps take it for granted that we will feel abandoned by God? All alone, except for the hand of him who is our Shepherd and who leads us on the right path, the only path, to our final goal? A path which he recognizes all too well as the right one because he himself has passed this way, from earthly life through earthly death, to life everlasting.

Through death to the light on the other side of the darkness.—Vincent Fecher

Topic: My Redeemer Lives

TEXT: Job 14:7–14; 19:23–27

Job was a good man who appears from nowhere and disappears into the mist of the Old Testament. His only claim to fame is the unreasonable suffering which he experienced. His story addresses the question of justice (Do people get exactly what they deserve in life?) and the question of hope (What is the point or goal of life?). Job does not provide us with better answers than we would find in the Gospel on Easter morning, but Job raises the questions to which the death and Resurrection of our Lord give response. Life does not run in rigid tracks of precise logic, and sometimes the answer is easier than the question. Like an algebraic equation, the missing element X is often on the left side of the equal sign. Job causes us to face the issues of life which we prefer to ignore. As punctuation marks, Easter is the exclamation for which Job provides the question.

I. Nature tends to torment our quest for hope. The route from my home to school was a comfortable walk which took me past a strange tree. Unlike its siblings pointing to the heavens and reaching out branches to receive the birds, this strange oak was growing along the ground, with a significant trunk rooted at both ends and branches only on the top side. I recall wondering about the history of this freak of nature. Had the tree been pinned to the ground by someone with a strange sense of humor and no sense of the landscape who was trying to prove the proverb, "as the twig is bent . . . ?" Was this a victim of one of nature's indiscriminate attacks on itself, a fall storm which indiscriminately rips out buildings and trees?

When is the last time you meditated on a tree and envied its place in creation? Joyce Kilmer gave us the line "I think that I shall never see / A poem as lovely as a tree." As a thing of beauty to behold with wonder, a tree is a magnificent creation of God. I agree with Kilmer: "Poems are made by fools like me, / But only God can make a tree." When life gets down to the dregs with Job, perhaps the longevity of a tree is appealing, but who would want to trade places with a tree? I am really impressed with the discovery of a fifteen-hundred-year-old, thirty-seven-acre mushroom field along the Wisconsin-Michigan border, but who would exchange the human three-score-and-ten for the millennium of a mushroom or a sequoia tree? No, Job, nature falls short of the promise you seek. You must look elsewhere to vindicate your life and justify your existence.

II. The sands of time wear away human memory. In desperation Job grasps for the straw of immortality in the archives of human history: "O that my words were written down!" Do we find our hope in the preservation of our thoughts? If so, Job lives on. The meditation of his heart and the anger of his spleen are vented to the view of all future generations. The poet fulfills his wish for literary immortality and demonstrates the ironic emptiness of fame when we become little more than a fading, distorted memory in the rush of time.

Percy Shelley's poem describes a mythical Egyptian statue erected as a monument for all future generations to behold. Shelley wrote: "My name is Ozymandias, king of kings; / Look on my works, ye Mighty, and despair! / Nothing beside remains. Round the decay / Of that colossal wreck, boundless and bare / The lone and level sands stretch far away." If our hope for immortality depends on our monuments, we are indeed a desperate lot. Books, which were once viewed as symbols of something lasting, have become as abundant and temporary as the birds.

III. Only in the eternal vigilance of a loving God is there hope for humankind. Job has most of the questions and none of the answers. An issue of *Christian Century* tells Job's story in a new way. Murray Joseph Haar is the son of a devout Jewish family. His parents were among the few relatives who survived the Nazi Holocaust, but they did not like to discuss the horrible experience with their son. As a young adult, Murray read about Auschwitz, Buchenwald, and Dachau. Not only did this raise questions for the young Jew but anger at a God who would stand in silence at the atrocities: "No God with an ounce of love or compassion could have watched children being burned alive and have remained silent." Murray met a Lutheran pastor who not only allowed his questions but suggested that good questions are holy, that questions and faith go together. He learned about the man who died on the cross shouting a question at God. When asked where Jesus was in the death camps of the Holocaust, the pastor replied, "He was with the dying, relentlessly and unceasingly, screaming the questions at God."

Haar became a Christian, was ordained as a Lutheran pastor, and now teaches at a Lutheran college. "To fail to question God after Auschwitz is blasphemy," Haar writes. "Faith after Auschwitz must be linked to questions."

Job seems to see through the fog of his suffering long enough to see Easter morning. Handel's interpretation of Job, "I know that my redeemer lives," is in line with early Christians. The *goel*, redeemer, of Job is an avenger in the family of one who has been wronged. In Job's state of despair, the redeemer is one who will vindicate him before God and perhaps even rescue him from God. Perhaps this traditional message of victory is really a whimper of defeat from Job, the final word of despair. The words, however, betray a hope which transcends the mind and time of Job. We do not live with simple answers to the profound questions of life. Sometimes we do not even know the right questions to raise. The Christian hope is in the God who is stronger than death. The loving God who raised the crucified is the redemptive hope of Job and all of his kind.

—Larry Dipboye

ILLUSTRATIONS

BY ROBERT C. SHANNON

PERPETUAL SUNRISE. Long before the Creek Indians came into Georgia, there lived there a nation of mound builders. In their city of Ocmulgee, now Macon, Georgia, they built their council house. It was an earth-covered mound that could be entered only by a long tunnel. That tunnel was oriented so that the rising sun would shine down the tunnel and directly into the face of the high priest on only two days out of the year: February 22 and October 22. Does the sunrise of Easter morning shine on us spiritually only one day of the year—or every day?

EASTER AFTERGLOW. In deference to the pluralism of our society the Easter holiday has now become the spring break and may not fall on Easter at all. England's King Alfred the Great appointed the week after Easter as a holy week. It was to be a time to rejoice in the Resurrection. But rejoicing easily becomes secular, and soon the week was characterized by sports and games. But then, one week is not really enough to bask in the afterglow of Easter. We need fifty-two weeks for that!

HE HAS RISEN. The great H poet Sandor Petofi was killed in tive revolt in 1848. He is honored in Budapest's Petofi bridge and in the music that composer Franz Liszt wrote in his honor. A legend says that Petofi still lives and will rise again to help his nation in some future hour of need. Of course, no one today takes the legend seriously. But the Resurrection of Jesus Christ is taken seriously by millions. He has risen to help them in their hour of need.

CREATIVE BEAUTY. A tulip changed the life of Charles Connick. He was living in Philadelphia when it was a dirty, smoky city. Looking out a dirty window into a dirty alley, he saw a garbage can. Out of the garbage can a red tulip was growing. He later said that that tulip reminded him that there could be much beauty in the world, even in ugly surroundings. He became an artist in stained glass, creating windows for the Chapel at Princeton, for the Cathedral of St. John the Divine, and for the American Church in Paris. The Easter lily will not necessarily change your life, but the Christ symbolized by the lily can—and will!

THE BREAD OF LIFE. In some parts of England it used to be the custom to keep a loaf of bread baked on Good Friday. It was considered a charm that would bring good luck and good health throughout the year. Today on Good Friday we honor no object but the Living Bread Jesus. He alone is the Bread of Life.

SECTION VI.
Advent and Christmas Preaching

SERMON SUGGESTIONS

Topic: Are You He Who Is to Come?
TEXT: Matt. 11:2–6

In Matthew 11, John the Baptist is pictured as a caged lion. The first-century prophet roamed the hills and plains of Judea announcing the coming of the Messiah. With unrelenting courage, John called for repentance among the Jews. He charged the religious leadership with hypocrisy. He confronted the people with their unfaithfulness. He was truly the voice that roared throughout the land. But now the lion was caged.

John charged Herod with an unlawful marriage. Never one to flinch at authority, John said to Herod, "It is not lawful for you to have her." And for this John was awarded permanent residence in Herod's jail.

The lion of the wilderness languished in prison. His roar had fallen away to a whimper. His vision had given way to doubt. Had he understood correctly his calling? Had he been right about Jesus?

In John's case everything hinged on Jesus. His whole life was a testimony for the Messiah. If he had been wrong about Jesus, much of his life had been wasted. He could endure imprisonment if he could just be sure about Jesus.

John could stand it no longer. So he sent his disciples to Jesus to ask, "Are you he who is to come, or shall we look for another?"

John had good reasons for asking this question of Jesus. In announcing the coming of the Messiah, he had emphasized judgment. He saw in the Messiah one who would move quickly to right the wrongs in the world. He stressed the Messiah's strength and power. Read Matthew's account (3:10–12).

Jesus hadn't done any of these things; quite the opposite was true. In one of his sermons, he said, "Blessed are the poor in spirit. . . . Blessed are the meek. . . . Blessed are the merciful. . . . Blessed are the peacemakers . . . ," and so on. Later he added, "You have heard that it was said, 'Eye for eye, and tooth for tooth.' But I tell you, do not resist an evil person" (Matt. 5:38, NIV). And also, "I tell you: Love your enemies and pray for those who persecute you" (5:44, NIV). His is hardly the rhetoric one would expect from a judge. Hence John's question, "Are you he who is to come, or shall we look for another?"

In a sense this question has been asked again and again, countless times, since John's disciples showed up on Jesus' doorstep. Is Jesus the One? Is he the deliverer we have been looking for?

We have a way of making Jesus into what we want or think we need. A Gallup poll asking what Americans think about Jesus yielded more than twenty descriptions of the personality of Jesus. Said a twenty-two-year-old mechanic, "I often think of [Jesus] as a smart older brother . . . who understands me and forgives me when I stray a bit. But he also encourages me and helps me do the right thing. I

252

never had a brother, but I sometimes wish I had."[1]

As we prepare for the coming of Christmas, we would do well to ask what we expect in Jesus. Is it the same Jesus who was born centuries ago? Jesus did not chasten John for his questioning. He gave a straight answer (vv. 4–5). He pointed to his actions as evidence of his messiahship. But it was just these actions that had given John trouble. He'd been looking for a divine equalizer, but Jesus was occupied with spreading peace and goodwill. John had expected Jesus to move on to Jerusalem, but he spent most of his time on skid row. Yet when Jesus answered John's disciples, he pointed to the same ministry which had confused them. He seemed to be saying: "This is what I am about. In spite of what you have expected, I have come to bring health and wholeness. I have come to bind up the broken and strengthen the weak. I have come to give hope to the hopeless. This is who I am. Take it or leave it."

Jesus will not conform to our expectations of him. We must bring our expectations in line with the truth about him. If conforming must be done, we will have to do it.

Wild distortions about Jesus are being perpetrated in our time. We are being told, for example, that Jesus is the god of wealth. He wants people to have everything they want. If they just ask for it and believe enough and give enough seed money, their wishes will come true. How does that idea square with Jesus' word to John?

The nature of Jesus' ministry is humble service. Jesus is the personification of God's mercy and love. His kingdom is not of this world; it is of peace and love and charity and respect and fellowship and compassion.

Frank Weston said, "You cannot claim to worship Jesus in the tabernacle if you do not pity Jesus in the slum. Now go out into the highways and hedges, and look for Jesus in the ragged and the naked, in the oppressed and the sweated, in those who have lost hope, and in those who are struggling to make good . . . and when you have found him, gird yourself with his towel and wash his feet in the person of his brethren."[2]

The last sentence of Jesus' answer to John has been called the tenth Beatitude. He said, "And blessed is he who takes no offense at me." The word translated "offense" in this sentence is the same word from which our word *scandal* comes. The idea is that the person who does not find Jesus a stumbling block has found the truth and joy that always comes with that discovery.

Jesus nearly became a stumbling block for John. And John had been looking for Jesus. From his childhood, he lived with the expectation that the Messiah would come. And when he did, John almost missed him. If anybody should have recognized Jesus as the Messiah, John should have. And for a time it appeared that he did. But late in the game, when time was running out and justice still had not been enforced, John needed reassuring.

If John had trouble recognizing Jesus, how much more trouble will we have if we aren't even looking for him? Can we really expect an occasional glance at a nativity scene to open our eyes to the real Jesus this Christmas? Is it reasonable to think that our presence at a Christmas Eve Communion service will be enough to put us face to face with the true Jesus this year? What makes us think we can do better than John the Baptist?

This is why Advent is important— because we will not be prepared for Christ's coming unless we discipline ourselves for it. We will mark the days with worship and prayer until that blessed night when Christ will come again and our hearts will be strangely moved because we know him.

[1]George Gallup, Jr., and George O'Connell, *Who Do Americans Say That I Am?* (Philadelphia: Westminster Press, 1986), 25.

[2]H. Richard Niebuhr and Daniel D. Williams, *The Ministry in Historical Perspectives* (San Francisco: Harper & Row, 1983), 174.

Russian writer Ivan Turgenev tells about visiting a village church surrounded by peasants when suddenly someone stepped in close behind him. He had the sensation that this person was Christ.

Turgenev was overcome with emotion, curiosity, and fear all at once. This man near him had a countenance like other people's. His eyes were looking softly and attentively upward. His lips were closed but not compressed. His beard was not long and was parted at the chin. His hands were folded and motionless. Even his apparel was like that of others.

"Can this be Christ?" Turgenev thought. Such an unpretending, perfectly simple person. It cannot be.

The Russian turned away, but scarcely had he withdrawn his glance from this plain man when it seemed to him that he who was standing by him must really be Christ. He looked at the man once more, and again he saw the same face that looked like the faces of all other men; the same everyday though unfamiliar features. Then, suddenly, it became clear that Christ really has just such a common human face.[3]

To the extent that we are prepared for his coming and are willing to set aside our expectations and let Jesus be Jesus, we will recognize him this Christmas.
—David Crocker

Topic: The Heart of Christmas
TEXT: 2 Cor. 4:5

The feeling of Christmas is in the air. The tinsel and the Christmas lights, the decorations and overstocked stores, the gifts under the tree and the remnants of wrapping paper on the floor, the ring of the cash register and the muffled sound of the charge-a-plate device, the reindeer pulling Santa's sleigh, and the nativity scenes: all of this reminds us that Christmastime is here again. It is the season of cranky clerks and jangled nerves, the season of quick trips to the mall, a season in which we spend more than we have, buy

more than we can afford, and eat more than we can hold. But Christmas is more than all of that. Christmas is first and foremost the celebration of the birth of our Lord.

When Pope Julius I authorized December 25 to be celebrated as the birthday of Jesus in A.D. 353, who would have ever thought that it would become what it is today?

When Professor Charles Follen lit candles on the first Christmas tree in America in 1832, who would have ever thought that the decorations would become as elaborate as they are today?

It is a long time since 1832, longer still from 353, longer still from that dark night brightened by a special star in which Jesus the King was born. Yet, as we approach December 25 again, it gives us yet another opportunity to pause, and in the midst of all of the excitement and elaborate decorations and expensive commercialization which surround Christmas today, to consider again the event of Christmas and the person whose birth we celebrate.

We must remember that Jesus Christ is the heart of Christmas. It is his birthday we celebrate. It is in his name we gather. As Paul reminds us in our text for today, it is about Jesus we preach.

The question that comes to our minds as we focus on the heart of Christmas is this: What kind of man was this whose birth is so significant that it splits time into B.C. and A.D.? Who is this one who is the heart of Christmas? Let's ask that question in four different forms.

I. What does the Bible say about him? The Bible is the sourcebook for the Christian, and therefore it provides our basic information about Jesus Christ. What does the Bible say about Jesus?

The biblical writers affirm, first of all, that Jesus was a man. We believe in the virgin birth of Christ, but it was not actually the birth which was supernatural. It was the conception which was supernatural. Jesus was conceived by the Spirit of God. After the supernatural conception, Jesus was born just as any other baby would be born. He was born of a

---

[3]Gallup, *Who Do Americans Say That I Am?*, 38–39.

woman when the time for delivery had come.

He also grew up just like any other person. While working as a carpenter in the city of Nazareth, Jesus experienced what other carpenters experienced. His hands were roughened by the tools of his trade. At evening, after a heavy day, he was tired just as other carpenters are.

When he became a man, Jesus experienced what other men experience. He had to walk along the roads of Palestine just like others had to do. When he did, his feet got tired and dirty, his mouth became dry, his feet blistered, and his legs chapped just like others.

Physically, intellectually, emotionally, and spiritually, Jesus lived the same life we all live. He worked. He played. He laughed. He cried. He could feel lonely. He became tired. He hurt. He was a man.

But there is more in the Bible's discussion of Jesus. The biblical writers could not talk of Jesus as a man without referring to a mysterious plus in him. Jesus was not just a man. Jesus was divine. Jesus was filled with the divine in such a unique way that the biblical writers referred to him as Emmanuel, which means "God with us."

What did these biblical writers mean when they called him Emmanuel, God with us?

They meant that in Jesus they felt God's presence as they had never felt it before in any other man. In Jesus they saw clearly what God was like. In Jesus they had experienced the unique presence of God in this world.

Jesus was a man, but he was different from any other man who ever lived. There had never been another man like him, nor would there be. The disciples were sure of this fact. But it strained the limits of their day to try to express this fact. He was the best that life had to offer. How could they express it?

They went to the realm of Jewish religion and took the term *Messiah,* the greatest title they knew of to use in reference to a man; and looking at Jesus they said, "He is the 'Messiah.'"

They went to the realm of Greek thought and found the term *logos,* mean-

ing "word", which was the greatest title they knew, and looking at Jesus they said "He is the 'Logos,' the 'Word.' "

What does the Bible say about Jesus? The Bible affirms he was the most unique man who ever lived—a man whose life can only be explained by declaring he was God in human flesh.

II. What did Jesus say about himself? When we consider what Jesus said in the New Testament, we see that he matched the claims the biblical writers made about him by the claims he made about himself.

He said that he was the way to God, that no one can come to the Father but by him.

He said that he had been with God since the beginning and that he brought a special message from God.

He said that to believe in him meant to have life but to refuse to believe in him meant to miss what life was all about.

He focused our attention beyond the shadow of the grave and said that if we wanted to make heaven and miss hell there was only one way and that was to make him the King of our lives.

He said that his connection with God was so close that to know him was to know God, to see him was to see God, to believe in him was to believe in God.

Those are fantastic claims Jesus made about himself. And the most incredible thing is that he backed up these claims with the life he lived.

He lived such a life of purity that those closest to him gave this testimony about his life: "He committed no sin. No guilt was found on his lips."

He exhibited such power over the lives of men that many were healed merely at the touch of his hand.

He showed such a depth of compassion that no one was outside the limits of his love.

He lived a life like no man has ever lived.

Then when he died, he died with such power that the man on the cross next to him said, "Lord, remember me when you come into your kingdom." And a bystanding centurion muttered, "Surely, this man must be the Son of God." As he lived and as he died, Jesus confirmed the claims he made about himself.

What did Jesus say about himself? That he had a unique relationship with God that no other person has ever had.

III. What does history say about him? Jesus has the unique ability to come across the centuries as a living Lord and to challenge men and women of all generations to follow him. Listen to their testimony.

David Livingstone, adventurous pioneer who labored long years in Africa, has said, "All that I am I owe to Jesus Christ."

Alfred Edersheim, Jewish historian and author of *The Life and Times of Jesus the Messiah,* said, "If Jesus Christ did not live, and he was not the Son of God and he is not the Messiah, then there never has been a Messiah and there never will be."

Dale Evans, movie star who in later life has become a spokesperson for Christ, said, "All my life I looked for a pot of gold at the end of the rainbow, and I found it at the foot of the cross."

Multiplied thousands of such testimonies can be given. These testimonies from history confirm the testimonies of the Bible about Jesus and the declarations of Jesus about himself. He was the most unique man who has ever lived, a man whose uniqueness can only be explained by the presence and power of God in his life.

IV. What do you say about him? This is really the most significant of the questions because the answer to this question will determine your eternal destiny. What do you say about Jesus? You only have two options.

You can accept him as being who he says he is. You can say, "I believe Jesus was the most unique man who ever walked the face of the earth, and I believe his uniqueness can be explained by the fact that he was God himself living among us."

Or you can explain him away by saying that he was the biggest liar in history and his lies laid the foundation for history's greatest farce.

No other alternatives are open to you.

You must receive him or reject him. You must decide that either he was a liar or he was telling the truth. Your response will determine whether or not you experience the true meaning of Christmas. — Brian L. Harbour

Topic: The Prince and the Pauper

TEXT: Luke 2:1–12

Reading: Luke 2:1–3. "In those days Caesar Augustus issued a decree that a census should be taken of the entire Roman world. (This was the first census while Quirinius was governor of Syria.) And everyone went to his own town to register."

"In those days Caesar Augustus . . ." Caesar, Augustus . . . emperor of the Roman Empire, grand poo-bah of the Western World, imperial potentate, lord of all he surveyed, the big cheese . . . Reverend—that's kind of what the word Augustus means in Latin—Reverend Gaius Octavius, born September 23, 63 B.C., to aristocratic parents and later adopted as son and heir by none other than Julius Caesar. If he had gone to high school, his class would have voted him most likely to succeed. Around the time Jesus was born, Augustus's friends threw a big birthday bash. They had a lot of testimonials and such and commissioned an inscription in his honor. Part of it read: "The birthday of the god was the beginning of the good news to the world on his account." The god (little G) they're talking about is Augustus. Nearly everyone, rich and poor alike, thought well of him. He did so much to unify the empire and bring peace and prosperity that some even called him savior.

So when God (big G) got ready to *really* save the world, it would have seemed appropriate to have come to Caesar Augustus and his wife and let them know that their first son was going to be God's son. That kind of a deal wouldn't have been a theological problem for a Roman. Augustus was practically divine already. It would have given Augustus's wife a good excuse to redecorate the nursery: refinish the floor and paint new frescoes. They could have gone out and bought a new, 24K gold layette set, plenty of soft blankets and silk sleepers, and a nice cradle with rockers on the bottom. The baby would be born with a silver spoon in his mouth, have the best education, and be in a position to really influence the world for good, building on the deeds and reputation of Augustus.

After all, if you're going to do the greatest good for the greatest number of people, you need to go to Rome (or Washington or Moscow) where the power and the money are. How can you change the course of history unless you're in the driver's seat? That's how we usually look at the world, isn't it? Today I invite you to hear the story of Jesus' birth from that point of view. Move back one thousand nine hundred and ninety-one years with me and listen to the story as if we were living in that time. Some things about people never change, so let's try to imagine ourselves reliving those events with the common prejudices and assumptions that condition our lives.

Let's pretend that I'm a Sadduccee, a Jewish landowner of the first century [put on prayer shawl]. I'm in cahoots with the Roman governor to see that my friends and I get all the advantages to maintain our wealth and our social status. I see that the right person is appointed high priest and that the *am ha'aretz*, the people of the land, who really have no land of their own, are kept in their place. I'm arrogant and selfish and opinionated. Religion for me is only skin deep. I attend worship to make myself look good and maintain my business connections. I have definite ideas about how God acts in the world and the people whom God favors. Many in my day are looking for the Messiah. I suppose I am, too.

Hymn: "O Come, O Come, Emmanuel"

Reading: Luke 2:4. "So Joseph also went up from the town of Nazareth in Galilee to Judea, to Bethlehem, the town of David, because he belonged to the house and line of David."

Joseph? Joseph who? Who's this guy Joseph? Roman official? Local politician? Jewish leader? Oh, Joseph the wealthy building contractor? No? No! Joseph, a carpenter from Nazareth. A yokel from Hicksville who makes his living, such as it is, working with his hands in wood. Oh, well, he's just one of the many who have to register for the census Caesar and Quirinius have ordered —not important, let's go on.

Hymn: "O Little Town of Bethlehem"

Reading: Luke 2:5. "He went there to register with Mary who was pledged to be married to him and was expecting a child."

Humph! Isn't that typical? These young people have no self-control. Not even married yet, and already there's a baby on the way. How's the world ever going to make any progress with all those ignorant folks out there having babies they can't afford? I'll bet they won't be able to offer a proper temple sacrifice for the kid after he arrives. Well, at least he does have a job. But they don't seem to be able to plan ahead very well. Look at this:

Reading: Luke 2:6–7. "While they were there the time came for the baby to be born, and she gave birth to her firstborn, a son. She wrapped him in cloths and placed him in a manger, because there was no room for them in the inn."

Now what's she doing going off on such a trip when her baby is due? They should have known the place would be crowded, considering how many wives and children David and Solomon had. That's the problem with a lot of poor people. They haven't got sense enough to come in out of the rain. Imagine having a baby in a barn. But then you can't just *give* them a nice place to stay because they won't know how to take care of it.

Hymn: "Away in a Manger" (verses 1, 2)

Reading: Luke 2:8. "And there were shepherds living out in the fields near by, keeping watch over their flocks by night."

Shepherds. Low-life. Unwashed. And I don't mean just dirt under the fingernails and forgot to brush their hair this morning. They've been sleeping on the ground and cooking over a campfire forever. Wood smoke and sweat and the smell of sheep all mixed together. Mmmmmm! You can't trust them either. Hold on tight to your purse when they're around. Roll up your windows and lock the doors when you drive through Shepherdsville. And never mind letting them in to worship at the Temple. It would take quite a lot of soap and water and sacrifice to make that bunch fit for communion with God. They deserve to be out there on the graveyard shift, minding a flock of dumb sheep. Helps keep them out of sight. Besides, somebody has to tend the animals for the temple sacrifices.

Reading: Luke 2:9. "An angel of the Lord appeared to them, and the glory of the Lord shone around them, and they were terrified."

Heh! Now they're going to get it. God's finally going to give them "what for." It's about time the Lord cleaned house. There are quite a few others who need the fear of God put in them, too. If somehow, for just one day, it was possible to make everyone obey the whole law, surely the Messiah would appear. God's kingdom would reign supreme. But how? How could we get everyone to clean up their act even for one day? It would take a miracle: an act of God.

Hymn: "The First Noel" (verse 1)

Reading: Luke 2:10–12. "But the angel said to them, 'Do not be afraid. I bring you good news of great joy that will be for all the people. Today in the town of David a Savior has been born to you; he is Christ the Lord. This will be a sign to you: you will find a baby wrapped in cloths and lying in a manger.'"

"Don't be afraid"? Good news? Joy for all the people? What's happening here? Well, yes, of course it's good news, I guess. I mean, I'm not sure why the shepherds, of all people, get told first, but YES, it is good news: a Savior has been born! Born in David's city, yes, that's where Isaiah said it would happen. But born to "you"—born to the shepherds? And the Christ, the Messiah, is a baby— lying in a manger?! Wait, come again, what did they say? City of David, a baby in a manger, wrapped in cloths. You don't mean it! That must be the child of those two hillbillies from Nazareth: Joseph and Mary. Well, I'll be. Who'd have thought?

But what about Augustus? What about the fancy layette in the nursery? How is a kid from Bread City ever going to make even a tiny dent in the armor of the Roman Empire? How will he get any legislation passed? Who's going to listen to some Jewish kid from East Overshoe? How's he going to get the Roman army and that maniac Herod off the backs of all the good Jews? If he starts bucking the system they'll snuff him out in no time flat. How's anyone going to save the world without an army, a fat bankroll, and a political platform? I can tell you I have my doubts. I wouldn't have done it that way. I sure hope God knows what he's doing!

Hymn: "Angels from the Realms of Glory" (verses 1, 2)

The first Christians had to explain what we now take for granted. In birth, in life, and in death Jesus broke the rules. He was born in a poor place, associated with lowly persons, touched the lepers, went to dinner with outcasts, and died the terrible and humiliating death of a robber and revolutionary. We've lost a genuine appreciation for how unusual it was. Perhaps this new year we can be more open to the surprising acts of God. I believe God is still at work in our world through the Holy Spirit, teaching and leading us. I think we still must look for God at work in unexpected places and unlikely persons, including you and me.

Healing this year's hurts: The year is almost over. What kind of year has it been for you? Has it been a good year or a difficult year? Did someone or something disappoint you? Jesus said he came that we might have life, abundant life, but sometimes it seems our hurts and our losses are more abundant than our pleasures and our gains. Sometimes life weighs us down, and the weight often feels heaviest at Christmastime. Jesus said, "Come to me, all you who are weary and burdened, and I will give you rest. Take my yoke upon you and learn from me, for I am gentle and humble in heart and you will find rest for your souls. For my yoke is easy and my burden is light." As we sing the soothing words and melody of "Silent Night," offer your pain and disappointment to God. Put down the burdens you've been carrying and take up the easy yoke of the gentle Jesus.

Hymn: "Silent Night"

Celebrating this year's joys: Let us also celebrate the good things of this year. New friends, new children or grandchildren; a new or remodeled place to live; the fact that we have survived our trials and times of testing and grown not only older but wiser. Let us give thanks for our hopes and dreams for the coming year. Jesus said he came that we might have life, abundant life, life to the full, and eternal life in the world to come. In a moment we'll sing a song of joy in celebration of the fact that Christ came into the world to defeat the powers of darkness, sin, and death that would otherwise claim our lives.

Jesus also said, "I am the light of the world. Whoever follows me will never walk in darkness, but will have the light of life." He said, too, that we who follow him are light to the world. As we sing the last hymn, Maurice and Harold will light their candles from the Christ candle in our Advent wreath. They will take the light to the first person in each pew. Each of you in turn can share the light with the person standing next to you until all the candles are lit.

Hymn: "Joy to the World"

Benediction: May the grace of the Lord Jesus Christ, the love of God, and the fellowship of the Holy Spirit be with you all, now and forever. Amen. —Alan Hoskins

Topic: Where Does Christmas Start?

TEXT: Matt. 1:1–17

Why in heaven's name does the minister read a tedious genealogy on the Sunday before Christmas? What a monotonous and unedifying list that is! Why not tell the Christmas story from Matthew or Luke with their allusions to grace and peace? Why not offer the angels and shepherds, the three kings and the crèche? When I told the staff last Monday I considered addressing Matthew's genealogy, one of them just leaned back in her chair and yawned. Boring!

Well, friends, don't despair. Don't give up. Don't go home. I've got some fantastic news to tell you this morning, news that's embedded in this so-called genealogy of Jesus. Like everything else in the New Testament it's telling us something important about meanings. And in this case it gives us some important clues about the meaning of Christmas; even more, it gives us some clues as to where the Christmas story starts and who tells and bears it today.

In the first place this isn't a genealogy like the one you've got in your family Bible at home. It's different. The one in our Bible, for instance, starts with my great-grandparents, Margaret Coalter and Francis Crawford, back in 1840 and traces us down through the marriages and deaths of their nine children through 1909. That's one kind of genealogy. Matthew's, however, is not a biological genealogy. He does not seek to trace bloodlines. He's not proving genetic successions. Matthew tells a story. It's Israel's messianic story. If you were to ask, where does the story of Jesus start, you'd probably be looking for date, place, and time, something that would sound like 2:37 A.M., at Bethlehem of Judea on December 25 in the year one. Not Matthew. Matthew starts at the beginning of a great saga. He starts with Abraham, and he follows the promise God gives to Abraham and his descendents to be a light to the nations. He tells us of those who bear the promise for thousands of years; he tells us how the promise finally crystalizes in the Bethlehem manger.

Let me give you an analogy. Suppose someone asked you where the story of Martin Luther King, Jr., starts. You could talk about his birth in Atlanta in 1929, his mother and father being ministers, his progress through Morehouse, Crozer, and Boston University. But in Matthew's terms—in Matthew's terms—Martin Luther King's story might look more like this:

The story of Martin Luther King, Jr., begins with Jesus Christ who wrought the Apostle Paul, and then (to use the language of the King James Version) Paul begat Martin Luther who begat John Wesley who begat Crispus Attucks who begat Thomas Jefferson who begat Sojourner Truth who begat Nat Turner who begat Frederick Douglas who begat Abraham Lincoln, president during the great war to abolish slavery and promote human rights. Abraham Lincoln begat Susan B. Anthony who begat W. E. B Dubois who begat Rosa Parks who begat Martin Luther King, Jr. That's not bloodlines. That's the story of freedom. That's not genetics. That's the bloodline of justice. Those names provide keys to a great saga telling about the meaning of who we Americans are as a people.

Just so with Matthew. He chooses names, beginning with Abraham, that tell the story of a people's hope for a new world of justice, grace, and peace. The names Matthew offers us are not necessarily related to one another by blood. They are, rather, bound by God's purpose in bringing into our broken and fragmented world a new community where, as the prophet says, "the wolf can lie down with the lamb, the leopard shall lie down with the kid, the calf, the lion and the fatling together . . . and a little child shall lead them." Or in contemporary terms, a world where the Croat can live with the Serb, the Czech with the Slovak, the Armenian with the Azerbijan, the Muslim with the Hindu, the Palestinian with the Jew, the black with the white, joy shall reign between them and us. What Matthew does, you see, is to march us through Israel's liberation history right up to the Christmas hope for a liberated human community blessed by joy, solidarity, and peace.

And Matthew puts some marvelous twists and ironies into his story. There's no tedium here. Let's take a closer look at some of those names in this morning's passage. They read like an eye-glazing, ear-blistering, inventory of unpronounceable male monikers—but look on down a little bit, and you'll see there the names of four women. Let's touch base with them for just a moment. See? Tamar, Rahab, Ruth, and "the wife of Uriah the Hittite"—whom we all know to be Bathsheba. These women will add some spice to your Christmas punch.

Take Tamar, for instance. She does something absolutely taboo in her own time and in ours. She connives to bear a son by her own father-in-law. Tamar's is the story of a dysfunctional family, and a father-in-law's failure to do his duty. In short, Judah, the father-in-law, doesn't produce additional husbands for Tamar when her first husband is slain, her second refuses to consummate the marriage, and the promised third Judah gives away to someone else. Tamar is left without children. But even more important for Matthew, Judah is left without grandchildren. The promise offered to Abraham to be "a light to the nations" is about to die. So Tamar does what Matthew believes, for God's sake, she has to do—she disguises herself as a prostitute and seduces Judah, her father-in-law. Nine months later she bears a child through what the law would call incest. Incredible! But hear this: By this incestuous seduction, according to Matthew, Tamar keeps the messianic promise alive, a promise which because of her guts, courage, and daring results centuries later in fulfillment in the Bethlehem manger.

Now friends, Tamar and her ilk may not be among those we would put front and center in our genealogies, but for Matthew, Tamar and her audacity are crucial to sustaining the Christmas promise. You dump Tamar; you dump Christmas.

Or take Rahab. Now, Rahab is not a prostitute in disguise—she's the real thing. That's what she does for a living. When Joshua and his crowd, out to conquer the Promised Land, go to reconnoiter Jericho, Rahab puts them up in her establishment. For Joshua's sake she lies to the cops about his whereabouts and sends them off on a wild goose chase. She is a foreigner, an alien, an outsider, a tainted woman, a traitor to her own people. Not the usual heroine in your genealogical gallery. But, my soul, there she is in Matthew's genealogy, a veritable forebear of the Christ! She saves the promise. Think of it: without the likes of Rahab, no Christmas!

Or Ruth. Again, the astounding story of an odd union between a man and a woman; again, a despised outsider whose bloodlines carry no status but who turns out to be, because of her own devotion to an alien Jew, the grandmother of King David—King David, the one who sets the contours for the Christmas hope. No Ruth; no Christmas!

Or Bathsheba: You know her story. King David simply commands her to his palace, they practice adultery, she gets pregnant, David plots to kill her husband, they get married, their love child dies, then she bears Solomon, and just when it looks as if a usurper will gain David's throne, Bathsheba intervenes with David for Solomon—and the Christmas promise is saved. Without Bathsheba, you can kiss Christmas goodbye.

And folks, the men involved are not cut from cloth any different. From Jacob, crafty, shrewd, a old master deceiver, through David, an old conniver and cynical politician, we've got a clique of ancestors most of us would slam into the closet. Some of them come right out of the *National Enquirer,* or with things as they are in the country right now, right off the front pages of your friendly morning newspaper or from behind the blue dot on CNN.

What's going on here? What's Matthew doing? Well, Matthew tells us the promise of Christmas makes its way through some rough scrapes; it comes to us in all too human hands, it's not immune to the terrors and traumas, the ironies and tragedies of human life. Christmas, Matthew says, comes into our world because those who hold the vision are no less frail than the rest of us; it comes because the promise of a new world is borne on the shoulders and suffering of winners and losers in this old world of ours. No sentimentality, no fairy tales, no Pollyannish fantasies, no simplistic goody-two-shoes characters here. Matthew's genealogical crowd sounds more like some people we know, maybe some people we are. What a parade, this gang who bear the message, who save the promise, who bring Christmas to fulfillment. Who was it that said, "God writes straight with crooked lines"?

And if you'll look at the next set of names, kings and prophets and mon-archs and hierarchs: the likes of Rehoboam, Asa, Jehoshaphat. Some of them more or less good, some of them corrupt, others incompetent, still others such failures that finally this people bearing the messianic promise is forcibly dragged out of its own land and left to die under a foreign tyrant. Whatever else that second series of names beginning with Solomon and ending with the disintegration in Babylon means, it means the promise is held in nations and peoples: it resides in political states and religious institutions—hear that? Religious institutions like Israel—religious institutions like churches.

That's right: churches! Matthew is alert to our type in his genealogy, saying simply, You churches, out there, yes, even you at Old South in Boston, the Christmas promise can come through your slow moving, inertia-bound, self-interested, myopic, hypocritical operation. Through all your muddle and mess, through your timid witness, your pathetic preaching, your floundering around, yes, through all of your good intentions and failed nerve, you, too, stand in that long line of nations and peoples who in all their frailty and self-deception seek to save and live the promise of the new kind of world breaking in among us at Christmastime. Without you—yes, you in the churches, you in Old South—it's Christmas. Sayonara!

But friends, it's that last crowd in Matthew's list that's truly incredible. It's Abi'ud, Eliakim, Azor, Zadok, Achim, Eliud, Eleazar, Matthan, and Jacob, the father of Mary's husband, Joseph. Do you know why that's a terrific list? Because every other name Matthew gives us in this Christmas genealogy can be found somewhere else in Israel's saga of salvation. But these names don't appear anywhere. They're anonymous. They're nobodies. They're the little people who don't get written up. They're the ones who bear the Christmas promise day by day, no big deals, no derring-do, no neon lights, no prominent headlines.

Scotty Wight, Rollie Stevens, Helen Boynton, Red Gramlich: Have you ever heard their names? Of course not. They were my Sunday school teachers. Anonymous bearers of the Christmas promise! And you've got a list of those names in your life, too. The ones who told you the Christmas story; the ones who bore the promise. Or look to the person on your left, the one on your right, the one in front of you, the one in back of you—hey, it's Abi'ud, Eliakim, Azor, Zadok, Eleazar! Right here in this church this morning, celebrating the Christmas story, carried by generations of men and women of all sorts, us included. We heard the promise from someone who got it from someone who experienced it through someone who saw it through someone who knew it through someone who grasped it through someone who caught it from someone—begat, begat, begat, begat.

So my friends, where does the Christmas story with its promise of hope, its heralding of peace, start? Well, according to Matthew, it starts with Abraham and, incredibly, it moves through imposters, whores, chiselers, and pretenders. It has come through monarchs, slaves, aliens, and even churches like this one. It has been borne by the John Does and Mary Roes of this world. With whom you identify in this grand procession I do not know. But here is what I do know: You've heard the Christmas story, you've been embraced by its grace; you've been renewed by its forgiveness; you've been included in its peace; you've been inspired by its promise of new life for the world and for you. My friends, where does Christmas start today? You know where. It starts, it continues, with you! —James W. Crawford

ILLUSTRATIONS

BY ROBERT C. SHANNON

KING WITH A DIFFERENCE. When Emperor Akihito received his crown in November 1990, there was a lavish ceremony. He stood on a spectacular purple and laquerware stage under a canopy twenty feet high. Flags waved and drums sounded as thousands marched in the procession. How different it was when Christ the King came into this world. The only canopy was a canopy of stars, the only stage a manger. No procession. No pomp. No ceremony. No cheers. "He came unto his own, and his own received him not."

LOW AND HIGH OFFER HOMAGE. Near Buckingham Palace in London is St. James Church. There are many services offered that are, to say the least, innovative and that seem to be quite secular. But a lovely custom continues there. Every Christmas dignitaries of the Church of England march in procession and present gifts of gold, frankincense, and myrrh. We are so accustomed to seeing youth from the congregation do that, and our custom is lovely, too. But there is something special about high-ranking churchmen playing the parts of the Magi.

A MISSING STAR. It sounds like a story that somebody made up, but someone remembered this event from his childhood. It was time for the class to read aloud. Each section to be read was marked by an asterisk. When it was one child's turn to read he hesitated. "I don't have a star," he said, "and I have lost my place."

BORN AMONG US. No one can be president of the United States unless he or she is born in the United States. Jesus could have been our Savior under different circumstances, but he chose to be born among us, born of a woman, before he became our Savior.

SECTION VII.
Evangelism and World Missions

SERMON SUGGESTIONS

Topic: Salvation in Three Tenses

Our salvation is in three tenses. We have been saved, we are being saved, and we shall be saved. Emil Brunner once said that to be a Christian is to share "something which has happened, which is happening, and which will happen." Let us look at these three time dimensions of our salvation.

I. *Salvation as past.* Salvation in the past has two meanings: Something has been done in the past that made salvation possible, and our initial experience of salvation is in the past.

We look back to the gracious actions of God, especially the death of Jesus Christ, for the sources of salvation. Jesus while on the cross said, "It is finished" (John 19:30).

Scriptures are plentiful that tell of the past tense of our salvation: "Christ redeemed us from the curse of the law, having become a curse for us" (Gal. 3:13); "He has delivered us from the dominion of darkness and transferred us to the kingdom of his beloved Son, in whom we have redemption, the forgiveness of sins" (Col. 1:13); "In Christ God was reconciling the world to himself" (2 Cor. 5:19).

Also we were saved in the past. Like all things personal and historical there must be a beginning. The new birth, as well as the physical birth, takes place sometime. We sing, "O happy day that fixed my choice / On thee my Savior and my God!"

Some people have very dramatic experiences. They can pinpoint it in the past. They can tell you the day, the hour, and the place when the great burden of guilt was rolled away and they knew the peace of God.

Paul could have done that. He could have taken us to a roadside near Damascus, given the date, and then said, "It happened here on this spot at noon." He had no experience more dated than that.

John Wesley could have done that. It was at Aldersgate at 8:45 in the evening when he knew God had forgiven his sins.

Many cannot do that. They are Christians although they cannot date the experience of grace so precisely. But that it has happened is the testimony of their lives.

II. *Salvation as present.* Paul felt that salvation is in the present. We are still being saved. "For the word of the cross," wrote Paul, "is folly to those who are perishing, but to us who are being saved it is the power of God" (1 Cor. 1:18). Or again, "Now I would remind you, brethren, in what terms I preached to you the gospel, which you received, in which you stand, by which you are saved, if you hold it fast—unless you believed in vain" (15:1–2).

Salvation in the present is a dynamic, vital experience, in which you are growing in grace.

I remember a bright young man we once had in our church. He became restless and unhappy with us, so I went to talk with him. He said something like this: "I don't like your concept of salvation. You think it is a point in the past, that it is static. I see it as being present, vital, living, growing." I was able to say to him: "I would not want to argue with you about this. There is much in the New Testament that supports your way of thinking."

This growing experience in salvation is what we have called sanctification. It is growing in grace, becoming more like Jesus, and maturing in Christ. Paul tells us that we are to come to "mature manhood, to the measure of the stature of the fullness of Christ. . . . Speaking the truth in love, we are to grow up in every way into him who is the head, into Christ" (Eph. 4:13, 15).

One of the finest things about being a pastor is seeing people grow spiritually. Here is a man about whom you can say, "He is so different from what he was ten years ago. He is really not the same person." This is a man who knows salvation as a present experience. He is being saved.

Maybe you can say about yourself, "I am not the person I want to be, but I am certainly not the person I was." You are being saved.

III. *Salvation as future.* We shall be saved. "Since therefore, we are now justified by his blood," Paul wrote, "much more shall we be saved by him from the wrath of God" (Rom. 5:9).

One-fifth of the 150 references to salvation in the New Testament have to do with salvation to be consummated in the last day. Full and complete salvation lies out there in the future. John tells us, "Beloved, we are God's children now; it does not yet appear what we shall be, but we know that when he appears we shall be like him, for we shall see him as he is" (1 John 3:2).

"You . . . were sealed," Paul wrote, "with the promised Holy Spirit, which is the guarantee of our inheritance now; we acquire possession of it, to the praise of his glory" (Eph. 1:13–14). The Holy Spirit is like a down payment which guarantees that God will eventually give us our inheritance in full.

We shall at last be fully saved from our sin and mortality, not here but there. We shall have a new life in a new dimension, free from pain, suffering, tears, and death. We shall have new bodies befitting the new order, and we shall live in a new city without shadows and darkness. There will be no sin and death there. Work will be worship and worship will be work, for we shall serve God day and night in his temple. We shall offer God perfect service, and we shall love our fellows with perfect love. Never before have we been able to do that. When all of this has come to pass, then can it be said that we have been fully saved. But we shall have to wait for it. It is out there in the future.

Do not forget that the most persistent religious question is, What shall I do to be saved? Speak often to that question.— Chevis F. Horne

Topic: The Conversion of an Unpromising Prospect

TEXT: Luke 19:1–10

I. Zacchaeus was not the kind of man most people would go out of their way to save. He had made a terrible mistake. It was unpardonable, if you look at it the way some of his fellow Jews saw it. He was a publican, a tax gatherer. This meant that he was a quisling, a traitor, a renegade. He was perhaps the most unpopular man in Jericho. To get and hold his job he had to collaborate with imperial Rome. He took up the cause of the enemy against his own people. Or so it seemed.

We all know how it works. Zacchaeus received the brunt of people's natural dislike of a cheat, an informer, a spy. Zacchaeus was an odious man not only because he cooperated with the enemy but, more than that, because he got rich doing it.

We do not have an exact equivalent of Zacchaeus in our society. But don't we treat many people as the Jews treated Zacchaeus? Jesus said that he came to save sinners, but don't we spend most of our time seeking out the respectable? Jesus said that it was his mission to draw all men unto himself, but don't we make some people feel unwelcome in our churches? Jesus said that he came not to bring peace but a sword, but don't we placate the man of the world and condemn the so-called fanatic? So Zacchaeus, with various aliases, is still among us.

II. Look again at the Zacchaeus of Jesus' time. He was a despised man, yes! But he had his compensations. Even some of his disdainful contemporaries could have said, "I could stand a lot of cold-shouldering if I had his kind of money." Many of them could have been easily tempted to sacrifice affection for power.

Zacchaeus was not universally despised. He had his little group to whom he looked for approval, perhaps even affection. There was the Roman government, his benefactor. And there were those scattered officials working under him, with him, and over him. From them he got little crumbs of approval that kept him from completely starving for human fellowship.

What a fantastic spot was Jericho, the home of Zacchaeus! Zacchaeus awoke every morning to smell the fragrance of the balsam trees that grew in profusion and made Jericho famous throughout the East. A story is told that this remarkable fragrance was carried by the winds across the wilderness of Judea and all the way to the Mediterranean Sea. For Zacchaeus the smell of the balsam trees was the smell of money. He loved it!

No place in the world enjoyed a better climate. It was only thirty miles east of high, windswept, often cold Jerusalem, right at the edge of the godforsaken wilderness of Judea. You could look to the south and see the dreadful but beautiful Dead Sea and to the east, the Jordan river. Jericho was a tropical paradise. Here Herod the Great and his son Archelaus had built their winter palaces. Here the wealthy built fabulous villas comparable to the expensive homes at Pompeii. Here a large number of the priests at Jerusalem chose to live. It was an ideal place for the assistant secretary of the treasury.

III. But Zacchaeus had a great emptiness in his life. He could hardly enjoy his money living every day under the frowns and disapproving eyes of his fellow citizens. What could a million dollars or ten cents mean to him if he had to lie awake at night worrying about how he got it? Lush, formal gardens, sparkling fountains, and marbled walls could scarcely beguile his dreams of children crying from hunger.

Every sacred feast, every family gathering reminded Zacchaeus of his great spiritual distance from his childhood neighbors, his old friends, and his own relatives. Yet he may have made a great pretense of indifference. People often do. What they cannot enjoy they scorn. What they cannot have in themselves, they laugh at in others. What their money cannot buy, they say they do not want anyway. But rare moments of insight dawn even in the most callous. The sound of carefree laughter, the haunting refrain of a song heard in childhood, the sight of an unexpected tragedy—any one of these was enough to shatter the walls of Zacchaeus's pride and send a chill of despair to his heart.

Could it be that the coming of Jesus to Jericho stirred some old, half-forgotten longings in Zacchaeus? Had Zacchaeus heard of other tax gatherers who had begun to follow Jesus? Surely word of these goings-on had been carried quickly to Jericho, and Zacchaeus was among the first to hear the news. Here was a Jew who had a kind word for a tax gatherer. Here was a Jew who did not take up the derisive chant of his fellow citizens.

IV. Whatever his motivation, Zacchaeus was determined to see Jesus. But it was not easy. Zacchaeus was short of stature. He might own the tax franchise in Jericho, but he didn't own the streets! No one would let him make an opening in the throng and get through to Jesus. This little incident in itself indicates how unpopular Zacchaeus was. Still he did not give up.

He ran on ahead of the crowd and scrambled up a sycamore tree where he could get a clear view when Jesus passed by. A thousand times he had compensated for his lack of height by asserting his legal power over the money and property of others. Now he did it again.

He had not gotten his wealth by timidity. He was aggressive. He was resourceful. If one thing did not work, he would try another, even if it meant climbing into a sycamore tree! You wouldn't have caught a Pharisee doing this, but Zacchaeus couldn't have cared less.

V. There Zacchaeus was, sitting on a branch of the tree. Jesus moved slowly along amid the chatter and tumult that surrounded him. Can you visualize it? One by one the faces intent on Jesus turned away until all eyes were fastened on the funny little man in the tree. Perhaps someone pointed toward Zacchaeus and snickered scornfully. It was a ludicrous sight. But Jesus did not join in their derision. He stopped. He made a gesture for silence. What was he going to say to this man? Was he going to put him in his place? Jesus spoke, and what he said was astounding. "Zacchaeus, make haste and come down; for I must stay at your house today" (Luke 19:5, RSV). Jesus completely ignored the prejudices of the crowd. By requesting his hospitality, he honored Zacchaeus. No doubt Zacchaeus was just as astonished as the crowd. Yet he was overjoyed.

VI. But the astonishment of the crowd quickly turned into resentment. "There are a hundred places in Jericho Jesus could have stayed without having to stay with him." "There's the Inn of the Good Samaritan only a little way off." "I'd rather sleep outside than share the house of a tax gatherer." You can imagine the kind of things they said. But they were traveling with Jesus, these disciples and other companions! And it was a large crowd! And Zacchaeus would set a good table! And it was about time somebody got some good out of all those hateful taxes they paid! And Jesus just might tell him what's what! So they gritted their teeth, and they, too, accepted Zacchaeus's hospitality.

Picture these people as they climbed step-by-step up to the house of Zacchaeus. Zacchaeus led the way and Jesus walked with him. The disciples and the others followed behind, talking in hushed but sometimes scornful tones as they viewed the costly appointments.

Then came mealtime. The tired, hungry travelers bathed their hands and faces and feet with the cold water brought in through aquaduct from the valley made famous by the Twenty-third Psalm. Now they were refreshed. They took their places on couches and the feast began. Jesus was next to Zacchaeus.

VII. The two had much to talk about. Zacchaeus was overwhelmed by the honor that had come to him. Therefore, I can imagine, he was all the more embarrassed by his occupation. Think of the explanations, the defenses, the rationalizations before Jesus had said a word to him about the way he made his living. No doubt Zacchaeus argued. The more he defended himself the weaker his case became. Did he finally give up as so many before and since have done and say, "Lord, what shall I do?"

As guest of honor at a long, lavish meal, Jesus had time and opportunity to say what he wished to his host. Perhaps the others were too busy eating the delightfully seasoned food—mouth-watering enough for a king—and talking among themselves to pay too much attention to what Jesus and Zacchaeus said quietly to each other.

I imagine that Jesus left no sensitive spot in the man's soul untouched. Did Jesus tell Zacchaeus of his own temptations? There, within sight, was the place in the wilderness where he was tempted of the devil. When Satan suggested that Jesus bow down and worship him and promised that if he did so all the world and its glories would be his, was Jesus then looking down on the fertile valley below with its dates and balsams, with Jericho and the palaces and the villas? This would have been a good place to start—the wealthiest spot in Palestine.

Now what did Jesus ask Zacchaeus? "Friend, has your wealth brought you happiness?" "Are there people whose lives could be better if you had helped them?" "Have you considered what God may think of you?" Whatever it was, the words of Jesus found their mark. Whatever searching and probing of conscience he did, Jesus talked at the same time of something so great, so exciting, and so rewarding that anything he had to say was welcome. For all of their sharp, astringent pain, Jesus' words were good news.

Of course Jesus might have played down the demands. He might have tried to flatter Zacchaeus and get him to give enough to the poor to put his conscience to sleep and then let it go at that. But if Jesus had done this, Zacchaeus would have been a lost soul still. He would have been no better off. The demand was unconditional surrender, and the reward was as great as the demand.

VIII. Here shines forth the glory of Jesus' ministry. Jesus dealt with people as individuals. Certainly the multitudes thronged about him. He did not drive the crowds away. But he sought out individuals within the crowd. He had love for these persons; he had time for them; he had a message tailored to their uniqueness. Some of the yearning faces that looked up at him were the lean faces of the poor; some the twisted faces of the suffering. Some of the eyes that sought him out were the frightened eyes of the persecuted and exploited; some the cold, calculating eyes of the proud and hardhearted. But Jesus read again and again the story told by the lines in those faces and by the looks in those eyes, and he went after the individuals they represented and helped them one by one.

A miracle happened! Zacchaeus was a changed man. A complete reversal of values shook his character to its foundations. The old motivation in life died. A new resolve was born. Life had a new center. The poor, the exploited were now his concern. His heart was strangely warmed by the mercy of God and by the "still, sad music of humanity."

It was time for a solemn avowal. Zacchaeus stood up. "Behold, Lord, half of my goods I give to the poor," he said. A whisper went among the guests. Their faces registered both pleasure and awe. "Do our ears deceive us?" you can imagine them saying. Then, not defiantly, but shaken by this transforming experience, Zacchaeus went on: "And if I have defrauded any one of anything, I restore it fourfold."

This was even more astonishing. The Jewish law required a man to pay back only twice what he had taken dishonestly. To pay back four dollars for every one was unbelievable!

Yet this kind of response should not be too surprising. And why? Because conversion is a miracle of God. The God who created the universe out of nothing, who brought Israel out of slavery in Egypt, who returned the exiles from Babylon, who raised Jesus Christ from the dead, this God takes a moral and spiritual nobody and gives him a new name and a new disposition. It is because we still believe in God that we go to the Zacchaeuses of the twentieth century, the social pariahs, the outcasts, and hold before them the prospect of a new life, a life full of miracle and meaning. The day of moral and spiritual miracles is not past.

Zacchaeus, the unlikely convert, was genuinely changed. Jesus saw that his experience ran deep. It was no passing fancy. It was no seed springing up quickly in shallow soil only to wither as quickly as it had sprung up. New life had begun. Jesus responded by saying, "Today salvation has come to this house." What had happened to Zacchaeus was what Paul described when he wrote: "If any man be in Christ, he is a new creature: old things are passed away, behold all things are become new" (2 Cor. 5:17).

In this incident was Jesus' philosophy of evangelism. Here Jesus showed us by what he did, what we ought to do. If we do not seek out the rejected, the morally homeless of this world, and if we do not see them as individual souls made for God, then we may discover that even in our "churchiness" we are working for ourselves, not for Jesus Christ; that custom and convention mean more to us than does the kingdom of God. Jesus declared that the "Son of man came to seek and to save the lost" (Luke 19:10, rsv). As those who represent him today, we have no greater task ourselves.—James W. Cox

Topic: Families Reaching Their Own

TEXT: Song of Solomon 1:6b

B. H. Carrol was a great Baptist leader

earlier in this century—an outstanding pastor, preacher, and educator. His son was killed in a senseless way while engaged in questionable behavior. Carrol was heard crying out as he walked back and forth wringing his hands, "They made me a keeper of the vineyards, but mine own vineyard have I not kept." Other families he had taken care of, but his own he had neglected. If such tragedy could come to such a great Christian, it can come to anyone.

Surely we must guard against giving primary attention to matters outside of our home to the neglect of our own family. We must realize the importance of reaching our own family. In fact, effectively reaching others depends to a large degree on how effectively we reach our own family. We can reach our family through witness, evangelism, nurture, and ministry.

I. *Through witness.* Jesus told his disciples that they were to be witnesses unto him everywhere in the world (Acts 1:6–8). Certainly that includes the family. A witness is someone who testifies concerning what he or she has experienced. A Christian witness bears testimony concerning his or her relationship to the Lord Jesus Christ. This testimony is by the quality of life lived as well as by words spoken. The Christian witness lives out before others, including the members of the family, the difference that Jesus makes.

Parents are to be witnesses—examples—to their children. Under normal circumstances no one has more influence on a child than parents, especially in a child's early years. A godly parent by deed and word demonstrates to a child what it means to be a Christian and how wonderful God is to his children. Of course, no parent or child is perfect and sometimes a profound witness comes at the point of forgiveness and reconciliation.

Children can be witnesses to parents, brothers, sisters, and others in their family. By relating to their parents in the way the Bible directs, they encourage their parents to follow God's way in their lives (Eph. 6:1–3). The Bible teaches that youth are to be an example to others: "Let no man despise thy youth; but be thou an example of the believers, in word, in conversation, in charity, in spirit, in faith, in purity" (1 Tim. 4:12). Adult children can also be effective witnesses to older parents.

Other members of the family can bear significant witnesses, such as grandparents. Many people can testify about the tremendous positive impact that their grandparent's example had on them. Timothy must have had such an experience because Paul wrote to him, "When I call to remembrance the unfeigned faith that is in thee, which dwelt first in thy grandmother Lois, and thy mother Eunice; and I am persuaded that in thee also" (2 Tim. 1:5).

II. *Through evangelism.* Example alone does not result in persons coming to have faith in Jesus Christ as Lord and Savior. Words also are necessary. People need to be told clearly of God's plan of salvation. As Timothy was to "do the work of an evangelist" (2 Tim. 4:5), so is each Christian. And evangelism begins at home.

Parents can lead children to understand God's plan of salvation. They can explain what sin, repentance, faith, conversion, and baptism mean and how we are saved from sin to life in Christ. All too often parents bring a child to the pastor and say, "We think he is ready"—meaning we think he is ready for the pastor to explain the way of salvation. How much better for a parent to lead a child to faith in Jesus Christ and then share the good news with the pastor. No more precious memory is possible than that of a parent being God's instrument in bringing a child to the throne of grace.

Children can lead unsaved parents to faith in Christ. Often a little child has led an adult to understand how to be saved. Sometimes a child does this by encouraging a parent to attend Sunday school or church or to visit with the pastor. However, in some cases the child has personally led a parent to faith in Christ.

Other members of the family can be evangelists to those who are lost. Grandparents, aunts, uncles, cousins, and others have been agents of redemption within families. Obviously family ties are greatly strengthened when family members reach their own for Christ.

III. *Through nurturing.* Conversion is only the beginning of the Christian life, the start of the race, not the end. Thus after a family member has come to faith in Christ and been saved, the process of Christian growth through nurture begins.

Parents clearly have a responsibility for the nurture of children: "And, ye fathers, provoke not your children to wrath: but bring them up in the nurture and admonition of the Lord" (Eph. 6:4). At least seven elements seem vital for the adequate nurture of children: love, discipline, supervision, worship, security, togetherness, and order or harmony. Parents can best provide these for children and youth.

The total family ought to be involved in nurture. Children can help parents grow in Christ. Brothers and sisters and members of the extended family can be part of the process. As families work together to grow in Christ, they not only strengthen one another but also the family itself. For one thing, family members can help one another discover, develop, and exercise spiritual gifts. All God's children are gifted, and when these gifts are utilized, the family is made stronger and more effective in reaching others.

IV. *Through ministry.* Ministry to family members by others in the family is essential for family strength. The Bible forcefully declares, "But if any provide not for his own, and specially for those of his own house, he had denied the faith, and is worse than an infidel" (1 Tim. 5:8). Caring for the needs of the members of the family is something that can be shared by all.

Effective ministry must be to all the needs of a person, not just a few or those we prefer to meet. Family members have many different kinds of needs—physical, mental, emotional, social, as well as spiritual—and care must be taken to meet each one. As the life of the family unfolds, certain members will be better equipped or positioned to meet a particular need of a family member. But ministry to need is every member's responsibility and opportunity. By so doing, the family is strengthened.

Families are to reach families, and one of the families to be reached is our own. If we neglect our own way, we may find ourself weeping, "Other vineyards I have kept, but mine own have I not kept." And certainly if we do not reach our own family, it will be not as strong as it could be and thus not as able to reach others. Dedicate yourself to reaching your own family through witness, evangelism, nurture, and ministry.—William M. Pinson, Jr.

Topic: If You're Tired of Sin, Come on In!

TEXT: Heb. 10:11–18

In the mountains of western North Carolina, people load their garbage into their cars and take it to the nearest dump site. We used to visit that area often. Every time we would go into town, we'd gather up all our garbage and stop off at the bank of garbage dumpsters that were located at various intervals along the side of the road.

On one or two occasions, however, I recall coming back home with the garbage. I ran my errands and conducted my business but forgot to leave the garbage at the dumpster. My forgetfulness either required that I make a second trip immediately or that I stockpile my garbage until the next convenient opportunity to dispose of it.

I remember reading something some time ago where the writer described worship—both personal and corporate—as an occasion for spiritual "garbage disposal," as well as time of celebration and praise. At first, I was a little offended at the analogy, but then I realized there was a valuable truth in what he suggested.

I. When I come to worship, I come with both gratitude and garbage. But most of the time, I only remember being encouraged to contribute my gratitude—and my tithe. Most of the time I trudge back home with my garbage still hidden in the closets and basements of my life.

But if worship accomplishes its true purpose, then it also must provide me with an opportunity to regularly dump my sins and failures, my spiritual garbage. If I understand the Bible correctly, he wants to collect it all and take it off my hands and get it out of my life.

The tragic truth of the matter, however, is that sin is a virtually ignored category—even in Christian worship. Many people believe that dealing with sin actually detracts from worship. "Preaching on sin sends out such negative signals," they suggest. "You know that people won't come if they hear too much about sin. It's too negative. You've got to keep the gospel positive if you want to reach people today."

Recently, a cartoon depicted a prophet figure decked out in sackcloth and ashes, carrying a sign which read, "Resist Temptation." A rather seedy-looking character walked up, looked at the sign, and said, "Personally, I'm not interested in resisting temptation. I'm just trying to find some."

Then, of course, there's the story of the bulletin board in front of the church which usually carried the title of the minister's sermon for the coming Sunday. One week, the board read, "If you're tired of sin, come on in." But with a brightly colored marker someone else scribbled on the glass door just underneath that message these words: "But if you're not, dial 555–1234."

II. Of course, there are some sins which are acceptable—indeed, required—to be periodically addressed during Sunday morning church.

(a) These are "cultural" sins—the sins which offend every one's sense of decency and good taste. For instance, almost everyone agrees that drug abuse, spouse and child abuse, pornography are sinful. But they are not generally the sins of the people who are in church. And that is what makes them safe to deal with on Sunday mornings.

(b) I have another way of classifying sin: crazy, mean, and stupid. Stupid sins are things you do that hurt yourself and others—usually out of ignorance. You do something and say afterward, "Boy, was

that dumb!" Being smart about what is good for you is important. But some things are simply dumb—from alcohol and drug abuse to laziness and procrastination.

Crazy sins are things you do that you know will hurt you, but you go ahead and do them anyway. For example, you lie, knowing that sooner or later you will be caught. Or you get involved in an extramarital affair, knowing that there is absolutely no future to it and that there is only bad news ahead.

Mean sins are just that: mean. They are what we used to call being ornery. We willfully inflict pain on other people: gossip's sharp tongue, greed's cold heart, envy's evil eye, and other acts of personal cruelty like prejudice and bias.

These are the sins—this is the spiritual garbage—you and I actually bring to worship with us every Sunday. We may be dressed in our Sunday best, all washed and scrubbed, all smiling and friendly. But we are not as pure as we like to think we are.

III. Worship is supposed to help us admit that. Worship is supposed to keep us tied to the facts about ourselves: the fact of our sin, our infidelity, our hypocrisy, our falsehood—all of which makes worship so desperately important for our survival and for the survival of our faith.

Occasionally, someone will confess that even though they know that worship is the most important thing a Christian can do, it's not all that important for them. "I don't come like I should," they will confess. "I get bored so easily in worship." "I just can't keep my mind focused and attentive." "I can't concentrate on the prayers, and I don't always understand the hymns or the sermon." "I feel so guilty about it. Tell me, pastor, what can I do?"

Let me tell you what I do when that happens to me. I look for all the garbage that I forgot to dump the last time I worshiped. When I have difficulty seeing God and feeling his power in my life, I usually discover that I need to confess my sin, repent of it, and experience God's forgiveness. When I give God my spiritual garbage regularly in worship—as well as my praise, my gratitude, and even my tithe—then the windows are cleared up so that I can usually discover that I need to confess my sin, repent of it, and experience God's forgiveness. When I give God my spiritual garbage regularly in worship—as well as my praise, my gratitude, and even my tithe—then the windows are cleared up so that I can see new visions of God and the doors are thrown open wide so that I can experience the freshness of his power in my life. When I dump my spiritual garbage regularly in worship, then I feel enormous relief and release. Praise and gratitude become spontaneous—I can't help myself! But until I deal with my sin, there is little joy or enthusiasm in any part of the worship experience.

IV. The sermon text reminds us that Christian worship is a call to dump all our spiritual garbage at the foot of the cross of Jesus. He offered the ultimate sacrifice for our sin on a strange, skull-like hill just outside the north gate of Jerusalem. Did you know that one of the reasons that Golgotha was chosen as the place for public crucifixions was because it was located next to the city garbage dump? It's ironic that we've never really noticed that before now, isn't it?

There's no need to take your garbage home with you. Leave it here. He knows what to do with it.

A father caught his teenage son coming home drunk late one night. "You know how disappointed I am in you right now, don't you, son? I've told you what I would do if I ever caught you drinking. Go to your room, and I'll be right there."

The father went to his bedroom and retrieved the widest, thickest belt he owned. He went to the son's room and told the boy that he was going to give him the three hardest licks he had ever experienced. But he only hit his son once and left the room.

The next day, the father and son spent the afternoon together. They stopped by a local ice cream parlor and began to talk about the night before. "Dad," said the son, "why did you hit me only once last night? I deserved all three licks."

"Son, that was mercy. I want to always remember what mercy is." Then, almost as an afterthought, the father said, "Are you enjoying your ice cream?"

"Yes sir, I am. Thank you very much."

Then the father said, "Son, the ice cream is grace. I always want to remember what grace is also."

Worship is the finest opportunity you will ever have to experience God's mercy and grace. He wants you to confess your sin—not to make you wallow in the despair of your own failure, not to shame and embarrass you, but so that you can be free of it, so that you won't have to take it with you when you leave this room and haul it around with you for the rest of the week, indeed, for the rest of your life.

So come to him, now, and leave all your sin right here.—Gary C. Redding

Illustrations

By Robert C. Shannon

PRIORITIES.   The January 19, 1992, issue of *Parade* magazine carried a cartoon showing a businessman speaking to his secretary. "Priorities?" he is saying. "I don't have time for that now!" We all know that evangelism is the first priority of the church, yet so many congregations are saying, "I don't have time for that!"

DRAWING OTHERS FOR CHRIST.   In 1781 Herschel discovered the planet Uranus. Then astronomers noticed a strong influence pulling at Uranus and discovered Neptune, discovered it before they could see it, because of the gravitational pull. Then Lowell noticed that another planet was also pulling at Uranus and discovered Pluto. So each Christian should exert a gravitational pull on his or her friends in the world. So the church in the evangelized world exerts its influence on the pagan world.

BETTER TO GIVE.   A Hungarian Christian came to study at a mission in Austria. He lost the equivalent of two hundred and fifty dollars. For him that was a lot of money. The director took up a collection among the mission staff and collected enough money to replace the missing funds. He said to one contributor. "That man has been so worried. He'll sleep better tonight." "So will I," said the giver.

BEYOND BOUNDARIES.   An airline magazine publishes a list of the routes its airline flies and, as most do, includes a route map. Recently one noted that the map no longer had any national boundaries. It said that history was moving faster then geography these days and the mapmakers couldn't keep up with the changes in national boundaries. People with a heart for missions have long believed in a map without boundaries. "This is our Father's world," they sang and believed that Christ really did mean for them to go into all the world.

SECTION VIII
Preaching from Hosea:
A Gospel for Broken Things

BY ROGER LOVETTE

Harry Crews in his autobiography, *A Childhood*, tells about his early fascination with the Sears, Roebuck catalogue. As a young boy he would spend hours looking at the happy, smiling models in the catalogue. They were different from the people Crews knew. For the people in the catalogue were picture perfect. Crews writes that everybody he knew personally had something missing. Fingers cut off. Toes split. Ears half-chewed away and eyes clouded with blindness from a glancing fence staple. He writes that those who had nothing missing were carrying scars. From barbed wire or knives or fishhooks. The people in the catalogue had no such hurts. They were not only physically perfect but were also beautiful.* Hosea would have understood Harry Crews' world. For the prophet had married a woman only to find her unfaithful. And if that were not enough, she left him and their children and went whoring after other men. So out of the broken things of his own life, Hosea began to write a great saga of redemption. Israel would take his words and see in them as the sad story of a bad marriage. But God's chosen people would see mirrored in his story their own lives, their own history. Painfully they found their own names written at the edges of that story.

Hosea, then, is a gospel for broken things, things too broken to mend. Out

of his own heartbreak, the prophet Hosea would spin a tale that would provide hope and redemption for the distraught people of God. So much was so wrong. Israel suffered from a long war with Assyria. The country was in virtual anarchy. After the death of Jeroboam II, four of the six Israelite kings had been assassinated in the short span of 14 years. The best and the brightest would soon be carried away in chains into Assyrian captivity. There was no way things could be put right again. Indeed, things seemed irreparably broken, too broken to mend.

Interestingly enough, Hosea saw in his own fractured history a painful reflection of the larger world around him. What had happened to him had also happened to God's people. They, like Gomer, had gone whoring after strange gods. The problems were two-fold: 1) The problems within of religious syncretism—of blending with the false gods of Baal something which would leave faith weak and diluted; 2) The problem without— the threat of the Assyrian army pounding at their doors. Israel was willing to do almost anything to make peace with the enemy.

The questions in Hosea are the old questions. Could Hosea find hope and meaning in such a terrible personal crisis? And the larger question: were things too broken to mend ever again? It was a time of grave political and cultural crisis for the prophet's people. The temptation was to hold on to the old order. Another temptation was to face the future unen-

*Harry Crews, *A Childhood: The Biography of a Place* (New York: Harper & Row, 1978), p. 54.

cumbered by no faith at all. For the great danger was to chuck faith once and for all as being irrelevant.

Using the motif of his own broken marriage, in chapters one through three, Hosea would point toward hope and redemption, for his own life and country as well. So he answered the brokenness of his own life and that of his people with a new word. There was no chasm too broken to mend. For what he discovered for himself and Gomer and his own people was that the divine redemption covered everything. For the redeeming love of God—this *chesed*—this loving-kindness redeems and heals everything it touches.

Thomas Mann said of great literature, It is, is always is, however much we say it was. And if this be true, it means that Hosea's old story is more than a story in a faraway land on the other side of the sea. No, this is our story. The story of our own broken relationships. With ourselves. With those we love. With our own religious commitments. We are no strangers to divorce or the flawed world view of Harry Crews. The people we know are broken or crippled in one way or the other. Most of them do not resemble the characters in the Sears, Roebuck catalogue.

Our age too is much like Hosea's. The old axioms simply do not hold. The old values we lived by have been challenged by advertisements and politics and culture itself. We are torn apart by many issues: black-white, rich-poor, conservative-liberal issues. Churches are split over doctrine and social pronouncements. The nation is divided over economics and rights of all kinds of people: poor, women, homosexual, the unborn, the handicapped.

Some days we feel like Hosea must have felt. There are some things too broken to mend. Many days the people in the pews must feel like Israel's beleaguered people. There seems to be little hope for the days ahead.

Hosea learned some powerful lessons in the broken relationship with his unfaithful wife, Gomer. Israel, in a time of exile and crisis, would learn some new lessons about their relationship with God. There are profound lessons here for the people of our time.

These were some of the issues. 1) Life and faith are relational in nature. If this relation is not tended, nothing works. So the relationship of God and his people is to be given primary attention. 2) The bridal motif is primary. As Hosea relates to Gomer, so God relates to Israel. They are bound together in a covenantal bond. This is primary. If the covenant is broken—it must be restored. 3) God is seen as husband and parent. They learned something about redemption from the face of this parent. 4) Harlotry was party of every life. The temptation to adulterate, to dilute, to compromise is ever-present. We must be careful lest we lose everything in this diluting process. 5) We discover something here concerning the nature of sin. The most urgent problem of their time was the linking of the Biblical faith with the faith of the Baals. This dilution was destroying the power and force of their faith. 6) The overarching image is the face of God—God as parent and God as lover. Here we see someone who will go to any lengths to win us back. This love that will not let us go is redemptive and healing in nature. Across every brokenness is the possibility for reconciliation and wholeness. 7) Hope is the last word in the book. Hope for Gomer and Hosea. Hope for exiled, fearful, and unfaithful Israel. Hope for us and our world and our time.

Topic: "The Broken Marriage—A Symbol"

TEXT: Hosea 1:1–3:5

A man passed a pawnshop one day and saw a strange sight in the window. A wedding band. The caption under the band bore a strange message: "Will sell cheap." The man was intrigued. He went into the store and asked to see the gold band. As he studied the ring closely he turned it so he could read an inscription on the inside. Sally loves John and the date 1–18–61. The man wondered what went wrong. What could possibly have caused this symbol of love to wind up in a pawnshop window?

Hosea could have provided an answer to this question. With high hopes, he hard married his beloved Gomer. Soon after the marriage, children came, one after another. The young couple seemed happy. But then something happened. Gomer distanced herself from her husband. Communication broke down and finally stopped. She turned away and left home. Gomer became unfaithful and there was no way to bring her back. Hosea, at home with the children, wondered what he had done and what had gone wrong.

As happens so often the prophet saw in his own tortured history a parable of his nation's plight. Israel had gone whoring after other husbands—false gods. She would not stay at home and be faithful to Yahweh. She left the marriage and sought other liaisons, other lovers. The covenant that bound people and God was shattered. So we come to the first sermon in Hosea. What are we to do with the broken things?

The problem of Israel's infidelity was long-standing. Hers was not an outright rejection. Her infidelity was more subtle, like ours. Like the relationship between Hosea and Gomer, Israel's defection happened slowly, over a period of time. At first there was no outright rejection. Israel never really renounced Yahweh. Rather, God's people simply inculcated into their worship and daily lives much of pagan Baal worship practices. Life became cheap. Sex and religion were blended. Faith became manipulative. They faced a watering down of their principles and faith. A dilution. We call it an adultery. For that word means to dilute, to make less potent or life-changing. They were left with a broken relationship, a watered-down contract which meant little.

What do we learn from this first sermon?

1. *We recognize the broken things.* Like Hosea we come to terms with the things of our lives. He had to give attention to the infidelities of Gomer. Hosea pointed out to his people that they had to look at the dilemma of their situation. Like Hosea's marriage, it was no surprise at the

brokenness that surrounded them. Kings had been murdered and assassinated one after another. The kingdom was in utter chaos. Insecurity and fear were everywhere. Assyria knocked at the gates. Everything was in disarray. Israel, as a people, had to face the fragmentation of their lives as did the broken-hearted husband, Hosea.

2. *We deal with the broken things.* Hosea placed a finger on the pulse of his marriage and country. What went wrong? Where did the trouble lie? As in any marriage, the answers were not simple. They were complicated. A multitude of layers of difficulties. So it was with Israel. They had to deal with the broken things of their national life. Walter Brueggemann has said that to rightly discern the crisis was the primary work of the prophet and people. This is also the task of the preacher as he/she opens the Bible to Hosea. What are the broken things that need attention in our world? Brueggemann has said we are a polarized people. Split, broken, and divided as a church, nation, and world on almost every issue. We must give serious attention to the broken things. Making a connection between then and now may be the most important service of the preacher today.

3. *Like Hosea, we must learn from the broken things.* Hosea was called to go and bring Gomer back home. Israel, in this story, learned from their own painful history something of redemption and forgiveness. Brokenness did not have the last word. Hosea 2:15–16 makes it clear that hope is a larger reality. After great suffering, healing really did come. After spiritual infidelity, of which we are all guilty, God takes us back. The unfaithful are made faithful. Our sins are forgiven. Hosea 3:5 holds out a great promise: "Afterwards the Israelites shall return and seek the Lord their God, and David their king: they shall come in awe to the Lord and to his goodness in the latter days."

Topic: "The Seeds of Brokenness"
TEXT: Hosea 4:1–19
After Hosea's moving autobiographical section, he turned toward his beloved

people, Israel. The rest of the book is addressed to his own people and their problems.

Pondering his own situation, Hosea must have asked, over and over, what went wrong with Gomer? Why did this happen to our marriage? And what we find at the beginning of the fourth chapter is this same question: What went wrong, Israel? In his questioning Hosea comes upon some answers.

In Hosea 4:1 he touches Israel's central dilemma. "There is no faithfulness or loyalty, and no knowledge of God in the land." A long list of Israel's misdeeds are found in 4:2. But the clue to all the brokenness can be traced back to this powerful word, knowing. He first dealt with "the spirit of harlotry" (4:12). The seeds of their brokenness rested with a lack of their knowledge of God. Confusion would flow out of misunderstanding. Misdeeds would follow a wrong spirit. Here the prophet dealt with the relationship of inner disposition to outward behavior. Hosea had stumbled upon an old truth. Evil hearts produced evil deeds. If a person or nation strayed too far from the living God they found themselves in serious trouble.

In 4:4–10 Hosea says that even the religious leaders were not immune to this trouble. Indeed, their casual syncretism had led the nation astray. In 4:13–14 he warned that a blending of Baal with Yahweh would simply not work. This sermon could very well be called the "The Seeds of Our Bewilderment." Brueggemann says that the problem was not a broken covenant as much as a bewildered covenant. Perhaps such a direction would be helpful for people in our time. Bewilderment characterizes our age. Ours is not a lack of knowing as much as it is a confusion of knowing. The seeds of our brokenness lie here. What we give ourselves to, what we truly know tells us much of our direction for the future.

Frederick Buechner tells the story of a man who had betrayed his wife and done terrible things to her. After great pain she divorced him. They went their separate ways. Years later the man had married again. He became a respected and honored member of the community. His former wife learned of his reputation and sought him out. She could not believe the evil man who had so hurt her could have changed. She decided to expose his hypocrisy. She would let everyone know the kind of person he was. And so, in a public gathering she challenged him. "Take your mask off and let everyone see who you are. You have lived a lie long enough." Slowly the man began to peel the mask away. People waited breathlessly as he performed this painful act. As he peeled the mask away, the former wife grew silent. He had become, through the years, the mask he wore. Hosea challenged his people to return to a knowledge of the one, true God. In giving themselves to Yahweh, something miraculous would happen to them, too. This knowledge of God changes from inside out.

Topic: "Where Is God?"

Text: Hosea 5:1–15

The key verse in this chapter is 5:6. "With their blocks and herds they shall go to seek the Lord but they will not find him; he has withdrawn from them." When trouble came to Hosea he asked the question all suffering believers have asked: "Where is God?" Israel, too, asked this question. The exile would soon claim many of the best in their land. The government was unstable. It looked like the end of the land and the promise that stretched all the way back to Abraham's day. Chaos reigned. No wonder they asked, again and again, Where is God?

Chapter four was an indictment against the religious leaders. They had led the people astray. Chapter five enlarged the circle. Hosea pointed to the political figures of his day. They, too, had sold out to the strange gods of Baal.

What we find here is a picture of God. Their understanding of God was unclear and fuzzy. Their adulterous relationship with the Canaanite god, Baal, had blurred their understanding of the one true God. Baal could be manipulated. Baal could be tricked to give them what they wanted. He was available at their beck and call.

But Yahweh was different. Hosea pointed out that the politicians could not claim God for their own partisan interests. The great danger to faith in every age has always been the same. To use the power and authority of God to benefit one's own interests. The religious leaders had tried this and it had dismally failed. The political leaders also tried to manipulate Yahweh. This did not work. Where was God? Why did he not answer when they called?

God was not really absent but he was not available to be used as the Israelites wished. If Yahweh did not come running at their beck and call—surely he was not there at all. Perhaps he did not even exist. The point was that *God was not at their disposal.*

Nazi Germany taught us a powerful lesson. Hitler used the established church to accomplish his terrible goals. Each nation has tried to wrap God in the colors of their own selfish interests. Chapter five says this will not work. Yahweh spoke: "I myself will tear and go away; I will carry off, and no one shall rescue. I will return again to my place until they acknowledge their guilt and seek my face" (5:14b–15). Let this be a warning. God cannot be manipulated or counted on to support our interests, our parties or our causes. God is not Baal. He will return only when we put away our sinful ways.

Topic: "Bridge Over Troubled Waters"

TEXT: Hosea 6:1–6

Charles Bracelen Flood wrote a great novel, *Love is the Bridge.* But Hosea gave this chapter a different title: Forgiveness is the bridge. For forgiveness becomes the span by which we are connected and reunited. Hosea learned in his own painful marriage that love alone could not span the chasm. Forgiveness is the bridge over the troubled waters.

So chapter six dealt with renewal. "Let us return," Hosea 6:1 proclaimed, "for it is he who has torn, and he will heal us; he has struck down, and he will bind us up." This was followed by a wonderful word in 6:2: "He will revive us . . . He will raise

us up." The analogy here is wonderful: "He will come to us like the showers, like the spring rains that water the earth" (6:3). So the bridge becomes a reality: "I desire steadfast love and not sacrifice, the knowledge of God rather than burnt offerings" (6:6).

Hosea took up the theme that first appeared in Hosea 2:7 and 3:5. The word is *turn.* They were challenged to leave the popular practices of Baal and re-turn to the original relationship with God they had in the wilderness.

The broken covenant was to be restored as they returned. That knowing of God became, for them, a state of being. And the turned Israel was taken back as Hosea took Gomer back. The past was forgiven. The future opened wide with possibility and hope. Forgiveness, then, becomes the bridge over the troubled waters of every age.

Topic: "Journey Inward—Journey Outward"

TEXT: Hosea 6:7–7:16

Hosea's time was an age of chaos. Brokenness could be seen at the highest levels. Four of the six kings had been murdered during the years that Hosea prophesied. Allegiances were made with foreign governments hoping to save the nation. Principles were compromised. Instability and discord ruled. Beginning with 6:7 Hosea ticked off the charges. God's people transgressed the covenant. They dealt faithlessly with Yahweh. The city was filled with evildoers and tracked with blood. Robbers were everywhere. Priests were unfaithful, murder and other crimes were daily occurrences. Hosea continually intoned one word as he look at the world around him. *Whoredom.*

What remedy was there for such chaos? There were no easy answers. They had looked to their kingly leaders only to find failure. They had looked to their ecclesiastical leaders only to find disappointment. Where were they to turn?

Many opted for a private faith that did not relate to public life. Pray, follow the principles of faith—forget the state. Turn inward. Spend quality time in the tiny circle of your own life. Journey inward. Others cast their lot with kings and government. Real lasting change would only come from public life. Many believed that through the all-too-human monarchy and its tributaries, would real change occur. Some looked to the outside for answers to their difficulties. The nation was in disarray—who could turn away from the challenges to help? Hosea, in his own life, had seen the pain of the personal and the agony of the larger picture. The prophet linked these two journeys—outward and inward in a beautiful way. Chapters 1–3 were personal—as personal as one could get. Chapters 4–14 dealt with the life of the nation.

Surely the journey inward cannot be ignored. Hosea could not ignore the shambles of his own marriage and his own family. He had to give enormous energy to the task of reconciliation and rebuilding. Yet he knew that he lived in the context of a larger world. His life and family would be doomed if the nation failed. And so he also turned outward with a message to the larger world.

History teaches us that faith can easily become fanaticism when linked with specific political causes. History also teaches us that politics cut off from moral roots is destitute and corrupt. The challenge for the people of God then and now is to link faith and politics. Faith cannot do it alone. Politics cannot do it all. Together we, too, must seek not faith *or* politics. We must seek both. Linking the inward and outward journeys, led by the power and presence of a very great God will lead us through a time of chaos and difficulty.

Topic: "Inherit the Wind"

TEXT: Hosea 8:1–14

One of the great plays of our time was entitled, "Inherit the Wind." It told the story of the Scopes Trial in Dayton, Tennessee. To that little town came two great men, William Jennings Bryan and Clarence Darrow. The issue was evolution. Could it be taught in the school system? Would a science teacher be put behind bars for teachings accepted as scientific evidence? The title of the play judges the

whole matter. If we sow the wind—we are likely to inherit a whirlwind.

In our text in Hosea 8:7 we deal with the cumulative power of evil. One of the great biblical themes is reaping and sowing (Gal. 6:7; 2 Cor. 9:6; Ps. 126:6). Jesus continually dealt with this theme. His parables began: "A sower went out to sow . . ." (Mark 4:3). Again and again the theme returns: we reap what we sow.

In the case of Israel, to sow the wrong seeds meant simply that the harvest would be flawed. Hosea 8:7 says that the "standing grain has no heads, it shall yield no meal. . . ." There would be growth but it would not produce the crops needed for sustenance. If Israel continued on this path of destruction she would be doomed.

The *Interpreter's Bible* talks about the outreach of the whirlwind as well as its intensity. The seeds of evil grow in strength and power. Israel could not ignore the consequences of the monarchs who reigned or the idolatry of her citizenry. Hosea's words were simple and sure. Tares do not produce crops that sustain. Poor seed can only lead to a bitter harvest.

Topic: "Dry Rot"

TEXT: Hosea 9:1–17

In 1884 water hyacinths were brought from South America to New Orleans as an exhibit at the cotton exhibition. People loved the orchid-like lavender blossoms. One story reports that a woman in San Mateo, Florida, put the plant in her fish pond and it grew so rapidly that she threw the surplus into the St. John's River nearby. Within ten years the plants had spread over a water area more than half the size of Manhattan. Today water hyacinths clog waterways in all the Gulf Coast states. In Florida alone cleaning hyacinths from the inland waters is a never ending job. The cleaning bill runs more than $650,000 a year.

Hosea would have understood this story. For chapter nine dealt with the consequences of sin. What we have here is a sermon on judgment. This word is a missing note in the church today. Little judgment is heard. Most of our messages deal with personal problems. The inward journey. But here Hosea dealt with the root causes of Israel's problems. Hosea harked back to his own personal situation. Israel, too, had "played the whore" and "departed from their God" (9:2). He talked about the destitution of their sacrifices and special religious feast days.

Perhaps the central part of the judgment message is seen in 9:16: "Ephraim is stricken; their root is dried up, they shall bear no fruit." If the root was dead—no fruit would come to the impotent tree. He also turned to the reproductive metaphor. No children would come to this people. The consequences of their whoredoms would affect not only them but generations to come. This was no new message for Hosea. These themes have already been dealt with in Hosea 4:1–3. Now they are repeated in a stronger measure in this chapter.

Menninger's *Whatever Became of Sin* might be a good place to begin as you study for this sermon. The church today is in need of Hosea's message of judgment and sin.

Topic: "Basics for Brokenness"

TEXT: Hosea 10:1–5

There hangs on the wall in my study a photograph from the sixties. In the picture a little black boy, about eight, runs through the ghetto streets. He is surrounded by large high-rise tenements. The streets are dirty and unkempt. You can tell by his clothes that he is poor and has little of the world's goods. Yet in his hands he carries, lovingly, an Easter lily. He looks up and his face radiates a smile of hope.

In this chapter Hosea wrote of abandoned altars where thistles grow (10:8) and broken fortresses that provide no real refuge (10:14). Surrounded by a crumbling kingdom and a corrupt religious system, the prophet returned to the basics as an antidote for the people's brokenness. Those basics are recounted in 10:12–13. The prophet gives us four imperatives. One could easily call this sermon: "Living by the Right Imperatives." These imperatives formed the basic antidotes for the brokenness of his hard age.

1) *Sow* righteousness (as opposed to the seeds that produce nothing substantial); 2) *Reap* the fruits of steadfast love (as opposed to the infidelities with false gods); 3) *Break up* the fallow ground (break up the old habits, leave the old road behind, change your ways); 4) *Seek* the Lord (as opposed to following Baal and his idolatries).

This is a proper antidote for any real brokenness. There is a real righteousness. In the middle of the ghetto there is a lily. It is pure and whole and living and real. There is a love that will not fail. There is good soil, even in unlikely places, if the rules of cultivation are followed. The Lord can be followed and lesser gods can be put aside. These are not sophisticated instructions. They are basic rules for the road.

Topic: "What Does God Look Like?"

TEXT: Hosea 11:1–11

If you were to draw a picture of God— what would you draw? Some pictures might be angry and cruel. God would have a scowl on his face. Some would paint God white and middle-class and maybe even looking like us. Those in other lands would paint God with black or yellow or red faces. Some would draw God as male and some would draw God as female. If you were to take a piece of paper and pencil—what would your picture of God look like?

J. B. Phillips years ago wrote a book called *Your God is Too Small*. In that book he wanted Christians to see that usually our pictures of God are too human, too earthbound, too provincial, and too weak. God is not male or white or female or middle-class or American or black. God is God.

Hosea was centuries ahead of his time in his understanding of God. In this sermon we come to some of the most beautiful literature in the Old Testament. For seven chapters (4–10) Hosea dealt with a long list of Israel's sins and wrongs—her whoredoms. But in this chapter Hosea tenderly returned to the theme which began in Hosea 1–3. That theme was the love of God as seen in the powerful metaphor of nurturing parent.

This is what God looks like. Yahweh speaks, and one can almost hear a catch in that voice, "When Israel was a child, I loved him, and out of Egypt I called my son ..." (11:1). "... It was I who taught Ephraim to walk, I took them up in my arms; but they did not know that I healed them" (11:3). "I was to them like those who lift infants to their cheeks. I bent down to them and fed them" (11:4). God is seen as parent. Father *and* mother. Male *and* female. Here, God pulls down the old photograph album and dusts it off and begins to point to the pictures. There are those early scenes of Egyptian slavery. There is the crossing of the Red Sea. See those pictures in the wilderness. They were not alone. There was a pillar of fire by night and a cloud by day. If you look closely when the water was given and the manna came—you can see, squinting your eyes, another figure in the background. There are pictures of Moses and encampments and forty years and Joshua and a ribbon of a river and a new land with promise and hope. There are scenes of crops and lush fields and smiling faces. But there are other pictures. Baal worship. Strange gods. False allegiances. Cruel kings. Pictures of injustice and ignoring the poor and mistreating the less fortunate. There are also pictures of foreign kings and exile and broken temples, monarchs, and hearts. But we come back to this picture of God as father *and* mother. God as parent. Weeping over Israel's foolish mistakes and sins and heartbreaks. Saying, with love, even after great disappointment, "How can I give you up, Ephraim?" (11:8a).

This is the picture of God we see in Hosea 1–3. Taking Gomer back after great sin. Forgiving her every wrong, redeeming her with a love that will never let any of us go. In chapter 11, we stand before a great painting of the loving face of God. This is only one side of the face. Stand close. Ponder the power of the picture.

As the father waited in the prodigal story, God waits for us. He will not twist our arms, he will not force our hands. He waits, with a light in the window, always waiting for his boy and girl to come home. Such a picture heals. And redeems. And renews. No wonder Gomer came back home and stayed. This love is a wondrous love. This God is a wondrous God.

Topic: "Learning from History"

TEXT: Hosea 12:1–15

A wise man said that the problem with history is that we learn nothing from history. Most persons and nations learn little from the mistakes of others. We keep repeating the same wrongs and errors.

As Hosea looked at his bleak age, he remembered one of the great names in Hebrew history, Jacob. Hosea linked his own eighth century to that ancient patriarch, Jacob.

In Hosea 12 Jacob is seen as self-seeking, greedy, cruel, and dishonest. The tribe of Ephraim in Hosea's time was an exact replica of Jacob, the conniving cheat. Once again Hosea illustrated the powerful connection between root and branch (9:16).

Hosea listed all the flaws of Jacob's character and alongside those he placed his own people. They, too, "have multiplied falsehood and violence" (12:1). They had made treaties with Assyria and made compromising allegiances with Egypt (12:1). Ephraim had been greedy and gained wealth only for himself (12:8). The people had given themselves over to iniquity (12:11) and sacrificed to false gods (12:11).

What connections can we find here with this text in Hosea? We, too, must study biblical history in order to learn from the mistakes of others. Must every age constantly reinvent the wheel? The great biblical word is remember. Remembering slavery and the Red Sea and the wilderness and the Promised Land did something for Israel. It brought them back. One might preach a sermon on "The Grace of Memory."

Nels Ferre told that when he was thirteen years old he left his homeland of Sweden to come to the United States. This was hard for he had little money and did not know English. The last family gathering before he left home was memorable. His family assembled and read from the New Testament. Then they prayed. After that all eight of the children and his mother and father walked him to the train station. At the station, the church choir had come to sing a wonderful hymn. But Ferre says that the memory that formed a motivating faith in his life was the memory of his mother. She wanted to say something that sad day as he left. She knew she might never see him again. She wanted to say something that would be right and real. Ferre watched as she tried to form words and nothing came from her mouth. Finally the conductor blew the whistle and the train started to pull away. Ferre said his mother ran along the platform, whispering to him, "Nels, remember Jesus; Nels, remember Jesus."

A wise person has written that the important things are what we remember after we have forgotten everything else. Hosea called his people back down history's lane until they stood before a portrait of Jacob. And pointing he said: "Remember." This is one of the great tasks of the church today.

Topic: "When Kingdoms Fall"
TEXT: Hosea 13:1–6
The death of a marriage is a terrible thing. To break up a house, to sort out one's treasures, to box up one's memories and pictures, to try to explain to the children why you are doing this is a heart-rending experience. Everybody loses. Nobody wins. There was something sad, indeed, to watch the cranes slowly hover over the statues and lift them from their established places in Russia. The symbols of a corrupt nation were erased one after another. Even good change is hard and difficult to endure.

In Hosea's thirteenth chapter he takes the darkest colors of his palette and paints a picture of the fall of a great nation. "Therefore they shall be like the morning mist or like the dew that goes away early, like chaff that swirls from the threshing floor or like smoke from a window." He continues this same, sad theme in 13:15–16: "... The east wind shall come, a blast from the Lord, rising from the wilderness; his fountain shall dry up,

his spring shall be parched. It shall strip his treasury of every precious thing. Samaria shall bear her guilt, because she has rebelled against her God they shall fall by the sword, their little ones shall be dashed in pieces, and their pregnant women ripped open."

These are terrible words of anguish and sorrow. Hosea believed that Gomer's lusting after strange lovers led to the disintegration of their marriage. The covenant was broken. The marriage contract was dissolved. That analogy now spills forth into the thirteenth chapter.

Hosea pointed his finger at the religious and political leaders of Israel throughout the book (13:9–11). What are we to say to the plagues of death and the destruction that Sheol brings here?

1. No nation is immune from judgment.

2. No nation is invincible.

3. Leaders, both religious and political, must be good stewards of the trust in their people.

4. Nations, like individuals, choose their destiny.

5. We must live with the consequences of our actions. There are many innocent victims of broken marriage. There are many innocent victims in national catastrophes. The ripples set loose in the streams go on and on.

Hosea believed that Assyria would be the instrument to bring about the destruction of the kingdom of Israel. The exile would be the logical conclusion to the misdeeds and idolatry of many years.

These words call us to ponder and to remember the painful lessons of history. We must learn the lessons from Israel (13:4–6). Kingdoms fall. Brokenness becomes the sad metaphor of a nation when it forgets its covenant responsibilities.

Topic: "Hope for Years to Come"
TEXT: Hosea 14:1–9
Dan Wakefield in his book, *Returning*, has written a great story of redemption. Wakefield is a bestselling novelist and screenwriter. After years of straying from the church, trying success, psychoanalysis, drugs, and alcohol, Wakefield

found himself at a church service on Christmas Eve. The book is the poignant story of his slow return to a faith he thought was gone forever. This is not the saga of going back. It is a re-turning to a road of spiritual enlightenment. This last chapter in Hosea begins with this powerful word, *return*. The second verse played on this theme a second time. What we find here is a call to repentance. We must remember that chapter 13 is a partial word. Chapter 14 is the last word. That word is hope for the days to come. Renewal and co-creation really can take place.

The chapter can be broken down into two parts:

1. God will heal his people's faithlessness (14:4).

2. Israel will flourish once more in the garden of God. Eden will be a possibility once more (14:5–7).

Who knew this truth better than Hosea? After her great sinning God told Hosea to take his wayward wife back. Here Hosea told his beloved people that God would take them back even after the terrible exile.

The last word does not stop with the broken things. The final words are reconciliation and redemption. Two beams span the chasm of any real brokenness. The first word is forgiveness. All the wrongs that make our journey so cumbersome and difficult are taken away. The second beam is love. That sturdy beam of kindness and grace provides our pathway to the future. Perhaps Charles Flood was right in his novel's title after all, *Love is the Bridge*.

For further resources see James M. Ward, *Amos/Hosea* (Atlanta: John Knox Press, 1981); Walter Brueggemann, *Tradition for Crisis* (Atlanta: John Knox Press, 1968); James Luther Mays, *Hosea* (Philadelphia: The Westminster Press, 1969); *The Interpreter's Bible*, Vol. VI (Nashville: Abingdon, 1956).

SECTION IX.
Preaching on "The Great Commission"

BY C. WELTON GADDY

The renowned Swiss missionary-theologian, Emil Brunner, likened the church's involvement in missions to the relationship between fire and burning. It is a matter of essence. The action-oriented verbs define the basic nature of the nouns. No burning, no fire. No missions, no church.

The entire sweep of Christian history as well as the central message of the Bible validates the truth of Brunner's observation. God's people are always—always! —a people on mission. Missions pulsate at the heart of a church's nature. Missions involvements reveal a church's true character. An absence of missions in a fellowship that claims to be a church signifies an impostor.

Preaching set in the context of a church's worship mandates exploring the biblical basis, theological nature, and personal challenge of the church's mission to the world.

Jesus sounded the missionary imperative unequivocally in his post-Resurrection, mountain-top words spoken, according to Matthew, just prior to the Ascension. Addressing all disciples, those within earshot and those in generations to come, Jesus joined a mandate to missions with a descriptive statement about the meaning of missions. Matthew's record of Jesus' words, commonly called "The Great Commission," provides invaluable insights related to missions.

A solid sermonic treatment of "The Great Commission" deserves no less than a month of Sundays devoted to it. Such preaching, always appropriate, is especially beneficial at the beginning of a new church year or during a season in which a church reflects on its priorities.

The most effective preaching on "The Great Commission" serves a singular purpose. No effort is made to raise a special offering, to elicit congregational support for a particular program, or even to call for intercessory prayer for missionaries. The preacher's attention is riveted on a declaration of the biblical challenge to missions.

Here are four sermon ideas related to "The Great Commission." Each builds upon the other. But each can stand alone. Effectiveness is enhanced if these four sermons are delivered on successive Sundays.

Each sermon should begin with a reading of the words of Jesus according to Matthew 28:19–20. The questions of why, where, what, and when relate directly to this declaration of Jesus and prompt a careful examination of its meaning.

Topic: The Great Commission: Why?
(The Question of Authority)

Why? Why are we to be going, discipling, teaching, and baptizing? Why must we take these ancient words preserved by Matthew any more seriously than the present avalanche of words coming from church council discussions, deacons' meetings, church conferences, and the innumerable offices of denominational headquarters?

The word "therefore" in Matthew 28:19 establishes the authoritative nature of "The Great Commission" by linking the content of the imperative to the person of Christ. Examine the text. Jesus said, "All authority in heaven and on earth has been given to me. Go *therefore*." Authority for "The Great commission" resides within the Incarnation—the revelation of God in Christ.

The Authority of Jesus Establishes the Priority of the Church. Speaking theologically and thinking ultimately, Jesus has authority over the church. Considering the matter practically and experientially, however, raises doubts about the authority of Jesus. Whether or not Jesus' authority is acknowledged and obeyed in a church depends upon the decisions and actions of each specific congregation.

Every church enjoys freedom in its decision-making. However, no church is free to reject the authority of Jesus and remain a church. Such a fellowship can exist as a superior charitable organization, a fine community agency, an attractive social institution, but not as a Christian church. The authority of Jesus establishes the priority of the church.

The Authority of Jesus Provides the Ability of the Church. Christ's authority not only establishes the priority of the church and thus provides the reason for all its work, Christ's authority provides the power by which a church can function as a church. Human strength, abilities, and resources alone cannot sustain the work of the church. Just as the church looks to Jesus' authority in order to know its highest priority, the church depends on Jesus' authority as the resource for its ability.

Recently I encountered an interesting question. "What has happened in the church that cannot be understood in human terms?" Frankly, the inquiry disturbed me. Is anything happening in the church that is not a product of people taking on more tasks, trying harder, and working more? Is the church charting its course in response to institutional principles of success, suggestions for good public relations, or data devised to assure popularity? How much does the church depend upon God?

The Authority of Jesus Shapes the Identity of the Church. All this talk about authority and missions may intimidate both individuals and churches. Whether verbalized or not, people think, "We will never be sufficient for such tasks." Caution. Don't form judgments of this nature too quickly.

Be instructed by an interesting comment in a verse immediately preceding the text of "The Great Commission" (Matthew 28:17) to be specific. The gospel writer observed that when the disciples saw Jesus "they worshiped him, but some doubted." Remember the occasion. The public ministry of Jesus was a matter of record. The time for Jesus' Ascension is at hand. Matthew's comment describes the people to whom Jesus will entrust the divine mission. "Some doubted!" Imagine that.

I am always impressed by the sheer humanity of the people Jesus chose to do his work. Then, and now, an honest look at Jesus' followers identifies strugglers, doubters, and failures in the crowd. But Jesus was not put off by this reality. Weaknesses, mistakes, and even sins were rejected as disqualifications for ministry. The identity of people on mission is shaped by the authority of Jesus.

The Authority of Jesus Demands Activity by the Church. God calls the church to be a people on mission. Not just a people, but a people on mission.

A church does well to sponsor educational studies related to missions, conduct weeks of intercessory prayer for missions, and raise special offerings in support of missions. None of that, however, suffices for a church doing missions. The authority of Jesus demands missionary activity by the church.

Dare to answer truthfully a few probing questions: What mission activity in the present makes our existence as a church an absolute necessity? What one ministry of our congregation most accurately reveals our fidelity to Jesus' authority and thus our identity as the people of God?

Share your faith with a spiritual struggler and your bread with one weakened by hunger. Teach the truths of Jesus' words just as you point out the proper streets to travel to people needing directions. Offer the strength which comes with Christian commitment to those with fatigued souls and make available a cup of God's grace for the guilty and acts of mercy for the lonely. Bear evidence of hope amid despair and extend acts of mercy for the lonely. Bear evidence of hope amid despair and extend comfort in confrontations with sorrow. On and on go the possibilities to be faithful to Jesus' commission about discipling, teaching, baptizing and caring.

Obedience to "The Great Commission" is not an option for people earnestly desiring to live and function as a church. The authority of Jesus shapes the very identity of the church, even its priorities, power, and ministry.

Topic: The Great Commission: Where?
(An Agenda for Pilgrims)

Where? Where does obedience to the words of Jesus send us?

In traditional translations of Matthew 28:19, the first word is "go." For that reason, many people have concluded that doing missions always necessitates going somewhere else. Subsequently, moving to another location to implement Christian ministry has been considered spiritually superior to behaving as a Christian where one lives.

Jesus' words of commissioning actually begin with a participle. Literally, Jesus said, "As you are going . . . ." Think of that. Geography does not determine authenticity in missions. Most important is not where, if anywhere, we are going but what we are doing as we go, even if our going involves no more than a walk around the neighborhood.

Within that powerful participle voiced by the One with all authority in heaven and earth you will find profound spiritual truths related to missions. They comprise an agenda for pilgrims. Note first as a reality . . .

The Shifting of Holy Ground. Biblical writers warned against a too-strictly prescribed concept of holiness in relation to a place. Certain kinds of buildings, art, symbols, and sounds do not necessarily provide conclusive evidence of the spiritual significance of a site. Throughout the scriptures, a holy place is a place where God is met, a spot where God is served—whether a temple or a lion's den, a sanctuary or a jail cell.

As he began to voice "The Great Commission," Jesus once and for all settled this matter of holiness in relation to a place. "As you are going," he said. In other words, all ground is potentially holy ground because God can be worshiped and served anywhere.

"As you are going," Jesus said, share a witness. And do ministry in Christ's name. "Where?" you ask. Everywhere. Literally everywhere—on a business trip to another city, walking with a friend to the meeting of a civic club, sitting in a classroom, shopping in a mall, picking up the children after school, jogging in the park, crossing the country on vacation.

The words of Jesus, "As you are going," also suggest . . .

Life-styles as Witness. With the words "As you are going," Jesus defined the how as well as the where of missions. All of life is a form of witness. A witness for Christ is to be shared as we are going—working, shopping, parenting, playing, budgeting, planning.

A friend from the former Soviet Union told me of a soldier's astonishing inquiries about the Christian faith. When the military man was asked what prodded his interest, he told of a woman laborer whom he had observed working on a state-owned farm. The soldier talked of how he and his comrades tried to reward this woman's hard work by encouraging her to take home more food than the government allowed. Repeatedly she refused to take advantage of their turned backs. She did her job faithfully with no sloughing off, no skimping. The military man reported that when this woman was asked to explain her behavior, she confessed that she was a Christian. That was the reason the soldier said he wanted to know about the Christian faith.

"As *you* are going." More hard questions need answers. What is the witness of your life-style? What does your church's budget reveal about a commitment to missions? While you are going, are you sharing the gospel, helping the hurting, feeding the hungry, comforting the broken-hearted, reclaiming failures? According to Jesus, what we do while we are going to and fro constitutes a powerful form of witness.

Jesus' words "as you are going" also set before us . . .

A Non-Parochial Gospel. Since the inception of the church, people have sought to capture the gospel in one tradition, religion, culture or nation. The New Testament book of Acts provides a stirring account of the vitality of the gospel in remaining free from such captivity.

Still, though, some people continue to measure the depth of Christian commitment in other people by the level of the others' conformity to their traditions, habits, economics, and politics. Syntheses of Christianity and culture and Christianity and nationalism produce missions aimed at reshaping people in a particular societal image rather than sharing with them the world-transcending good news of the gospel.

When William Carey proposed taking the gospel to foreign lands, self-acclaimed theologians instructed him that God would convert the heathen in God's own time. Such reasoning is not dead. Only the words have changed. Listen to conversations in the church: "We must take care of our own first. We do not need to go dabbling in other people's lives. Those folks are just too different from us to appreciate our ministry. We don't have any business trying to take on too many ministries in our church."

John Wesley modeled the spirit of the New Testament when he embraced the world as his parish. Certainly that is the vision commended to us in "The Great Commission." The content of the gospel of Jesus Christ must not be confused with cultural etiquette, national patriotism, or policies established by majority votes. Christ is the content of the gospel. And Christ is for all people.

What a powerful participle! And an urgent demand. "As you are going." Here are our orders for the day, for all days.

Within these words we find the where and the how related to Christian missions. No area of life is off limits as a place in which Christ can be served. No believer is excluded from the mission.

Topic: The Great Commission: What?
(Mandates for Ministry)

What? What do these words from Jesus mean for us?

Every congregation has the option of deciding whether or not to be a church. However, after resolving to be a church, no congregation has the option of deciding what to do. "The Great Commission" clearly defines the church's agenda for action. Jesus outlined the mandates which must govern a church's ministry.

Note the terminology. Mandates! Not options, not possibilities, not alternatives, not referendums. The words of Jesus in Matthew 28:19–20 carry the force of commandments. His directives are non-negotiables among Christian disciples. Here are our orders for mission, mandates for our ministry.

Making Disciples. How do we make disciples? How do we lead people into total allegiance to Jesus? Those questions are best answered by a careful analysis of the actions of Jesus and the methods of ministry extant in the early church.

Love is the first requirement. Discipling with integrity requires loving people unconditionally and comprehensively.

Those whom we would disciple can read us like a grammar-school book. They will not believe statements of our concern for them or listen to us speak of God's love if we do not love them enough to try to do something about the gnawing pains of hunger in their stomachs, the sharp throbs of stress in their chests, the unhealthy conditions of their poverty housing, and the burning desire in the psyches for someone to affirm them without wanting something from them.

Discipling begins with loving—loving in deeds as well as through words. Then, *then*, comes the sharing of the gospel with an invitation to discipleship. Our credibility in speaking about the gospel depends upon the visibility of the gospel in our lives.

Making disciples also means lovingly telling God's story as our story. Please do not cause that act to be more difficult than it needs to be. In order to share a witness you do not have to memorize anything so that you can mechanically repeat a particular program of persuasion and set in motion a prescribed sequence of events involving laws to be endorsed, specific sentences to be repeated, and petitions to be prayed. Offering a witness for Christ means speaking in your own words about the redemptive activity of God in the world and in your life. You need say no more than what you have experienced—"This is what happened to me." But, you dare not say less.

Discipling also involves nurturing spiritual growth. The New Testament contains even more admonitions about growing in Christ than about coming to Christ. Spiritual maturation is just as important as spiritual conversion.

Jesus spoke first about making disciples. Then, he pointed us toward . . .

Baptizing. Please understand right off that in the mind of Jesus baptizing had as much to do with getting right as with getting wet. Throughout the New Testament, comments on baptism focus much more on putting on Christ than going under water. Look at the imagery in Paul's baptismal theology as spelled out in Romans 6:1–11 and Galatians 3:25–28.

According to Paul, being baptized meant deciding to be good, taking on the character of Jesus, refusing to discriminate between people because of their race, sex, or social status, caring for widows and orphans, working for liberation, and building up the church. The best evidence of a baptized believer, in Paul's opinion, is a commitment to fleshing out Christian ethics in that believer's life.

Jesus set us to the tasks of making disciples, baptizing, and . . .

Teaching. Jesus charged his followers to teach his disciples all that he had commanded. A church is not faithfully on mission unless it is integrally and responsibly involved in Christian education. The curriculum is not a matter of insti-

tutional or personal preference. God's people teach the truths of Christ.

The Word of God, the basic substance of Christian education, is born out of relationships between biblical texts and contemporary situations. Knowing what the Bible says is crucial. Equally important, though, is understanding how the message of the Bible impacts individuals' lives.

Bible study demands a consideration of how obedience to the inspired scriptures impacts a response to the needs of citizens in a Third World nation, the justification of grain reserves in one place while people are starving in another place, appropriate counsel for couples bound by law but devoid of love, decisions about professional careers, and economic priorities in family budgets.

Neither individual Christians nor institutional churches have to decide about the importance of outreach, evangelism, and nurture—about discipling. The same is true of baptizing and teaching. Jesus has already established the proper conclusions about those priorities for us. The only decision we must make is whether or not to be Christ's followers, God's people.

Topic: The Great Commission: When?
(The Promise of Presence)

When? When are we to take action implementing "The Great Commission"?

Answering those questions involves little more than looking back to the introductory phrase of Jesus' statement. "As you are going," Jesus said. Now is the time for discipling, baptizing, and teaching. Obedience to Christ is the order of the day, *today.*

People's protests are predictable. "I cannot do that by myself." "I will never be able to sustain obedience to Christ's commands on my own." Precisely. All such comments are accurate. Jesus knew the difficulty of obeying the commission he declared. That is why he said in closing, "I am with you always."

Ponder the implications of Christ's promise of the divine presence. Here is assurance of . . .

Security in Adversity. Jesus offered no guarantees to his disciples. In fact, sometimes he seemed to go out of his way to warn of difficulties.

Jesus viewed adversity as a near certainty in the lives of all who serve him. Disciples of Jesus can count on labels of ridicule—"fanatic," "clown," "goody-goody." Both the wisdom and values of Christ's followers will be questioned. In some cases adversity may even take the form of physical suffering.

Jesus said, "I am with you always." Contained in that promise is the certainty that temporary adversity does not nullify the hope of ultimate victory. Christ's promise of presence is also a guarantee of . . .

Encouragement Amid Complexity. Obedience to "The Great Commission" pummels us headlong into energy-draining complexity. Discipling involves far more than merely showing up somewhere, hurling a gospel word at a group of people, and quickly pressing for decisions. We minister to people and they turn on us in anger. We teach about a God of love and a listener spits out words about a God who sends a killer tornado. We commend fellowship and listen to charges of prejudice within a church.

Complexity can wear us out. We cannot implement "The Great Commission" alone. But we don't have to be alone. Jesus offered astounding encouragement when he said, "I am with you." His strength is sufficient to sustain us even on our most difficult days. Jesus' statement endorses . . .

Ministry for Eternity. In relation to "The Great Commission," answering the question of "when" with "now" probably prods an inquiry of "How long?" Do any time boundaries bracket Jesus' words? How long are we to be about this missionary task? The answer to the latter question is always. Forever.

That realization may strike fear with us. Ministry without a stopping point in sight seems overwhelming. Intimidation and fear might reign were it not for the promise of Christ—"I am with you." Note carefully that the extent of our ministry never reaches beyond the extent of God's care. Though our mission has no point of termination, neither does the promise of God's presence with us.

Beware of being blinded by immediacy. Set the Christian mission in an eternal context. In the lives of people obedient to the divine will, God can work even in unwanted failures, disappointments, and tragedies to accomplish redemptive purposes. That truth, screamed from Golgotha, resounds through the centuries. As long as God is with us, even the worst moments imaginable can be wombs from which hope springs. And God has promised to never leave us. "I am with you always."

David Livingstone pointed to these last words of Jesus in explaining what had sustained him during his mission work in Africa. When Livingstone's wife died, he personally prepared her body for burial, dug the grave, and buried her remains. Then, he read the last verse of Matthew's Gospel and in the presence of the onlooking natives claimed the promise of God's presence.

The One who gives rise to the mission sustains all who take it up with a presence that is sheer power, love, and grace.

Most of us have heard all this before. You probably have preached similar sermons. So, these four messages could be written off as just another series of sermons, a way of fulfilling homiletical demands for an entire month. Wait, though.

The authority behind these words cannot be ignored. In "The Great Commission," we find an indisputable statement of the agenda for the Christian mission. These words define the work incumbent upon all who intend to live as God's people.

The spirit with which these sermons should be preached is captured in the words with which this essay ends. First, from Jesus:

"As you are going make disciples of all nations, baptizing them in the name of the Father and of the Son and of the Holy Spirit, teaching them to observe all that I have commanded you; and lo, I am with you always, to the close of the age."

Then from Livingstone: "Let us get on with the task."

SECTION X.
Children's Sermons and Stories

January 2: The Greatest Gift of All

TEXT: 1 Cor. 13

How many of you have pets? What kind of pets do you have? Sometimes I wonder why people like to have pets— why do you think people like pets? I bet part of the reason is that people like to love and to be loved. Do you think that is true? We can love and hug and talk to our pets, and many of them will love us right back, won't they?

When I was a child about your age I used to make up stories with my older brother. We would pretend we had all kinds of things we wanted, like a big black motorcycle that would go 120 miles per hour in neutral. We gave ourselves about a million billion dollars spending money, and we could turn invisible when we wanted to. Then when we had ourselves all fixed up we would go off on adventures, like maybe' catching turtles, and things like that.

But now I guess I'm about the age the Apostle Paul was when he wrote the first letter to the Corinthians. You are going to be surprised when I tell you that Paul did something a little like what I did when I imagined all the things I would like to have when I was a child. When he was writing that letter he asked himself what would be the greatest gift a person could ever have. He thought about a lot of things—probably not motorcycles— things like being famous, being rich, being a great speaker. I think an angel whispered the answer in his ear. Do you

know what Paul said was the greatest gift of all? Love.

Would you believe that? He said it was the greatest thing in the world. Right now you love your pets and your families and your friends. As you grow up it will be your challenge to love more and more people. And do you know what? You won't run out of love, because God will give it to you. It's a gift.—Stuart G. Collier

January 9: Finding the Way Home

I want to tell you a story. This story really did happen when I was the pastor of another church. One Sunday morning before our worship service was to begin the custodian told me that there was a bird trapped in the sanctuary trying to fly to freedom. The two of us tried everything we could to convince that bird to escape through an open window. But the bird didn't understand what we were saying. It would wing its way to a bright, colorful light that seemed to be the opening that led to safety. Yet, as it flew toward the light, it would time after time go crashing into one of the great stained-glass windows. Can you imagine two grown men running around the sanctuary flapping their arms faster than the bird was moving its wings? We were frantically trying to keep the bird from harming itself and help it find the way home. If I could have become a bird, I could have made the poor little creature understand and lead the way home. I had heard stories like this before, but it was the first time I was in one! I knew why God became a person; it was the only way we could know what God wanted to say to us and to find our way home. That's really the reason we celebrate Christmas. God came in Jesus. Now God can speak to us through what Jesus said and did. "For God so loved the world, he gave his only son . . . ." That's the truest story I know.—Gary D. Stratman

January 16: Love Lights
TEXT: 1 John 4:19
Here is a light which can never shine by itself. That is the bad news. But this little light is not sad because it cannot shine with its own light. It does something other lights can't do. It can shine in total darkness.

We call this a reflector light. A reflector is much like a mirror. It reflects whatever light comes to it. It can be placed on a mailbox beside the road or on a gate across the road so people will not run over the mailbox or into the gate when driving at night. If this place were totally dark right now, someone could shine a light from far away. When that light strikes this reflector lamp, it returns every bit of the light back to the source. It shows light because someone first gave it light.

Love is like a light. The love that we feel in our hearts for God shines forth. But that love did not begin within us. We do not create love. We reflect it. The Bible says that "We love, because he first loved us."

The love which we have for God and for others came first of all from God. So we ought to be like a reflector light which takes that light and bounces it back. That way others can see God's love in us.—C. W. Best

January 23: Living for Something
Dr. Fosdick once told me of a cruise he took along the coast of Maine. One day he stopped at a desolate little island where a tall lighthouse sent out its bright rays over the sea. He sat with the lighthouse keeper, and in their conversation the lighthouse keeper told how he lived alone there, but that once in two weeks a

Coast Guard vessel brought him his necessary supplies. Amazed at the isolation within sight of land, Fosdick said: "Don't you get lonesome and bored out here all by yourself day after day? You seem to have very little in your life."

Then the old weather-beaten man turned to Fosdick—and I shall always thrill to his simple reply: "Not since I saved my first life!"—William Stidger

January 30: I Can Follow Jesus
TEXT: Matt. 4:18–22; 9:9
Peter and his brother, Andrew, were fishermen. Their fishing business was located on a beautiful lake called the Sea of Galilee.

On this particular day, Peter and Andrew were fishing with a big net. Peter and Andrew would wade out into the shallow water of the lake and throw the big, heavy net out into the deeper water. The net had lead weights on it, so it would sink. The fishermen would then pull the net through the water and trap the fish in the net.

During the day, Peter and Andrew were joined by a man who was walking on the seashore. He was no stranger to the fishermen because they had seen him and had talked with him before.

"Follow me," Jesus said to the fishermen, "and I will make you fishers of men." That meant that Jesus would teach Peter and Andrew how to help men, women, boys, and girls.

Being the busy fishermen they were, Peter and Andrew could have said, "Not today, Jesus. We are much too busy."

The Bible says that they left their nets and followed Jesus. They decided that the most important thing in life for them was to learn from Jesus.

Jesus and his new followers walked further on the seashore. Soon they saw three men. James and John were sitting with their father Zebedee in a boat. They were busy mending their fish nets.

Jesus said the same thing to them as he had said to Peter and Andrew. He called to them and asked them to follow him.

Although they were busy fishermen, James and John left their boat and followed Jesus.

Jesus called other men to be his followers. Each man was different from the other. In fact, Jesus called one man who was a tax collector. Most everyone hated the tax collectors because they usually charged more money for taxes than they were supposed to charge. Many of them became rich by doing so.

Matthew was a tax collector. As he sat at his tax collector's table one day, Jesus came by. He looked at Matthew and said to him the same words he had said to Peter, Andrew, James, and John. Matthew left his tax collector's table and went with Jesus.

Before Jesus finished, he had called twelve men to be his followers. Jesus taught them about God so they could tell others about him. They became Jesus' good friends and helpers. — Leon W. Castle

February 6: Not Ordinary, but Special

TEXT: Luke 4:21–32

Good morning, boys and girls. You've all seen an egg before. How many of you had some kind of eggs for breakfast? (Wait for show of hands.) You probably had eggs either scrambled or fried. Do you know that there are dozens of ways to fix eggs? (Let them respond.) There are poached eggs and eggs on a biscuit and egg salad and deviled eggs and omelets. Have you heard of all of those? (Let them respond.) Most of you have. Some of you even like some of those kinds of eggs. Those ways to fix eggs are pretty ordinary. But there are some more ways that you probably haven't heard of. There are creamed eggs and pickled eggs and egg croquettes and egg souffle and egg foo yung and eggs à la king! Do any of you ever eat all those special kinds of eggs? (Let them respond.) I haven't eaten very many of those kinds of eggs. Then there are eggs Benedict, eggnog, custard, crepes, and even pizza eggs. There's even a recipe for a punch called Spitzzerinktum! That's a funny name, isn't it! Did you ever imagine that you could do all those things with an egg? (Let them respond.) My all-time favorite is a recipe where you put cake on the bottom and ice cream on top and then you beat up egg whites with a little sugar and spread it all over the top of the ice cream and cake, pop it in a very hot oven and when you take it out, it's called baked Alaska. It's just delicious! And all those recipes are from an ordinary egg!

Our lesson today is about Jesus in his hometown. He had moved away for a long time. When he came back to visit, the people couldn't believe it was the same Jesus all grown up. They expected him to talk the same and act like the same ordinary person he used to be like this ordinary egg. But Jesus read part of the Bible and explained it to them and they were very surprised. They thought he should say things like they were used to hearing. Instead he told them some very new special things that they weren't ready to hear. They wanted ordinary and he gave them special! So Jesus didn't stay in his hometown. He went to towns where people were tired of ordinary things and were excited when he told them special things about God. Those people were ready to hear the special stories about God's love that Jesus told. — *Children's Sermon Service, Plus*

February 13: God's Love

TEXT: Rom. 5:8

Here is a Valentine Day card complete with a pretty red heart on the cover to symbolize love. Millions of Valentine Day cards like this will be bought and given during this season because people want to express their feelings to those they love. But what is love? Perhaps we should spend a few moments thinking about real love.

When a boy gets a crush on a sweet little girl, we adults joke about it being a case of puppy love. You know why? Because we worry that puppy love leads to a dog's life!

Perhaps you didn't understand that joke, but your parents did. Here is how a ten-year-old explained his feeling of love represented by this red heart:

Love is a funny thing;
It's just like a lizard.
It curls up round in your heart,
And jumps in your gizzard!

That boy's father had his own poem:
Love is like an onion:
We taste it with delight.
But when it's all gone,
We wonder what made us bite!

Now those are funny ways to explain love, but the Bible points us in a better direction. It teaches us that God gave the best example of love. More than just saying, "I love you" or even sending a card about love, God showed us his love by dying for us on a cross. In Romans 5:8 we learn "But God shows his love for us in that while we were yet sinners Christ died for us."

That means God loved us before we ever started loving him. He did not wait for us to become pretty or nice to love us. While we were still sinners, he showed his wonderful love by dying on the cross.

I'm going to draw something on this Valentine Day card which helps explain God's love. Watch now as I draw the sign of a cross. The next time you see a valentine, think about the cross. That's how God proved his love to us.—C. W. Bess

February 20: Setting Things Right

When someone says you have made a mistake, what do they mean by that . . . ? (You did something wrong.) And what do you do when you make a mistake? (You say you are sorry and if you can you try to set things right.)

Now what do you think you should do if you find that someone else has made a mistake? (Wait for possible answers. If there are no right answers, continue.) Suppose you went home after church and found that someone had knocked over all the chairs around your kitchen table, what would you do? (Set them up right so that you could sit on them to eat.) Suppose you saw someone sitting on a curb, holding his head and his head was bleeding; what would you do? (Call for help so that they could set things right for that person.)

Jesus called such a person a Good Samaritan. He told a story about a man who was from Samaria. He found an injured person and he helped him, even though he did not know him.

Whenever we see someone who needs help, we can set things right for that person by offering to help if we can. That is an important lesson for every Christian to remember. Thank you for coming up here today.—Kenneth Mortonson

February 27: The Power of Loving Jesus

A little dog lives at our house. She is a black and white cocker spaniel named Lady. Now, you may think this is strange, but I often think she is a better Christian than I am. She always loves me, no matter what I do or don't do, she never holds grudges, or forgets to wag thank you, or acts as if she is more important than she is—I could go on.

But she does have one problem, which I have spoken to her about many times. She is slightly greedy. I'm not sure she is working on improving, either. When we throw food into the yard for her she tries to eat every bite so that no other animal will get anything. When we throw food to the cat she tries to eat every bite. When we throw crumbs to the birds, she vacuums the ground to get every one. She even eats birdseed that falls from the bird feeder. Sometimes we throw pancakes into the yard, or other food that she really hates; then she won't eat it but will lie in the yard all day guarding it so nothing else can get it.

We joke that we would never need to chain her in the yard; we could just throw out a pancake and she would be a prisoner all day. She reminds me of the way you and I can become prisoners of the things we want too much. If the truth were known, we really are prisoners to many things we don't need. A job may pay so well that we aren't free to move residences when we should. You long for bigger allowances. Adults have dreams that we chase until we realize we have missed a lot of life by spending too much time with butterfly nets. We get "addicted" to things that harm us. Whatever we give our hearts to makes us prisoner and puts chains on us.

You will understand this better as you grow up, but remember that Jesus really does free us from all these things when we love him more than anything else. You will be surprised at how many cares of the world melt away when you love Jesus more than anything or anyone else.—Stuart G. Collier

March 6: Riding a Train

Have any of you ever ridden on a train? . . . It is an interesting experience. When I was a child, people bought a ticket from a person in the station and when they got on the train, they gave the ticket to a conductor. But that is not the case on some trains today. For example, if you were to ride a train into Philadelphia, this is what would happen. At the train station, you would find a machine that would take a $5 bill and give back to you five silver dollars. Then you would find another machine into which you would put a certain number of the coins and out would come a plastic ticket. Then you would use the plastic card to unlock a gate that would let you into the station to get the train. When the train stopped, you would get on. When it stopped again at the place you were going, you would get off and use the plastic ticket to open a gate to get out of the station. You would have no contact with anyone operating the transportation system. There would be no one to check up on you, but if you wanted to ride the train, you would have to follow the rules.

That is a lesson that applies to life also. If you want to get the most out of life, you need to follow the rules. To have a friend, be a friend. Do unto others as you would have them do unto you. Part of growing up is to learn about the rules of life that work; and Jesus is the best teacher in that regard.—Kenneth Mortonson

March 13: Running a Race

Text: Heb. 12:1-2

Object: Ankle weights

What do I have in my hands? Maybe you would like to hold them. They are heavy, aren't they? People use them when they exercise, when they jog or practice basketball. They are called ankle weights, and some of you have seen your parents or older brothers and sisters use

them. But let's imagine for a moment that you are going to run a race. It is very important for you to run this race. You know that you can win it if you run as fast as you can. (I see several of you are getting ready to run right now.) If you wanted to win, would you put these heavy weights on your legs to run the race? No, I don't think you would. I wouldn't either. We would take off all the extra weights that we didn't need so that we could run the best race possible.

In our Bible story today, life is compared to a race. We are to run the race, live our lives with patience and faith. That means we sometimes will go through hard and difficult turns in the race, but if we keep our eyes on Jesus who has run the race before us, he will give us the strength to win. To win is to know and enjoy God forever. Since the prize is ours through Jesus, we do not want to be weighted down with the "ankle weights" of hatred, jealousy, prejudice or cruelty. We are to let any of these weights drop off as we run the race of life with joy and thanksgiving.—Gary D. Stratman

March 20: Slippers

Have any of you ever visited a foreign country? (Let them tell which ones, if any.) Every country has special things that the people do. For example, in Austria, when you enter the home of a family there you will probably see several pairs of objects that look like these in the hallway by the door. Do you know what they are? (Slippers) How many of you have slippers? . . . And where do you keep your slippers? . . . I keep mine in the bedroom, so I would be surprised to see the slippers of the people in Austria out in the hall by the door. The reason the Austrians do this is because they have the practice of taking their shoes off and putting on their slippers as soon as they enter the house. They do this for a very practical reason: It helps to keep the house clean. Any dust or dirt on the shoes is not carried through the whole house.

I like that idea, for it shows that they care about the place where they live. I am not saying that you should do the same thing in your house, but the lesson is important for us all. Be it your own room, or your house or even your church and school; helping to keep it clean is an important job for everyone.

So, the next time you put on your slippers, remember what they do in Austria and remember to do what you can to keep your living space looking nice.—Kenneth Mortonson

March 27: Whose Side Is God On?

There is an old saying, "God is on the side with the biggest battalions." What that means is that God is on the side of the most powerful people. But it isn't true, is it? Many times God is on the side of the weakest, the underdogs, the ones who are up against the toughest odds.

Do you remember the story of Gideon? Who can tell me something about Gideon? God wanted Gideon to get some soldiers together to do something. Gideon called for men to volunteer to be soldiers, and he raised a big army. I'm sure Gideon was proud of himself, but God said, "That's too many." Now Gideon was going to war, and God said to send most of those soldiers home. Why would God possibly have done that?

Most likely, God wanted Gideon and the Israelites to know that God would give the victory, and it was not the big army at all that would win. It is an important story for you to remember, because there are times when you will be trying to do something when the odds are all against you. You need to remember that God will give you power to do good things, to do God's will, and you shouldn't be afraid to try to do big things for God. Jesus said that many things are impossible for us to do, but that with God all things are possible.—Stuart G. Collier

April 3: Symbols of Easter

Look at the congregation. This must be a special day with so many people here. And so it is. This is Easter. Now, you may have noticed that Easter comes on a different date each year. That is because the time of Easter is set by the moon. Once it is spring, Easter is the first Sunday after the full moon. Last week (or whenever) spring started and the full moon was on Wednesday. (Give the correct day for the current year.) Today is the first Sunday after that full moon and so it is Easter.

There are some special symbols in that. When we have a full moon, it is as bright as it can be at night; it is a bright light shining in the darkness. And Jesus is the light of the world. Spring is the time when life returns to our earth, as things start to grow again. And Jesus is our source of true life.

The Easter egg is also a special symbol. Do you know why? What comes out of the egg? The egg is like a tomb, and then it breaks open and a little chick, full of life, comes forth.

We color our eggs in bright colors to remind us of the joy of Easter. Today I have a little treat for you in the form of a chick that reminds us of the new life that comes from the egg. This is indeed a happy day as we remember God's love for us all.—Kenneth Mortonson

April 10: Living in a Special Time
(For use at the time of baptism)

Today we will be doing something very special. We are going to baptize someone. This person will not be baptized again, because we believe each person needs to be baptized only once. So something will happen here in our church today that will never happen again and that makes this a very special day. But you know what? Every day is a very special day for all of us. You will never be in church again on the last Sunday in July (or whatever Sunday it is) at your present age. Hopefully, you will be in church again next year on this Sunday, but by then you will be a year older.

So, the lesson I want you to learn today is very simple, yet very important. EACH DAY IS A SPECIAL DAY IN YOUR LIFE FOR THERE WILL NEVER BE ANOTHER DAY LIKE THIS. And I hope you will look for the special things in each day.

I tried to think of something I might give you to help make this a special day for you. I decided to share with you . . . (Use whatever is appropriate. Balloon,

candy, homemade cookie, etc.)—
Kenneth Mortonson

April 17: Thankfulness

Let's play a game this morning. I will
name something, and you tell me how it
is a gift from God. Cheerios (God gives
us grain, fire to cook with, intelligence to
make the dry cereal). Toothpaste (God
helps us protect our teeth). Clothes
(clothing fibers, mills, colors). Air (plenty
of it, free, necessary). Family (love, companionship).

When you think about all the things
God provides for you, do you feel overwhelmed that all this has been done for
you? We have so much.

Once I worked with a man who was
critical of everything, including the company that had given him the job. He
made others unhappy because he was always complaining about all the things
that were wrong. He didn't make enough
money, he had to come into work during
his free time, his family was lousy, all the
people running for president were
dummies—I didn't like being around this
man because he was so unhappy.

What do you think could have helped
him be happy? One thing I have discovered is that when I am thankful, I am
happy. Sometime try praying and telling
God how thankful you are for as many
things as you can think of, and at the
same time try to feel miserable. Try to
frown while you are praying, "Dear
Lord, thank you for the air that is so free
and good, thank you for the breakfast I
had this morning, for these pretty clothes
I'm fortunate enough to have, for my
family who surrounds my life with love,
for all the little things like toothpaste that
makes my life easier." Keep naming
things for about five or ten minutes, then
see if you don't feel good. Thankfulness
is beautiful in a person, and it makes
beautiful persons. In all things, you really
can be a thankful person.—Stuart G.
Collier

April 24: Beware of Imitations

This morning I want to show you
something that I received in the mail (or
wherever you might have obtained a cu-

bic zirconia simulated diamond). What
does it look like? (A diamond) But it is
not a diamond and I would be tricked by
someone if they sold it to me as a diamond, for diamonds are very expensive,
and this cost me nothing. (If you cannot
find a zirconia stone omit this part.)
What is this? (A rose) But it is not a real
rose, for it is made out of cloth and wire.
It reminds me of a rose, but I cannot say
that it is a rose for only God can create a
real flower. Imitations help us to remember what something is like, but we must
be careful not to think that the imitation
is the real thing. Here is a picture of Jesus but that is not Jesus. It is used to remind us of him.

One of our goals in the church is to
find the real life that God wants us to
live. That requires hard work and a lot of
learning. There are no shortcuts to the
real thing. Anything less than the real life
God desires for us is an imitation.

So, remember that one of the reasons
why you come to church is to strive to
find the real life God wants you to have.
Your Sunday school teachers and everyone else who is with you each Sunday has
that goal in mind for you and you can
help them help you by listening to them
and doing what they teach you.—
Kenneth Mortonson

May 1: Parents Dedication Sunday
(Give each child a small plant or a few
seeds.)

Congratulations! You each have in
your hands the start of a wonderful
plant. I hope you take this seriously, because your attitude and your effort will
have a great deal to do with how your
plant will grow. Do any of you have experience in raising plants? Do you know
the kinds of things you need to do to get
started? Some of you are a little nervous
right now. You've never raised a plant.
You're not sure you will be able to keep
it alive. Most plants take some work on
your part. You have to care for them.
You have to make sure that you give
them what they need to live and grow—
things like good soil, water, and sun. You
do all those things that you know to do,
and then you do something else. You

wait. Even with all your good work, you can't really make that little seed sprout. It just happens on its own. It's part of the wonderful mystery of nature. We help it along, but that is all we do.

Today we are having a dedication service for the new parents in our church. They have in their hands little babies that will someday be wonderful children, and then teenagers, and then adults. Some of them have raised children before. Some of them are brand new. They're a little nervous. They all know that there are certain things they must do for their babies if they are to grow and be healthy. They need to give the babies food and clothes, and keep them warm. They need to talk to the babies and love and teach them. They need to introduce their children to God and help them in their faith. These parents will do everything they know to do, and then they will wait. Just like you with your plant, they know that no matter how much they help, they can't make their children become everything God wants them to be. That's one of the reasons they are here today. They realize that to be good parents, they must understand that their children are really God's children. They know that God will have to help them a great deal over the years. They are telling us that they want him to be part of their new family.

Over the next few weeks, as you're taking care of your little plants, remember these new families in our church. Maybe you could even say a prayer for them. Why don't we do that right now?—Carol Younger

May 8: You Belong

This morning I have a special picture I want to show you. Last summer, all my children were home at one time and all their children were with us too. We had our picture taken and here you can see my wife and my children and my grandchildren. (Use whatever family picture you have.)

Now, suppose something nice happens to one of the people in the picture, what effect do you think it would have on the other people in our family? (They would be happy.) And suppose something unpleasant happened to one of the people in this picture, what effect do you think that would have upon the other people in the family? (They would be sad.)

You see, we sometimes forget that we belong to a family and what happens to us affects the other people in that family. Also, since we are part of a group, we should be concerned about the things that happen in that group. For example, if you like to live in a nice clean house, and you see a piece of paper on the floor, that you did not drop, what should you do? (If you want a clean house, and you are part of that family, you should pick it up.) Today I have for you the material to make a picture frame, with the help of your parents. In that frame, I would like you to put a picture of your family so that it will remind you that you are a part of a special group of people. We want you to do your part to make your home a happy place to live. (Two pieces of light cardboard can be used to make a frame. Decide on the size of the photo to be used and cut out a square for the picture in one piece, slightly smaller than the intended photo. The second piece of cardboard will serve as the back.)—Kenneth Mortonson

May 15: You and I in Heaven

Object: An apple seed

Not long ago an adult Sunday school class got into a big argument. Can you believe adults do that? You can? Well, they did. They were trying to understand what resurrected people look like. Could one of you help them out?

They were trying to understand what kind of body they would have in heaven. That is a mystery to us, and God leaves it a mystery for now. Do you know what a mystery is? The dictionary says a mystery is a religious truth which we can know only as God reveals it to us, but which we don't fully understand. Our bodies in heaven are a mystery to us, but we do know some things. We will still be exactly who we are. I will be me and you will be you. We will keep our personalities— maybe a little improved!

But what about our bodies? Well, Paul says we will have spiritual bodies. The

Sunday school class wanted to know all about spiritual bodies—do you know anyone who just can't leave a mystery alone, and just has to know all about it? As if we understood this body well enough to be worrying about one we haven't even seen! All Paul could tell us was that we would be changed—flesh and bones would become spiritual. Our bodies would still be our bodies, but very different in substance.

We don't understand that, but we know it can happen, because things change like that all the time. Look at this seed. If you knew nothing about seeds, hadn't even heard about them, then I showed you this seed and said that it can change from this little thing into something about fifty feet high, with delicious fruit on it every year, you would think I was bananas, even though you didn't know where bananas came from. But you know it is true. And so we know that other things we don't really understand—mysteries, like our heavenly bodies—can be true. That is a wonderful mystery, isn't it?—Stuart G. Collier

May 22: Sending and Receiving

This morning I want to show you something which we use every Sunday and that is very important to what we do. This is called a wireless mike. When a person speaks into the little mike here, the sound is sent out this wire and in a back room of the church there is a receiver that sends the sound through an amplifier and then out to the speakers so that people can hear what is said. I'd like you to try it. Tell me your name . . . (Let each child use the mike.)

Now, what makes this work is a little battery inside. Without the power of the battery, nothing would happen. But the battery itself needs to be recharged or replaced so that it can work. If it simply gives of its power, it will soon be no good.

One of the reasons why we say that people should come to church regularly is to receive new power for living. It is like getting our spiritual battery recharged or replaced so that we can take what we receive here and go out and share it with others.

Here we remember that God loves us, and, therefore, we can go out and love others. Here we learn about forgiveness so that we can go out and forgive others. Here we learn about all the good things God has done for us and so we can go out and do good things for others. We receive so that we can give, like this wireless mike. Its purpose is to be a sender for the good of others. We hope you will learn to be like that too.—Kenneth Mortonson

May 29: Three Ways God Loves Us

TEXT: 2 Cor. 13:11–14

Object: a letter that says "I love you"

Boys and girls, have you told anybody how much you love them lately? (Let them answer.) You know, since we belong to Jesus, and because Jesus wants us to show God's love to everybody we can, we need to find a lot of ways to do it. What are some ways we can say "I love you" to somebody? (Talk about it.) Well, you're right. One way is to just open your mouth and say the words: "I love you." Sometimes we forget to do that even when we really do love the person we are talking to. We should say it to our mom or dad, or to our brother or sister, or maybe the people who live next door whom we want to be our friend.

Are there any other ways to say "I love you"? (Let them think.) How about this way? (Reach out and hug somebody.) Now, I didn't say a word, but I said something by what I did. You can say "I love you" by doing that, can't you? Yes, you really can.

Here's still another way to do it. (Show them the letter that has big letters inside.) You see, this letter is from me to you and it is only three words long. Can you read it? (Let them read it to you.) That's a way to say "I love you" when you aren't there to say it in words or to give a hug.

Now we know three different ways to say "I love you." And I want to tell you today that sometimes God uses three different ways to talk to us. Sometimes we talk about God as our Father in heaven. We read about his words and promises in the Bible. That's like getting a letter, just like this one, straight from heaven. Other times God talks to us in person. In the Bible we read a lot of stories about Jesus, God's son. When Jesus was living in our world he didn't have to send a letter telling people about God's love. He just did it by opening his mouth and saying it. We can hear Jesus doing that for us when we read the stories about Jesus in the Bible. And then sometimes God uses his Spirit to show his love. His Spirit gets into people like you and me and we help other people. That's like giving them a hug from God. God shows his love to people in three ways.—*Children's Sermon Services, Plus*

June 5: "When Do I Croak, Doc?"

Jimmy Chubb, as we minister friends call him, one of our great rural preachers, told me the story of a young boy who was called upon to give his small brother a blood transfusion because of a serious accident in which he had a dangerous loss of blood.

The older brother was called to the hospital suddenly and was hurriedly prepared for the transfusion. His father had driven the boy to the hospital but, as is the way of even thoughtful parents, doctors, and nurses in an emergency, had not explained what a transfusion meant.

The boy donned the hospital garb, and lay down beside his brother. The needle was inserted in the left arm, and he watched his pallid brother lying unconscious beside him. He looked up at the doctor who was making the transfusion, and said, as seriously as a young boy could say anything: "When do I croak, Doc?"

He knew nothing about transfusions, and as no one had explained to him that it was a harmless experience to a healthy body, he had actually felt during all the hurried trip to the hospital and the transfusion itself that they were asking him to give his life for his younger brother. That one question, "When do I croak, Doc?", revealed to the doctor, nurses, and his parents that he had never raised a question about it. A dramatic moment!— William L. Stidger

June 12: Snap Your Fingers

What do you usually do when you meet someone? You say hello or shake hands. That is the way we greet people.

But there is a country far away from here called the Sudan. They snap their fingers, like this.

In that country, our greeting at the beginning of worship would sound like this. (Snap . . . get congregation to snap back.)

As these people translated the Bible into their own language, they had to find a way of expressing what the Bible says in ways the people could understand. The word "reconciliation" means being united with God again as a friend, so they translated their ideas as: "Meet, snapping fingers together again."

This is a very important idea for us to remember. God wants to be our friend. He wants to snap fingers with us. And more than that, God wants to be like a parent to us, loving us and helping us—if we will let him.

Let's snap our fingers once more, and remember God wants to be our friend.— Kenneth Mortonson

June 19: Our Church Home

(Show them a key.) Do you know what this is? . . . What is a key used for? . . . Why do people lock up a car or a house or anything else that is important to them? . . . (To protect it, that is, to take care of what they have.) The key is a good symbol of a very important lesson we all need to remember. It is part of what we call stewardship. We are to take care of what we have and this is especially important in our church, for what we have here, we have received from others.

They took care of it and passed it on to us and we are to do the same. Now, how do you think you boys and girls can help do this? If you come into the church with dirty shoes, would that be taking care of the church? If you made crayon marks on the tables in the Sunday school rooms, would that be taking care of the church? . . . If you took a pencil and scribbled in the worship book, would that be taking care of the church? . . .

So, remember, you are part of the church family and we want you to do all you can to take care of our church home just as we expect your parents and these other adults to help take care of this church for you and for others who will come after us all.—Kenneth Mortonson

June 26: Understanding

All of you have been to a doctor before, haven't you? A doctor delivered almost all of us. We might say a little prayer of thanksgiving sometime for the doctors and nurses who delivered us without pulling our toes off. Do each of you have all your toes? You should have ten.

Doctors can do wonderful things for us because they know so much about the human body and how it gets sick and well. I bet when you go to your doctor you expect her to fix you right up. But they can't always make us well, can they? What are some reasons why doctors can't always do that?

Whether we know it or not, doctors hurt inside when they can't do anything for sick people. One doctor wrote a story about that. She wrote a lot about death and dying. A child she was caring for was dying and she couldn't prevent it. She said something to the child that I hope I never forget. She sat on the child's bed and simply listened as the little girl talked, then she took the child's hand and said, "I can't keep you from dying. But I can try to understand." She later wrote that next to helping a person to live, understanding was the greatest gift she could give.

I remember that when I am with people who are in trouble, or sad, or discouraged, or angry. I try to understand. It is difficult to do, but it is a very great gift to give. You will know what I mean if you think of how you have felt when no one understood you. Maybe your parents or your friends didn't understand what you were feeling inside when you did something, or what you needed from them but weren't able to put into words.

There are many people around you everyday like that. If you try to understand, you will be a friend to them and not someone else who could have helped but just didn't understand. You will be like the Good Samaritan who took time out to check on the wounded man by the road. Come to think of it, understanding someone *is* a way to help someone live!— Stuart G. Collier

July 3: Put Back in Shape

TEXT: Luke 4:16–19

Object: A small rubber ball imprinted with a map of the world

Who can tell me what a "habit" is? That's right, it is something you do over and over again until it becomes a part of you. Can you give me some examples of habits? Did you notice that a lot of the habits we thought of this morning were bad habits? They are the kinds of things people want to quit doing. Now, can you think of some good habits? One good habit that I know you have is regularly being part of worship and our "Time for Children." In our Bible story this morning, we learn that Jesus was in the habit of going to a place of worship on the Sabbath. This habit helps us remember who we are and whose we are.

What do I have in my hand? That's right, it is a ball. (Open your hand.) What kind of ball? That's right, it looks like our world. In my hand, it got all squeezed out of shape, didn't it? Now look at it. It reminds me of the way our lives and the lives of others in the world get pressed and squeezed out of shape by things that happen to us during the week. We need regular times of worship to hear God's words to us . . . to pray together . . . and to let our lives be reshaped again by God's love. Now look at the "world." I want you to remember all week, "God's got the whole world in his hand." (Lift the re-shaped ball up in the palm of your hand.) Thank you for coming, it's a good habit.—Gary D. Stratman

July 10: Growing in a Different Way

TEXT: Col. 1:1–14

Object: A balloon

Good morning, boys and girls. How many of you like balloons? (Wait for show of hands.) What do you like to do with balloons? (Let them respond.) People put them up for decorations for parties or birthdays. There's a game played

...d onto everyone's ankle ... pop everyone's balloon ...ing your own get popped. It's ... game. You can put regular air in ...alloons or you can have them filled with helium, a special gas that keeps the balloon up in the air. How many of you like to fill balloons with water and throw them at each other? (Wait for show of hands.) You usually get very wet when you get hit with a water balloon! What happens to it? (Let them respond.) It breaks! As you begin to blow air into a balloon, what happens to it? (Let them respond.) It begins to grow, doesn't it! As you keep on blowing air into it, what happens? (Let them respond.) It gets bigger and bigger. What would happen if you kept on blowing and blowing and blowing? (Let them respond.) It would pop! The balloon can only hold so much air. If you fill it too full, it will explode.

Our lesson today talks about growing in the knowledge of God. When we learn more about God, we are growing in our knowledge of God. When I think about growing in knowledge, I think of putting all the things we learn about God into a balloon. The balloon gets bigger and bigger. (Blow up the balloon.) Every time we hear a Bible story at home, the balloon gets bigger. (Blow some more.) If we keep putting all those stories into the balloon, what will happen to it? (Let them respond.) That's right, the balloon will pop. We need to keep telling others the stories about God. (Let a little air out of the balloon.) When we tell others about God, our balloon won't be so full that it will pop. (Let a little more air out.) That's why we come to church—to hear the stories of God. (Blow up balloon a little.) Just like our bodies grow over the summer, our minds grow with the knowledge of God.—*Children's Sermon Service, Plus*

July 17: Reading Faces

One of the most important things you can do is to learn to read faces. Let me show you what I mean. When you see a face like this, what does it mean? (Look happy) And this? (Look sad) And this? (Look tired) The face of another person helps you to know how they are feeling

and then you can respond to that message. If someone is sad and you are concerned about that person, you can try to make them feel better. Maybe your father and mother look tired at the end of a day and when you see their face, you may decide it is not the time to ask them to come and play with you. Maybe you can even do something to help them. Reading faces helps us to consider how other people feel and that is an important part of being a Christian.

Today I would like to share a smiling face sticker with you. You can use it to share happiness with someone else. I suggest you take this home and write a letter or draw a picture for your grandparent or another relative and send it to them with this sticker, to make them happy. And remember to watch the other people in your home and your friends. Try to read their faces and respond to what you see. Thank you for coming up here today. (Give them a big smile.)—Kenneth Mortonson

July 24: Feeling Loved and Special

TEXT: Eph. 1:3–14

Object: pictures of homeless people and refugees

Good morning, boys and girls. I brought some pictures of some people for you to see this morning. What can you tell me about these pictures? (Show them the pictures and let them respond. Your conversation may include some of the following.) They look poor. They're homeless. They live on the street. They're dirty. They look unhappy or sad. What do you think these people need? (Let them respond.) They need the same thing all of you need every day. They need food. They need clothes to wear. They need shelter or a house to live in. But we've left out one of the most important things that all people need. Does anyone know what it is? (Let them respond.) They need love. Love is what makes each one of us feel like we're special. When we feel special and loved, then we can love other people. Where do we get love? (Let them respond.) We get love from other people. Sometimes it's from a mom or dad or grandma or grandpa and sometimes it can be from a friend.

What happens to a baby who is born and for some reason the mommy and daddy can't take care of the baby? (Let them respond.) Sometimes the baby is adopted by another mommy and daddy. When the baby gets older the mommy and daddy tell the baby how special that baby was and that the mommy and daddy picked that baby to be theirs.

Our verse today says that God picks us specially to love. It says God adopts us. Now if we already have parents, we have more than enough love to share with others. How can we help these people in the pictures feel like they are loved? (Let them respond.) We collect cans of food sometimes at church. We save used clothing and give it to poor people. We collect offerings at church and some of that money goes to help needy people. Some of your families have adopted a child who is poor in another country and send money each month to that child. When people are sad or don't have enough to eat or a place to live, we try to make them feel special by helping them to see that someone cares. God adopts us and tells us we're special and loved and God wants us to help others feel loved and special, too. When we care, we show them that God cares. — *Children's Sermon Service, Plus*

July 31: A Special Treasure

TEXT: Matt. 13:44–52

Object: Some shiny coins

Good morning, boys and girls. Today I have some shiny coins to put in a special place. Where would you put these coins? (Let them respond.) You might put them in a piggy bank. Would you save them to see how many you could get? (Let them respond.) Some of you would save them and some of you would want to spend them right away. Where else would you put them? (Let them respond.) You could put them in a savings account at the bank. How many of you have a savings account at the bank? (Wait for show of hands.) If you put coins in the bank, you might have a special bank book that tells you how large your treasure is. Is this many coins a treasure? (Let them re-

spond.) That's right, a treasure is a lot of money that's put away. Or it could be a lot of jewels, like diamonds and gold and rubies that are worth a lot of money. So are this many coins a treasure? (Let them respond.) Probably not this many. We'd need a lot more for most people to think it's a treasure. If you went to the place where they make all these coins, then you would really see a treasure. We call someone who takes care of the money for a group of people a treasurer. This person has to collect money, put it in the bank, and pay bills with it. We have a treasurer at this church. When we collect the offering on Sunday, the treasurer writes the amount collected down in a book. That's another thing we could do with these coins; we could put them in the offering. (Drop them in the offering plate.) Now are they a treasure? (Let them respond.) Yes, I think even one of these coins is a treasure when we give it to help do God's work.

But, boys and girls, none of these treasures is what our Gospel lesson is about today. Matthew tells us that Jesus said that heaven is like a special treasure. That means that heaven is very special, so special that we might think of heaven like a very expensive treasure. We would do anything to have this treasure. Do we have to have lots of money to go to heaven? (Let them respond.) No, even millions of coins won't get us to heaven. All we have to do is love God, and then that special treasure will be ours. — *Children's Sermon Service, Plus*

August 7: Is God Funny?

May I ask you a question about God? You just say whatever comes to mind. If I asked the adults they would give me some long, boring answers about immutability, about God not being put together like people — someone would say it is a stupid question, then we'd get into a big fight about it. So I'm asking you, because God said that we don't know as much as we think, and we ought to be more like you children. So tell me, "Is God funny?"

When I was younger I had this idea that God stomped around muttering about this lousy world, dressed in pure black, with a hat pulled down low over his eyes and his mouth turned down like this all the time. When I prayed I would always be very serious and talk in a low tone of voice, as if my last friend in the world had just died. Then I started wondering where in the world I got such a lousy idea of God. I started looking around me. I noticed really neat people—they could be so happy and beautiful and good. I started looking at the rest of what God created. I wondered if God didn't want to tell me, "Lighten up a little bit! And quit depressing me always with all the troubles you have. Let me hear about some of the good stuff."

Now I understand that there are tigers and snakes around, there is a lot of pain in life, and the world is a mess, but what about the rest? Think of some animals that you would have laughed your head off if you had made them up. Have you looked at a hippopotamus lately? How about a fat, waddling porcupine? Would you have put a mask on the raccoon? Who ever heard of birds like the hummingbird flying backwards? Where did God find a neck long enough to reach the giraffe's head? Come to think of it, why do we even think it all is funny? Where did our laugh come from?—Stuart G. Collier

August 14: Some Heavenly Blessings

If one should give me a dish of sand, and tell me that there were particles of iron in it, I might look for them with my eyes and search for them with my clumsy fingers and never detect them; but let me take a magnet and sweep it through that dish of sand, and that magnet would draw those tiny particles of iron to it through the power of its attraction! The unthankful heart, like my finger in the sand, discovers no mercies; but let the thankful heart sweep through the day, and, as the magnet finds the iron, so it will find in every hour some heavenly blessings, only the iron in God's hand is gold!—Henry Ward Beecher

August 21: He Gives More Than We Need

TEXT: John 6:1–15

Object: Any flower or vegetable plant that has gone to seed

Boys and girls, there are a lot of growing things in the world that did not get planted by you or me. How did they get planted? (Talk it over.) You're right. A plant makes new seeds so that it can make sure there will be more of them later on. Here is an example. (Show them your plant.) Look how many new seeds there are on this plant. If all of these seeds would grow, there would be almost too many of this plant, wouldn't there! And remember, every other plant that's growing right now does the same thing. Now you and I know that there are many of these seeds that will never get planted and will never grow. But some of them will. God has given the plant the power to scatter all these seeds so that some will be sure to grow. In other words, God gives the plant far more seeds than it needs, doesn't he!

Remember how many seeds you found the last time you ate watermelon? It's the same thing. God could make new watermelons from all those seeds. There are far more than we need. God does it because he wants to be generous.

In the Bible story for today God did the same thing. He took only five loaves of bread and he fed five thousand people. Imagine what could have happened if there had been a hundred loaves! God is generous. He gives us more than we need.

In the Bible story, we learn that Jesus didn't want any of the leftover bread thrown away. Is that surprising to us? Why not throw it away if God can make so much so easily? (Talk it over.) Right. God is generous, but he doesn't want us to waste what we have. He wants us to use it wisely, and to share it with people who are still hungry. Do you know anybody who is hungry because they don't have enough food? Maybe we could find a way to help them get enough.—*Children's Sermon Service, Plus*

August 28: Jesus Has a "Buddy System"

TEXT: Mark 6:7–13

Object: A pair of swimming trunks

Boys and girls, do you like to go swimming? (Wait for answers.) How many of you have been swimming this summer? When it gets hot out it's great to go in the water, isn't it?

When you look at this pair of swimming trunks it almost makes you want to walk right out of church and head for the nearest lake or swimming pool, doesn't it! Just imagine with me for a minute that you're at a lake on a warm summer afternoon. There's a wonderful sandy beach and, out where the water gets deep, they have a rope floating to tell you not to go any farther because it isn't safe. There's also a lifeguard, and the lifeguard tells you you can't go in the water unless you use the "buddy system." What's the "buddy system"? (Let them tell you.)

Right. The buddy system is a way of giving every swimmer a partner. From time to time the lifeguard blows his or her whistle and everybody finds their buddy, takes their hand and holds it up. It shows that nobody is getting lost or is in trouble in the water. It's really a good idea, isn't it.

Jesus gave you and me a "buddy system" too. He started it when he first sent out his disciples to tell the good news to people about God. He didn't send them out one at a time. He sent them out in pairs, two at a time, in a sort of "buddy system." That way, if one of them got discouraged—or ran into a lot of complaints or trouble with the people they would talk to, the buddy would encourage them so they wouldn't give up and quit. When we try to do what God asks us to do—things like helping people, showing God's love, telling other people how wonderful Jesus is, we should use the buddy system too. We should find a friend to talk to sometimes. Our buddy can help us to be a faithful follower of Jesus when we get discouraged. And we can help our buddy too.—*Children's Sermon Service, Plus*

September 4: What Is Work?

Tomorrow is a special day in our country. Do you know what it is called? . . . (Labor Day) Do you know why we have a Labor Day? . . . It is to honor all the people who work.

On your feet are shoes that I assume your parents bought for you at the store. Now the people in the store did not make those shoes; someone else did. That was their work; just as the people in the store work to help you buy things. Working is a very important part of our life together. It is what you do to accomplish something that needs to be done.

One of the difficult lessons of life that boys and girls have trouble learning is that there is joy in working to accomplish something. Coloring a picture with crayons is work, but it is also fun when you feel the pleasure of having a finished picture nicely colored. Learning to ride a bike is hard work; but once it is accomplished, it helps you travel fast and far. Cleaning up your room is hard work, but when it is done, it looks nice and usually you are better able to find your things when you need them.

So, don't be afraid of work. It is an important part of the true life. Thank you for coming up here so that we could share this time together.—Kenneth Mortonson

September 11: Seven Hundred Things That Will Not Work

I knew intimately Francis Jahl, who for many years was Thomas Edison's assistant in experimental work on the phonograph and the incandescent electric light.

While they were working on the filaments for the incandescent light Jahl became discouraged and indifferent. They had tried to make filaments out of thread, wood, wire—everything imaginable. But all of them proved futile because they would burn out.

"Well, I guess you better give up trying to work out an incandescent light, Mr. Edison," young Francis Jahl said after hundreds of failures.

"No, I am not ready to stop and give it up just yet."

"We'll never make it."

"I think we will," replied Edison.

"Where has all this experimental work gotten us?" asked the younger, less mature worker.

"At least now we know over seven hundred things that will *not* work," said Edison, with a smile. Young Francis saw the point, so they continued their experiments through another seven hundred things that would not work, until, at long last, they found the thing that *would* work. And we now have the perfected incandescent lamp as a result of that patience.

"At least we now know over seven hundred things that will *not* work." — William L. Stidger

September 18: The Little Things Do Count

TEXT: Luke 16:1–13

Object: A large children's toy such as a wagon or tricycle

It's good to see you today, boys and girls. I hope you have a really good Sunday. How many of you would like to be able to drive a car someday? (Ask for a show of hands and get their comments.) I see most of you would like to do that and some of you even know what kind of car you would like to be able to drive.

Today I want to tell you a way that will almost guarantee that you will be able to drive someday. The secret is this: take good care of your wagon. (Wait for their response.) Some of you are snickering. Why? You are wondering what taking good care of your wagon has to do with driving a car. But think about it this way: when you start driving, someone is going to have to loan you a car. Whose do you think it will be? (Let them answer.) More than likely one of your parents' car. Your mom or dad will have to hand you the keys. They will know a lot about you by then. They will remember how you took care of your wagon and other toys. If you are really reckless with them, you may have a hard time getting the family car.

In our Bible lesson today, Jesus taught us that we learn how to do the important things in life by the way we learn to do the little things. If you learn how to share your toys, you are much more likely to be able to help a friend when you get older. If you attend Sunday school every Sunday, you are much more likely to continue going to church every Sunday when you get old enough to decide for yourself what you will do. If you learn how to help around the house and do a good job mowing the lawn, you are likely to get a very good job when you get old enough to hold one. It is also true that if you learn to treat your brothers and sisters with love and respect, you will be much more likely to do the same for your husband or wife someday.

You see, boys and girls, your childhood days are very important. I hope you really enjoy your days now and learn many good things which you can use later. You will have a much happier life and God will be there to guide you. Have a good week learning to do what you do well. — *Children's Sermon Service, Plus*

September 25: All We Need

TEXT: Rom. 13:1–10

Object: A mirror

Good morning, boys and girls. I have a picture here, of somebody I think is one of the neatest, most special people I know. Do you know who it might be? (Let them offer some answers.) No, I'm not thinking of Jesus this morning, although he is certainly somebody special too. I want you to take a look at the picture right now. I'm going to pass it around. And when you look at this person, then you tell me if you agree with me that this person is really somebody pretty special.

(Pass around the mirror. Let each one look in. Be prepared for some chuckles. When they are all finished and you have the mirror back, have them share their reactions with you.)

Well, I really think everybody here is one of the most special people I know. And do you know why I think so? It's because God thinks so too. God made every one of us special. He loves us a lot. He loves us so much he gave us his son Jesus, and allowed Jesus to die on the cross for us.

If God loves us that much, what do you think God wants us to think about ourselves? (Discuss it.) Right. God wants us to love ourselves because we already know that God does. And sometimes we forget to do that, don't we. We think we aren't very important. Or we think we don't matter. Or we think everybody is worth more than we are. Or we think we don't need to take care of our bodies. But God loves us and wants us to think of ourselves as really special. He wants us to love ourselves as much as God loves us. Now there is one more thing we can do. We can also love the other people around us. And how much does God love those people? (Let them answer.) Right. God loves everybody else as much as God loves us. That means when we love ourselves, we know how to love other people. We can do it in exactly the same way. We don't need a lot of help figuring out how to love other people. All we need is to look in the mirror and remember how wonderful we are in God's eyes. And that will tell us how wonderful other people are in God's eyes too. And then when we try to be good to other people, we can use that special rule called "love." God uses love to help us. God wants us to use the same thing with other people. Love always tries to find out what will help somebody the most. — *Children's Sermon Service, Plus*

October 2: Out of the Ordinary

TEXT: Matt. 26:26–29

Main Truth: Sometimes what you see isn't the most important thing but what becomes of it.

Object: A rather large piece of wood, like a two-by-four about two or three feet long. Any large stick or piece of wood will do.

If I asked you, "What do I have in my hand?" you'd probably answer, "A stick or a piece of wood." And you'd be right. What if I told you, though, that this is a baseball bat or a chair leg or one thousand toothpicks? You might scratch your head and wonder if I'm crazy.

But in the hands of a skilled woodworker, with time and loving care, this piece of wood could become just about anything!

The same thing is true with us. People look at you or you look at yourself and see just a little boy or a little girl. But when I look at you, I see tomorrow's doctors, lawyers, teachers, mothers, fathers, and presidents. You can become anything you want to be and are willing to work hard enough to become.

I thought about that in relation to this piece of wood and ourselves this week in preparing for the Lord's Supper.

In the first Lord's Supper, told in Matthew 26:26–29, Jesus took ordinary bread and wine and made it symbolize, or stand for, something wonderful. The bread stood for his body. The fruit of the vine stood for his blood. Together they remind us that Jesus died on the cross for our sins, our salvation. His body and blood, symbolized in the bread and juice of the Lord's Supper, mean our sins are forgiven through Jesus.

Sometimes what you see is not the most important thing, but what becomes of it. Think about that this morning as we remember Jesus in the Lord's Supper.

Note: You could also use this idea with baptism, changing the analogy from bread and wine to ordinary water. — Roy E. DeBrand

October 9: Stability

(For use at the start of a new church school year.)

This morning, I would like each one of you to stand up. Now, please stand on one foot, for as long as you can, while you listen to me. As soon as you lose your balance and have to touch the floor with the other foot, sit down.

Some people find that they can stand on one foot for a long time. Such people usually have to really concentrate on what they are doing to maintain their balance. It is much easier for us to stand or move about when we use both feet. Our feet give us a special stability in life when we use them properly.

Today marks the beginning of a new church school year. All of you are expected to go to public school, or some other type of school that will teach you the things you need to learn to be an educated person. But in the church family, we believe that to be a complete person, you also need to learn the things that are offered to you in the church school program. That is like the second foot that gives stability to your life.

So, I hope you will remember how important it is to come to Sunday school and that you will pay attention so that you can learn those important things that you need for life. And I hope all the people here this morning will remember that Christian education is important to life, no matter what your age. I hope all of them will take advantage of the opportunities offered to them to keep on learning.

Thank you for coming up here this morning.—Kenneth Mortonson

October 16: Mind and Body

TEXT: Luke 17:11–19

Object: A variety of first aid items—bandages, gauze and tape, first aid cream, and a relaxation tape

Good morning, boys and girls. I brought a first aid kit this morning so we could talk about healing. Let's see what I have in here. (Show the items as you talk about them.) Here's a bandage. There are lots of different sizes of bandages. There are large ones for hurt knees. There are little round ones for tiny cuts. There are bandages to go on knuckles so you can bend them. Here's some first aid cream. What do we use it for? (Let them respond.) We put it on before we put the bandage on. It puts special healing medicine right into the cut. Here is some gauze and some tape. What do we use this for? (Let them respond.) This is to make what we call a dressing. It's a larger bandage for a larger cut or sore. Sometimes a dressing is put over where a person has had surgery. It protects the surgery place so it can heal just like a tiny bandage protects a tiny cut. Here's a cassette tape. Does anyone have any idea why this tape might be in our first aid kit? (Let them respond.) This tape is called a relaxation tape. It has special music and words to help you relax. Some people call it an imagining tape. You close your eyes and while you listen a voice helps your mind imagine things like a walk in the forest or a pretty waterfall or the ocean waves. Now you're still

probably wondering what a tape has to do with bandages. It's because doctors are finding out that music and imagining help our bodies heal. People with a disease called cancer imagine that the cancer is being destroyed and doctors find out what it is. Our bodies and our minds work together to heal us.

Our lesson today is about ten people who had a skin disease. They had large sores all over them and people were afraid of them. Jesus made them well again. Nine of them went away, but one of them turned around to thank Jesus. Jesus told him that his faith made him well. Jesus knew that the man believed he was going to get well. Do you think the man was happy not to have sores all over him any more? (Let them respond.) I think he was very happy. Jesus said we have the power to believe that we can be well and healthy. We need to remember that God made us with that power to let our minds and our bodies work together.—*Children's Sermon Service, Plus*

October 23: Something's in the Way

TEXT: Mark 10:17–27 (28–30)

Object: A television program guide

Boys and girls, do you like to watch television? (Let them answer.) Which is better, watching television or doing things your parents want you to do? (Let them answer.) Actually that's not a very fair question, is it? Doing both things can be good. But it depends on which is more important at the time, doesn't it?

Let's suppose you have a television set in your bedroom. Now I don't really recommend this because it might encourage you to spend too much time watching television when you could be doing other more important things. But some boys and girls have TV sets in their rooms.

Now let's suppose your mother tells you she wants you to be sure to clean up your room, make your bed, take out the trash, and do the dishes. She says you can do these things any time you want to, just as long as they get done in the next three or four days. You agree to do them, but every time you go into your room you see this copy of the *TV Guide*. And when you look inside, you remember there's a really neat program you wanted to watch. So you start watching TV while your mother waits for you to start doing your assignments. What will happen? (Discuss it.)

Right. Your mother is going to get very angry very quickly. Now, if you have good discipline, you'll do the work. But maybe what you should do is take the TV out of your room because it's in the way of doing more important things. God says we should try to find out what things in our life—like too much money, or a TV set in our room, or anything that might become too important to us—what things are stopping us from doing God's work. When we find out, we need to get them out of the way. Then we can do what God really wants from us. Is there anything in your life like that just now?— *Children's Sermon Service, Plus*

October 30: God's Time

Does anyone know what this is? (Show them an actual sundial, or a picture of one.) It is used to tell the time by the position of the sun in the sky and the shadow that is cast on the plate. But if the sun is not shining, it will not work. What time is it on this clock? (Use a big clock drawing, or an actual clock.) Is it night time or day time? Can you tell that by looking at the clock? (No, you need to think about time in the setting of the day.) And as time passes, we call each twenty-four hours a day and the days make up the weeks and the weeks become months and then years. And all of time is a gift from God.

Now, the true meaning of a gift is found in the way the gift is used. If someone gives you a book and you do not read it or look at the pictures in it, then that gift has little meaning for you. If someone gives you a toy and you never play with that toy, it has no value for you. So, if we believe that time is a gift from God, then the way we use time will show how we feel about that gift. Remember, we all have the same amount of time each day. A wise person, therefore, is one who learns to make good use of time.— Kenneth Mortonson

November 6: Taking Care of God's World

You are not too young to know something important that churches all over the world are doing these days. Churches are learning that they have forgotten something. They have forgotten words from the story of the Garden of Eden in Genesis. In that story God says that people are to enjoy all the wonderful delights of creation, but they are to take care of the earth. They are to take care of it in God's name, for God's sake.

We really have forgotten all about God saying that to us long ago. Because we forgot, we have all participated in harming the earth. The air is unhealthy, the streams are full of poison, precious and beautiful things of nature have been destroyed forever—those are just a few of the problems we have with the environment in which we live. And, remember, it is not just people's environment, but it belongs to all the plants and animals too. We share God's world with the rest of God's creatures.

Just recently many nations of the world met in Brazil to talk about what to do. Leaders from governments everywhere are trying to cooperate to stop the harmful things we've all been doing. The churches are also trying to understand what we should do. What do you think we could do?—Stuart G. Collier

November 13: The Meaning of Stewardship

This morning I want to use a paper towel to remind you of something very important. I want each one of you to have one of these. (Give each child a section of paper towel.)

Now, what could you do with this piece of a paper towel? (Wash windows, clean up a mess, help to keep your lap clean when you eat, shine your shoes, dry your hands after they have been washed, etc.)

There are a lot of uses for a paper towel and most of them are to help us take care of things or of ourself. The paper towel helps us to do what we call stewardship. Stewardship means taking care of what you have and making good use of it. It means using what you have for the good of others as well as for your own good.

Today, your parents and the other adults here will be asked to think about the stewardship of their money. That means they need to think about how they will use their money and how much they will give to our church to help support our church family. It is a big decision for them to make. It is also very important to our church family.

Now, I want you to take this piece of paper towel home and try to be a good steward with it. See what good thing you can do with it there. Then remember to take good care of all that you have, for that is the meaning of stewardship.

Thank you for coming up today.—Kenneth Mortonson

November 20: Look to the Bible

May I ask you a question? What should you do when your family gets lost on the highway as you are trying to get somewhere in your car? You could stop and ask for directions, couldn't you? How many of you would do that? Or you could do what a friend of mine does—just drive faster and faster! Do you know anyone who does that? Or you could just say, "Well, let's see where this road will come out. I think it is going in the right direction." Have you ever heard that one?

Now, imagine that living your life is like going somewhere on a highway. You don't know what is coming next, do you? You don't really know what the future holds for you, or where the highway you are on goes. Can you get some answers about how to live your life? Where would you get answers about how to live? Television? A counselor? Friends? Families?

Where is the best place? The Bible. It is the best place, because God, who knows all about life and about us, will guide us when we look to the Bible for answers. But will you remember this about the Bible? The Bible doesn't have easy answers to all our questions. We have to live with questions, too. For example, Job wanted to know why bad things happen to good people, and he didn't get an answer. God is mysterious, and we can't know every-

thing about God. We can't know everything about life, or death, or heaven. If we think the Bible tells us everything, one day we will be disappointed, and we may just quit reading it completely.

But the Bible tells us more than enough to help us live wonderfully joyful lives. Without the Bible we are simply on a road that we don't know much about, and our lives can get into a lot of trouble that we could have avoided if we looked to the Bible.—Stuart G. Collier

November 27: Love Needed

Most of you were in Sunday school this morning, weren't you? If you missed it, please come next Sunday because we are doing something important. Do you know what that is? We are learning about God!

I knew a young lady who didn't think Sunday school was for her. She would wake up Sunday mornings and ask herself, "Do I want to go to Sunday school today?" Then she would think about all the things she could do instead—like sleep a little longer, watch some TV, eat two breakfasts, things like that. Every Sunday she had to make the decision again, "Am I going to Sunday school today?" And guess what! Just about every Sunday she decided, "No, I think I'll sleep a little longer, watch some TV, and eat two breakfasts."

One day a friend invited her to Sunday school, and she went, and she loved it, mostly because everybody was happy to see her there, and she loved being with those people. She knew those people loved her. Before long, when she asked herself that question on Sunday mornings—what was the question she asked herself?—she would say, "No, I can sleep late, watch some TV, and eat two breakfasts on Saturday. On Sundays I'm going to Sunday school."

Before long, she quit asking herself that question every Sunday morning, because it was all settled. She knew she was going to be with her Christian friends in Sunday school. Now she is a Sunday school teacher. It all really started when she discovered that people loved her in Sunday school, and wanted her to be with them. That is something each of you can do for God—you can love people. It's a funny thing, but when people know you care about them, they somehow feel the love of God for them. Love comes from God right through you to them. Wham! When they feel the love of God, they begin to love God back. Isn't it wonderful to know that your love is so important? Remember that God and a lot of people need your love.—Stuart G. Collier

December 4: Bigger and Brighter

TEXT: Rom. 15:4–13

Object: An Advent wreath

Good morning, boys and girls. We are in the Advent season now. Advent is a time to get ready, isn't it! What are we getting ready for? (Let them answer.) Yes, we're waiting for Christmas to come. Christmas is a fun time to get ready for. There are special things that happen. Special people come to visit. And maybe you will go on a trip to visit some people. People give gifts of love to each other. We have special decorations and special programs and worship services at church. In fact, one of the decorations we use at Christmas is something we first use in Advent. Here it is. (Have them look at the Advent wreath with you.)

The Advent wreath is a special way to look forward, isn't it? Every week we light another candle. Today we have two candles burning. Next week we will have three, then on the fourth Sunday we will have four. After that, Christmas comes! So our hope burns brighter and brighter every week, doesn't it! The more flames we have burning on the wreath, the bigger and brighter our excitement gets.

That's something like the way God works inside our hearts. God puts a fire burning inside you and me. The fire is God's love and we can share it with other people. As we grow older, and get to know Jesus better and to love him more and more, our love for him grows bigger and brighter. It's like lighting more and more candles on the Advent wreath.

Sometimes when we talk to people who are very old they will tell us that they have had a long and happy life and they are hoping God will let them die soon

and go to live with him. Their hope is burning even brighter than ours is. They know that God will take them to be with him and they know it will be soon. If they know and love God, they will have a big and bright hope that God will let it happen soon. That's the way God will build trust and hope inside of you and me. It's like lighting still one more candle on the wreath each week, and seeing more and brighter light than before.—*Children's Sermon Service, Plus*

December 11: Watch the Clock!

TEXT: 2 Pet. 3:8–14

Object: Photo illustration of a clock

Good morning, boys and girls. How many of you know how to tell time? (Let them answer.) Telling time is something we need to learn to do. Sometimes our parents teach us how to do it at home. Some of us learn how to tell time in the classroom when we go to school.

Here is a clock. (Show them the picture.) Can you tell me what time the clock says? (Let some who know how to tell time tell you.) Very good. That's the correct time, according to the clock in this picture.

Sometimes when we say to someone, "What time is it?" they will say "Three o'clock" or "a quarter past two" or "ten-thirty." But other times they may say "Time to get going" or "Time for lunch." For answers like those you don't really need a clock, do you! Or, somebody might say, "It's about time something got done around here!" Or, if you come late to supper or to get into the car to come to church, somebody who has been waiting might just say, "Well, it's about time!" Usually we don't feel very good when they say it then, because they are impatient and have been waiting for us to hurry up and come.

God is interested in time, just as we are. In fact, God has told us that we only have a certain amount of time. After that it will be all gone and it will be too late to do any more of the things we want to do. We wonder how much time God will give us. Nobody knows except God. We need to remember that time is a special gift to us from God. When we look at a clock, like the one in this picture, we could say, "Well, the hands on the clock just keep going round and round so time never really runs out." But we need to be careful not to think like that, because time does run out. And sometimes the clock will even stop. Then there is no more time.

God has a lot of time, but we don't. The Bible says "for God, one day and a thousand years are the same thing." But for you and me, the clock is running down. God wants us to use our time carefully. Some day we will get surprised. The clock will stop and we will run out of time to do good things for God. In one way, that will be wonderful, because then we can go to live with God. But before that happens, we have a lot of work to do, don't we. Watch the clock!—*Children's Sermon Service, Plus*

December 18: What Do You Want from Christmas?

I have a very important question to ask of you this morning. What do you want from Christmas? (Wait for any answers.) Remember, I asked what do you want *from* Christmas, not what do you want *for* Christmas. There is a big difference. What we want from Christmas are the good things we can experience during this season and on Christmas Day. Let me tell you what I want from Christmas. I want Christmas to bring peace and happiness and love to all these people. I want Christmas to help us all know how beautiful life can be and I want Christmas to be a time when I can share my love of God and life with others. I guess what I want from Christmas is to be able to share.

Now, I'd like you to experience this sharing in Christmas and so today I am going to give you a piece of plain paper that has been folded into a card. You can draw on it and color it or paste a Christmas picture on it; and inside you can write your own message to someone. If you cannot write yet, I am sure your mother or father will help you.

Thank you for sharing this time with me.—Kenneth Mortonson

December 25: My Favorite Things

Each of us has his or her own special "favorite things." One of my favorite movies is "The Sound of Music." Julie Andrews sings about her favorite things. She lists such things as cream-colored ponies, sleighbells and snowflakes.

Some of my favorite things are covered bridges, Christmas ornaments, grist mills, choo-choo trains, churches, and good books. (You may have object lessons such as pictures or models of your favorite things.)

Ask the children, "What are some of your favorite things?" (Give them time to respond.)

Ask the children, "What do you think are some of God's favorite things?"

Did you know that God gave us his most favorite thing? A man named John tells us, "For God so loved the world that he gave his only Son, that whoever believes in him should not perish but have eternal life" (John 3:17, RSV).

Of everything and everyone special to me, Jesus Christ tops them all as my favorite. He is my closest and best friend. He even makes all my other favorite things even better. I hope Jesus is as special to you as he is to me.—Ron R. Blankenship

SECTION XI.
A Little Treasury of Sermon Illustrations

LEGALISM. There is no tyranny more intolerable than a conscience unrestrained by love. Like an ill-loaded gun, it recoils at the breech and kills at the muzzle. A conscience unsubdued by love torments the owner, and bruises those upon whom he lets it loose.—Henry Ward Beecher

CHURCH. Bruce Larsen tells of hearing about a girl in his congregation who had left town, due to being pregnant, to go live with her brother. He asked if he could go see her, but was told he was the last person she wanted to know what happened. Larsen says: "That's what's wrong with the church in our time. It's the place you go when you put on your best clothes; you sit in Sunday school, you worship, you have a potluck dinner together—*but you don't bring your life!* You leave behind all your pain, your brokenness, your hopes, even your joys."—C. Neill Strait, in *Leadership*

STRUGGLING WITH GOD. At the beginning of Swiss history stands William Tell, the great warrior against the tyrants. At the beginning of the history of Israel stands Jacob, the great fighter against God who because of his character received the name Israel. Therefore, Israel saw itself as a nation that from the time of its ancestor had continually fought *against* God, not for God. If you want to find God's people, the church, you will find them engaged in a struggle with God from the very beginning. Complete

resignation to the will of God, imperturbable and unruffled calm, was practiced much more effectively by the Greek and Roman Stoics than by the people of the Bible. In the Bible, people remonstrate and complain; they suffer every injustice and abysmal need of this world. Rebellious, remonstrating prophets fling it all into the face of God, for they do not like what is going on and do not find it easy to resign themselves to the will of God.— Eduard Schweizer

GOALS. Vance Havner asked a preacher, "How are you getting along?" "We are living in idolatry—just sitting around admiring our new church. We have arrived; we have it made—no more worlds to conquer. What ought to be a *milestone* has become a *millstone*. We have run out of goals."—C. Neil Strait

NEW LIFE. "From my confinement here I want to send you, over the walls of my exile, these words of joy that come from my heart. I am 29 years old, and I was condemned to life imprisonment for murder back in 1977. At that time I did not know that Jesus really existed. But today, after years of grief and anguish, I am starting to live my life anew.

"What happened was that while I was depressed and miserable, my heart just about breaking, a friend gave me a small book. It was the Gospel of Luke.

"As I read through the Gospel, it was as if every word touched my heart profoundly. At the end I knelt down in my cell and, in tears, I confessed my sin to Jesus.

"For the first time in my life I felt his presence. I know I was born anew and I want to help others to find this wonderful peace that I now have in Christ. The Gospel has given me a zest for life." — *American Bible Society Record*

GOOD PEOPLE? You know yourselves that there are some kinds of good people whom you would walk blocks to avoid meeting. There are the conventionally good who, through a long lifetime of having observed little rules of respectability, immoderately admire themselves in consequence, like the Pharisee in Jesus' parable: "I fast twice in the week; I give tithes of all that I get." There are the negatively good whose goodness consists in having kept the lid clamped tightly down on their insurgent badness so that they are repressed and dried up and sour. How dreadful they are! There are the censoriously good whose morality is all for export, who in endless interferences with other people's business try to do us good. There are the narrowly good, who make an infinite to-do about infinitesimal matters of behavior which do not matter much and who never get their eyes on the great ethical issues of their day, on economic justice and international peace. — Harry Emerson Fosdick

POISON IN THE ENVIRONMENT. When Clare Booth Luce was appointed U.S. Ambassador to Italy, she established residence in a beautiful 17th-century villa. Soon her health began to deteriorate. She lost weight. She had little energy. Her doctors discovered that she was suffering from arsenic poisoning; but the source of the deadly substance remained a mystery until, finally, they traced it to the ceiling of her bedroom. Some beautiful rose designs, ornately done in bas relief, had been painted with a paint that contained arsenic lead. A fine dust fell from those roses. Completely unaware of it, Mrs. Luce was slowly being poisoned as she lay in her bed. — James E. Carter

PERSPECTIVE. Sometimes when we feel dejected about our time we need to look to another time to get a perspective. College students in our time are derided by some for being activists and later as being incipient yuppies. In Harvard's long history we need to remember that Harvard tried to stifle antislavery agitation. In fact, in 1848 the rising Whig politician Charles Summer, himself a Harvard graduate, was to criticize slavery in a speech to the student body. Henry Wadsworth Longfellow records that "the shouts and hisses and the vulgar interruptions grated on my ears" and the poet finally left the hall. — David W. Richardson

HOPE FOR FAMILY. Many who are distressed by what is happening — or not happening — in families and the rootlessness of our time might just be given hope by looking at history. Harvard University Press has published a book, *Greek Religion*, by Walter Burkert in which Burkert stresses that it was the coming of the very large and amorphous cities, in which local roots and family connections were lost, that Christianity triumphed: "It was in the megalopolis of the ancient world that Christianity would most easily find a foothold." What happened once could surely happen again. — David W. Richardson, citing *The New York Review of Books*

TROUBLES. Troubles are often the tools by which God fashions us for better things. Far up the mountain side lies a block of granite, and says to itself, "How happy am I in my serenity — above the winds, above the trees, almost above the flight of the birds! Here I rest, age after age, and nothing disturbs me."

Yet what is it? It is only a bare block of granite, jutting out of the cliff, and its happiness is the happiness of death.

By and by comes the miner, and with strong and repeated strokes he drills a hole in its top, and the rock says, "What does this mean?" Then the black powder is poured in, and with a blast that makes the mountain echo, the block is blown asunder, and goes crashing down into the valley. "Ah!" it exclaims as it falls, "why this rending?" Then come saws to cut and fashion it; and humbled now, and willing to be nothing, it is borne away from the mountain and conveyed to the city. Now it is chiseled and polished, until, at length, finished in beauty, by block and tackle it is raised, with mighty hoistings, high in the air, to be the top-stone on some monument of the country's glory.

So God Almighty casts a man down when he wants to chisel him, and the chiseling is always to make him something finer and better than he was before. — Henry Ward Beecher

ENTHUSIASM.   Ralph Waldo Emerson in a lecture stated, "Every great and commanding moment in the annals of the world is the triumph of some enthusiasm." In every person's and every church's life there come moments when we need enthusiasm. At such times it helps to know how wrong some unenthusiastic people have been. Charles H. Duell, the director of the U.S. Patent Office, in 1899 declared, "Everything that can be invented has been invented." Grover Cleveland in 1905 said, "Sensible and responsible women do not want to vote." Robert Milliken, winner of the Nobel Prize in physics, in 1923 said, "There is no likelihood man can ever tap the power of the atom." Lord Kelvin, president of the Royal Society, said in the 1890s, "Heavier than air flying machines are impossible." The great baseball player Tris Speaker in 1921 said, "Ruth made a big mistake when he gave up pitching." And Harry M. Warner, the Warner of Warner Bros. Pictures, about 1927 stated that people did not want to hear actors talk. While some supposedly intelligent people were saying one thing, others were smart enough to be enthusiastic. — David W. Richardson, citing *Forbes*

FIRST THINGS FIRST.   A man bought one of Whistler's paintings and asked that great artist to assist him in finding the right place for it in his home. The artist agreed to help and walked patiently from place to place while the man held the picture up in various locations. No place seemed exactly right. Finally, Whistler said: "You are going about this all wrong. What you need to do is move all the furniture out, hang the picture where you want it, and then arrange all the furniture in relationship to the picture."

INDEPENDENCE IN QUESTION.   In a Peanuts comic strip, Lucy is saying, "It's my life." Later, she adds: "It's my life and I'll do whatever I want with it. I'm my own person. It's my life and I'm the one who has to live it." In the last frame she grins and adds, "WITH A LITTLE HELP." — C. Neil Strait

ATTITUDE.   The story is told by Dr. Norman Vincent Peale about walking by a tattoo parlor along one of Hong Kong's narrow streets. In the shop window there was a display of decorations that could be imprinted on one's skin — flags, patriotic slogans, anchors, daggers, skulls, crossbones, and mermaids.

There was one, however, which caught Dr. Peale's eye with the somber phrase: "Born to Lose." He was curious and went into the shop; he found the proprietor spoke a little English. He asked if people really did have that message permanently imprinted on themselves. Yes, was the answer. The last customer who wanted it had it emblazoned across his chest. "Why on earth would anyone want to be branded with a gloomy slogan like that?" Dr. Peale asked.

The old Chinese man shrugged his shoulders and said, "Before tattoo on chest, tattoo already on mind." — Charles DeHaven in *The Clergy Journal*

THE MASTER'S TOUCH.   Mendelssohn once visited a cathedral in Europe that housed an almost priceless organ. He sat quietly and listened as the organist practiced. When the organist finished playing, Mendelssohn asked permission to play the instrument. The organist replied that strangers were not allowed to play the organ. Mendelssohn persisted in his request, and the organist was finally persuaded that no harm would be done. The cathedral was filled with magnificent sounds as Mendelssohn played. With tears in his eyes the organist lightly touched Mendelssohn on the shoulder and asked his name. "Mendelssohn," was the reply. The organist, of course, was overcome with embarrassment and hung his head as he said, "To think I nearly forbade Mendelssohn to play on my organ!"—Mary Frances Bailey

CHURCH-SUPPORT GROUP. Robert Schuller explains that the root system of most trees is as wide and deep as the leaf line is wide and high. That is not true, however, of the redwood, which has roots that spread out in all directions but not very deep.

That creates a problem for a redwood standing alone, for it can easily be blown over because the lack of deep roots gives it no stability.

But when several redwoods grow together, their root structures intertwine with each other and help support the whole group. Though weak as separate trees, they become strong as a group.

The church brings us together as individual Christians and provides the strength of love and support from one another.—C. Neil Strait

CHURCH—BEST TIMES. Terry Muck, editor of *Leadership*, describing the best times the churches have had with which he was affiliated, says: "The best times have come when we all focused our conversations on our passion for Jesus Christ and the consequences that passion has for our present church and the church we want to be in the future."—C. Neil Strait

GOALS. A 96-year-old lady died, and her family found a note on her desk. The note contained her goals for the next eight years!—C. Neil Strait

PSYCHOTHERAPY IN THE BEAUTY PARLOR. This unlikely institution may be the new frontier of psychotherapy, unwittingly demonstrating that beauty is not "only skin deep." Women, spending hours with their operators, pour out stories of trouble with the children, the struggle of money management, thoughtless husbands, and the complexities of a modern woman's life. The intimate details of the most personal aspects of husband-wife relations are enough to make the hair dryer blow a fuse!

And all of this takes place because of the listening ear of a beauty operator!

Sometimes with a limited formal education, but with wide experience of life and senses not too easily shocked, she is well remunerated for her work. Her rate of pay is justified by her possession of unwitting psychotherapeutic skills plus the fact that she need have no professional scruples about accepting a tip. Madam's feeling of well-being as she leaves the salon may in no small measure be related to the operator's capacity to listen.—John W. Drakeford

SUFFERING WITH. To suffer with another person does not mean to drown oneself in the other's suffering; that would be as foolish as jumping in the pool to save a sinking swimmer only to drown oneself. More to the point, I doubt that it is even possible to enter fully into another person's pain, for suffering is a profoundly solitary experience. To suffer with another person means to be there in whatever way possible, to share the circumstances of the other's life as much as one can—not to add to the world's pool of suffering, but to gain intimate understanding of what the other requires.

What we usually learn, once we are there, is that there is no "fix" for the person who suffers, only the slow and painful process of walking through the suffering to whatever lies on the other side. Once there, we learn that being there is the best we can do, being there not as cure but as companion to the person who suffers on his or her slow journey. There is no arm's-length "solution" for suffering, and people who offer such only add to the pain. But there is comfort and even healing in the presence of people who know how to be with others, how to be fully there.—Parker J. Palmer

ON BEING RECEPTIVE.   I have put down on paper many times (articles and a book) my deep obligation to William Carlos Williams, my affectionate memory of him. I simply state it again here, as I conclude twenty-five years of work. "Catch an eyeful, catch an earful, and don't drop what you've caught," he'd tell me as he pushed himself from building to building, that doctor's black bag in his hand, and the feverish brain working at full speed, waiting for the evening to set it down, scratch in those lines of poetry, those astonishing doctor stories, or in a novel, perhaps, which also drew upon a doctor's working experiences. Those of us who rather obviously lack his talents can at least be glad for his sanction, his encouragement, his example.—Robert Coles

TRUE LOVE.   It is love in old age, no longer blind, that is true love. For love's highest intensity doesn't necessarily mean its highest quality. Glamour and jealousy are gone; and the ardent caress, no longer needed, is valueless compared to the reassuring touch of a trembling hand. Passersby commonly see little beauty in the embrace of young lovers on a park bench, but the understanding smile of an old wife to her husband is one of the loveliest things in the world.—Booth Tarkington

AS GOD SENDS THE RAIN.   Perhaps a person owns a small business. Should she refuse to hire people who are not "born-again" Christians? Or should she actively promote religion on the job? Perhaps one man fires anyone who does anything contrary to his moral ideas. Do you think this man's policy is right? Another man gives preference to Christians when he is hiring. He does not "harass" his employees or try to interfere in their private lives. He treats them fairly, pays them well, and runs his business in a way that glorifies God. Which of these two men is more likely to be a good witness to the Lord?—Carlton Myers

THE ULTIMATE IDOL.   The gift of the gospel is, in great part, a gift of courage to see the world for what it is—a world ruled by powers and forces that derive their strength from our natural human fear of destruction and our natural need for self-preservation at any cost. Governments have gained such power over our lives because they offer us security in exchange for truth and freedom. Luther calls security the ultimate idol. We have demonstrated, over and over again, that we will exchange anything for a taste of security.—William H. Willimon

BIBLE.   A writer in *The New Yorker* tells of an unnamed person working in Madrid over a very boring 1909 chronicle. However at the very end of the book he discovered this jewel: When some primitive people were first exposed to paper, they called it "the skin of God." What a wonderful image for us to think of the Bible as "the skin of God."—David W. Richardson

RESOURCES FOR THE JOURNEY.   One New Year's Day, in the Tournament of Roses parade, a beautiful float suddenly sputtered and quit. It was out of gas. The whole parade was held up until someone could get a can of gas.

The amusing thing was this float represented an oil company. With its vast oil resources, its truck was out of gas.—C. Neil Strait

CHRISTIAN LIVING.   A true Christian is a sign of contradiction—a living symbol of the Cross. He or she is a person who believes the unbelievable, bears the unbearable, forgives the unforgivable, loves the unlovable, is perfectly happy not to be perfect, is willing to give up his or her will, becomes weak to be strong . . . and finds love by giving it away.—Joseph Roy in *Leadership*

LESSONS OF THE YEARS.   Take a sharp-cut young saint, just crystallized, as many-pointed and as clear as a diamond, and how good he is! How decided for the right, and how abhorrent of wrong! He abhors evil rather than loves good. He has not yet attained to the meekness and gentleness of Christ. But years will teach him that love is more just than justice; that compassion will cure more sins than condemnation; and that summer will do more, with silent warmth, to redeem the earth from barrenness, than winter can, with all the majesty of storms and the irresistible power of her icy hand.—Henry Ward Beecher

DEVOTIONS. Paul Cho, in his book *More than Numbers*, tells of stopping by a building project near his home in Seoul. As he observed the deep hole the men were digging, he inquired why there was such a deep hole. One of the men smiled back and said, "They are going deep because they plan to build high."—C. Neil Strait

THE SUPER-WORLD. Pascal long ago remarked that the branch can never grasp the meaning of the whole tree. Modern biology has shown that each living creature is locked within its specific environment and is unable to break out of it. For all that humans may occupy an exceptional position, for all that they may be unusually receptive to the world, and that the world itself may be their environment—still, who can say that beyond this world a super-world does not exist? Just as the animal can scarcely reach out of its environment to understand the superior world of humans, so perhaps we can scarcely ever grasp the super-world, though we can reach out toward it in religion—or perhaps encounter it in revelation. A domestic animal does not understand the purposes for which we employ it. How then could humans know what "final" purpose their life has, what "super-meaning" the universe has.

We will, then, visualize the relationship of the human world to a super-world as analogous to the relationship between the animal's "environment" and ours. Schleich has most cogently and beautifully expressed this relationship where he says: "God sat at the organ of possibilities and improvised the world. Poor creatures that we are, we men can only hear the vox humana. If that is so beautiful, how

glorious the Whole must be."—Viktor Frankl

PRAYER. Leonardo da Vinci, the great painter, was accustomed to long pauses as he painted. When someone inquired about these long pauses, he replied: "When I pause the longest, I make the best strokes."—C. Neil Strait

THE WORTH OF PRAYER. Clemenceau was violently atheistic. But one day he sought conference with Marshal Foch and was told the old warrior was at prayer. "Well, don't disturb him, then," the tiger snarled, "let him keep at it. The thing seems to work for him."—Frederick B. Speakman

THE NEED OF GRACE. Give up trying to live on your own moral fat. If true goodness were dependent wholly on your will, would you not have been good a long time ago? Most of us are like men locked in airtight compartments, breathing in the same air we breathe out; we are suffocating, because we are trying to live on our own exhalation. Such is the fallacy of Humanism; flat tires cannot fix themselves; no analysis of a rotted acorn can make an oak. As your eyes need light to see, as your ears cannot hear without waves of sound, and your lungs cannot breathe without air, so neither can you be all we could be, unless you receive the grace of God.—Fulton J. Sheen

THE LIMITS OF FREEDOM. When I was a youth I dreamed of being twenty-one years old and therefore free. I wanted to be free of parental control and I fought that control in both legal and illegal ways. I wanted to be free of having to do homework, and my rebellion against it cost me the loss of a respectable academic record. I resented financial control, and my rebellions kept me broke. The lesson I had to learn was that there is never a freedom that does not have to respect some limitation.—Reuel L. Howe

THE USE OF A PREACHER. Reading the Bible is like listening to a symphony. The music is made up of a blending of individual notes and instruments. It cannot be reduced to a single note or instrument. Meaning in the Bible is much the same. It results from the harmonious communion of author, text, reader, and world. When they all blend together, the beauty of meaning is present. A symphony needs a conductor, and a community needs a preacher to proclaim the living voice of the Scriptures.—Bernard Brandon Scott

WHEN LIFE GOES CRAZY.   Over the entrance of the campus library at a university, the following sign appeared some time ago: "Due to reorganization the basement will be on the second floor, one half of the second floor will be on the first floor, but one half will remain on the second. We suggest you ask for help."

Unfortunately, life is often like that. The pieces just do not fit together. The best thing to do is to ask for help.—C. Neil Strait

COOPERATION.   A man wandered aimlessly in an Alaskan blizzard, preparing himself for an inevitable death. Most parts of his body were numb with cold. So he decided to give up without resistance. But just before he slumped over into a snowbank, he heard a faint whimper. At his feet lay a small puppy that faced the same predicament as he. Forgetting his own misery, he picked up the dog and vigorously rubbed his fur. The dog revived and the man also felt warmer. By helping the dog he was able to last through the night.—Jon Johnston

TAMING THE TRUTH.   There is a story in *Sinbad the Sailor* of a ship which sailed so near to the magnetic mountain that all the nails which held its parts together were drawn out by the magnetism of the mountain and the ship sank. It is possible for a church to come into such close proximity to a magnetic mountain whose pull consists not in iron but in silver and gold, that the principles which hold it together as a church of Christ are drawn out. A church which forgets or does not take seriously the uncompromising ideal and teaching of Jesus must be content with a watered-down adaptation of Jesus.—Halford E. Luccock

THE OLD-TIME RELIGION.   The old-time religion was the religion of Moses—a religion of social revolution. Perhaps "revolution" is a strong word. So be it. The religion of Moses was a strong thing. It was a blazing conviction which thundered at the established order in Egypt, on behalf of the depressed, defrauded, exploited people, the command, "Let my people go!" The familiar hymn of praise to the old-time religion has one line which declares, "It was good enough for Moses." That is an unmitigated slander. After his vision of God in the desert Moses was not content with any worn conventionalities. He had learned that the will of God meant the release of the toilers, those in bondage. The social gospel is not any new thing. It is one of the oldest things in the Bible. It was one of the first results of the vision of God which came to Moses. And any religion which does not have that social vision and throbbing sympathy for human beings at its very center cannot have any claim to being an old-time religion. It is a pale, bloodless modern substitute.—Halford E. Luccock

COMMITMENT.   There's a difference between interest and commitment. When you're interested in doing something, you do it only when it's convenient. When you're committed to something, you accept no excuses, only results.—Kenneth Blanchard

REVIVAL.   Sometimes your medicine bottle has on it, "SHAKE WELL BEFORE USING." That is what God has to do with some of his people. He has to shake them well before they are ever usable. Paul wrote to Timothy, "Stir up the gift of God, which is in thee."—Vance Havner

THE REALITY OF EVIL.   And there were religious voices—or were they pseudoreligious ones? Indeed they had been heard already for some time, saying: "There is no evil! Look for the positive value which is to be found within everyone and everything. Do not countenance negative thoughts or feelings, they are wrong. Everything is beautiful. We are not fettered by the past, nor by sin, nor by diseases, nor by wrong social orders. There is no darkness; just believe in the light." It was a powerful message; and it seemed to work. Many people became much happier.

But—cities were raided, thousands of women and children were maimed. "Everything is beautiful, there is no darkness." Millions of soldiers were killed in action, nations reduced nations to starvation. "We are not fettered by sin." Are we not? Is there no evil in our world? Should we not do something about it?

Religion without a thorough study of sin, religion without awareness of conscious and unconscious, individual and collective darkness, evil and deviation, is not religion but blind idolatry. Let us be aware, as honestly and objectively as we can, of our dangers and negativities. Let us bring to consciousness this terrible "unconscious of the past," let us face the task as depth psychology reveals it. Let us acknowledge our individual and collective debts. And, knowing that there is no other possibility, let us look for the really religious way out.—Fritz Kunkel

SURRENDER.   One of the paradoxes of the Christian faith is that freedom from self comes only with surrender of the self. When self is surrendered to God, the Holy Spirit frees it to realize its highest potential. George Matheson wrote: Make me a captive, Lord, and then I shall be free; force me to render up my sword, and I shall conqueror be.—Kenneth Cain Kinghorn

TIME TO CELEBRATE.   I met a young clergyman who was twenty-five and looked sixty-five. His face was set. He could repeat the New Testament impeccably, but there was no joy in his life. I remember after we prayed together, we got up from our knees and I taught him how to do a Scottish fling.

It was the first time he had ever let go enough to enjoy himself!

There was a point when David loved the Lord so much that there was nothing to do but dance before the Ark. I believe that's what ought to happen to the people of God when the inner experiences of grace so possesses them that infectious joy radiates in their fellowship.—Lloyd John Ogilvie

GOD'S PRESENCE.   God is "really present" in the world. He is admittedly not a part of the world, and it might be more accurate to speak of his presence to the world than his presence in the world. Nevertheless, the world is the object of his continuing care and concern, and the affairs of man and nations are under his providence and control. To those who have ears to hear and eyes to see are given signs of his present and continuing activity. A hidden God he may be, an absent God never.—Peter Baelz

A FATHER'S TASK.   The task of a father can be summed up in a few words. He must prove himself a good fellow man to his wife, to his children, and to society. He must meet in a good way the three problems of life—occupation, friendship, and love—and he must cooperate on an equal footing with his wife in the care and protection of the family. He should not forget that the woman's part in the creation of family life can never be surpassed. It is not his part to dethrone the mother, but to work with her. Especially with regard to money we should emphasize that if the financial support of the family comes through him it is still a common affair. He should never make it appear that he gives and the others receive. In a good marriage the fact that the money comes through him is only a result of the division of labor in the family.—Alfred Adler

PRESENCE AND CARING.   Near the end of the musical play 1776 a discouraged John Adams, having arrived early in the room where the divided colonial delegates have been meeting, steps toward the front of the darkened stage and poses a question to the audience. "Is anybody there? Does anybody care?" he asks plaintively. "Does anybody see what I see?" In many ways, modern man, peering into the darkness of his future, is placing the same questions. Is anybody there? Does anybody care?—Eugene C. Kennedy

POTENTIAL.   Goethe said that if we take man as he is, we make him worse; if we take him as he ought to be, we help him become it.—Victor Frankl

ECSTASY.   I was guest in a home in Texas one time when the phone rang announcing the discovery of oil. Now there was a form of ecstasy that could be trusted! Nobody in the local chamber of commerce or Rotary Club was agitating for the removal of these enthusiasts from their rolls.

Nor do we feel out of place in a football stadium when the home crowd goes wild as a desperation pass in the final seconds wins the conference championship against a traditional rival. Ecstasy because of one's alma mater is safe; it's ecstasy become of our heavenly Father that is suspect!—Jack W. MacGorman

REVELATION.   But though God freely wills to reveal himself to creatures he does it only progressively. He does not immediately draw the veil that hides his august majesty. He merely gives his creatures little glimpses and reserves the full vision for heaven. As centuries whirl around into space, he permits us to catch a few and furtive glances of his ineffable greatness. And each new revelation has made him better known and better loved. Have we not sometimes seen the sunlight passing through a prism and noticed how it was broken up into the seven colors of the spectrum varying from deep red to deep violet? In just such a fashion as this the wonderful nature of God is broken up for our intelligence in the three-fold diffusion of divine life: creation, the incarnation and, the church; God shines through the prism of creation and reveals his existence and his attributes; he shines through the prism of the incarnation and reveals his inmost nature; he shines through the prism of the church

and reveals the life of his incarnate son. If God had never chosen to reveal himself by these progressive manifestations, we should never have been able to know him well, just as we could never have seen the colors hidden in the white light of the sun unless they had passed through the prism.—Fulton J. Sheen

POWER OF WORDS.   Wilfred Funk, noted lexicographer and dictionary publisher, suggests the ten most impressive words in the English language. Note their illustrative value:

- "Alone"—the bitterest word
- "Mother"—the most revered word
- "Death"—the most tragic
- "Faith"—brings greatest comfort
- "Forgotten"—saddest
- "Love"—most beautiful
- "Revenge"—cruelest
- "Friendship"—warmest
- "No"—coldest
- "Tranquility"—most peaceful
—Robert J. Hastings

HOPE FOR HUMANITY.   Many years ago when I was a student, I walked in Times Square, in New York, with a friend. We were commenting on the drab and dull faces of the city dwellers whom we met on the street. And then there came along the street a young lady of such beauty, poise, and charm, that my friend—rather susceptible in such matters—suddenly said, "Look at her. I guess there's something worthwhile after all." In my more mature years I have found that that incident points to a truth of much deeper significance. When I ride in the New York subway or on a bus, I am inclined to think how drab and dull, how stupid and inane, much of life is; how hopeless most of the people one meets seem to be. And then, with a turn of the mind, I think of the flaming figure of Jesus Christ, who wore our humanity like a royal garment, who turned the curse of life into a cross bravely borne, who triumphed not so much over strife as in the midst of strife. And when I think of him, I can look again at the people around me and the world in which they and I live; and then

I find that I have for these people and for that world a strange love, a deep concern, an inescapable care. If he lived in our world, if he wore our human nature, then indeed there is hope.—W. Norman Pittenger

SACRIFICE.   Every evangelist knows, especially if he has a scholar's brain and a scholar's heart, what sacrifices he must make for his evangelism. Outside the church, the evangelist is often regarded as a humbug or (at the best) deluded, and inside the church he is often sneered at as a "hot-gospeler." Certainly he exposes himself to the charge of being shallow-minded, though he may be (like Dwight L. Moody) a man with a first-class brain. He will be regarded by some as a dealer in unintelligent emotionalism, though his mind, like that of John Wesley, may be of logic all compounded.

Mrs. Hugh Price Hughes was once asked what was the greatest sacrifice her husband ever made, and she said, "He could have been a scholar but he chose, under God, to be a simple preacher of the gospel."

You may not think that a very great sacrifice, but that would only prove that you have not the scholar's heart. The greatest sacrifice some men have made for evangelism has been to obey the voice of God when he called them to abandon the delights of scholarly research and tell plain people, in plain words, the things which belong to their peace.—W. E. Sangster

A DREAM OF HEAVEN.   As—in some summer's morning which wakes with a ring of birds, when it is clear, leagues up into the blue, and everything is as distinctly cut as if it stood in heaven and not on earth, when the distant mountains lie bold upon the horizon, and the air is full of the fragrance of flowers which the night cradled—the traveler goes forth with buoyant and elastic step upon his journey, and halts not till in the twilight shadows he reaches his goal, so may we, who are but pilgrims, go forth beneath the smile of God, upon our homeward journey. May heaven lie upon the horizon, luring us on; and when at last we sink to sleep, and dream that we behold again those whom we have lost, may we wake to find that it was not a dream, but that we are in heaven; and may the children for whom we have yearned, and the companions who anticipated us and gained heaven first, come to greet us. Then, sweeter than all, may we behold the face of the Lord Jesus, our Master, our Life, and cast ourselves before him, that he may raise us up with great grace, to stand upon our feet forevermore!—Henry Ward Beecher

ANY BUSINESS ENTRIES?   John Woolman's *Journal* is one of the classics of the devotional life, a book, about which Charles Lamb said: "Get the *Journal* of John Woolman by heart." In part of the *Journal* there is a mournful item that is repeated over and over. On a trip during which he visited the Friends' Societies in North Carolina, he felt a deep distress over the frequent occurrence in the minutes of the Societies' meetings of the words: "No business that required entry." Sometimes he felt heartbroken. Sometimes he grew angry, feeling: "In God's name, why was there not some business that required entry and strong action? With the sin of slavery and its cruelties all around them, and the sin of war impending, how could they say, 'No business that required entry'?"—Halford E. Luccock

CRITICISM.   A young musician's concert was poorly received by the critics. The famous Finnish composer Jean Sibelius consoled him by patting him on the shoulder and saying, "Remember, son, there is no city in the world where they have erected a statue to a critic."—Haddon Robinson in *Leadership*

REVERENCE FOR LIFE.   Existence depends more on reverence for life than the law and the prophets. Reverence for life comprises the whole ethic of love in its deepest and highest sense. It is the source of constant renewal for the individual and for mankind.—Albert Schweitzer

SUFFERING. A woman who was very ill said to her minister: "I have to suffer a lot, and often it is very hard. Yet I do not want to return to the state I was in before God visited me in this sickness, for I know my inward self has been enriched by this suffering." Doesn't that tell the truth of Jesus' saying? When I am lifted up, I will draw all men unto me.—Albert Schweitzer

TEMPTATION. Satan, as the master counterfeiter, is trying to do something that looks like the will of God, but isn't. This fact is especially important for Christians to grasp. Satan knows that if he puts something in a Christian's path which is obviously not the will of God, the Christian is likely to be alert to the temptation and resist it. But if Satan can offer something which, though good in itself, is not the best, the Christian is more likely to accept Satan's offer.—Charles C. Ryrie

PLURALISM OF BIBLE. One of the reasons the Bible has lasted so long and given survival power to synagogue and church at numerous crucial junctures in their histories is surely its pluralism, its inherent depths of ambiguity (in the right sense of that term) and especially its adaptability as canon. There is nothing built upon what it says that can escape the challenge of something else in it: it contains its own built-in correctives. Every program of obedience which has issued from genuine dialogue with the Bible but then goes on to become a rigid, oppressing structure itself eventually comes under the judgment of the very canon out of which that structure had first blossomed.—James A. Sanders

PEOPLE ARE REDEEMABLE. Some years ago I was visiting in the Fiji Islands and heard the story of John Hunt, a young Methodist missionary from England who converted the cannibal tribes. He writes in his journal about the lying and immorality of the chiefs. He speaks of the stench of burning human flesh when the warriors returned from their raids and prepared for the feast. But he bore his witness bravely and patiently, although when he died in 1848 there was little sign of any general repentance or conversion. But some years after his death the main chief, Thakombau, became a Christian and led a great movement into the church.

One day in a little church on the little island of Baa, I saw a rough stone with the top hollowed out. It was used as a baptismal font. They told me it was the old killing stone upon which Thakombau had killed his victims. It had been stained with human blood. Now the sacrament of baptism is the symbol of entrance into the new life of Christ. And I said to myself, wouldn't it be great if every church could have something to remind the people of what they were in their sin and what they can become when Christ finds them. This symbol of the worst and the best spoke to me that day of the realism of Christianity. Men are bad enough, as God knows, but they are redeemable and we are in the world to bear witness to that truth.—Gerald Kennedy

SPEAKING UP. In Germany, the Nazis first came for the Communists, and I didn't speak up because I wasn't a Communist. They came for the Jews, and I didn't speak up because I wasn't a Jew. Then they came for the trade unionists, and I didn't speak up because I wasn't a trade unionist. They came for the Catholics, and I didn't speak up because I was a Protestant. Then they came for me, and by that time there was no one left to speak for me.—Martin Niemoeller

THE CROSS: FAITH'S PARADOX. The cross of Christ became for all time the supreme symbol of faith's paradox. The Crucifixion was the worst and saddest thing that ever happened through the wickedness of men, yet also the best and most glorious thing that ever happened through the wisdom and power and love of God. . . . It was the Passion of Christ that thus became a crucial instance, driving Christian faith, from its very beginnings in the New Testament, not only to regard suffering more than ever as an evil and an enemy against which God calls us to fight, but also, paradoxically, to find room for the mystery of suffering in God's holy and perfect and acceptable will and purpose for our Good. Christianity "pointed to Jesus with the terror of death upon Him in Gethsemane; with a cry of desolation upon the Cross on Calvary; it allowed the soul, it encouraged the soul, to sob itself out. It not only taught men frankly to face and to recognize physical and mental pain, death, and all other, especially all moral evils and sufferings as very real; it actually showed men the presence and gravity of a host of pains, evils, and miseries which they had, up to then, quite ignored, or at least greatly minimized. And yet, with all this—in spite of all such material for despair, the final note of Christianity was, and is still, one of trust, of love, of transcendent joy."—D. M. Baillie

ANSWERS TO PRAYER.   A man who knew empirically that an event had been caused by his prayer would feel like a magician. His head would turn and his heart would be corrupted. The Christian is not to ask whether this or that event happened because of a prayer. He is rather to believe that all events without exception are answers to prayer in the sense that whether they are grantings or refusals the prayers of all concerned and their needs have all been taken into account. All prayers are heard, though not all prayers are granted. We must not picture destiny as a film unrolling for the most part on its own, but in which our prayers are sometimes allowed to insert additional items. On the contrary; what the film displays to us as it unrolls already contains the results of our prayers and of all our other acts. There is no question whether an event has happened because of your prayer. When the event you prayed for occurs your prayer has always contributed to it. When the opposite event occurs your prayer has never been ignored; it has been considered and refused, for your ultimate good and the good of the whole universe.—C. S. Lewis

MEMORY.   How do we store good memories? We might be helped by a study made which showed that grade-school children were helped by asking, "What did you learn that is so important that you want to remember it always?" rather than "What did you read that you should remember for a test?"—David W. Richardson

MOTHER'S DAY.   Erich Fromm has shown us an important insight into the love a mother should have. Fromm wrote, "In erotic love, two people who were separate become one. In motherly love, two people who were one become separate. The mother must not only tolerate, she must wish and support the child's separation." Ellen Cantarow has shown how important it is to decide to have a child. She writes, "Making a decision to have a child—it's momentous. It is to decide forever to have your heart walking around outside your body."—David W. Richardson

LOVE.   Bishop Elvind Berggrave was a great Norwegian Lutheran churchman during World War II. He was kept prisoner under heavy Nazi guard. We are told that his witness was so effective and his deeds and words of love so compelling that his eleven-man guard was constantly changed to keep them from coming under his strong spiritual leadership.—C. Neil Strait

IDENTIFICATION.   When I was pastor of a small church in the bluegrass section of Kentucky, a mother of a fourteen-year-old boy brought him to me after the evening service. She said to me: "What am I going to do with Gordon? He would not come to church this afternoon. He wanted to play. He got mad. He said, 'Church, church, church! That's all I hear!' Now, Mr. Oates, what do you think of him?" The boy was terribly embarrassed. I said to him: "Gordon, I know exactly how you feel. All I hear is 'church,' and sometimes I get tired. And when I get real tired of church the next time, I am coming to see you, because I know you will understand." Then I turned to his mother and said: "Anybody who has never gotten tired of church just

never has been to church much."—
Wayne Oates

CHRIST IMPLIED.   It is significant that
the higher developments in Greek religion, such as in Aeschylus' dramas, show
a movement toward marriage with the
Hebrew view of sin as pride. The cause
of human evil in Aeschylus is *hybris*, the
pride which leads one to set oneself up as
God; and this causes the destruction of
Agamemnon and Clytemnestra, and almost of Orestes. Aeschylus begins the
tragic circle of his *Orestia* with the more
popular Greek view of "fate," which sets
up an unbreakable circle of retribution;
but through humility and suffering
Orestes is able to get forgiveness and reconciliation. This achievement of divine
forgiveness and grace points up toward a
higher flowering of religion which implies the Christ.—Rollo May

UNDERSTANDING THE SCRIPTURES.   The
bells of the scriptures ring clearly in your
life when you try to love. What may once
have been random events are now understood as the feasts and friendships, the
loneliness and separation, the small
deaths and resurrections through which
we sense the mystery of Jesus in our own
lives.—Eugene C. Kennedy

BITTERNESS.   Leo Buscaglia tells of a
lady in Florida who was raped, shot in
the heart, brutally mutilated, and left to
die. Astoundingly, she survived. Her
head wound left her blinded. A television
host, while interviewing her, reflected on
the bitterness she must feel because of
the scars she would have to deal with the
rest of her life. Her reply: "Oh, no! That
man took one night of my life; I refuse to
give him one additional second!"—C.
Neil Strait

ACKNOWLEDGMENTS

Acknowledgment and gratitude are hereby expressed to the following for kind permission to reprint material from the books and periodicals listed below:

BROADMAN PRESS: Excerpts from C. W. Bess, *Children's Sermons for Special Times*, pp. 18–19, 77, © 1988, Broadman Press; Excerpts from Charles B. Bugg, *Getting on Top When Life Gets Us Down*, pp. 41–45, © 1990, Broadman Press; Excerpts from Leon W. Castle, *Fifty-Two Children's Sermons*, pp. 82–83, © 1988, Broadman Press; Excerpts from Roy E. DeBrand, *Children's Sermons for Special Occasions*, pp. 39–40, © 1983, Broadman Press; Excerpts from Jerry Hayner, *Yes, God Can*, pp. 136–137, © 1985, Broadman Press; Excerpts from Herschel H. Hobbs, *Basic Bible Sermons on John*, pp. 59–64, © 1990, Broadman Press; Excerpts from Chevis Horne, *Basic Bible Sermons on Easter*, pp. 121–26, © 1990, Broadman Press; Excerpts from Chevis F. Horne, *Preaching the Great Themes of the Bible*, pp. 215–18, © 1986, Broadman Press; Excerpts from Nolan P. Howington, *A Royal Priesthood*, pp. 87–94, © 1986, Broadman Press; Excerpts from William C. Lacy, *Bitter Weeds and Burning Bushes*, pp. 65–77, © 1990, Broadman Press; Excerpts from Hugh Litchfield, *Sermons on Those Other Special Days*, pp. 128–33, © 1990, Broadman Press; Excerpts from Roger Lovette, *Questions Jesus Raised*, pp. 105–09, © 1986, Broadman Press; Excerpts from H. Stephen Shoemaker, *Strength in Weakness*, pp. 41–42, © 1989, Broadman Press; Excerpts from Ralph M. Smith, *Basic Bible*

Sermons on the Church, pp. 51–58, © 1990, Broadman Press.

C.S.S. PUBLISHING COMPANY: *Selections* from *Children's Sermon Service, Plus!*.

CONVENTION PRESS: Excerpts from Robert J. Hastings, in *Adult Life and Work Lesson Annual (1991)*, pp. 286–87, © 1990, Convention Press; Excerpts from Ernest L. Holloway, Jr., in *Adult Life and Work Lesson Annual (1991)*, pp. 171–72, © 1990, Convention Press; Excerpts from Gary Parker, in *Adult Life and Work Lesson Annual (1991)*, p. 263, © 1990, Convention Press.

HARPERCOLLINS PUBLISHER'S INC.: Excerpts from Karl Barth, *Deliverance to the Captives*, © 1961, Harper & Brothers; Excerpts from William Sloane Coffin, *Living the Truth in a World of Illusions*, © 1985, Harper & Row; Excerpts from Fred B. Craddock in James W. Cox, *Best Sermons 1*, © 1988, Harper & Row; Excerpts from Edgar DeWitt Jones, ed., *The Best of John A. Hutton*, © 1950, Harper & Brothers; Excerpts from D. W. Cleverley Ford, *An Expository Preacher's Notebook*, © 1960, Harper & Brothers; Excerpts from Harry Emerson Fosdick, *A Book of Public Prayers*, © 1959, Harper & Brothers; Excerpts from Harry Emerson Fosdick, *Riverside Sermons*, © 1958, Harper & Brothers; Excerpts from Harry Emerson Fosdick, *What Is Vital in Religion*, © 1955, Harper & Brothers; Excerpts from Arnold H. Lowe, *The Importance of Being Ourselves*, © 1948, Harper & Brothers; Excerpts from Arnold H. Lowe, *Power for Life's Living*, © 1954, Harper & Brothers;

Excerpts from Arnold H. Lowe, *When God Moves In*, © 1952, Harper & Brothers; Excerpts from Robert E. Luccock, *If God Be for Us*, © 1954, Harper & Brothers; Excerpts from Halford E. Luccock, *Unfinished Business*, © 1956, Harper and Brothers; Excerpts from Samuel H. Miller, *Prayers for Daily Use*, © 1957, Harper & Brothers; Excerpts from Joseph Fort Newton, *Live, Love, and Learn*, © 1943, Harper & Brothers; Excerpts from Parker J. Palmer, *The Active Life*, © 1990, Harper & Row; Excerpts from Paul Scherer, *The Word God Sent*, © 1965, Harper & Brothers; Excerpts from V. L. Stanfield, ed., *Favorite Sermons of John A. Broadus*, © 1959, Harper & Brothers; Excerpts from Helmut Thielicke, *The Waiting Father*, © 1959, Harper & Brothers.

SUNDAY SCHOOL BOARD OF THE SOUTHERN BAPTIST CONVENTION: Excerpts from Mary Frances Bailey in *Adult Bible Teacher*, January-March, 1987, for March 8, © 1986, The Sunday School Board of the Southern Baptist Convention; Excerpts from Michael Brooks in *Proclaim*, April-June, 1992, p. 35, © 1992, The Sunday School Board of the Southern Baptist Convention; Excerpts from David Crocker in *Proclaim*, October-December, 1990, pp. 6–7, © 1990, The Sunday School Board of the Southern Baptist Convention; Excerpts from Harold E. Dye in *Open Windows*, April-June, 1992, for June 19, © 1992, The Sunday School Board of the Southern Baptist Convention; Excerpts from Walter M. Fox in *Open Windows*, January-March, 1992, for January 4, © 1991, The Sunday School Board of the Southern Baptist Convention; Excerpts from Brian L. Harbour in *Proclaim*, October-December, 1991, pp. 9–10, © 1991, The Sunday School Board of the Southern Baptist Convention; Excerpts from Brian L. Harbour in *Proclaim*, July-September, 1992, p. 18, © 1992, The Sunday School Board of the Southern Baptist Convention; Excerpts from John C. Howell in *Open Windows*, October-December, 1991, for December 27 and 28, © 1991, The Sunday School Board of the Southern Baptist Convention; Excerpts from William Pinson, Jr., in *Proclaim*, April-June, 1991, pp. 9–10, © 1991, The Sunday School Board of the Southern Baptist Convention; Excerpts from Cecil Taylor in *Proclaim*, April-June 1992, pp. 18–19, © 1992, The Sunday School Board of the Southern Baptist Convention.

INDEX OF CONTRIBUTORS

SERMON TITLE INDEX

(Children's stories and sermons are identified as **cs**; *sermon suggestions as* **ss**)

SCRIPTURAL INDEX

INDEX OF PRAYERS

INDEX OF MATERIALS USEFUL AS CHILDREN'S STORIES AND SERMONS NOT INCLUDED IN SECTION X

INDEX OF MATERIALS USEFUL FOR SMALL GROUPS

TOPICAL INDEX